D1601946

UNIVERSITY CASEBOOK SERIES®

BANKRUPTCY

AND CORPORATE REORGANIZATION

LEGAL AND FINANCIAL MATERIALS

FOURTH EDITION

MARK J. ROE
Harvard Law School
David Berg Professor of Corporate Law

FREDERICK TUNG
Boston University School of Law
Howard Zhang Faculty Research Scholar and Professor of Law

444 Cedar Street, Suite 700
St. Paul, MN 55101
1–877–888–1330

Printed in the United States of America

ISBN: 978–1–60930–426–3

PREFACE

With these materials we hope the student will learn not only the major elements of corporate reorganization in chapter 11 of the Bankruptcy Code, but also the major facets of bankruptcy that influence financing transactions. After all, what counts most in a financing transaction is what will happen if the firm does badly and cannot repay its debt, because for the most part a simple I.O.U. would suffice otherwise. Much of the documentation that accompanies complex financing transactions is drafted and negotiated in anticipation of a possible reorganization in chapter 11, or a private reorganization accomplished in its shadow.

We hope the student will acquire another skill while mastering these materials. Good lawyers can advise clients about financial complexity and these financial skills aren't always front and center in law school courses. Indeed, if we can over-generalize, the hidden message in many first-year (and upper-year) law school courses is that students need to understand how to distinguish one judicial decision from another. And the hidden message in some upper-level courses, like taxation and maybe securities regulation or a commercial law course, is to teach the student how to read and construct a complex regulatory or statutory system. Our message behind these materials is how to understand complex financial deal-making and how to integrate finance with law, in the context of bankruptcy. These deal-making skills are usually picked up by the young lawyer working in the law firm, but there's no reason why young lawyers shouldn't get a head start in law school.

With these financial and deal-making skills in mind, we've approached the subject of bankruptcy differently from how it's approached in most bankruptcy casebooks. Most bankruptcy courses provide an anatomy-of-a-bankruptcy. That's the better approach for a course designed primarily for budding bankruptcy practitioners, but a less useful approach for budding deal-makers and financiers (or for advisors to deal-makers and financiers). An anatomy-of-a-bankruptcy course might begin with the requirements for a petition and end with the confirmation of a plan of reorganization. But to a financier, the content of the plan—and how bankruptcy can affect my contract is more important than the largely formal prerequisites to filing a petition. So early on in these materials we focus on the contents of a plan, the bargaining context of plan formation, and the principal warps in the bargaining process.

The goals here also affect the type of materials we've chosen to include. When feasible, we use not just judicial opinions, but materials that financing lawyers use day-to-day: bond indentures, prospectuses, materials about drafting loan agreements, and SEC submissions. The result is that the materials are less black-letter law oriented, more conceptual and more deal-oriented than typical. And, although finance theory might be thought the province of academics, the student or young lawyer who understands the basic concepts from finance theory—not just the sine qua non basics of discounting, present value, risk, and diversification, but also principal-agent theory, monitoring, information incompleteness, and so on—will be a better lawyer, will be better able to advise clients, and will be better able to structure deals.

MARK J. ROE
FREDERICK TUNG

December 2015

ACKNOWLEDGMENTS

Apcar, Leonard & Caleb Solomon, *Going for Broke: Hunt Brothers Pin Hopes for Comeback on 'Crapshoot' in Oil*, Wall Street Journal, July 13, 1988, © Wall Street Journal, permission conveyed through Copyright Clearance Center, Inc.

Baird, Douglas, *The Uneasy Case for Corporate Reorganization*, Journal of Legal Studies (1986), © University of Chicago Press, reprinted by permission.

Baird, Douglas & Robert K. Rasmussen, *Chapter 11 at Twilight*, Stanford Law Review (2004), © Stanford Law Review, permission conveyed through Copyright Clearance Center, Inc.

Baker, Donald W., *A Lawyer's Basic Guide to Secured Transactions* (1983), © American Law Institute–American Bar Association Committee on Continuing Professional Education, reprinted by permission.

Berlin, Mitchell, *Bank Loans & Marketable Securities: How Do Financial Contracts Control Borrowing Firms?*, Federal Reserve Bank of Philadelphia Business Review (1987), © Federal Reserve Bank of Philadelphia, Business Review, reprinted by permission.

Brealey, Richard, Stewart Myers, and Franklin Allen, *Principles of Corporate Finance* (2014), © The McGraw-Hill Companies, reprinted by permission.

Brudney, Victor & Marvin Chirelstein, *Corporate Finance: Cases and Materials* (1987), © Foundation Press, reprinted by permission.

Callison, J. William, *Partnership Law & Practice: General & Limited Partnership* (1997), © WestGroup, reprinted by permission.

Clark, Robert C., *The Interdisciplinary Study of Legal Evolution*, Yale Law Journal (1981), © Yale Law Journal, reprinted by permission.

Cook, Michael L. & Jessica L. Fainman, *No Time for Bankruptcy Venue Hypocrisy*, © Law Journal Newsletters (2005), reprinted by permission.

Dewing, Arthur S., *The Financial Policy of Corporations* (1953), © John Wiley & Sons, Inc., reprinted by permission.

Farnsworth, Allan, *Disputes over Omission in Contracts*, Columbia Law Review (1968), © Columbia Law Review, reprinted by permission.

Fortgang, Chaim & Lawrence King, *The 1978 Code: Some Wrong Policy Decisions*, New York University Law Review (1981), © New York University Law Review, reprinted by permission.

Frank, Peter H., *Hunts' Tactics May Pay Off*, New York Times, July 17, 1987, © New York Times, reprinted by permission.

Glenn, Garrard, *Fraudulent Conveyances & Preferences* (1940), © Baker, Voorhis & Co., Inc., reprinted by permission.

Goetz, Charles & Robert Scott, *Principles of Relational Contracts*, Virginia Law Review (1981), © Virginia Law Review, reprinted by permission.

Jackson, Thomas H., *The Logic & Limits of Bankruptcy Law* (1986), © Harvard University Press, reprinted by permission.

Kimhi, Omer, *Chapter 9 of the Bankruptcy Code: A Solution in Search of a Problem* (2010), © Yale Journal on Regulation, reprinted by permission.

Kuney, George W., *Hijacking Chapter 11*, Emory Bankruptcy Developments Journal (2004), © Emory Bankruptcy Developments Journal, reprinted by permission.

Loeys, Jan, *Low-Grade Bonds: A Growing Source of Corporate Funding*, Federal Reserve Bank of Philadelphia, Business Review (1986), © Federal Reserve Bank of Philadelphia, Business Review, reprinted by permission.

LoPucki, Lynn M. & Christopher R. Mirick, *Strategies for Creditors in Bankruptcy Proceedings* (2007), © Aspen Publishers, reprinted by permission.

Markowitz, Harry M., *Markets & Morality: Or Arbitragers Get No Respect*, Wall Street Journal, May 14, 1991, © Harry M. Markowitz, reprinted by permission.

McCoid, John C., *Setoff: Why Bankruptcy Priority?*, Virginia Law Review (1989), © Virginia Law Review, reprinted by permission.

Mnookin, Robert H. & Robert B. Wilson, *Rational Bargaining & Market Efficiency: Understanding Pennzoil v. Texaco*, Virginia Law Review (1989), © Virginia Law Review, reprinted by permission.

Posner, Richard, *The Rights of Creditors of Affiliated Corporations*, University of Chicago Law Review (1976), © University of Chicago Law Review, reprinted by permission.

Roe, Mark J., *Bankruptcy and Debt: A New Model for Corporate Reorganization*, Columbia Law Review (1983), © Columbia Law Review, reprinted by permission.

Roe, Mark J., *Bankruptcy, Priority and Economics*, Virginia Law Review (1989), © Virginia Law Review, reprinted by permission.

Roe, Mark J. & David Skeel, *Assessing the Chrysler Bankruptcy*, Michigan Law Review (2010), © Michigan Law Review, reprinted by permission.

Salpukas, Agis, *Court Gives Eastern Air $135 Million: Trustee Is Allowed Use of Escrow Funds to Keep Line Going,* The New York Times, November 28, 1990, © The New York Times, reprinted by permission.

Skeel, David A., *The Past, Present and Future of Debtor-in-Possession Financing*, Cardozo Law Review (2004), © Cardozo Law Review, reprinted by permission.

Skeel, David A., *The Story of Saybrook: Defining the Limits of Debtor-In-Possession Financing*, in *Bankruptcy Law Stories*, Thomson Reuters (2007), © Thomson Reuters, reprinted by permission.

Slain, John J. & Homer Kripke, *The Interface Between Securities Regulation & Bankruptcy Allocating the Risk of Illegal Securities Issuance Between Security holders & the Issuer's Creditors*, New York University Law Review (1973), © New York University Law Review, reprinted by permission.

Sloane, Craig A., *The Sub Rosa Plan of Reorganization: Side-stepping Creditor Protections in Chapter 11*, Bankruptcy Developments Journal (1999), © Craig A. Sloane, reprinted by permission.

Sontchi, Christopher S., *Valuation Methodologies: A Judge's View*, American Bankruptcy Institute Law Review (2012), © American Bankruptcy Institute Law Review, reprinted by permission.

Squire, Richard, *Strategic Liability in the Corporate Group.*, University of Chicago Law Review (2011), © University of Chicago Law Review, reprinted by permission.

Tung, Frederick, *Confirmation and Claims Trading*, Northwestern University Law Review (1996), © Northwestern University Law Review, reprinted by permission.

Veasey, Norman E., *Counseling the Board of Directors of a Delaware Corporation in Distress*, American Bankruptcy Institute Journal (2008), © American Bankruptcy Institute, reprinted by permission.

SUMMARY OF CONTENTS

TABLE OF CONTENTS

TABLE OF CASES

TABLE OF STATUTES

TABLE OF AUTHORITIES

UNIVERSITY CASEBOOK SERIES®

BANKRUPTCY

AND CORPORATE REORGANIZATION

LEGAL AND FINANCIAL MATERIALS

FOURTH EDITION

CHAPTER 1

INTRODUCTION

¶ 101: Introductory Note

This course is about debt.

Companies borrow money to finance expansion of their factories, to purchase inventory and raw materials, to pay workers to produce goods, to replace cash lost in poor operations when their products do not sell profitably, and to refinance prior loans already in place but coming due.

Oftentimes the borrowing, especially when of a significant sum of money, is documented by more than a simple IOU. Frequently, the lender will seek protection beyond a handshake and a firm's promise to repay. Lawyers often become involved, drafting and negotiating the documents and advising lenders and borrowers of risks and pitfalls.

When the company fails to produce sufficient cash to repay the loan, lenders can invoke legal institutions. Lenders and their lawyers scrutinize the lending agreement for its terms and conditions. They may sue the company to be repaid. The company may have many creditors, all of whom demand to be repaid. The cliché is that outside of bankruptcy, state law contract and property rights lead to the creditors "racing to the courthouse," each seeking to reduce its claim to a judgment, which entitles the creditor to have the sheriff levy on the company's property (if it comes to that). The out-of-bankruptcy rule is largely a first-in-time race to sue, obtain a judgment, and levy on that judgment.

One common type of creditor has additional rights. It is secured and has rights in a piece of the debtor's property under state law. Typically it acquires these rights via Article 9 of the Uniform Commercial Code for goods, and via state mortgage law for realty. If the debtor company fails to pay, the secured lender can typically seize the property securing its loan, sell the property, and apply the proceeds to pay off the loan (returning the excess, if any, to the debtor company).

A federal super-structure sits atop the state-based contract, property, tort, and judicial institutions that lead to this race-to-the-courthouse. The super-structure is of course bankruptcy. The debtor company can file for bankruptcy in a federal bankruptcy court, at which point, the bankruptcy automatically enjoins all of the state-based lawsuits against the debtor company. No one can collect from the bankruptcy debtor outside of the bankruptcy proceedings.

While the bankruptcy institutions' injunction against creditor action is in place (called the bankruptcy "stay"), the business is usually restructured to best reflect the realities of what products the company can and cannot sell. Operationally, the worst divisions are shut down. Financially, the debtor and its creditors redo their contracts. At the same time, a redistribution of the value of the debtor company is planned. Bankruptcy law's distributional rules inside bankruptcy displace the outside-of-bankruptcy, state-based, first-in-time, race-to-the-courthouse rules with distributional principles that accord value first to priority creditors (according to a hierarchy) and then, when value runs out, proportionately to the lower ranking creditors. This priority and proportionate system deserves considerable attention, which it will get in these materials.

Bankruptcy comes in two varieties, liquidation and reorganization. In a liquidation, a court-appointed bankruptcy trustee sells the firm—traditionally in a piecemeal fashion that shuts down the firm's ongoing operations. The trustee collects the sale proceeds and then disburses the cash to the creditors. When the usual liquidation (which turns the firm's solid assets into "liquid" cash) is completed, the business ceases to exist. The second variety, reorganization, is more complex and, for businesses of any significant size, more common. In a reorganization, the firm's debt payments are deferred or reduced, its capital stock is reallocated, and the firm continues to operate. These—liquidation and reorganization—are the two polar cases; hybrids exist and are common.

The reorganization statute vitally affects the nature, meaning, and enforceability of basic contract terms of any business financing. Accordingly, although some corporate finance lawyers might see bankruptcy as a specialist's task, most quickly learn that lawyers who draft and negotiate financing documents must be familiar with the ramifications of their drafting and negotiating should a bankruptcy come to pass. Creditors looking to be repaid by the debtor firm typically enforce their contracts not in a local court that applies state contract law, but in a bankruptcy court operating under the Bankruptcy Code. And bankruptcy law often overrides contracts and corporate charters; the statute gives the court authority to rewrite the debtor company's financial and other contracts and to redo the debtor corporation's charter:

§ 1141. Effect of confirmation.

(a) . . . the provisions of a confirmed plan bind . . . any entity acquiring property under the plan [of reorganization], and any creditor, equity security holder, or general partner in the debtor, whether or not the claim or interest of such creditor, equity security holder, or general partner is impaired under the plan *and whether or not such creditor, equity security holder, or general partner has accepted the plan.*[1]

(b) Except as otherwise provided in the plan or the order confirming the plan, the confirmation of a plan vests all of the property of the estate in the debtor.

(c) . . . the property dealt with by the plan is free and clear of all claims and interests of creditors, equity security holders, and of general partners in the debtor.

(d)(1) Except as otherwise provided in this subsection, in the plan, or in the order confirming the plan, the confirmation of a plan—

(A) discharges the debtor from any debt that arose before the date of such confirmation . . . whether or not . . . the holder of such claim has accepted the plan; and

(B) terminates all rights and interests of equity security holders and general partners provided for by the plan.

§ 1123. Contents of plan

(a) Notwithstanding any otherwise applicable nonbankruptcy law, a plan shall—

(1) . . .

(2) specify any class of claims or interests that is not impaired under the plan;

(3) specify the treatment of any class of claims or interests that is impaired under the plan;

(4) . . .

(5) provide adequate means for the plan's implementation, such as—

(A) . . .

(B) . . .

(C) merger or consolidation of the debtor with one or more persons;

(D) . . .

(E) satisfaction or modification of any lien;[2]

(F) cancellation or modification of any bond indenture or similar instrument;

(G) curing or waiving of any default;

(H) extension of a maturity date or a change in an interest rate or other term of outstanding securities;

(I) amendment of the debtor's charter; or

(J) . . .

(6) [amend the corporate charter in several respects; and]

---

[1] [Emphasis supplied.—Roe & Tung.]

[2] [A lien is the right a secured creditor has in the debtor's property.]

(7) contain only provisions that are consistent with the interests of creditors and equity security holders and with public policy with respect to the manner of selection of any officer, director, or trustee under the plan and any successor to such officer, director, or trustee . . . .

(b) Subject to subsection (a) of this section, a plan may—

(1) impair or leave unimpaired any class of claims, secured or unsecured, or of interests;

(2) . . . provide for the assumption, rejection, or assignment of any executory contract or unexpired lease of the debtor not previously rejected under such section;

(3) provide for—

(A) the settlement or adjustment of any claim or interest belonging to the debtor or to the estate; . . .

(B) . . .

(4) provide for the sale of all or substantially all of the property of the estate, and the distribution of the proceeds of such sale among holders of claims or interests;

(5) modify the rights of holders of secured claims, . . . or of holders of unsecured claims, or leave unaffected the rights of holders of any class of claims; and

(6) include any other appropriate provision not inconsistent with the applicable provisions of this title.

Chapter 11 of the Bankruptcy Code, from which the above provisions are drawn, obviously anticipates the court rewriting a debtor's contracts, re-drafting its corporate charter, selling its assets, and modifying the rights of the parties contracting with the debtor corporation.

While understanding modern chapter 11 reorganization is obviously relevant to practicing law today—not just when representing the firm and its creditors in bankruptcy, but also when representing creditors and others dealing with a firm that might go bankrupt—it is helpful to first put the problem of corporate reorganization into historical perspective to better see why we have a system of reorganization that overrides contract.

Reorganization problems link to technological and engineering changes that came to prevail in the United States at the end of the nineteenth century. Early in the nineteenth century, business finance and reorganization were simple, since an entrepreneur typically financed his or her own operations from savings and earnings. But by the end of that century, large enterprises required commitments of capital larger than that which any single saver (or small group of savers) could provide. The capital built not simple operations that could be shut down nearly costlessly, but long-lived assets such as steel mills, oil refineries, and railroads, which even when currently unprofitable might have long-run value. The long-lived nature of large-scale capital assets, and the complex arrangements needed to finance the assets, formed the basis for the complex reorganization institutions that arose toward the end of the nineteenth century—called equity receiverships at the time—and that developed further during the twentieth century.

¶ 102: The Shift in Business Technology at the End of the Nineteenth Century

When manufacturing firms were small proprietorships with generic machinery, such as a simple lathe or a forge, the essential problems of modern reorganization had yet to appear. The firm's creditors were few: a local bank, a few suppliers, and several employees. A firm might fail, but closing it was simple. The entrepreneur collected his or her assets, received and held all the payments due him or her, and then distributed the receipts to the creditors. (Sometimes a court-appointed official, aptly named a "receiver," gathered the debtor's incoming receipts of cash for the bankrupt's creditors, who feared what the debtor might do with the cash.) With the ordinary assets sold and the cash due to the debtor collected, the receiver could then distribute the funds to the debtor's creditors. Because the firm usually had very few creditors, the creditors had little problem coordinating their collection actions.

Businesses changed in scale and scope toward the end of the nineteenth century. Advances in engineering technologies made it possible to manufacture goods much more cheaply in huge enterprises than in small ones. Steel mills and oil refineries were built, and railroads crisscrossed the nation. These large specialized assets—mills, refineries, railroad tracks—had no obvious alternative use to their intended use as a mill, refinery, or railroad, unlike the simple lathe or forge. The difference between their scrap value and their value in a reorganized firm was seen to be large and worth preserving. Moreover, the large enterprises were financed by many creditors, who had trouble coordinating their actions when their debtor failed. Lastly, many large failed businesses at the end of the nineteenth century were railroads, which were seen as critical to regional economies. Courts—operating without a bankruptcy law—developed a reorganization apparatus to keep the railroads running, even when the railroads failed to make as much money as anticipated and could no longer pay off their creditors.

¶ 103: The Equity Receivership

The first large scale bankrupts in the United States were major railroads, which grew rapidly and then collapsed financially during the deep depression of the 1890s. Until 1898, there was no continuing American bankruptcy statute; yet, during the 1890s, companies owning a majority of the railroad track in America were reorganized. The receivership was the judicial means of reorganization. It was a long-standing common law device, originally designed for simpler times and simpler companies. Federal judges adapted the receivership to reorganize the railroads. Over the next century the equity receivership developed into chapter 11.

David A. Skeel, Jr., *The Past, Present and Future of Debtor-in-Possession Financing*, 25 Cardozo Law Review 1905, 1908-10 (2004)

* * *

The classic equity receiverships involved moderately large railroads—railroads whose tracks crossed several state lines, and which had issued common stock, preferred stock, and several different mortgage bonds[3] to raise money over the years. If the railroad encountered financial distress, and failed to make the requisite interest payments on its bonds, a creditor would first file a "creditor's bill" asking the court to appoint a receiver to oversee the defaulting railroad's property. The principal reason for appointing a receiver was that doing so technically shifted control of the railroad's assets to the receiver and out of the reach of prying creditors. If a creditor tried to obtain a lien against railroad property, for instance, the receiver would simply ask the court for an injunction.

The next step was to file a second "bill," the foreclosure bill. In form, the foreclosure bill asked the court to schedule a sale of the property. In reality, the sale would be put off for months, and often years, while the parties negotiated over the terms of a reorganization plan.

In the meantime, the investment banks that had underwritten the railroad's bonds would quickly form a bondholders' committee to represent bondholders in the negotiations. If the firm had issued more than one class of bonds, several committees might form; there might also be committees of common stockholders and preferred stockholders. The virtue of forming a committee was that it centralized the bargaining process and theoretically gave thousands of widely scattered bondholders a champion—which, in large receiverships at the turn of the century, usually meant J.P. Morgan and Company, Kuhn, Loeb, or one of a small group of other Wall Street banks.

To ensure their authority, the committee representatives asked investors to "deposit" their bonds (or stock, for a stockholders committee) with the committee. By depositing their bonds, investors gave the committee complete control over the bonds for the duration of the negotiations, with one limitation: bondholders would have the right to withdraw their bonds if they disapproved of the plan that the committee negotiated on their behalf.

The goal of the negotiations was to rework the railroad's capital structure, reducing its obligations so that it could get back on track financially after the receivership. Often this meant converting fixed obligations into variable ones, or reducing interest rates, or extending the payback period. Once they had agreed to an overall plan, the committees were combined to form a single super-committee called the "Reorganization Committee." It was the Reorganization Committee that "purchased" the railroad's assets at the foreclosure "sale." Since the Reorganization Committee had all of the deposited securities at its

[3] [Mortgage bonds are bonds — publicly-issued debt — that have property securing the bonds. If the debtor doesn't pay, the creditors can get to the assets given as security.]

disposal, and could bid the face value of the securities as a substitute for cash, no one else bothered to bid at the auction. In the words of Paul Cravath, one of the leading receivership lawyers: "[c]ounsel who have acted frequently for reorganization committees have spent a great many anxious hours preparing for the unexpected bidder, but in my own experience he has never appeared. . . . Manifestly in most sales where the security holders . . . have . . . placed their interest in the hands of a committee there is not likely to be serious competition at the sale."

As soon as the Reorganization Committee purchased the assets, it transferred them to a shell corporation that had been set up for just this purpose. The stock and other securities of the new corporation were then distributed to the old investors on the terms laid out in the reorganization plan.

The dry recitation of facts that I have just given doesn't even begin to convey the ingenuity of the receivership process. The biggest marvel of all was where it came from: in form, the equity receivership was a dramatic elaboration of the traditional foreclosure procedure, the humble device that had been used for generations, and is, of course, still used by secured creditors to force a sale of the debtor's collateral after the debtor has defaulted on his or her obligations. The development of the equity receivership was one of the great innovations of the common law in nineteenth-century America.

¶ 104: A Brief Anatomy of a Bankruptcy

These materials are not organized to replicate the legal path of a bankruptcy chronologically from its beginning to its conclusion. That path begins when the debtor files a bankruptcy petition, continues with the gathering of the debtor's property into the bankruptcy estate, culminates with the debtor and its creditors forming a plan of reorganization, and then ends with the court confirming a plan of reorganization.

Nor are these materials designed as a tour of the Bankruptcy Code, beginning, say, with chapter 1 of the Code (which contains the definitions and general provisions), then proceeding to chapters 3 (which deals with the administration of bankruptcy proceedings) and 5 (which establishes creditors' claims and defines what goes into the debtor's estate), footnoting chapters 9 (which deals with the bankruptcy of municipalities), 12 (for farmers), and 13 (for individuals), and then concluding with the finale: chapters 7 (which liquidates a debtor firm) and 11 (which reorganizes a debtor firm).

Instead, these materials allow the student to deeply analyze the financially salient features of bankruptcy, mostly relating to priority, that are critical both inside a bankruptcy and to financiers and managers (and, most importantly, their lawyers) when they finance enterprises (which they hope will never go into bankruptcy). Hence, we will begin at the end, with the priority system that chapter 11 sets out, asking who gets what and who comes first under the Bankruptcy Code. From there we will work backwards to fill in the definitions and concepts needed to understand priority, generally moving back through to the beginning of the chapter 11 proceeding and eventually, via the book's focus in chapter 22 on the leveraged buyout, to a time-frame that precedes bankruptcy. The topics we cover are designed to do double-duty: to be important both to those of us who will practice bankruptcy *and* to those of us who work on financing transactions and other business deals.

Still, a quick beginning-to-end overview of the modern reorganization of a public firm is useful to get us started. Here it is: The prebankruptcy scenario will have the firm borrowing to finance its operations, to build new factories, to acquire other enterprises, and to expand. Then the firm earns less than expected from its operations and cannot service its debt. Markets for its products fall, or operating expenses go up. Or both. Sometimes the firm's financial decline happens due to no fault of its own; it was unlucky. Sometimes the firm is mismanaged.

If the cash pinch persists and becomes a severe cash crunch, the company files for bankruptcy in chapter 11. Although the Bankruptcy Code allows *creditors* to force the bankruptcy, it's been rare for creditors to formally force a firm into bankruptcy. And overall, the Code's traditional provisions help the debtor and its managers, so chapter 11 is typically used defensively by debtors, not offensively by creditors. In the past decade, however, more creditor-friendly features and practices have arisen.

Chapter 11's central organizing feature is that it gathers all of the firm's assets and debts, and then allows a comprehensive reorganization plan to be formulated and implemented. This global settlement contrasts with what happens outside of bankruptcy, where state law rules generally govern creditor collection efforts: each creditor has an incentive to rush to sue the debtor individually, get a judgment, and levy on that judgment (seizing debtor assets to satisfy the judgment), because state law favors the first creditor to emerge from the courthouse with a judgment in hand.

But as soon as the petition for bankruptcy is filed, all lawsuits against the debtor are automatically stayed. Bankruptcy imposes a collective proceeding. No one can sue the debtor, levy on an existing judgment against the debtor, or seize security from the debtor under a prebankruptcy security agreement. The debtor's managers, who felt pressured before the filing, now can breathe more easily, because creditors are no longer individually pressing managers hard to be repaid. The Bankruptcy Code allows the judge to lift the bankruptcy stay, and a good deal of bankruptcy litigation arises from creditors seeking to get the stay lifted so that they can sue the debtor or, more frequently, so that they can seize assets securing their loans.

A debtor newly in bankruptcy typically needs fresh cash to keep operating. It needs to pay its employees and its suppliers. Occasionally, it gets enough from operations to pay them, but more typically it must borrow yet more cash. Just before the bankruptcy, that borrowing was often impossible because of infighting among the creditors about who would be first in line for repayment. The Bankruptcy Code resolves the infighting that could stymie new credit; it also permits the *new* financing, usually called debtor-in-possession or DIP financing, to be repaid first, once the plan of reorganization is made final. The DIP financer is repaid before prebankruptcy unsecured creditors.

Who runs the debtor firm? Incumbent managers typically run the firm when bankruptcy begins. The court could appoint a bankruptcy trustee to run the firm for the benefit of the firm's creditors; the firm's managers could be ousted. But this kind of formal ouster is rare. When the incumbent managers run the firm, as is usual, the debtor is said to remain in possession of its own assets. Hence, the term "debtor-in-possession." But these debtor-in-possession managers do face an official committee of unsecured creditors, which gets to review major actions, and the committee can complain to the judge if it's unhappy. The debtor-in-possession is typically authorized to run its business in the ordinary course, but must get court approval for out-of-the-ordinary-course actions. Sometimes major creditors press to replace the prebankruptcy managers.

Other creditors may form committees as well. Committees hire lawyers and other professional advisers to help negotiate a plan of reorganization with the debtor. Under a plan of reorganization, creditors are grouped into classes, roughly based on the similarity of their claims.

During the reorganization case, the committees, the debtor, and the court scrutinize prebankruptcy asset grabs by individual creditors, aiming to bring those assets back into the reorganization for the benefit of creditors as a group. That is, to nullify the state law race to the courthouse among creditors, the Bankruptcy Code allows the debtor to recover assets that the debtor dissipated on the eve of bankruptcy. The two critical recovery provisions are *fraudulent transfer* law (which exists under state law as well as the Bankruptcy Code and which we shall see does not require outright fraud and deception) and *preference* law.

When a debtor transfers an asset to another party for less than reasonably equivalent value, or with intent to hinder its other creditors, then a prima facie case is made for the debtor to recover this "fraudulent" transfer for itself and for the benefit of all of its creditors. The term "fraudulent" is in quotation marks because while actual fraud on the creditors is sufficient for the debtor to recover the prebankruptcy transfer, it is often unnecessary. If the debtor received less than equivalent value, as long as some other baseline conditions are met, the debtor can recover the transfer even in the absence of actual fraud.

Preference law allows the debtor company to recover payments made to creditors within 90 days *before* the bankruptcy. Preference law allows all creditors, and not just the debtor's favored creditors, to share in the eve-of-bankruptcy payments from the debtor. It also discourages eve-of-bankruptcy creditor races to seize the debtor's assets. Another remedy, *equitable subordination,* sends misbehaving, overreaching creditors to the end of the bankruptcy priority line.

The debtor can reject many of its unperformed contracts. While the contracting party will typically have a claim against the debtor for breach of contract, that claim becomes just another unsecured creditor's claim in the bankruptcy. The amount of the claim equals the damages from the debtor's breach. In effect, parties with unperformed contracts can be made into creditors of the firm. And most creditors are not paid in full in a bankruptcy reorganization.

The debtor firm and its managers enjoy the opportunity to propose the first plan of reorganization. During the first 120 days after the filing of the bankruptcy petition, a court will not listen to others proposing reorganization plans until management gets to show the court its plan. Creditors cannot formally solicit agreement to their own plan until management has revealed and sought formal acceptance of its own plan. Managers' ability to control the bankruptcy agenda during its initial stage puts great power in the hands of the incumbent managers and their allies in the reorganization. That authority may shift, particularly to new creditors providing new cash, but that's the Code's baseline.

A full-scale chapter 11 proceeding for a public firm typically takes a year and a few months. The well positioned creditors try to come first in priority and to conclude the proceeding quickly (so that they can get their money back); the debtor and its managers seek to survive. They all usually settle their disputes and agree to a plan of reorganization; if they don't agree, the judge can "cram down" a plan of reorganization. A cram-down typically requires the judge to value the firm—to see how much value there is in the firm to distribute. Because the cram-down is the ultimate judicial weapon in chapter 11 and affects renegotiations even in the many reorganizations in which the debtor and its creditors quickly settle, this is the first feature of bankruptcy we will examine, even though it is nearly the last act in the bankruptcy play. Although the bankruptcy players usually make a deal, and usually don't invoke bankruptcy's ultimate weapon, their fears (or hopes) of how a judicial cram-down would be employed influence what they accept, or what they insist on, when making a deal.

CHAPTER 2

THE VALUE OF THE DEBTOR IN BANKRUPTCY

A. HOW VALUE AFFECTS DISTRIBUTION

¶ 201: Is Bankruptcy "Just" a Valuation Institution?

Consider the entrepreneur who borrows $200 million to finance a firm that's worth much more than that, maybe $1 billion. But the business persistently loses money and runs out of cash. It files for bankruptcy. Core to the bankruptcy process will be assigning a value to the firm. One can see this intuitively. If the firm is worth $250 million, then the owner has a case to make that, although there's no cash left, the business has long-term value for the owner, because it's worth $250 million and owes "only" $200 million. As such, says the owner, the entrepreneur should continue owning the firm. But if the firm is worth less than $200 million, the amount it owes the creditors, then creditors have an intuitive case to make that the firm belongs to them and the entrepreneur's interest in the firm should unfortunately be wiped out.

In essence, bankruptcy seeks to solve for X in the simple balance sheet below. X was once equal to $1 billion, but now it's much less. If X is less than $200 million, then the creditors should own the firm.

Firm	
X	Creditors owed $200 million
	Stockholders

How could bankruptcy "solve" for X? Under the state law process, no court formally finds a number for X: creditors race to the courthouse to get judgments and then levy on them. If the firm's value is exhausted before all creditors are paid in full, then we know implicitly that X was less than $200 million. The bankruptcy process could be more formal in finding a number for X, in that the bankruptcy authorities could take briefs from litigants, get their own experts to advise the court, and then come to their own expert, administered conclusion on the value of X. Or, the creditors and the owner could make a deal on their own. Or, lastly, the authorities could seek market bids on the firm, with the highest bid determining the value of X. That gives us three alternatives to the race to the courthouse: an administered system, a deal among the parties, and a sale. As we shall see, all three are embedded in the Bankruptcy Code.

We focus in the next few chapters on the administered means. It's the mechanism that long prevailed in reorganizations of large firms in the United States. Even though the Bankruptcy Code now uses a more deal-oriented framework, the administered valuation is the backup if the parties to the bankruptcy cannot come to a deal among themselves.

¶ 202: Schematic of Controls on the Corporation

One can think of the corporation as a collection of cash flows. Creditors provide funds and goods and services to the corporation. Banks and other creditors lend funds and expect to be repaid, with interest. Trade creditors ship goods or provide services to the corporation and expect to be paid for them. A secured creditor gets a promise from the corporation that it, the secured creditor, can collect its debt by seizing specific assets of the corporation (the "security") if the corporation cannot get the cash together to pay the secured creditor. The security might be real estate, governed by mortgage laws in the state; or the security might be the machines, inventory, or accounts receivable of the corporation, governed typically by the Uniform Commercial Code. Not all debtors give, and not all creditors receive, security. Creditors without security—unsecured creditors—collect from the company out of the company's unencumbered assets, which are the debtor's assets that are not subject to any security interest (or collect from what's left after the secured creditors get paid). The company normally generates cash to pay the creditors by using its factory and machines to produce products to sell. The sale generates an account receivable from a customer, which is essentially a promise from the customer to pay the debtor later. When the customer pays the firm, the firm has cash to pay its creditors. If there's any cash left over, the firm might pay a dividend to its stockholders.

These cash relationships can be represented with a schematic, as shown below. A more standard way to represent the relationships is with financial statements, which follow on the next page.

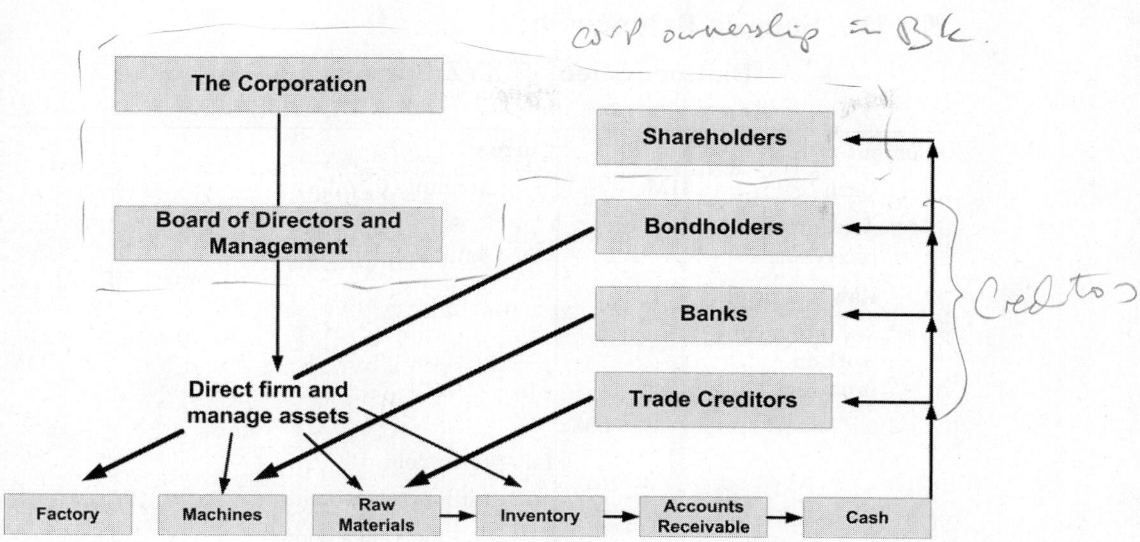

A prebankruptcy scenario:

1. The corporation, its board, and its managers borrow from bondholders and banks to build the factory, buy the machines, and fund its day-to-day operations. The bold lines represent funding by borrowing. The trade creditors ship in raw materials, with a promise from the corporation to pay for the materials 30 days later.
2. The board and managers try to run the factory and machines to turn the raw material into inventory—goods held for sale. Upon sale, they generate accounts receivable that, when paid, yield cash.
3. The cash is used to pay off the creditors. If there's more cash than needed for operations and creditor repayment, the excess cash is turned into profits and dividends for shareholders.
4. If bondholders aren't paid from the cash generated, they attempt to seize the factory.
5. If the secured banks aren't paid they sue the company or attempt to seize accounts receivable or inventory.
6. If the firm is in distress, its assets will be insufficient to pay all creditors in full, so each creditor hopes to be paid earlier than the others.
7. Contractual arrangements with creditors or suppliers may constrain the firm's latitude to use its cash or limit other decision-making authority of the board and management.

¶ 203: Sample Balance Sheet

Balance Sheet of XYZ Corp. at 12/31/1X

Assets			Liabilities		
Current			Current		
Cash	$1M		Accounts payable	$1M	
Accounts receivable	1M		Bank demand note	1M	
Raw materials	1M				2M
Inventory & work-in-progress	2M				
		5M			
			Long-term debt		
			1st mortgage bonds	2M	
			2nd mortgage bonds	1M	
			Debentures	1M	
			Equipment financing	1M	
					5M
Plant and Equipment			Shareholders' equity		
Plant	3M		Preferred	1M	
Machines	2M		Common	2M	
		5M			3M
		10M			10M

¶ 204: Seniority, Security, and Valuation

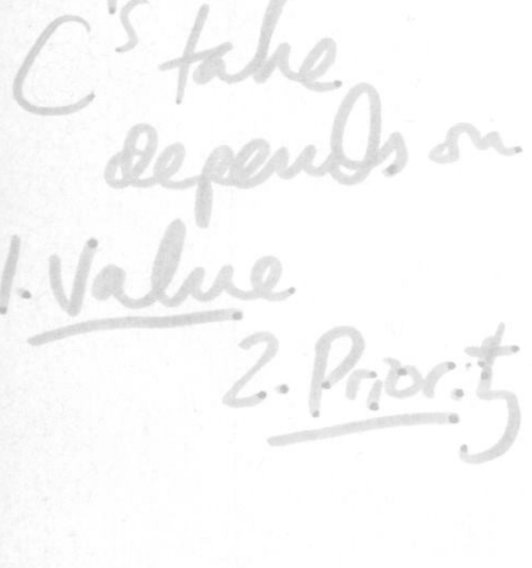

The two central variables in determining a creditor's "take" in a bankruptcy are the value of the enterprise and the priority ranking of the creditor's claim.

Priority in chapter 11 will command several weeks of our attention after we discuss valuation. But before we look in depth at valuation, we ought first to know a little about how ranking is determined and preserved, because priority and valuation interact.

Financiers seek to have their borrowers agree to contractual terms that will best assure that the financiers will be repaid if disaster strikes. If a financier cannot assure itself of repayment, it increases the price of its credit (usually in the form of a higher interest rate) to account for the risk of nonpayment.

Creditors use loan agreements to protect themselves. The core obligation of the debtor company under a loan agreement is to repay the loan with interest. Lenders to a company that makes enough money to pay all of its creditors need little protection. But not all companies will make enough money. Anticipating that possibility, creditors seek various protections. The most common protection usually known to law students is security: the lender gets the borrower company to commit that if it cannot pay off the loan, the lender can seize a specific asset of the company and can do so to the exclusion of the firm's other creditors. In its pure form the financier is fully paid out of the security that the borrower gave. If the security is worth enough to cover the loan, the financier is paid in full and the excess is returned to the debtor to satisfy its other creditors. If the security is insufficient to pay the lender in full, the lender's claim is split in two—a secured claim for the amount of the security and an unsecured claim for any deficiency. The filing and notice provisions in the state-enacted Uniform Commercial Code and in real estate mortgage laws protect other lenders from secret deals. These arrangements are the subject of commercial law, debtor-creditor, and secured transactions courses.

But security is far from the only protection that lenders seek. Many lenders seek to limit (1) the amount of dividends that the company can pay (because money that the company pays out as a dividend is unavailable to the lender when the company's cash gets tight), (2) the amount of other debt that the debtor company can incur (so that the creditor doesn't have to share with too many other creditors), and (3) the ratios of debt to equity (limiting the amount the debtor can borrow, based on a multiple of the amount shareholders have at risk). Lenders often insist on acceleration clauses, so that if the debtor fails to comply with one term or another of the loan agreement, the lender can demand to be repaid everything, immediately.

Debentures are certificates representing loans to the company. They are typically unsecured and long-term. The debentureholders' "loan agreement" is called an indenture. The indenture specifies the obligations of the company to the debentureholders and the circumstances under which the debentureholders may sue the company. A trustee, which is usually a bank, acts on behalf of all debentureholders, ideally as if it were itself the lender. The trustee enforces the company's obligations to the debentureholders and is usually the entity that sues on behalf of wronged debentureholders. When the indenture trustee takes security from the company on behalf of the creditors, the debt instruments are often called bonds instead of debentures, although in common usage in finance circles, the two terms have become largely interchangeable.[1]

Financiers will prioritize themselves. Some will insist on being paid first. They usually agree to a lower interest rate than those who agree to a lower priority, since a first-priority creditor faces less risk that the debtor cannot pay off the loan. Some will insist that the borrower not issue new debt, nor issue debt beyond a specified amount, nor issue debt if an agreed-upon formula would not be satisfied, nor give security to any other creditors. A creditor who agrees to come last usually is compensated for that risk with a higher interest rate. More precisely, the creditor agrees to wait to be paid until this or that condition comes to pass (usually that a "senior" creditor is paid in full). This agreement,

[1] The vocabulary we have here is impoverished. Two types of trustees concern us, the trustee for the bondholders, who operates outside (and inside) bankruptcy, and the trustee of the debtor's estate in bankruptcy, who, if the judge appoints one, runs the debtor company for the creditors. The two have the same name, but they're very different people with very different roles.

called a subordination agreement, became a central financial instrument in the 1980s and is still important: most "junk" bonds are subordinated to other creditors. The subordinated creditor agrees not to accept any payment in the event of a bankruptcy—or, occasionally, in any event—until the specified "senior" creditors are repaid.

These intercreditor relationships can complicate priority, and they also make the outcome of a valuation decision even more important. Consider this firm, which resembles the firm in ¶201, the one that owed $200 million and went bankrupt. For that firm, if X is less than $200 million, the creditors had an intuitive case that the firm belongs to them.

But now consider the possibility that the firm's $200 million in loans have inter-creditor priorities, with $100 million coming first and another $100 million coming next in priority:

Firm	
X	First: $100 million
	Second: $100 million
	Stockholders

With this capital structure, the valuation authorities need to find out more than whether X is less than $200 million. They also need to find out how much less. If X is less than $100 million, then intuitively the firm belongs to the Firsts. If it's between $100 and $200 million, then the Firsts and the Seconds both get a piece of the bankruptcy pie.

These intercreditor arrangements can be complex. Hybrids are possible. One secured creditor can obtain the "first" mortgage in a property. Other creditors can obtain the "second" mortgage in the same property. They agree that the first mortgage holder will be paid first out of the value of the mortgaged property; the second mortgage holder will get whatever is left over. Such "second lien" loans became popular in the past decade or two. Or, one creditor can be subordinated to a particular set of loans, but not to another set. Another creditor may be subordinated to a creditor that is itself subordinated to other loans. A subordinated creditor may agree to be subordinated only in the event of a bankruptcy or other reorganization, expecting to receive payments in the interim. Other subordination agreements may be "complete": the creditor agrees not to receive a dime until the senior creditor — to which the junior creditor has subordinated itself — is paid in full.

Several other valuation and operational difficulties arise in reorganization. The property may be worth less if severed from the enterprise than if kept embedded inside it. Imagine a mortgage covering some of the track of a failed railroad system. Ripping the track out may have little value to the mortgage holder: the cost of ripping out old track may exceed the sale value of the track. And the cost to the enterprise of losing that track could be very high: the railroad may not be able to run without it. Courts then need to value the track to determine the secured creditor's and the firm's entitlements. Is the track "worth" its scrap value or its value to the running railroad? Are the financier's rights to seize the security determined solely by the contract or by the overarching bankruptcy law? Defining the limits of what secured creditors can do with their security, and determining the value of the security under such circumstances is critical in bankruptcy reorganization. Such problems justify the creation of a government apparatus to reorganize companies under a framework that may differ from what the parties—financier and borrower—agreed to in their contract.

¶ 205: Who Gets What When the Business Sours?

Posit again a company that was worth $1 billion. It borrowed $100 million, secured by a mortgage on its principal factory. It also borrowed $100 million via unsecured debt. The company fails and files for bankruptcy. The company as a whole is now worth only $150 million, and its factory could be sold for $50 million.

Who gets what in the bankruptcy?

Allocating the $150 million might at first seem straightforward: $50 million to the secured creditor for its security, leaving $50 million of the secured creditor's loan unsatisfied. This $50 million "deficiency"—the amount by which the debt exceeds the value of the collateral—is treated as unsecured debt, which generally gets paid pro rata with the rest of the debtor's unsecured debt. That is, all unsecured debt shares proportionally in the value of the debtor's remaining assets (in this case, $100 million). The $50 million deficiency and the unsecured $100 million share proportionally in the remaining $100 million of the firm's value. With $150 million of unsecured debt sharing $100 million in assets, each dollar of unsecured debt is paid two-thirds of its face value, or 66.6 cents. So the $50 million deficiency claim receives a total of $33.3 million, while the $100 million unsecured debt receives $66.6 million, as shown below.

Who Gets What?

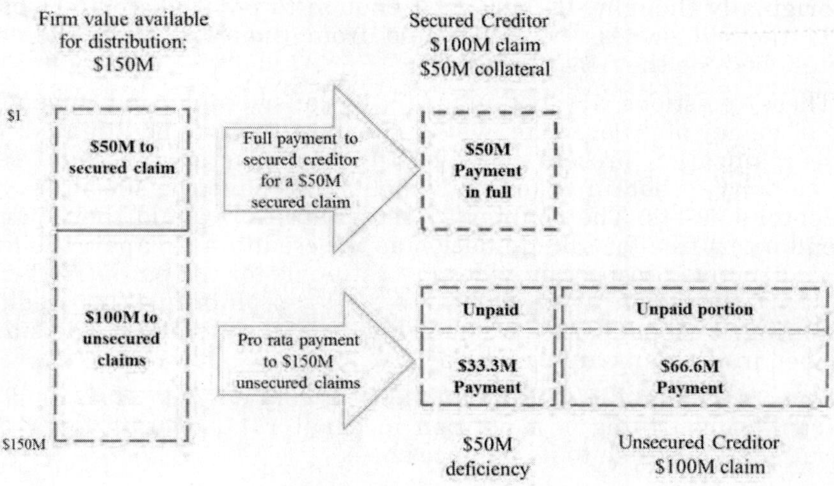

Easy. At least conceptually easy.

¶ 206: A Brief Introduction to Reorganization in Chapter 11

When the firm is unable to meet its financial obligations or owes more than it owns, it may declare bankruptcy. The form of that bankruptcy might be a liquidation, in which the business is discontinued. Its assets could be sold off, piecemeal or in separate operating units, one-by-one, if the units have some value. Although this could theoretically be accomplished by arrangement among the creditors, judicial supervision may lead to the business being liquidated in a more orderly way than creditors could negotiate on the fly. Supervision for such a liquidation occurs today primarily under chapter 7 of the Bankruptcy Code: assets are sold, the cash gathered, and then the cash is distributed to the creditors in the order of their priorities.

But in some instances, the firm, although unable to meet current financial obligations, is still worthwhile as a continuing enterprise. (Or at least that prospect of profitable continuance is a question for exploration and litigation.) The scrap value of a steel mill is low: it cannot readily be retasked to a different location or a different purpose. But once the economy pulls out of the recession, the steel company might earn a good return. Say the company owes $100 million and the mill is worth (in terms of its expected net cash flows) $50 million, but the next best use for the mill (scrap metal and real estate with an unsightly structure) is only $25 million. The preexisting $100 million debt burden is no longer supportable, but liquidation—scrapping and closing the $50 million mill—is wasteful because scrapping it would garner only $25 million.

The legal structure in which we reorganize the company is chapter 11 of the Bankruptcy Code. The firm's operations and assets are held together, neither liquidated piecemeal under judicial supervision nor dismembered by creditors trying to seize parts of the firm, but the ownership interests in the firm are reallocated. Two considerations are central: Should some of the prebankruptcy ownership interests and loans be eliminated or cut down? The firm is worth so much less than was originally thought. If there isn't enough to pay the creditors back, should the old owners be eliminated from the firm? And shouldn't creditors become the firm's owners?

These questions are not immediately answerable and, given the sums of money often at stake, we could expect them to be litigated. But the reorganization process could be thwarted if creditors could seize their security or obtain default judgments and have the sheriff levy on the debtor's assets. The chapter 11 reorganization would then quickly descend into a free-for-all liquidation as the creditors rip apart the firm. This destructive prospect provides the rationale for the bankruptcy stay (really an injunction against the creditors), prohibiting the creditors from trying to collect from the firm when it is in chapter 11. The stay is described in the Bankruptcy Code, § 362.

The stay is automatic, quite broad, and very effective. It is as if the firm could, upon filing of a petition in chapter 11, operate for a time without a liability side to its balance sheet.

§ 362. Automatic stay

(a) [A bankruptcy petition] operates as a stay, applicable to all entities, of—

(1) the commencement or continuation, including the issuance or employment of process, of a judicial, administrative, or other action or proceeding against the debtor that was or could have been commenced before the commencement of the case under this title, or to recover a claim against the debtor that arose before the commencement of the case under this title;

(2) the enforcement, against the debtor or against property of the estate, of a judgment obtained before the commencement of the case under this title;

(3) any act to obtain possession of property of the estate . . . or to exercise control over property of the estate;

(4) any act to create, perfect, or enforce any lien[2] against property of the estate;

(5) any act to create, perfect, or enforce against property of the debtor any lien to the extent that such lien secures a claim that arose before the commencement of the case under this title;

(6) any act to collect, assess, or recover a claim against the debtor that arose before the commencement of the case under this title;

(7) the setoff of any debt owing to the debtor that arose before the commencement of the case under this title against any claim against the debtor; and

(8) the commencement or continuation of a proceeding before the United States Tax Court concerning a tax liability of a debtor that is a corporation. . . .

¶ 207: Christopher S. Sontchi,* *Valuation Methodologies: A Judge's View*, 20 American Bankruptcy Institute Law Review, Spring 2012, at 1–2

At heart, chapter 11 is a simple exercise. In bankruptcy parlance, it is to gather the property of the estate, determine the amount and nature of the claims; and confirm a plan of reorganization that distributes the property of the estate to the creditors in accordance with the requirements of the Bankruptcy Code. Inherent in this process is determining the value of the property of the estate and the claims. Understanding the methodologies used to determine value is critical for any attorney or judge in this field. The goal of this article is to provide the reader with a basic understanding of the methodologies used to value an asset.

What is the value of an asset or a firm? The standard definition is that the value of an asset is its material or monetary worth, i.e., "the amount of money, goods, etc., for which a thing can be exchanged or traded." Of course, the easiest and most accurate way to determine the

---

[2] [A lien is the claim that a creditor asserts against specific property.—Roe & Tung.]

* United States Bankruptcy Judge for the District of Delaware.

amount of money for which an asset can be exchanged is to do just that—exchange the asset for money or, put more plainly, sell it. When one does not wish to sell the asset or simply cannot do so it becomes more difficult to determine the asset's value. Nonetheless, in determining an asset's value the ultimate goal remains the same—to determine as accurately as possible what the sale price would be.

The most obvious method for estimating an asset's potential sale price is to consult the current market price for that asset. Of course, not all assets can be readily bought and sold in a market. For example, while there is a ready market for trading in bushels of wheat there is no such market for wheat farms (if for no other reason that each farm is unique) such that one could consult a market price to determine the farm's value. Even when there is a market it may not fairly estimate the potential sale price of an asset if the market is inefficient, disrupted or dysfunctional.

Financial academics and professionals have established a variety of methodologies to determine the value of assets that are not readily valued by reference to a market. Broadly speaking, a firm, its assets and/or its equity can be valued in one of [three basic] ways: (i) asset-based valuation where one estimates the value of a firm by determining the current value of its assets, (ii) discounted cash flow or "DCF" valuation where one discounts cash flows to arrive at a value of the firm or its equity, [and] (iii) relative valuation approaches, which include the "comparable company analysis" and the "comparable transaction analysis" that base value on how comparable assets are priced . . . . [A]ll of these valuation methodologies, either individually or in various combinations, are routinely presented to bankruptcy courts in valuation hearings. No matter which methodology is used, however, the purpose remains the same—to determine as accurately as possible what the sale price would be, which is referred to as "price discovery."

¶ 208: Winners and Losers

Who wins and who loses in chapter 11? The initial answer will turn on how much the firm is worth. The more value there is in the firm, the further down the capital structure pecking order can value be distributed.

The distributional question will depend on estimates of the future cash flows of the debtor and which valuation story the judge accepts. That is why we must master the basic concepts of present value and why we will examine the valuation proceedings in one bankruptcy proceeding.

¶ 209: The Limits of Judicial Expertise: Reliance on the Parties?

The bankruptcy judge will not ordinarily be an expert at valuation techniques. Judges are not usually trained for valuation; financiers are. Like good business lawyers, bankruptcy judges know valuation fundamentals, but not every nuance.

The expertise problem is deeper than a question of technical expertise. Since valuation is a guess about future states of the economy, future prices of the company's product, and future costs of the company's production, even a good business lawyer's knowledge of the tools for valuation (discounting, variance, diversification, etc.) may not be enough. Knowledge or a feel for the particular industry and sometimes the particular company is required.

Financial analysts will themselves come up with differing valuation figures. The economic analysts at Merrill Lynch might tell the industry analyst to assume a 2% growth rate in the gross national product. The economists at Goldman Sachs might be more optimistic and assume a 3% growth rate. Merrill Lynch's oil analyst could conclude oil will be at $100 per barrel next year, while Goldman's projects $50 per barrel. These differences would lead Goldman (or its client) to buy the oil property from Merrill Lynch's client. Usually we have no need for a judicial second guess; in a market economy, the project goes to the higher bidder.

And, there is a problem with judicial valuation that lies deeper. Because the judge has no financial stake in her valuation, she might more easily make a mistake or let nonfinancial considerations infect the valuation determination.

Could the court effectively use experts? That is, could the court rely on the parties to produce experts who will present the relevant valuation data? Consider the district court opinion in In re New York, New Haven and Hartford RR, 4 Bankr. 758 (D. Conn. 1980). Consider the experts' testimony, as reported, and their incentives.

¶ 210: In re New York, New Haven and Hartford RR Co., 4 Bankr. 758 (D. Conn. 1980) (Zampano, J.)

[The New Haven Railroad went bankrupt in 1961 and was later absorbed into Penn Central. Years later, at the time of confirmation of the New Haven plan of reorganization, the principal issue for resolution in the plan of reorganization was the value of the New Haven Railroad.]
. . .

A. THE PARTIES' VALUATION OF THE NEW HAVEN ESTATE

A valuation of the assets of the New Haven is a necessary prerequisite to the design of a fair and equitable plan of reorganization for the enterprise. Once that valuation is ascertained, it is then translated into a new set of securities of the reorganized New Haven which, in turn, is distributed to creditors in accordance with the absolute priority rule. As Collier [the long-standard bankruptcy treatise] explains:

> If the court is to pass upon the proposed distribution of the debtor's assets, the classes of creditors and stockholders to be granted participation, the allocation of new securities or other compensation, the allocation of voting control, and the like, as well as upon the soundness of the proposed capital structure of the rehabilitated enterprise with regard to its ability to meet future charges and to furnish an adequate return to creditors, *the court obviously must have before it a complete and reliable evaluation of the debtor's assets.* Absent the requisite valuation data, the court is in no position to exercise the informed judgment required of it in assessing

the fairness, equity and feasibility of a plan, either upon approval or confirmation thereof.

6A Collier on Bankruptcy, P11.05 at 184–85 (1977); see also Consolidated Rock, [312 U.S. 510, 524 (1941),] (a determination of the value of the debtor's assets is required . . . to determine an appropriate allocation of new securities between bondholders and stockholders).

The main controversy in this case . . . [is the] valu[e of] the assets of the New Haven. . . . *The parties urge acceptance of the valuation procedures for th[ose] securities* which best conform to their views of the applicable law and *which, coincidentally, establish the most favorable standing with respect to their own cause.* In support of their positions, the parties have submitted considerable evidence by way of affidavits, expert testimony, exhibits, moving papers, and briefs. *Each of the varied and conflicting opinions of the experts was the subject of extensive and, at times, exhaustive cross-examination; hardly a material representation on valuation submitted by one party went unchallenged by another party. The voluminous record in the proceedings speaks eloquently of the tireless efforts of counsel on behalf of their clients.*[3]

The Trustee's Methodology

The trustee contends that, for reorganization purposes, the Court is required to measure the worth of the New Haven by evaluating its earning power as a going concern. Under this methodology, the securities held by the New Haven must be appraised by estimating their "intrinsic" or "reorganization" value, rather than by reference to their current market value. . . .

* * *

Utilizing the intrinsic value concept . . . , the trustee concludes that, with the cash on hand, the value of the New Haven estate for reorganization purposes is within a range of $120 million to $150 million, and that the value of the equity of the reorganized New Haven is commensurate with this value. At the high end, this valuation would provide compensation to the First Mortgage Bondholders to the full extent of their claim, as computed by the trustee, i.e., approximately $135.7 million ($76,819,900 in principal plus $58,895,251 in interest to date), as well as affording a present equity in the estate for the Income Bondholders. In practical effect, the Amended Plan affords the First Mortgage Bondholders 93.1%, and the Income Bondholders 6.9%, of the reorganized New Haven.

* * *

The First Mortgage Bondholders' Methodology

In marked contrast to the trustee's position, the basic argument of the First Mortgage Bondholders is that fair market value [is much less.]

* * *

[Based on market value, the First Mortgage Bondholders' expert testified that the New Haven Railroad was worth $71 million.]

---

[3] [Emphasis supplied here and elsewhere, typically without our notations.—Roe & Tung.]

* * *

The Income Bondholders' Methodology

The Income Bondholders [expert] . . . testified that in his view the reorganization value of the New Haven is in the range of $174.5 million to $246 million, that the trustee's Amended Plan was not fair and equitable, and that the Income Bondholders' proposed plan of reorganization was the only one feasible and equitable.

B. THE COURT'S RULINGS ON VALUATION

The disputed issues of fact and law relating to the applicable methodology for the valuation of the assets of the New Haven have been fully litigated in a trial on the merits. *The validity of every opinion expressed on the subject was contested to the minutest detail.*[4] After a careful review and consideration of the extensive evidence and voluminous briefs, the Court is of the opinion that no party's valuation procedures can be accepted in toto as the basis for a fair, equitable and feasible plan of reorganization.

* * *

In the instant case, the Court finds that the market in general is somewhat unsettled because of the social, political, and economic stresses current on the domestic and international scenes. Yet, it is neither in disarray nor in a panic state which in and of itself would warrant a rejection of the investors' perceptions of the value of securities . . . .

Use of a substitute "reorganization value" [instead of the market value of the firm's assets] may under the circumstances be the only fair means of determining the value of the securities distributed.

In addition, it is reasonable to assume that much more time is necessary for the marketplace to absorb, digest and react rationally to the available information concerning the [underlying railroad's] Asset Disposition Program . . . and the complex capital structure of the Penn Central with its tiers of securities, cascades, lien priorities and the utilization of tax losses.

[The court then valued New Haven as worth $150 million.]

¶ 211: The Implications of Valuation

1. How does valuation of the firm in reorganization determine who gets what? Imagine that the New Haven Railroad will be recapitalized with 100 shares of common stock and no debt. These 100 shares of common stock therefore represent the entire value of the railroad. Suppose further that this common stock of the reorganized railroad is the only currency to be used to pay the railroad's prebankruptcy creditors, who will be paid in priority order. Because the First Mortgage Bondholders are secured, their claims are paid prior to the claims of Income Bondholders, as long as the

[4] [Emphasis supplied.—Roe & Tung.]

mortgaged property is worth enough to cover the Firsts' claims. That is, Mortgage Bondholders are entitled to be paid in full out of the value of the mortgaged properties before Income Bondholders receive anything.

If the judge values the railroad at $71 million, as the First Mortgage Bondholders contended was proper, how would the shares of stock be divided? (How much were the First Mortgage Bondholders owed?)

Judge values RR at 71M	Firsts get: ___ shares	Seconds get: ___ shares
If true value is 71M, then . . .	Value of Firsts' stock is:	Value of Seconds' stock is:
If true value is 246M, then . . .	Value of Firsts' stock is:	Value of Seconds' stock is:
Judge values RR at 246M	Firsts get: ___ shares	Seconds get: ___ shares
If true value is only 71M, then . . .	Value of Firsts' stock is:	Value of Seconds' stock is:
If true value is 246M, then . . .	Value of Firsts' stock is:	Value of Seconds' stock is:

If the judge values the railroad at $246 million, as the Income Bondholders contended was proper, how would the shares of stock be divided? The First Mortgages Bondholders are senior to the Income Bondholders.

The judge concluded that the railroad was worth $150 million. How would a new 100–share capital structure be divided up?

2. The judge noted that the players in the New Haven Railroad reorganization contested "the validity of every opinion expressed on the subject . . . to the minutest detail." See italicized text on p. 23. Why did the parties fight so vociferously over the railroad's valuation, a number that is just the judge's opinion of the railroad's value, one that need not be the real value of the railroad and often is not?

3. Is valuation solely a matter of concern as it determines the allocation of the bankruptcy pie? How does (or could) valuation determine the operational decision of whether to liquidate or reorganize the firm? Must the bankruptcy system explicitly or implicitly find the value of the firm if liquidated, find the value if reorganized, and then compare the two?

4. To answer these questions well, to represent clients well in a bankruptcy, to judge a bankruptcy well, and to evaluate the success of a reorganization system, the lawyer will have to understand the basic techniques of valuation.

B. HOW BANKRUPTCY CAN ENHANCE VALUE

Bankruptcy, when done well, can enhance the value of the firm. In the language of social science, bankruptcy can be said to solve, or at least reduce, a "common pool" problem among creditors.

¶ 212: The Common Pool Problem in General

The creditors' and stockholders' scrambling for position in reorganization (and the resulting deterioration of the firm as managers' time is diverted and relations with suppliers and customers deteriorate) can be analogized to what economists call a "common pool" problem. When there's a common pool, people may overuse the pool, to the detriment of everyone. Each person deciding whether to use the pool could rationally calculate that their own benefits exceed their own costs, because others bear most of the costs. X pollutes the stream, although X lives next to the stream. The full costs of X's pollution are borne by X, Y, and Z. If the convenience to X of polluting exceeds 1/3 of the costs of the pollution (the share of the pollution that X absorbs), then X has an incentive to pollute despite the fact that it's socially wasteful. So do Y and Z.

The idea, when applied to bankruptcy, is that when creditors pursue their individual remedies, they may destroy common value in a going concern. To preserve that common value—often called going concern value in the bankruptcy vocabulary—they either need a framework via which they can negotiate a deal among them all or have a resulted imposed on them. The excerpt below elaborates.

Bankruptcy as a Common Pool Problem: Thomas H. Jackson, The Logic and Limits of Bankruptcy Law 10–19 (1986)[5]

* * *

The basic problem that bankruptcy law is designed to handle, both as a normative matter and as a positive matter, is that the system of individual creditor remedies may be bad for the creditors *as a group* when there are not enough assets to go around. Because creditors have conflicting rights, there is a tendency in their debt-collection efforts to make a bad situation worse. Bankruptcy law responds to this problem. . . . [One way to characterize the problem] is as a species of what is called a *common pool* problem. . . . [6]

---

[5] Reprinted by permission of the publisher from The Logic And Limits of Bankruptcy Law by Thomas H. Jackson, Cambridge, Mass.: Harvard University Press, Copyright 1986 by the President and Fellows of Harvard College.

[6] See Hardin, "The Tragedy of the Commons," 162 Science 1243 (1968): Libecap & Wiggins, "Contractual Responses to the Common Pool: Prorationing of Crude Oil Production," 74 Am. Econ. Rev. 87 (1984). . . .

This role of bankruptcy law is largely unquestioned. . . . [I]t is worth considering the basics of the problem so that we understand its essential features before examining whether and why credit may present that problem. The vehicle will be a typical, albeit simple, common pool example. Imagine that you own a lake. There are fish in the lake. You are the only one who has the right to fish in that lake, and no one constrains your decision as to how much fishing to do. You have it in your power to catch all the fish this year and sell them for, say, $100,000. If you did that, however, there would be no fish in the lake next year. It might be better for you—you might maximize your total return from fishing—if you caught and sold some fish this year but left other fish in the lake so that they could multiply and you would have fish in subsequent years. Assume that, by taking this approach, you could earn (adjusting for inflation) $50,000 each year. Having this outcome is like having a perpetual annuity paying $50,000 a year. It has a present value of perhaps $500,000. Since (obviously, I hope) when all other things are equal, $500,000 is better than $100,000, you as sole owner, would limit your fishing this year unless some other factor influenced you.

But what if you are not the only one who can fish in this lake? What if a hundred people can do so? The optimal solution has not changed: it would be preferable to leave some fish in the lake to multiply because doing so has a present value of $500,000. But in this case, unlike that where you have to control only yourself, an obstacle exists in achieving that result. If there are a hundred fishermen, you cannot be sure, by limiting your fishing, that there will be any more fish next year, unless you can also control the others. You may, then, have an incentive to catch as many fish as you can today because maximizing your take this year (catching, on average, $1,000 worth of fish) is better for you than holding off (catching, say only $500 worth of fish this year) while others scramble and deplete the stock entirely.[7] If you hold off, your aggregate return is only $500, since nothing will be left for next year or the year after. But that sort of reasoning by each of the hundred fishermen will mean that the stock of fish will be gone by the end of the first season. The fishermen will split $100,000 this year, but there will be no fish—and no money—in future years. Self-interest results in their splitting $100,000, not $500,000.

What is required is some rule that will make all hundred fishermen act as a sole owner would. That is where bankruptcy law enters the picture in a world not of fish but of credit. The grab rules of nonbankruptcy law and their allocation of assets on the basis of first-come, first-served create an incentive on the part of the individual creditors, when they sense that a debtor may have more liabilities than assets, to get in line today (by, for example, getting a sheriff to execute on the debtor's equipment), because if they do not, they run the risk of getting nothing. This decision by numerous individual creditors, however, may be the wrong decision for the creditors as a group. Even though the debtor is insolvent, they might be better off if they held the assets together. Bankruptcy provides a way to make these diverse individuals act as one, by imposing a *collective* and *compulsory*

---

[7] . . . [T]his [example] assumes that you are selfish, not altruistic. . . .

proceeding on them. Unlike a typical common pool solution, however, the compulsory solution of bankruptcy law does not apply in all places at all times. Instead, it runs parallel with a system of individual debt-collection rules and is available to supplant them when and if needed.

. . . Exactly how does bankruptcy law make creditors as a group better off? To find the answer to that question, consider a simple hypothetical example involving credit, not fish. Debtor has a small printing business. At the point of insolvency. . . the business is expected to be worth $50,000 if sold piecemeal. Creditors also know that each of them will have to spend $1,000 in pursuit of their individual collection efforts should Debtor become insolvent and fail to repay them. Under these circumstances Debtor borrow[ed] $25,000 from each of four creditors, Creditors 1 through 4. . . .

If the creditors have to protect themselves by means of a costly and inefficient system, [with costly individual action,] Debtor is going to have to pay more to obtain credit. Thus, when we consider them all together—Creditors 1 through 4 and Debtor—the relevant question is: would the availability of a bankruptcy system reduce the costs of credit?

* * *

. . . [First] the case for bankruptcy's advantages. The common pool example of fish in a lake suggests that one of the advantages to a collective system is a larger aggregate pie. Does that advantage exist in the case of credit? When dealing with businesses, the answer, at least some of the time, would seem to be "yes." The use of individual creditor remedies may lead to a piecemeal dismantling of a debtor's business by the untimely removal of necessary operating assets. To the extent that a non-piecemeal collective process (whether in the form of a liquidation or reorganization) is likely to increase the aggregate value of the pool of assets, its substitution for individual remedies would be advantageous to the creditors as a group. This is derived from a commonplace notion: that a collection of assets is sometimes more valuable together than the same assets would be if spread to the winds. It is often referred to as the surplus of a going-concern value over a liquidation value.

Thus, the most obvious reason for a collective system of creditor collection is to make sure that creditors, in pursuing their individual remedies, do not actually decrease the aggregate value of the assets that will be used to repay them. In our example this situation would occur when a printing press, for example, could be sold to a third party for $20,000, leaving $30,000 of other assets, but the business as a unit could generate sufficient cash so as to have a value of more than $50,000. As such it is directly analogous to the case of the fish in the lake. Even in the case in which the assets should be sold and the business dismembered, the aggregate value of the assets may be increased by keeping groups of those assets together (the printing press with its custom dies, for example) to be sold as a discrete unit.

This advantage, however, is not the only one to be derived from a collective system for creditors. Consider what the creditors would get if there were no bankruptcy system (putting aside the ultimate collection costs). Without a collective system all of the creditors in our example know that in the case of Debtor's insolvency the first two creditors to get to (and through) the courthouse (or to Debtor, to persuade Debtor to pay voluntarily), will get $25,000 [each], leaving nothing for the third and fourth. . . . A collective system, however, would ensure that they would each get $12,500.

* * *

One other possible advantage of a collective proceeding should also be noted: there may be costs to the individualized approach to collecting (in addition to the $1,000 collection costs). For example, since each creditor [would] know [that, absent bankruptcy] it must "beat out" the others if it wants to be paid in full, it will spend time monitoring Debtor and the other creditors to make sure that it will be no worse than second in the race (and therefore still be paid in full). Although some of these activities may be beneficial, many may not be; they will simply be costs of racing against other creditors. . . . Each creditor has to spend this money just to stay in the race because if it does not, it is a virtual certainty that the others will beat it to the payment punch. . . .

* * *

. . . The single most fruitful way to think about bankruptcy is to see it as ameliorating a common pool problem created by a system of individual creditor remedies. Bankruptcy provides a way to override the creditors' pursuit of their own remedies and to make them work together.[8]

This approach immediately suggests several features of bankruptcy law. First, such a law must usurp individual creditor remedies in order to make the claimants act in an altruistic and cooperative way. Thus, the proceeding is inherently *collective*. Moreover, this system works only if all the creditors are bound to it. To allow a debtor to contract with a creditor to avoid participating in the bankruptcy proceeding would destroy the advantages of a collective system. So the proceeding must be compulsory as well. But unlike common pool solutions in oil and gas or fishing, it is not the exclusive system for dividing up assets. It, instead, supplants an existing system of individual creditor remedies, and as we shall see, it is this feature that makes crucial an awareness of its limitations.

* * *

[8] As such, it reflects the kind of contract that creditors would agree to if they were able to negotiate with each other before extending credit. . . .

CHAPTER 3

PRIORITY

A. THE CONCEPT: ABSOLUTE PRIORITY

¶ 301: Contractual Priorities in Reorganization

The ordering of liabilities in reorganization will now command our attention. In general, priorities in bankruptcy track creditors' contractual priorities arranged outside of bankruptcy. However, Chapter 11 adds a negotiation framework through which creditors and the debtor bargain over a plan of reorganization. Creditors may consent to receiving less in reorganization than their strict priority entitlements, but absent consent, each creditor class is entitled to "absolute" priority treatment (explained below). When creditor consent and/or absolute priority requirements are met, along with a number of other important constraints, the judge may "confirm" (approve) a plan of reorganization, which then becomes the blueprint for the debtor's emergence from bankruptcy.

To understand this interplay of priority entitlements with creditor consent, we have statutory intricacies to master. Upon doing so, we shall again see that the distribution to creditors in reorganization importantly depends on the value assigned to the firm in reorganization. With that value in mind, lawyers can advise clients on what to expect in reorganization, thereby facilitating a quick reorganization settlement. However, if the value assigned in reorganization is unpredictable (because courts will not use objective measures or because objective measures, like the market, are highly mutable during the year or two of a typical chapter 11 proceeding), then the players will find it harder to settle than if value were fixed and certain. From a public policy perspective, we might ask whether a framework can be designed to achieve quick corporate reorganization settlements.

From a more practical perspective, some financiers will seek priority in position when they lend. This priority position would aid them in any subsequent collection efforts should the borrower encounter financial distress (whether the firm enters a bankruptcy proceeding or not). Other financiers will accept lower priority if compensated for the added risk. Contractual mechanisms exist to set priorities among competing creditors. In this Chapter, we focus primarily on the two most common devices: contractual subordination and security interests.[1]

The mechanisms of contract formation and acquisition of a secured position are subjects for other courses in law school. What will concern us in this Chapter is how bankruptcy treats properly formed subordination contracts and security interests. Again, the effects of these arrangements on priority in bankruptcy generally track priority rules outside of bankruptcy, which are typically a matter of state law. These prebankruptcy arrangements therefore demand our attention. Their treatment in bankruptcy is at the core of the legal framework for corporate reorganization.

¶ 302: The Setting of Reorganization

Although we will be primarily concerned in the next few chapters with priority, valuation, and the core requirements of plan confirmation, we should be aware of the typical chronological sequence of a chapter 11 reorganization.

First, the debtor files its petition with the bankruptcy court, and the Bankruptcy Code's automatic stay (§ 362) enjoins all attempts to collect from the debtor. No creditor can sue, seize collateral, continue a lawsuit, levy on a judgment, or even demand repayment.

For large companies, the company's prebankruptcy management almost invariably initially continues as the management of the firm in bankruptcy.[2] The bankrupt entity is called a debtor-in-possession (DIP). Occasionally but rarely, creditors do seek to oust management and

[1] Subsequent chapters will address other private priority-setting devices, including the negative pledge clause and structural subordination through incorporation of subsidiaries, as well as the court-created doctrines of equitable subordination and substantive consolidation.

[2] While the statute does not require a change in management, managerial turnover is frequent, sometimes before the bankruptcy, and often after the filing. By the time the judge confirms a plan of reorganization, the debtor is more likely than not going to have a new team of managers.

appoint a trustee under § 1104 ("for cause, including fraud, dishonesty, incompetence, or gross mismanagement of the . . . debtor by current management . . . [or] if such appointment is in the interests of creditors"). But this is rare.

Many bankrupt companies need financing for ongoing operations. The *new* post-petition lender usually gets a superpriority above prebankruptcy lenders.

Meanwhile, the prebankruptcy lenders are unhappy with the bankruptcy stay. Secured creditors often ask the court to lift the stay, so they can foreclose on their collateral. In order for the stay to remain in place—and for the secured creditor's collateral to remain in the bankruptcy estate under the debtor's control—the debtor must provide the secured creditors with "adequate protection" of their security interests (§ 362(d)). That is, the secured creditor must be protected from any deterioration in the value of its collateral while the debtor retains the collateral for its reorganization efforts. Adequate protection typically comes in the form of periodic cash payments. Sometimes the secured property produces cash, which could be subject to a creditor's lien (which makes this cash "cash collateral"). The debtor often would like to use this cash during the reorganization and usually asks the court to find some other adequate protection for the secured creditor.

While the stay, new debtor-in-possession financing, and fights over the disposition of cash collateral are going on, a creditors' committee is appointed, usually of the seven largest creditors of the debtor. Negotiations for a plan of reorganization begin. For the first four months of the case, the debtor enjoys the exclusive right to propose a plan. Typically bankruptcy judges extend this period of exclusivity, at times in the 1980s and 1990s for years.[3] This agenda control gives the debtor some leverage in getting its favored result.

Some operations are closed, some sold, some continued. Managers of the debtor-in-possession—can make all "ordinary course" decisions for the business. But the court must approve out-of-the-ordinary-course decisions.

Eventually a plan is proposed and confirmed by the court.

B. THE STATUTE TODAY: BASICS

¶ 303: Statement by the Hon. Dennis DeConcini, Chairman of the Subcommittee on Improvements in Judicial Machinery . . . , Upon Introducing the Senate Amendment to the House Amendment to H.R. 8200, 124 Congressional Record S 17406 (Oct. 6, 1978)

The record of [our] hearings . . . is replete with evidence of the failure of the reorganization provisions of the existing Bankruptcy Act

[3] The 1994 bankruptcy amendments sought to keep the period of incumbent management's monopoly over proposing a plan shorter. The 2005 amendments sought to do so again.

to meet the needs of insolvent corporations in today's business environment. Chapter X was designed to impose rigid and formalized procedures upon the reorganization of corporations and, although designed to protect public creditors, has often worked to the detriment of such creditors. As the House report has noted:

> The negative results under [the old] chapter X have resulted from the stilted procedures, under which [1] management is always ousted and replaced by an independent trustee, [2] the courts and the Securities and Exchange Commission examine the plan of reorganization in great detail, no matter how long that takes, and [3] the court values the business, a time consuming and inherently uncertain procedure.

* * *

The primary problem posed by chapter X is delay. The modern corporation is a complex and multifaceted entity. . . . Over and over again, it is demonstrated that corporations which must avail themselves of the provisions of the Bankruptcy Act suffer appreciable deterioration if they are caught in a chapter X proceeding for any substantial period of time.

* * *

One cannot overemphasize the advantages of speed and simplicity to both creditors and debtors. . . .

. . . [C]hapter X has been far from a success. Of the 991 chapter X cases filed during the period of January 1, 1967, through December 31, 1977, only 664 have been terminated. Of those cases recorded as "terminated," only 140 resulted in consummated plans. This 21 percent success rate suggests one of the reasons for the unpopularity of chapter X.

¶ 304: Absolute Priority and Consent: The 1978 Bankruptcy Code Changes

From 1938 onward, with the passage of the Bankruptcy Act and follow-on Supreme Court decisions—often written by Justice William O. Douglas in the few years after 1938—the reorganization of a public company required a judicial valuation, typically done with an advisory opinion from the Securities and Exchange Commission. Judicial valuation was required under the 1938 Act in order to assure that the bankruptcy distribution followed strict absolute priority: junior claimants could take nothing until senior claimants had been paid in full.

But by the 1970s, this process—particularly the mandated judicial valuation—was seen as time consuming and inaccurate, in need of updating and upgrading. Congress sought a way to reorganize in bankruptcy without a mandated valuation hearing. Congress passed a new Bankruptcy Code in 1978, with its major corporate reorganization reform being to rely on creditor consent in place of a mandated judicial valuation and inquiry into whether absolute priority had been adhered to. If creditor classes approved a proposed bankruptcy distribution, then no formal judicial valuation was required under the new statute.

(Creditors also voted under the 1938 Act, but creditor approval was an independent requirement from judicial valuation and scrutiny for adherence to absolute priority; until 1978, creditor approval did not obviate the Act's required judicial valuation.)

The unhappiness with Douglas's system led Congress to set up a Bankruptcy Commission, which reported back to Congress in Report of the Commission on the Bankruptcy Laws of the United States, House Doc. 93–137, 93d Cong., 1st Sess 257 (1973):

> The heart of the application of the absolute priority rule is the valuation of the business. The participation of junior creditors and equity security holders depends upon the finding of a value in the business over and above that of the claims of the senior interests.
>
> * * *
>
> . . . Since valuation, which is at the heart of the absolute priority rule, is at best an educated guess, the courts and the parties (including the Securities and Exchange Commission) have considerable freedom to overcome the strait jacket of the absolute priority rule. [By] a slight change of the capitalization rate, an insolvent company in which equity security holders are denied participation becomes a solvent company in which equity security holders are entitled to an interest. [The choice of a capitalization rate might just] rationalize a predetermined result [about whom the decision-maker wanted to participate, or not participate, in the reorganization]. There is ample inducement for the trial court to choose a valuation which will eliminate controversy.
>
> . . . Courts, writhing under conflicting and plentiful testimony on valuation, may be impelled, therefore, to circumvent the spirit of the *Los Angeles Lumber* case by making generous estimates of the valuation of assets. . . . [V]aluation is so inexact a process and so much a matter of discretion. . . .

The legislative history to the Bankruptcy Code says (in H.R. Report No. 595, 95th Cong., 1st Sess. (1977)):

* * *

> The premise of the bill's financial standard for confirmation is the same as the premise of the securities law: parties should be given adequate disclosure or relevant information, and they should make their own decision on the acceptability of the proposed plan. . . . The parties are left to their own to negotiate a fair settlement. The question of whether creditors are entitled to the going-concern or liquidation value of the business is impossible to answer. It is unrealistic to assume that the bill could or even should attempt to answer that question. Instead, negotiation among the parties after full disclosure will govern how the value of

> the reorganizing company will be distributed among the creditors and stockholders. The bill only sets the outer limits on the outcome: it must be somewhere between the going-concern value and the liquidation value.
>
> Only when the parties are unable to agree on a proper distribution of the value of the company does the bill establish a financial standard. If the debtor is unable to obtain the consents of all classes of creditors and stockholders, then the court may confirm the plan anyway on request of the plan's proponent, if the plan treats the nonconsenting classes fairly. . . . [T]he bill permits senior classes to take less than full payment, in order to expedite or insure the success of the reorganization.

¶ 305: Absolute Priority Today: Understanding § 1129(a)(8)

Under the Bankruptcy Code, enacted in 1978, the court need not determine that the plan follows absolute priority—a determination that will typically require the judge to assign a value to the debtor—as long as the creditors consent to the proposed plan. Put differently, creditors (or some of them) can demand a valuation and ruling on absolute priority by voting against the proposed plan. But if creditors can make a deal among themselves, the judge will not second-guess them.

While this concept of creditor consent obviating the requirement for a valuation makes conceptual and policy sense, its application is not straightforward. The central consent provision is in § 1129(a)(8), but its apparent simplicity is belied by the fact that it is laden with specialized terms defined elsewhere in the Code, and that there is a major alternative to § 1129(a)(8)'s consent, namely § 1129(b).

To get some of the definitional flavor, consider the following questions while studying the statute: What is a "class" of claims or interests? It's their consent that counts under 1129(a)(8). Why is the concept of class consent important? Cf. § 1122, 1126(c). How does a class consent to a plan of reorganization? When is a class impaired and when is it not impaired under the plan? See § 1124. If a creditor class does not accept the plan, what recourse does it have? Can it insist on absolute priority? See § 1129(b), which introduces two seemingly open-ended terms, "fair and equitable" and "unfair discrimination." What do those terms mean?

¶ 306: Core Reorganization Statutory Provisions

One way to read a statute is to read it straight through, from start to finish. A better way for us to read the bankruptcy statute is to start with § 1129(a)(8) and then see how other sections give content to the key terms that § 1129(a)(8) uses—acceptance and nonimpairment, in particular—and how other sections act as alternatives to (a)(8). Perhaps an even better way to read the core priority terms of the Code is to read them against a set of (seemingly) simple problems, such as those in ¶307. Here are the core statutes.

---

§ 1129. Confirmation of plan

(a) The court shall confirm a plan only if all of the following requirements are met:

* * *

(3) The plan has been proposed in good faith and not by any means forbidden by law.

* * *

(8) With respect to each class of claims or interests—

(A) such class has accepted the plan; or

(B) such class is not impaired under the plan.[4]

* * *

(10) If a class of claims is impaired under the plan, at least one class of claims that is impaired under the plan has accepted the plan, determined without including any acceptance of the plan by any insider.

(11) Confirmation of the plan is not likely to be followed by the liquidation, or the need for further financial reorganization, of the debtor or any successor to the debtor under the plan, unless such liquidation or reorganization is proposed in the plan.

(b) (1) . . . if all of the applicable requirements of subsection (a) of this section other than paragraph (8) are met with respect to a plan, the court, on request of the proponent of the plan, shall confirm the plan notwithstanding the requirements of such paragraph if the plan does not discriminate unfairly,[5] and is fair and equitable,[6] with respect to each class of claims or interests that is impaired under, and has not accepted, the plan.

(2) For the purpose of this subsection, the condition that a plan be fair and equitable with respect to a class includes the following requirements:

* * *

(B) With respect to a class of unsecured[7] claims—

(i) the plan provides that each holder of a claim of such class receive or retain on account of such claim property of a value, as of the effective date of the plan, equal to the allowed amount of such claim; or

---

[4] [Acceptance is defined in § 1126. A definition of impairment is in § 1124. An alternative to compliance with § 1129(a)(8) is in § 1129(b).

[Section 1122(a) requires that claims in a single class be substantially similar and § 1123(a)(4) requires that the claims in a single class be treated equally, unless any poorly-treated claimants agree. The court in In re Dow Corning Corp., 244 B.R. 634 (Bankr. E.D. Mich. 1999), stated that "substantially similar claims may not be classified separately when it is done for an illegitimate reason."]

[5] [Unfair discrimination is exemplified, although not defined, in the legislative history to the Code, reproduced in ¶ 309.]

[6] [Fair and equitable is defined in § 1129(b)(2).]

[7] [Subsection (A) sets out the conditions that the plan be fair and equitable to secured creditors. We examine this subsection below, in ¶314, at p. 55.]

(ii) the holder of any claim or interest that is junior to the claims of such class will not receive or retain under the plan on account of such junior claim or interest any property. . . .

§ 1124. Impairment of claims or interests

[Unless a holder of a claim or interest agrees to less favorable treatment] a class of claims or interests is impaired under a plan unless, with respect to each claim or interest of such class, the plan [either]—

(1) leaves unaltered the legal, equitable, and contractual rights to which such claim or interest entitles the holder of such claim or interest; or

(2) notwithstanding any contractual provision or applicable law that entitles the holder of such claim or interest to demand or receive accelerated payment of such claim or interest after the occurrence of a default—

(A) cures any such default that occurred before or after the commencement of the case under this title, other than a default of a kind specified in section 365(b)(2) of this title . . . ; [and][8]

(B) reinstates the maturity of such claim or interest as such maturity existed before such default; [and]

(C) compensates the holder of such claim or interest for any damages incurred as a result of any reasonable reliance by such holder on such contractual provision or such applicable law; [and]

(D) if such claim or such interest arises from any failure to perform a nonmonetary obligation . . . , compensates the holder of such claim or such interest . . . for any actual pecuniary loss incurred by such holder as a result of such failure; and

(E) does not *otherwise* alter the legal, equitable, or contractual rights to which such claim or interest entitles the holder of such claim or interest.

§ 1126. Acceptance of plan

(c) A class of claims has accepted a plan if such plan has been accepted by creditors . . . that hold at least two-thirds in amount and more than one-half in number of the allowed claims of such class held by creditors. . . [that vote].

* * *

(f) Notwithstanding any other provision of this section, a class that is not impaired under a plan, and each holder of a claim or interest of such class, are conclusively presumed to have accepted the plan, and solicitation of acceptances with respect to such class from the holders of claims or interests of such class is not required.

(g) Notwithstanding any other provision of this section, a class is deemed not to have accepted a plan if such plan provides that the claims or

[8] [Section 365(b)(2) lists these items: (A) the insolvency or financial condition of the debtor at any time before the closing of the case; (B) the commencement of a case under this title; [or] (C) the appointment of . . . a trustee in a case under this title. . . .]

interests of such class do not entitle the holders of such claims or interests to receive or retain any property under the plan on account of such claims or interests.

¶ 307: Absolute Priority and Consent in the Code: Plan Confirmation Problem 1

Better than reading the statute cold is to work through problems. The core statutory sections needed are in ¶ 306. The critical sections are § 1129(a)(8), § 1126(c), § 1124, and § 1129(b).

A. XYZ Corp. has a capital structure of (a) $1 million of secured debt due in 10 years, (b) $1.2 million in unsecured debentures due in a few months, and (c) common stock. XYZ Corp. defaults on an interest payment to the unsecured debentureholders. They elect, through their trustee, to accelerate their debt. (How can they do this? See infra ¶ 703, the prospectus of Drum Financial Corporation under "Description of Debentures—Events of Default and Notice Thereof" at p. 149 in ¶ 703.) The debentureholders sue and obtain a judgment. XYZ Corp., not having any cash, cannot and does not pay. Under a cross-default provision in the secured creditor's indenture, the secured debt's maturity is accelerated; the secured creditor demands payment. (What is a cross-default provision? See id.) XYZ Corp., still without cash, refuses (because it has no cash). The debentureholders begin attachment proceedings on XYZ Corp.'s unsecured property. The secured creditor begins proceedings to arrange for a sheriff's sale of the property (about one-half of the property of XYZ Corp.) on which it has a lien; the proceeds of such a sale would be used to satisfy its claim.

XYZ Corp. files a bankruptcy petition. The debentureholders' and secured creditor's proceedings stop. (Why? Does any section of the Bankruptcy Code require this? See § 362.)

The company proposes the following reorganization plan:

1. The secured creditor will have her maturity reinstated and interest payments will be paid when due under the old indenture. Her lien on XYZ Corp.'s property will continue. One interest payment was missed during the reorganization proceedings. She will be paid the missed interest payment with an added premium for the delay.

2. The unsecured creditors will receive 6 annual installments of $300,000 each.

3. The common stockholders will remain as such. (XYZ Corp. is, or would be, valued at $2 million, if that is important to know.)

Assume, first, that both the secured creditor and the unsecured creditors accept the plan. What result under § 1129(a)(8)? Any valuation of the firm?

B. Same facts and plan as A, but this time the secured creditor objects to the plan. The others accept the plan. Can the court confirm the plan over the secured creditor's objection? Are all of the standards of § 1129(a) met? Does § 1124 have any bearing on whether § 1129(a)(8) is satisfied?

C. Same facts and plan as A, but this time one debentureholder (out of the 100 debentureholders in all, holding 25% of the principal amount of the voting outstanding debentures) objects. (The secured creditor and the other 99 debentureholders accept the plan.) Is § 1129(a)(8) satisfied? See § 1126.

D. Same facts and plan as A, but this time all debentureholders object. (The secured creditor accepts the plan.) Can the plan be confirmed? Does the plan comply with § 1129(a)(8)? Does § 1129(b) provide an alternative if the plan fails under § 1129(a)(8)? Is it an alternative to noncompliance with every requirement of § 1129(a), or just noncompliance with (a)(8)?

What did the balance sheet of XYZ Corp. look like? What would it look like if the plan is confirmed?

How does one calculate the present value of the six annual payments of $300,000 per year to the debentureholders? How is the present value of the payment promised important?

Even if the plan could be crammed down on the debentureholders, could the judge confirm it? Is § 1129(a)(11) relevant? What would you argue if you represented the plan proponents? If you represented the plan's opponents?

C. CONTRACTUAL PREDICATES TO CODE PRIORITY

¶ 308: Subordination

Thus far we have seen creditors come first by having security: the debtor gives the lender an interest in the debtor's property. If the debtor defaults, the secured creditor seeks to obtain the security to realize repayment of its loan.

Security is not the only way for creditors to get priority ahead of other creditors. Particularly for large, public companies, intercreditor agreements, typically called subordination agreements, can order intercreditor priority. The next reading describes subordination basics and the following materials set up several subordination priority problems.

The American Bar Foundation drafted a model sample indenture, with typical terms, and provided a commentary on these typical terms. American Bar Foundation, Corporate Debt Financing Project (1971). The following commentary comes from the Foundation's chapter on subordination provisions.

I. Introduction

Although present day subordination provisions contained in indentures are a complex of legal refinements, the underlying concept of subordination can be stated quite simply: it is the agreement by the holder of certain debt (the "subordinated debt") that the holder of certain other specified indebtedness of the same debtor (the "senior debt") will receive prior payment in full of that Senior Debt. Put another way—to illustrate the operation of subordination—in the circumstances specified in the subordination provisions, payments or distributions on the subordinated debt are turned over to the holders of senior debt for application thereon until the senior debt is paid in full. It should be emphasized that, so far as the debtor is concerned, subordinated debt is just as truly debt as is the senior debt, and, in the event of the bankruptcy of the debtor, [the debtor is obligated to repay] both subordinated debt and senior debt . . .. [But] by virtue of the subordination provisions[,] . . . the holders of the subordinated debt are not entitled to retain payments or distributions thereon and, as a practical matter, are placed in a junior position with respect to the holders of the senior debt.

* * *

[Discussion of Model Indenture Provisions]

C. Senior Debt

[The debtor and its creditors—the latter usually via the underwriter on behalf of the creditors if the subordinated debt is publicly issued—will carefully] negotiat[e] the definition of "Senior Debt," i.e., the indebtedness which is to be entitled to the benefits of the subordination. A review of currently outstanding indentures will reveal wide variations among such definitions. . . . All other things being equal, the greater the senior debt, the less attractive the subordinated debentures.

* * *

It should go without saying that a careful analysis of what is or is not included in the definition of "Senior Debt" is of paramount importance to any potential lender, senior or junior. The exact wording of the definition will determine the type and amount of senior debt which will be entitled to the benefits of the subordination.

These model indenture terms have been updated intermittently, with accompanying discussion of relevant case law, statutory law, and transactional innovations. The latest version was published in the year 2000, as Revised Model Simplified Indenture, 55 Business Lawyer 1115 (2000).

¶ 309: Trade Creditors and Unfair Discrimination: Legislative History with Examples

You'll have noticed that § 1129(b) requires that the plan both be fair and equitable (the priority standard among classes) and that the plan not discriminate unfairly (within the same priority). Section 1129(b) must be satisfied if § 1129(a)(8) is not. Thus, functionally, § 1129(b) is the third subsection of § 1129(a)(8). If subsection (A) or (B) of (a)(8) is satisfied, the court need not turn to § 1129(b) to cram down a plan on a dissenting class.

The fair and equitable concept is carefully defined in § 1129(b)(2) and normally would require a valuation hearing, unless the lower-ranking claimants and interests are wiped out. "The phrase 'fair and equitable' is not a vague exhortation to bankruptcy judges that they do the right thing; rather, it implements the so-called absolute priority rule under which an objecting class must be paid . . . in full before any claim or interest junior to it gets anything at all." In re Perez, 30 F.3d 1209, 1212 (9th Cir. 1994).

"Unfair discrimination" also turns out to be a carefully worked out concept—pro rata, equal treatment, after giving effect to side-deals. But it's left undefined in the Bankruptcy Code; instead, it's worked out by being exemplified in the Code's legislative history. For each of the five plans illustrated in the legislative history, we could fill in these numbers in the chart that follows the legislative history. Read the legislative history below and, as you do so, fill in the five charts on p. 45. Once you've done the five charts, do you see a pattern?

H.R. Rep. No. 95–595, at 415–18 (1977)

While *§ 1129(a) does not [require] valuation of the debtor's business*, such a valuation will almost always be required under § 1129(b) in order to determine the value of the consideration to be distributed under the plan. Once the valuation is performed, it becomes a simple matter to impose the criterion that no claim will be paid more than in full.

* * *

. . . [W]hen an impaired class [of unsecured claims] that has not accepted the plan is to receive less than full value under the plan . . ., the plan may be confirmed . . . if the class is not unfairly discriminated against with respect to equal classes and if junior classes will receive nothing under the plan. The second criterion is the easier to understand. It is designed to prevent a senior class from giving up consideration to a junior class unless every intermediate class consents, is paid in full, or is unimpaired. This gives intermediate creditors a great deal of leverage in negotiating with senior or secured creditors who wish to have a plan that gives value to equity. One aspect of this test that is not obvious is that whether one class is senior, equal, or junior to another class is relative and not absolute. Thus from the perspective of trade creditors holding unsecured claims, claims of senior and subordinated debentures may be entitled to share on an equal basis with the trade claims. However, from the perspective of the senior unsecured debt, the subordinated debentures are junior. This point illustrates the lack of precision in the first criterion which demands that a class not be unfairly discriminated against with respect to equal classes. From the perspective of unsecured trade claims, there is no unfair discrimination as long as the total consideration given all other classes of equal rank does not exceed the amount that would result from an exact aliquot[, fractional] distribution. [**The first plan.**] Thus if trade creditors, senior debt, and subordinated debt are each owed $100 and the plan proposes to pay the trade debt $15, the senior debt $30, and the junior debt $0, the plan would not unfairly discriminate against the trade debt nor would any other allocation of consideration under the plan between the senior and junior debt be unfair as to the trade debt as long as the aggregate consideration is less than $30. [**The second plan.**] The senior debt could take $25 and give up $5 to the junior debt and the trade debt would have no cause to complain because as far as it is concerned the junior debt is an equal class.

However, in this latter case the senior debt would have been unfairly discriminated against . . . ;[9] of course the plan would also fail unless the senior debt was unimpaired, received full value, or accepted the plan, because from its perspective a junior class received property under the plan. [**The third plan.**] Application of the test from the perspective of senior debt is best illustrated by the plan that proposes to pay trade debt $15, senior debt $25, and junior debt $0. Here the senior debt is being unfairly discriminated against with respect to the equal trade debt even though the trade debt receives less than the senior debt. The discrimination arises from the fact that the senior debt is entitled to the rights of the junior debt which in this example entitle the senior debt to share on a 2:1 basis with the trade debt.

Finally, it is necessary to interpret the first criterion from the perspective of [the] subordinated debt. The junior debt is [only junior] to the rights of senior debt [until] the senior debt is paid in full. Thus, while the **[third]** plan that pays trade debt $15, senior debt $25, and junior debt $0 is not unfairly discriminatory against the junior debt, a [**fourth**] plan that proposes to pay trade debt $55, senior debt $100, and junior debt $1 would be unfairly discriminatory. In order to avoid discriminatory treatment against the junior debt, [**under a fifth plan**] at least $10 would have to be received by such [junior] debt under those facts. The criterion of unfair discrimination is not derived from the fair and equitable rule [now found in § 1129(b)(2)] or from the best interests of creditors test [now in § 1129(a)(7)]. Rather it preserves just treatment of a dissenting class from the class's own perspective.

---

[9] [I deleted this phrase from the excerpt: "because the trade debt was being unfairly overcompensated." But isn't it the subordinated, not the trade, that was unfairly overcompensated?—Roe.]

First Plan

	Amount owed	Actual compensation under plan	Hypothetical pro rata compensation	The fair, non-discriminatory compensation
Trade				
Senior				
Subordinated				

Second Plan

	Amount owed	Actual compensation under plan	Hypothetical pro rata compensation	The fair, non-discriminatory compensation
Trade				
Senior				
Subordinated				

Third Plan

	Amount owed	Actual compensation under plan	Hypothetical pro rata compensation	The fair, non-discriminatory compensation
Trade				
Senior				
Subordinated				

Fourth Plan

	Amount owed	Actual compensation under plan	Hypothetical pro rata compensation	The fair, non-discriminatory compensation
Trade				
Senior				
Subordinated				

Fifth Plan

	Amount owed	Actual compensation under plan	Hypothetical pro rata compensation	The fair, non-discriminatory compensation
Trade				
Senior				
Subordinated				

¶ 310: Trade Creditors and Unfair Discrimination: Plan Confirmation Problem 2

The following problems allow you to work through how unfair discrimination works. Again, remember that the "fair and equitable" absolute priority standard generally covers vertical fairness among differing priorities; "unfair discrimination" generally deals with horizontal fairness among creditors with the same priority.

A. XYZ Corp. has outstanding $1 million in subordinated debentures with the same subordination provision as described in the Drum Financial Corporation prospectus (¶ 703) under "Description of Debentures—Subordination of Debentures." It has $1 million of bank debt issued under an indenture designating the bank debt as superior in right of payment to the subordinated debentures. It also has $1 million of trade debt on open account for raw materials shipped to XYZ Corp.'s plant 20 days ago. (Trade debt arises when a supplier sends the debtor supplies and expects payment after delivery.) Is the trade debt "senior" to the subordinated debentures? (I.e., does the subordination provision on p. 149 of ¶ 703 contemplate that Senior Indebtedness be anything other than financial debt?) Does the trade debt share equally and ratably with the subordinated debentures? With the senior bank debt? With the two combined?

B. XYZ Corp. goes bankrupt. Its business is valued at $990,000. What does XYZ Corp.'s balance sheet look like prior to reorganization?

C. The plan proposes that the bank get property worth $600,000, the trade creditors $330,000, the subordinated debentureholders $60,000. The stockholders are wiped out. The seniors and subordinated consent under § 1126 and § 1129(a)(8)(A). The trade creditors reject the plan.

   i. Can the plan be confirmed under § 1129(a)(8)(A)?

   ii. Can the plan be confirmed as fair and equitable? Under § 1129(b)(2)(B)(i)? Under (b)(2)(B)(ii)?

   iii. Does the plan discriminate unfairly against the trade creditors?

D. Same facts as A. XYZ Corp.'s value is $990,000. The plan proposes that the bank debt get $675,000 and the trade debt get $315,000. Can the plan be confirmed over either the bank's or the trade creditors' objection?

   i. Can the plan be confirmed under § 1129(a)(8)(A)?

   ii. Can the plan be confirmed as fair and equitable? Under § 1129(b)(2)(B)(i)? Under § 1129(b)(2)(B)(ii)?

   iii. Does the plan discriminate unfairly against the trade creditors? Again, see the legislative history in the next section of these materials.

   iv. Return to Plan C. Does it discriminate unfairly against the seniors? Is it fair and equitable to the seniors? Is Plan D fair and equitable to the seniors?

E. Same facts as A. XYZ Corp. is worth $1.8 million. The plan proposes that the bank creditor get $1 million, the trade creditors

$750,000, and the subordinated debentures $50,000. Is anyone the victim of unfair discrimination? Who?

¶ 311: "Fair" Discrimination and Trade Creditors

Although the legislative history's parsing of trade, senior, and subordinated creditors is mechanical, the statute's express words require that the plan not discriminate *unfairly*. The statute does not necessarily prohibit plans that discriminate, but it requires that any discrimination must be fair. Some courts have picked up on the open-ended nature of "unfairly" and allowed plans that compensate equal-ranking creditors differently. Often times the favored are trade creditors, with the rationale for favoring the trade creditor being that further compensation for the trade creditors will facilitate the bankrupt's recovery, particularly if the creditor contributes specific and new value to the bankrupt company. Bruce A. Markell, *A New Perspective on Unfair Discrimination in Chapter 11*, 72 American Bankruptcy Law Journal 227 (1998); City Bar Ass'n, Committee on Bankruptcy and Corporate Reorganization, *Making the Test for Unfair Discrimination More "Fair": A Proposal*, 58 Business Lawyer 83 (2002). The court could split the two rationales: the contributing creditor could be well paid separately for the new contribution, while being compensated mechanically and ratably on its old debt.

In Detroit's bankruptcy case, its Chapter 9 plan treated pension claims and certain bondholder and employment-related claims more generously than general unsecured claims. In the face of an unfair discrimination challenge, Judge Rhodes considered but rejected previous courts' various articulations of the unfair discrimination standard as being too constraining: "The test . . . is only whether the discrimination is unfair. Congress certainly could have established . . . a more specific standard . . . , including any of the standards that the cases adopt or that the commentators propose. It did not." Judge Rhodes held instead that "fairness is a matter of relying on the judgment of conscience. That is all that Congress intended in so broadly articulating the unfair discrimination test . . . ." For Detroit's specific plan, this judgment of conscience was informed by "the circumstances in the case that bear upon the fairness of the discrimination in light of the purpose of chapter 9," as well as the court's "experience and sense of morality." Noting that Chapter 9 leaves the municipality in control of its affairs while it restructures its debt, so that the municipality can provide adequate municipal services, the court held that "a more flexible standard of unfair discrimination in Chapter 9 cases is appropriate." Needless to say, Judge Rhodes rejected arguments that the discrimination was unfair. In re City of Detroit, 524 B.R. 147 (Bankr. E.D. Mich. 2014).

¶ 312: Dieglom: Plan Confirmation Problem 3

And now one more problem to tie all these priority issues together:

Dieglom, Inc. is a diversified manufacturing company making automobile parts (used principally in large, fuel-inefficient cars), steel, rubber tires (nonradial only), shoes, and domestically-produced inexpensive sweaters.

Its balance sheet as of December 31, 2010, and results of operations for the twelve-month period ending December 31, 2010 were:

DIEGLOM, INC.
Balance Sheet
(as of December 31, 2010)

Assets			Liabilities and shareholders' equity		
Current Assets			Current Liabilities		
Cash	$10M		Bank debt due within one year	$10M	
Accounts receivable	1M		Trade accounts payable	10M	
Inventory and raw materials	1M				
		12M			20M
Plant and Equipment[1]	100 M		Long-term Debt		
Less depreciation	(52M)		7% senior debentures (issued 1996), due 2012	20M	
			3% mortgage bonds due 2020 (issued 1969) mortgaging principal plants	20M	
		48M			
			14% subordinated debentures due 2011 (issued 1991)	30M	
			Total long-term debt		70M
			Total liabilities		90M
			Accumulated shareholders' deficit		(30M)
Total assets		60M	Total liabilities and shareholders' equity		60M

1. The bulk of the plant and equipment was acquired in 1994 for $100 million, with a then-expected life of 20 years. Changes in the nature of the markets in which Dieglom operates make it uncertain what the continuing value of the plant or associated equipment is. Management estimates a scrap value of $5 million and a replacement value of $10 million.

DIEGLOM, INC.
Results of Operations
(for the year ending December 31, 2010)[2]

Gross sales	$100M
Less cost of goods sold	(90M)
Net sales	10M
Less depreciation	(5M)
Income before interest expense	5M
Less interest expense	(8M)
Net Loss	(3M)

2. Income statements for the previous five years have had results similar to the above. Assets have been sold to meet interest payments.

1. For purposes of reorganization valuation in 2010, the value of Dieglom's assets on its accounting books is, as the balance sheet shows, $60 million. But book value is not necessarily the market value of the company, and typically is not. Businesspeople will see the value of the company not primarily as a function of the accounting entries for the company's assets, which are typically based on historical costs of the assets, and more as a function of the cash that the company can produce in the future. We shall see more of this "discounting of future cash flows" in the next chapter.

2. Assume for the remainder of this problem that the judge has valued or would value Dieglom at $50 million. Further assume that the replacement value of the mortgaged properties is $10 million, because the assets have declined in value, just as the value of company overall has declined in value (scrap value, if relevant, is $5 million). How would value be distributed in a manner consistent solely with § 1129(b)? Cf. § 506. Ignore the possibility of consented-to deviations from § 1129(b) or of nonimpairment.

---

§ 506. Determination of secured status

(a)(1) An allowed claim of a creditor secured by a lien on property in which the estate has an interest . . . is a secured claim to the extent of the value of such creditor's interest in the estate's interest in such property . . . and is an unsecured claim to the extent that the value of such creditor's interest. . . is less than the amount of such allowed claim. *Such value shall be determined in light of the purpose of the valuation and of the proposed disposition or use of such property,* and in conjunction with any hearing on such disposition or use or on a plan affecting such creditor's interest.

In Associates Commercial Corp. v. Rash, 520 U.S. 953 (1997), the debtor retained the collateral and the question presented was whether the value of the collateral would "be determined by (1) what the secured creditor could obtain through foreclosure sale of the property . . . ; [or] (2) what the debtor would have to pay for comparable property . . . [or] (3) the midpoint between these two measurements[.]" The secured creditor said that the debtor would have to pay $41,000 to replace the collateral, a truck. But the debtor said that the secured creditor would only realize $32,000 if it repossessed the truck and sold it. The lower court fixed the value at $32,000, as did the Fifth Circuit, because, said the Fifth Circuit, under state law, the secured creditor could only obtain $32,000 of value from the collateral. For a bankruptcy court to allow more than the state rights would be incorrect unless such a result was "clearly compelled" by the Bankruptcy Code.

What does § 506(a)(1) compel? The Supreme Court concluded that it compelled replacement value, but it's not all that easy to reach that conclusion.

The first sentence in § 506 speaks of the secured party's interest, which, since the secured party's interest is determined under state law, militates for a state-determined value, i.e., liquidation value. Although courts and commentators have usually interpreted the state-law value to the secured as being the security's liquidation value, to so conclude is to move too fast.

Is the state-law value to the secured creditor the asset's liquidation value? What if the property is worth more to the company than it is to the secured creditor? If so, the two have incentives to make a deal somewhere in between.

Or would they? If the asset's replacement value is high, and the debtor wants it, does it have to pay more than liquidation value under state law? Under state law, the asset would be sold at a sheriff's auction, presumably at its liquidation value. But the debtor could stop the sheriff from ripping the asset out the debtor's factory by out-bidding the best bidder at the auction sale by a dollar or two. So the deal between the debtor and the secured creditor would only reflect whatever additional costs a sheriff's sale inflicted on the debtor.

The second sentence of § 506 says that the value of the security "shall be determined in light of the purpose of the valuation and of the proposed disposition or use of such property." This sentence would seem to demand a going concern, replacement value attributed to the secured party's claim. The Supreme Court said that the second sentence dominates the first one, making the secured claim the replacement value of the secured property.[10]

More recently, in In re Residential Capital, LLC, 501 B.R. 549 (Bankr. S.D.N.Y. 2013), the court confirmed the importance of the second sentence of § 506, albeit in a slightly different context. Junior secured noteholders (JSNs) claimed that their collateral had diminished in value between the filing of the debtor's Chapter 11 petition and the effective date of the debtor's proposed plan. Accordingly, they asserted a superpriority failure-of-adequate-protection claim for $515 million under § 507(b) noted in ¶302 and a provision we will deal with in Chapters 14 and 16. This required the court to value their collateral as of the petition date. The court rejected the debtor's argument that the JSNs were entitled only to the foreclosure value of their collateral on the petition date. Instead, because all parties understood that the debtor would be marketing and selling its properties as a going concern, the court decided that the appropriate valuation benchmark was "fair market value in the hands of the Debtors."

3. How do we know which Dieglom creditors are subordinated and to whom they're subordinated? Wouldn't the company have had an incentive in 1991 to avoid designating the subordinated as being subordinated to the mortgage bondholders? Why? But could the 3% bondholders have previously constrained the company by, say, getting the company's promise that all future debt be subordinated?

NO, pay for subordin (higher r)

[10] For individual debtors, Congress later indicated that a vehicle's cramdown value would be its replacement value.

Will the company have had an incentive when negotiating loan terms with the bank creditor to designate that loan as senior to the subordinated debentures? Could the company have been constrained in the subordination agreement not to designate the bank as senior? How? Why? How can the lawyer know what is subordinated to what?

4. Assume for the rest of the problem that the subordinated debentures are subordinate to the senior debentures, that they're subordinate only to the senior debentures, and that no other creditor has agreed to subordinate itself to another creditor. Outline a distribution that could withstand attack under § 1129(b)(2) from any single dissenting class.

   Now that you have a plan satisfying § 1129, check for its realism. Describe the considerations that the various parties would raise while negotiating a plan of reorganization.

   i. Will stockholders accept the plan as is, one giving them nothing?
   ii. If the firm declines in value during a delay, who loses?
   iii. If the firm rises in value during a delay, who profits?
   iv. If the firm's operational value neither rises nor falls during a delay, but the judge overvalues the firm under § 1129(b), who profits?
   v. If the firm's operational value neither rises nor falls during a delay, but the judge undervalues the firm under § 1129(b), who profits?

5. Bankruptcy accelerates the claims to the present. Do any of the creditors want to push any of the claims back to the original maturity, with their original interest rate? Do stockholders or creditors have a financial reason to invoke § 1124(2)? Against whom? How could § 1124(2) make a distributional difference?

6. Who bears the costs of the deterioration if the stockholders (or subordinated creditors) insist on a valuation hearing?

7. Who profits if the firm unexpectedly is worth a lot more than its current $50 million?

8. Who profits if the judge (mistakenly) values the firm at $65 million?

9. Why would the non-mortgagee creditors want to reinstate the mortgage bondholders under § 1124(2)? How could they possibly prefer that the debtor pay the bondholders $20 million (on the bond's original maturity date in 2020) to the company paying the bondholders $15 million in value on the plan's confirmation date? (That $15 million is the number you should have come up earlier with when evaluating an absolute priority plan for Dieglom.) The answer lies in the (low) interest rate from the original deal. We'll return to this question below, when we'll precisely analyze the valuation issues embedded in § 1124(2).

D. SECURED CREDIT PREDICATES TO CODE PRIORITY

The following readings explain the basics of security interests and the theory of what security interests do. Basically, a creditor seeks assurance that if the debtor cannot pay the loan back, the creditor can seize property of the debtor. The fundamental legal problems are of priority and notice: when two creditors have security interests in the property, usually the creditor who filed notice first wins.

The property to be secured could be realty. Realty interests are generally governed by state realty mortgage statutes. They set up a local realty filing system, with mortgage priority accorded to the first filer in the realty records. Non-realty interests (in machinery, inventory, raw materials, patents, etc.) are governed by Article 9 of the Uniform Commercial Code. The UCC sets up a filing and notice system, not all that different from the mortgage system. The UCC's mechanics are described in the next reading, after which appears the basic UCC Form 1.

¶ 313: Secured Transactions: Donald W. Baker, A Lawyer's Basic Guide to Secured Transactions 18–24, 67–69, 89–90 (1983)[11]

§ 1-3. An Overview of Secured Transactions under Article 9

* * *

B. Significance of a Security Interest; Unsecured Creditors and the Process of Obtaining a Judicial Lien

Assume that Debtor Corporation purchases business equipment from Supply Company on "open account," that is, "on its signature" alone, that is, on unsecured credit. When Debtor fails to [ ]pay Supply Company at the appropriate time, may Supply Company simply repossess the equipment? No; as an *unsecured* creditor, Supply Company cannot retake the equipment until it has first gone through the sometimes lengthy, expensive process of obtaining a "judicial lien." In many states this process, sometimes called the "collection process," requires that the unsecured creditor file suit on the debt, obtain a judgment, and—if the defendant debtor does not voluntarily pay the judgment—obtain from the court a writ of execution ordering the sheriff to seize whatever property of the debtor is available. After seizing the property—called levying—the sheriff sells it at a public sale, whereupon the proceeds are paid to the creditor to satisfy the debt. By contrast, had Supply Company taken a valid Article 9 security interest, it would generally be entitled to repossess and sell the collateral itself, without resort to judicial proceedings.

A second major advantage to having a security interest arises when a third party, such as a competing creditor, lays claim to the property covered by the security interest. When the rules of Article 9 give the secured creditor priority, he has sole claim to the collateral, meaning he

[11] Copyright 1983 by The American Law Institute. Reprinted with the permission of The American Law Institute–American Bar Association Committee on Continuing Professional Education.

can use it to fully satisfy his loan before the competing party has any rights. This advantage is apparent, for instance, when the debtor has gone into bankruptcy. Assume the bankrupt's sole asset is a machine having a resale value of $10,000, against which X, who took an Article 9 security interest, loaned $9,000. The bankrupt debtor has two unsecured creditors, Y and Z, each of whom he owes $10,000. If X satisfies the appropriate requirements of Article 9 (and the Bankruptcy Act), he will be entitled to $9,000, leaving Y and Z to share in the remaining $1,000. On the other hand, if X were an unsecured creditor, he would share pro rata with Y and Z, in this case receiving less ($3,103) than the latter two parties ($3,448 each).

C. Basic Concepts and Terminology of Article 9

The parties to a secured transaction are the "debtor" and the "secured party." The "debtor" is the person who owes performance of the obligation secured—usually payment of a debt. The "secured party" (also commonly referred to in the literature as the secured creditor) is the party in whose favor the security interest exists. A "security interest" is an interest in personal property or fixtures that secures payment or performance of an obligation. The "collateral" is the property covered by the security interest. The debtor usually grants the security interest to the secured party in a written contract called a "security agreement."

A security interest is not enforceable by the secured party against anyone—either the debtor or third parties—unless and until it "attaches," which generally requires that the debtor ha[s] executed a written security agreement, that the secured party ha[s] given value, and that the debtor ha[s] acquired rights in the collateral. Upon execution of the security agreement and satisfaction of the other requirements for attachment, the security interest becomes enforceable against the debtor, meaning that should the debtor "default"—as by failure to pay the debt owed the secured party at the appropriate time and in the appropriate manner—the secured party can . . . repossess the collateral and either retain it or sell it to satisfy the debt.

In many instances the secured party will be in conflict with a third party asserting a claim to the collateral, rather than with the debtor. The third party may be an unsecured creditor of the debtor with a judicial lien on the collateral, a buyer who has purchased the collateral from the debtor, another Article 9 creditor with a security interest in the collateral, or a bankruptcy trustee representing the debtor's unsecured creditors. When the debtor has sold the original collateral covered by the security interest, the conflict with the third party may concern the cash or other items received by the debtor upon the sale—called proceeds—rather than the original collateral. In conflicts of the foregoing types, the Article 9 "rules of priority" dictate whether the secured party or the third party prevails. These rules . . . generally provide (with important exceptions) that the secured party has priority only if he "perfects" his security interest before the third party's interest arises or (in the case of a competing secured creditor) is perfected. . . [P]erfection usually entails either taking possession of the collateral or filing a public notice of the security interest—called a financing statement—in the appropriate state office (the latter method being the most common).

§ 1–4. Applicability of Article 9

The first question one must always ask is whether the problem at hand is governed by Article 9. The answer will usually be found in the rules set forth in Sections 9–[109], 1–201[(b)(35)]), and 9–104, as discussed infra.

A. Basic Aspects of Coverage

Section 9–[109](a)(1) provides that . . . Article 9 applies ["to a transaction, regardless of its form, that creates a security interest in personal property. . . by contract]." This language makes it clear that the determinative factor is the intent of the parties to create a security interest, rather than the particular form in which they cast their transaction. Taken together with the broad definition of "security interest" in Section 1–201[(b)(35)], it also indicates that Article 9 is sufficiently flexible to encompass not only traditional forms of secured transactions . . . but also new arrangements that may be invented by innovative lawyers. . . .

* * *

The major advantage in having an Article 9 security interest has previously been discussed, namely that the secured party who has previously perfected his interest will usually prevail against an adverse party, such as a competing creditor or judicial lienor, who lays claim to the collateral.

UCC FINANCING STATEMENT

FOLLOW INSTRUCTIONS

A. NAME & PHONE OF CONTACT AT FILER (optional)

B. E-MAIL CONTACT AT FILER (optional)

C. SEND ACKNOWLEDGMENT TO: (Name and Address)

Print Reset

THE ABOVE SPACE IS FOR FILING OFFICE USE ONLY

1. DEBTOR'S NAME: Provide only one Debtor name (1a or 1b) (use exact, full name; do not omit, modify, or abbreviate any part of the Debtor's name); if any part of the Individual Debtor's name will not fit in line 1b, leave all of item 1 blank, check here ☐ and provide the Individual Debtor information in item 10 of the Financing Statement Addendum (Form UCC1Ad)

1a. ORGANIZATION'S NAME				
OR 1b. INDIVIDUAL'S SURNAME	FIRST PERSONAL NAME	ADDITIONAL NAME(S)/INITIAL(S)		SUFFIX
1c. MAILING ADDRESS	CITY	STATE	POSTAL CODE	COUNTRY

2. DEBTOR'S NAME: Provide only one Debtor name (2a or 2b) (use exact, full name; do not omit, modify, or abbreviate any part of the Debtor's name); if any part of the Individual Debtor's name will not fit in line 2b, leave all of item 2 blank, check here ☐ and provide the Individual Debtor information in item 10 of the Financing Statement Addendum (Form UCC1Ad)

2a. ORGANIZATION'S NAME				
OR 2b. INDIVIDUAL'S SURNAME	FIRST PERSONAL NAME	ADDITIONAL NAME(S)/INITIAL(S)		SUFFIX
2c. MAILING ADDRESS	CITY	STATE	POSTAL CODE	COUNTRY

3. SECURED PARTY'S NAME (or NAME of ASSIGNEE of ASSIGNOR SECURED PARTY): Provide only one Secured Party name (3a or 3b)

3a. ORGANIZATION'S NAME				
OR 3b. INDIVIDUAL'S SURNAME	FIRST PERSONAL NAME	ADDITIONAL NAME(S)/INITIAL(S)		SUFFIX
3c. MAILING ADDRESS	CITY	STATE	POSTAL CODE	COUNTRY

4. COLLATERAL: This financing statement covers the following collateral:

5. Check only if applicable and check only one box: Collateral is ☐ held in a Trust (see UCC1Ad, item 17 and Instructions) ☐ being administered by a Decedent's Personal Representative

6a. Check only if applicable and check only one box:
☐ Public-Finance Transaction ☐ Manufactured-Home Transaction ☐ A Debtor is a Transmitting Utility

6b. Check only if applicable and check only one box:
☐ Agricultural Lien ☐ Non-UCC Filing

7. ALTERNATIVE DESIGNATION (if applicable): ☐ Lessee/Lessor ☐ Consignee/Consignor ☐ Seller/Buyer ☐ Bailee/Bailor ☐ Licensee/Licensor

8. OPTIONAL FILER REFERENCE DATA:

FILING OFFICE COPY — UCC FINANCING STATEMENT (Form UCC1) (Rev. 04/20/11) International Association of Commercial Administrators (IACA)

William H. Lawrence, William H. Henning & R. Wilson Freyermuth, Understanding Secured Transactions (2d ed. 1999)*

[A] The Security Concept

An unsecured creditor . . . who wishes to enforce its rights following . . . a breach must proceed through judicial action. The process can be long and expensive, requiring a lawsuit to reduce the claim to judgment, and then perhaps an execution on the judgment. To execute on a judgment, the successful litigant must procure a writ of execution, which the sheriff will attempt to execute by levying on property of the debtor. . . . [T]he sheriff will conduct an auction sale, which generally yields low prices, and distribute the proceeds to the creditor in satisfaction of the judgment. The expense and delay associated with these procedures leaves lenders and sellers reluctant to rely solely upon their rights under debt or sales law.

Lenders and credit sellers can enhance their positions in several ways. They can, for example, insist that their obligor obtain a promise from a third person to act as surety and repay the obligation in the event of default. They can also insist that their obligor grant them an interest in real or personal property as security. This latter technique gives the creditor a special property interest in the identified property. One of the great advantages of this enhanced position is that, in the event of default, the creditor can proceed directly against the security without having first to reduce the claim to judgment. Costs and delays in enforcing the rights of secured creditors thus can be reduced significantly.

Although mortgage financing and secured financing are analogous operations, with respect to real and personal property, respectively, they are governed by separate bodies of law. . . . [S]ecured personal-property financing [is governed by] Article 9 of the Uniform Commercial Code. . . . There are overlaps [between Article 9 and real estate mortgages]. . . .

In Article 9 terminology, the creditor's special property interest is called a "security interest," and it is created through the consent of the debtor. Absent a security [interest, a creditor has no property interest in any particular asset of its debtor. An] unsecured seller of goods does not retain a property interest even in the goods sold;[12] in the event of a breach, the seller's basic remedy is its Article 2 claim for the unpaid balance of the purchase price.[13] Acquiring a consensual security interest adds the rights available to secured parties under Article 9.

---

* [While there is a 2012 edition of this book, the later edition lacks this excerpt's overview.—Roe.]

[12] . . . Unless the seller and buyer agree otherwise, the goods belong to the buyer and the seller receives in exchange only a legally enforceable right to the purchase price. U.C.C. §§ 2–607(1), 2–709(1).

[13] A creditor seller may also have a right to reclaim the goods themselves from [a bankrupt] buyer, but such rights are extremely limited. The seller must ascertain that the buyer received the goods while insolvent, and even then the seller generally must notify the buyer of its intent to reclaim them within ten days following their receipt. See U.C.C. § 2–702[; Bankruptcy Code § 546(c)].

Although a security interest gives a secured party a property interest in identified assets of the debtor, the interest is unique. Two primary features of the property interest define its essential nature. First, the secured party does not have any right to proceed against the property unless the debtor is in default. . . . [S]uch action would constitute conversion. Second, even following a default, the secured creditor's disposition of the collateral is only for the purpose of satisfying the outstanding indebtedness of the debtor. Generally, the secured creditor will sell the collateral and apply the proceeds against the amount of the debt still owed. The secured creditor cannot retain any surplus realized upon the sale, but rather must account for it to the debtor. Security is thus designed to allow a lender or credit seller to proceed, after default and without judicial process, directly against specific assets of the debtor to satisfy the outstanding indebtedness.

[B] An Organizational Overview of Article 9

. . . Article 9 is organized around five major conceptual areas: the scope of Article 9; attachment of security interests; perfection of security interests; priorities in collateral; and default. . . .

Scope questions focus on identification of the transactions to which Article 9 applies. Although, generally, the applicability of Article 9 is eminently apparent, the issue has proved to be one of the most litigated areas under the U.C.C. Certain transactions may be labeled as something other than a security interest by the parties (e.g., a lease or consignment) yet be the functional equivalent of an Article 9 secured transaction and thus within its scope. In addition, certain outright sales transactions also fall within the scope of Article 9.

"Attachment" of a security interest addresses how security interests are created. The process is contractual, because security interests are consensual in nature and thus must be created by agreement. The essential requirements are quite simple, although troublesome questions inevitably arise in some specific contexts. Enforceability of the agreement is also relevant through the inclusion in Article 9 of a statute-of-frauds provision.

Although the Article 9 relationship between a secured party and a debtor is established through the contract embodied in their security agreement, the secured party should also be concerned about the prospect of competing third-party claims to the collateral. In particular, courts are sympathetic with third parties who enter into relationships with the debtor on the mistaken belief that the debtor holds unencumbered ownership of the assets in its possession. This problem is sometimes referred to as an "ostensible ownership" problem. To enhance their position against such claimants, secured parties must ordinarily "perfect" their security interests, generally by taking steps that will publicize their interests. The most effective mechanism for overcoming the ostensible ownership problem is for the secured party to take possession of the collateral. . . . Possession is often impractical, however, and the most commonly used alternative method of perfection is the public filing of a financing statement. . . .

When the interests of claimants conflict with respect to particular property, the law must have rules by which it can prioritize the competing interests. When one of the competing claimants is a secured party, most of these priority rules are contained in Article 9.

"Default" is a pivotal concept because it opens the opportunity for the secured party to enforce its security interest against the collateral. The enforcement phase of a transaction is sometimes referred to as the "foreclosure process."

¶ 314: The Secured Creditor Under the Code: Cram-down and the Avoiding Power

The Bankruptcy Code generally respects state-created security interests. Nevertheless, while that's the baseline, specific bankruptcy rules alter the putative secured creditor's state-based rights. For example, § 506 of the Code divides a secured loan into a secured portion to the extent of the value of the security, and an unsecured portion for the remainder.

For the secured portion, the nonconsenting secured creditor can be "crammed down," in a manner parallel to what we saw for unsecured creditors in § 1129(b)(2)(B). Section 1129(b)(2)(A) of the Code describes the required fair and equitable treatment of secured creditors, which enables plan confirmation over the dissent of an impaired secured class):

§ 1129. Confirmation of plan

* * *

(b)(2) For the purpose of this subsection, the condition that a plan be fair and equitable with respect to a class includes the following requirements:

(A) With respect to a class of secured claims, the plan provides—

(i)(I) that the holders of such claims retain the liens securing such claims, whether the property subject to such liens is retained by the debtor or transferred to another entity, to the extent of the allowed amount of such claims; and

(II) that such holder of a claim of such class receive on account of such claim deferred cash payments totaling at least the allowed amount of such claim, of a value, as of the effective date of the plan, of at least the value of such holder's interest in the estate's interest in such property;

(ii) for the sale . . . of any property that is subject to the liens securing such claims, free and clear of such liens, with such liens to attach to the proceeds of such sale . . . ; or

(iii) for the realization by such holders of the indubitable equivalent of such claims.

Under state law, the secured creditor could liquidate the security and apply the proceeds of the sale to the creditor's loan. Under the

Code, the secured creditor is stayed, must participate in the proceeding, and can be crammed down.

Secured creditors are not just those who provided cash to finance the debtor. Mechanics' liens for work done on construction projects and tax liens under tax statutes are respected under § 545 if they would be valid under state law against a bona fide purchaser of the underlying property.

Three sections of the Bankruptcy Code can directly upset an otherwise valid security interest. A security interest given to a prebankruptcy creditor on the eve of the debtor's filing for bankruptcy may be a "preference," one that can be recovered to benefit the bankruptcy estate (and, hence, all of the debtor's unsecured creditors). See § 547 and chapter 9 for extensive discussion. A security interest that is given for inadequate consideration could be a fraudulent transfer. See § 548 and chapter 8 for extended discussion. Some security interests could also be avoided under what's known as the strong-arm power, in § 544.

§ 544. Trustee as lien creditor . . .

(a) The trustee shall have, as of the commencement of the case . . . the rights and powers of, or may avoid any transfer of property of the debtor or any obligation incurred by the debtor that is voidable by—

(1) a creditor that extends credit to the debtor at the time of the commencement of the case, and that obtains, at such time and with respect to such credit, a judicial lien on all property on which a creditor on a simple contract could have obtained such a judicial lien, *whether or not such a creditor exists;*

(2) a creditor that extends credit to the debtor at the time of the commencement of the case, and obtains, at such time and with respect to such credit, an execution against the debtor that is returned unsatisfied at such time, *whether or not such a creditor exists;*. . . .

What does § 544 do? "The purpose of [§ 544,] the 'strong arm clause[,]' is to cut off unperfected security interests, secret liens and undisclosed prepetition claims against the debtor's property. . . ." Collier on Bankruptcy ¶ 544.03 (15th ed. 2009). The effect of the trustee's strong-arm power is as follows. A creditor lends money to the firm and takes a security interest in the firm's inventory, but neglects to perfect the security interest, because, say, it forgot to file the UCC financing statement with the state authorities. The filing would have given public notice of the security interest. During the bankruptcy, the trustee can set aside the security interest (even if no real creditor could do so), because the trustee takes on the power of a hypothetically ideal creditor, whether or not such an ideal creditor exists.

E. FURTHER ON THE STATUTE: NEW VALUE, GIFT PLANS

¶ 315: New Value, Gift Plans

Consider this possibility: The Debtor borrows $100 million, then goes bankrupt. There's no doubt that the firm is insolvent and worth less than $100 million. The stockholder-managers concede that the firm is insolvent and that they are not entitled to any property under the plan of reorganization. Nevertheless, the Debtor's managers propose a plan that promises the creditors $80 million, with new stock to be issued to the managers, for which they'd pay $10 million. Creditors reject the plan. But, say the stockholder-managers, this $10 million in new value justifies the court cramming down the creditors, who are entitled, the stockholders say, only to $80 million in value.

If the firm is indeed worth $80 million, and if the new stock layer is indeed worth no more than $10 million, and if everyone involved, including the judge, know this, then there is little to dispute here.

But how does the judge know that the firm is worth only $80 million and that the new stock is worth no more than $10 million? The valuation hearing is one means for the court to reach such a conclusion. If the court found that the plan violated § 1129(b)(2)(B), it could value the firm to find out if the firm was worth no more than $80 million.

1. *Absolute Priority*. Did the stockholders' purchase of the firm's stock violate § 1129(b)(2)(B)? Clearly the plan doesn't satisfy (B)(i), as the creditors aren't getting $100 million in property. Does the plan satisfy (B)(ii)? The stockholders are junior, and they aren't wiped out. But are they "receiv[ing] . . . under the plan *on account of such junior . . . interest* any property[?]"

2. *New Value?* Douglas wrote in *L.A. Lumber* in 1939: "[T]here are circumstances under which stockholders may participate in a plan of reorganization of an insolvent debtor[.] Where . . . the old stockholders make a fresh contribution and receive in return a participation reasonably equivalent to their contribution, no objection can be made. . . ."

   How can the judge tell whether the fresh contribution is reasonably equivalent to the participation that the old stockholders receive? Must the judge value the firm?

3. "*On account of*". Well, it depends. If the stockholder-managers would receive the stock on account of, *and solely on the account of*, the check they write out for $10 million, then the statutory standard is met. But, if, on account of their old interest in the debtor, the stockholders got to propose the plan, and, if on account of their old interest, the stockholders could take advantage of the period of exclusivity (§ 1121(b), which gives the debtor the exclusive right to propose a plan for the first 120 days of bankruptcy), and, if on account of their old stock interest, the stockholders had access to all of the firm's inside information, then perhaps they got the best deal possible because they were the stockholders and had a position of power. They, in short, got a good deal because of their stockholding interest. What they got—or at least some of it—was, hence, "on account of [their] junior interest."

Similar facts came up in the reorganization of the 203 North LaSalle Street partnership in the 1990s. The bankruptcy court approved the plan, cramming it down at the stockholders' request under § 1129(b)(2)(B) over the creditor's objection. The Seventh Circuit said that as long as the old owners infused new capital into the bankrupt debtor firm reasonably equivalent to the value of the stock, the cram-down could be confirmed.

But the Supreme Court concluded that the stockholder-managers could not show that they weren't receiving property on account of their junior interest, unless they showed that third parties had had an opportunity to buy the bankrupt debtor's new equity. If no one else was ready to buy, then the bankruptcy court could cram down the plan under § 1129(b)(2)(B). But the bankruptcy court couldn't be sure that the stockholder-managers weren't getting a special deal until the equity interest was shopped. The very fact that the old owners got an "exclusive" gave them value on account of their old interest in the insolvent firm. "On account of" means no more or less than "because of." And "because of" the old stockholders' interest and power over the firm, they got first crack at the new equity, and thus the plan violated § 1129(b)(2)(B). Bank of America v. 203 North LaSalle Street Partnership, 526 U.S. 434 (1999). See Barry E. Adler & George G. Triantis, *The Aftermath of North LaSalle Street*, 70 University of Cincinnati Law Review 1225 (2002).

4. *Gift Plans*. A related practice arises in "gift" plans. Stockholders receive something under the plan of reorganization. A senior creditor, however, says that it made a gift to the stockholders. The senior creditor would have received more, it asserts, had it pursued its full rights to absolute priority. Instead, it ceded some of its bankruptcy entitlement to the shareholders.

Does the purpose of the gift matter? If the purpose of the gift was, say, to encourage stockholders to propose a plan that favored the gifting creditor, what result under § 1129(b)(2)(B)? What if the purpose of the gift was to help retain stockholder-managers as company employees, to motivate them to manage better post-reorganization? I.e., what if the gift was an employment bonus? How can the judge tell whether the motivation for the gift was a bonus or to facilitate a plan favorable to the senior creditor? (By the way, in either case—plan facilitation or employment contract—is "gift" the correct descriptive here?)

This gifting practice has been common and bankruptcy courts were regularly approving gifting plans until 2011, when the Second Circuit, in *In re* DBSD North America, Inc., 634 F.3d 79 (2d Cir. 2011), stated that gift plans were suspect in general and that the specific gift plan at issue violated the absolute priority rule in § 1129(b)(2). Perhaps the gift in *DBSD* was particularly suspect, as the bankruptcy court viewed the gift as facilitating the shareholder's "continued cooperation and assistance" in the chapter 11 proceeding—something useful to the senior creditor only because of the shareholder's position as equity holder.

In addition, the *DBSD* "gift" was to be made as part of the formal distribution scheme in the plan of reorganization, to which a creditor objected. The generous creditor was not giving some of its bankruptcy receipts to the shareholder *after* a *completed* reorganization. For these reasons, the court held that the shareholder received "property," "under the plan," and "on account of" its junior interest, in violation of § 1129(b)(2)(B)(ii).

Should the timing make any difference? Should it matter whether the parties had concluded a separate formal deal before confirmation or just had an informal understanding? Should it matter if the shareholders would not continue to manage the company?

Consider this century-old Supreme Court pronouncement:

> It is one thing for a [mortgagee] who has acquired absolute title by foreclosure to mortgaged property to thereafter give of his interests to others, and an entirely different thing whether such [mortgagee] . . . to secure a waiver of all objections on the part of the stockholder, and consummate speedily the foreclosure, may proffer to [the mortgagor stockholders] an interest in the property after foreclosure. The former may be beyond the power of the courts to inquire into or condemn. The latter . . . deserves the condemnation of every court, and should never be aided by any decree or order thereof. It involves an offer, a temptation[,] . . . [because] the purchase price thereof to be paid, [is] not [to be paid] by the mortgagee, but in fact [paid] by the unsecured creditor.

Louisville Trust Co. v. Louisville, New Albany & Chi. Ry. Co., 174 U.S. 674, 5889 (1899). Cf. Ralph Brubaker & Charles Jordan Tabb, Bankruptcy Reorganizations and the Troubling Legacy of Chrysler and GM, 5 Illinois Law Review 1375, 1403 (2010).

¶ 316: Other Creditors With Statutory Priority

The Code sets up several priorities that are independent of state-created priorities. Each prioritized creditor comes ahead of general unsecured creditors, but remains junior to secured creditors.

Section 507(a) sets up these bankruptcy priorities in the following order:

1. Administrative expenses, which include not just the costs of paying the attorneys, accountants, trustees, and professionals who administer the bankrupt firm and preserve it, but also include the bankrupt's payments to new post-petition lenders and to trade creditors who ship it merchandise or provide it services during the bankruptcy proceeding.
2. "Gap" creditors, who are trade creditors whose claim arose during the moments after a bankruptcy petition was filed, but before the court granted an "order of relief."
3. Back wages to the debtor's employees, limited in amount and time.
4. Monies due to employee benefit plans, again limited in amount and time.
5. Special provision for grain facilities.

6. Return of deposits to those who paid the debtor for goods or services that weren't delivered, but limited in amount.
7. Some taxes.

After these priority claims are paid, general unsecured creditors are paid.

¶ 317: Miscellaneous Code Provisions

Additional relevant Code provisions:

§ 502. Allowance of claims or interests

(a) A claim or interest . . . is deemed allowed, unless a party in interest . . . objects.

(b) . . . [T]he court, after notice and a hearing, shall determine the amount of such claim in lawful currency of the United States as of the date of the filing of the petition . . . except to the extent that—

(2) such claim is for unmatured interest[.]

The legislative history of § 502 states: "Section 502(b) thus contains two principles of present law. First, interest stops accruing at the date of the filing of the petition, because any claim for unmatured interest is disallowed under this paragraph. Second, bankruptcy operates as the acceleration of the principal amount of all claims against the debtor."

§ 1125. Postpetition disclosure and solicitation

(a) In this section—

(1) "adequate information" means information of a kind, and in sufficient detail, as far as is reasonably practicable in light of the nature and history of the debtor and the condition of the debtor's books and records . . . and a hypothetical investor typical of the holders of claims or interests in the case, that would enable such a hypothetical investor of the relevant class to make an informed judgment about the plan, but adequate information need not include such information about any other possible or proposed plan . . . ; and . . .

(b) An acceptance or rejection of a plan may not be solicited after the commencement of the case . . . unless . . . there is transmitted to such holder the plan or a summary of the plan, and a written disclosure statement approved, after notice and a hearing, by the court as containing adequate information. The court may approve a disclosure statement without a valuation of the debtor or an appraisal of the debtor's assets.

* * *

(d) Whether a disclosure statement [under (b)] contains adequate information is not governed by any otherwise applicable nonbankruptcy [securities] law, rule, or regulation, . . .

(e) A person that solicits acceptance or rejection of a plan, in good faith and in compliance with the applicable provisions of this title . . . is not liable, on account of such solicitation . . . for violation of any applicable [securities] law, rule, or regulation governing solicitation of acceptance or rejection of a plan. . . .

F. A NOTE ON PURPOSES

¶ 318: Fresh Starts

The purposes of bankruptcy, one might think, should be easy to find and state. Individual bankruptcies seem suffused with the purpose of offering people a "fresh start." On moral grounds, crushing debt should not burden people for their entire lives. And on efficiency grounds, once debt is crushing, the individual's incentives to work off that debt can dissipate. Bankruptcy relief can thus be both fair and efficient.

But one cannot readily apply this fresh start principle to corporate reorganization in chapter 11. Bankruptcy can wipe out shareholders' interests without crushing the individual shareholder, who typically, particularly for shareholders of a public company that's gone bankrupt, has a diversified portfolio that cannot be wiped out by the failure of a single firm. Creditors are similarly diversified and thus not in need of a fresh start.

It's easy to see how a fresh start mentality might have historically suffused business bankruptcy. Individuals get the benefit of the fresh start. Individuals in business might similarly get its benefit. When individuals (or families, or small, tight partnerships among friends) were the principal business owners, the fresh start policy could suffuse business bankruptcies. From there, the principle might spread to corporate reorganizations in chapter 11 of public firms with diversified shareholders, although if corporate reorganizations had been the first bankruptcies to occur when constructing a bankruptcy system, the fresh start principle might not have been primary, or even operative.

The purposes of business bankruptcy can be seen as falling into two large bins. One bin looks at creditor wealth maximization, and can be seen as analogous to the shareholder wealth maximization norm from corporate law, modulated to recognize that in bankruptcy it's usually the creditors who become the residual claimants. In another large bin are the other social interests, the most obvious of which are the interests of the bankrupt firm's employees and the surrounding community.

People beginning from premises in the first bin will tend to favor market-based solutions to chapter 11. People beginning from premises in the second bin will tend to see slow reorganization and props to the decaying firm as justified in softening the pain to employees of the decaying firm. Because chapter 11 has historically worked more slowly than it seems that it has to, and worked more slowly than other similar corporate transactions, the real world of bankruptcy seems to have been built with premises, implicitly or explicitly, from the social interests bin.

While these two camps might seem to be at war[14]—creditor wealth maximization contrasting with caring about employees—the market-bin supporters could assert that market solutions are best for employees and communities as a whole.

That is, in the abstract, a utilitarian seeks the greatest good for the greatest number. Creditor wealth maximization in chapter 11 is not a goal in itself, but serves as a rough proxy for the utilitarian norm. A bankruptcy system that pays creditors back best facilitates the fluidity of capital—a fluidity that market-based theorists usually think improves overall employment. The practical problem though is two-fold here: First, when jobs are lost, the visible lost job is politically painful to eliminate, even if the abstraction says that unidentified jobs are preserved or created elsewhere in the economy. Second, a utilitarian has trouble comparing the pain felt by the job loser to the gains felt elsewhere in the system. Sometimes, after all, the local pain may exceed the diffuse gains; the market norms then depend on the value of generality and the high costs of assessing when the local pain is so great that reducing it deserves primacy.

¶ 319: The Historical Development of Absolute Priority: *Los Angeles Lumber*

Los Angeles Lumber Products was the major historical absolute priority case. The decision had two priority prongs. For the first, which should be familiar: priority was absolute. The creditors were to be paid in full before stockholders could receive value in the reorganization. The second is less familiar, given the current statutory structure: judicial review of the priority structure was a necessary requirement, not a fallback if the parties couldn't come to terms.

¶ 320: Case v. Los Angeles Lumber Prods. Co., 308 U.S. 106 (1939)

MR. JUSTICE DOUGLAS delivered the opinion of the Court.

These cases present the question of the conditions under which stockholders may participate in a plan of reorganization under . . . the Bankruptcy Act where the debtor corporation is insolvent. . . .

. . . [The plan] provides for the formation of a new corporation, which will acquire the assets of Los Angeles Shipbuilding and Drydock Corporation, and which will have a capital structure of 1,000,000 shares. . . .

. . . 641,375 shares of the preferred are to be issued to the bondholders, 250 shares to be exchanged for each $1000 bond. The [old] Class A stockholders will receive the 188,625 shares of common stock, without the payment of any subscription or assessment. . . .

[14] E.g., Donald R. Korobkin, *The Role of Normative Theory in Bankruptcy Debates*, 82 Iowa Law Review 75, 103, 105 (1996).

The plan was assented to by approximately 92.81% of the face amount of the bonds. Petitioners own $18,500 face amount of the bonds. They did not consent . . . [a]nd . . . they objected that the plan was not fair and equitable to bondholders.

The District Court found that the debtor was insolvent both in the equity sense and in the bankruptcy sense[;][15] the total value of all assets of Los Angeles Shipbuilding and Drydock Corporation was $830,000. . . . Yet in spite of this finding, the court . . . confirmed the plan . . . despite . . . that the old stockholders, who have no equity in the assets of the enterprise, are given 23% of the assets and voting power in the new company without making any fresh contribution. . . . The court, however, justified inclusion of the stockholders in the plan . . . because it apparently felt that the relative priorities of the bondholders and stockholders were maintained by virtue of the preferences accorded the stock which the bondholders were to receive and the fact that the stock going to the bondholders carried 77% of the voting power of all the stock presently to be issued under the plan . . . .

[Moreover, i]f the bondholders were able to foreclose now and liquidate the debtor's assets, they would receive "substantially less than the present appraised value" of the assets. [And, the bondholders cannot now foreclose without "long and protracted litigation" which would be "expensive and of great injury" to the debtor. . . .

* * *

[We conclude that] as a matter of law the plan was not fair and equitable.

[W]here a plan is not fair and equitable as a matter of law it cannot be approved by the court [under chapter X] *even though the percentage of the various classes of security holders required by [the Bankruptcy Act] for confirmation of the plan has consented*. . . . Congress has required *both* that the required percentages of each class of security holders approve the plan *and* that the plan be found to be "fair and equitable."[16] The former is not a substitute for the latter. The court is not merely a ministerial register of the vote of the several classes of security holders. All those interested in the estate are entitled to the court's protection. Accordingly the fact that the vast majority of the security holders have approved the plan is not the test of whether the plan is a fair and equitable one. . . . [17]

Hence, in this case the fact that 92.81% in amount of the bonds . . . have approved the plan is as immaterial on the basic issue of its

[15] [I.e., the debtor was unable to meet its debts as they came due and the debtor's liabilities were more than its assets. Insolvency is not a prerequisite for a debtor to file bankruptcy under the 1978 Bankruptcy Code.—Roe.]

[16] It provides in part: "After hearing such objections as may be made to the plan, the judge shall confirm the plan if satisfied that (1) it is fair and equitable and does not discriminate unfairly in favor of any class of creditors or stockholders, and is feasible; . . . (3) it has been accepted as required by the provisions of subdivision (e), clause (1) of this section; . . ." [Textual italics added for "and."—Roe.]

[17] [Both the court's finding and a creditors' vote play a role in today's chapter 11, but not the same role that they had in Los Angeles Lumber. If there's consent today, the court does not also decide whether the plan is fair and equitable. I.e., a vote and approval is today a substitute for the judge finding that the plan is fair and equitable.—Roe & Tung.]

fairness as is the fact that petitioners own only $18,500 face amount of a large bond issue.

* * *

[Bondholders entitled to more than liquidation value of assets]

. . . The District Court's further finding that if the bondholders were to foreclose now they would receive "substantially less than the present appraised value" of the assets of the debtor corporation is no support for inclusion of the old stockholders in the plan. The fact that bondholders might fare worse as a result of a foreclosure and liquidation than they would by taking a debtor's plan . . . can have no relevant bearing on whether a proposed plan is "fair and equitable" under [the Act]. . . . To hold that in a [bankruptcy] reorganization creditors of a hopelessly insolvent debtor may be forced to share the already insufficient assets with stockholders because apart from rehabilitation under that section they would suffer a worse fate, would disregard the standards of "fair and equitable"; and would result in impairment of the Act to the extent that it restored some of the conditions which the Congress sought to ameliorate by that remedial legislation.

* * *

[Compromise of legitimate legal disputes allowable]

. . . The holding of the District Court that the value to the bondholders of maintaining the debtor as a going concern and of avoiding litigation with the old stockholders justifies the inclusion of the latter in the plan is likewise erroneous. . . . Of course, this is not to intimate that compromise of claims is not allowable under [the Act]. . . . Thus, ambiguities in the wording of two indentures may make plausible the claim of one class of creditors to an exclusive or prior right to certain assets as against the other class in spite of the fact that the latter's claim flows from a first mortgage. Close questions of interpretations will give rise to honest doubts as to which security holders have first claim to certain assets. Settlement of such conflicting claims . . . is a normal part of the process of reorganization. In sanctioning such settlements the court is not bowing to nuisance claims; it is administering the proceedings in an economical and practical manner. But that is not the situation here. . . .

* * *

We therefore hold that the plan is not fair and equitable and that the judgment below must be and is Reversed.

¶ 321: Notes on Los Angeles Lumber

1. *Los Angeles Lumber* is at the heart of modern bankruptcy doctrine. Prior to the decision, debate was fierce as to whether absolute priority, sometimes called strict priority, ought to govern in reorganization proceedings. First, hadn't all of claimants made a bad investment? Shouldn't they all share the pain of the common disaster?

Second, if the creditor had agreed to bad investment features when it lent to the debtor, such as an interest rate that now, because of the firm's sad shape, is a low one, shouldn't their bad deal be reflected in their compensation if the firm is continued? If the firm is continued, shouldn't the bad deal be continued as well? Wouldn't anything else provide the creditors with a windfall?

But, third, did the creditor bargain for liquidation value? Its non-bankruptcy remedy was to seize security (or levy on a judgment). If there's an excess of going concern value over liquidation value, is it clear who's entitled to it, the creditors or the stockholders?

Fourth, and most importantly, if the creditor class *agreed* in the reorganization proceeding to give up their strict priority, why should a court not accede to the class's will?

And, fifth, does strict priority follow directly from the language of the statutory requirement (that the plan be fair and equitable, see *Los Angeles Lumber*, 308 U.S. at 114, at p. 64)? Isn't the standard quite open-ended?

Several elements of the absolute priority rule in the old chapter X were interconnected: (a) creditors have "absolute" priority over stockholders, i.e., they are to be paid in full before stockholders receive anything, (b) creditor consent to accept a plan deviating from that priority via a creditor vote is not dispositive, (c) when there are intermediate creditors, creditors cannot skip over an intermediate class to consent to a lower class's participation.

Today, (a) and (c) persist, if the creditors insist. But they can compromise now under § 1129(a)(8).

2. Recall that it's the statute's fair and equitable standard that is the basis for the doctrinal result. Isn't it relevant in determining whether the result was fair and equitable to note, as the lower court had, that the creditors took the bonds under a bond indenture that allowed a majority vote to compromise the claim of the bonds and that the bondholders had given an approving vote prior to the reorganization of Los Angeles Lumber? See In re Los Angeles Lumber Prods., 24 F. Supp. 501, 504 (S.D. Cal. 1938), rev'd sub. nom. Case v. Los Angeles Lumber Prods. Co., 308 U.S. 106 (1939).

3. Presumably a strong basis for strict priority is that priority is what the parties bargained for. Is that strong basis vitiated if the parties *also* bargained to allow a majority vote of the bondholders to recapitalize the bonds and the reorganization proponents obtain that majority vote?

4. Is the stockholders' hindrance value a persuasive reason to bar creditors from giving the stockholders something? 308 U.S. at 129. A partnership agrees to take most actions by a 2/3 vote. A customer of the partnership defaults in payment for $1000 of goods sold and delivered. The partnership votes to accept $900, because the litigation process is slow, uncertain, and expensive. Could similar considerations have motivated the bondholders in *Los Angeles Lumber*? I.e., could it make sense even for a majority of non-conflicted, fully-aware bondholders to compromise their claim?

Douglas says that mere nuisance value cannot support the settlement. If the stockholders have a colorable legal claim, can they dispute with the bondholders, then settle?

5. *Los Angeles Lumber* was decided toward the end of the great depression; markets were distrusted, administrators trusted. At the heart of the decision was a faith in the valuation process. Courts could quickly and accurately value the firm. Claims could then be compensated. That New Deal faith in the administrative valuation process seems to have been misplaced, and by 1978 Congress sought to *avoid* the valuation hearing in chapter 11. See infra Bankruptcy Code § 1129. When you go through the following priority problems, ask yourself how much of *Los Angeles Lumber* survives the new Bankruptcy Code.

¶ 322: Section 1129(a)(7)—The Best Interests Test

Thus far we have paid little attention to the so-called best interests requirement for plan confirmation, namely, that no complaining creditor does less well under the chapter 11 plan that it would have done in a liquidation. As you can see, this test isn't subject to the class consent. Every creditor can use it to (in theory) scuttle an objectionable plan.

§ 1129. Confirmation of plan

(a) The court shall confirm a plan only if all of the following requirements are met:

* * *

(7) With respect to each impaired class of claims or interests—

(A) each holder of a claim or interest of such class—

(i) has accepted the plan; or

(ii) will receive or retain under the plan on account of such claim or interest property of a value, as of the effective date of the plan, that is not less than the amount that such holder would so receive or retain if the debtor were liquidated under chapter 7 of this title on such date; . . .

---

1. William Douglas's individualized-consent framework for reorganization in Los Angeles Lumber lives on in weakened form in § 1129(a)(7), which allows each impaired claimant to complain and not be bound by the consent of a holder's class. The holder can complain if the class has voted to give away so much that the holder would have received more in a liquidation. In effect, the class can negotiate to give away the "going concern" value of its claim, but the majority can give away from a dissenter's pocket no more than the difference between the going concern value and the liquidation value. This test became known as the "best interests" test, i.e., the plan would be seen as in the best interests of the creditors,

because it got them at least what they would have gotten if the firm had been liquidated.

2. Review the problems in ¶¶ 307 and 312 to see how § 1129(a)(7) could affect the judge's authority to confirm those plans.

3. Section 1129(a)(7) seems easy for plan proponents to meet. If the judge concludes that the firm's liquidation value is a pittance, and its going concern value much higher, then the § 1129(a)(7) hearing could be finished quickly.

4. But potential interpretive ambiguities lurk in § 1129(a)(7). In an efficient market the firm could be sold at a price representing, in the aggregate, the present value of the firm.

5. Would a sale of the entire bankrupt firm be a liquidation?

6. If so, could § 1129(a)(7) override the bargain framework of class consent in § 1129(a)(8)(A)? Would Douglas' framework rise up to dominate all of bankruptcy once again?

7. Return to the Dieglom problem in ¶ 312. The lower-ranking claimants and interests plan to seek reinstatement of the mortgage bonds under § 1124(2). They calculate that the present value of an 10–year promise to repay $20 million at 3% interest annually is $11.4 million. Can the mortgage bondholders invoke § 1129(b)(2)(A) to upset the plan?

   The mortgage bondholders calculate (contrary to the original $5 million or $10 million in the problem) that the value under § 506 of their security interest is $14 million. Can they invoke § 1129(a)(7) to upset the plan?

   Consider this alternative plan: The plan proponents would like to cut down the company's post-reorganization debt. They ask the bondholders to accept stock in place of their reinstated bonds. Indeed, they offer $13 million in value (in cash, stock, and other securities) to the bondholders, most of whom prefer the revised offer to reinstatement (because $13 million is more than $11.4 million). Two-thirds of the bondholders (by dollar amount) and more than one-half in number vote to accept the $13 million plan. Can a dissenting bondholder upset the plan under

   § 1129(a)(8)(A)–(B)?

   Under § 1129(b)(2)(A)?

   Under § 1129(a)(7)?

CHAPTER 4

VALUATION IN PRINCIPLE

A. BASIC VALUATION

To understand the fundamentals of valuation, we need to understand two core concepts: (i) the time value of money, or discounting to present value; and (ii) risk.

¶ 401: Discounting to Present Value: The Time Value of Money

The value of a firm to a financier will usually be the value of the cash the firm can throw off over time. Because the firm will throw off cash both immediately and in the future, some method must be found to value that future cash in terms of today's dollars. Money to be received years from now is not as valuable as the same dollar amount received today, not just because of the risks of non-receipt but because money today can be put into a bank, which will pay interest. So a sure $1000 a year from now will be worth less than $1000 today, because a smaller sum of money can be put into the bank and yield the $1000 a year from now.

Assume an interest rate of 10%. How much must be deposited today, so that the money deposited today, accruing 10% interest for the year, will yield $1000 a year from now? Thus:

(1) X+10% of X = $1000

Or:

(2) 1.1 X = $1000

(3) X = $1000/1.1

(4) X = $909.09

That is, $909, deposited today at 10% interest, will give the depositor about $1000 in the bank a year from now.

¶ 402: Present Values in More Detail

Richard A. Brealey, Stewart C. Myers, and Franklin Allen, Principles of Corporate Finance 18–25 (11th ed. 2014)

Future Values and Present Values

Calculating Future Values

Money can be invested to earn interest. So, if you are offered the choice between $100 today and $100 next year, you naturally take the money now to get a year's interest. Financial managers make the same point when they say that money has a time value or when they quote the most basic principle of finance: *a dollar today is worth more than a dollar tomorrow.*

Suppose you invest $100 in a bank account that pays interest of r = 7% a year. In the first year you will earn interest of .07 x $100 = $7 and the value of your investment will grow to $107:

Value of investment after 1 year
= $100 x (1 + r) = 100 x 1.07 = $107

By investing, you give up the opportunity to spend $100 today, but you gain the chance to spend $107 next year.

If you leave your money in the bank for a second year, you earn interest of .07 x $107 = $7.49 and your investment will grow to $114.49:

Value of investment after 2 years
= $107 x 1.07 = $100 x 1.072 = $114.49

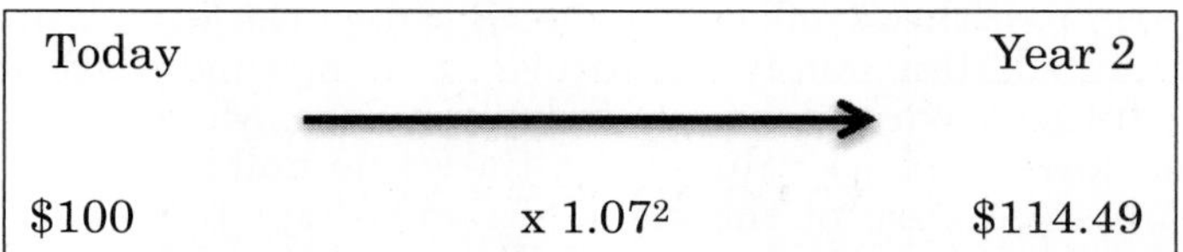

Notice that in the second year you earn interest on both your initial investment ($100) and the previous year's interest ($7). Thus your wealth grows at a *compound rate* and the interest that you earn is called **compound interest**.

If you invest your $100 for *t* years, your investment will continue to grow at a 7% compound rate to $\$100 \times (1.07)^t$. For any interest rate *r*, the future value of your $100 investment will be:

$$\text{Future value of } \$100 = \$100 \times (1+r)^t$$

The higher the interest rate, the faster your savings will grow. The figure below shows that a few percentage points added to the interest rate can do wonders for your future wealth. For example, by the end of 20 years $100 invested at 10% will grow to $\$100 \times (1.10)^{20} = \$672.75$. If it is invested at 5%, it will grow to only $\$100 \times (1.05)^{20} = \$265.33$.

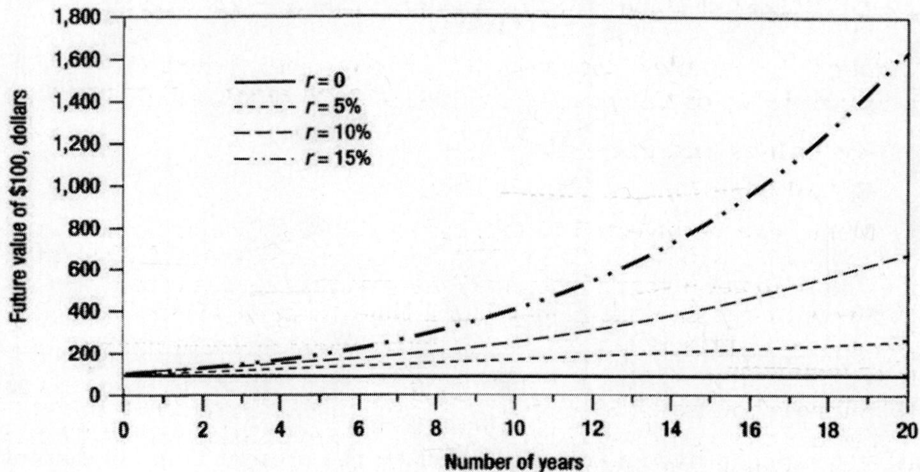

Calculating Present Values

We have seen that $100 invested for two years at 7% will grow to a future value of $100 \times 1.07^2 = \$114.49$. Let's turn this around and ask how much you need to invest *today* to produce $114.49 at the end of the second year. In other words, what is the present value (PV) of the $114.49 payoff?

You already know that the answer is $100. But, if you didn't know or you forgot, you can just run the future value calculation in reverse and divide the future payoff by $(1.07)^2$.

$$\text{Present value} = \text{PV} = \frac{\$114.49}{(1.07)^2} = \$100$$

Today		Year 2
	←	
$100	$\div 1.07^2$	$114.49

In general, suppose that you will receive a cash flow of C_t dollars at the end of year *t*. The present value of this future payment is

$$\text{Present Value} = \text{PV} = \frac{C_t}{(1+r)^t}$$

The rate, *r*, in the formula is called the discount rate, and the present value is the discounted value of the cash flow, C_t. . . . The longer you have to wait for your money, the lower its present value. This is illustrated in [the next figure]. Notice how small variations in the

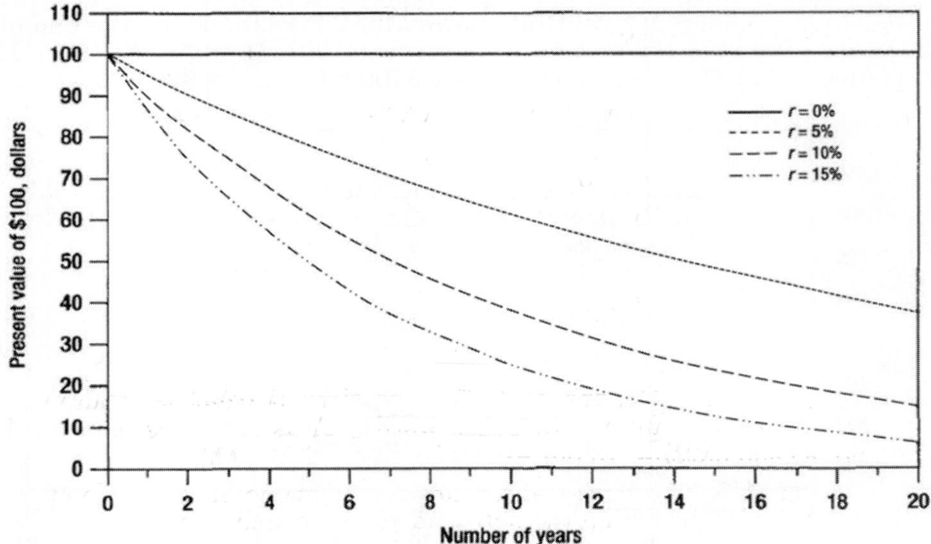

interest rate can have a powerful effect on the present value of distant cash flows. At an interest rate of 5%, a payment of $100 in year 20 is worth $37.69 today. If the interest rate increases to 10%, the value of the future payment falls by about 60% to $14.86.

Valuing an Investment Opportunity

How do you decide whether an investment opportunity is worth undertaking? Suppose you own a small company that is contemplating construction of a suburban office block. The cost of buying the land and constructing the building is $700,000. Your company has cash in the bank to finance construction. Your real-estate adviser forecasts a shortage of office space and predicts that you will be able to sell next year for $800,000. For simplicity, we will assume initially that this $800,000 is a sure thing. . . . We assume that [you] can earn a 7% profit by investing for one year in safe assets (U.S. Treasury debt securities, for example). [So for present purposes, we'll assume a discount rate of 7%.] . . .

[H]ow much is [the office block project] worth and how much will the investment add to your wealth? The project produces a cash flow at the end of one year. To find its present value we discount that cash flow by the opportunity cost of capital:[1]

[1] [For our purposes, the discount rate.—Roe & Tung.]

$$\text{Present Value} = PV = \frac{C_1}{1+r} = \frac{800{,}000}{1.07} = \$747{,}664$$

* * *

Net Present Value

The office building is worth $747,664 today, but that does not mean you are $747,664 better off. You invested $700,000, so the net present value (NPV) is $47,664. Net present value equals present value minus the required investment:

$$NPV = PV - \text{investment} = 747{,}664 - 700{,}000 = \$47{,}664$$

In other words, your office development is worth more than it costs. It makes a *net* contribution to value and increases your wealth. The formula for calculating the NPV of your project can be written as:

$$NPV = C_0 + C_1/(1 + r)$$

Remember that C_0, the cash flow at time 0 (that is, today) is usually a negative number. In other words, C_0 is an investment and therefore a cash outflow. In our example, $C_0 = -\$700{,}000$.

When cash flows occur at different points in time, it is often helpful to draw a time line showing the date and value of each cash flow.

* * *

Calculating Present Values When There are Multiple Cash Flows

One of the nice things about present values is that they are all expressed in current dollars—so you can add them up. In other words, the present value of cash flow (A + B) is equal to the present value of cash flow A plus the present value of cash flow B.

[An extended series of annual cash flows, with the first three years cash expressed as individual formulas, would look like:]

$$PV = \frac{C_1}{1 + r_1} + \frac{C_2}{(1 + r_2)^2} + \frac{C_3}{(1 + r_3)^3} + \ldots$$

[In principle there can be a different interest rate for each future period. We will generally assume that the interest rate in each period is the same.]

* * *

. . . [So far all our examples could be worked out fairly easily by hand or] required just a few keystrokes on a calculator. Real problems can be much more complicated . . . [sometimes requiring] financial calculators especially programmed for present value calculations or to computer spreadsheet programs.

¶ 403: Perpetuities

Let's say a firm will produce a $100 per year forever and with certainty. How much is this firm worth? This is simply a special but not uncommon flavor of present value problem—valuing a perpetuity. Assume a 10% rate of interest. We can then frame the question as follows: how much must be deposited in the bank today to yield $100 per year forever, given our 10% interest rate. The answer of course is $1000, so the value of this firm must be $1000, the amount that would yield $100 per year forever.

This perpetuity is equivalent to taking the value of $100 one year from now, discounting it to present value, then taking the value of $100 two years from now, discounting it to present value, then taking the value of $100 three years from now, discounting it to present value, etc. When this infinite process is completed, the present values of $100 in each year would be added up, giving us the present value of this firm.

The process of discounting the perpetual income stream is usually called "capitalizing" an income stream. We simply multiply the annual income stream by a capitalization multiplier, which is the *inverse* of the discount rate. So with a stream of $100 per year forever, discounted at 5%, the multiplier is 20, which gives us a present value of $2000 for the perpetuity, or 20 times the expected annual income. When we're dealing with a perpetuity, we often call the discount rate for the income stream its capitalization rate.[2]

As will be apparent once we get a feel for the numbers, the choice of a capitalization rate can be crucial to the valuation outcome. The same expected income can yield widely variant present values, depending on the choice of the discount rate. As we've just seen, a $100 perpetuity at 10% yields a present value of $1000; $100 at 5% yields a present value of $2000. If the discount rate were 20%, the present value would plummet to $500.

Lastly, while discounting a perpetuity to present value has an unreal air to it—we can barely predict income for next year, so how can we have any assurance of income twenty years down the road?—the problem is less critical than it might seem. In most valuations, all of the income from twenty years on out in perpetuity will be a small part of the present value of most industrial firms.

The following excerpt from Brealey & Myers elaborates.

Richard A. Brealey, Stewart C. Myers, and Franklin Allen, Principles of Corporate Finance 26 (11th ed. 2014)

Looking for Shortcuts—Perpetuities and Annuities

Sometimes there are shortcuts that make it easy to calculate present values. Let us look at some examples.

---

[2] The discount rate incorporates not only the time value of money but also the riskiness of the cash stream, with the riskiness reflecting that the expected value of the stream might not be realized.

On occasion, the British and the French have been known to disagree and sometimes even to fight wars. At the end of some of these wars the British consolidated the debt they had issued during the war. The securities issued in such cases were called consols. Consols are **perpetuities**. These are bonds that the government is under no obligation to repay but that offer a fixed income for each year to perpetuity. The British government is still paying interest on consols issued all those years ago. The annual rate of return on a perpetuity is equal to the promised annual payment divided by the present value:

$$\text{Return} = \frac{\text{cash flow}}{\text{present value}}$$

$$r = \frac{C}{PV}$$

We can obviously twist this around and find the present value of a perpetuity given the discount rate *r* and the cash payment C:

$$PV = C/r$$

The year is 2030. You have been fabulously successful and are now a billionaire many times over. It was fortunate indeed that you took that finance course all those years ago. You have decided to follow in the footsteps of two of your heroes, Bill Gates and Warren Buffet. Malaria is still a scourge and you want to help eradicate it and other infectious diseases by endowing a foundation to fund research to combat these diseases. You aim to provide $1 billion a year starting next year. So, if the interest rate is 10%, you are going to have to write a check for

$$\text{Present value of perpetuity} = C/r = \$1\text{ billion}/.1 = \$10\text{ billion}$$

Two warnings about the perpetuity formula. First, at a quick glance you can easily confuse the formula with the present value of a single payment. A payment of $1 at the end of one year has a present value of 1/(1 + r). The perpetuity has a value of 1/r. These are quite different.

Second, the perpetuity formula tells us the value of a regular stream of payments starting one period from now. Thus your $10 billion endowment would provide the foundation with its first payment in one year's time. If you also want to provide an up-front sum, you will need to lay out an extra $1 billion.

¶ 404: Present Value Problems

The Construction Company in Bankruptcy

Your client, a construction company, is in bankruptcy. It has one available project. The project is covered by a draft contract, which has been drafted by counsel for the manufacturing company. You review the draft of the contract. Your client will build an addition to a factory at a price of $550,000. The manufacturer will pay $50,000 down, when construction commences. Construction will take five years. The completed factory will be delivered at the very end of five years; the buyer will make the final payment of $500,000 on the next day, which would be five years from the signing of the contract.

Your client, the debtor construction company, expects construction to cost $500,000 and take 5 years. It has $500,000 cash, an asset which is somewhat unusual for a debtor in bankruptcy. (But this is a law school hypothetical.) Expenses (which to simplify will include the normal profits the client would expect) will be incurred annually at a rate of about $100,000 per year. So, the debtor will incur $100,000 of expenses in the first year. Another $100,000 of expenses will be incurred in the second year, and then $100,000 again in the third year, and so on. (We'll assume that the expenses are incurred at the very end of each year so that we can keep the arithmetic tractable.)

The client says "$550,000 is coming in; $500,000 is going out. Fifty thousand dollars profit on a project like this one isn't bad. Sure, I'll make less than $50,000, because of the timing discrepancies. But how much less?"

Do you have any further comments for your client? Assuming the risk of non-payment by the manufacturer upon completion is nil and assuming that your client's next best use of its funds would earn it 10% per year (so we can assume a 10% discount rate), how might you outline the contract's payment terms to your client, or to the valuing authority?

Value of Construction Project

	Now	End of Year 1	End of Year 2	End of Year 3	End of Year 4	End of Year 5	Total
Receipts (actual)							
Expenses (actual)							
Receipts (present value)							
Expenses (present value)							

After valuing the company, would you have an operating recommendation to make to the construction company? If you were the judge making the valuation in bankruptcy, might you consider whether the debtor should go ahead and finish the deal to construct the factory?

The Bond Valuation Problem

We need to find the value of a bond, which is a loan to the debtor and a promised stream of cash payments to each bondholder. The amount lent is the principal. The time until the bond's maturity, when the debtor must pay back the loan, is the loan's term. The debtor pays interest to the bondholders during the loan's term, at the end of each year, at the (typically) fixed interest rate specified in the bond. The appropriate discount rate applicable to the promised cash stream at any given time is the going rate of interest in the market for bonds of a similar term and quality. The price of the bond is what someone else in the market would be willing to pay to a bondholder to receive that stream of interest payments and the principal when the bond matures.

Summary of the bond's terms:	
Principal:	$1000
Term:	10 years
Interest Rate:	3%

1. Assume that the appropriate discount rate for the bond's principal amount and all of the annual interest payments is 3%, just like the bond's promised interest rate. What is the value of the bond? (Assume you are valuing the bond on New Year's Day and interest is paid on the last day of each year.)

2. Consider the bond's value if the discount rate appropriate for this bond has risen to 10%.

Notice that the promised stream of interest payments on the bond is fixed on the day the bond is issued. The amount of each annual interest payment is predetermined based on the principal amount and the specified interest rate. In this example, the bondholder receives $30 each year in interest (3% of $1,000). However, the appropriate discount rate—the rate we use to discount this stream of annual $30 payments—may change over the life of the bond. The discount rate might rise above the promised 3% interest rate if interest rates across the economy have risen generally after the bond was issued or because the company is now riskier than a 3% annual payment justifies.

What is the present value of the principal on the bond alone? What is the present value of the interest payments alone? What is the value of the bond?

¶ 405: Application: Reinstatement in Dieglom

Let's revisit the last question we asked in ¶ 312. Why would the non-mortgagee creditors want to reinstate the mortgagee bondholders under § 1124(2)? Why could they possibly prefer that the company pay the bondholders $20 million (on the maturity date in 2020) to the company paying the bondholders $15 million in value when the plan of reorganization is confirmed? (That $15 million is the number you should have come up with in the exercise in ¶ 312.)

$20 million in value today versus reinstatement:

First consider a 2010 plan that would have given the bondholders $20 million in value. (That is, for a few moments, ignore the mortgage bondholders' deficiency—they'd not be paid in full—and Dieglom's insolvency.) Also, think about the company paying the bondholders their $20 million under § 1129(b)(2) upon the completion of the reorganization. I.e., it's either a $20 million cramdown under § 1129, or $20 million under the bond's original terms.

Remember that the bond's original terms promised annual 3% interest payments on a $20 million principal amount, or $600,000 per year. Let's say that at the time of plan formulation, 10% is the appropriate discount rate for a stream of income with features similar to that which the reinstated bondholders would enjoy. One might set up a simple spreadsheet for the debtor's payments on the reinstated debt and their present value:

Year	2011	2012	2013	2014	2015	2016	2017	2018	2019	2020
Payment	600K	600K	600K	600K	600K	600K	600K	600K	600K	600K+20M
PV	545K	496K	451K	410K	373K	339K	308K	280K	254K	231K+ 7.7M

The present value of this $20 million, 10–year promise, at 3% per year interest is about $11,400,000, which comes from discounting each annual $600,000 payment to present value (at a 10% discount rate), discounting the final $20 million repayment in year 10 to present value (also at a 10% discount rate), and then adding up all the present values in the bottom row of our spreadsheet. Because $11.4 million is less than $20 million, the other impaired creditors prefer to reinstate the bondholders, because reinstating the bondholders gives the other creditors an extra $8,600,000 to divide up among themselves.

Think about what the company would have to promise the bondholders under § 1129(b) if the company sought *under § 1129(b)* to force the bondholders to wait until 2020 to be paid off.

For the property given to the bondholders to have a value equal to the allowed amount of the claims, the present value of the promise to pay $20 million in 2020 will have to have an interest rate equal to the market interest rate for such a debt, and that rate we'll assume is about 10%. So now: if the non-bondholder creditors seek to repay the bondholders in 2010 *using § 1129(b),* we look to the last line below:

Year	2011	2012	2013	2014	2015	2016	2017	2018	2019	2020
1124(2)	600K	600K	600K	600K	600K	600K	600K	600K	600K	600K+20M
1129(b)	2M	2M	2M	2M	2M	2M	2M	2M	2M	2M+ 20M

To prefer using § 1124(2) over § 1129(b) against the bondholders, the non-bondholder creditors only have to know that $2 million is more than $600,000. By using § 1124(2), the other creditors gain $1,400,000 each year to divide up among themselves (or even to throw a little to the shareholders to buy their quick assent to the plan, or to gain their help in proposing the plan).

$15 million in value today versus reinstatement:

It's only a little harder to see why the nonbondholder creditors might prefer to promise $20 million in 2020, on the original terms, over $15 million today (the amount we promised to the mortgage bondholders based on our original absolute priority distribution in

¶ 312, where we wiped out junior interests). As we calculated above, the present value of reinstatement of the 2020 maturity date is $11.4 million, because the interest rate is so low, only 3%.

Therefore any plan that compensates the bondholders with $15 million in true value (either cash today, or cash tomorrow with a proper rate of interest) would give the bondholders *more* than the $11.4 million that reinstatement would give them. The other creditors, preferring to give the bondholders as little in true value as is possible, therefore prefer to reinstate them at their 3% interest rate and original maturity date.

¶ 406: Nonimpairment

From the legislative history:

> A claim or interest is unimpaired [under §1124(2)] by curing the effect of a default and reinstating the original terms of an obligation when maturity was on or accelerated by the default. The intervention of bankruptcy and the defaults represent a temporary crisis, which the plan of reorganization is intended to clear away. The holder of a claim or interest who under the plan is restored to his original position, when others receive less or get nothing at all, is fortunate indeed and has no cause to complain. Curing of the default and the assumption of the debt in accordance with its terms is an important reorganization technique for dealing with a particular class of claims, especially secured claims.

S. Rep. No. 989, 95th Cong., 2d Sess 120, reprinted in 1978 U.S. Code Cong. & Ad. News 5787, 5906.

B. RISK AND DIVERSIFICATION

¶ 407: Risk

To understand discounting of cash flow to present value, we've generally assumed that the future returns are fixed and certain, and the only issue is how much it's worth to delay their realization. The problem in the prior paragraph requires the discounting of a sum certain back to present value.

But investments are fraught with risk. The economy might change, the debtor's business might change, management might fail.

We now come to the concept of expected value—a quick and dirty way to capture the range of expectations on a risky investment.

As a baseline example, consider a prospective investment with a certain chance of producing $1 million in one year's time. Calculating the expected value of such an investment is easy. If that was the only return expected, it would be $1 million in expected value. (Its discounted expected value would account for the one-year delay in realization.) If the investment truly was a sure-thing, its dispersion of potential outcomes would be a vertical single line on the graph on p. 81.

But suppose we discover a prospective investment today that has the following potential outcomes a year from now. The actual outcome depends on whether the general economy turns out to be hot, cold, or lukewarm, with the respective probabilities for each state of the economy as shown below:

Investment A

Economy	Hot	Lukewarm	Cold
Probability	33%	33%	33%
Outcome	$2M	$1M	$0

Calculating the expected value of Investment A is straightforward. We simply multiply the value of each potential outcome by its probability, and then we add up all the resulting possibilities:

EV = (33% x $2M) + (33% x $1M) + (33% x $0)
= $0.66M + $0.33M + $0
= $1M

We adjust each potential outcome by its probability because no prospective outcome is a sure thing. Adjusting gives us a weighted average of all possible outcomes. To finish up, we then would discount that $ 1 million in expected value to present value.

Suppose we found an alternative $1,000,000 investment, Investment B, an agricultural investment whose value in one year depends on the amount of rainfall over the year.

Investment B

Rainfall	High	Medium	Low
Probability	10%	80%	10%
Outcome (total value of investment one year from now)	$1.25M	$1M	$0.75M

Calculating the expected value of Investment B, we find:

EV = (10% x $1.25M) + (80% x $1M) + (10% x $0.75M)
= $.125M + $0.8M + $0.075M
= $1M

Note that Investment A and Investment B have the same expected value. However, Investment A, standing alone, is riskier than Investment B. The best and worst outcomes for Investment A are more dramatic than for Investment B. They are farther apart and farther from the expected value of $1 million than are the best and worst outcomes for Investment B. The range of potential outcomes is greater. In addition, the probability of receiving something besides the expected value of $1 million are greater for Investment A (66%) than for Investment B (20%). Finally, the expected value of the best outcome for A ($2M) is larger than for B ($1.25M), but the expected value of the worst outcome for A ($0) is also smaller than for B ($0.75M).

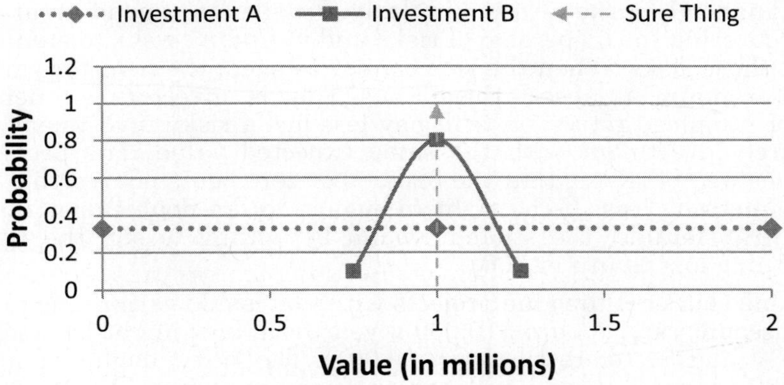

If we represent the range of probabilities above, we see that for B, the safer bet, the range of outcomes is more tightly concentrated around the expected value, while for risky bet A, the probability distribution is more widely dispersed. We can say that the *variance* of Investment A is higher than for Investment B, or that A exhibits greater *volatility* than B. Note that the sure investment, represented by the vertical line in the center of the figure, has a probability of 1 (on the left-axis) of having a value of $1 million (on the horizontal axis), i.e., a 100% chance of being worth $1 million. The sure investment will be worth $1 million always. It has zero variance; its outcome is certain.

Another way to see the problem of risk: the value of a risky project is not necessarily the same as a riskless one with the same expected value. Consider the student with $10,000, asked to invest in a project expected to yield $10,000, plus a small profit. The distribution of that profit, or the shape of the probability distribution (see the figure above) will be of intense interest to the student. If the project will yield $10,000 with certainty (plus the small profit), the project will allow continued enrollment in law school. If the project yields zero or $20,000 with equal probability (plus a small profit), then the expected monetary value is still $10,000 [from (.5 x $20,000) + (.5 x 0)].

But the usefulness (or expected utility, in the economic jargon) of the double-or-nothing bet—despite its identical expected dollar value of $10,000—is less than that of the sure thing $10,000. Why? Because the risky project means there's a 50% chance that the student will be forced to drop out of law school. True, the good outcome yields an extra $10,000, which would enable the student to take a vacation or buy a car, attractive prospects no doubt, but which the student finds less worthwhile than the certainty of being able to go to law school.

The net effect is that the risky investment will be worth less than $10,000 to the student. A 50–50 chance of $20,000 or nothing is overall not worth $10,000, but something less, perhaps considerably less. Like most individuals, the student displays *risk aversion*. She would rather take a risk-free bet than a risky one with the same expected value.

Financial markets work similarly. Financiers expend great energy in discovering the dispersion of risks and in finding ways to eliminate or offset these risks. When the risk cannot be shed, the investor will insist on a "premium" to absorb these risks. That is, investors will demand a higher promised return on (will pay less for) a risky investment than a risk-free investment with the same expected value. The premium is another way of saying that the $20,000 or zero bet is not worth $10,000, but something less. If the right to engage in the double-or-nothing bet were transferable, the student would be willing to sell the right for something less than $10,000.

One short-cut to value projects with noticeable variance is to adjust the discount rate. A sure $10,000 a year from now might be discounted at 10% (and therefore be worth $9,091). The risky, double or nothing, $20,000 or zero outcome still has an expected outcome of $10,000, but the expected outcome is discounted at, say, 20%, yielding a value of $8,333. The discount rate does double duty: paying for the time delay in receiving money and accounting for risk.

¶ 408: Variance and Diversification

Risky returns will demand a premium. How does this play out when there are many risky investments in the economy? The answer lies in the next key concept for valuation: diversification. So far, we have focused on isolated investments, each standing by itself. Multiple, different investments, however, can be combined. Some combinations can reduce the overall risk of the pooled investments. This strategy is diversification.

An investor can construct a portfolio of investments to lower the overall risk of the portfolio compared to any single investment. Imagine investing in an ice cream shop. The earnings from the shop will fluctuate with the weather: more people like to eat ice cream on hot days than on rainy days. So there is weather risk in the ice cream business: the ice cream store investor hopes for hot sunny days and long, hot summers. One way to diversify away some of this risk of bad weather is to find another investment with the opposite risk profile—one that is more profitable on rainy days. The ice cream shop investor might invest in an umbrella factory, which profits when it's rainy.

While the earnings of each business separately may fluctuate wildly, depending on whether there's sun or rain, overall earnings of the combined investments in both businesses will be much more stable than either investment standing alone.

Let's look at a more detailed and sophisticated example.

The sure-thing railroad. A riskless railroad, originally worth more, has fallen on hard times. It has filed for bankruptcy but still has a solid core business. It is expected to have certain income of $1 million per year for the foreseeable future. The riskless rate of interest is 10%. Accordingly, this railroad, Railroad A, the sure-thing railroad, would be worth $10 million. (Review the discussion of perpetuities *supra* if this valuation is unclear.) The judge accepts the $1 million projection and the 10% discount rate. She turns the whole railroad over to the railroad's one creditor, owed $10 million.

The risky railroad. Now with risk: Another railroad goes into bankruptcy, but we don't know how good the railroad will be. On average, we expect the railroad to yield $1 million. But we don't know for sure. It could earn $2 million per year, or it might earn nothing every year.

The problem is that the railroad runs from the oil fields to munitions plants. If there's war, the railroad makes a lot of money, $2 million per year. If there's peace, the railroad is useless and makes nothing. If there's tension, this Warco Railroad makes $1 million per year.

Risky Warco Railroad

Peace	Tension	War
.33	.33	.33
–0–	$1 million	$2 million

The expected income in any year will still be $1 million. To establish the present value of this risky income stream would presumably require a higher discount rate than 10%. Say that market participants insist on an extra 2%, as a risk premium for this kind of variance. A 12% discount rate would yield an enterprise value of $8.3 million. This is no different than the law student worried that if the investment turns out badly, this would force her withdrawal from law school.

This railroad, Railroad B—the risky warrior railroad—has an expected income of $1 million and a value of $8.3 million because the income is uncertain. Accordingly, the judge values the railroad at $8.3 million and gives it to Railroad B's $10 million creditor.

Railroad A—the sure-thing railroad—also has an expected income of $1 million, but because its assured income will not force any investor to face the risk of dropping out of law school, its value is $10 million. After emerging from bankruptcy, both railroads have publicly offered their stock to law school students and recent law school graduates. One thousand law school students invest $10,000 in the sure-thing railroad, which will yield each of them $1,000 in the next year. They sell their stock when they have to meet tuition bills. Stock of Railroad B—the risky railroad—sells for $8,300, but it's taken up by recent law school graduates with salaried jobs—people who can handle some of the risk.

Diversification: Railroad C and an uncorrelated income stream. Bored with schoolwork and looking at investment reports, you discover a third railroad, railroad C. Railroad C's road runs from wheat fields and infrastructure factories to cities. If there's war, it will be worthless, because the products it transports will not be made in the factories or sold in the cities. If there's tension, some of its products will be made, shipped, and sold. But if there's peace, it will boom, because demand for the products it ships will zoom, and it will be able to raise its rates.

If there's peace, this Peaceco Railroad makes a lot of money, $2 million per year. If there's war, the railroad is useless and makes nothing. If there's tension, the railroad makes $1 million per year.

Risky Peaceco Railroad

Peace	Tension	War
.33	.33	.33
$2 million	$1 million	–0–

Again, although the expected income in any year will still be $1 million, investors insist on a premium, of say 2%, for this kind of variance. A 12% discount rate would yield an enterprise value of $8.3 million. You notice that each of the 1,000 shares of Railroad C, the Peaceco Railroad, sells for $8300. Recent law school graduates, your steadily employed friends, own the stock.

Are you on your way to making a fortune? How?[3] Hint: can you construct a risk-free investment from two risky investments? Do the Peaceco and Warco Railroads remind you of ice cream and umbrellas?

C. LITIGATION IMPLICATIONS OF VALUATION IN THEORY

¶ 409: Bankruptcy Implications of Risk and Diversification

Which railroad stock would you rather own, the sure-thing railroad (worth more), or the risky one (worth less)? Posit that all three railroads (Sure–Thing, Warco, and Peaceco) had been capitalized with $10 million of bonds. All three railroads go into bankruptcy. Six months from now we'll know whether there'll be war or peace, or something in-between. Right now, each result seems equally likely (war, peace, or tension), but in six months we'll have a very good idea what the world will look like for the next several years. Which railroad's stockholders

[3] Measuring firm-specific, unsystematic risk, and the techniques for constructing a portfolio to reduce such risk is a key financial goal. Some risks are not firm-specific, but systematic. Risks to which the whole economic system is subject—a general decline in the economy, for example—are called systematic risks. In the financial formulas, systematic risk is measured by a term called "beta," which you will hear about from time to time in financial circles, but is not critical for this course. Beta is a measure of how sensitive a particular company, or its stock, is to general changes in economic conditions. To get the story on beta and systematic risk, consult any good Corporate Finance textbook, like Brealey, Myers, and Allen.

should do better when the smoke clears and the reorganization is completed: stockholders of the sure-thing railroad or stockholders of one of the risky railroads? Does your answer depend on whether the underlying risk of the railroad is diversifiable? Or is that irrelevant in these bankruptcies? Could an initially lower-value railroad end up being *more* valuable to stockholders than an initially higher-value railroad?

Why? Consider the Hunt's maneuvering, next.

Leonard Apcar & Caleb Solomon, *Going for Broke: Hunt Brothers Pin Hopes for Comeback on 'Crapshoot' in Oil*, Wall St. J., July 12, 1988, at 1

Green Canyon, Gulf of Mexico — As storm-driven 21–foot–seas rocked the Penrod 72 oil rig last winter, work had to stop for as long as a week at a time.

Every delay heightened fears that the well it was to drill in Green Canyon would never be completed — and for the three Hunt brothers of Dallas, heirs and squanderers of an oil empire, completing the well was imperative. A deckhand recalls the order of the day: "Move it, move it, move it!"

* * *

So goes the Hunt brothers' frantic effort to rebuild in oil a fortune largely lost in oil—and in silver, sugar and real estate. The Hunts need the money to help pay people they owe and secure the future of their anemic former money-gusher, Placid Oil Co. It owes $1 billion and has been mired in Chapter 11 Bankruptcy proceedings in federal court in Dallas for nearly two years. The Hunts believe that the richest rewards of Green Canyon and nearby oil-and-gas reservoirs will go to those who exploit the area first.

Big rewards imply big risks. . . .

The Hunts are betting the ranch, encumbered as it is, on one of the world's riskiest ventures. At 1,522 feet, Green Canyon's depth, this will be the deepest water off American shores that has ever produced oil. At a cost of $340 million, it is a high-stakes crapshoot. . . . N. Bunker, W. Herbert and Lamar Hunt and their partners in the Green Canyon venture are relying on an untested, one-of-a-kind, floating drilling and production system to get oil and gas from a place that some specialists believe lies barely within the industry's technological reach.

. . . [T]he Hunts' bankers have tried to lace them into financial straitjackets, and their other creditors have dogged their every step. . . . At one point, banks even proposed that the bankruptcy court auction off the Hunts' flagship company, Placid Oil, to pay off its debts.

* * *

The water in Green Canyon's Block 29 is deeper than the Sears Tower is tall. Above the water, rigs must withstand hurricane gusts of up to 150 miles an hour. Below it, drilling and production grow more complex with every additional foot. There's no consensus among major oil companies about how to begin the effort, which in any case, some oil men say, isn't worth it. "Green Canyon doesn't have enough oil and gas to fool with," says R. Paul Wickes, a lawyer for Placid's lead bank, First Republic Bank Dallas.

Five experts looked at Green Canyon Block 29, where the production apparatus is anchored, and at two nearby drilling blocks, the sites for satellite wells to pump oil to the main production center. Each expert had a different estimate of the oil and natural gas in these three blocks, covering 27 square miles. The lowest came from Netherland, Sewell & Associates, a Dallas consulting firm hired by the Hunts' banks. The firm called Placid Oil's estimate of 70 million barrels of oil and its equivalent in natural gas—medium-size, as oil deposits go—wildly optimistic. As for drilling, says Frederic D. Sewell, an executive vice president of Netherland Sewell, "going forward wouldn't be economically viable."

The banks' hired guns are out to torpedo the project by pooh-poohing it, Hunt men say. The Hunts believe that their three blocks plus huge additional acreage they have leased in the Green Canyon area all together contain way more than a half billion barrels of oil.

Peter H. Frank, *Hunts' Tactics May Pay Off*, N.Y. Times, July 17, 1987, at D2

The . . . Hunt [family] trust . . . , [under] Chapter 11 bankruptcy protection [in 1987], has repeatedly used extraordinary legal tactics. The reorganization plan filed last Wednesday by the trust's attorneys was more of the same, according to lawyers involved in the case.

* * *

In August 1986, the Hunts' Placid Oil Company . . . filed for Chapter 11 bankruptcy in an effort to thwart foreclosure proceedings by the Hunts' 23 banks. Attorneys agreed that the move damaged the already acrimonious relationship between the Hunts and their bank lenders. . . .

* * *

Beyond the disagreement about who should be paid how much and by whom, lawyers agreed that at stake was which side should be granted operational control of the Hunt trust and its companies.

* * *

A reorganization plan also submitted on Wednesday by the banks called for . . . a trustee who has no connection to the Hunts to operate the Hunt companies. . . .

Some lawyers for the banks said privately that the legal quagmire had worked as the Hunts had hoped. With the recent rise in oil prices—to more than $20 a barrel—the Hunt companies' revenue and the value of their holdings have increased substantially, making it probable that the bankruptcy cases will soon be settled, some observers said. "They wanted to hang on until the oil prices went up without losing control," said Peter Winship, a law professor at Southern Methodist University who has followed the case. "There is much more optimism now, and some sort of plan that can be approved by the court is more likely."

¶ 410: Value Uncertain: Practical Lawyers, Modern Delay, and the Advantages of the Valuation Hearing for Shareholders

Consider the following report from attorneys who represented the stockholders' committee in the reorganization in chapter 11 of Saxon Industries. In 1981 Saxon was a Fortune 500 company. The chapter 11 audit showed that its net worth was a negative $200 million. Creditors were owed $320 million.

> [Creditors] argued that the . . . stockholders had no further interest in the company. Because liabilities appeared to so greatly exceed assets, it did not seem likely that [even] the unsecured creditors would get paid in full under any reorganization plan. . . . Saxon's stockholders [might have] seemed doomed to getting nothing for their stock.
>
> . . . [U]nder the reorganization plan ultimately confirmed by the bankruptcy court, however, the Saxon shareholders weren't wiped out. They received convertible stock with a total value of $9 million [or almost 10% of the company's book value as shown in the bankruptcy audit].
>
> How did the shareholders do so well? Mainly because [they] formed a committee, utilized their rightful leverage under the bankruptcy laws, and negotiated with Saxon's creditors and the company itself.
>
> Today, in almost every instance in which a public company seeks protection under Chapter 11, the shareholders are faced with the same argument that Saxon's [shareholders] encountered—that the debtor is insolvent and, therefore, their equity no longer exists. In effect, the creditors claim they own the company.
>
> As the Saxon shareholders—and creditors—found out, however, just saying that a company is insolvent doesn't make it so under the bankruptcy laws. In order for shareholders to have their interest eliminated, the bankruptcy court must go through a complicated fact-finding trial [under § 1129(b)(2)] to determine whether the company is insolvent. The court must take extensive testimony on the actual value of the company's assets, listen to experts from opposing sides, and come to some supportable conclusion itself.
>
> Such trials are very time-consuming. When they are undertaken, confirmation of a plan of reorganization for a company operating under Chapter 11 is delayed. . . .
>
> It's not in [the unsecured creditors'] best interest . . . to engage in a lengthy battle, especially if the outcome is uncertain. And it usually is very difficult to know in advance whether a court will decide that a bankrupt company is solvent or insolvent under the bankruptcy laws. The unsecured creditors' experts will testify that

the corporation is insolvent and that the shareholders' interests should be eliminated. The shareholders' experts will testify that the corporation is clearly solvent and the shareholders should maintain their stock ownership, or have it diluted minimally.

Creditors, though, will be willing to negotiate only if there are some shareholders with whom they can negotiate. [S]hareholders must . . . form a committee [to] negotiate to protect their interests."

Barry Radick & Stephen Blauner, *Shareholders, Unite!—What To Do When a Firm Goes Bankrupt*, Barron's, Apr. 14, 1986, at 22–24.

Lynn LoPucki and William Whitford examined many chapter 11 reorganizations of the 1980s and found substantial deviation from absolute priority, benefiting stockholders. When the court appointed an equity holders' committee, equity was nearly certain to get something, averaging about 7 or 8%, in the § 1129(a)(8) settlement. Lynn LoPucki & William Whitford, *Preemptive Cram Down*, 65 American Bankruptcy Law Journal 625, 626 (1991). Similar, although sometimes smaller shareholder retentions of value were found in Elizabeth Tashjian, Ronald C. Lease & John McConnell, *Prepacks: An Empirical Analysis of Prepackaged Bankruptcies*, 40 Journal of Financial Economics 135 (1996).

Although hold-up value, uncertainty, and creditors' desire to keep shareholder-managers on board helped equity, LoPucki and Whitford believe many firms would quickly have been found insolvent if an early solvency hearing apart from the late-stage cram-down hearing under § 1129 were readily available under the Code. Why then wasn't cram-down used against the shareholders? They speculate "that the difficulty of cram-down was in large part a convenient myth that served the interests of the relatively small group of lawyers who repeatedly play important roles in major reorganization cases. Because these lawyers appeared against each other so often, they had an interest in preserving their reputations as reasonable and responsible negotiators." Id. at 630–31.

Although creditors still often complain about juniors' capacity to delay proceedings, and surely such delays continue today, most observers see the strategic delay issue as more attenuated now, with creditors having more influence in the proceedings. We see this shift further in Chapter 16, where we examine the role of the so-called "DIP lender," who lends to the debtor early in the proceeding.

¶ 411: Rule 11

The Federal Rules of Civil Procedure provide:

> By presenting to the court a pleading, written motion, or other paper—whether by signing, filing, submitting, or later advocating it—an attorney. . . certifies that to the best of [the attorney's] knowledge, information, and belief, formed after an inquiry reasonable under the circumstances[,] it is not being presented for any improper purpose, such as to . . . cause unnecessary delay. . . ; [the] claims, defenses, and other legal contentions are warranted by existing law or by a

> nonfrivolous argument for extending, modifying, or reversing existing law or for establishing new law; [the] factual contentions have evidentiary support. . .

This rule might worry bankruptcy lawyers for the stockholders of an apparently insolvent firm. But if valuation in bankruptcy is elastic, need an attorney's conscience or sense of professional responsibility be troubled when he or she asserts that the stockholders have an interest in the firm pursuant to § 1129(b)(2)?

Rule 11 sanctions have only infrequently been asserted in private commercial cases; they have usually been invoked in civil rights cases and occasionally in federal income taxation suits. Note, *Plausible Pleadings: Developing Standards for Rule 11 Sanctions*, 100 Harv. L. Rev. 630 (1987). Bankruptcy courts have their own rules; Bankruptcy Rule 9011 is substantively similar to Rule 11.

¶ 412: Standards of Professional Responsibility

RULE 3.1 of The American Bar Association's Model Rules of Professional Responsibility: Meritorious Claims and Contentions

A lawyer shall not bring or defend a proceeding, or assert or controvert an issue therein, unless there is a basis in law and fact for doing so that is not frivolous, which includes a good faith argument for an extension, modification or reversal of existing law. . . .

Comment

The advocate has a duty to use legal procedure for the fullest benefit of the client's cause, but also a duty not to abuse legal procedure. The law, both procedural and substantive, establishes the limits within which an advocate may proceed. However, the law is not always clear and never is static. Accordingly, in determining the proper scope of advocacy, account must be taken of the law's ambiguities and potential for change.

The filing of an action or defense or similar action taken for a client is not frivolous merely because the facts have not first been fully substantiated. . . . Such action is not frivolous even though the lawyer believes that the client's position ultimately will not prevail. The action is frivolous, however, if the lawyer is unable to either make a good faith argument on the merits of the action taken or to support the action taken by a good faith argument for an extension, modification or reversal of existing law. . . .

RULE 3.2 Expediting Litigation

A lawyer shall make reasonable efforts to expedite litigation consistent with the interests of the client.

Comment

Dilatory practices bring the administration of justice into disrepute. . . . [F]ailure to expedite [is un]reasonable if done for the purpose of frustrating an opposing party's attempt to obtain rightful redress or repose. It is not a justification that similar conduct is often tolerated by the bench and bar. The question is whether a competent lawyer acting in good faith would regard the course of action as having some substantial purpose other than delay. *Realizing financial or other benefit from otherwise improper delay in litigation is not a legitimate interest of the client.*

CHAPTER 5

VALUATION IN PRACTICE

So valuation is easy, right? At least conceptually—get the number and apply it to the debtor at hand in the bankruptcy court. See how far down the liability side of the balance sheet the number goes. And then the bankruptcy is complete.

Maybe it's not so straight-forward to value the firm. Indeed, to many observers, key bankruptcy problems like valuation tend towards intractability. To better understand why, we need to see the complexities entailed in a full-scale judicial valuation of a bankrupt debtor and the difficulty of getting to the valuation number. A modern case might have some advantages. But few cases are as good at revealing the difficulties of judicial valuation as is the SEC's advisory opinion for *Atlas Pipeline* in 1941, a case that for quite some time has been at the heart of finance-oriented law school casebooks. We start by examining the difficulty of judicial valuation with an excerpt from the SEC's Advisory Opinion in *Atlas Pipeline*. Studying *Atlas* gives us a window into valuation mechanics in action, the parties' conflicts and biases in valuation, the potential for judicial inexpertise, and the possibility that value in the marketplace can change rapidly as the bankruptcy proceeding moves along. It also embeds alternatives to the judicial valuation: a deal among the parties or a sale of the firm, or its major assets.

A. FAILURE

¶ 501: Background to *Atlas Pipeline*

Atlas was an oil refiner and transporter, which failed in a series of reorganizations in the 1930s. It filed for relief under old chapter X of the Bankruptcy Act of 1938. (Today's Chapter 11 was enacted in 1978 to replace the old Chapter X.) Under chapter X, the court appointed a trustee—a person unaffiliated with the company—to run the company and propose a plan of reorganization, and the SEC wrote an advisory opinion to the court administering the proceeding, a process that gave the court the benefit of the SEC's financial expertise. The court was required under the statute to set a value for the bankrupt firm and to determine whether the plan of reorganization proposed by the trustee met certain requirements: the plan had to be "fair and equitable" and "feasible." The court decided (implicitly or explicitly) whether to liquidate or reorganize, and then distributed claims on the reorganized firm to the bankrupt's creditors.

Today's chapter 11 operates somewhat differently. Today, the debtor typically operates without a trustee; the prebankruptcy managers run the debtor firm and they (or their successors) get first crack at proposing the plan of reorganization.[1] The major difference for present purposes is that today, a valuation of the firm is not mandatory; it is required only when creditors do not approve the proposed plan. A great deal of the current chapter 11 was designed to avoid the harsh difficulties of a valuation hearing, as exemplified in *Atlas Pipeline*. To see what Congress and the reorganization establishment sought to avoid in 1978, and to understand the ugly valuation hearing cloud that the parties to today's chapter 11 fear and under which they negotiate, we study *Atlas Pipeline*.

¶ 502: The Distinction Between Financial Failure and Economic Failure

Consider the following when reading *Atlas Pipeline*.

1. In March 1941, was Atlas Pipeline an economic failure, a financial failure, or both? An economic (or operating) failure doesn't generate enough cash from its operations to pay the costs of its ongoing operations—its materials, payroll, factory lease payments, etc. A financial failure (in this setting) is unable to pay back its creditors even if its operations generate enough cash to pay its ongoing operating expenses. Will an economic failure always go into bankruptcy? Not if it has no debt and owes nothing: it closes up without invoking bankruptcy law.
2. Will a financial failure always close up? Not necessarily. A financial failure can arise from the firm having borrowed too much. It does less well than expected, and it can't pay back its debts. It tries

[1] And the Securities and Exchange Commission—a key actor in Atlas Pipeline in particular and chapter X generally—has no formal role in assessing the modern plan of reorganization.

to renegotiate with its financiers. Sometimes it succeeds; sometimes it doesn't and it files for bankruptcy. But some of these firms, even though they are in bankruptcy, are economically worth continuing in business and should be saved from closing up, because their operations are viable. They can still make enough money to cover their operating costs and maybe more. They've done worse than expected but still have viable operations.

3. Consider how businesses deal with failure outside of bankruptcy. Not every failure closes up. "Failure . . . does not necessarily mean that the resources will be withdrawn from the industry and that production will cease. Whether or not this result will follow will depend upon the degree to which it is possible in the instant case to disinvest the capital entirely or adapt it to the production of alternative products or services. Many capital goods are technologically so highly specialized that they are not adaptable to uses other than those for which they were designed. . . ." A steel company builds a steel mill, but the market for steel isn't there. However, once the mill is built, the mill can only make steel. Firms will often continue in business even when earning only "a negligible return on the basis of past historical capital investment. Yet the equipment[,] being highly specialized[, makes it] next to impossible to adapt . . . to other uses and its scrap value net after disinvestment costs [is] very small. As a consequence such enterprises continue to operate so long as they succeed in securing an income . . . greater than the direct out-of-pocket costs involved in produc[tion] by an amount at least equal to a fair return on the net scrap value of the equipment. When the returns fall below that the [assets] are torn up and . . . sold for . . . scrap . . . ." Norman S. Buchanan, The Economics of Corporate Enterprise 332–35 (1940).

4. Consider two identical firms, each of whose operations are expected to be worth about $20 million. Firm A is financed completely with common stock; Firm B borrows $10 million and raises the rest with common stock. Both firms unexpectedly decline in value to $10 million. Which one needs to reorganize in bankruptcy? Which one is a financial failure (in a bankruptcy sense)? Aren't both economic failures?

5. To get us ready for the conflicts over valuation, consider the following questions: How do you conceptualize the corporation? What images or metaphors come to mind when you think of the word "corporation"? A businessperson? An entrepreneur? A board of directors? A bundle of sticks? Who owned Atlas Pipeline?

B. VALUATION OF ATLAS PIPELINE

Atlas Pipeline is factually complex. It introduces us to (or reminds us of, if we have already been introduced) a variety of terms and corporate financial actors, and we should be sure we understand this vocabulary. What is an indenture trustee?[2] A first mortgage bond?[3] A second mortgage bond?[4] A trade creditor?[5] A sinking fund?[6] Preferred stock? Liquidation value?[7] Going concern value?

The following readings abbreviate the SEC's report on the Trustee's reorganization plan. The SEC report has been divided into four parts to allow reflection on several key elements of Atlas Pipeline's valuation—the expertise of the judicial valuer and the judge's advisor, the stability of valuation over time, the relative speed of the judicial process and market changes, the decision on operational disposition of Atlas Pipeline's business, and the conflicts of interest embedded in every key operational and valuation decision.

¶ 503: Early in the Proceeding: First Trust Co. of Phil. v. Atlas Pipeline Corp., 29 F. Supp. 32 (W.D. La. 1939) (Aug. 7, 1939) (Dawkins, District Judge)

Upon the application of the First Trust Company of Philadelphia, Trustee, under the first bond mortgage, on May 26, 1939, a . . . receiver for all property and effects of the Atlas Pipeline Corporation was appointed. . . .

The property has been administered and the business carried on as a going concern since that time. Subsequently, *the said Trustee applied to have the receiver sell the entire assets as a going concern*, publication was made and notice sent out to all creditors, and on July 26, 1939, hearing was had, at which, *informal or oral objections* to granting the order of sale and for an adjournment or postponement of thirty days *[were] made in open court by counsel representing some of the second mortgage creditors. . . .*

---

[2] The entity, usually a bank, that acts for the many bondholders. Note our impoverished vocabulary. An indenture trustee works for bondholders (in and out of bankruptcy). The trustee in bankruptcy runs the bankrupt company. They're two different entities, with different functions. They have the same name, however.

[3] A debt secured by a mortgage, often on the company's plant or equipment. If the debtor defaults, the bondholders can then, usually acting through their trustee, seize the mortgaged properties from the debtor under state law, sell the properties, and use the proceeds to pay down their loan.

[4] A second mortgage bond gets paid out of the mortgaged property after the first mortgage bondholder is paid.

[5] A supplier sells merchandise to the firm; the firm pays the supplier after the supplier has delivered the merchandise to the firm. During the gap between when the supplier delivers the goods and the debtor pays for them, the supplier is a trade creditor of the debtor.

[6] A fund established by a company to repay debt before the debt's final maturity date.

[7] Usually the value from the quick sale of pieces of the firm, occurring as the firm's operations are shut down. However, it's plausible to imagine the quick sale of the firm, intact, with the buyer then deciding after the sale what to shut down and what to keep in business. The former owners would have "liquidated" their position in the firm, by turning their ownership interests into liquid cash (or other consideration). More on that when we study § 363 sales in Chapter 6.

* * *

¶ 504: The rejected sale: *Atlas Pipeline*

1. Think about the following questions as you read this chapter. Pay attention to the dates on which the court or the SEC speaks. How much was Atlas Pipeline worth? On August 17, 1939? On September 1, 1939? In September 1941? On December 8, 1941? After 1945?
2. On August 17, 1939, Judge Dawkins put the company up for sale, with the minimum acceptable bid set at $1.2 million. No bids came in. Why? Did Dawkins want too much for Atlas?

¶ 505: In re Atlas Pipeline Corporation, SEC Advisory Opinion, Under the Corporate Reorganization Act, June 7, 1941, 9 S.E.C. 416 (1941): Part I

REPORT OF THE SECURITIES AND EXCHANGE COMMISSION ON PROPOSED PLAN OF REORGANIZATION

HISTORY AND BUSINESS OF DEBTOR

A. Debtor's Business and Principal Assets

The Debtor is presently engaged in refining petroleum and marketing the products thereof. It owns an inland refinery located near Shreveport, Louisiana, and an oil pipeline system connecting its refinery with oil fields in East Texas, Arkansas and Louisiana. . . .

* * *

B. History of Debtor and Predecessor Corporations

* * *

In November 1934, Atlas Pipeline Company, Inc., and its subsidiary, Spartan, both went into receivership.[8] This was followed by a reorganization proceeding under . . . the Bankruptcy Act. A plan was confirmed in that proceeding. . . .

. . . Thereafter the Debtor defaulted on . . . interest payments . . . and a receivership proceeding was instituted . . . by the indenture trustee for the first mortgage bondholders. *On August 17, 1939, the court directed a public sale of the mortgaged properties, and fixed an upset price of $1,200,000.*[9] *No bids were received*[10] and on September 20, 1939, the present proceeding was instituted by the filing of the Debtor's petition for reorganization under Chapter X.

[8] [In a receivership, a court appoints a person, or occasionally a bank, to gather a weak firm's assets for the benefit of the firm's creditors. The receiver "receives" payments due the firm, holds the receipts for the creditors, and prevents unwise disbursement of these receipts. The modern reorganization apparatus—chapter 11 of the Bankruptcy Code and its pre–1978 predecessor, chapter X—grew out of the common law receivership mechanism and has largely replaced it.—Roe.]

[9] [An upset price is a price below which bids will not be accepted.—Roe.]

[10] [Emphasis supplied here and elsewhere where italicized.—Roe & Tung.]

PRESENT CAPITALIZATION

The present capitalization of the Debtor is as follows:

First Mortgage 6% Sinking Fund Convertible Bonds [with unpaid interest] $961,400

Second Mortgage 6% Sinking Fund Convertible Bonds [with unpaid interest] $1,500,750

Common Stock, par value $10 .... 268,800 Shs.

* * *

SUMMARY OF PLAN

A. Distribution of Cash and Securities

The [trustee's] proposed plan provides for the organization of a new company to take over the assets of the Debtor. The new company will have the following capitalization:

4½% First Mortgage Bonds	$1,011,400
4% Preferred Stock	435,000
Common Stock ($20 par value)	100,000

Under the plan Federal [and state] tax claims aggregating approximately [$105,000] will be paid in cash. . . . General unsecured claims aggregating approximately $400,000 will receive 10% in cash without interest. . . .

The first mortgage bondholders will receive $961,400 of the new 4½% first mortgage bonds, which corresponds to the principal amount of their claims plus accrued interest to May 1, 1941. The remaining $50,000 of new first mortgage bonds will be sold at par to the American Locomotive Company[11] subject to a purchase agreement with the Producers Group hereinafter described. The second mortgage bondholders will receive the new $435,000 issue of preferred stock, corresponding to one-third of the principal amount of their claims, "in exchange not only for the security of their mortgage but for their interest as ordinary creditors in the unmortgaged assets."[12] In view of the Debtor's insolvency, as found by the Court, its common stockholders are excluded from participation in the plan.

The common stock of the new company is to be purchased for $100,000 by a group of oil producers (hereinafter called the "Producers Group" or "Group") who own or control substantial oil production in the Magnolia Oil field in Arkansas. . . . [T]he common stock cannot be divested of control for at least the first 3 years of the company's existence because of failure to pay preferred stock dividends. . . .

C. Summary

The plan, in brief, gives all the common stock and virtually complete control of the Debtor to a group of oil producers who will have

[11] This company holds $765,000 of the Debtor's second mortgage bonds. . . .

[12] . . . It appears to be generally agreed that the first and second mortgages do not cover any of the current assets of the Debtor, except for certain materials and supplies with a book value of $41,573. It has also been held in this proceeding that the 10–mile pipeline from Gilark, Louisiana to the Cotton Valley Oil Field is not subject to either lien. In re Atlas Pipeline Corp., 39 F. Supp. 846 (W.D. La. 1941).

a 3–year contract to sell crude oil to the Debtor, under which the latter is obligated to purchase all of its requirements. . . .

The first mortgage bondholders are required to take a reduction in interest from 6% to 4½%, to extend the maturity of their bonds for 15 years and to give up their lien on approximately $150,600 in cash held by the indenture trustee. . . .[13] The second mortgage bondholders are required to accept new 4% preferred stock having a par value equal to one-third of the principal amount of their claims.

¶ 506: Questions about Atlas Pipeline: Part I

1. Why did the judge try to sell the company initially? Why did the court set an upset price? Is there any sense why it picked that price? What does the balance of the opinion, that follows, suggest about that upset price? Was it too high? Too low?
2. In the trustee's proposed plan, how much are the debt payments reduced? Who receives control? How much did they pay for control?

¶ 507: Atlas Pipeline SEC Advisory Opinion: Part II—Atlas's Earnings

In order to pass on the fairness and feasibility of a plan of reorganization [and thereby ascertain whether the reorganized Atlas will be able both to pay the debts contemplated in the reorganization plan and to survive as a going concern], it is necessary to determine the prospective earnings and value of the reorganized property. The capitalization of prospective earnings is the basic element in the latter determination. In estimating prospective earnings we may turn to the past earnings record of the Debtor which, after adjustment for unusual conditions and reasonably foreseeable changes, here provides a guide to what may be anticipated in the future.

A. Debtor's Past Earnings

In none of [the past five] years did the Debtor earn a profit. . . . It is to be noted also that the refining division reported a deficit . . . every year and that such profits as were shown by the Debtor were contributed by the pipeline division.

[Changed Operations]

As a result of . . . significant changes in the character of the Debtor's operations and in the conditions affecting them, [particularly the shutdown of Atlas's profitable pipeline division,] it appears that the five year record of earnings as such does not constitute a satisfactory basis for the calculation of prospective earnings.

B. Trustee's Estimate of Prospective Earnings

As the basis of his estimates the Trustee has adopted the 5–month period from November 1940 through March 1941. To the Debtor's

---

[13] [Elsewhere in the opinion, the SEC said "that the annual sinking fund requirements will be met by the purchase of $50,000 face amount of bonds at $25,000." This suggests the trustee and SEC believe the bonds' market value would be 50% of what they say the bonds are valued at in this plan.—Roe & Tung.]

earnings of this period he has applied various adjustments in arriving at his determination of prospective earnings. The use of this period as a base has certain advantages; it is a recent period, it follows the increase in refinery capacity and in operating efficiency which occurred in October 1940, it gives effect to the cessation of pipeline transportation for the account of others and reflects the predominant use of Magnolia crude on which the refinery would operate during the life of the proposed purchase agreement. . . .

TABLE II
Trustee's Estimate of Prospective Earnings
(Before Bond Interest, Bond Discount and Depreciation)

Actual Earnings (12 Months Basis)		$26,500
Adjustments Increasing Earnings		
	Sales of Refined Products	$90,314
	Purchases: Crude Oil	78,733
	Purchases: Ethyl Lead	45,444
	Refinery Fuel	29,798
Total Adjustments Increasing Earnings		$244,289
Adjustment Decreasing Earnings		
	Pipeline Operation	7,873
Net Adjustments Increasing Earnings		236,416
Trustee's Estimated Earnings (12 Months Basis)		$262,916

. . . [A]ctual earnings during the five months ended March 31, 1941, were [only] $11,042 before depreciation, bond interest and discount. Without allowance for seasonal variation these earnings are at the rate of $26,500 for a full year. To these earnings the Trustee has applied a number of adjustments as set forth in [Table II].

[Freight Reductions]

. . . The increase of $90,314 in "Sales of Refined Products" represents the Trustee's estimate of the amount by which the Debtor's [profits on] gasoline sales will be increased by certain freight rate reductions ordered by the Interstate Commerce Commission effective June 11, 1941. These rate reductions apply to shipments of refined petroleum products from all the points in the midcontinent field to western trunk-line territory.

. . . [But] the marketing of gasoline in the western trunk-line territory is highly competitive [and] there is a substantial possibility that midcontinent refiners will reduce their prices . . . , thus passing on . . . part of the savings in transportation costs. . . . [Competition will erode the freight savings] in sales of refined products [to] $51,469, or $38,845 less than the Trustee's estimate of $90,314.

* * *

C. Other Adjustments to Earnings

* * *

The Trustee has also adopted without adjustment the average refining margin. . . . The record indicates that [margins] during the base period were the lowest in the Debtor's history but also indicates that earnings during the period showed substantial improvement as compared with the preceding 18 months.

Since the close of the base period on March 31, 1941, . . . advances [have] occurred in the prices of crude oil and gasoline. . . . [T]here have been wide fluctuations in the refining margins, and although at the present time they show improvement it is not possible to determine what they will be when prices of crude and refined products become more stable. Furthermore, the recent fluctuations do not appear to be of great significance in a consideration of the Debtor's prospective earnings over the remaining economic life of its refinery. The immediate cause of the advance in gasoline prices has been a *"record breaking increase in gasoline demand"*[14] *reflecting*, at least in part, *the stimulus of the defense program.* Although the initial effect has been favorable to the Debtor's operations, the extension of the defense program may result in offsetting developments such as diversion by the Government of means of oil transportation, reduction in automobile output and measures affecting prices. Under all the circumstances, we believe that the Trustee's adoption of the Debtor's refining margin during the base period is reasonable.

* * *

D. Summary

In arriving at his estimate of prospective earnings the Trustee has taken the actual earnings of the five months period which were at the annual rate of $26,500. To this he has added certain net adjustments in the amount of $236,416 representing estimated improvements which have not yet been realized. Total estimated earnings so arrived at amount to $262,916 before depreciation [of $90,000 of Atlas's physical facilities] and bond interest. . . . [The net annual earnings came to $170,600.]

. . . [I]t is our opinion that the Trustee's [$263,000] forecast is excessive by at least $135,000 and that the Debtor's reasonably prospective earnings for reorganization purposes do not exceed $130,000 annually before depreciation and bond interest.

Even such an estimate, however, requires substantial qualification. Initially it is to be noted that the Debtor's operation is a marginal one. Prospective earnings of $130,000 represent a profit of only 5.2 [cents] per barrel of crude processed before allowance for depreciation. Thus, *a continued decline in refining margin equivalent to 3/16 cents per gallon of gasoline sold would come near to eliminating all earnings*, before depreciation, reducing them by $115,000. Because of the small margin of profit any such estimate of earnings is subject to a high degree of uncertainty.

[14] Oil and Gas Journal, April 17, 1941, p. 39.

* * *

¶ 508: Questions about Atlas Pipeline's: Part II—Earnings

1. In the section entitled "Other Adjustments to Earnings", the SEC mentions stimulus of gasoline demand by a defense program. How does the SEC interpret that information as affecting Atlas's valuation? As a positive for its valuation? As a negative? As too difficult to assess? Do you agree with its overall interpretation? Was there a "market" opinion on the impact of the defense program?
2. Evaluate the impact of the narrow 3/16 cent per gallon margin, as discussed above.

¶ 509: Atlas Pipeline SEC Advisory Opinion: Part III—Operational Disposition and the Discount Rate

VALUATION [AND LIQUIDATION VS. REORGANIZATION]

In valuing this marginal enterprise it is necessary to consider what may be obtained from the Debtor's assets on the basis of two alternative courses of action, a) liquidation and sale of the property and b) continuation of the Debtor as an operating entity.

A. Liquidating Value

* * *

... [T]he net liquidating value of the Debtor's assets is $1,189,600[.]

* * *

B. Value as Operating Entity

The value derivable from this Debtor as an operating entity is dependent in large part upon the amount of earnings to be obtained from the property as reorganized and the length of time for which such earnings will be available. ... We turn now to a consideration of the remaining economic life of the enterprise.

1) Economic Life

The [Trustee's estimate] of the remaining life of the present plant facilities [was 10 years and] he computed annual depreciation for the reorganized company['s present facilities] on th[at] basis[.]

* * *

[But in] view of the age of the equipment and the trend of technological advance in the industry it is our opinion that substantial investment in plant facilities will be required before the end of the 10 year period in order to keep the enterprise competitive. If this point is reached in ... 5 years, as it very well may, the Debtor's earnings would have provided for this purpose a total of ... $328,000 at the end of five years. ...

Even though the Debtor could continue to operate for the next five years there is substantial reason to doubt that $328,000 should be adequate to make competitive the cracking units, which cost $900,000 and which at that time will be 11–12 years old, and the other equipment most of which will be over 20 years old. *If at the end of the economic life of the present facilities, the Debtor has been unable to earn sufficient funds above its debt service requirements to re-equip its plant and maintain its competitive position the Debtor's existence as an operating entity will cease.*[15] . . .

2) Determination of Value

[Choosing a capitalization rate]

The Trustee has estimated the going concern value of the reorganized Debtor at approximately $1,700,000. . . . In arriving at this value the Trustee deducted an annual depreciation charge of $90,000 from his estimated prospective earnings of $262,000. The balance of $170,000, representing his estimated prospective earnings before bond interest and income taxes, was capitalized at 10%.

In our opinion this value is predicated on an estimate of prospective earnings which is overstated by $135,000, [on] the depreciation charge[16] [which] is calculated on the assumption of a 10 year remaining life for the present facilities . . . and *for the reasons set forth subsequently, [on a] 10% [capitalization rate which] is too low a rate of capitalization in the light of the risks inherent in this enterprise.*

We believe a more appropriate approach to the valuation of this Debtor would be one which recognized the company's uncertain tenure of existence as an operating entity. In our opinion, it is improbable that this Debtor will be able during the remaining economic life of its present properties to obtain sufficient funds from earnings to meet its debt service and to make the necessary plant replacements to maintain its competitive position. On this basis the elements of value derivable from the reorganized company consist of the present worth, at an appropriate discount rate, of the cash profits that may be produced during its remaining operating life and the present worth of the values realizable at the end of that life from the disposition of its assets.

The Trustee has testified that in his opinion the proper rate of return[17] to apply in valuing the Debtor ranged from 8% to 20%. The General Manager testified that in his opinion the rate should be 8% to 12% or possibly 14%. The rate used by them was 10%.

---

[15] Because of the excessive issuance of debt and preferred stock provided for in the proposed plan, the Debtor will be effectively foreclosed from entering the capital markets for the necessary funds. [Why would this excessive, overhanging debt foreclose Atlas from raising capital even if it could use the new capital for a good, profitable project? We examine the reasons in Chapter 19, at ¶ 1923.—Roe.]

[16] The depreciation charge of $90,000 compares with an average depreciation charge of $236,000 for the last five years.

[17] [The rate of return is usually the percentage that an investment will return. If a $1,000,000 investment will return $100,000, then the rate of return is 10%. The SEC is using rate of return and discount rate synonymously.—Roe.]

The determination of an appropriate rate must be predicated on the risks inherent in the enterprise.[18] The Debtor is operating in a highly competitive field. Furthermore it has the weaknesses characteristic of a small inland refinery. In addition to the general risks arising from the nature of the industry and the Debtor's position in it, there are numerous hazards affecting the realization by the Debtor of the prospective earnings estimated herein. These have been set forth earlier in the report. *In the light of the risks inherent in the enterprise it is our opinion that the proper rate of return to be applied to the Debtor's prospective earnings before income taxes would be 15%, certainly not less than 12%.*[19]

* * *

[Scrap value at the end of Atlas's expected life]

. . . [W]e have shown the liquidating value of the Debtor's assets as indicated by the record. [But t]his value is applicable only to a liquidation undertaken by the Debtor at the present time. The realization that may be obtained in a liquidation several years hence is a speculative and uncertain matter. The testimony is clear that present conditions provide an *unusually favorable opportunity* for the disposal of the Debtor's fixed assets. *There is a scarcity of new and used pipe, and prices advanced considerably in the 60 or 90 days preceding the hearing on the proposed plan. How long these unusual conditions may be expected to continue is a matter of speculation.*

* * *

[Conclusion on liquidation vs. reorganization value]

In our opinion, a reasonable estimate of the operating life of the reorganized company should be taken at approximately five years for purposes of valuation. . . . [T]he value of the reorganized company as an operating entity, on the basis of a five-year life and the other factors set forth above, ranges between $1,144,000 and $1,230,000 before allowance for capital improvements and reorganization expenses. From this must be deducted $110,000 representing the cost of necessary capital improvements. . . .

[I]t appears that the value of the reorganized Debtor . . . would be $1,100,000 before reorganization expenses. . . .

¶ 510: Atlas Pipeline SEC Advisory Opinion: Part IV—Conclusion

FEASIBILITY AND FAIRNESS

The . . . salient facts are that (a) the Debtor's value upon present liquidation may well equal, if not exceed, its value as a continued

[18] Dewing, The Financial Policy of Corporations (3d ed. 6th reprinting 1939) at 145: ". . . the rate at which a business shall be capitalized, to obtain its value, will depend on the relative uncertainty or certainty, the relative risk, of the continuation of the earnings. The greater the risk, the greater the doubt of continued earnings and the lower is the capitalized value of these earnings; and conversely, the lower the risk, the greater the value."

[19] . . . General Motors is selling (after taxes) on a 10% basis. . . . [T]he contrast between General Motors and the Debtor points up the inadequacy of the Trustee's rate.

operating entity; (b) its earnings prospects are subject to substantial fluctuation, and as a going concern it would operate as a marginal enterprise; (c) its remaining economic life is limited by reason of advancing obsolescence of its refining facilities *and its apparent inability to earn the substantial investment to be required within a few years if the enterprise is to be kept competitive.*

* * *

We have emphasized in the preceding section that the company will have an uncertain tenure of existence as an operating unit. . . . [I]t is improbable that the new company will be able during the remaining economic life of its present properties to obtain sufficient funds from earnings to meet its debt service and make the necessary plant replacements to maintain its competitive position. *The effort to do so alternatively from the sale of securities would appear doomed to failure,* in view of the nature of the proposed capitalization. With its property grossly overbonded and subject to the other deficiencies we have discussed, *the plan thus contains the seeds of another early reorganization, or liquidation. . . .*

* * *

To summarize, *the plan allocates to the first mortgage bondholders new bonds which, it was testified, will have a value materially less than their face amount. . . .* In addition, as next discussed, they are to place the fate of their investment in the hands of the Producers Group despite the latter's conflicting interests . . . , leading in our opinion to the conclusion that the plan cannot be considered fair.

* * *

[The SEC then describes this part of the trustee's plan: The debtor must purchase all the crude oil it needs from the Producer Group alone for 3 years, even though it has access to many fields. In addition, the price it will pay is limited both up and down. The SEC observes in addition that crude oil supply problems have never troubled Atlas.]

* * *

CONCLUSION

We believe that the proposed plan cannot be approved as feasible or fair. It has been suggested that the interests of the Debtor's security holders require an agreement with the Producers Group, and that the plan embodies the most favorable terms which could be obtained from them. It is our view that the risks to the Debtor's security holders entailed by disapproval of the plan are outweighed by the sacrifices they are asked to make under the plan, and by the probable existence of alternative courses of action which are not subject to these same objections.

(a) On the assumption that continuation of the Debtor's operations would be in the interests of its security holders, . . . the Producers Group's contribution is not shown to be essential to continuation of operations. . . .

(b) . . . [T]here has been interest in the Debtor's property [from other oil companies].[20] [The record suggests that] the parties have unduly restricted their efforts by attempting to work out a plan [with the Producers Group] which would produce a maximum face amount of new fixed obligations for the bondholders.

(c) Finally, if it develops that no reorganization can be effected on a fair and feasible basis, a liquidation of the enterprise may be necessary. In our opinion it is entirely possible that the Debtor's bondholders will fare as well, if not better, in such event than they would under the present plan. We have already considered at length the factors which point in that direction, such as the marginal nature of the enterprise, its necessarily limited life in view of the age of its equipment and the technological advances in the industry, the fact that liquidation will be probable in a relatively few years, and the indications that favorable liquidation possibilities exist at the present time which may not be present later.

By the Commission. . . .

¶ 511: The Judicial Verdict: In Re Atlas Pipeline Corp., 39 F. Supp. 846 (W.D. La. 1941) (July 15, 1941) (Dawkins, District Judge)

The Trustee has presented to the court for tentative approval and *submission to creditors a plan of reorganization for this corporation, which already has the approval of representatives of all classes of creditors.* However, the Securities and Exchange Commission, to whom it was submitted under provisions of the Bankruptcy Act, . . . , has filed a report to the effect that the plan is neither fair nor feasible.

* * *

Since it has been in the hands of this court, . . . [t]he court has judicially declared it insolvent, eliminated participation of common stock and the proposed plan therefore attempts to provide for the claims of creditors only. . . .

* * *

The report of the Commission consisting of some sixty odd pages, criticized the figures of the Trustee in calculating or estimating the prospective earnings and consequent success of the new company in numerous respects, and of course, speaks for itself. I shall not undertake to discuss these in detail, but think it sufficient to say that while no one can be certain as to such matters, I believe that the Trustee has adopted a reasonable and conservative basis for his calculations, which are being borne out by his own experience over the period since certain improvements and changes in operations were instituted in the fall of 1940. The feasibility of the plan would seem to be further attested, if not assured, by the fact that the Purchasing Group, [a group of oil producers that generally use Atlas's pipeline to

[20] . . . Lion Oil Company in December of 1939 was "willing to negotiate an agreement for the purchase of the [Debtor's] properties" on a basis [that] . . . Mr. Boenning described . . . as "a very satisfactory deal from the viewpoint of the bondholders."

transport their oil] who will have charge of the new management, are men of large means with an assured supply of crude oil, which they agree to furnish upon a reasonable basis, so as to keep the refinery operating at something near capacity. Their investment of $100,000 in the common stock and willingness to extend addition credit or cash for another $200,000 is very tangible evidence of the faith of these experienced operators in the success of the undertaking. When this is considered, along with the fact that bankers and business men of wide experience acting for and interested with the present first and second mortgage bondholders, have unqualifiedly approved the plan, the court would hesitate to turn it down and adopt the suggestion of the Commission that the properties be scrapped and liquidated as junk.

I am impressed that the views of the Commission are somewhat cold blooded and are based on the theory that no new security should be issued which is not worth, at the time, its face value. . . . [B]ut [it is] the duty of the court to try to protect the interest of all creditors as far as the assets and circumstances of the debtor permit. . . .

* * *

Under all the circumstances, I think that the plan is both fair and feasible, and should be submitted to the creditors for their consideration.

Proper decree should be presented.

¶ 512: Atlas Pipeline: More on the Decision

Consider the Atlas opinions in terms of valuation, liquidation vs. reorganization, and distribution to creditors.

1. *Valuation*. The SEC's advisory opinion notes at p. 95 that on August 17, 1939, the court directed a public sale of the pipeline properties, but required that the minimum bid be $1.2 million. The court refused to consider bids that were any lower. No bids came in, and the reorganization began. How might the judge have determined the minimum bid? If the value of the company was as high as the Trustee thought, at $1.7 million, why did no one bid on the company? Should the court have taken the best bid it could have found?

   Recall the questions posed before the Atlas readings. How much was Atlas Pipeline worth on August 17, 1939? On September 1, 1939? In September 1941? On December 8, 1941? After 1945?

2. *Liquidate or Reorganize?* Should the fact that Atlas staggered through the 1930s, unable to repay its debt, have suggested to the judge that Atlas was a candidate for liquidation? Or should that history, in theory, tell us very little about whether Atlas's operations should have been liquidated in 1939?

   The decision on whether to liquidate or reorganize the firm can involve valuation, of course: if liquidation would be worth X, but reorganization would be worth Y, then the question could simply be whether X or Y is greater

   Liquidation—conventionally the piecemeal sale of the firm's assets—would have ended the firm's existence. Reorganization lets it try again. In reading Atlas Pipeline, consider the reasons why a court should decide whether to liquidate or reorganize Atlas Pipeline. (Why not let the parties decide? And, if so, which parties?)

Usually such business decisions on closing or continuing a business are made in the American economy by those running the enterprise, without any judicial intervention. If, say, General Motors is losing money on an auto assembly plant, then, once it satisfies whatever contractual and statutory obligations it has to its employees, it can decide to close the unprofitable factory. Isn't this basic to corporate law's business judgment rule? What justifies the business judgment rule? Are the rule's justifications inapplicable to the reorganization of Atlas Pipeline?

Is judicial intervention solely an act of sympathy for the bankrupt debtor's satellite interests (such as its employees, suppliers, and local businesses that rely on the bigger firm)? If so, why not intervene when factories close, whether inside or outside of bankruptcy? Do the opinions evince such sympathy for the bankrupt firm's satellite interests?

3. *Distributional Consequences of the Plan*. Using the figures on page 96, complete the following chart for the *Atlas Pipeline* plan. What percentage return does each layer get, and how much is the value accorded to each layer? Does the trustee's proposal make sense? What explanations are there for the result?

	Value	Income	Percentage return
Bondholder			
Preferred			
New shareholders			
Overall company			

Could these results, particularly the percentage return you just came up with for the new shareholders, explain why the SEC opposed the trustee's plan? But why don't the Firsts, or their representatives, object?

How much does the trustee expect the First's new bonds to trade at after the reorganization? See p. 97 (footnote).

Is there any way to justify the plan as beneficial to the Firsts? If the Firsts reject the trustee's plan, what follows? Another plan? Another two years of process? Another SEC advisory opinion? A court confirmation hearing? Appeals? When was the last time the Firsts received interest on their bonds? Could well-informed, sensible bondholders approve the trustee's plan?

4. *Structure: Sale or Reorganization?* Was Atlas reorganized or was it sold to the Producers Group? If sold, how much did the Producers Group pay?

5. *Administration*. The SEC, the trustee, and the judge all have radically different senses of the valuation of Atlas Pipeline, yet all are government officials and all are ostensibly neutral. Either value

isn't obvious or each official has a reason to reach a particular result.

¶ 513: After the Reorganization: The Historical Verdict

Victor Brudney & Marvin Chirelstein, Corporate Finance 30–31 (3d ed. 1987): The Aftermath of the Atlas Pipeline Case

Atlas Pipeline Corporation emerged from reorganization as Atlas Oil and Refining Company in January 1942. The prices at which its bonds sold are as follows:

	1942	1943	1944	1945	1946	1947
High	88	95	100	99½	103¾	102½
Low	62	80	92½	90	98	92

The enterprise apparently succeeded beyond all expectations. The following are its earnings before taxes and interest, after taxes and interest, and per share of preferred stock and of common stock for the years ended November 30, 1943 and 1944, the only years for which figures are available:

	1943	1944
Before taxes & interest	$515,422	$966,955
After tax & interest	134,818	242,093
Per preferred (4350 shares outstanding)	30.99	60.06
Per common (5000 outstanding)	23.48	45.19

Atlas's common stock was purchased by Standard Oil (Ohio) periodically; by the end of 1945 Standard Oil owned 28% of the common stock, by the end of 1946 it owned 57% of the common stock, and in 1948 the bonds and the preferred stock were retired. As of the end of 1943 only $513,200 . . . of the bonds was outstanding. The bonds in Atlas' treasury had been acquired by the company at a discount of approximately 11%.

¶ 514: After the Reorganization Questions

1. What happened after the reorganization? How did Atlas Pipeline become such a success? What can drive success in a business like refining oil?
2. How did the SEC get it so wrong? Did the SEC just pick a low earnings number, reflecting the depression-era economy, and then justify the number inadequately? Did the SEC fail to anticipate the subsequent success of Atlas Pipeline? Should it be faulted for doing so? Is there evidence in the case that people familiar with the oil mar-

ket at the time of the advisory opinion believed that those with oil distribution and refining facilities had a valuable resource? Why was there "an unusually favorable opportunity for the disposal of the Debtor's fixed assets"? (p. 102.) Why was there a "record breaking increase in gasoline demand" after March 1941? (p. 99.) Did the judge foresee any better? Should he be praised?

3. How did the economic outlook of the oil refinery and transportation business change between 1939 and 1941? Who benefited under the plan that was confirmed? Who would have benefited if the company had been sold in 1939?

4. Equity stock in a company is sometimes described as an option. If the value of the stock is above zero, the stock is valuable, but if the value of the stock is below zero (that is, the company is insolvent), the stockholders are not liable for the deficit—limited liability of the corporate shareholder. This is the basic result of limited liability of corporate stockholders. The relationship is asymmetric: full profit-sharing without full loss-sharing. Equity's "option," therefore, is the option to walk away and lose only what it has invested, but no more than what it has invested. Is that "option" valuable? If stockholders (and managers who are sometimes closely allied with them) share in the profits but aren't liable for exceptional losses, what incentives does that give them when a business venture is struggling? What sort of risk profile might they prefer? In Atlas Pipeline the stockholders were all wiped out and replaced, but could you see it ending differently if they had managed to delay resolution until the market turned around?

C. CREDITOR CONFLICT

The Atlas Pipeline valuation was highly contested. The length and detail of the SEC Advisory Opinion seemed to negatively influence the judge, and ultimately three competent, supposedly neutral government parties (the judge, the trustee, and the SEC) were not able to find a consensus. Yet, when we looked at valuation in the last chapter, it seemed relatively straightforward, even somewhat dry. Why was this valuation so hard? We will explore one of the key obstacles in this section.

1. Will each party to the reorganization scientifically calculate the value of the firm if liquidated and if reorganized and then present such dispassionate valuations to the judge? See *Hartford Railroad*, supra.

2. What if Atlas Pipeline's first mortgagee bondholders (owed $961,400) knew the pipeline and refinery could be scrapped for a little under $1 million? They also knew, we hypothesize, that the firm's going concern value was $1.2 million (equal chances of earning enough to be worth $.6 million, $1.2 million, or $1.8 million). What operational decision would the Firsts want, especially if they could not easily make a deal with the second mortgagees? To what extent would the operational decision depend upon the type of com-

pensation given the first mortgagee (stock, debt, cash, or some hybrid) if the company were reorganized instead of liquidated for cash?

3. Is the second mortgagee necessarily more trustworthy? (The second mortgagee was owed $1,500,750 but would be paid only after the first mortgagee bondholders were paid.) If Atlas Pipeline's liquidation value was $1 million, but it's going concern value was $800,000—made from equal chances of turning out to be worth 0, $800,000, and $1.6 million—what would the second mortgagee want (assuming that reorganization would keep the first mortgagee's debt in place)?
4. Is there any party to the reorganization to whom the judge can turn?
5. After thinking through questions 3 and 4, consider whether the judges in the early Atlas Pipeline decision or the Eastern Air Lines bankruptcy (below) could have deferred to one of the parties.

¶ 515: Eastern Air Lines

Valuation-judgment-driven conflicts are not just a thing of the distant past or the old Chapter X. In the Eastern Air Lines case, the issue was not the sale of assets, but the release of restricted cash, yet the issue was still (implicitly) whether liquidation or reorganization would be better.

Bankruptcy courts make what are in effect liquidation versus reorganization decisions at several points during the proceeding. They may do so without formally valuing the firm and deciding on whether liquidation value exceeds reorganization value. But once made, the decisions will affect the value of the firm. One decision point is obvious: a creditor may ask that the company be liquidated, usually by requesting that the chapter 11 proceeding (a reorganization) be converted to chapter 7 (a liquidation).

Another point when the bankruptcy court is really making a liquidation versus reorganization decision is less obvious: At the very beginning of the bankruptcy case, when the typical debtor enters chapter 11, it has run out of cash. If it can't get new money soon, it won't be able to pay its employees on their next payday. If it fails to meet its payroll (or fails to get new inventory, or fails to buy the necessary new machine, etc.), then the debtor will be forced to self-liquidate. Under the Code, the firm can borrow and give a new creditor a superpriority, but must get court approval to do so. If the court doesn't approve, the firm would usually then have to liquidate.

A third, rarer scenario: some firms have cash but need court approval to use it. If they cannot use their cash, they again will typically be forced to liquidate.

Consider the following news summary of part of the Eastern Air Lines bankruptcy. The unsecured creditors seemed sympathetic to the firm being liquidated, which would have yielded them 2 cents on each dollar of debt they were owed (according to Eastern's trustee). Should the judge have been reluctant to turn them down, if he or she were only interested in maximizing the value to Eastern's financial owners?

Agis Salpukas, *Court Gives Eastern Air $135 Million: Trustee Is Allowed Use of Escrow Funds To Keep Line Going*, N.Y. Times, Nov. 28, 1990, at D1, col. 1*

A Bankruptcy Court judge yesterday allowed Eastern Airlines to draw up to $135 million in escrow funds to help assure that the airline can keep operating through early next year.

In his decision, Judge Burton R. Lifland backed up the business judgment of Martin R. Shugrue, the trustee appointed by the judge in April to try to make the airline viable.

A relieved Mr. Shugrue said the money would enable Eastern to attract advance bookings again. In his testimony yesterday Mr. Shugrue said it was impossible to run an airline by being kept on such a short financial leash.

"Through the floor"

He said advance bookings went "through the floor" after Nov. 14, when a committee of unsecured creditors urged Judge Lifland to shut the airline down and liquidate it.

At the hearing the judge granted Eastern $30 million out of the funds being held in escrow, with $15 million being made available right away to keep the airline operating.

* * *

Warning to Creditors

The unsecured creditors, in this round, did not specifically urge a liquidation; although in their motion they said Eastern "is not and cannot be a viable stand-alone airline." They also warned that "further withdrawal of the magnitude now requested throws into doubt the ability of the estate to conduct an orderly liquidation."

Of the $135 million granted yesterday, $120 million can be used at the discretion of Mr. Shugrue, while $15 million would be set aside by the court as a fund to reassure suppliers. Eastern would have to get the court's permission to use the $15 million.

Mr. Shugrue has predicted that Eastern could begin to break even by March if fuel prices moderated and if its program to attract business passengers continued to work.

Joel Zweibel, the attorney representing the unsecured creditors, repeated many of the same arguments presented at the last hearing, when the committee had urged a liquidation. He said Mr. Shugrue was attempting a turnaround at a time of great Mideast uncertainty. Jet fuel prices have skyrocketed since Iraq's invasion of Kuwait in August, although they have declined recently.

He added that Eastern had continually been unable to meet its own projections and has had to come back to the court for more money from the escrow fund to keep operating.

Mr. Zweibel also said that Mr. Shugrue had estimated that only $40 million, or about 2 cents for every dollar of debt, would go to the unsecured creditors if the airline was liquidated. He said that at the current rate of losses this could be wiped out in less than a month.

* * *

¶ 516: Practice Points: Psychology

Could the psychology of practicing law contribute to the deadlocks and costs of corporate reorganization? Consider the following readings.

> In cases of civil liability, attorneys frequently fail to negotiate a settlement until well after they have spent enormous amounts of their client's resources. If a case is going to settle, economic rationality would dictate that the parties resolve the dispute before incurring the burdensome costs of pretrial posturing. Why is it that attorneys only rarely achieve this efficient outcome? Several cognitive biases in perception of their cases may prevent attorneys from achieving an early settlement. . . . Prospect Theory, a psychological theory of the perception of chance events, predicts that all defendants will systematically undervalue the expected utility of the case against them. This undervaluing can lead defendants to reject otherwise acceptable settlement offers and gamble on the outcome at trial. . . .
>
> Part of an attorney's job is [to] generate arguments which advance his position. The process of generating such arguments may lead the attorney to believe more strongly in his case. In research on story-generation, cognitive psychologists have found that *when a person generates reasons and stories to support a position, they come to believe in that position.* . . . [E]ven if the parties do not feel an enormous need to litigate the case because of some hatred for the other party or desire to have one's day in court, cognitive biases impede the negotiation and settlement process.

Jeffrey Rachlinski, Prospect Theory and Civil Negotiation, Stanford Center on Conflict and Negotiation, Working Paper No. 17, Oct. 1990.

Consider the possibility that uncertain standards in chapter 11 (and uncertain valuation) could lead each party to differ on their notion of what settlement would be "fair":

> A major unsolved riddle facing the social sciences is the cause of impasse in negotiations. The consequences of impasse are evident in the amount of private and public resources spent on civil litigation, the costs of labor unrest, the psychic and pecuniary wounds of domestic strife, and in clashes among religious, ethnic and regional groups. Impasses in these settings are not only pernicious, but somewhat paradoxical since negotiations typically unfold over long periods of time, offering ample opportunities for interaction between the parties.
>
> Economists . . . typically attribute delays in settlement to incomplete information. Bargainers possess private information about factors such as their alternatives to negotiated agreements and costs

> to delay, causing them to be mutually uncertain about the other side's reservation value. Uncertainty produces impasse because bargainers use costly delays to signal to the other party information about their own reservation value. . . .
>
> [A] different and relatively simple psychological mechanism [can also] cause . . . bargaining impasse. This is the tendency for parties to arrive at judgments that reflect a self-serving bias—to conflate what is fair with what benefits oneself. Such self-serving assessments of fairness can impede negotiations and promote impasse in at least three ways. First, if negotiators estimate the value of the alternatives to negotiated settlements in self-serving ways, this could rule out any chance of settlement by eliminating the contract zone (the set of agreements that both sides prefer to their reservation values). Second, if disputants believe that their notion of fairness is impartial and shared by both sides, then they will interpret the other party's aggressive bargaining not as an attempt to get what they perceive of as fair, but as a cynical and exploitative attempt to gain an unfair strategic advantage. Research in psychology and economics has shown that bargainers care not only about what the other party offers, but also about the other party's motives. Third, negotiators are strongly averse to settling even slightly below the point they view as fair. . . . If disputants are willing to make economic sacrifices to avoid a settlement perceived as unfair and their ideas of fairness are biased in directions that favor themselves, then bargainers who are "only trying to get what is fair" may not be able to settle their dispute.
>
> . . . [This] self-serving bias, and the impasses it causes, occurs even when disputants possess identical information. . . . The bias is also present when bargainers have incentives to evaluate the situation impartially, which implies that the bias does not appear to be deliberate or strategic.

Linda Babcock & George Loewenstein, *Explaining Bargaining Impasse: The Role of Self–Serving Biases*, 11 Journal of Economic Perspectives 109, 109–10 (1997).

D. THE MANAGERS

¶ 517: The Role of Managers in Chapter 11

Los Angeles Lumber paints a picture of managers as allied with shareholders of the bankrupt. Because the Code gives managers the power to present the first plan, due to the 120–day exclusivity period, regularly extended, during which only the debtor can present a plan, an alliance of incumbent managers with shareholders could be powerful.[21]

While such alliances surely still occur, and perhaps occur often, a modern chapter 11 of a public company can be more complex. First, managers of the public company often do not have a lot of their own

[21] Section 1121(b): "only the debtor may file a plan until after 120 days after the date of the order for relief . . . ."

wealth tied up in the company, nor do they own a substantial fraction of the bankrupt's stock. Second, managerial turnover in chapter 11 is fairly high.[22] Third, the orientation of the new managers can be uncertain. In a few cases the new managers wanted to keep the enterprise going, even when liquidation seemed warranted. Eastern Airlines used up its enormous cash reserves, illustrating how managers (even a manager who was a court-appointed trustee) might prefer to take a chance to be a hero who saves the company. But, fourth, there now is a cadre of professional "turnaround" managers who move from chapter 11 to chapter 11, turn the company around, often with partial liquidations, and then move on. Creditors are often instrumental in bringing these chapter 11 veterans into the reorganizing company.[23]

On the issue of delay, over time, incentives could make a difference. David Skeel reports: "key executives are increasingly given performance-based compensation packages in Chapter 11. The most common strategy is to promise the executives a large bonus if they complete the reorganization quickly; likewise, executives face ever-smaller bonuses if the case takes longer." David A. Skeel, *Creditors' Ball: The "New" New Corporate Governance in Chapter 11*, 152 University of Pennsylvania Law Review 917 (2003).

[22] Stuart Gilson, *Bankruptcy, boards, banks, and blockholders*, 27 Journal of Financial Economics 355 (1987) (more than half of the bankrupt's board of directors is gone by the end of a chapter 11).

[23] Lynn M. LoPucki, *Strange Visions in a Strange World*, 91 Michigan Law Review 79, 96 (1991).

CHAPTER 6

THE § 363 SALE

A. SELLING

¶ 601: Sale of the Firm to Provide a Value?

Could the firm in its entirety be put up for bids? Why would that not solve the valuation problem? Instead of allowing the firm to be dismantled piecemeal outside of bankruptcy, and instead of having a bankruptcy-based one-year or longer renegotiation, the court could solicit bids for the debtor's entire operations, seeking to sell the operational side of the firm intact.

The sale would not only provide a bottom-line valuation of the firm, but would provide cold cash to then distribute to the creditors. Perhaps surprisingly, the Code did not anticipate such whole-firm sales and the statutory provisions that govern such sales are rather thin.

Nevertheless, such going concern sales are today common in bankruptcy. One study finds that more than 20% of public companies filing for Chapter 11 from 2002 to 2011 were restructured by a sale of substantially all their assets as going concerns.[1] The figure below illustrates the steadily increasing trend in going-concern sales, effectuated

[1] Stuart Gilson, Edith Hotchkiss, and Matthew Osborn, Cashing Out: The Rise of M&A in Bankruptcy, Working Paper (2015), available at http://ssrn.com/abstract=2547168.

under § 363, as a percentage of public company Chapter 11s from 1989 through 2013.[2]

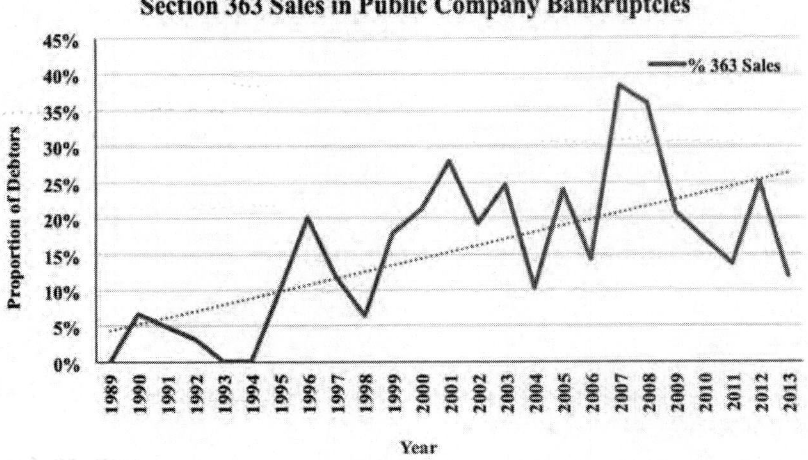

The increasing number of bankruptcy restructurings via a sale of the entire firm, intact, may be due to (i) the depth of the merger market, which expanded in the 1980s, after the Code became law, (ii) the wider availability of financing for potential buyers, and (iii) the increasing number of firms that enter Chapter 11 with substantial secured debt. The secured creditor can more readily bring about a sale than other creditors. Such going concern sales can proceed under § 363 of the Code, under a Chapter 11 plan, or even—at least theoretically—under Chapter 7, the liquidation chapter.

¶ 602: The § 363 Sale

Section 363 authorizes the debtor-in-possession to use, sell, or lease estate property. It does not specifically focus on going concern sales of the entire firm's operations. Dispositions out of the ordinary course of business require notice and a hearing. § 363(b). The statute provides no standard for the judge to apply, so judges fashioned a common law for whole-firm § 363 sales. A major legal issue for such sales is whether the sale transaction short-circuits the process and creditor protections embedded in § 1129's plan confirmation requirements. Claimants with differing stakes and priorities will typically have conflicting interests, as our earlier reorganization discussion illustrates. Section 363 does not build in devices for resolving claimant conflicts, unlike § 1129.

Could creditors use § 363 to sidestep the reorganization negotiations under § 1129? Could the judge allow the trustee to sell all of the company's assets and operations, shorn of the debtor's liabilities? If so, the judge would then take the cash proceeds from the sale and distribute the cash to the claimants as soon as priority issues were resolved and a § 1129 plan confirmed.

[2] AMERICAN BANKRUPTCY INSTITUTE COMMISSION TO STUDY THE REFORM OF CHAPTER 11, 2012-2014 FINAL REPORT AND RECOMMENDATIONS 203 (2014). The figure is based on data from the UCLA-LoPucki Bankruptcy Research Database. *Id.* at n.750.

Who would oppose such a sale? Who would favor such a sale?

Section § 363(b)(1) is simply drafted, saying that: "The trustee, after notice and a hearing, may use, sell, or lease, other than in the ordinary course of business, property of the estate[.]"

In lieu of a trustee, the court usually leaves the prebankruptcy debtor as a debtor-in-possession, allowing its prebankruptcy management to continue running the company. It's thus typically the debtor-in-possession that must move the court to make the sale. Creditors cannot move under § 363 on their own. One might presume that ongoing managers would not be highly motivated to sell the entire company, since a sale would put their jobs in jeopardy. Think of the incentives of managers of firms targeted for hostile takeovers. And think of the incentives of managers, if they're allied with equity-holders (because they are themselves substantial stockholders), if the firm's value becomes fixed and certain. While managers might be wary of a § 363 sale, the senior or secured creditor would prefer it and would have reason to try to align managers' incentives (via pay or otherwise) to facilitate whole-firm, § 363 sales.

If creditors dislike the debtor-in-possession's decision to forgo a § 363 sale, they can move the court to replace the management of the debtor-in-possession with a trustee friendly to the creditors and amenable to a sale. But trustee appointment is rare.

> [A]necdotal evidence suggests that chapter 11 trustees are the rare exception rather than the rule. The paucity of cases in which chapter 11 trustees serve may suggest that the overall system is working and that stakeholders either have confidence in the debtor's management or have replaced troublesome managers prior to or shortly after the petition date. Parties in interest may also be using the possibility of seeking the appointment of a trustee in negotiations with the debtor in a way that fosters meaningful results and eliminates the need for a trustee. . . . Parties in interest also may fear retribution by the debtor or other stakeholders if the court denies the motion, or may prefer having individuals with whom they are familiar (even if they do not like or necessarily trust them) rather than an individual they do not know.[3]

Under § 1104, the standard for trustee appointment is "for cause, including fraud, dishonesty, incompetence, or gross mismanagement of the . . . debtor by current management . . . [or] if such appointment is in the interests of creditors."

Creditors seeking a sale could negotiate a plan of reorganization under § 1129(a)(8), with the plan contemplating such a sale. But, since creditors presumably want a sale in order to *avoid* negotiating, cramming down, and valuing under § 1129, the last alternative isn't much of a benefit.

---

[3] ABI 2014 REPORT, supra note 2, at 27.

¶ 603: Statutory Provisions

§ 363. Use, sale, or lease of property

(b)(1) The trustee, after notice and a hearing, may use, sell, or lease, other than in the ordinary course of business, property of the estate. . . .

* * *

(c)(1) . . . [U]nless the court orders otherwise, the trustee may enter into transactions, including the sale or lease of property of the estate, in the ordinary course of business, without notice or a hearing, and may use property of the estate in the ordinary course of business without notice or a hearing.

§ 1107. Rights, powers, and duties of debtor in possession.

(a) . . . a debtor in possession shall have all the rights . . . and powers, and shall perform all the functions and duties . . . of a trustee serving in a case under this chapter.

The next three judicial decisions involve efforts to sell a firm in its entirety (or a substantial part of it) in chapter 11. In the first case, creditors sought the sale of the debtor's principal asset, stock in an electronics firm. The company and its managers agreed, but equity holders objected and appealed when the bankruptcy court ordered the sale.

¶ 604: In re The Lionel Corp., 722 F.2d 1063 (2d Cir. 1983)

PRIOR HISTORY: Appeal from . . . an order . . . approving a sale of property of the debtor's estate pursuant to 11 U.S.C. § 363(b).

Reversed and remanded. Judge Winter dissents in a separate opinion.

Before: MANSFIELD, CARDAMONE and WINTER, Circuit Judges.

CARDAMONE, Circuit Judge:

This expedited appeal is from an order . . . authoriz[ing] the sale by Lionel Corporation, a Chapter 11 debtor in possession, of its 82% common stock holding in Dale Electronics, Inc. to [another company] for $50 million.

I—FACTS

On February 19, 1982 the Lionel Corporation—toy train manufacturer of childhood [memory]—. . . filed . . . for reorganization under Chapter 11 of the Bankruptcy Code. Resort to Chapter 11 was precipitated by losses totaling $22.5 million that Lionel incurred in its toy retailing operation during the two year period ending [the prior] December. . . .

* * *

Lionel's most important asset and the subject of this proceeding is its ownership of 82% of the common stock of Dale, a corporation engaged in the manufacture of electronic components. . . . Public investors own the remaining 18 percent of Dale's common stock, which is listed on the American Stock Exchange. Its balance sheet reflects . . . [a] shareholders' equity of approximately $28.0 million. Lionel's stock investment in Dale . . . is Lionel's most valuable single asset. Unlike Lionel's toy retailing operation, Dale is profitable. . . .

On June 14, 1983 Lionel filed an application under section 363(b) seeking bankruptcy court authorization to sell its 82% interest in Dale. . . . Four days later the debtor filed a plan of reorganization conditioned upon a sale of Dale with the proceeds to be distributed to creditors. Certain issues of the reorganization remain unresolved, and negotiations are continuing; however, a solicitation of votes on the plan has not yet begun. On September 7, 1983, following the Securities and Exchange Commission's July 15 filing of objections to the sale, Bankruptcy Judge Ryan held a hearing on Lionel's application. At the hearing, Peabody emerged as the successful of three bidders with an offer of $50 million for Lionel's interest in Dale.

The Chief Executive Officer of Lionel and a Vice–President of Salomon Brothers were the only witnesses produced and both testified in support of the application. Their testimony established that while the price paid for the stock was "fair," Dale is not an asset "that is wasting away in any sense." Lionel's Chief Executive Officer stated that there was no reason why the sale of Dale stock could not be accomplished as part of the reorganization plan, and that the sole reason for Lionel's application to sell was the Creditors' Committee's insistence upon it. The creditors wanted to turn this asset of Lionel into a "pot of cash," to provide the bulk of the $70 million required to repay creditors under the proposed plan of reorganization.

In confirming the sale, Judge Ryan made no formal findings of fact. He simply noted that cause to sell was sufficiently shown by the Creditors' Committee's insistence upon it. *Judge Ryan further found cause—presumably from long experience—based upon his own opinion that a present failure to confirm would set the entire reorganization process back a year or longer while the parties attempted to restructure it.*

The Committee of Equity Security Holders, statutory representatives of the 10,000 public shareholders of Lionel, appealed this order claiming that *the sale, prior to approval of a reorganization plan, deprives the equity holders* of the Bankruptcy Code's safeguards of disclosure, solicitation *and acceptance [under § 1129(a)(8)]* and divests the debtor of a dominant and profitable asset which could serve as a cornerstone for a sound plan. The SEC also appeared and objected to the sale in the bankruptcy court and supports the Equity Committee's appeal, claiming that approval of the sale side-steps the Code's requirement for informed suffrage which is at the heart of Chapter 11.

The Creditors' Committee favors the sale because it believes it is in the best interests of Lionel and because the sale is expressly authorized by § 363(b) of the Code. Lionel tells us that its ownership of Dale, a non-operating asset, is held for investment purposes only and that its sale will provide the estate with the large block of the cash needed to fund its plan of reorganization.

From the oral arguments and briefs we gather that the Equity Committee believes that Chapter 11 has cleared the reorganization field of major pre-plan sales . . . [,] relegating § 363(b) to be used only in emergencies. The Creditors' Committee counters that a bankruptcy judge should have absolute freedom under § 363(b) to do as he thinks best. Neither of these arguments is wholly persuasive. . . . [T]he policies underlying the Bankruptcy Reform Act of 1978 support a middle ground—one which gives the bankruptcy judge considerable discretion yet requires him to articulate sound business justifications for his decisions.

II—DISCUSSION

The issue now before this Court is to what extent Chapter 11 permits a bankruptcy judge to authorize the sale of an important asset of the bankrupt's estate, out of the ordinary course of business and prior to acceptance and outside of any plan of reorganization. Section 363(b), the focal point of our analysis, provides that "[t]he trustee, after notice and a hearing, may use, sell, or lease, other than in the ordinary course of business, property of the estate."

On its face, section 363(b) appears to permit disposition of any property of the estate of a corporate debtor without resort to the statutory safeguards embodied in Chapter 11. . . . Yet, analysis of the statute's history and over seven decades of case law convinces us that such a literal reading of section 363(b) would unnecessarily violate the congressional scheme for corporate reorganizations.

[The court then examined the sales standard under prior bankruptcy statutes and found it permitted sales of perishable or wasting assets, but usually not otherwise.]

The Third Circuit took an even stricter view in In re Solar Mfg. Corp., 176 F.2d 493 (3d Cir. 1949). Acknowledging that a sale of corporate assets could occur outside and prior to a plan, . . . the court concluded that pre-confirmation sales should be "confined to emergencies where there is imminent danger that the assets of the ailing business will be lost if prompt action is not taken." . . .

. . . In In re Sire Plan, Inc., 332 F.2d 497 (2d Cir. 1964), corporate owners of a seven-story skeletal building then under construction filed for reorganization. . . . [We noted] that the evidence demonstrated that in its exposed state a "partially constructed building is a 'wasting asset' [that] can only deteriorate in value the longer it remains uncompleted." *Id.* at 499.

More recently, other circuits have upheld sales prior to plan approval under the Bankruptcy Act where the bankruptcy court outlined the circumstances in its findings of fact indicating why the sale was in the best interest of the estate. E.g., In re Equity Funding Corporation of America, 492 F.2d 793, 794 (9th Cir.), cert. denied, 419 U.S. 964 (1974) (finding of fact that because market value of asset was likely to deteriorate substantially in the near future, sale was in the estate's best interests); . . . . In essence, these cases evidence the continuing vitality under the old law of an "emergency" or "perishability" standard. As we shall see, the new Bankruptcy Code no longer requires such strict limitations on a bankruptcy judge's authority to order disposition of the estate's property; nevertheless, it does not go so far as to eliminate all constraints on that judge's discretion.

C. The Bankruptcy Reform Act of 1978

Section 363(b) of the Code seems on its face to confer upon the bankruptcy judge virtually unfettered discretion to authorize the use, sale or lease, other than in the ordinary course of business, of property of the estate. Of course, the statute requires that notice be given and a hearing conducted, but [no] reference is made to an "emergency" or "perishability" requirement nor is there an indication that a debtor in possession or trustee contemplating sale must show "cause." Thus, the language of § 363(b) clearly is different from the terms of its statutory predecessors. And, while Congress never expressly stated why it abandoned the [prior] "upon cause shown" terminology . . . , arguably that omission permits easier access to § 363(b). Various policy considerations lend some support to this view.

First and foremost is the notion that a bankruptcy judge must not be shackled with unnecessarily rigid rules when exercising the undoubtedly broad administrative power granted him under the Code. . . . To further the purposes of Chapter 11 reorganization, a bankruptcy judge must have substantial freedom to tailor his orders to meet differing circumstances. This is exactly the result a liberal reading of § 363(b) will achieve.

Support for this policy is found in the rationale underlying a number of earlier cases that had applied [the old "upon cause shown" standard. Emergency or perishability standards have not always been in play; sometimes] a good business opportunity was . . . available, so long as the parties could act quickly. In such cases therefore the bankruptcy machinery should not straitjacket the bankruptcy judge so as to prevent him from doing what is best for the estate.

Just as we reject the requirement that only an emergency permits the use of § 363(b), we also reject the view that § 363(b) grants the bankruptcy judge carte blanche. Several reasons lead us to this conclusion: the statute requires notice and a hearing, and these procedural safeguards would be meaningless absent a further requirement that reasons be given for whatever determination is made; similarly, appellate review would effectively be precluded by an irreversible order; *and, finally, such construction of § 363(b) swallows up Chapter 11's safeguards*. In fact, the legislative history surrounding the enactment of Chapter 11 makes evident Congress' concern with rights of equity interests as well as those of creditors.

Chapter 5 of the House bill dealing with reorganizations states that the purpose of a business reorganization is to restructure a business' finances to enable it to operate productively, provide jobs for its employees, pay its creditors and produce a return for its stockholders. The automatic stay upon filing a petition prevents creditors from acting unilaterally or pressuring the debtor. The plan of reorganization determines how much and in what form creditors will be paid, whether stockholders will continue to retain any interests, and in what form the business will continue. Requiring acceptance by a percentage of creditors and stockholders [under § 1126] for confirmation [under § 1129] forces negotiation among the debtor, its creditors and its stockholders. [House Report] at 221. . . .

The Senate hearings similarly reflect a concern as to how losses are to be apportioned between creditors and stockholders in the reorganization of a public company. [Senate Report] at 9. *Noting that "the most vulnerable today are public investors," the Senate Judiciary Committee Report states that the bill is designed to counteract "the natural tendency of a debtor in distress to pacify large creditors with whom the debtor would expect to do business, at the expense of small and scattered public investors."* S. Rep. No. 95–989 at 10. The Committee believed that investor protection is most critical when the public company is in such financial distress as to cause it to seek aid under the bankruptcy laws. *Id.* The need for this protection was plain. Reorganization under the 1938 Act was often unfair to public investors who lacked bargaining power, and these conditions continued. Echoing the conclusion of the House Committee, the Senate Committee believed that the bill would promote fairer and more equitable reorganizations granting to public investors the last chance to conserve values that corporate insolvency has jeopardized. *Id.* at 10–11.

III—CONCLUSION

The history surrounding the enactment in 1978 of current Chapter 11 and the logic underlying it buttress our conclusion that there must be *some articulated business justification, other than appeasement of major creditors,* for using, selling or leasing property out of the ordinary course of business before the bankruptcy judge may order such disposition under section 363(b).

The case law under section 363's statutory predecessors used terms like "perishable," "deteriorating," and "emergency" as guides in deciding whether a debtor's property could be sold outside the ordinary course of business. The use of such words persisted long after their omission from newer statutes and rules. The administrative power to sell or lease property in a reorganization continued to be the exception, not the rule. . . . In enacting the 1978 Code Congress was aware of existing case law and clearly indicated as one of its purposes that equity interests have a greater voice in reorganization plans—hence, the safeguards of disclosure, voting, acceptance and confirmation in present Chapter 11.

Resolving the apparent conflict between Chapter 11 and § 363(b) does not require an all or nothing approach. Every sale under § 363(b) does not automatically short-circuit or side-step Chapter 11; nor are these two statutory provisions to be read as mutually exclusive. Instead, if a bankruptcy judge is to administer a business reorganization successfully under the Code, then . . . some play for the operation of both § 363(b) and Chapter 11 must be allowed for.

The rule we adopt requires that a judge determining a § 363(b) application expressly find from the evidence presented before him at the hearing a good business reason to grant such an application. In this case the only reason advanced for granting the request to sell Lionel's 82 percent stock interest in Dale was the Creditors' Committee's insistence on it. Such is insufficient as a matter of fact because it is not a sound business reason and insufficient as a matter of law because it ignores the equity interests required to be weighed and considered under Chapter 11. The court also expressed its concern that a present failure to approve the sale would result in a long delay. . . . [I]t is easy to sympathize with the desire of a bankruptcy court to expedite bankruptcy reorganization proceedings for they are frequently protracted[, but this is not a basis for abandoning proper standards]. Thus, the approval of the sale of Lionel's 82 percent interest in Dale was an abuse of the trial court's discretion.

In fashioning its findings, a bankruptcy judge must not blindly follow the hue and cry of the most vocal special interest groups; rather, he should consider all salient factors pertaining to the proceeding and, accordingly, act to further the diverse interests of the debtor, creditors and equity holders, alike. He might, for example, look to such relevant factors as the proportionate value of the asset to the estate as a whole, the amount of elapsed time since the filing, the likelihood that a plan of reorganization will be proposed and confirmed in the near future, the effect of the proposed disposition on future plans of reorganization, the proceeds to be obtained from the disposition vis-a-vis any appraisals of the property, which of the alternatives of use, sale or lease the proposal envisions and, most importantly perhaps, whether the asset is increasing or decreasing in value. This list is not intended to be exclusive, but merely to provide guidance to the bankruptcy judge.

Finally, we must consider whether appellants opposing the sale produced evidence before the bankruptcy court that such sale was not justified. While a debtor applying under § 363(b) carries the burden of demonstrating that a use, sale or lease out of the ordinary course of business will aid the debtor's reorganization, an objectant, such as the Equity Committee here, is required to produce some evidence respecting its objections. Appellants made three objections below: First, the sale was premature because Dale is not a wasting asset and there is no emergency; second, there was no justifiable cause present since Dale, if anything, is improving; and third, the price was inadequate. No proof was required as to the first objection because it was stipulated as conceded. The second and third objections are interrelated. Following Judge Ryan's suggestion that objections could as a practical matter be developed on cross-examination, Equity's counsel elicited testimony from the financial expert produced by Lionel that Dale is less subject than other companies to wide market fluctuations. The same witness also conceded that he knew of no reason why those interested in Dale's stock at the September 7, 1983 hearing would not be just as interested six months from then.[4] The only other witness who testified was the Chief Executive Officer of Lionel, who stated that it was only at the insistence of the Creditors' Committee that Dale stock was being sold and that Lionel "would very much like to retain its interest in Dale." These uncontroverted statements of the two witnesses elicited by the Equity Committee on cross-examination were sufficient proof to support its objections to the present sale of Dale because this evidence

[4] As noted, the bidding for Dale started with a $43 million offer from Acme–Cleveland and has since jumped to $50 million. There is no indication that this trend will reverse itself.

demonstrated that there was no good business reason for the present sale. Hence, appellants satisfied their burden.

Accordingly, the order appealed from is reversed and the matter remanded to the district court with directions to remand to the bankruptcy court for further proceedings consistent with this opinion.

WINTER, Circuit Judge, dissenting:

* * *

The following facts are undisputed . . . : (i) Lionel sought a buyer for the Dale stock willing to condition its purchase upon confirmation of a reorganization plan. It was unsuccessful since, in the words of the bankruptcy judge, "the confirmation of any plan is usually somewhat iffy," and few purchasers are willing to commit upwards of $50 million for an extended period without a contract binding on the other party; (ii) every feasible reorganization plan contemplates the sale of the Dale stock for cash; (iii) a reorganization plan may be approved fairly soon if the Dale stock is sold now. If the sale is prohibited, renewed negotiations between the creditors and the equity holders will be necessary, and the submission of a plan, if any, will be put off well into the future; and (iv) the Dale stock can be sold now at or near the same price as it can be sold later.

The effect of the present decision is thus to leave the debtor in possession powerless as a legal matter to sell the Dale stock outside a reorganization plan. . . . This, of course, pleases the equity holders who, having introduced no evidence demonstrating a disadvantage to the bankrupt estate from the sale of the Dale stock, are now given a veto over it to be used as leverage in negotiating a better deal for themselves in a reorganization.

The likely result[ ] of today's decision [is that] notwithstanding the majority decision, the Dale stock will be sold under Section 363(b) for exactly the same reasons offered in support of the present proposed sale. However, the ultimate reorganization plan will be more favorable to the equity holders, and they will not veto the sale.

It seems reasonably obvious that [this] result . . . is contrary to the purpose of the reorganization provisions in causing delay and further economic risk [and] also suffers from the legal infirmity which led the majority to reject the proposed sale, the only difference between the two sales being the agreement of the equity holders.

The equity holders offered no evidence whatsoever that the sale of Dale now will harm Lionel. . . . The courts below were quite right in not treating their arguments seriously. . . . [5]

The equity holders argue that Chapter 11's provisions for disclosure, hearing and a vote before confirmation of a reorganization

[5] . . . [T]he problem of statutory interpretation is entirely straightforward and not deserving of a lengthy exegesis into legal history. The language of Section 363(b) is about as plain as it could be and surely does not permit a judicial grafting of stringent conditions on the power of trustees. As for its legislative history, the words "upon cause shown" were dropped by the Congress from the predecessor to Section 363(b) in 1978, a signal clearly dictating that Congress meant what it said.

plan stringently limit the authority of trustees under 11 U.S.C. § 363(b). However, a reorganization plan affects the rights of the parties as well as the disposition of assets, and there is no inconsistency in allowing the disposition of property outside the confirmation proceedings. Arguably, *some transactions proposed under Section 363(b) would, if carried out, eliminate a number of options available for reorganization plans and thereby pre-ordain a particular kind of plan or preclude a reorganization entirely. In such a case, a colorable claim can be made for a limitation on a trustee's power under Section 363(b)* narrowly tailored to prevent such a result in order to effectuate the core purposes of Chapter 11. However, it is not disputed that in the present case the final reorganization plan will include a sale of Dale stock. A sale now thus does not preclude any feasible reorganization plan.

¶ 605: Questions on *Lionel*

1. Managers' incentives. Lionel managers managed the toy company, which held stock in Dale, the electronics company, for investment. Does the operational structure explain why managers consented to sell Dale? Would managers as readily have agreed to sell the entire debtor company? Would Lionel's managers have as readily agreed to a sale of the toy company? What statutory hurdles would creditors have to overcome if they could not get the debtor's managers to back the sale? Wouldn't they need to get their own trustee appointed, or get the reorganization moved to chapter 7 for liquidation?

2. Is every debtor a wasting asset? The court says that showing perishability suffices to justify a sale, but that it isn't a sine qua non for sale under § 363. But the judge does not have carte blanche to sell. Under the wasting asset doctrine of the *Lionel* opinion, couldn't creditors argue that every bankrupt firm is a wasting asset, and that a quick sale reduces the waste? As such, they'd argue, sales under § 363 are always warranted.

   Such an argument would be harder to make if the sale would destroy significant private value of the estate. If markets for entire companies are weak and mergers difficult to engineer, then judges might believe that the sale produces inadequate value for the estate, and accordingly even if the asset were "wasting" a sale wouldn't eliminate the waste. Such a view became harder to hold after the merger wave of the 1980s.

3. Protecting equity through negotiations. Lionel had already filed a proposed plan of reorganization, although the plan had not yet been consented to, and open issues remained. The equity holders argued that the sale should proceed under the plan of reorganization, not under a § 363 motion. Obviously, compliance with § 1129(a)(8) (including *shareholder* consent or a valuation hearing under § 1129(b)) was a prerequisite to selling Dale under the plan route, but not under the § 363 route.

   The court cites the Senate Judiciary Committee Report, which articulates a general concern with "the natural tendency of a debtor in distress to pacify large creditors . . . at the expense of small and scattered public investors." While there are scattered public investors today, there are also institutions, hedge funds, and individual investors who buy up stock or debt of bankrupt debtors if they think they can make a profit. Scattered, silent stockholders seem to be less an issue today than it seemed to have been in 1978.

The court privileges negotiation under § 1129, using the statute's preference for negotiation to inform the court how to interpret § 363. But did Congress prefer negotiation for its own sake? See the legislative history in ¶¶ 303 and 304. Or did Congress prefer negotiated solutions only as a device to avoid an *Atlas Pipeline*-type valuation hearing? If a sale would moot a valuation hearing under § 1129(b), does the legislative history necessarily condemn it as loudly as the *Lionel* court believes? Might the legislative history in fact be stretched to *favor* the sale?

Note that the Bankruptcy Code was enacted in 1978. By the mid–1980s American businesses were going through a huge merger wave.

4. *A business justification standard for a § 363 sale?* Is the court's interpretation of § 363 that a sale would scuttle § 1129(a)(8)'s scheme of acceptance and therefore cannot proceed unless proponents of the sale offer a business justification, with creditor preference not allowed to justify the sale? Subsequent decisions followed *Lionel*, with some courts imposing a higher burden under § 363. Lee R. Bogdanoff, *The Purchase and Sale of Assets in Reorganization Cases*, 47 Business Lawyer 1367, 1391–92 esp. n.90 (1992). (Note that even a sale with a business justification would scuttle bargaining, disclosure, and acceptance under § 1129; presumably though we'd have a "justified" scuttling.)

5. *Aftermath*. After the Lionel court struck down the proposed sale, the company went to market again. Eventually it sold Dale for $78,000,000. The equity holders consented when they were included in the proposed plan of reorganization, as Judge Winter, the dissenter, anticipated. For several years, bankruptcy players thought that firms could be sold under the Code, but only in the context of a § 1129 plan.

B. THE SUB ROSA § 1129 PLAN VIA A § 363 SALE

¶ 606: Side Deals Under § 363

What if the creditors trying to effectuate the § 363 sale made side deals with creditors and stockholders, gaining the acquiescence of potential opponents? What if they planned to "earmark" for some creditors or stockholders some of the consideration to be received in the sale and thereby "buy" those creditors' or stockholders' acquiescence to a § 363 sale? Would that enhance the chance of the deal going through under § 363?

In re Braniff Airways, Inc., 700 F.2d 935 (5th Cir. 1983)

On May 13, 1982, Braniff . . . filed [a] petition[ ] for reorganization under Chapter 11 . . . [and] continued in the management and operation of [its] businesses and properties as debtors-in-possession pursuant to §§ 1107 and 1108 of the Code. No trustee or examiner was appointed.

* * *

On December 23, 1982, Braniff [sought] . . . [court] approval of a proposed agreement between Braniff and PSA. On December 30, 1982, Braniff filed with the Bankruptcy Court a "Memorandum of Understanding" as a basis for a proposed settlement and compromise of all claims, counterclaims, and potential litigations by and among Braniff, certain unsecured creditors, and certain secured creditors.

Between December 30, 1982, and January 3, 1983, various notices of hearings on the proposed agreements were mailed or published. These documents gave notice of a hearing to be held on January 14, 1983, to consider the matters set forth in the PSA Agreement and the Memorandum of Understanding. As stated in these notices, a hearing commenced. . . .

* * *

The Bankruptcy Court [and district court] approved . . . the PSA [transaction]. . . . [But] was the district court's approval of the PSA transaction authorized under Section 363(b) of the Bankruptcy Code, 11 U.S.C. § 363(b)? . . .

I.

The courts below approved the PSA transaction pursuant to Section 363(b) of the Bankruptcy Code, which provides:

> The trustee, after notice and a hearing, may use, sell, or lease, other than in the ordinary course of business, property of the estate. 11 U.S.C. § 363(b).

The appellants [the unsecured ticketholders' committee, Continental Airlines, and the U.S. Pension Benefit Guaranty Corporation] contend that § 363(b) is not applicable to sales or other dispositions of all the assets of a debtor, and that such a transaction must be effected pursuant to the voting, disclosure and confirmation requirements of the Code. Braniff responds that cases decided before and after promulgation of the Code authorize a § 363(b) sale of all of a debtor's assets.

We need not express an opinion on this controversy because we are convinced that the PSA transaction is much more than the "use, sale or lease" of Braniff's property authorized by § 363(b). Reduced to its barest bones, the PSA transaction would provide for Braniff's transfer of cash, airplanes and equipment, terminal leases and landing slots to PSA in return for travel scrip, unsecured notes, and a profit participation in PSA's proposed operation. The PSA transaction would also require significant restructuring of the rights of Braniff creditors. Appellants raise a blizzard of objections to each of these elements of the deal. It is not necessary, however, to decide whether each individual component of the PSA transaction is or is not authorized by § 363 because the entire transaction was treated by both courts below as an integrated whole. Since certain portions of the transaction are clearly outside the scope of

§ 363, the district court was without power under that section to approve it. Its order must be reversed.

[One] example[ ] will illustrate our rationale. The PSA Agreement provided that Braniff would pay $2.5 million to PSA in exchange for $7.5 million of scrip entitling the holder to travel on PSA. *It further required that the scrip be used only in a future Braniff reorganization and that it be issued only to former Braniff employees or shareholders or, in a limited amount, to unsecured creditors. This provision not only changed the composition of Braniff's assets, the contemplated result under § 363(b), it also had the practical effect of dictating some of the terms of any future reorganization plan.* The reorganization plan would have to allocate the scrip according to the terms of the PSA agreement or forfeit a valuable asset. *The debtor and the Bankruptcy Court should not be able to short circuit the requirements of Chapter 11 for confirmation of a reorganization plan by establishing the terms of the plan sub rosa in connection with the sale of assets.*

* * *

For these reasons, we hold that the district court was not authorized by § 363(b) to approve the PSA transaction and that its order is reversed. In any future attempts to specify the terms whereby a reorganization plan is to be adopted, the parties and the district court must scale the hurdles erected in Chapter 11. See, e.g., 11 U.S.C. § 1125 (disclosure requirements); id. § 1126 (voting); id. § 1129(a)(7) (best interest of creditors test); id. § 1129(b)(2)(B) (absolute priority rule). Were this transaction approved, and considering the properties proposed to be transferred, little would remain save fixed . . . equipment and little prospect or occasion for further reorganization. These considerations reinforce our view that this is in fact a reorganization.

¶ 607: A Simple § 363 Sale

Consider a debtor owing $10 million to a secured creditor and $4 million to trade creditors at time (1). It has assets and operations ("X") that an auction reveals to have a market value of $12 million. The court cannot readily and assuredly determine the collateral's value.

Time (1)	OldCo (before sale)		
	X	Secured	$10M
		Trade	$ 4M
		Stockholders	–

NewCo, the top bidder at the auction, has $12 million in cash. It buys OldCo's assets and operations for $12 million at time (2). After it makes the purchase, at time (3) it has the assets and operations ("X"), while OldCo has $12 million in cash in the bank.

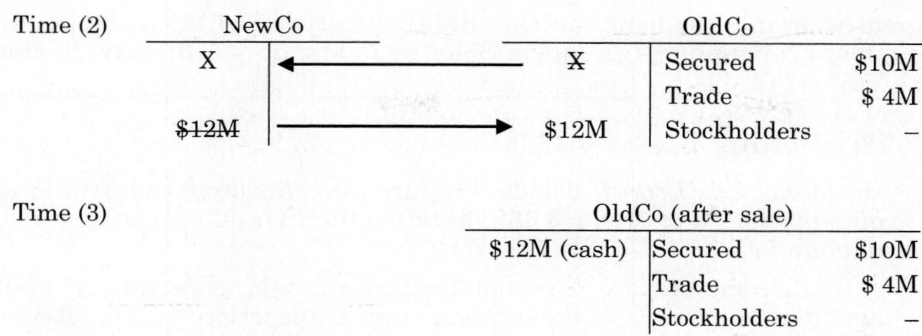

OldCo then liquidates at time (4). Misvaluing $12 million of cash in the bank is difficult, so the valuation problem from Atlas and potentially in § 1129(b)(2) is avoided. While $12 million can be misinvested, it's easier for the court to check whether wild risks are being taken with cash than it is for the court to check the riskiness of the debtor firm's business.

So, if the security was worth $10 million, the secured creditors' security interest carries over as a claim on the first $10 million in proceeds of the sale. As such, the $10 million in cash goes to the secured creditors at time (4) and the remaining $2 million would go to the unsecured trade creditors.

But what if the security wasn't worth $10 million? If it was worth less than the total allowed claim, then the secured creditors get the value of the security and, for the deficiency, share ratably with the unsecured trade creditors. If the security was only worth $6 million, for example, the secured creditors get a check for $6 million in satisfaction of their secured claims. They would have $4 million deficiency, which via § 506(b) would drop down to share pro rata with the trade creditors' unsecured $4 million claim. The two unsecured claimants (one for the secureds' deficiency and one from the trade creditors) each have claims of $4 million and would share the post-security $6 million. The secured creditors would get a second check for $3 million, giving them a total of $9 million. The trade creditors would get a check for $3 million.

OldCo, no longer with any assets at time (5), ends its existence. Its one-time operations, X, continue on, in NewCo.

Some texture on the sales process, which will be familiar in broad outline to those who handle mergers and acquisitions: Typically, "the debtor corporation 'identifies a stalking horse or initial bidder, usually after a marketing process of some kind, and enters into a definitive agreement to purchase the company's assets with the understanding that the agreement will be shopped around to other prospective purchasers who will be solicited to top its deal.' [source omitted] [The] bankruptcy court—specialized in dealing with such matters—is then asked to approve this stalking horse bid, the auction date and bidding procedures, which set the rules of the auction. The bidding procedures will generally include built-in protections for the stalking horse, including minimum bidding increments, an approved form of purchase agreement for competing bids, standard bidder qualifications, a 'break[-up] fee' to be paid to the stalking horse if it is outbid, and some form of expenses reimbursement for the stalking horse if outbid." Stephanie Ben–Ishai & Stephen J. Lubben, Sales or Plans, 56 McGill Law Review 591, 600–01 (2011).

¶ 608: Selling Under § 363?

1. Do *Lionel* and *Braniff* decide the pure case: a sale of the firm in its entirety for cash under § 363, because the firm is operating poorly in chapter 11?
2. Although the statute does not facilitate a sale, especially if management opposes one, its economic and transactional fit is often so good that the business pressure to sell overcomes resistance. Frequently incumbent managers resign just before or after bankruptcy. The new managers—often turnaround specialists—are less afraid of selling than the incumbents were. Chapter 23 brings forward rationales for using market sales instead of negotiated deals.
4. In light of § 363, *Braniff*, and *LaSalle*, consider this alternative Dieglom transation. It contrasts with the § 1129 disposition we analyzed earlier in ¶312. Dieglom's senior managers (who are also the company's principal shareholders) see creditors' efforts to use § 363 and in reaction try to coopt use of that section. They promote their own § 363 sale, first organizing a new company, LiveGlom, in which they will own the equity, to purchase Dieglom's assets. They arrange for the new company to borrow $15 million, with which LiveGlom will buy all of Dieglom's assets via § 363. LiveGlom's capital structure will be:
   - (i) An obligation to the old bank lender in the amount of $8 million; assumption of all the obligations to the old trade creditors, who'll be paid in full; an obligation to the original mortgage bondholders, for $15 million; and a new $15 million obligation to the old subordinated debentureholders. Each of these creditors forgive Dieglom, cancelling their obligation from Dieglom.
   - (ii) A new obligation of $15 million to the bank (which provides the $15 million to buy Dieglom's assets).
   - (iii) And a stock issue to Dieglom's management.

LIVEGLOM, INC.
(pre-December 31, 2011)

Cash $15M	New borrowing $15M
	Common stock —

LIVEGLOM, INC.
Balance Sheet
(as of December 31, 2011)

Assets		Liabilities and shareholders' equity		
		Current Liabilities		
		Bank debt due within one year	$ 6M	
		Trade accounts payable	6M	
		New borrowing	15M	
			20M	
		Long-term Debt		
		3% mortgage bonds due 2020	15M	
		New debentures [for old subordinated]	6M	
Operational value	50M	Total long-term debt	21M	
		Total liabilities		48M
		New equity		2M
Total assets	50M	Total liabilities and shareholders' equity 50M		

DIEGLOM, INC.
Balance Sheet
(as of December 31, 2011)

Assets		Liabilities and shareholders' equity	
Current Assets		Liabilities	
Cash	$15M	7% senior debentures	$20M
	——	Equity	——

We've simplified the left-hand side of LiveGlom's balance sheet. While LiveGlom would own all of Dieglom's prebankruptcy assets, here we simply reflect the operational value of the assets as a whole. The right-hand side has much less debt than Dieglom's pre-sale balance sheet. LiveGlom is, after this management-led § 363 sale, solvent, although barely so, and controlled by Dieglom's former managers.

Are there distributional and priority problems with this transaction under *Braniff* or *LaSalle*? As a practical matter, who will complain about the transaction? Reexamine the original Dieglom balance sheet in ¶312.

¶ 609: Section 363 Sales and § 1129 Priority: Craig A. Sloane, The Sub Rosa Plan of Reorganization: Side–Stepping Creditor Protections in Chapter 11, 16 Bankruptcy Developments Journal 37 (1999)

The first mention of a plan sub rosa was in an opinion by the Fifth Circuit Court of Appeals, issued in the early 1980s, in the case of Pension Benefit Guaranty Corp. v. Braniff Airways, Inc. (In re Braniff Airways, Inc.). A sub rosa plan has also been referred to as a "de facto plan" or a "creeping plan of reorganization." Essentially, the concern regarding a plan sub rosa arises when a debtor in bankruptcy seeks to enter into a transaction outside of a plan of reorganization that could have a significant effect upon the bankruptcy case and the bankruptcy estate. Some courts and practitioners believe that these transactions should be prohibited by the courts because they will have "the practical effect of dictating some of the terms of any future reorganization plan" of the debtor and will "short circuit the requirements of chapter 11 for confirmation of a reorganization plan."[6]

Although a relatively unused doctrine, a plan sub rosa creates a genuine threat, and courts should recognize that certain transactions ought to be voted on by creditors and not merely approved under the court's discretionary powers. However, at the same time, when the effect of a transaction is not significant, the courts are entitled to, and should, exercise their right to approve, or disapprove, these transactions. An especially fine line has been drawn by Congress in allowing asset sales preconfirmation, especially considering that the courts generally permit a debtor to sell all of its assets prior to filing a plan and disclosure statement. For these reasons, courts must carefully balance their discretion to approve certain transactions with the need to subject certain others to the plan process.

¶ 610: In re Continental Air Lines, Inc., 780 F.2d 1223 (5th Cir. 1986)

In *Braniff* we recognized that a debtor in Chapter 11 cannot use § 363(b) to sidestep the protection creditors have when it comes time to confirm a plan of reorganization. Likewise, if a debtor were allowed to reorganize the estate in some fundamental fashion pursuant to § 363(b), creditor's rights under, for example, 11 U.S.C. §§ 1125, 1126, 1129(a)(7), and 1129(b)(2) might become meaningless. Undertaking reorganization piecemeal pursuant to § 363(b) should not deny creditors the protection they would receive if the proposals were first raised in the reorganization plan. [citation omitted] At the same time, we fully appreciate the post-petition, pre-confirmation transactions outside the ordinary course of business [which] may be required and that each hearing on a § 363(b) transaction cannot become a mini-hearing on plan confirmation. Balancing these considerations, we hold that when an objector to a proposed transaction under § 363(b) claims that it is being denied certain protection because approval is sought pursuant to § 363(b) instead of as part of a reorganization plan, the objector must specify exactly what protection is being denied. If the court concludes that there has in actuality been such a denial, it may then consider fashioning appropriate protective measures modeled on those which would attend a reorganization plan.

¶ 611: A Less Simple § 363 Sale

Consider this transaction. Will it pass muster under *Lionel*, *Braniff*, and *Continental*?

[6] Pension Benefit Guar. Corp. v. Braniff Airways, Inc. (In re Braniff Airways, Inc.), 700 F.2d 935, 940 (5th Cir. 1983).

The company has a secured creditor due $10 million and trade creditors due $4 million. Its stockholders also manage the company.

OldCo (before sale)

X=$10M	Secured	$10M
	Trade	4M
	Stockholders	—

Secured creditors and the stockholder-managers propose that the company be sold for $10 million to NewCo, which they have organized. Secured creditors assert that the assets, worth $10 million, belong to them. But because the secured are not adept at running the firm's operations, they intend to give 80% of the stock to the old stockholders; the secured will take a $9 million debt obligation from the buying firm.

So, the buying firm looks like this after it's set up, but before the purchase:

NewCo (before sale)

$10M cash	Secured	$9M
	Stockholders	1M

NewCo then buys the assets from OldCo for $10 million. The resulting post-sale balance sheets look like this:

OldCo (after sale)

$10M cash	Secured	$10M
	Trade	4M
	Stockholders	—

NewCo (after sale)

$10M assets	Secured	$9M
	Stockholders	1M

Since OldCo's assets now consist of $10 million in cash, they go to the Secured. (As a technical matter, secured creditors get an interest in the cash proceeds from sales of their assets.) Who should be expected to complain about this proposed sale?

How would the *Braniff* court evaluate the sale? Doesn't it determine the distribution in bankruptcy and, therefore, isn't it inappropriate for a § 363 sale?

But what would the *Continental* court do? Might the sale succeed under *Continental*? A minor priority issue might have been distorted, the proponents concede. But the trade must come forward under *Continental* to complain if they want to upset the sale. If the court agrees with those objecting to the sale, the court would, if faithful to *Continental*, try to fashion a makeshift remedy, rather than go through a full-scale § 1129 hearing. Under § 1129, the plan proponents need to come in with class consent (after disclosure of OldCo's condition and financial state), or show nonimpairment, or satisfy § 1129(b).

The sale proponents would be confronted with a serious hurdle if they had to show full § 1129(b)(2)(B) compliance: the trade creditors could argue that stockholders would receive something "on account of" their stock interest in OldCo, a potential vulnerability under § 1129, see

LaSalle, supra, without the trade being paid in full. (The sale proponents would argue that the old stockholders receive stock in NewCo "on account of" their managerial skills, not on account of their interest in OldCo.)

What's there really to be afraid of under the proposed sale? Won't the sale reposition the company quickly in a way that makes enough business sense? Doesn't it also clear the judge's docket and get a company's operations out from bankruptcy quickly? Hence, isn't it operationally just about what we want from bankruptcy?

And, say the sales proponents, we shouldn't let some procedural niceties hold up a good business plan when it's obvious that the firm belongs to the secureds.

How should we evaluate the sales proponents' two arguments in favor of the sale? The disposition of the firm's assets indeed makes operational sense (although less so in the hypothetical at hand than usual, because the capital structure is only moderately reconfigured from $14 million in debt down to $9 million).

But do we really know whether the procedural niceties are minor or not? Is the fact that the secureds are re-hiring the stockholder-managers the only major motivation for them to propose the sale and subsequent split with the old stockholders?

Private information about firm value. First, consider the possibility that the shareholders and secureds know the real value of the firm, because they're closest to the firm and really understand its potential, while no one else does. It's really worth $15 million, but no one could figure that out without a full valuation hearing, or full disclosure of the company's business situation and prospects, or access to the company's inside information.

Private information about asset value. Alternatively, consider the possibility that the company is really worth $10 million, just as the two say. But the shareholders and secureds know that the security is insufficient to cover the full amount of the claim. The security is worth only $6 million, but it's not so easy to find out that there's a deficiency unless one looks very carefully, with sales and valuation data at hand, or unless the court tries to sell the assets (and finds no one willing to pay more than $6 million for the assets alone).

In an absolute priority reorganization under § 506(a) and § 1129, what would the distribution be under those values? Wouldn't the secureds get $8 million (from $6 million for their secured claim and $2 million for their deficiency's share of the remaining $4 million in cash to distribute), the trade $2 million, and the stockholders nothing?

Compare that distribution with the values that will be distributed in the proponents' § 363 sale. Doesn't making that comparison allow us to understand another explanation—less laudable than fast operational repositioning alone—for why the secureds and the stockholders form a united front in court in support of the sale?

The policy issue here then is that the quick sale has business justifications, but poses § 1129–type distributional risks.

¶ 612: Chrysler's 2009 Reorganization: Mark J. Roe & David Skeel, Assessing the Chrysler Bankruptcy, 108 Michigan Law Review 727 (2010)

[Automakers' shrinking market share combined with the 2009 recession drove two of the Big Three American automakers into chapter 11. They received significant government assistance before and during the reorganization. Consider this summary of the Chrysler transaction:]

One of the larger American industrial companies entered chapter 11 and exited 42 days later. Clearly speed was achieved because of the governments' cash infusion of $15 billion on noncommercial terms into a company whose assets were valued at only $2 billion. The influx came at a time when the American economy was sinking, financial institutions were weakened, and the government feared that a collapse of the auto industry would have grave consequences for the rest of the economy. Never before had the government used bankruptcy to bail out a major industrial corporation. As a matter of bankruptcy technique, the rapidity of the Chrysler chapter 11 was a tour de force.

The economic policy and political background is worthy of its own analysis, but . . . it will not be our focus, except as it interacts with the Bankruptcy Code. Briefly, Chrysler was a weak producer, making cars that had limited consumer acceptance, in an industry suffering from substantial domestic and world-wide over-capacity. Industries facing such pressure normally need to shrink and their weakest producers, like Chrysler, are the first candidates for shrinkage.

* * *

The deal's basic structure is straightforward to summarize. Prebankruptcy, Chrysler was a private firm, owned by Cerberus, a large private equity fund. As of the bankruptcy, its two largest creditors were secured creditors owed $6.9 billion and an unsecured employee benefit plan, owed $10 billion. It also owed trade creditors $5.3 billion, and it had warranty and dealer obligations of several billion dollars.

The government created and funded a shell company that, through a § 363 sale, bought substantially all of Chrysler's assets for $2 billion, giving the secured creditors a return of 29 cents on the dollar. FIAT was brought in to manage the new firm and was given a slice of the new company's stock. New Chrysler (formally: New CarCo Acquisition LLC) then assumed the old company's debts to the retirees, most dealers, and trade creditors. The unsecured claims of the retirees' benefits plan were replaced with a new $4.6 billion note as well as 55% of the new company's stock.

* * *

The Chrysler § 363 transaction can be charted, as it is below.

Old Chrysler		New Chrysler	
Secured Debt		Secured Debt	
First Lien	$6.9B		
Second Lien (prior shareholders)	$2B		
Third Lien DIP (government)	$4.5B	Government	$6B
Unsecured Debt		Unsecured Debt	
TARP Loan	$4B		
Trade Debt	$5.3B →	Trade Debt	$5.3B
Warranty and Dealer	$4B →	Warranty and Dealer	$4B
Underfunded Pensions	$3.5B →	Underfunded Pensions	$3.5B
VEBA Obligations*	$10B →	VEBA Note	$4.6B
Shareholders' equity	↘	Shareholders' equity	
Cerberus		VEBA	55%
		Fiat	35%
		U.S. Treasury	8%
		Canadian government	2%

* VEBA is the acronym for voluntary employee benefit association, which handles Chrysler's obligations to its retirees, mostly for health benefits. TARP is the government program under which the U.S. Treasury advanced Chrysler funds.

¶ 613: Chrysler Appeal and § 363(m)

1. Should the transaction have best been analyzed as a § 363 sale or a § 1129 reorganization? How would *Braniff* and *Continental* apply to the *Chrysler* facts?
2. In the sales document, Old Chrysler required that New Chrysler pick up the obligations indicated by the arrows in the diagram above. Under the plan, New Chrysler paid Old Chrysler $2 billion for its main assets. The $2 billion was then distributed to the Chrysler's $6.9 billion secured creditors. Future claimants for defective Chrysler cars on the road at the time of the sale had to bring their lawsuit against Old Chrysler, which would presumably soon be without assets.
3. The unsecured creditors supported the sale. While the secured creditors holding the first lien on Chrysler's assets originally insisted on receiving $6.9 billion, the bulk of them, including several banks with large positions in the secured facility and large rescue loans from the U.S. Treasury, came to support the plan. Several secured creditors opposed the plan as violating § 1129, particularly by not providing them § 1129(a)(7) liquidation value. Unsecured creditors received nothing from Old Chrysler.
4. How does the *Chrysler* § 363 sale fit with *Lionel*, *Braniff*, and *Continental*?
5. The structure of the Chrysler § 363 sale was not unprecedented, but it was unusual. A majority of the public firm § 363 sales before

Chrysler's bankruptcy were done just for cash, without the buyer assuming any of the bankrupt debtor's debt. On average, only 10% of the prebankruptcy debt moved over to the buying company; the fraction of prebankruptcy debt that moved to the buyer was much higher in the Chrysler bankruptcy. Mar J. Roe & Joo-Hee Chung, *How Different Was Chrysler's Reogranization?*, 5 Journal of Legal Analysis 400 (2013).

6. After the bankruptcy court approved the sale, the sale was stayed pending appeal. The Second Circuit affirmed the sale, but stayed its completion so that the Supreme Court could consider whether to review it. The Court did not, the stay was lifted, and the sale was completed quickly afterwards. Later, an ordinary appeal from the sale (after it was completed) reached the Supreme Court. The Court granted certiorari and then, in a short opinion, vacated the Second Circuit's opinion. *Ind. State Police Pension Trust v. Chrysler, LLC*, 556 U.S. 960 (2009). The vacatur's impact was unclear. Some thought the Court signaled displeasure with the disposition of the Chrysler bankruptcy. Others thought that since the sale was completed and irreversible, the Court just had no basis to effectively review the Second Circuit's opinion, and was signaling nothing more than that. Section 363(m) is relevant to the latter possibility:

§ 363. Use, sale, or lease of property.

(m) The reversal or modification on appeal of an authorization under [§ 363](b) or (c) . . . does not affect the validity of a sale . . . to an entity that purchased . . . such property in good faith, whether or not such entity knew of the pendency of the appeal, unless such authorization and such sale or lease were stayed pending appeal.

Section 363(m) makes completed sales judicially unreviewable. When there's controversy, the sales order is typically temporarily stayed for an appeal. The appeal then occurs in a high pressure business atmosphere, as proponents of the sale argue that the firm's operations are deteriorating every minute that the sale is delayed.

7. Bankruptcy Rule 6004(h) provides that "[a]n order authorizing the use, sale, or lease of property other than cash collateral is stayed until the expiration of 14 days after entry of the order, unless the court orders otherwise." Fed. R. Bankr. P. 6004(h). So absent a court order, a dissenting party has 14 days to appeal; otherwise the sale order is final.

¶ 614: Credit Bidding and § 363(k)

Secured creditors may use their debt to bid if the property securing their claim is sold under § 363. They are thereby saved the inconvenience and cost of raising, or allocating, funding to any bid they make (but only up to the amount of their allowed secured claim):

§ 363. Use, sale, or lease of property.

(k) At a sale under subsection (b) . . . of property that is subject to a lien . . . , unless the court for cause holds otherwise the holder of such [a secured] claim may bid . . . , and, if [it] purchases such property, [it] may offset [its] claim against the purchase price. . . .

The secured creditor's § 363(k) right to credit bid helps to protect the secured creditor from a sale of its collateral at too low a price. Markets for the asset may be thin or financing may be scarce. In those situations, a secured creditor has the option to buy its own collateral from the estate by credit bidding its debt as currency. Relieving the secured creditor from having to pay cash for its bid makes sense insofar as the secured creditor would otherwise essentially be paying itself with the cash derived from its own cash bid. In winning the auction, the secured creditor would get both the collateral (as the winning bidder) and the cash (because as a secured creditor, its security interest in the sold collateral would transfer to the cash proceeds of the sale). By paying itself with its cash bid, the secured creditor's claim is extinguished. This same result is achieved more cheaply and directly with credit bidding.

Potential Costs. While credit bidding economizes on the secured creditor's financing costs in bidding, credit bidding can deter prospective outside bidders from participating in any auction. The credit bidder bids with dollars already lent to the debtor, IOU dollars rarely worth 100 cents, whose value can be recovered if at all only in the bankruptcy. By contrast, outside bidders must bid with new money—real cash—for which they may have to incur financing and other transaction costs that the bidding secured creditor does not face. Some courts see this difference as important: "[A]n auction sale in which one bidder is an existing lender who does not have to put up new money, but can rely on money previously advanced and which the lender has no other actual way to recover, is not a sale in which the bidders are on a level playing field."[7]

Outsiders are also typically less informed than the secured creditor is on the quality and value of the assets up for bid. That information disparity can make prospective bidders wary, especially when the collateral's value is uncertain and not readily marketable. An outsider would have to incur the costs of doing due diligence—investigating and valuing the assets—and this investment in due diligence goes for naught if the outsider's bid does not win. It may well fear that if it wins a bid against the insider, it will win because the insider-secured creditor concludes that the collateral is not worth what the outsider bid. These information and cost considerations suggest that credit bidding may deter outside bidding in some contexts.

Cause to Restrict Credit Bidding. The statute authorizes the court to restrict the secured creditor's bid for "cause," but the Code does not define "cause." A cook's tour of recent cases, however, gives some flavor of the factors courts consider when constraining or prohibiting credit bidding. The Third Circuit said that "a court may deny a lender the right to credit bid in the interest of any policy advanced by the Code,

---

[7] In re Antaeus Technical Services, Inc., 345 B.R. 556, 564 (Bankr. W.D. Va. 2005).

such as to ensure the success of the reorganization or to foster a competitive bidding environment." The factors that courts have cited in finding cause include (i) the presence of likely cash bidders who would be deterred from bidding in the face of an unconstrained credit bid,[8] (ii) the existence of a bona fide dispute as to the validity of the putative secured creditor's lien[9] or uncertainty as to which assets were covered by the secured creditor's lien,[10] (iii) interested secured creditors did not receive notice of the proposed sale,[11] and (iv) inequitable conduct meant to dampen interest in an auction.[12] Some of the cases where courts have found cause to restrict credit bidding have involved "loan-to-own" creditors—investment funds or strategic buyers that purchase secured debt before or during the case, typically at a deep discount, for the express purpose of purchasing the debtor's assets by credit bidding their purchased debt at face value.[13]

Credit Bidding in Chapter 11 Cramdown Sales. Asset sales, including whole-firm sales, can also occur under a Chapter 11 plan. When a secured creditor's collateral is being sold under a plan, and the secured creditor opposes the plan, this triggers the cramdown provisions of § 1129(b)(2)(A).

Until recently, the conventional wisdom was that such sales were governed by subsection (ii) of § 1129(b)(2)(A), which permits the debtor to sell the secured creditor's collateral free and clear of its lean, with the lien attaching instead to the sale proceeds. Subsection (b)(2)(A)(ii) also clearly preserves the secured creditor's §363(k) right to credit bid in the cramdown sale.

Two recent circuit court decisions upended this conventional wisdom, denying secured creditors the right to credit bid in sales of their collateral under Chapter 11 cramdown plans. *In re Philadelphia Newspapers, LLC.*, 599 F.3d 298 (3d Cir. 2010), *In re Pacific Lumber Co.*, 584 F.3d 229 (5th Cir. 2009).

These decisions turned on the interpretation of § 1129(b)(2)(A). While subsection (b)(2)(A)(ii) authorizes a free and clear sale "subject to section 363(k)"—i.e., a sale in which a secured creditor gets to credit bid—subsection (b)(2)(A)(iii) offers an alternative cramdown treatment: the plan may provide for the secured creditor's "realization . . . of the indubitable equivalent of [its] claim." In both *Pacific Lumber* and *Phil-*

[8] In re Fisker Automotive Holdings, Inc., 510 B.R. 55 (Bankr. D. Del. 2014).

[9] In re Octagon Roofing, 124 B.R. 522 (N. D. Ill. 1991), had a Chapter 7 trustee claiming that the secured creditor's lien was voidable. The § 363 sale occurred before this avoidance issue was resolved, and the court required the secured creditor to post a letter of credit in order to effect its credit bid in case its lien was later avoided.

[10] Id.

[11] In re Takeout Taxi Holdings, Inc., 307 B.R. 525 (Bankr. E.D. Va. 2004); In re Free Lance–Star Publ'g Co., 512 B.R. 798 (Bankr. E.D. Va. 2014).

[12] 512 B.R. 798.

[13] "The credit bid mechanism that normally works to protect secured lenders against the undervaluation of collateral sold at a bankruptcy sale does not always function properly when a party has bought the secured debt in a loan-to-own strategy in order to acquire the target company." In re Free Lance–Star Publ'g Co., 512 B.R. 798, 806 (Bankr. E.D. Va. 2014). The *Fisker* court, without expressly casting aspersions on loan-to-own credit bidders, limited the secured creditor's bid to the amount it had paid for its secured claim. In re Fisker Automotive Holdings, Inc., 510 B.R. 55, 61 (Bankr. D. Del. 2014).

adelphia Newspapers, the plan proposed to cram down the secured creditor by selling its collateral free and clear of any liens, but without allowing it to credit bid. Instead, the debtors argued successfully that paying the sale proceeds over to the secured creditor gave the creditor its "indubitable equivalent" under subsection (iii), relieving the plan from having to comply with subsection (ii).

These decisions offered debtors a convenient end-run around § 363(k). Instead of selling under § 363, a debtor could instead impose a cramdown plan on a secured creditor (as long as other confirmation requirements are met), selling the secured creditor's collateral to a favored cash bidder at a price below that amount of the secured creditor's claim, leaving the secured creditor with a large deficiency.

The Supreme Court, however, soon returned us to the conventional understanding that credit bidding applies in plan sales of secured creditors' collateral under § 1129(b), just as it applies to sales under § 363 sales. *Radlax Gateway Hotel, LLC v. Amalgamated Bank*, 132 S.Ct. 2065 (2012). The Court concluded that the more general "indubitable equivalent" locution in subsection (iii) should not be read to govern or render superfluous the more specific provision in subsection (ii) requiring credit bidding.

¶ 615: Claims Trading

A party interested in acquiring the debtor may make strategic purchases of bankruptcy claims against the debtor. That is, a bidder might make simultaneous offers for the various credit and stock claims of the debtor. Consider an offeror who plans to buy up two-thirds majorities of each class and then to propose a plan that will sell the firm to the highest bidder. If successful, the bidder owns the claims, votes them under § 1129(a)(8), and, hence owns the company as long as it makes the high bid.

Or what if the offeror tenders for 2/3 of each class of debt, with its obligation to "close" and actually buy up the debt being contingent on each class of creditors and interests approving a plan of reorganization that contemplates a third-party sale?

Such efforts have run into problems. See generally In re Allegheny Int'l, 118 Bankr. 282 (Bankr. W.D. Pa. 1990), amended on reconsideration, 1990 Bkrtcy LEXIS 1759 (1990). See generally Chaim J. Fortgang & Thomas Mayer, *Trading Claims and Taking Control of Corporations in Chapter 11*, 12 Cardozo Law Review 1 (1990).

Under § 1126(c)–(e), class acceptance does not include acceptance by "any entity whose acceptance or rejection of such plan was not in good faith, or was not solicited . . . in good faith[.]"

§ 1126. Acceptance of plan

(c) A class of claims has accepted a plan if such plan has been accepted by creditors, *other than any entity designated under subsection (e) of this section,* that hold at least two-thirds in amount and more than one-half in number. . . .

(d) [Similar standard for interests.]

(e) On request of a party in interest, . . . the court may designate any entity whose acceptance or rejection of such plan was not in good faith. . . .

Will a buyer of the claims vote all classes based on maximizing the value of that class of claims? Won't the buyer of the claims be interested in its total take in the reorganization, and be prepared to take less on one level if it gets more on another?

What if the bidder proposes a plan and, to help get the plan accepted, makes a tender offer for one class of claims? It intends to buy up those claims that accept the tender offer and vote the tendered claims in favor of the plan. Can it make the tender offer at a slight premium above the plan amount? See § 1123(a)(4): "[A] plan shall . . . provide the same treatment for each claim or interest of a particular class, unless the holder . . . agrees to a less favorable treatment. . . ." Would the plan also unfairly discriminate under § 1129(b)(1)? In re Allegheny Int'l, 118 Bankr. 282, 295–96 (Bankr. W.D. Pa. 1990). Is the tender offer a payment to creditors to buy their votes? Is that bad faith, which warrants exclusion of the purchased vote from the tally? Is the bidder-proponent thereby acting in bad faith, making the plan unconfirmable under § 1129(a)(3) ("The plan has been proposed in good faith and not by any means forbidden by law.")? *Allegheny* interpreted the good faith requirement expansively.

In In re DBSD North America, Inc., Dish, the satellite TV company, acquired a block of bonds in the bankruptcy of a competitor that it wished to acquire. The Second Circuit designated Dish under § 1126(e), because it purchased the bond claims not to vote for their best value but to use as leverage to serve its strategic objective of acquiring the bankrupt competitor. 634 F.3d 79 (2nd Cir. 2011). Presumably if its merger-oriented strategy was more important than its bondholding claims, it wouldn't have been motivated to vote the bonds for their basic return in bankruptcy, but to facilitate Dish's merger goals. It might have voted against a reorganization that was good for creditors overall, but that wouldn't have resulted in a merger with Dish.

Claims trading occurs not only in the context of bankruptcy acquisitions. It may also have strategic value in traditional reorganizations. However, claims trading may affect the reorganization deal structure embedded in Section 1129(a)(8), as the next excerpt explains.

¶ 616: Frederick Tung, Confirmation and Claims Trading, 90 Northwestern University Law Review 1684 (1996)

[C]laims trading has the potential to impede reorganization, imposing costs on the debtor company and its creditors. Because of Chapter 11's collective nature and the significant role of creditors in the [plan formation] process, instability in the creditor constituency may be disruptive. Throughout the course of a case, parties make significant reorganization-specific investment. They develop relationships with each other and acquire specialized knowledge about the business. They learn to cooperate. In this context, participants may not be fungible; the identities of particular creditors may matter. Creditor turnover may therefore destabilize the process. A significant creditor's exit from, or entry into, the process may render other parties prior investment [in understanding the company and developing working relationships] worthless, or may require significant additional investment by the parties. Even the *potential* for trading may impose costs on the parties by deterring cooperation.

While instability among creditor constituencies may hinder reorganization efforts, claims trading can also facilitate reorganization by coalescing a class into a useful bargaining position. Claims sellers may happily sell at a discount to secure an early exit from a case, while purchasers may harbor longer-term plans for engagement with the debtor. A claim purchaser may therefore be able to assemble a class with a unified view of the debtor's prospects for reorganization and the structure of a promising plan.

C. CHAPTER 7 LIQUIDATIONS AS SALES

¶ 617: Conversion to Chapter 7?

If senior creditors are dissatisfied with the plan proposed, can they do more than reject the plan and battle against cram-down under § 1129(b)? Couldn't they ask the court to convert the proceeding from chapter 11 to chapter 7, where the firm would be liquidated? Presumably the trustee would maximize the sales proceed by selling the firm in its entirety if the firm were worth more kept together than sold off piecemeal? Consider § 1112. Conversion to chapter 7 has been seen as an extraordinary event. The relevant conversion provisions have been amended several times since 1978, most recently in 2010 and there's more leeway now, at least doctrinally.

Consider the current formulation.

§ 1112. Conversion or dismissal

(b)(1) . . . [O]n request of a party in interest . . . , and after notice and a hearing, the court *shall* convert [a chapter 11 proceeding to] chapter 7 . . . for cause unless the court determines that the appointment under section 1104(a) of a trustee or an examiner is in the best interests of creditors and the estate.

(2) The court may not convert a case . . . to a case under chapter 7 . . . if the court finds and specifically identifies unusual circumstances establishing that converting or dismissing the case is not in the best interests of the creditors and the estate, and the debtor or any other party in interest establishes that—

(A) there is a reasonable likelihood that a plan will be confirmed . . . within the timeframes established in section[]1121(e)

. . . or if such section[] do[es] not apply, within a reasonable period of time; and

(B) the grounds for converting or dismissing the case include an act or omission of the debtor other than that under paragraph (4)(A) . . . for which there exists a reasonable justification . . . and . . . that will be cured within a reasonable period of time. . . .

(3) . . .

(4) . . . [T]he term "cause" includes

(A) substantial or continuing loss to or diminution of the estate and the absence of a reasonable likelihood of rehabilitation;

(B) gross mismanagement of the estate;

(C) . . .

(D) unauthorized use of cash collateral . . . ;

* * *

(I) failure . . . to pay taxes owed . . . ;

(J) failure to file a disclosure statement . . . ;

* * *

(N) material default by the debtor with respect to a confirmed plan. . . .

§ 1104. Appointment of trustee . . .

(a) . . . on request of a party . . . the court shall order the appointment of a trustee—

(1) for cause, including fraud, dishonesty, incompetence or gross mismanagement . . . ; or

(2) if such appointment is in the interests of creditors, any equity security holders, and other interests of the estate.

---

1. Congress rewrote § 1112 in 2005 (and again in 2010), ostensibly making it easier for creditors to win conversion or dismissal motions. Prior to 2005, the statute was phrased as permissive ("may") if the standards were met. As amended in 2005, the rule is phrased as a mandatory one, once the requesting party establishes cause, unless "the court finds and specifically identifies unusual circumstances establishing that converting or dismissing the case is not in the best interests of the creditors and the estate."
2. The amended § 1112 lists specific debtor wrong-doing that would justify conversion to chapter 7. (Not all of the specifics are listed above.) If the debtor committed none of the specifics, the creditor may still find each of the general standards difficult to meet. The estate may not be diminishing in size, but just not growing fast enough to provide financiers a normal rate of return. Low operating profit doesn't seem to satisfy (b)(4)(A). That is, slowness in formulating a plan may mean that the debtor fails to maximize its value,

but doesn't necessarily create a continuing loss. And even if the estate were diminishing, "a reasonable likelihood of rehabilitation" could well still exist, although one at a value lower than the maximum attainable. Subsection (b)(4)(A) requires both loss and no realistic chance of rehabilitation.

3. Similarly, sub-section (b)(4)(B) requires not just that the debtor has mismanaged the estate but that the mismanagement is gross mismanagement.

4. Note that in § 1112(b)(2), it's the opponents of conversion who need to show that a plan is likely to be confirmed in a timely manner.

5. Bankruptcy courts regularly extended the debtor's period of exclusivity for proposing a plan in the decades after the 1978 Code became law. With the 2005 amendments, Congress sought to cut those extensions down. And, by making conversion easier, perhaps Congress sought to force the parties to agree more quickly to a plan.

   While the 2005 version of § 1112 provides a wedge for senior creditors, Congress sought similar tightening in the past, but it did not work out that way. Conversion from chapter 11 to chapter 7 has usually been seen as drastic, as a sign of failure. The new § 1112 seems to want to make conversion more routine.

CHAPTER 7

JUNK BONDS

Introduction: Priority among financial claimants

Priority is determined not only by the statute but by contract. The creditors can order themselves, making deals at the time that they lend as to who would come first and who would come second. Generally speaking, the Bankruptcy Code enforces these deals among the creditors. These deals could depend on which creditor takes security. The creditor who gets a mortgage on the debtor's real property or a security interest on the debtor's equipment and inventory under the Uniform Commercial Code would be paid out of that asset and, usually, become a general unsecured creditor of the company for any deficiency. Or the creditors could in these deals just say who would come first and who would come last. The creditor who comes last presumably is paid to do so, getting a higher promised interest rate and, hence, more compensation if the firm doesn't run into trouble. Such creditors who agree to stand aside until another creditor gets paid are said to subordinate themselves to the creditor who will come first. That creditor who comes first is said to be "senior" to the "subordinated" creditor. The most famous of those creditors who agree to take a place near the end of the priority line are junk bondholders.

In this chapter, we analyze the main means of contractual ordering of priority, looking at what limits creditors put on how far back in line they can be placed, mostly via financial covenants.

A. BOND INDENTURES AND THEIR COVENANTS

¶ 701: Background to the Bond Indenture

The bond indenture is the bondholders' loan agreement. Its core establishes the interest rate, maturity date, and amount loaned. With it, the debtor can provide security to the creditor bondholders. It can control the level of debt claims that will be superior to or inferior to the subject bondholders, set up the mechanisms by which the debt will be assumed in the event of a merger, constrain the dividends that the firm can pay, require sinking funds to pay back the debt little by little, and restrict the type of investments the firm can make.

Bonds, in the classic notion, are long-term corporate debt obligations, issued under an indenture, under which a trustee takes title to, or a lien on, property of the corporation. Debentures are also issued under an indenture, but the trustee takes no security. The trustee's job is to ascertain corporate compliance with various financial covenants (usually via certificates from the company), to collect and disburse the money to the debentureholders, and to bring legal action against the corporation for the debentureholders, if it is wise to do so. In common usage among finance people, no distinction is made between the two and debentures are often also called bonds. Corporate notes are debt obligations not issued under an indenture.

The bond indenture (a term used for both secured bonds and unsecured debentures), seeks to govern conflict between the creditors and the stockholders. In this chapter, after we read background material, we'll focus on the interplay among three key priority elements: seniority and subordination, negative pledge clauses, and security interests. First, some background from Smith & Warner:

> [T]here are four major sources of conflict . . . between [creditors] and stockholders:
>
> Dividend payment. If a firm issues bonds and the bonds are priced assuming the firm will maintain its [current] dividend policy, the value of the bonds is reduced by [the firm's] raising the dividend rate and financing the increase by reducing investment. At the limit, if the firm sells all its assets and pays a liquidating dividend to the stockholders, the bondholders are left with worthless claims.
>
> Claim dilution. If the firm sells bonds, and the bonds are priced assuming that no additional debt will be issued, the value of the bondholders' claims is reduced by issuing additional debt of the same or higher priority.
>
> Asset substitution. If a firm sells bonds for the stated purposed of engaging in low [risk] projects and the bonds are valued at prices commensurate with that low risk, the value of the stockholders' equity rises and the value of the bondholders' claim is reduced by substituting

projects which increase the firm's variance rate [i.e., high risk projects].

Underinvestment. [A] substantial portion of the value of the firm is composed of intangible assets in the form of future investment opportunities. A firm with outstanding bonds can have incentives to reject projects which have a positive net present value if the benefit from accepting the project accrues to the bondholders.

[To reduce these conflicts, the creditor asks the debtor for covenants that specify what risks the debtor can take:]

Covenants which directly restrict the shareholders' choice of production/ investment policy . . . restrict[ ] the firm's holdings of financial investments, [its] disposition of assets, and . . . the firm's merger activity. [Although specific limits on investments are rare,] covenants which restrict dividend and financing policy also [have the effect of] restrict[ing] investment policy.

Bond covenants which directly restrict the payment of dividends [usually do] not take the form of a constant dollar limitation. Instead, the maximum allowable dividend is a function of both accounting earnings and the proceeds from the sale of new equity. . . .

Financing policy covenants . . . restrict not only the issuance of senior debt, [but also] the issuance of debt of any priority, [and the granting of security]. In addition, the firm's right to incur other fixed obligations such as leases is restricted. . . .

[Other] covenants . . . include the [promise to provide] audited financial statements, the specification of accounting techniques, the required purchase of insurance, and the periodic provision of a statement, signed by the firm's officers, indicating compliance with the covenants.

[Some conflicts cannot be anticipated. Fearing risks it cannot anticipate, the creditor will also insist that the debtor pay for extra risk with a higher interest rate.]

Clifford Smith & Jerold Warner, *On Financial Contracting: An Analysis of Bond Covenants*, 7 Journal of Financial Economics 117 (1979).

¶ 702: Dewing, The Financial Policy of Corporations (5th Ed. 1953)[1]

[The contents of the bond indenture can be summarized:]

This rather elaborate document has, ordinarily, [four] important sets of provisions, some of which are mere recapitulations or elaborations of statements made in the primary contract, the bond [formerly a simple piece of paper stating that the company owes, and will pay the specified sum of money and the specified interest, on the specified due dates, and now more typically a computer entry—Roe], and some provisions only indirectly referred to in the bond.

[1] As reproduced in Victor Brudney and Marvin Chirelstein, Corporate Finance (3d ed. 1987).

There is, first, the set of provisions summarizing the amounts [due and the] future date of payment, the interest rate and the time of interest payment—provisions which acknowledge that the bondholder is a creditor of the corporation entitled to the payment of his loan with interest. Furthermore, if the payment of the debt may be anticipated by the corporation [i.e., paid by the debtor in advance of maturity—Roe], the fact will be clearly stated, together with the specific mechanism of prepayment which shall insure fairness to all the scattered bondholders. The second set of provisions describes the character and the extent of property against which the bondholder may levy in order to satisfy his debt. If there is no such property, the agreement will categorically state that fact. Thirdly, there is a set of provisions which defines with a high degree of precision the exact course the bondholders, acting individually or together, must pursue in order to levy on the corporation, as general creditors, or to levy on the specific property, if any, set aside for the security of the bonds issued under the indenture.

Again, [fourthly], there are provisions describing the duties and the obligations of the trustee. These clauses define with precision what he can and what he cannot do, on behalf both of the corporation and of the individual and collective bondholders.

Victor Brudney & Marvin Chirelstein, Corporate Finance: Cases and Materials 166 note e, 171 (3d ed. 1987):

The impetus for the early long-term corporate debt securities, the mortgage bonds issued by railroads in the 19th century, came from entrepreneurs who were forced to sell mortgage notes to many persons, since no one person was willing or able to furnish all of the funds to be raised.[2] The problem was to give the numerous and widely dispersed purchasers of these mortgage notes, or bonds, the security of a mortgage on the railroad's assets without conveying individual fractional interests in the collateral to each bond purchaser. At the same time, the bonds were to be marketable and to carry along the lien on the mortgaged property. The solution was to convey the mortgaged assets, under a trust indenture, to someone as trustee, for the equal and ratable benefit of each of the bondholders.

* * *

The mortgage bond is an obligation secured by specified property which either is made subject to the obligee's lien by the mortgage (although technically title continues to be held by the obligor) or, in some states, is technically transferred to the obligee to be held solely as security for the repayment of the debt. In theory, the mortgagee of a corporate mortgage, like the mortgagee of a simple home mortgage,

---

[2] [The substance behind the phrase "since no one person was willing or able to furnish all of the funds to be raised" derived not just from the fact that big firms' capital needs were so much greater than the wealth of businesspeople, but also from the structure of America's 19th century financial institutions. Banks, the prime financial institutions of the time, could not operate across state lines. Industry went big, and national, at the end of the 19th century, but finance stayed (more or less) local. This structure of American financial institutions then affected the capital structure of American firms. See Mark J. Roe, Strong Managers, Weak Owners: A Political Theory of American Corporate Finance (1994).]

applies the security in payment of the defaulted debt by foreclosure on the mortgaged property in a proceeding which results in a sale. [If the debtor defaults, the property is usually sold under state law and t]he mortgagee may purchase the property at the sale which ideally is an auction at which competitive bidding is designed at least formally, to assure a fair price. Whether the property is sold to the obligee or otherwise, its proceeds are applied in payment of the obligation. The historical inadequacy of the foreclosure procedure to protect the corporate bondholders has been the subject of considerable literature and has resulted in the development of bankruptcy reorganization procedure under federal legislation.

To the extent that the property subject to a corporate mortgage is an integral part of a going concern, it generally has a higher monetary value if it continues to be a part of the going concern than if it is sold for cash, piecemeal or *in toto*. Hence, even when [bondholders could foreclose, they typically obtained] new participations in the continuing enterprise [They rarely forced or were able to] force the sale of the liened property to third persons for cash. When reorganizations thus were consummated through the process of mortgage foreclosure—principally in the case of railroads—the value of the property subject to the mortgage was theoretically available to pay the debt it secured to the extent thereof. If the pledged property was "worth" more than the amount of the debt, the surplus was available to second or even more junior mortgagees or to general creditors. On the other hand, if the property was not "worth" enough to pay the debt, the unpaid balance became an unsecured claim against the borrower, and the mortgage bondholders shared with other general creditors in the borrower's unsecured assets. The principle of allocating the full "value" of the mortgaged property to satisfy the mortgage bondholder before any other creditor could receive any part of the proceeds was imported into the statutory procedure for bankruptcy reorganization. . . .

B. THE JUNK BOND

¶ 703: Drum Financial Prospectus

Prospectus **$20,000,000**

DRUM FINANCIAL CORPORATION

12⅞% Senior Subordinated Debentures due September 15, 1999

Interest payable March 15 and September 15

* * *

The Debentures will be subordinated to all Senior Indebtedness (as defined) of the Company. As of June 30, 1979, after giving effect to the sale of the Debentures and the application of the estimated net proceeds therefrom, the Company's Senior Indebtedness would have been $480,713. See "Use of Proceeds." The Debentures will rank senior to the Company's 5½% Convertible Subordinated Debentures due May 1, 1988. For a discussion of restrictions in the indenture upon the creation of Senior Funded Debt and debt ranking pari passu with the Debentures, see "Description of Debentures—Certain Covenants."

DREXEL BURNHAM LAMBERT INCORPORATED **THE ROBINSON-HUMPHREY COMPANY, INC.**

September 26, 1979

SELECTED FINANCIAL INFORMATION

(Dollars in thousands)

Consolidated Operating Summary

[edited]

	Year Ended December 31					Six months Ended June 30	
	1974	1975	1976	1977	1978	1978	1979
						Unaudited	
Income (loss) from continuing operations before realized investment gains (losses) and extraordinary items	(6,237)	(7,939)	737	3,615	5,487	2,137	3,254
Realized investment gains (losses) less federal income taxes	647	140	50	2,044	(121)	(48)	(499)
Loss related to discontinued operations	(1,302)	(15,496)	(1,855)	(1,855)	(53)	(25)	—
Extraordinary items Net income (loss)	398	—	8,446	3,543	3,130	1,404	1,180
Income (loss) from continuing operations before realized investment gains (losses) and extraordinary items	(6,494)	(23,295)	7,378	(1,557)	8,443	3,468	3,935

Summary of Consolidated Balance Sheet

(Unaudited)

[edited]

	June 30, 1979 Actual
Total Assets	$141,538
Stockholders' Equity	22,088

THE COMPANY

Drum Financial Corporation (formerly Fidelity Corporation) is an insurance holding company engaged through its subsidiaries in the sale, underwriting and servicing primarily of property and casualty insurance as well as of credit life insurance, both group and individual. In 1978, approximately 70% of the Company's net insurance premiums written arose from consumer credit transactions originated by banks, finance companies, credit unions and retail merchants.... For a description of estimated recent losses resulting from Hurricanes David and Frederic, see "Business—Property and Casualty Insurance—Mobile home insurance."

During the late 1960s and early 1970s the Company was engaged in an expansion and diversification program which included the acquisition of several businesses, primarily in the insurance and financial service fields and the marketing of insurance lines not previously included among the Company's principal insurance products. This program ... resulted in substantial losses for the Company, most of which were realized between 1973 and 1975. Of significance were the following: (i) a $23.5 million loss in 1973 on the Company's investment in Equity Funding Corporation of America [and] (ii) [substantial losses in the firm's other insurance businesses]. In view of these adverse developments, *changes in senior management of the holding company were initiated in late 1975.* Since that time the Company has emphasized, and plans to continue to emphasize, those insurance product lines which have historically been profitable.

* * *

General

The Debentures are to be issued under an Indenture (the "Indenture") to be dated as of September 15, 1979, between the Company and The Omaha National Bank, as Trustee (the "Trustee"). The Debentures will bear interest from September 15, 1979 at the rate shown on the cover page of this Prospectus payable on March 15, 1980. (Section 2.02.)

* * *

Certain Definitions

The following summarizes certain definitions to be used in the Indenture.

"Consolidated Net Income" shall mean net income of the Company and its Subsidiaries determined in accordance with generally accepted accounting principles.

"Consolidated Net Worth" shall mean the excess of the Company's and its Subsidiaries' assets over their liabilities.

"Consolidated Senior Funded Debt" shall mean the aggregate Senior Funded Debt of the Company and its Subsidiaries....

"Funded Debt" ... shall mean any Indebtedness with a stated maturity more than one year from the date of determination....

"Indebtedness" shall mean any indebtedness for borrowed money or evidenced by bonds, notes, debentures or similar instruments, or the deferred and unpaid balance of the purchase price of any property which would appear as a liability upon a balance sheet prepared in accordance with generally accepted accounting principles and shall also include capitalized lease obligations and equity convertible into debt.

"Insurance Subsidiaries" shall mean any Subsidiary [now owned or subsequently] acquired or organized that engages, directly or indirectly, in the insurance business and any successor to any of the foregoing.

"Pari Passu Funded Debt" shall mean the Debentures and all other unsecured Funded Debt of the Company that both (i) ranks, as to payment of principal, premium, if any, and interest, pari passu [i.e., at the same level—Roe] with the Debentures and (ii) is subordinated to Indebtedness that is Senior Indebtedness under the Indenture. Unsecured Funded Debt that ranks pari passu with the Debentures would share ratably with the Debentures should there be funds insufficient to discharge both the Company's obligations on such unsecured Funded Debt and the Debentures.

* * *

"Senior Funded Debt" shall mean all Funded Debt other than Pari Passu Funded Debt and Subordinated Funded Debt.

"Subordinated Funded Debt" shall mean (i) the Company's unsecured Funded Debt if designated by the Company to be subordinate in right of payment to the Debentures and (ii) the Company's 5½% Convertible Subordinated Debentures due May 1, 1988.

"Subsidiary" shall mean any corporation of which at least a majority in voting power of the outstanding stock shall be owned by the Company directly or through Subsidiaries.

Certain Covenants

Limitation on Senior and Pari Passu Funded Debt. The company will not, and will not permit any Subsidiary to, incur any Senior [or Pari Passu] Funded Debt . . . unless after giving effect thereto, the aggregate [of the value of these Debentures, other Pari Passu Funded Debt, and the] Consolidated Senior Funded Debt . . . of the Company and its Subsidiaries shall be less than the sum of Consolidated Net Worth and Subordinated Funded Debt. . . .

At June 30, 1979, after giving effect to the sale of the Debentures and the use of a portion of the net proceeds to retire bank debt, an additional $7,939,957 aggregate principal amount of Senior and Pari Passu Funded Debt could have been incurred.

Limitation on Dividends, Stock Purchases and Restricted Investments. The Company will not (i) pay dividends or make distributions on its capital stock (other than in shares or stock rights), (ii) purchase or redeem, or permit a Subsidiary to purchase or redeem, capital stock of the Company . . . if the sum of . . . the amount[s] expended for any such purpose . . . would exceed the sum of (1) 50% of Consolidated Net Income accrued subsequent to December 31, 1978; (2) the net proceeds received by the Company after December 31, 1978 from the sale of its capital stock, other than to a Subsidiary, for cash or upon certain conversions of Indebtedness (other than the 5½% Convertible Subordinated Debentures) and (3) $2,000,000. . . .

Limitations on Dispositions of Insurance Subsidiaries. The Company will not, and will not permit any Subsidiary to, dispose (except to the Company) of any capital stock of any Subsidiary that was, or is the successor to, an Insurance Subsidiary on the date of the Indenture, or of any options therefor, except for sales for fair value of 100% of the capital stock of such an Insurance Subsidiary. (Section 6.08.)

Limitation on Investments. . . .

Limitation on Guarantees and Other Contingent Liabilities. . . .

Limitation on Mergers and Dispositions of Assets. . . .

Subordination of Debentures

The payment of the principal of and premium, if any, and interest on the Debentures is subordinated in right of payment, as set forth in the Indenture, to the prior payment in full of all Senior Indebtedness of the Company, as defined in the Indenture, whether outstanding on the date of the Indenture or thereafter created, incurred, assumed or guaranteed. Upon (i) the maturity of Senior Indebtedness by lapse of time, acceleration or otherwise or (ii) any distribution of the assets of the Company upon any dissolution, winding up, liquidation or reorganization of the Company, the holders of Senior Indebtedness will be entitled to receive payment in full before the holders of Debentures are entitled to receive any payment. If in any of the situations referred to in clause (ii) above a payment is made to the Trustee or to holders of Debentures before all Senior Indebtedness has been paid in full or provision has been made for such payment, the payment to the Trustee or holders of Debentures must be paid over to the holders of the Senior Indebtedness.

Senior Indebtedness is defined as the principal of and premium, if any, and interest on indebtedness (other than the Debentures and the Company's 5½% Convertible Subordinated Debentures), whether outstanding on the date of the Indenture or thereafter created, (i) incurred or guaranteed by the Company for money borrowed from lending or financing institutions [or] (ii) evidenced by notes, bonds or debentures of the Company issued under the provisions of an indenture or similar instrument; provided the terms of the instrument creating or evidencing such future indebtedness provide that such indebtedness is superior in right of payment to the Debentures. (Article 4.)

By reason of such subordination, in the event of insolvency holders of the Debentures may recover less than the general creditors of the Company.

Priority of Debentures

Under the indenture relating to the Company's 5½% Convertible Subordinated Debentures due 1988, the Debentures will be "Senior Debt" (as defined therein). As a result, the Company's obligations with regard to those debentures will be subordinate to the Company's obligations with regard to the Debentures.

Events of Default and Notice Thereof

The term "Event of Default" when used in the Indenture shall mean any one of the following: failure to pay interest for thirty days, or principal (including premium, if any) or any sinking fund or other redemption installment when due; *failure to perform any other covenant for sixty days after notice*; acceleration of other indebtedness of the Company under the terms of the indenture or instrument evidencing such indebtedness unless rescinded or annulled within ten days after notice; final judgment for the payment of more than $100,000 rendered against the Company and not discharged within sixty days after the judgment becomes final; and certain events of bankruptcy, insolvency or reorganization. (Section 7.01.)

The Indenture provides that the Trustee shall, within ninety days after the occurrence of a default, give to the Debentureholders notice of all uncured defaults known to it (the term "default" to include the events specified above without grace or notice). . . . (Section 10.03.)

In case an Event of Default shall occur and be continuing, the Trustee or the holders of at least 25% in aggregate principal amount of the Debentures then outstanding, by notice in writing to the Company (and to the Trustee if given by Debenture holders), may declare the principal of all the Debentures to be due and payable immediately. Such declaration may be annulled and past defaults (except, unless theretofore cured, a default in payment of principal of and interest or premium, if any, on the Debentures or failure to make any sinking fund payment) may be waived by the holders of a majority in principal amount of the Debentures, upon the conditions provided in the Indenture. (Section 7.02.)

The Indenture includes a covenant that the Company will file annually with the Trustee a statement regarding compliance by the Company with the terms thereof and specifying any defaults of which the signers may have knowledge. (Section 6.12.)

The Company will furnish to the holders of the Debentures annual reports containing financial statements certified by independent public accountants.

Modification of the Indenture

Under the Indenture, the rights and obligations of the Company and the rights of the holders of the Debentures may be modified by the Company and the Trustee only with the consent of the holders of 66⅔% in principal amount of the Debentures then outstanding; provided, however, that, among other things [no (i)] change in the time of payment of principal of, or any installment of interest on, any Debenture, or (ii) reduction in the principal amount thereof or the rate of interest thereon or any premium payable upon the redemption thereof, or (iii) reduction in the aggregate principal amount of Debentures required to be redeemed pursuant to the sinking fund, or (iv) impairment in the right to institute suit for the enforcement of any such payment, or (v) reduction in the percentage required for modification of the Indenture or the consent for any waiver provided for in the Indenture, may be made without the consent of the holder of each outstanding Debenture affected thereby. (Section 14.02.)

The Trustee

The Omaha National Bank will be the Trustee under the Indenture.

The Indenture contains certain limitations on the right of the Trustee, should it become a creditor of the Company, to obtain payment of claims in certain cases, or to realize on certain property received in respect of any such claim as security or otherwise. (Section 10.08.) The Trustee will be permitted to engage in certain other transactions; however, if it acquires any conflicting interest (as described in the Indenture) it must eliminate such conflict or resign. (Section 10.05.)

Subject to certain limitations, the holders of a majority in principal amount of all outstanding Debentures will have the right to direct the time, method and place of conducting any proceeding for exercising any remedy available to the Trustee. (Section 7.06.) The Indenture provides that in case an Event of Default has occurred and is continuing the Trustee must exercise such of the rights and powers vested in it by the Indenture, and use the same degree of care and skill in their exercise, as a prudent man would exercise or use under the circumstances in the conduct of his own affairs. (Section 10.01.) Subject to the foregoing, the Trustee will be under no obligation to exercise any of its rights or powers under the Indenture at the request or direction of any of the holders of Debentures, unless they shall have offered to the Trustee reasonable security or indemnity against the costs, expenses and liabilities which might be incurred by it in compliance with such request or direction. (Section 10.01.) Except for the right to collect principal, premium if any, and interest on the Debentures when due, no holder of any Debentures has the right to institute any action, suit or proceeding at law or in equity for the enforcement of any remedy under the Indenture, unless the holders of 25% in principal amount of Debentures shall have submitted written requests to the Trustee to take action and shall have afforded the Trustee satisfactory security and indemnity against costs, expenses and liabilities, and the Trustee shall not have taken such action for 60 days thereafter. (Section 7.07.)

¶ 704: Questions on the Drum Financial Indenture, Subordinated as Guarantor?

1. Do the creditors rely on state dividend statutes to protect them from the debtor paying out high dividends, which would make the debentures riskier than if the dividends were not paid out?
2. Can Drum Financial incur an unlimited amount of senior funded debt? That is, the compensation of the debentureholders is capped (see the cover page of the prospectus) at 12⁷⁄₈ percent.
3. Consider Drum Financial with the following balance sheet:

Assets	Liabilities and Shareholders' Equity	
$100M	Senior Funded Debt	$30M (A)
	The Debentures	$20M (B)
	Further Subordinated	$10M (C)
	Common Stock	$40M (D)

   The $10 million of "Further Subordinated" debt is debt that is subordinated to the debentures. The creditors are organized in three layers of priority. Could another $20 million of Senior Debt be issued under the debentures' indenture? Could any Senior Debt be issued?
4. Is there any Senior Indebtedness that is not Senior Funded Debt?
5. Is there any Senior Funded Debt that is not Senior Indebtedness? Can future creditors come before the subordinated debentures without being designated as "Senior Indebtedness"? If a creditor

obtains a mortgage but Drum doesn't designate it to be senior, is it "Senior Indebtedness" under "Subordination of Debentures"? Is it "Senior Funded Debt"? How are "Certain Covenants" drafted?

6. If Drum Financial merely issues a lot of long-term debt, *without* designating the debt as senior, do Drum's chief financial officer and its lawyers need to run that debt incurrence through any covenants to check for compliance? That is, if the company issued lots of basic debt and lost money, there'd be lots of creditors chasing the remaining assets. The debentureholders' claims would be diluted by the claims of the other creditors. See the definition of "Senior Funded Debt" and the "Limitation on Senior . . . Funded Debt."

7. Are the subordinated debentureholders guarantors? Of whom? To what extent?

C. FINANCIAL MARKETS AND JUNK BONDS

¶ 705: Jan Loeys, *Low–Grade Bonds: A Growing Source of Corporate Funding,* Federal Reserve Bank of Philadelphia, Business Review, Nov./Dec. 1986

In recent years, a growing part of corporate borrowing has taken the form of "low-grade bonds." Called "junk bonds" by some, and "high-yield bonds" by others, these bonds are rated as speculative by the major rating agencies, and they are therefore considered more risky than high- or investment-grade bonds. [In the 1980s] low-grade bonds . . . received a lot of public attention because of their use in corporate takeovers. But in fact, most low-grade bond issues are not [and were not] used for this purpose. Corporations that now issue low-grade bonds are firms that, because of their lack of size, track record, and name recognition, used to borrow mostly via bank loans or privately placed bonds. Recently, investors have become more willing to lend directly to smaller and less creditworthy corporations by buying these low-grade bonds. There are several reasons for the new popularity of these bonds. But before discussing those reasons, it is useful to examine in more depth exactly what low-grade bonds are and how their market first developed.

WHAT ARE LOW–GRADE BONDS?

Low-grade bonds represent corporate bonds that are rated below investment grade by the major rating agencies, Standard & Poor's and Moody's. These ratings, which firms usually request before issuing bonds to the public, reflect each agency's estimate of the firm's capacity to honor its debt (that is, to pay interest and repay principal when due). The highest rating is AAA (for firms with an "extremely strong" capacity to pay interest and repay principal), and then AA ("very strong"), A ("strong"), and BBB ("adequate"). Bonds rated BB, B, CCC, or CC are regarded as "speculative" with respect to the issuer's capacity to meet the terms of the obligation. Firms generally strive to maintain at least a BBB rating because many institutions or investment funds cannot, because of regulation, or will not, because of firm policy, invest in lower grade bonds. This explains why bonds rated below BBB are also known as "below-investment" grade bonds.

* * *

THE MARKET FOR LOW–GRADE BONDS

Low-grade bonds have received widespread attention from the press in recent years, largely because of their association with ... corporate takeover[s]. But low-grade bonds have been around for a long time. In fact, during the 1920s and 1930s, about 17 percent of domestic corporate bond offerings (that is, new issues) were low grade. Furthermore, as the Depression of the 1930s wore on, many bonds that were originally issued with a high-grade rating were downgraded to below-investment grade. These so-called "fallen angels" were bonds of companies that had fallen on hard times. By 1940, as a result of both these downgradings and the earlier heavy volume of new low-grade offerings, low-grade bonds made up more than 40 percent of all bonds outstanding.

* * *

In 1977, Drexel Burnham Lambert, an investment bank that was already making a secondary market in fallen angels, started an effort to revitalize the market for original-issue low-grade bonds by underwriting new issues and subsequently making a secondary market in them. . . . By the end of 1985, the total stock of low-grade bonds outstanding reached about $75 billion (or 14 percent of the total), less than a third of which consisted of fallen angels. To compensate investors for th[e default] risk they bear by holding low-grade debt ... rather than (presumably) default-free Treasury securities, firms promise to pay higher yields on their debt than the Treasury does. This difference between yields is called a "risk premium." . . .

* * *

The recent revival of the low-grade bond market raises the question of why this product has become successful again. One popular misconception is that these bonds are used solely to finance corporate takeovers. But . . . the market had taken off well before the first major use of low-grade bonds in corporate takeover attempts in 1983. And even in 1985—a year of unprecedented merger activity—low-grade bonds issued for takeover purposes made up only about 38 percent of total low-grade bond issuance. . . . Rather than reflecting a rise in one particular use for low-grade bonds, the reemergence of the market paralleled more fundamental changes in financial markets that made low-grade bonds relatively more attractive compared with other forms of financing.

WHY DID THE MARKET GROW?

The main alternative to issuing public debt securities directly in the open market is to obtain a loan from a [bank or insurance company] that issues securities (or deposits) of its own in the market.

Before the reemergence of original-issue low-grade bonds, only large, well-known firms with established track records found it economical to raise money by issuing their own debt securities in the public capital markets. For smaller, relatively new or unknown firms, the expense was usually prohibitive. Because of the risk of underwriting low-grade bonds, investment bankers would demand hefty underwriting fees. Also, less creditworthy issuers would have had to pay a very high premium on their debt because investors perceived them as particularly risky investments.

Such borrowers thus found it more economical simply to obtain a loan from a bank or to place a private bond issue with a life insurance company. . . .

The reemergence of a market for public original issue low-grade bonds suggests that this situation is changing. . . . As with many financial innovations, it is impossible to identify all the factors responsible for this development. But it is possible to suggest several important ones that may have made a contribution to the reemergence of original-issue low-grade bonds, and three seem particularly noteworthy—a greater demand by investors for marketable assets; lower information costs; and changes in investors' risk perceptions.

Marketability vs. Covenant Restrictions. . . . [B]uyers of privately placed bonds have become more willing to trade some of the safety they found in the contractual restrictions they placed on borrowers in return for the marketability and higher yields of publicly issued low-grade bonds. Private placements are bilateral, customized loan agreements with complex contractual restrictions on borrowers' actions. However, the lack of standardization of these covenants and the frequent need for renegotiation when borrowers want to transgress the covenant restrictions make it very costly to have a lot of lenders per issue, or to change the identity of the lenders. As a result, there is not much of a secondary market for private placements. That is, they are not marketable.

Low-grade bonds, in contrast, are public securities and are issued with relatively simple, standardized contracts without cumbersome restrictions on borrowers' actions, in order to facilitate their trading in a secondary market. And in exchange for the added freedom from covenant restrictions, borrowers pay a higher yield on low-grade bonds than on private placements. . . .

* * *

Information Costs. A second factor contributing to the growth of the low-grade bond market is that, in recent years, it has become much easier for individual and institutional investors to obtain and maintain information about the condition of corporate borrowers. Thus lenders are now more likely to find it cost-effective to lend directly to smaller and less well-known corporations, rather than indirectly through financial intermediaries such as commercial banks.

Indeed, recent technological improvements in such areas as data manipulation and telecommunications have reduced greatly the costs of obtaining and processing information about the conditions—whether international or domestic, industry-wide or firm-specific—that affect the value of a borrowing firm. Any analyst now has computerized access to a wealth of economic and financial information at a relatively low cost. New information reaches investors across the world in a matter of minutes. Given the reduction in information costs, the cheapest method of lending to certain smaller and less creditworthy borrowers may no longer require a specialized intermediary as the sole lender to these borrowers, especially after recognizing the other expenses of using the intermediary.[3] . . .

Figure 1

New Domestic Corporate Bond Issues: 1978–1985

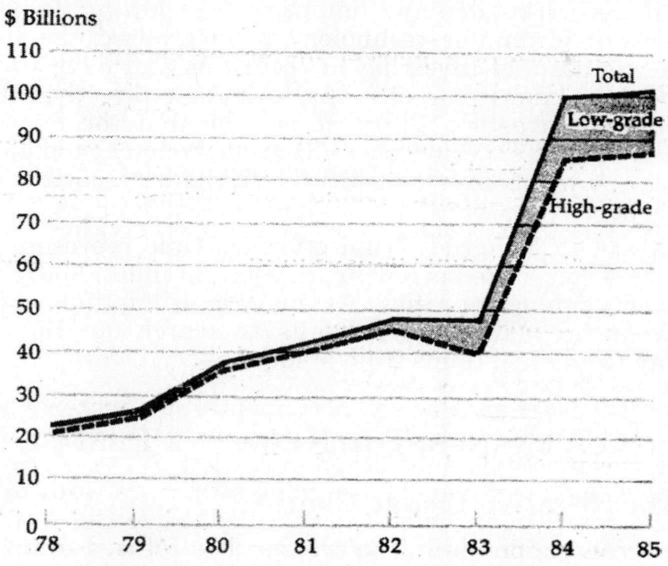

Source: Edward I. Altman and Scott A. Nammacher, "The Anatomy of the High Yield Debt Market: 1985 Update," Morgan Stanley (June 1986).

Risk Perceptions. A third explanation of the growth in low-grade bond offerings is more on the psychological side. Investors [may not have become any] better informed about the risks they take on, but they may have also become more willing to invest in risky securities. After the 1930s, the market for newly issued low-grade bonds shrank as most investors—with the losses incurred during the Depression still vividly in mind—turned to high-grade securities and left it to financial intermediaries to manage the risk of lending to less creditworthy borrowers. But as time passed[,] . . . the memory of the 1930s faded[.] . . .

SUMMARY

Low-grade bonds are bonds that are rated "speculative" by the major rating agencies and that are therefore considered very risky investments. These bonds are either corporate bonds that have been downgraded, or, more recently, bonds that are issued originally with a rating below investment grade. Original-issue low-grade bonds are issued mostly by corporations that previously borrowed in the form of commercial loans or privately placed bonds.

---

[3] These added costs of using a financial intermediary instead of lending directly to a firm by buying its debt securities involve, for example, taxes, administration costs, and the costs of monitoring the condition and behavior of the intermediary.

Several factors seem to have contributed to the growth in low-grade bond offerings. For one, increased volatility in their sources of funds and a worsening of interest rate and credit risk have forced life insurance companies, which are the major buyers of private placements, to shift their investment focus towards assets that are somewhat more marketable and liquid, such as low-grade bonds. Also, improvements in computer technology have lowered the information and monitoring costs of investing in securities and have thus allowed smaller and less known corporations to borrow directly from private and institutional investors. Third, it may be that the favorable post-World War II default experience on low-grade bonds has made investors more receptive towards investing directly in riskier securities, including low-grade bonds.

The growth in low-grade bond offerings thus represents mostly a rechanneling of corporate borrowing, away from individually negotiated loans, towards public securities. As such, it exemplifies a continuing effort by financial market participants to search out the most cost-effective way to channel funds from lenders to borrowers.

D. BOND COVENANTS: THE NEGATIVE PLEDGE CLAUSE

¶ 706: The Negative Pledge Clause

1. You represent a creditor. The creditor has refused to take a subordinated position. You have advised the creditor that if it lends, it cannot be contractually subordinated without its consent, but will *effectively* be subordinated (i.e., will come second in a distribution in bankruptcy) if the company has granted security interests under Article 9 of the U.C.C. or realty mortgages. You check with the county clerk's office and find no filings.
2. Have you adequately protected the client's position? Will the client necessarily share ratably with all creditors at the time of a bankruptcy even if there are no security arrangements now?
3. In 1979 Chrysler—then America's third largest car manufacturer—neared bankruptcy, gasping for funds to keep it alive, and the government sought to support it. It couldn't borrow in ordinary markets, but then Congress authorized the administration to guarantee creditors of repayment of more than $1 billion of new loans to Chrysler. The act that enabled the administration to guarantee repayment of new loans to Chrysler in 1979 and 1980 also required the responsible administrators to be reasonably assured of repayment. To implement that requirement, the government board sought a security interest in Chrysler's manufacturing facilities, which were subject to negative pledge clauses in Chrysler's preexisting loan agreements.
4. What is a negative pledge clause? See the Chrysler Consent Solicitation, next.
5. Would the preexisting creditors have been able to enforce the negative pledge clauses against Chrysler's creditors in a Chrysler bankruptcy? What if Chrysler ignored the clauses and mortgaged its Principal Automotive Plants to new creditors despite the contrac-

tual bar in Chrysler's bond indentures? That is, what if Chrysler decided that with its back to the wall, it had to do something? A bank—or a government—came along and offered new debt, but only if it could obtain security. Chrysler in this hypothetical gave the security despite the preexisting negative pledge clauses. (As the consent solicitation says at p. 164: "Should Chrysler's efforts to obtain Consents be unsuccessful, Chrysler would seek alternative means to remove the need for the Consents in order to satisfy the conditions . . . for federal loan guarantees.") Then, unlike the historical result, no import quotas stifled competition from Honda and Toyota, the economy didn't pull out of the 1981 recession so quickly, and Chrysler's new car models did not obtain sufficient consumer acceptance. Chrysler then went bankrupt.

In this hypothetical bankruptcy, the last creditor—the big bank or the government—seeks priority based upon its security. The debentureholders argue that their contract and its negative pledge clause protect them. They, the debentureholders, must be brought along equally and ratably by giving effect to, by enforcing, the negative pledge clause.

The big creditor says its security interest and mortgage are valid; it has priority, notwithstanding the negative pledge clause.

6. Who wins? Consider *Kelly* and the U.C.C. provisions in the following paragraphs. But first make sure you understand how a negative pledge clause works by reading the Chrysler negative pledge, which follows next. Why did Chrysler seek to amend the clause? Who made them seek the amendment?

¶ 707: Chrysler Solicitation of Consents

Chrysler Corporation

February 23, 1980

To the Holders of Chrysler's

8⅞% Sinking Fund Debentures Due 1995

8% Sinking Fund Debentures Due 1998

Dear Debentureholders:

The United States Congress has passed, and the President has signed, the Chrysler Corporation Loan Guaranty Act of 1979. Under that Act, Chrysler may receive commitments for federal guarantees of up to $1.5 billion of loans. To obtain these commitments, which are essential to Chrysler, Chrysler must satisfy certain conditions under the Act.

As part of Chrysler's efforts to satisfy these conditions, Chrysler requests your Consents to Supplemental Indentures [to] amend the Indentures under which your Debentures were issued. Your Consents must be received by March 31, 1980, unless that date is extended by Chrysler.

The Supplemental Indentures become effective only after the Loan Guarantee Board has issued the first federal commitment for guaranteed loans. Before that commitment may be issued, Chrysler must have a . . . financing plan that includes at least $1.43 billion of assistance not guaranteed by the government and employee concessions of $587.5 million. Also, the Loan Guarantee Board must determine that Chrysler's financing plan is adequate and that its operating plan is realistic. . . .

The attached Explanatory Statement contains information concerning Chrysler, the consents and Indentures. You should read it carefully.

* * *

Your Consents are extremely important to our efforts. I urge you to send in your Consents as soon as possible.

Very truly yours,

/s/ LEE IACCOCA

Chairman of the Board

Chrysler Corporation

Solicitation of the Holders of

8⅞% Sinking Fund Debentures Due 1995

8% Sinking Fund Debentures Due 1998

You are urged to read carefully this Explanatory Statement, including the attached financial statements of Chrysler, the notes thereto, and the report of the certified public accountants of Chrysler relating thereto, Management's Discussion and Analysis of the Consolidated Statements of Operations, and the Attached Exhibits. The Explanatory Statement contains important information with respect to the business, management and financial condition of Chrysler which should be considered in reaching a decision as to whether to execute the Consents sought by Chrysler.

Your Consent must be received by March 31, 1980. . . .

Introduction

This Explanatory Statement is furnished by Chrysler Corporation . . . in connection with Chrysler's solicitation of Consents ("Consents") to Supplemental Indentures (the "Supplemental Debentures") to amend certain covenants in the indentures pursuant to which the 8⅞% Debentures and the 8% Debentures were issued.

Background

Chrysler is faced with pressing financial problems which have significantly weakened its financial condition. Chrysler had a loss of approximately $1.1 billion for 1979 and a loss of approximately $205 million for 1978. . . . Chrysler's loss for the fourth quarter of 1979 was approximately $376 million and Chrysler estimates that losses are continuing at approximately that rate in the first quarter of 1980.

Chrysler's working capital[4] has decreased from approximately $1.1 billion at December 31, 1978, to a negative position of approximately $111 million at December 31, 1979. Chrysler is in default under the agreements covering most of its institutional indebtedness and could not pay its institutional indebtedness if the lenders accelerated their loans. In that event, Chrysler also could not pay its indebtedness in respect of the Debentures. . . .

Chrysler's ability to continue operations is dependent at this time on its ability to obtain interim financing and cash flow from operations sufficient to permit it to meet its cash requirements until it can fulfill the conditions for a United States guaranteed loan. . . . If Chrysler cannot obtain sufficient interim financing or fails to meet the conditions for guaranteed loans, Chrysler would probably have to seek relief under the federal Bankruptcy Code, either seeking to reorganize Chrysler or, if reorganization is not possible, to liquidate Chrysler's assets. Even if Chrysler meets the conditions for guaranteed loans, its longer term viability is not assured.

Reasons for Solicitation

The Loan Guarantee Act generally requires that Chrysler grant [to the government as a guarantor of the loans to Chrysler] security in connection with the guaranteed loans. . . .

[But] Sections 1004 and 1005 of each of [Chrysler's preexisting] Indentures limit the ability of Chrysler to borrow money secured by liens on, or through the use of sale and leaseback transactions affecting, its Principal Domestic Automotive Plants . . . unless the Debentures are equally and ratably secured. However, under the Loan Guarantee Act it may not be possible to secure the Debentures equally and ratably with the federally guaranteed loans [because the government loan board must find that the government loans will in all likelihood be repaid and, unless Chrysler gives nearly all of its assets as security, it may not be possible for the government board to make a finding that repayment is likely]. In addition, as is often the case in workouts or companies with financial problems, any extensions of credit . . . [including those] required under the Loan Guarantee Act, will probably be made available only if secured ahead of the Debentures. Chrysler is seeking the Consents to authorize the Trustee to enter into the Supplemental Indentures which will amend each of the Indentures to permit Chrysler without equally and ratably securing the Debentures, to use Principal Domestic Automotive Plants to secure the federally guaranteed loans and nonfederally guaranteed assistance.

Chrysler is not seeking any other concessions from the holders of the Debentures. It is not asking the Debentureholders . . . to waive or defer interest or sinking fund payments. . . .

[4] [Working capital is the difference between short-term assets (inventory, raw materials, accounts receivable) and short-term liabilities (short-term loans, accounts payable, trade credit). The working capital of most firms is positive.—Roe.]

Supplemental Indentures

* * *

The Supplemental Indentures would permit Chrysler's Principal Domestic Automotive Plants to be mortgaged or otherwise used as security, without the Debentures being equally and ratably secured, for . . . federally guaranteed loans. . . .

Should Chrysler's efforts to obtain Consents be unsuccessful, Chrysler would seek alternative means to remove the need for the Consents in order to satisfy the conditions for obtaining the first commitment for federal loan guarantees. However, Chrysler has no way of knowing whether or not these efforts would be successful. Failure to obtain the commitment for loan guarantees would probably result in Chrysler seeking relief under the Bankruptcy Code.

CHRYSLER CORPORATION

Trustee

SUPPLEMENTAL INDENTURE

Dated as of __, 1980

to Indenture between

CHRYSLER CORPORATION

and

BANK

Dated as of ___, 19

_____ % Sinking Fund Debentures due _____

THIS SUPPLEMENTAL INDENTURE, dated as of ______, 1980, between CHRYSLER CORPORATION, a Delaware corporation (the "Company"), and ______ Bank, a New York banking corporation (herein together with its predecessor and any future successor or successor, sometimes referred to as the "Trustee"), as successor to ______ Bank.

WITNESSETH

(Here insert appropriate recitals.)

NOW, THEREFORE, THIS SUPPLEMENTAL INDENTURE WITNESSETH:

That in order to enable the Company to meet certain of the conditions required under the Loan Guarantee Act to obtain the loan guarantees of the United States contemplated thereby, the parties hereby agree as follows:

* * *

Section 1004 of the Indenture is hereby amended to read as follows:[5]

SECTION 1004. Limitation on Liens. The Company will not itself, and will not permit any Subsidiary to, incur, issue, assume, guarantee or suffer to exist any notes, bonds, debentures or other similar evidences of indebtedness for money borrowed, secured by a Mortgage on any Principal Domestic Automotive Plant, or on any shares of stock of or indebtedness of any Subsidiary which owns or leases a Principal Domestic Automotive Plant, without effectively providing that the Debentures . . . shall be secured equally and ratably with (or prior to) such secured indebtedness, so long as such secured indebtedness shall be so secured, unless, after giving effect thereto, the aggregate amount of all such secured indebtedness plus all Attributable Debt of the Company and its Subsidiaries in respect of sale and leaseback transactions . . . would not exceed 5% of [Chrysler's] Consolidated Net Worth: provided, however, that this Section shall not apply to indebtedness secured by:

[List of exceptions]

and, provided, further, that, . . . this Section shall not apply to indebtedness secured by Mortgages if such indebtedness . . . has been guaranteed by the United States under the Loan Guarantee Act.

¶ 708: Questions About Chrysler's Negative Pledge

1. Why did Chrysler have negative pledge clauses in its preexisting loan agreements and bond indentures? What were the previous creditors concerned about?
2. What problem did these negative pledge clauses present to Chrysler's new prospective creditor in 1980?
3. What if Chrysler ignored the negative pledge clause and mortgaged its principal automotive plants anyway, without having obtained sufficient consents to modify the indenture? The new creditor would have taken a mortgage and security interest in Chrysler's principal automotive assets. In the subsequent bankruptcy, the bondholders and lenders with negative pledge clauses argue that they should share ratably with the secured creditor. What would the result have been? See *Kelly* and the U.C.C., next.

   Similarly, what if Drum Financial issued too much debt under "Certain Covenants" and then went bankrupt. How would the violation of the covenants affect the bankruptcy distribution? See Chrysler, supra, and *Kelly*, next.

¶ 709: Kelly v. Central Hanover Bank & Trust Co., 11 F. Supp. 497, Rev'd 85 F.2d 61 (2d Cir. 1936)

OPINION: MACK, Circuit Judge.

These class suits were brought by a debenture holder of the Insull Utility Investments, Inc. (hereinafter referred to as I.U.I.), after the latter's adjudication in bankruptcy. . . . Plaintiff asks, on behalf of . . .

[5] *[Italicized]* material at the end of Section 1004 indicates changes from Section 1004 of the existing indenture.

all . . . debenture holders . . . that stock pledged to defendants by I.U.I. as collateral to certain loans made by each of them in 1931, be returned or that the debenture holders share equally and ratably with those defendants in such securities.

* * *

I.U.I. was incorporated in December, 1928. . . . In January, 1929, $6,000,000, 20–year 6 per cent debentures (series A) were issued. . . . Then followed a period of short-term borrowing, largely from the Continental Illinois Bank & Trust Company of Chicago. . . .

* * *

As the company was already largely indebted to the Chicago banks, the officers of the company turned their attention to the New York banks. . . . Negotiations with each of the defendant [New York] banks resulted in loans by them to I.U.I. totaling $17,000,000, made between March 14, 1931, and August 12, 1931. . . . Each of the loans was secured by pledges of stock of Insull group companies, held in the I.U.I. portfolio. . . .

* * *

Plaintiff[s, who are previous, unsecured creditors,] base the[ir] suits against each defendant on the charge that the defendant therein made and renewed the loan and received and held the original and the subsequent collateral as security therefor, with knowledge or charged with notice that each of the transactions was in violation of . . . the "negative pledge clause"[6] . . . contained in the I.U.I. debentures. . . .

Immediately following the covenant[ ], there is, in each debenture of each series, [an acceleration] clause. . . .

Each defendant denies that it had actual knowledge or is chargeable with notice of the existence and/or text of the restrictive covenants. While contending that under a proper interpretation of the covenants, neither the loan nor the pledge transactions constituted a breach thereof, it alleges that, in any event, it had no actual knowledge and is not chargeable with notice of any such breach. Each defendant further contends that *even if any of the transactions had constituted a breach of [the negative pledge] covenant[ ] and if such transaction had been made with actual knowledge that it did involve such a breach, defendant nevertheless would not be liable because it did not induce and is not charged with having induced I.U.I. to violate the covenant.*[7]

---

[6] The negative pledge clause reads: "The Company hereby covenants and agrees with the holder hereof that . . . it will not mortgage or pledge any of its property unless the instrument creating such mortgage or pledge shall provide that this debenture shall be secured thereby equally and ratably with all other obligations issued or to be issued thereunder, except that the company without so securing this debenture (a) may at any time mortgage or pledge any of its property for the purpose of securing loans to the Company contracted in the usual course of business for periods not exceeding one year, and (b). . . . "

[7] Knowledge is sought to be imputed and notice charged to defendants in many ways. . . . It was also established at the trial that annual statements of I.U.I., revealing the existence, though not the terms of the debentures, were in the credit files of each of the banks prior to the loans, and were consulted by most of the loaning officers. Plaintiff and cross-plaintiff urge that, due to the prevalence of restrictive covenants in debenture issues, knowledge that there

[The court held that as drafted the negative pledge clause did not apply to the subject transaction. Although perhaps ambiguous, the clause did not bar the firm from pledging assets to secure short-term borrowings. But even if it did bar them, the beneficiaries of the clause could not seek remedy by following the assets into the hands of the pledgee. The debentureholders had no equitable servitude in the asset; they held—if the clause were applicable at all—only a claim against the bankrupt for breach of a covenant.]

* * *

By the negative pledge clause, I.U.I. agrees not to mortgage or pledge any of its assets "unless the instrument creating the mortgage or pledge" provides for equal and ratable security to the debenture holders with "obligations issued or to be issued thereunder."

* * *

[The plaintiffs argue]: (1) That the issuance of the debentures created an equitable lien for the benefit of the debenture holders on all of the assets of I.U.I., whether held by the company at that time or thereafter acquired; (2) that the covenants created "something in the nature of an equitable servitude" on all such assets of I.U.I.; (3) that defendants are constructive trustees of the pledged collateral for the benefit of the debenture holders, either because they participated in a breach of trust or knowingly and unjustifiably interfered with the debenture holders' contract rights; (4) that the debenture holders had a right, enforceable in equity, to continued performance of their contract by I.U.I., and consequently now have an equitable right of reparation against those who knowingly invaded that right, even though they did not induce the breach of contract.

. . . The claim of an equitable lien on all of the assets of I.U.I then held and subsequently acquired, created by the issuance of the debentures, is without foundation. This claim, as well as that of "something in the nature of an equitable servitude" is rested on the negative pledge clause, for that covenant alone purports to restrict the use of property. . . . [N]o equitable lien can be created out of that prohibition. . . .

[T]he I.U.I debenture covenants created only personal rights against the company, not a present security interest in its assets. Furthermore, the company at all times, whether before or after breach of the covenant, had the right while solvent to sell all of the stock in its portfolio to a purchaser with knowledge of the restrictive covenants and of their violation. That right, although not contradictory to the

are outstanding debentures puts defendants on inquiry as to whether there are restrictive covenants therein, and, if so, what the terms thereof are. . . .

Only one of the witnesses called by plaintiff and cross-plaintiff, was asked on direct examination whether he knew of the existence of the restrictive covenants at the time that a defendant for which he had acted made its loan; his answer was in the negative. Most of the other bankers were asked, on cross-examination, whether they had such knowledge at the time of the respective loans and renewals made by them, and all of them, except McGee of the Bankers Trust, asserted that they had no such knowledge. McGee testified that he had no such knowledge at the time of the original advance made by Bankers Trust, but that he learned about the covenants prior to the date of renewal.

restrictive covenants, is inconsistent with a right to an equitable lien on the assets. It therefore compels the rejection of the equitable lien theory.

* * *

... The contention that the covenants created "something in the nature of an equitable servitude" is also, in my judgment, unfounded, even as applied to the negative pledge covenant. . . .

* * *

Plaintiff and cross-plaintiff also seek to charge defendants as constructive trustees on the theory that receipt of property with knowledge that the transfer is in violation of a contractual obligation creates a liability in equity in favor of the obligee. But the cases do not support this broad proposition. [One cited case] is not in point. All that it holds is that where A, by fraudulent means, *induces* B to break his contract with C, as a result of which A obtains property which would otherwise have gone to C, A holds that property in constructive trust for C. No such case is before me; defendants are charged neither with actual fraud nor with inducing a breach of contract.

* * *

At the time of the original loans by these defendant banks, I.U.I. was abundantly solvent; therefore, if a debenture holder had known of any violation, he could have recovered at law the full amount of the debentures, certainly a perfectly adequate remedy. . . .

¶ 710: The UCC, *Kelly*, and the Negative Pledge Clause

1. The district court decision was reversed and remanded in a one paragraph opinion, directing the lower court to "pass upon the questions presented, (a) whether the loans were made in the ordinary course of business and (b) whether the banks had knowledge of the restrictive covenants in the debentures." Kelly v. Central Hanover Bank & Trust Co., 85 F.2d 61, 63 (2d Cir. 1936). The appellate opinion is cryptic, with instruction (a) probably directed toward interpretation of the actual clause and instruction (b) directed toward other doctrines, such as fraudulent conveyance or equitable subordination, matters to be discussed in Chapters 8, 9, 11, and 18, or fraudulent inducement.

   Is the negative pledge clause a secret lien, not publicly recorded, and accordingly unenforceable against third parties?

   Does the Uniform Commercial Code also speak to the issues dealt with in *Kelly*?

2. Consider the following excerpts of the Uniform Commercial Code:

   § 9–109. Scope.

   (a) Except as otherwise provided . . . this article [of the U.C.C.] applies to:

   (1) a transaction, regardless of its form, that creates a security interest in personal property or fixtures by contract; . . .

(3) a sale of accounts, chattel paper, payment intangibles, or promissory notes. . . .

The official comment says "this Article applies regardless of the form of the transaction or the name that parties have given to it." It also says that it derives from § 9–102 of the prior U.C.C., with "[n]o change in meaning . . . intended." That prior provision's official comment said "[t]he main purpose of this Section is to bring all consensual security interests in personal property and fixtures under this Article[.]" In general, Article 9 is a filing and notice statute: one acquires security interests usually by public filing and without a public filing one usually cannot defeat a subsequent creditor who publicly files notice of its own security interest. Moreover:

§ 9–401. Alienability of Debtor's Rights.

(b) **[Agreement does not prevent transfer.]** An agreement between the debtor and secured party which prohibits a transfer of the debtor's rights in collateral or makes the transfer a default does not prevent the transfer from taking effect.

Comment 5 to UCC § 9–401 states:

5. Negative Pledge Covenant. Subsection (b) . . . makes clear that in secured transactions under this Article the debtor has rights in collateral (whether legal title or equitable) which it can transfer and which its creditors can reach. It is best explained with an example.

Example 2: A debtor, D, grants to SP, the Secured Party, a security interest to secure a debt in excess of the value of the collateral. D agrees with SP that it will not create a subsequent security interest in the collateral and that any security interest purportedly granted in violation of the agreement will be void. Subsequently, in violation of its agreement with SP, D purports to grant a security interest in the same collateral to another secured party.

Subsection (b) validates D's creation of the subsequent (prohibited) security interest, which might even achieve priority over the earlier security interest. . . . [However,] subsection (b) does not provide that the agreement restricting assignment is "ineffective." Consequently, the debtor's breach may create a default.

§ 9–322. Priorities Among Conflicting Security Interests in . . . [the] Same Collateral.

(a) (1) Conflicting perfected security interests . . . rank according to priority in time of filing or perfection. . . . [8]

3. Debtor borrows $1000 from creditor X and offers X security worth $5000. X fails to file a notice of the security agreement. Later, Y gets a security agreement in the same property and files its security agreement. In bankruptcy, who wins?

4. Same debtor borrows $1000 from creditor X and gives X a security agreement (this time properly filed) on security worth $5000. Debt-

[8] Perfected security interests "beat" the claims of other creditors against the security. Perfection is typically obtained under the Uniform Commercial Code by a filing in the Secretary of State's office.

or would like to give the remaining $4000 as security to creditor Y. Can the debtor do so under § 9–401? Would the debtor be any less able to give security to Y if the secured interest of X were never recorded? If X had never taken any security interest in the $5000 of collateral, could the debtor give a security interest in all of it to Y? If X had never taken any security interest in the $5000 of collateral, but debtor promised never to give a security interest to anyone, could debtor still give a security interest in all of it to Y?

5. "Despite the reversal by the Second Circuit . . . in *Kelly*, most lawyers have assumed [even before § 9–401 became part of the U.C.C.] that negative pledge clauses and other covenants in transactions involving personal property are not enforceable against third parties. . . . The effectiveness of negative pledge clauses and other covenants would seem to be very limited because Article 9 purports to be the exclusive means by which a creditor can create a consensual property interest to ensure repayment of his debt. Comment 5 to 9–203 [of the prior form of the U.C.C.] says explicitly that the concept of the equitable mortgage has been abandoned. Given the role of ostensible ownership in Article 9, isn't this conclusion the one most consistent with the structure of Article 9?" Douglas Baird & Thomas Jackson, Security Interests in Personal Property 929–30 (1984).

   And, from commercial law leaders: "The case law [for negative pledge clauses] is rather thin and in general dates from the depression. It indicates that a purely negative covenant creates no security interest in the property described. Such a covenant obviously lacks the customary provisions invoking enforcement remedies as well as other attributes of security." Peter F. Coogan, Homer Kripke & Fredric Weiss, *The Outer Fringes of Article 9: Subordination Agreements, Security Interests in Money and Deposits, Negative Pledge Clauses, and Participation Agreements*, 79 Harvard Law Review 229, 262 (1965).

   The more recent Restatement (Third) of Property: Mortgages § 3.5 (1997) states that "a promise by a debtor to a creditor not to encumber or transfer an interest in real estate does not create a mortgage, equitable lien, or other security interest in that real estate." More than a negative covenant is needed for an effective mortgage.

6. A modern U.S. District Court interpreted New York law to protect the negative pledge clause holder more than *Kelly* and the above excerpt indicate. The court said that New York law recognized equitable liens "notwithstanding the failure of a creditor and debtor to observe the formalities of perfecting a proper security interest." And this "survived the adoption of the Uniform Commercial Code. . . . " But the court couldn't find any post-U.C.C.—or even post-*Kelly*—case in which negative pledge clause holders got an equitable lien. The court concluded that "[t]o obtain an equitable lien under New York law, plaintiff has the burden of demonstrating both the breach of the Negative Pledge . . . *and knowledge by the defendants of both the clause and its breach*." Note that knowledge is a lower standard than inducement, which was an important part of *Kelly*. If followed, the case would give more hope in bankruptcy

than otherwise thought to the negative pledge clause holders. In re Hechinger Investment Co., 2004 WL 724960 (D. Del. 2004).

7. For further doctrinal discussion, see Carl S. Bjerre, *Secured Transactions Inside Out: Negative Pledge Covenants, Property and Perfection*, 84 Cornell Law Review 305 (1999); Robert K. Rasmussen, *The Uneasy Case Against the Uniform Commercial Code*, 62 Louisiana Law Review 1097 (2002).

8. Is a negative pledge clause valuable to a creditor, even if it is unenforceable against the party that receives the pledge in violation of the clause?

   First, note once again that there are other noncontractual doctrines that might be available to the lender with a negative pledge clause. Equitable subordination (Chapter 11), fraudulent transfer law (Chapters 8 and 22), and preference law (Chapter 9) might be useful to the wronged creditor. (Tort doctrine might give the early lender a cause of action against the later, knowing lender, particularly if it induced the debtor to breach its contract with the prior creditor.)

   But is the contract containing the negative pledge clause directly valuable to the creditor in keeping the property free from security interests? What rights does it give the offended creditor outside of bankruptcy? How does a contract with the negative pledge clause affect the incentives and strategizing of the offending creditor who would lend in violation of the preexisting negative pledge clause? That is, even if knowledge would not (or would not necessarily) create an equitable lien or other remedy in the debtor's eventual bankruptcy, how would the incentives of the negative pledge clause creditor affect the offending creditor's judgment on whether or not to lend?

9. Time (1): Debtor borrows and uses a negative pledge clause at Time 1.

10M in assets	10M unsecured debt with NPC

Time (2): Later, at Time 2, the debtor borrows from another creditor, and gives the new creditor security in all of the debtor's assets.

20M in assets	10M secured debt (all assets) 10M unsecured with NPC

In the next year, the company suffers serious reverses, declines in value, and files for bankruptcy.

Time (3): Bankruptcy after decline in value of firm and assets

10M in assets	10M secured debt (seeking all assets) 10M unsecured with NPC

The NPC creditors seek an equitable lien at Time 3. What result? Should the NPC creditors seek equitable subordination? What are the arguments in favor? And the arguments against? What should the NPC creditor have done at Time 2?

E. FINANCE THEORY OF SECURITY AND PRIORITY

¶ 711: Security and Priority in Theory

The theoretical explanation why public firms use security and priority is not abundantly clear. The intuitive notion explaining security is that the secured party takes less risk by obtaining security. Taking less risk, it requires a lower interest rate. Or stated more practically, whether or not the creditor takes a security interest depends on its negotiating power.

But analysis shows weaknesses in this explanation. The risk sought to be avoided by the secured or prioritized party is not eliminated. It is shifted to other shoulders. If the secured party takes less risk, someone else takes more. If, for example, the potentially secured party will give 2 per cent off of its interest rate if it takes the security, and the risk it avoids is placed on the shoulders of, say, creditor A, why doesn't creditor A insist on a 2 per cent interest premium? If the gains are offset by the costs, why does the public corporation bother?

Perhaps there's room for a mutually worthwhile deal. The secured party takes less risk and gives up 2 per cent, while creditor A takes more risk but only asks for a 1% premium, perhaps because it can institutionally handle that risk better. But even if such a deal were obtainable, why should the parties use security interests and mortgages to reflect the shifting of risk? A contractual seniority/subordination agreement is cheaper to negotiate; after all, it's just a few clauses in the loan agreements. Neither cumbersome security interests, nor mortgages, nor the resultant policing of the security are necessary.

In fact, many (but not all) public firms never use security, perhaps because of these considerations. They do use negative pledge clauses or debt limitation covenants, so that once a credit commitment is made, the creditor knows it will not be made inferior to new creditors (or at least knows the range of inferiority it will face). Morey McDaniel, *Are Negative Pledge Clauses in Public Debt Issues Obsolete?* 38 Business Lawyer 867 (1983). Some public firms may prefer to use unsecured loans because the unsecured lender investigates the firm before lending, thereby sending a signal to distant public stockholders that managers are doing a good enough job, a signal that is stronger coming from the unsecured lenders than it would be if it came from a low-risk secured lender. See Barry E. Adler, *An Equity–Agency Solution to the Bankruptcy–Priority Puzzle*, 22 Journal of Legal Studies 73 (1993); George Triantis, *Financial Slack Policy and the Law of Secured Transaction*, 29 Journal of Legal Studies 35 (2000).

Why then is security used at all? The efficiency explanations rely on monitoring, screening, and other priority explanations. First, the secured creditor can monitor the security offered and thereby sometimes stop the debtor from substituting riskier projects than it anticipated at the time it lent to the debtor. Second, the creditor may cut down on its own information gathering: it understands one part of the debtor's business and lends on the assets in the business it understands; or, similarly, the creditor can assess with confidence the value of the physical asset, but it has less confidence in its estimate of the cash flows that the debtor can generate from that asset. Third, the first creditor is worried that the debtor could borrow and dissipate the proceeds of future loans. The debtor would then owe more but own less. That kind of borrowing and dissipation would leave the first creditor with a diluted claim that it must share with other creditors.

Another explanation is that, like the explanation given by some analysts for all property, security is theft. The secured party takes less risk. That risk is shifted to the shoulders of others in an equal and offsetting transfer. But those others are unable (because they are uninformed or do not bargain with the firm) to insist on compensation (via a higher interest rate) for the increase in risk. Who are these hapless victims? Tort claimants, consumer claimants, labor claimants, (some, usually smaller) trade creditors, and previous lenders with gaps in their loan agreements.

This explanation tells a story consistent with the observation that public firms tended until recent decades not to use security. Why? Substantial tort and labor claimants in bankruptcies of public firms have until recent decades been unusual. Trade creditors are more substantial but still not overwhelming in the public firm bankruptcy.

If analysis indicates that security is theft, why not prohibit it? The answer is that the theft analysis is incomplete. Efficiency explanations for security, usually outside of the public firm context, have been given: the security device helps creditors monitor debtor misbehavior (i.e., reduce the chances that the debtor steals from the creditor in question), the security helps make sure that the debtor stays in the same business (or gets the creditor's consent before selling the machinery that is subject to the security), or the security helps screen bad credit risks from good credit risks at the time the loan is negotiated.

These results (or the indeterminacy of whether efficiency or theft considerations predominate) lead economically-oriented policy-thinkers to suggest a superpriority for the uninformed (tort claimants, consumer claimants, and maybe some trade creditors). But then one would leave room for security to sort the results out for those creditors that really bargain (i.e., financial institutions and some large trade creditors).

The basic weakness in the intuitive explanation for security was first analyzed in Alan Schwartz, *Security Interests and Bankruptcy Priorities: A Review of Current Theories*, 10 Journal of Legal Studies 1 (1981). Additions to this analysis can be found in Thomas Jackson & Anthony Kronman, *Secured Financing and Priorities Among Creditors*, 88 Yale Law Journal 1143 (1979); Saul Levmore, *Monitors and Freeriders in Commercial and Corporate Settings*, 92 Yale Law Journal 49 (1982); Alan Schwartz, *The Continuing Puzzle of Secured Debt*, 37 Vanderbilt Law Review 1051 (1984); Robert Scott, *A Relational Theory of Secured Financing*, 86 Columbia Law Review 901 (1986); Frank Buckley, *The Bankruptcy Priority Puzzle*, 72 Virginia Law Review 1393 (1986); Lucian Bebchuk & Jesse M. Fried, *The Uneasy Case for the Priority of Secured Claims in Bankruptcy*, 105 Yale Law Journal 857 (1996).

F. LOW PRIORITY

What are the business reasons why some creditors take low priority and agree to subordinate their own repayment to other creditors? True, they'll be paid to take the additional risk, but why does the debtor want to pay them to take the added risk?

Creditors with a large stake in the debtor's performance are unlikely to sit idly by, hoping passively to be repaid, if their debtor stumbles. Low priority creditors in particular have incentives to monitor the firm's and its managers' results and to intervene if they think they can help improve poor performance.

¶ 712: Background Bases for Contractual Subordination

Why would the firm want to pay new creditors to take the risks of subordination?

One easy case is when previous creditors have insisted on the subordination of future creditors. They may insist upon future creditors' subordination via a covenant, like that in the Drum Financial indenture, in which the firm promises not to issue new debt at the same level, unless certain financial ratios are met. Or the previous creditors may simply insist that no new debt come in at the same level. One substantial reason why both the firm and the previous creditors would find it worthwhile to limit the firm's future ability to borrow is that the previous creditor may have feared that the firm would have future risky projects that might be substituted, subjecting the previous creditor to added risk. This possibility of asset substitution is outlined at the end of Chapter 4; it's exemplified in the Hunts' bankruptcy in ¶ 409, the risk of asset substitution is mitigated (but not eliminated) by the firm promising the previous creditor priority.

But this last scenario does not help explain why the firm would find it valuable to pay for subordination when it doesn't *already* have senior, priority debt in its capital structure. True, it may wish to keep a reserve for a rainy day, a financial insurance policy. And institutional considerations may make marketing subordinated "junk" bonds relatively cheap at times: some financial institutions might not be allowed to buy equity; the low-grade bonds could be priced by bondbuyers as near-equity for the regulated who cannot buy equity. Or the junk bonds may allow insured institutions like banks to take on pernicious risk at deposit-holders' or government-guarantors' expense. Similarly, the tax advantages of debt, via the deductibility of interest payments, may lead those seeking new capital to disguise a risky equity-type interest as debt.

If the firm doesn't have the super-high-risk asset substitution potential that drives the first scenario from Chapter 4 (in which the first creditor insists on priority), then this cost to the creditor (i.e., the risk of substitution) of forgoing priority is absent. Or, as long as the lender expects that the firm will have lots of good projects with a value to the stockholders that will be higher than the value to them of substituting a high-risk project, then the lender won't fear substitution and dissipation of the second loan, so it won't need to pay for priority.

In this setting of lots of good projects, the cost to the first creditor and to the firm of forgoing priority is absent. But where's the gain to voluntary subordination? Or, seen from the firm's perspective, why would the stockholders pay extra to the first creditor to agree to come last? The intuition is that the firm will do so because subordinating the first creditor makes it easier to finance the second project.

If the firm finances the first project, a risky one, with regular debt, it will find that it cannot borrow to finance the second project when and if the second one becomes available. The *second* lender will refuse to lend unless *it* can get priority because it would find itself supporting the previous, regular debt if it did lend, because its loan would make it more likely that the previous debt would be paid off. But if the initial creditor had been subordinated, the new lender would know it would take priority and would thus more readily finance the second project.

More detail: If the initial creditor is not subordinated, then any subsequent creditor will have to share, *pari passu*, with the original non-subordinated creditor. As a result, if the firm is looking for a new creditor to fund a project, the new creditor may refuse to lend if there is a strong possibility that the project will fail to generate enough return to repay both the first and the new creditor. In this situation, because of the first creditor's non-subordinated rights, both creditors have to share whatever returns are generated, thus resulting in a decreased expected return for the new creditor. But if the original creditor had been subordinated, then the new lender only needs to see that the next project is expected to be profitable enough to pay off the new lender and does not need to see that the firm will be able to pay off both lenders.

Thus, by paying to subordinate the first creditor, the stockholder can get financing for the second project but wouldn't be able to get financing otherwise.

¶ 713: Data on the Growth of the Junk Bond Market

The junk bond was not important before the 1980s. It has grown since then.

Quarterly and Annual Moving Average of Issued Bond Default Rates of Bonds

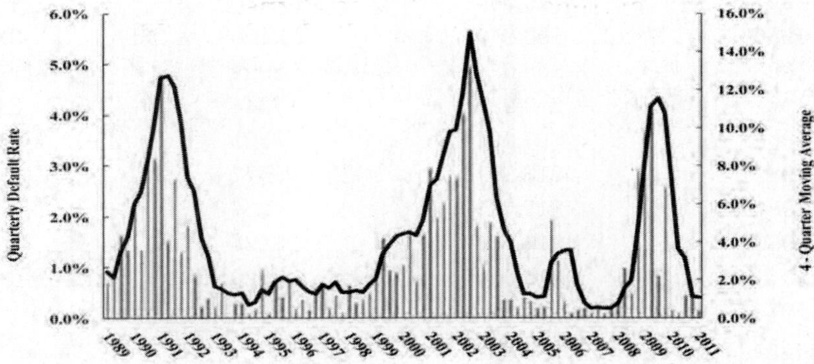

Source: Edward I. Altman & Brenda J. Kuehne, Defaults and Returns in the High-Yield Bond Market 6 (Feb. 3, 2012).

Junk Bond Default Rates and Losses (1978–2014)

Year	Outstanding ($MMs)	Par value of defaulted debt ($MMs)	Default Rate
2014	$1,496,814	$31,589	2.11%
2013	$1,392,212	$14,539	1.04%
2012	$1,212,362	$19,647	1.62%
2011	$1,354,649	$17,813	1.33%
2010	$1,221,569	$13,809	1.13%
2009	$1,152,952	$123,824	10.74%
2008	$1,091,000	$50,763	4.65%
2007	$1,075,400	$5,473	0.51%
2006	$993,600	$7,559	0.76%
2005	$1,073,000	$36,209	3.38%
2004	$933,100	$11,657	1.25%
2003	$825,000	$38,451	4.66%
2002	$757,000	$96,858	12.79%
2001	$649,000	$63,609	9.80%
2000	$597,200	$30,295	5.07%
1999	$567,400	$23,532	4.15%
1998	$465,500	$7,465	1.60%
1997	$335,400	$4,200	1.25%
1996	$271,000	$3,336	1.23%
1995	$240,000	$4,551	1.90%
1994	$235,000	$3,418	1.45%
1993	$206,907	$2,287	1.11%
1992	$163,000	$5,545	3.40%
1991	$183,600	$18,862	10.27%
1990	$181,000	$18,354	10.14%
1989	$189,258	$8,110	4.29%
1988	$148,187	$3,944	2.66%
1987	$129,557	$7,486	5.78%
1986	$90,243	$3,156	3.50%
1985	$58,088	$992	1.71%
1984	$40,939	$344	0.84%
1983	$27,492	$301	1.09%
1982	$18,109	$577	3.19%
1981	$17,115	$27	0.16%
1980	$14,935	$224	1.50%
1979	$10,356	$20	0.19%
1978	$8,946	$119	1.33%
Weighted Average 1978–2014:			3.34%

Source: Edward I. Altman & Brenda J. Kuehne, The Investment Performance and Market Dynamics of Defaulted and Distressed Corporate Bonds and Bank Loans 21 (Mar 5, 2015).

During the two decades or so from 1978 to 2001, the junk bond market promised a yield that averaged 12.87 per cent per year, while similar maturity United States Treasury bonds promised a yield of 8 per cent, for a "spread" between the two of 4.86 per cent. Many junk bonds defaulted; the United States did not. The net-of-default "spread" was about 1.86 per cent.

¶ 714: Practice Point: Drafting a Bond Indenture

How should one begin the task of drafting a bond indenture? Consider the following advice from a prominent lawyer about drafting a similar deposit agreement (for bondholders participating in a workout). The excerpt comes from Paul Cravath, The Reorganization of Corporations, *in* Some Legal Phases of Corporate Financing, Reorganization and Regulation 153, 164–65 (1917):

> I will not attempt to indicate in any detail what should be the provisions of a [bond indenture], whether it be for bonds or unsecured obligations . . . , but I will tell how you may simplify your task in preparing such an agreement if you pursue the course most lawyers do. Do not attempt to evolve the agreement out of your own consciousness, for it would take you days to work out clauses covering half of the contingencies for which provision should be made. If you have not a model for such an agreement in your own office, go to some friend, a lawyer or banker or broker, and get from him a copy of the deposit agreement used in some previous transaction of such magnitude and dignity that the agreement must have been the workmanship of some experienced and competent counsel. You can, without much difficulty, find a model which, with some change, will fit almost any situation. It is then a comparatively simple task to eliminate the provisions which are inapplicable to your situation and to add the provisions required by its special circumstances.
>
> I do not intend to give you the impression that the greatest care is not required in the preparation of such an agreement, for few instruments call for greater care or more painstaking attention to detail. . . .
>
> There will be no opportunity to correct mistakes, because there will be . . . many parties to the agreement . . . and the agreement cannot be changed without the[ir] consent. . . .

CHAPTER 8

RERANKING: FRAUDULENT TRANSFERS AND SUBSTANTIVE CONSOLIDATION

A. PREBANKRUPTCY TRANSFERS WITHIN CORPORATE GROUPS

Businesses sometimes organize themselves as a corporate group. One company, the headquarters company, owns several separate corporations; the headquarters company is the parent and owns the shares of its subsidiary companies. Sometimes the subsidiaries are in related aspects of the same business; one subsidiary may sell in one region and another in another region, or one subsidiary may manufacture the product and another distributes it. This structure might facilitate organizational decentralization. It might be the legacy of a history of corporate acquisitions. Traditionally, when the subsidiaries were in different businesses, the group was called a conglomerate.

Affiliated companies within a corporate group quite commonly transfer assets among themselves in the ordinary conduct of their businesses. When one or more affiliates find themselves in financial distress, however, it may turn out that pre-distress transfers within the corporate group have worked to the prejudice of certain creditors trying to recover in bankruptcy. In this Chapter, we study various creditor-protective doctrines that address this situation.

The most important of these doctrines is that of the fraudulent transfer, which allows the wronged creditor to reverse a transfer. While for concreteness we shall focus on a typical business pattern—a corporate group of inter-related companies—fraudulent conveyance law also captures transfers that do not involve corporate groups. All that is needed is that the transfer is "fraudulent," in statutory terms. And, as shall be seen, while fraud in the sense of misrepresentation can create a fraudulent conveyance, actual fraud is not always necessary.

¶ 801: Introduction

When a parent and its subsidiaries are all in bankruptcy, who gets first crack at the subsidiary's value in a reorganization? Who gets first crack at the parent company's value?

Because the parent and its subsidiaries are each separate legal entities, the parent's creditors would normally be entitled to the parent's assets, and each subsidiary's creditors would get that subsidiary's assets. Remember, however, that the parent's assets include the common stock of its subsidiaries. So if a subsidiary is solvent, its common stock would have value to the parent and the parent's creditors. The parent's creditors have access to the parent's assets and those assets include the stock of the subsidiaries; that stock will have value if a subsidiary is solvent. And, only when the parent's creditors were paid in full would parent stockholders receive any bankruptcy distribution.

Parent, Inc.	
Parent's Assets	Creditor of Parent
Stock of Sub One	Stockholders of Parent
Stock of Sub Two	

Sub One	
Assets	Creditor One
	Stockholder–owner (parent)

Sub Two	
Assets	Creditor Two
	Stockholder–owner (parent)

Separate Corporate Entities

What remedy for the creditor of a subsidiary if the subsidiary lacks enough value to fully pay off the subsidiary's creditor? Without more, these creditors generally could not claim against the parent company or any of its other subsidiaries, even if the parent or another subsidiary were solvent and able to pay off all of *its* creditors. This result follows directly from the corporate law baseline of corporate limited liability.

The parent is the insolvent subsidiary's sole stockholder and enjoys limited liability with respect to the subsidiary's debts, just as any other stockholder would.

The subsidiary's creditors could have obtained a guarantee from the parent company when they lent to the subsidiary. But if they didn't, they would lack a contractual claim against the parent in bankruptcy. Similarly, a solvent affiliate of the insolvent subsidiary is an independent legal entity separate from the insolvent sub. Ordinarily, each affiliate is liable only for its own debts and not those of its affiliated companies. Unless the insolvent subsidiary's creditors could invoke some protective doctrine, they collect against the insolvent subsidiary only. They are not paid in full if the subsidiary is insolvent, but need more than the affiliation standing alone to claim against an affiliate for any deficiency.

Pre-distress transfers among affiliated companies within a corporate group, however, can trigger creditor-protective doctrines, the most important of which is fraudulent conveyance doctrine. If an inter-group transfer is a fraudulent conveyance, the wronged creditors can have their debtor-subsidiary reverse the transfer, or they can collect directly against the transferee. The most common scenario involves a transfer of assets after which the transferor company goes into bankruptcy—and does so without having received reasonable consideration for the transfer. From the business group's overall perspective, this intercorporate transfer may make perfect business sense. But the transfer reduces the transferring subsidiary's ability to repay its own creditors, who complain.

For example, suppose that Transferor and Transferee are both subsidiaries of Parent. If Transferee sees an expansion opportunity, because the time is right for it to build a new factory in its business line, but hasn't the capital to pursue the opportunity, then Parent could direct Transferor, which has extra cash because its winding down its own businesses, to supply the cash to Transferee. The Parent expects that the transfer will make the corporate group more profitable overall, but it will also render Transferor less creditworthy, because it will have less cash after the transfer. This is a problem for Transferor's creditors and, if the transfer meets the standards for fraudulent conveyance liability, the Transferor's creditors can attack the transfer. Transferor, and Transferee are separate legal entities, even though they have a common owner (Parent). The lender to Transferor has no general right to collect its debt from any entity but Transferor, and Transferee's brighter future from Transferor's cash transfer strengthens Transferee but weakens Transferor, degrading it's ability to repay Transferor's creditors.

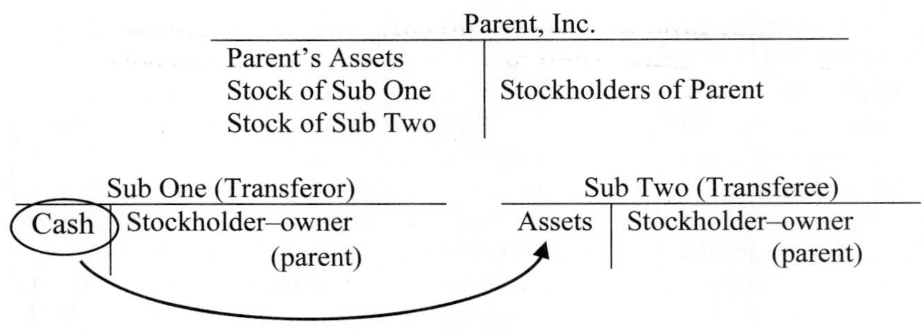

Affiliate Transfer

Not surprisingly, creditors often use contracts to restrict asset transfers among related, co-owned businesses. But noncontractual doctrines are also available for the harmed creditor. In addition to fraudulent conveyance law, veil piercing, dividend statutes, and substantive consolidation doctrines are potentially useful to that creditor. Next, we briefly outline these doctrines.

Fraudulent Transfer. If the transfer of assets in the example above is sufficiently large and poorly timed, that may imperil Transferor's creditors' repayment prospects. For this reason, the transfer may be a fraudulent transfer,[1] in which case, Transferor's creditors can pursue the transferred assets to satisfy their debts, even though those assets have moved over to Transferee. If the transfer wasn't made for reasonably equivalent value (Bankruptcy Code § 548(a)(1)(B)(i); Uniform Fraudulent Transfer Act §§ 4(a)(2), 5(a)), *and* the debtor firm was rendered insolvent (or was already insolvent), then the wronged creditors may attack the recipient of this so-called "constructively fraudulent" transfer, including an affiliate firm or the parent firm.

Alternatively, even if the transfer did not render the transferor insolvent, but was done with *intent to hinder, delay, or defraud* its creditor, the wronged creditors may attack the transfer as actual fraud. Bankruptcy Code § 548(a)(1)(A); U.F.T.A. § 4(a)(1). If Transferor is in bankruptcy, the debtor-in-possession would pursue the fraudulent transfer claim against Transferee, Inc. for the benefit of Transferor's estate. Outside of bankruptcy, state law offers a similar remedy, enabling Transferor's individual creditors to pursue collection against Transferee, Inc. to the extent of the assets fraudulently transferred.

Veil Piercing and Dividend Statutes. Besides the transfer between affiliated subsidiaries described above, assets might be transferred from a subsidiary up to a parent company or from a parent company down to a subsidiary. An "upstream" transfer—from subsidiary to parent—in addition to raising possible fraudulent transfer and breach of fiduciary duty claims by the subsidiary's creditors, might also trigger veil piercing doctrine. As a matter of corporate law, sometimes creditors can "pierce the veil" of shareholder limited liability and hold controlling shareholders liable for the corporation's debts. If the controllers operate

[1] It might also count as a breach by Transferor's directors of their fiduciary duties to run their corporation properly.

the firm in a way that fails to respect the corporation's separateness—for example, by commingling their own assets with the corporation's and ignoring corporate formalities—the controlling shareholders may lose their limited liability with respect to wronged creditors. In the parent-subsidiary context, veil piercing allows the subsidiary's creditors to claim directly against the parent. Cf. *Deep Rock,* infra.

An upstream transfer may also be deemed an illegal dividend. Dividend statutes enforce the general priority of creditors over equity holders by forbidding the payment of a dividend to stockholders if that would impair the company's capital. These statutes typically hold directors personally liable for illegal dividends, and they allow the wronged creditors to force the corporation to recover the dividends from stockholders. E.g., Del. Gen. Corp. L. § 174.

Substantive Consolidation. Though legally separate, affiliated entities are sometimes economically integrated. That is, the various functions of one economically integrated business are housed in separate corporate affiliates. Perhaps manufacturing is housed in A Corp., research and development in B Corp., and finance in C Corp., with Parent Corp. owning all three. Especially in this situation, intercompany transfers may be frequent and internal record keeping may be weak. When this corporate group enters bankruptcy, one can easily imagine the difficulty and high cost of attempting to identify and then unwind the numerous prebankruptcy transfers that might be fraudulent as to creditors of each separate entity. Some creditors might also have been misled as to the separateness of the entities; they thought they were dealing with an integrated business and are then surprised that they were only dealing with the corporate R&D arm of the business, with no access to the value in the separately–incorporated manufacturing facilities. In that scenario, it might make sense to treat the parent and its subsidiaries as a single entity, collapsing the separate corporations into one single pool of assets and liabilities. This result—substantive consolidation—would disrespect the separate corporate entities and cancel all intercorporate contracts and claims (including state law fiduciary duty, veil-piercing, and fraudulent transfer claims that one affiliate might have against another).

Special Purpose Vehicles. SPVs are entities created to hold specialized assets—typically in practice financial assets—that would ordinarily be held with a company in a corporate group, but which the group hopes to insulate from any bankruptcy of the rest of the group. And if bankruptcy must include the SPV, the group would hope to avoid the consolidation of the SPV with the rest of the group. Using an SPV for "bankruptcy-remoteness" gives comfort to lenders willing to lend against the SPV assets. Because the lender expects not to bear the risk of the rest of the business, and does not have to understand that business, it often lends at a lower interest rate than it would otherwise, and the SPV structure can thereby reduce the group's overall borrowing costs.

Preferences. Eve-of-bankruptcy payments to the debtor's favored creditors may frustrate the ameliorative purpose of the automatic stay, as well as the bankruptcy distribution scheme. The Bankruptcy Code enables recovery of these preferential payments. Prebankruptcy transactions involving corporate groups may also raise special preference problems. The next chapter deals with preference law.

B. FRAUDULENT TRANSFER AND CORPORATE GROUPS

¶ 802: The Origins of Fraudulent Transfer Law

The Anglo-Saxon law of fraudulent transfer enjoys a long pedigree that, going back to the 16th century, pre-dates both bankruptcy law and corporate groups. It responds to the age-old human instinct to hide one's assets when creditors are closing in. For example, suppose you have finally decided that you can't keep up on all your credit card payments and your rent. All the phone calls and emails from collection agencies have convinced you that your creditors are serious about collecting. So rather than let them seize your prized stamp collection—your only valuable asset—you give it to your cousin for safekeeping. She's happy to claim it as her own, at least until the heat dies down and your creditors stop calling. You reason that your creditors won't be able to seize assets you don't own to satisfy your debts.

Fraudulent transfer law is designed to thwart this common debtor strategy. It enables a creditor to pursue fraudulently transferred assets in the hands of the debtor's transferee—in our example, your accommodating cousin. The law catches actual fraud—transfers made with "actual intent to hinder, delay, or defraud" a creditor. U.F.T.A. § 4(a)(1); Bankruptcy Code § 548(a)(1)(A). The Uniform Fraudulent Transfer Act also includes a helpful list of "badges of fraud," factors that may be useful in inferring the presence of actual intent. U.F.T.A. § 4(b)).

We can see the corporate group analogy: The Transferor subsidiary is failing. The Parent concludes that the subsidiary will soon need to file for bankruptcy. But before it files, the Parent forces the Transferor subsidiary to transfer cash and other valuable assets, without being paid, to a sister corporation, which the Parent owns and which is solvent. That transfer hurt's Transferor's creditors and makes the stock of Transferee sister corporation more valuable, without making the stock of the Transferor company, which is insolvent, less valuable. If the smoking gun memo is found in the Parent's files ("let's pull assets out from Transferor before it tanks, so that we can gain value from those assets when they're moved to Transferee"), then the Transferor's creditors can readily make the case for actual fraud.

Fraudulent transfer law also catches constructive fraud, which does not require actual intent. Instead, constructive fraud involves a transfer of assets by the debtor (a) for "less than reasonably equivalent value" and (b) that was made while the debtor was in financial straits. Bankruptcy Code § 548(a)(1)(B); Uniform Fraudulent Transfer Act §§ 4(a)(2), 5(a).

Constructive fraud turns not on the debtor's intent, but on the financial harm done to the transferor's creditors: a transfer for less than reasonably equivalent value may be a good deal for the transferee, but when the debtor is insolvent or otherwise financially shaky, it is clearly not a good deal for transferor-debtor's creditors seeking to collect, since the debtor is essentially giving more than it gets.

Garrard Glenn, Fraudulent Conveyances and Preferences 79–87 (1940)

[The Act of 1571 (13 Eliz. c. 5) as the Basis of American Fraudulent Conveyance Law]

Our notion of the fraudulent conveyance traces to a statute of Elizabeth, cited in the above caption, and commonly called the Statute of Fraudulent Conveyances. This . . . was largely due to the restatement of the law which was made by Sir Edward Coke. . . .

The statute . . . became part of our [American] inheritance. We find colonial enactments repeating its words with more or less fullness and certainly emphasizing its principle. After the Revolution it was reenacted in some States, and in others the courts considered it as part of the common law in force. Of course there have been divergences in form; but fundamentally, with some variations . . . , this legislation has remained pretty true to the original mold. . . .

The Act of Elizabeth aided the creditor in his pursuit of legal assets that were attainable only under the process of equity. But courts of equity took care of this situation. And the courts, both of law and equity, also settled other open questions, viz: as to one who *bona fide* purchases from a guilty grantee, the rights of debtor and grantee as between themselves, and the methods of asserting creditors' rights under the Act.

The result was that at the beginning of [the 20th] century, the law of fraudulent conveyances was a mosaic of statutes and decisions, which had been developed around the statute of Elizabeth. In such circumstances legislation of a modern type was to be expected.

* * *

[Imprisonment for Debt, and Sanctuary, with Resulting Statutes]

To get the point, we should recall that England had certain sanctuaries into which the King's writ could not enter, with the result that if a debtor should gain the precincts of such a place, his creditors could not take his body in execution. This right, and the abuses of it, were well known in the bankruptcy legislation of Europe, for the Church, in sanctioning the right, was fortified by the custom of the Empire and certain passages of the Old Testament. Hence sanctuary meant, not so much the interior of a church with its altars, as certain precincts which were defined by custom or royal grant; and so the sanctuary of Westminster, for instance, embraced many nests and rookeries. Taking sanctuary was enumerated as an act of bankruptcy in the general bankruptcy laws which England enacted in 1542 and again in 1571. . . . [S]anctuary was abolished in 1623. . . .

Now, the association of sanctuary with fraudulent conveyance appeared on the face of the medieval legislation above discussed. In these statutes Parliament recited the common practice by which a debtor would transfer his assets to some friend but in trust for the debtor; and, that accomplished, the rascal would take himself to sanctuary and there "live a great time with a high countenance" until his creditors, being unable to reach the property which was held in trust for the debtor, would compromise their claims at a low figure, whereupon the delinquent would resume the ordinary course of life, and doubtless run up more bills. The idea of these statutes, as outlined by Bacon's Reading, was to make the debtor's lands and goods liable to his creditor's execution, despite the previous transfer. Here, then, we have the germ of the idea . . . that the judgment creditor may ignore the fraudulent conveyance and levy upon its subject matter.

* * *

¶ 803: Key Statutory Provisions

1. *Uniform Fraudulent Transfer Act*. Key provisions that will trigger a fraudulent conveyance claim are §§ 4 and 5 of the Uniform Fraudulent Transfer Act:[2]

§ 4. Transfers Fraudulent as to Present and Future Creditors.

(a) A transfer made or obligation incurred by a debtor is fraudulent as to a creditor, whether the creditor's claim arose before or after the transfer was made or the obligation was incurred, if the debtor made the transfer or incurred the obligation;

(1) with actual intent to hinder, delay, or defraud any creditor of the debtor; or

(2) without receiving a reasonably equivalent value in exchange for the transfer or obligation, and the debtor:

(i) was engaged or was about to engage in a business or a transaction for which the remaining assets of the debtor were unreasonably small in relation to the business or transaction; or

(ii) intended to incur, or believed or reasonably should have believed that [the transferor] would incur, debts beyond his [the transferor's] ability to pay as they became due.

(b) In determining actual intent under subsection (a)(1), consideration may be given, among other factors, to whether:

(1) the transfer or obligation was to an insider;

(2) the debtor retained possession or control of the property transferred after the transfer;

(3) the transfer or obligation was disclosed or concealed;

(4) before the transfer was made or obligation was incurred, the debtor had been sued or threatened with suit;

[2] The Uniform Fraudulent Transfer Act succeeded the Uniform Fraudulent Conveyance Act. By 2006, forty-five states adopted the U.F.T.A., but the U.F.C.A. is still used in some important jurisdictions, such as New York state. The two statutes are substantively very similar. The uniform laws commission has recently proposed a new replacement, The Uniform Voidable Transfer Act.

(5) the transfer was of substantially all the debtor's assets;

(6) the debtor absconded;

(7) the debtor removed or concealed assets;

(8) the value of the consideration received by the debtor was reasonably equivalent to the value of the asset transferred or the amount of the obligation incurred;

(9) the debtor was insolvent or become insolvent shortly after the transfer was made or the obligation incurred;

(10) the transfer occurred shortly before or shortly after a substantial debt was incurred; and

(11) the debtor transferred the essential assets of the business to a lienor who transferred the assets to an insider of the debtor.

§ 5. Transfers Fraudulent as to Present Creditors.

(a) A transfer made or obligation incurred by a debtor is fraudulent as to a creditor whose claim arose before the transfer was made or the obligation was incurred if the debtor made the transfer or incurred the obligation without receiving a reasonably equivalent value in exchange for the transfer or obligation and the debtor was insolvent at that time or the debtor became insolvent as a result of the transfer or obligation.

(b) A transfer made by a debtor is fraudulent as to a creditor whose claim arose before the transfer was made if the transfer was made to an insider for an antecedent debt, the debtor was insolvent at that time, and the insider had reasonable cause to believe that the debtor was insolvent.

§ 7. Remedies of Creditors.

(a) In an action for relief against a transfer or obligation under this Act, a creditor . . . may obtain:

(1) avoidance of the transfer or obligation to the extent necessary to satisfy the creditor's claim;

(2) an attachment or other provisional remedy against the asset transferred or other property of the transferee in accordance with the procedure prescribed by [other statute];

(3) subject to applicable principles of equity and in accordance with applicable rules of civil procedure,

(i) an injunction, against further disposition by the debtor or a transferee, or both, of the asset transferred or of other property;

(ii) appointment of a receiver to take charge of the asset transferred or of other property of the transferee; or

(iii) any other relief the circumstances may require.

(b) If a creditor has obtained a judgment on a claim against the debtor, the creditor, if the court so orders, may levy execution on the asset transferred or its proceeds.

Notice that §§ 4(a)(2) and 5 require that the debtor be insolvent and that the consideration for the transfer not be reasonably equivalent; § 4(a)(1) does not require either insolvency or a failure of equivalent consideration. Notice that §§ 4(a)(1) requires actual intent while §§ 4(a)(2) and 5 do not.

2. *Fraudulent Transfer and the Bankruptcy Code*. Section 544(b) of the Bankruptcy Code authorizes the trustee to avoid any transfers by the debtor that an unsecured creditor with an allowable claim could avoid under state fraudulent transfer law. Just to be sure, the Bankruptcy Code has its own mini-version of the Uniform Fraudulent Transfer Act, although with a shorter two-year statute of limitations. Section 548 of the Bankruptcy Code states:

§ 548. Fraudulent transfers and obligations

(a) (1) The trustee may avoid any transfer (including any transfer to or for the benefit of an insider under an employment contract) of an interest of the debtor in property, or any obligation (including any obligation to or for the benefit of an insider under an employment contract) incurred by the debtor, that was made or incurred on or within 2 years before the date of the filing of the petition, if the debtor voluntarily or involuntarily—

(A) made such transfer or incurred such obligation with actual intent to hinder, delay, or defraud any entity to which the debtor was or became, on or after the date that such transfer was made or such obligation was incurred, indebted; or

(B)(i) received less than a reasonably equivalent value in exchange for such transfer or obligation; and

(ii) (I) was insolvent on the date that such transfer was made or such obligation was incurred, or became insolvent as a result of such transfer or obligation;

(II) was engaged in business or a transaction, or was about to engage in business or a transaction, for which any property remaining with the debtor was an unreasonably small capital;

(III) intended to incur, or believed that the debtor would incur, debts that would be beyond the debtor's ability to pay as such debts matured; or

(IV) made such transfer to or for the benefit of an insider, or incurred such obligation to or for the benefit of an insider, under an employment contract and not in the ordinary course of business.

* * *

(c) . . . a transferee or obligee of such a transfer or obligation that takes for value and in good faith has a lien on or may retain any interest transferred or may enforce any obligation incurred, as the case may be, to the extent that such transferee or obligee gave value to the debtor in exchange for such transfer or obligation.

¶ 804: Transfer Between Sister Companies

We now evaluate the affiliate transfer diagram on page 182, primarily as a fraudulent conveyance. Recall our basic transfer scenario.

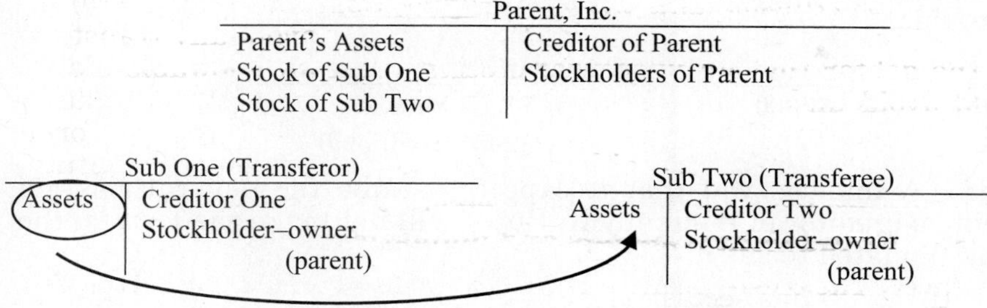

Transfer Between Sister Companies

This transfer makes Sub One worse off. It makes Creditor Two and, if Sub One was insolvent but Sub Two not insolvent, it also can make Parent, Inc. better off.

1. *Highly solvent scenario*. The Transferor firm is flush with cash and is highly solvent. But the managers at the Parent see the Transferor as having fewer new business opportunities requiring cash than the Transferee subsidiary. The Transferor is about to declare a formal dividend to the Parent company when the Parent instructs the Transferor to send the cash directly to Transferee. Transferor is still highly solvent (and indeed eventually pays the Creditor back.) Is the transfer an illegal dividend? A fraudulent conveyance?
2. *Weakened Transferor scenario*. The Transferor is sinking fast and the Parent company managers expect its operations to be without value in a few months; Transferee company, in contrast, has plausible business prospects. Transferor has $1 billion in cash in its bank account. The board of directors of Sub One approvers a transfer of the cash to Sub Two. The minutes of the board meeting state: "resolved, that our $1 billion in cash be transferred to Sub Two, for the benefit of Sub Two and our common Parent and to the detriment of our Creditor. This transfer is done to hinder, delay and defraud our very large creditor." A few months later, Transferor files to reorganize in chapter 11; neither Parent nor Sub Two file for bankruptcy. Evaluate the transfer under §548.
3. *Second weakened Transferor scenario*. As in the prior paragraph, the Transferor is sinking fast. It is insolvent, with assets less than its debts. The board of directors of Sub One approves a transfer of the cash to Sub Two. The minutes of the board meeting state: "Resolved, that our $ 1 billion in cash be transferred to Sub Two." Neither the minutes nor records of any surrounding discussion provide information or statement of justification for the transfer. A few months later, Transferor files to reorganize in chapter 11; Neither Parent nor Sub Two file for bankruptcy. The Creditor of the Transferor is upset. Evaluate the transfer under §548.

¶ 805: The Corporate Group and Structural Seniority

1. You represent Bank A, a prospective creditor of Company X. Company X has $3000 of assets. Your client expects to lend $1000, lifting the company's assets to $4000. After giving effect to the contemplated transaction, the loan, the company's balance sheet looks like this:

Company X	
$4000	$1000 Bank A
	$2000 Creditor B

Bank A informs you that it expects to take the general risks of being a creditor of Company X. But it will not make the loan on the contemplated terms if:

(i) B has security;

(ii) B is contractually senior to Bank A; or

(iii) future security can be granted to creditors.

You check; B has no security. You also inform Bank A that without its consent, B cannot be contractually senior. Finally, you draft a negative pledge clause (see Chapter 7 for the structure and bankruptcy impact of negative pledge clauses) to insert into the loan agreements (and inform Bank A of the consequences of a violation of the negative pledge clause if there is a subsequent bankruptcy).

Have you done enough?

2. One year after Bank A disburses the loan, X declines in value to $2000 and recapitalizes. Operations are sent down into an operating subsidiary. X becomes a holding company. B cancels its $2,000 note from X in exchange for a new $2,000 note from the subsidiary.

X's balance sheet looks like this:

Company X	
C/S of Subsidiary	$1000 Bank A
	Common stock

The subsidiary's balance sheet looks like this:

Subsidiary	
$2000	$2000 Creditor B
	Common stock

Is B effectively senior to Bank A? (In a more realistic transaction, A and B would remain as creditors of the parent and the subsidiary would take on a new creditor, Creditor C.) What kind of financial covenants could Bank A obtain if it fears this sort of maneuver (called "structural subordination")? How is debt of a subsidiary treated in the Drum Financial indenture?

3. Is the transfer from X to the subsidiary a fraudulent transfer?

(i) Is the transfer by an insolvent? (U.F.T.A. § 5.) Does it render X insolvent? Is reasonably equivalent value given?

(ii) Is the transfer made with intent to defraud? (§ 4.)

4. Suppose the restructuring is done when X is still worth $4000. Consider two possibilities at that time. First, what if there were no purpose to the transfer other than to obtain a better interest rate from B? Second, what if the purpose was to have operations run in a separate company and "headquarters" operations run in the parent company? Many companies, you are told, do this, including many companies about which there is not even a whisper of insolvency and bankruptcy. Incidental to this, creditor B might offer a better interest rate.

   Read and apply each of §§ 4 and 5 of the Uniform Fraudulent Transfer Act. See ¶ 803.

These examples should give you some sense of reach and limits of fraudulent transfer law in protecting creditors in the context of corporate groups. Creditors often rely on contract provisions to further restrict the transfer of assets among affiliated companies.

¶ 806: Richard Posner, The Rights of Creditors of Affiliated Corporations, 43 University of Chicago Law Review 449, 507–09 (1976)

* * *

[The excerpt below explains basic reasons why corporate parents typically incorporate several subsidiaries, and it argues why limited liability of each corporate entity within the group should generally be respected.]

B. The Economic Effects of Corporation Law

[S]pecific doctrines of corporation law should not be expected, in general, to have a profound impact on the credit system or to alter the balance of advantage between debtor and creditor. If corporation law did not provide for limited shareholder liability, then in situations where the parties desired to limit that liability in exchange for a higher interest rate the loan agreement would contain an express provision limiting liability. Conversely, under existing law a firm asked to lend money to a corporation in which it lacks confidence can insist as a condition of making the loan that the shareholders agree to guarantee repayment personally; of course, the interest rate will be lower than it would have been without such a guarantee.

Similarly, if the rules of corporation law limiting the payment of dividends to the amount of "earned surplus" shown on the corporation's books effectively protect creditors against attempts by firms to increase the risk of default after the loan has been made, well and good. But if corporation laws were amended to drop all limitations on the payment of dividends, the major consequence would be that those creditors who wanted dividend limitations would have to ask that they be written into the loan agreement.

* * *

C. Creditor Protection: The Problems of Information and Supervision

Let us take a closer look at the types of protection that creditors would normally insist upon and that would therefore be found in an efficient corporation or bankruptcy statute. It is convenient to divide the sources of risk faced by the creditor into two types. . . . The first is the risk of default based on circumstances known or anticipated when the loan is made. The creditor's interest is not necessarily in minimizing this risk; since it is compensated for risk, any measures taken to reduce it will also reduce the interest rate. The creditor's interest lies rather in forming an accurate idea of the risk, for otherwise he cannot determine what interest rate to charge. Assessment of the risk of default requires accurate information about the existing and expected assets and liabilities of the borrowing corporation and of anyone else who may be liable for the corporation's debts, insofar as those assets and liabilities affect the creditor's ability to obtain repayment. Coping with this risk presents the problem of information. Measures that increase the creditor's costs of information are prima facie undesirable. A good example of such a measure would be misrepresentation by the borrower of his solvency.

The second source of risk to the creditor is the possibility that the corporation will take steps to increase the riskiness of the loan after the terms have been set. The problem of coping with this risk is the problem of supervision; the creditor must supervise or regulate the corporation's disposition of its assets to the extent necessary to prevent any deliberate attempts to reduce the assets available to repay the loan. Dividend limitations are an illustration of the supervision type of credit term.

Obtaining information and supervising a corporation's internal affairs are costly undertakings. Economizing on these costs is one objective, social as well as private, of the provisions in a credit instrument. The first question to ask about any existing or proposed creditor's right under corporation or other laws is whether it actually reduces the creditor's information or supervision costs. It is often a difficult question to answer, because of differences in the costs of information and supervision to financial, trade, and nonbusiness creditors, because of the debtor's ability to increase those costs by various acts and omissions, and because of differences in the nature of the collateral put up by different debtors (e.g., land versus inventory).

The analysis, moreover, cannot stop with a consideration of the creditor's costs. The goal is to minimize not just the administrative costs of the credit transaction but its total social costs. Even if a rule abrogating the limited liability of corporate shareholders would lower the costs of credit administration by reducing the risk of defaulting on a loan and thereby decreasing the optimal level of expenditures on supervision and information,[3] it would probably be an uneconomical rule because it would prevent a type of risk shifting (from shareholders

[3] It is not certain that it would reduce those costs overall, however, since creditors of individuals exposed to unlimited liability for the debts of corporations in which they had invested might, in consequence, have to make a more extensive investigation of such individuals' creditworthiness.

to creditors) that is apparently highly efficient, judging by its prevalence. To the extent that—paradoxical as it may seem—risk can often be borne more cheaply by creditors than by shareholders, a rule that prevented the shifting of risk from the latter to the former would impose costs in undesired risk that might be much greater than the savings in reduced costs of credit administration. Similarly, a rule that forbade any payment of dividends to corporate shareholders would reduce supervision costs by increasing the assets available for the payment of creditors' claims, but it would also reduce the attractiveness of owning stock to those investors who do not consider appreciation a perfect substitute for periodic income.[4] It would probably not be an optimal rule considering all the relevant costs and benefits of corporate activity.

The ultimate objective of the credit process is to minimize the overall social costs of capital through a complex allocation of costs, including the disutility of risk, between borrower and lender. Measures that minimize the risk borne by the creditor will lower interest rates both directly and by reducing the creditor's optimum expenditure on obtaining information and supervising the debtor's business.[5] But beyond a certain point the cost to the investors of the added risk they are made to bear may well exceed the reduction in interest rates. It is of no benefit to a corporation to be able to borrow at six percent on condition that its shareholders personally guarantee repayment of the loan, if the expected earnings of the corporation are insufficient to compensate the shareholders for giving such a guarantee. An efficient corporation law is not one that maximizes creditor protection on the one hand or corporate freedom on the other, but one that mediates between these goals in a fashion that minimizes the costs of raising money for investment.

¶ 807: Fraudulent Transfers, LBOs, and Finance Companies

1. Leveraged Buyouts. An acquiring company might borrow to purchase a target company. The acquirer could obtain financing to buy the target, contingent on the acquirer offering the target's assets as security for the acquisition loan. To accomplish the deal, the acquirer could form an empty "shell" corporation as a subsidiary and then merge the target (that is, transfer all of the target's assets and liabilities) into the shell company. The acquire could then cause the target (now a subsidiary) to pledge its assets to the acquisition lender as security. Does that create a fraudulent transfer problem? See Chapter 22, The LBO.

---

[4] The transaction costs involved in selling stock in order to convert appreciation into cash income may make periodic income preferable to appreciation for some investors. [Also, some owners prefer that a firm commit a large portion of its expected cash flow to debt repayment, because the commitment increases the chance that managers will produce that cash. If the ownership is all in stock, managers may relax more than if ownership is largely in debt.—Roe & Tung.]

[5] Capital requirements imposed by the lender on the borrower are to be understood in this light: the more heavily capitalized the borrower is, the less likely he is to dissipate assets necessary to repay the loan by withdrawing capital from the enterprise in the form of dividends or otherwise.

2. *Financing Subsidiaries*. In the 1960s and 1970s many industrial firms set up finance companies. The finance subsidiary was used to provide credit to purchasers of the industrial company's product. Unlike its industrial company parent, whose assets consisted primarily of machinery, factories, and the like, the financing subsidiary's assets consisted primarily of its accounts receivable. The reasons for using this kind of a financing structure were often those offered by Posner, above. Separating industrial from financial assets enabled the finance company to approach a set of specialized creditors that understood how to value and monitor accounts receivable. While creditors of the industrial company parent would monitor its creditworthiness, based in large part on the robustness of the markets for the parent's products and the parent's competitive position, creditors of the separate financing subsidiary need only monitor the financial health of the specific customers of the parent who purchased products on credit, and who are therefore the obligors on the accounts receivable held by the subsidiary. By reducing these specialized creditors' monitoring costs, the finance company can borrow at a cheaper rate than if the financing operations and assets had not been segregated from the industrial company parent's operations and assets. Also, there might have been operating efficiencies in having a separate division or subsidiary with its own personnel who would be or become expert in financing activities.

Industrial	
Industrial Assets	Creditor of Parent
Stock of Finance Sub	Stockholders of Parent

Finance	
Accounts Receivable	Creditors
	Stockholder – owner (parent)

Finance Subsidiary

Since the financing company was a new and unexpected business development in the 1960s and 1970s, preexisting creditors of the operating company generally had no covenants to deal with the formation of a finance subsidiary. Did they have any reason to? If a creditor lent to an industrial firm and did not want to be subordinate to any other creditor, what protections did it need? A prohibition on any subordination agreement? A prohibition on lending to a subsidiary with a limited set of assets? A negative pledge clause to protect against security?

3. *Example of a Financial Subsidiary*. International Farm Machinery Company forms a finance subsidiary in the 1960s, when its operations are borderline profitable. Since the receivables of the finance subsidiary are good quality, short-term credits, it can borrow through the finance subsidiary at prime quality rates. Since the creditors of the industrial company, the parent, obviously can no longer get first crack at the receivables, those credits are perceived as being slightly more risky than they had been. They decline in value a fraction of a percent.

Finance economists note that the preexisting debt of industrial firms that formed finance subsidiaries declined in value, although only slightly. E. Han Kim, John McConnell & Paul Greenwood, *Capital Structure Rearrangements and Me-first Rules in an Efficient Capital Market*, 32 Journal of Finance 789 (1977).

In the 1970s, the bottom falls out of the farm machinery market. Creditors of the finance subsidiary, although unhappy, expect that in any bankruptcy they will be paid close to in full. The short-term receivables are about 90 per cent collectible.

Creditors of the industrial parent are less happy. They believe that if they collect only out of assets of their beleaguered debtor, they will receive 30 cents on the dollar.

Can creditors that lent to the industrial firm before the finance subsidiary was established attack the subsidiary's formation as a fraudulent transfer? Did the transfer render International Farm Machinery Company insolvent? Or was it the collapsing farm machinery market of the 1970s that rendered it insolvent? Was the transfer made with actual intent to hinder, delay or defraud? Prime-grade credits, including companies such as General Electric, formed finance subsidiaries for operating or lending efficiencies.

¶ 808: Upstream Guarantees

A creditor lending to a parent company often wants to be able to claim directly against the parent's subsidiaries, as it does not want to take value last, after the subsidiary pays off all of its own creditors and dividends up the remaining value to the parent, which then pays off its own creditors. Subsidiary guarantees of parent company debt are common.

A core bankruptcy problem here is that the guarantee, or payment on the guarantee, could be a fraudulent transfer. Upstream subsidiary guarantees are more susceptible to attack as a fraudulent transfer than downstream parent guarantees of subsidiary debt, because the subsidiary that guarantees the parent's debt typically receives consideration, if any, only indirectly. To limit fraudulent transfer problems, the lender to the parent often has the subsidiary limit its guarantee to its own net worth, thereby reducing the chances that the "render insolvent" prong of constructive fraud liability could be brought into play. Some creditors' efforts are more tailored and conceptual, limiting the subsidiary's guarantee to whatever extent is necessary to insulate the financing from any potential fraudulent transfer liability.

The theory and bases for intragroup guarantees is analyzed below. Noting the widespread use of intragroup guarantees, Richard Squire adds to, or offers an alternative to Posner's explanation, *supra*, for the existence of corporate groups.

¶ 809: Richard Squire, Strategic Liability in the Corporate Group. 78 University of Chicago Law Review 605, 606-07 (2011)

When a business firm gets big enough, it reliably does two things. First, it reconfigures itself into a corporate group by dividing itself into a multitude of commonly owned subsidiaries. Second, it causes the various entities in this group to guarantee each other's major outside debts. Previous scholarly theories of the corporate group can explain either the subsidiaries or the guarantees, but not both. Thus, [Posner's] theory argues that firms form subsidiaries in order to compartmentalize credit risk, thus reducing the cost of information for creditors by enabling them to lend against only those divisions of the firm they understand best. But this theory is contradicted in practice by the heavy use of the intragroup guarantee, which causes the creditors of one group member to bear the risk that another member will fall insolvent. Meanwhile, a second theory argues that firms issue intragroup guarantees because the guarantees permit creditors to ignore the subsidiary structure, lending instead based on the creditworthiness of the group as a whole. This second theory, however, raises the question of why firms form so many subsidiaries in the first place, and why they maintain them in a manner that, but for the guarantees, makes it harder rather than easier for creditors to evaluate risk.

There are other intercorporate issues. The subsidiary's creditor will not just be concerned with the subsidiary guaranteeing the parent's debts. It will also be concerned with dividends leaving the subsidiary and with other transfers to the parent company or other subsidiaries. What will fraudulent transfer law do for it? How protective is fraudulent transfer law if there are transfers and the subsidiary thereafter declines in value?

Consider the advice you must give a client in a holding company position analogous to Creditor B in ¶ 805. Creditor B considers the fraudulent transfer protections inadequate and would like to control the subsidiary's dividends more tightly. Would the dividend covenant in Drum Financial, ¶ 703, be of use? How would it help Creditor B?

The subsidiary is in the chemical business. Creditor B understands the subsidiary's chemical business, but it doesn't understand all of the holding company/conglomerate's other businesses. It wants most of the subsidiary's earnings retained inside the subsidiary. The creditor and the managers of the subsidiary agree to this. Often that is the end of the legal and financial inquiry.

But this time the managers of the parent company come back and say they'll need to water down the dividend covenant. One of the rationales for this kind of conglomerate organization—sometimes called the M-form or multiform organization in business schools—is this: the holding company is run by superstar strategic business planners. They don't supervise, manufacture, or market anything. But they see big picture trends and allocate capital among the holding company operations based on their strategic view of where the economy is going. They need flexibility to pull money out of the chemical subsidiary and put it into the steel subsidiary or go into the computer business.

The parent company's managers say they can't anticipate how much and when they'd change their strategic vision for the subsidiary's business. They don't want to be too tied down. They say they understand that our client, Creditor B, has two worries about not having a tight dividend covenant. Creditor B is worried that even if the parent company managers come to honestly believe that the subsidiary's business is going nowhere, their yanking money out of the subsidiary would nevertheless make Creditor B's loans riskier. They want to be repaid *before* the parent company yanks money out of the subsidiary, and not risk the non-repayment afterward. (Fraudulent transfer law would only bite if at the time of the transfer, the subsidiary was insolvent, there was actual intent to hinder, or the subsidiary was left with capital too small. That kind of protection isn't good enough for Creditor B.) That is, your client understands that if the subsidiary is rendered insolvent it will have fraudulent transfer protection. But the client is worried that the parent will yank the money out, and the subsidiary wouldn't thereby be rendered insolvent, but thereafter the subsidiary's value would decline, leaving the client unpaid.

Moreover, the parent company managers say they understand Creditor B's worries. Without constraints, the managers might pull funds out of the subsidiary, even if the subsidiary's business is passable, if financial problems elsewhere in the organization demand a transfer of cash.

To maintain flexibility and still give Creditor B protection, the parent company strategic managers propose to keep the dividend covenant, but to water it down. B will still, they say, be primarily lending on the credit-worthiness of the subsidiary and its understanding of the subsidiary's chemical business. But don't let the weaker dividend covenant induce you, B, to raise the interest rate, they say, because the parent company will guarantee repayment of the loan. So if the parent yanks too much money out, and the chemical company later collapses, B will have a claim not only on the chemical subsidiary but also against the parent company. Double protection.

There's a business problem with this. Creditor B says the reason it was willing to lend at this low rate to the chemical subsidiary was that it understood the chemical business and didn't have to get smart about the company's steel business or computer business and this company's position in each. The parent company is now proposing a hybrid, based on the credit-worthiness of both. The principal credit risk is still the chemical subsidiary, but B would be relying at least in part on the strength of the conglomerate's other businesses. This reduces the benefit of lending to a targeted subsidiary.

The trade-off might work or it might not work. This time, so that we can move on to the next section, it works. All the business-people at the bank, at the subsidiary, and at the parent company accept the trade-off.

C. SUBSTANTIVE CONSOLIDATION

¶ 810: Introduction

Within a corporate group, commingling of assets among affiliated entities is not uncommon. After all, it may be the profitability of the entire group that matters most to its senior management, so that assets may move to their best use within the corporate group without much company-level formality or record keeping about which company owes what to which affiliated company. When members of the group wind up in bankruptcy and creditors come to collect against their individual corporate borrowers, it might be difficult to retrace the movement of assets among affiliates on a transfer-by-transfer basis. Though a number of prebankruptcy transfers within the group might plausibly be attacked, either as fraudulent transfers, illegal dividends, or otherwise, the sheer number may make it difficult and costly to unscramble them all in order to do perfect justice to each creditor of each affiliated company. Leaving such transfers untouched, though, may leave some creditors better off and some worse off.

In this situation, in order to do some rough justice, courts may treat the affiliated debtors as a single entity, collapsing the affiliates into one pool of assets, with their respective claims all being paid out of the single pool. This substantive consolidation ignores the separate existence of each corporate affiliate and cancels all intercorporate contracts and claims. What are the justifications for substantive consolidation? The next two cases illustrate.

¶ 811: Consolidated Rock Prods. Co. v. DuBois, 312 U.S. 510 (1941)

MR. JUSTICE DOUGLAS delivered the opinion of the Court.

This case involves questions as to the *fairness* . . . of a plan of reorganization for a parent corporation (Consolidated Rock Products Co.) and its two wholly owned subsidiaries—Union Rock Co. and Consumers Rock and Gravel Co., Inc. The District Court confirmed the plan; the Circuit Court of Appeals reversed. We granted the petitions for certiorari. . . .

The stock of Union and Consumers is held by Consolidated. Union has outstanding in the hands of the public . . . a total mortgage indebtedness of $2,280,555. Consumers has outstanding in the hands of the public . . . a total mortgage indebtedness of $1,358,715. Consolidated has outstanding . . . preferred stock and . . . common stock.

The plan of reorganization calls for the formation of a new corporation to which will be transferred all of the assets of Consolidated, Union, and Consumers free of all claims. The securities of the new corporation are to be distributed as follows:

> Union and Consumers bonds held by the public will be exchanged for . . . bonds and preferred stock of the new company. . . . Union bondholders for their claims of $2,280,555 will receive . . . bonds and preferred stock in the face amount of $1,877,000; Consumers bondholders for their claims of $1,358,715 will receive income bonds and preferred stock in the face amount of $1,137,000. Each share of new preferred stock will have a warrant for the purchase of [some new common stock].

Preferred stockholders of Consolidated will receive one share of new common stock ($2 par value) for each share of old preferred or an aggregate of 285,947 shares of new common.

A warrant to purchase one share of new common for $1 within three months of issuance will be given to the common stockholders of Consolidated for each five shares of old common.

* * *

The bonds of Union and Consumers held by Consolidated, the stock of those companies held by Consolidated, and the intercompany claims (discussed hereafter) will be canceled.

. . . The average of the valuations (apparently based on physical factors) given by three witnesses at the hearing before the master were $2,202,733 for Union as against a mortgage indebtedness of $2,280,555; $1,151,033 for Consumers as against a mortgage indebtedness of $1,358,715. Relying on similar testimony, Consolidated argues that the value of its property, to be contributed to the new company, is over $1,359,000, or exclusive of an alleged good will of $500,000, $859,784. . . . [But] the earnings record of the enterprise casts grave doubts on the soundness of the estimated values. . . . [E]xcept for the year 1929, Consolidated had no net operating profit, after bond interest and amortization, depreciation and depletion, in any year down to September 30, 1937. Yet on this record the District Court found that the present fair value of all the assets of the several companies, exclusive of good will and going concern value, was in excess of the total bonded indebtedness, plus accrued and unpaid interest. And it also found that such value, including goodwill and going concern value, was insufficient to pay the bonded indebtedness plus accrued and unpaid interest and the liquidation preferences and accrued dividends on Consolidated preferred stock. It further found that the present fair value of the assets admittedly subject to the trust indentures of Union and Consumers was insufficient to pay the face amount, plus accrued and unpaid interest of the respective bond issues. In spite of that finding, the District Court also found that "it would be physically impossible to determine and segregate with any degree of accuracy or fairness properties which originally belonged to the companies separately"; that as a result of unified operation properties of every character "have been commingled and are now in the main held by Consolidated without any way of ascertaining what part, if any thereof, belongs to each or any of the companies separately"; and that, as a consequence, an appraisal "would be of such an indefinite and unsatisfactory nature as to produce further confusion."

The unified operation which resulted in that commingling of assets was pursuant to an operating agreement which Consolidated caused its wholly owned subsidiaries to execute in 1929. Under that agreement the subsidiaries ceased all operating functions and the entire management, operation and financing of the business and properties of the subsidiaries were undertaken by Consolidated. The corporate existence of the subsidiaries, however, was maintained and certain separate accounts were kept. Under this agreement Consolidated undertook, inter alia, to pay the subsidiaries the amounts necessary for the interest and sinking fund provisions of the indentures and to credit their current accounts with items of depreciation, depletion, amortization and obsolescence. Upon termination of the agreement the properties were to be returned and a final settlement of accounts made, Consolidated meanwhile to retain all net revenues after its obligations thereunder to the subsidiaries had been met. It was specifically provided that the agreement was made for the benefit of the parties, not "for the benefit of any third person." *Consolidated's books as at June 30, 1938, showed a net indebtedness under that agreement to Union and Consumers of somewhat over $5,000,000. That claim was canceled by the plan of reorganization,* no securities being issued to the creditors of the subsidiaries therefor. The District Court made no findings as respects the amount or validity of that intercompany claim; it summarily disposed of it by concluding that any liability under the operating agreement was "*not made for the benefit of any third parties and the bondholders are included in that category.*"

We agree with the Circuit Court of Appeals that it was error to confirm this plan of reorganization.

I.

On this record no determination of the fairness of any plan of reorganization could be made. Absent the requisite valuation data, the court was in no position to exercise the "informed, independent judgment" which appraisal of the fairness of a plan of reorganization entails. Case v. Los Angeles Lumber Products Co., 308 U.S. 106. There are two aspects of that valuation problem.

[Intercorporate debt as an asset of the subsidiary]

In the first place, there must be a determination of what assets are subject to the payment of the respective claims. This obvious requirement was not met. The status of the Union and Consumers bondholders emphasizes its necessity and importance. According to the District Court the mortgaged assets are insufficient to pay the mortgage debt. There is no finding, however, as to the extent of the deficiency or the amount of unmortgaged assets and their value. It is plain that the bondholders would have, as against Consolidated and its stockholders, prior recourse against any unmortgaged assets of Union and Consumers. The full and absolute priority rule of . . . Case v. Los Angeles Lumber Products Co. would preclude participation by the equity interests in any of those assets until the bondholders had been made whole. *Here there are some unmortgaged assets, for there is a claim of Union and Consumers against Consolidated—a claim which according to the books of Consolidated is over $5,000,000 in amount.* If that claim is valid . . . , then the entire assets of Consolidated would be drawn down into the estates of the subsidiaries. In that event . . . it would render untenable the present contention of Consolidated and the preferred stockholders that they are contributing all of the assets of the Consolidated to the new company in exchange for which they are entitled to new securities. On that theory of the case they would be making a contribution of only such assets of Consolidated, if any, as remained *after* any deficiency of the bondholders had been *wholly* satisfied.

[State law claims]

. . . Consolidated makes some point of the difficulty and expense of determining the extent of its liability under the operating agreement and of the necessity to abide by the technical terms of that agreement in ascertaining that liability. But equity will not permit a holding company, which has dominated and controlled its subsidiaries, to escape or reduce its liability to those subsidiaries by reliance upon self-serving contracts which it has imposed on them. A holding company, as well as others in dominating or controlling positions (Pepper v. Litton, 308 U.S. 295), has fiduciary duties to security holders of its system which will be strictly enforced. See Taylor v. Standard Gas & Electric Co., 306 U.S. 307. In this connection Consolidated cannot defeat or postpone the accounting because of the clause in the operating agreement that it was not made for the benefit of any third person. The question here is not a technical one as to who may sue to enforce that liability. It is merely a question as to the amount by which Consolidated is indebted to the subsidiaries and the proof and allowance of that claim. *The subsidiaries need not be sent into state courts to have that liability determined.* The bankruptcy court having exclusive jurisdiction over the holding company and the subsidiaries has plenary power to adjudicate all the issues pertaining to the claim. The intimations of Consolidated that there must be foreclosure proceedings and protracted litigation in state courts involve a misconception of the duties and powers of the bankruptcy court. The fact that Consolidated might have a strategic or nuisance value . . . does not detract from or impair the power and duty of the bankruptcy court to require a full accounting as a condition precedent to approval of any plan of reorganization. The fact that the claim might be settled, with the approval of the Court after full disclosure and notice to interested parties, does not justify the concealed compromise effected here through the simple expedient of extinguishing the claim.

[Substantive consolidation and veil-piercing]

So far as the ability of the bondholders of Union and Consumers to reach the assets of Consolidated on claims of the kind covered by the operation agreement is concerned, *there is another and more direct route* which reaches the same end. There has been *a unified operation* of those several properties by Consolidated pursuant to the operating agreement. That operation not only resulted in extensive commingling of assets. All management functions of the several companies were assumed by Consolidated. The subsidiaries abdicated. Consolidated operated them as mere departments of its own business. *Not even the formalities of separate corporate organizations were observed*, except in minor particulars such as the maintenance of certain separate accounts. In view of these facts, Consolidated is in no position to claim that its assets are insulated from such claims of creditors of the subsidiaries. To the contrary, it is well settled that *where a holding company directly intervenes in the management of its subsidiaries so as to treat them as mere departments of its own enterprise, it is responsible for the obligations of those subsidiaries* incurred or arising during its management. . . . We are not dealing here with a situation where other creditors of a parent company are competing with creditors of its subsidiaries. If meticulous regard to corporate forms, which Consolidated has long ignored, is now observed, the stockholders of Consolidated may be the direct beneficiaries. *Equity will not countenance such a result. A holding company which assumes to treat the properties of its subsidiaries as its own cannot take the benefits of direct management without the burdens.*

We have already noted that no adequate finding was made as to the value of the assets of Consolidated. In view of what we have said, it is apparent that a determination of that value must be made so that criteria will be available to determine an appropriate allocation of new securities between bondholders and stockholders in case there is an equity remaining after the bondholders have been made whole.

* * *

Affirmed.

¶ 812: Questions on *Consolidated Rock*

1. As argued by the stockholders and bondholders of Consolidated Rock, what were the balance sheets of Consolidated Rock (the parent company) and each of its subsidiaries? What was each subsidiary and each creditor and stockholder contributing to the reorganization?

   Complete these balance sheets, as the stockholders would have wanted the bankruptcy court to complete them:

   Consolidated Rock (parent only)

Assets + goodwill	300,000 preferred shares
Stock of Union	400,000 common shares
Stock of Consumers	

   Union

Plant	$2.3M bondholders
	Common stock (owned by Consolidated Rock)

   Consumers

Plant	$1.4M bondholders
	Common stock (owned by Consolidated Rock)

   Complete these balance sheets as the *bondholders* would have wanted the bankruptcy court to complete them:

Union	
Plant	$2.3M bondholders
Other asset?	Common stock (owned by Consolidated Rock)

So, the bondholders would argue that the balance sheet of Consolidated Rock (parent only) should be completed to look like:

Con. Rock (parent only)	
$1.4 assets + goodwill	Debts due to?
Stock of Consumers	Preferred
Stock of Union	Common

If the entire holding company structure were substantively consolidated, how would the balance sheet look?

Con. Rock (consolidated)	
$1.4 assets + goodwill	Debts due to?
Plants?	
Stock of Consumers?	Preferred
Stock of Union?	Common

What distribution results if absolute priority is respected, but the corporate group is substantively consolidated?

2. In a reorganization consistent with absolute priority, who would get what, if both the holding company is respected and the inter-company debt is enforced? What if the holding company is respected and the intercompany debt canceled?
3. How did the properties become commingled? Did the original arrangement blending together the operations also blend together the subsidiaries' debts?
4. The inter-corporate contract says that it's not for the benefit of third parties, presumably meaning not for the benefit of the subsidiaries' creditors. Does that mean that the court must ignore the contract to the extent it gives the *subsidiaries themselves* a cause of action against the parent company?
5. What is the source of law by which Douglas instructs the lower courts to consider a direct action by the creditors against the parent company? State law? If so, which state and what provision? Dividend statute, veil-piercing, or fraudulent transfer?
6. Or does the authority to consolidate come from the bankruptcy requirement that the plan of reorganization be fair and equitable? Or is it from the "nature" of bankruptcy administration, either as a court of equity or as a practical court trying to get a reorganization completed?

7. If it will cost $500,000 to parse out the value of Consolidated Rock's separate subsidiaries, does it make sense to do so, given the overall value of the enterprise? Does the *Consolidated Rock* opinion, like that in *Atlas Pipeline,* evince an unstated faith in the valuation process?

¶ 813: Complex Corporate Structures and Seniority

What if the parent company in *Consolidated Rock* had its own outstanding indebtedness? If so, then substantive consolidation might harm an "innocent" bystander, the parent's creditor, who expected to get first crack at the parent's assets. Presumably then, substantive consolidation would hurt that creditor and be disfavored. The values of the subsidiaries and parent would have to be sorted out, a sorting Douglas sought to require in *Consolidated Rock.*

But what if it turned out that sorting out the intercompany accounts was especially expensive? For a corporate group more complex than that in *Consolidated Rock,* there could have been multiple transfers up and down from parent to subsidiary, from subsidiary to parent, and from one subsidiary to another subsidiary of assets, opportunities, guarantees, and managers. For a court to value each transfer would be hard, expensive, and inaccurate. Does Douglas in *Consolidated Rock* contemplate this case? (Indeed, he rejected the lower court's protestations that a sorting would have been too hard.)

In *In re Augie/Restivo Baking Company, Ltd.*, 860 F.2d 515 (2d Cir. 1988), Judge Winter stated:

> Substantive consolidation has no express statutory basis but is a product of judicial gloss. Substantive consolidation usually results in . . . pooling the assets of, and claims against, the two entities; satisfying liabilities from the resulting common fund; eliminating intercompany claims; and combining the creditors of the two companies for purposes of voting on reorganization plans. The effect in the present case is . . . [to pay one creditor less than another]. Because of the dangers in forcing creditors of one debtor to share on a parity with creditors of a less solvent debtor, we have stressed that substantive consolidation "is no mere instrument of procedural convenience . . . but a measure affecting substantive rights."
>
> . . . [Substantive consolidation is based] on two critical factors: (i) whether creditors dealt with the entities as a single economic unit and "did not rely on their separate identity in extending credit" . . . ; or (ii) whether the affairs of the debtors are so entangled that consolidation will benefit all creditors. . . .
>
> With regard to the first factor, creditors who make loans on the basis of the financial status of a separate entity expect to be able to look to the assets of their particular borrower for satisfaction of that loan. Such lenders structure their loans according to their expectations regarding that borrower and do not anticipate either having the assets of a more sound company available in the case of insolvency or having the creditors of a less sound debtor compete for the borrower's assets. . . .

The second factor, entanglement of the debtors' affairs, involves cases in which there has been a commingling of two firms' assets and business functions. Resort to consolidation in such circumstances, however, should not be Pavlovian. Rather, substantive consolidation should be used *only* after it has been determined that *all* creditors will benefit because untangling is either impossible or so costly as to consume the assets. Otherwise . . . a series of fraudulent conveyances might be viewed as resulting in a "commingling" that justified substantive consolidation. That consolidation, because it would eliminate all inter-company claims, would prevent creditors of the transferor from recovering assets from the transferee. . . .

The evidence of commingling of assets and business function in the state case in no way [was hopelessly obscure in the case at hand.] . . . [R]ecords exist of all transactions. . . .

¶ 814: In re Commercial Envelope Mfg. Co., 3 Bankr. Ct. Dec. 647 (Bankr. S.D.N.Y. Aug. 22, 1977)

[Four interrelated corporations, each of which had filed a separate Chapter XI petition, moved for substantive consolidation, asserting that a merger of all their assets and liabilities was the only way to viably formulate a Chapter XI plan. The debtors were interrelated through ownership of their common stock and there were intercorporate guarantees and intercorporate credit arrangements. Two creditors filed objections to consolidation asserting that substantive consolidation would jeopardize their claims.]

[The court determined that since the objectants had failed to establish that the consolidation would have an adverse effect on their claims and because consolidation would benefit all creditors in that the debtors would operate profitably together, consolidation should be allowed.]

BABITT, Bankruptcy Judge: The movants are four related corporations, each of which filed its own separate petition seeking the relief contemplated by Chapter XI of the Bankruptcy Act, on October 20, 1976. [T]hese cases are being jointly administered. [J]oint or procedural administration in the interest of economy of judicial and clerical time [does not] affect . . . substantive rights. . . . The relief sought by the motion now before the court is for a substantive consolidation which *does* deal with the rights of the debtors' creditors. Substantive consolidation, as will be seen, is now part of the warp and woof of the fabric of the bankruptcy process involving related debtors, though to be used sparingly. *It has no statutory or rule basis:* rather it is the product of judicial gloss in the face of *changes in the makeup of companies involved with the country's insolvency laws.*

Although each of the debtors is a separate corporation, all four are related by virtue of common stock ownership. . . .

The debtors are convinced, and hope to convince the court, that the only way a meaningful Chapter XI plan can be presented to creditors is for that plan to be a single, unitary one affecting all of the debtors and all of their creditors. To achieve this result, the debtors have moved for a multi-faceted order authorizing and directing the consolidation of all four cases into a single one with a concomitant merger of all of the assets and liabilities of the four corporations into the consolidated entity. As a necessary corollary of such relief the debtors ask that all claims filed in each of the individual cases be treated as having been filed in the consolidated case; that all duplicate claims for the same indebtedness filed in more than one case be expunged; that all intercompany claims be eliminated and disallowed; that all cross-corporate guarantees of these debtors be eliminated and disallowed; and finally, that all the consolidated debtors be authorized to file a single set of schedules and a single plan in the consolidated proceeding. In a matter as pregnant with consequence to all concerned as is substantive consolidation and alert to the frequent reminders that the grant is to be given only on a proper showing of the criteria the courts have engrafted on the power, the court is to scrutinize the evidence offered. This is particularly so here where a creditor claims he would be prejudiced by the favorable exercise of this court's power to achieve what the debtor seeks.

* * *

At the trial, the debtors elicited testimony from an accountant, one Abraham Nowick, a member of the firm of accountants authorized in these proceedings to conduct an audit of the debtors' books and records.

* * *

Nowick testified as to the difficulty of isolating and ascertaining the individual assets and liabilities of each of the debtors. This was due to the arbitrary and inaccurate system of bookkeeping maintained by the companies. No separate accounting was had nor were separate records kept. Financial statements were issued on a consolidated basis. Each debtor had cross-guaranteed obligations of the others. Mr. Nowick went on to describe the astronomical cost of performing such audit as might be necessary to permit one to distinguish between the assets and liabilities of the debtors. However, this witness continued, because of the complexity and length of time over which the intercorporate transactions had taken place, he could give no guarantee that such an audit would be successful. He also testified that it was impossible to determine whether or not the individual operations of each of the debtors were even profitable. He expressed his opinion that physical consolidation into a single location would probably improve the profitability of the entire operation.

* * *

There are numerous cases emanating from this circuit which have dealt with consolidation. Although none of these cases has described conclusively the criteria that must exist before a case for consolidation is established, the cases do describe the common ingredients that seem to be present in all instances where consolidation was permitted. It is the opinion of this court that those elements exist in the present context and that therefore consolidation should proceed.

I turn to the cases. In Soviero v. Franklin National Bank of Long Island . . . the court authorized consolidation upon the finding of extensive co-mingling of assets and business functions and the existence of a unity of interest and ownership common to all the debtor companies. All the debtors in Soviero had been engaged in the same business, and gratuitous transfers of assets were made from one debtor to another. Guarantees to purchasers had been given in the parent's name.

In Matter of SeaTrade Corporation, 255 F. Supp. 696 (S.D.N.Y. 1966), the debtors, almost entirely owned by one family, operated with frequent disregard of the corporate formalities usually observed in independent corporations. *The court found that it would have been unreasonable in terms of time and cost to attempt to separate the assets and liabilities of this corporation, and even if audit steps were to be taken, there was no assurance that the true situation of the debtors would fairly be reflected.* The court also found that there was *no evidence that particular creditors would be unfairly dealt with on a consolidated basis.* There also existed inter-corporate guarantees and frequent transfers of assets without formal observance of accounting proprieties. Again, that court authorized consolidation of the debtors.

In Chemical Bank, N.Y. Trust v. Kheel . . . the Court of Appeals for this Circuit, for the first time relying on Soviero, set forth an additional criterion to justify consolidation. That criterion turned on the findings that the inter-relationship of the group of debtors was hopelessly obscured and that the time and expense necessary to even attempt to unscramble them was so substantial that it would threaten the realization of any net assets for all creditors. The court felt that if such findings could be made, an equitable base existed for the invocation of the court's broad equity powers to consolidate even in the absence of a showing that the creditor dealt with the bankrupt and its affiliates as one.

* * *

The essence of the objecting creditor's resistance to consolidation is that it could adversely affect the substantive rights of the holders of the First Mortgage Revenue Bonds, since such consolidation will render assets of [their debtors, which may be in better financial shape than the other companies in the complex] subject to the claims of creditors of the other debtors, thereby reducing the amounts available to satisfy the bonded indebtedness.

* * *

When all is said and done, there is a practicability to authorizing consolidation here. In effect, by this consolidation, all of the assets of all of the debtors are to be treated as common assets, and claims of all creditors against any of the debtors are to be treated as claims against this created common fund. This would eliminate duplicated claims filed against several of the debtors by creditors uncertain as to where the liability should be allocated. There appears to be no feasible alternative to consolidation from a practical standpoint, particularly where, as here, all of the companies are already before the court[.]

This court cannot read [precedent] as a mandate that consolidation must inevitably be refused where some creditor might be marginally injured. All conflicting interest must be balanced. Here the balance is decidedly in favor of all of the creditors of all of the debtor companies and in favor of achieving that debtor rehabilitation which Chapter XI contemplates and which cannot be achieved unless consolidation is granted. So much is implicit in the words of the Chemical Bank case that consolidation may be had in order

> "to reach a rough approximation of justice to some rather than deny any to all." 369 F.2d at 847.

It is, therefore, the judgment of this court that in order that a meaningful plan might be proposed and accepted and found to be in the best interests of creditors . . . consolidation is warranted. The motion is Granted and the objection Overruled.

Submit an Order.

The Third Circuit emphasized how "sparingly" substantive consolidation should be used in *In re Owens Corning*, 419 F.3d 195 (3rd Cir. 2005). Several banks had made an unsecured loan of $2 billion to Owens–Corning. The loan was partially guaranteed by Owens Corning's wholly-owned subsidiaries, giving the banks a direct claim against the guarantors, which other creditors of Owens Corning—including many tort claimants—did not have. The District Court had approved substantive consolidation, citing the guarantees and the common management of corporate cash as important centralizing factors to justify the consolidation. The court combined the assets and liabilities of the parent and subsidiaries for the purposes of figuring out the size of the proper bankruptcy distribution to the creditors.

The Third Circuit reversed the consolidation:

> In our Court what must be proven (absent consent) concerning the entities for whom substantive consolidation is sought is that (i) prepetition they disregarded separateness so significantly their *creditors relied* on the breakdown of entity borders and treated them as one legal entity, or (ii) postpetition their assets and liabilities are so scrambled that separating them is prohibitive and hurts all creditors.

The court further explained the two rationales:

> Proponents of substantive consolidation have the burden of showing one or the other rationale for consolidation. . . . A prima facie case for [the first rationale] typically exists when, based on the parties' prepetition dealings, a proponent proves corporate disregard creating contractual expectations of creditors that they were dealing with debtors as one indistinguishable entity. . . . Proponents who are creditors must also show that, in their prepetition course of dealing, they actually and reasonably relied on debtors' supposed unity. . . . Creditor opponents of consolidation can nonetheless defeat a prima facie showing under the first rationale if they can prove they are adversely affected and actually relied on debtors' separate existence. . . .
>
> [As for the second rationale,] commingling justifies consolidation only when separately accounting for the assets and liabilities of the distinct entities will reduce the recovery of every creditor—that is, when every creditor will benefit from the consolidation.

The Third Circuit court based its reversal of the District Court's judgment on its simple understanding of the loan to Owens–Corning:

> [T]he Banks did the "deal world" equivalent of "Lending 101." They loaned $2 billion to [Owens–Corning] and enhanced the credit of that unsecured loan indirectly by [obtaining] subsidiary guarantees covering less than half the initial debt. What the Banks got in lending lingo was "structural seniority"—a direct claim against the guarantors (and thus against their assets levied on once a judgment is obtained) that other creditors of [Owens–Corning] did not have. This kind of lending occurs every business day [and therefore the rare remedy of substantive consolidation should not be available].

Those with extensive experience in this lending world might restructure the Third Circuit's analysis here. Lenders aren't always looking to enhance their own credit by getting structural seniority, but want to prevent new creditors from jumping ahead of them. William Widen states:

> My analysis of the difference between a wealth transfer and a wrong suggests that the Third Circuit made an error in Owens Corning when it found loan syndicate reliance on intercompany guarantees. . . . A lending syndicate typically employs a web of intercompany guarantees defensively, rather than offensively. A defensive use of intercompany guarantees ensures that no subsidiary creditor has structural seniority over the syndicate's loans. This protection allows the syndicate to rely confidently upon consolidated financial statements and consolidated financial tests to monitor the corporate group as a single economic unit. Testimony from lending syndicate representatives suggests the defensive use of guarantees in the Owens Corning credit agreement, though the Third Circuit drew the opposite conclusion from its understanding of what it called "Lending 101."[6]

Does it make a difference to the result or reasoning that the complainants seeking substantive consolidation were tort claimants? How do tort claimants rely on separate or consolidated structures?

D. CONTRACTUAL ANTI–CONSOLIDATION: SPECIAL PURPOSE VEHICLES

¶ 815: Enron and the Special Purpose Vehicle

You are counsel to a lender who will finance a company's accounts receivable. The debtor will give your client a security interest in the accounts receivable, but the lending officer at the bank asks for even more. First off, she says, the bankruptcy stay is rather inconvenient. If the debtor deteriorates, she'd like to seize the security, sell it, and be

[6] William H. Widen, Corporate Form and Substantive Consolidation, 75 George Washington Law Review 237 (2006).

done with the matter. The CFO at the debtor would be happy to allow the bank to do so, even saying it would waive § 362. But you advise the loan officer that the bankruptcy court will not respect the waiver: the stay after all exists to enable an inquiry as to whether there's enough value inside the firm to make it worth continuing. It's as much for the benefit of the other creditors as it is for the debtor's management and stockholders. And the bank loan officer has other complaints about the typical bankruptcy: she doesn't like the idea that the bankruptcy court could, via § 364 (see Chapter 16) allow new loans ("DIP loans" or "debtor-in-possession loans") to come ahead of her bank's prebankruptcy loans (which could happen even if her bank's loan agreement bars such priority jumps outside of bankruptcy).

You have an idea. You tell the loan officer that the bank could just buy the accounts receivable from the debtor. If the bank owns the accounts receivable outright, the bankruptcy court cannot grab them back. Bankruptcy wouldn't stay the bank from collecting from the debtor, because the debtor would have already *sold* the accounts receivable, well before the bankruptcy. They wouldn't belong to the debtor when it files for chapter 11.

That sale structure might work, says the loan officer, but for this company she doesn't like an absolute sale. The accounts receivable might be uncollectible. The debtor might pass off some bogus accounts receivable. She wants the bank to have recourse to the debtor if too many of the accounts receivable turn out to be uncollectible. She doesn't want to have all—or any of—the credit risk of non-collection of the accounts receivable.

You have another idea. The debtor will sell the accounts receivable, but it will guarantee their collectability to a sufficient extent. Moreover, the debtor could sell the accounts to a new entity, a new firm, that would be the borrower from not just the loan officer's bank, but the bank syndicate she's putting together.

It'd work like this: A new corporation will be formed. The bank and the lending syndicate will own it. This new firm—the special purpose vehicle or SPV—will have one function, that of buying accounts receivable from the debtor. The debtor will make a residual guarantee to this special purpose entity to pay up to, say, 5% of the accounts that aren't fully collectible. The debtor will sell the accounts to the special purpose entity on a daily basis, and the special purpose entity would get funding from the banking syndicate overnight based on, say, 90 per cent of the value of the accounts receivable. A little care would be needed to make sure the transfer of the accounts receivable to the special purpose entity would be a true sale. A law firm would opine that the strings that enabled the bank to effectively put the risk of non-collection back onto the debtor were not so powerful that there was no sale. In fact, in time the bank syndicate might be replaced as the SPV's funder by the special purpose vehicle selling bonds to investors. Moreover, the debt wouldn't show up on the balance sheet of the originating company, because the special purpose vehicle, not the originating company, borrowed the money from the banks (or the bond market). (Even better: although the accounts receivable would be off the originator's books, the cash proceeds of the sale would be on the books.)

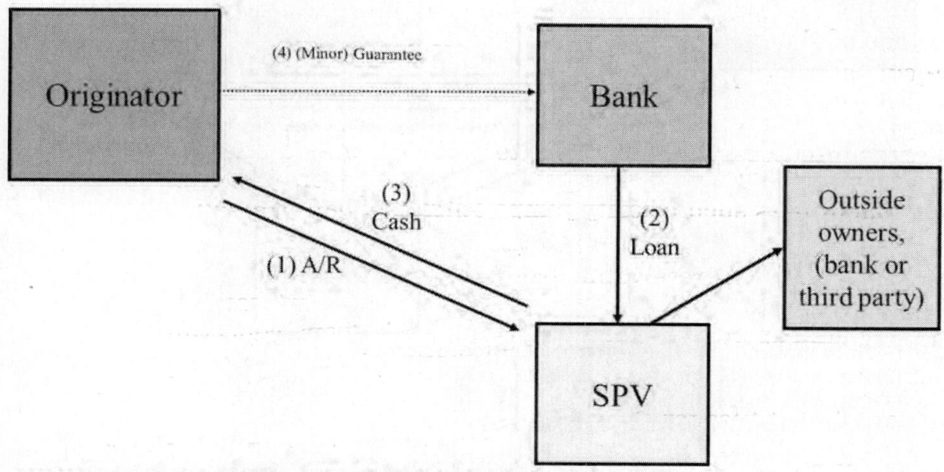

(1) Originator transfers Asset to SPV (True Sale Opinion needed).
(2) Bank loan to SPV.
(3) Cash distribution to Originator.
(4) Originator agrees to take back small number of uncollected A/R.

The SPV Buys Accounts Receivable from the Originator

And what would happen in a bankruptcy of the debtor? Well, if the sale-to-a-SPV all held up:

(a) The stay applicable to the debtor-originator would not apply to the SPV, which would be a separate company from the debtor, and it would also hopefully remain solvent and therefore not in bankruptcy.

(b) The bank with the loan to the SPV would not fear subordination to new DIP loans in the debtor-originator's bankruptcy under § 364, because the new lenders' claim would be against the debtor, not against the SPV.

(c) Even if the SPV went bankrupt, the bank syndicate wouldn't be competing against any other creditors. Indeed, it'd own the entity.

It'd be like a security interest, you tell the bank's loan officer. Only better.

Consider next the possibility that the parties are so happy with the structure that they expand its use. In some transactions, the SPV lender requests and obtains a substantial guarantee of SPV performance from the originator, Enron. If such a full guarantee is in place, what are the true economics of the transaction. Is the SPV lender really lending to the SPV or to Enron? Is Enron really selling the assets to the SPV (regardless of whether the sales document says they've been sold?)

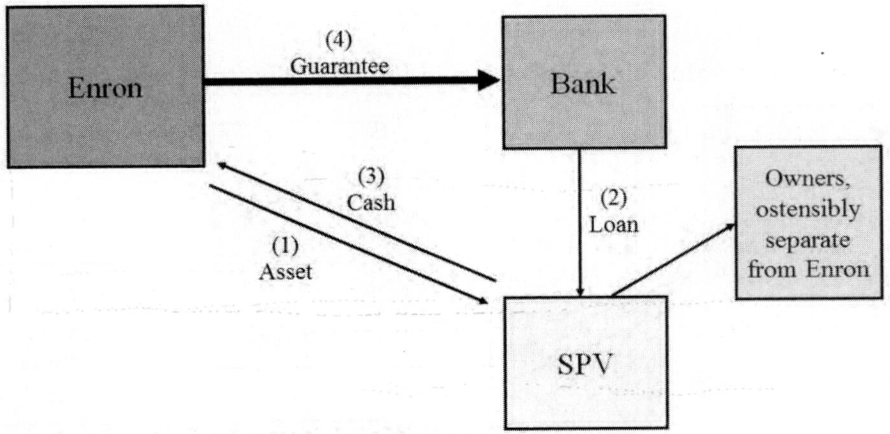

Has the SPV Truly Purchased the Originator's Accounts Receivable?

¶ 816: The Special Purpose Vehicle

Financiers of an SPV want the SPV kept separate from the originating firm, expecting that the SPV will not only be free from the risk of substantive consolidation in a bankruptcy of the originator (because it is so clearly a separate entity), but also that the SPV will be "bankruptcy remote:" even if the originator goes bankrupt, the SPV will not, allowing the SPV's own creditors to collect directly from the SPV.

Some analysts, however, see the SPV's bankruptcy remoteness as contestable. If the originating company is obliged to back up the SPV debt, then the SPVs could—and should, they say—be folded into the originator's bankruptcy and substantively consolidated. Or, if as a business matter, the originator's operations cannot be readily separated from the SPV's operations, then their interconnectedness could lead a bankruptcy court to pull the SPV into the originator's bankruptcy as well. (For example, the originator and the SPV could be viewed as partners, as joint venturers, see ¶ 1007, infra, or as inextricably connected.)

In LTV's bankruptcy, the bankruptcy remoteness of the steel company's SPV was challenged, but the case settled without a definitive result. In re LTV Steel, Inc. 2001 Bankr. LEXIS 131 (Bankr. N.D. Ohio Feb. 5, 2001). Nevertheless, the LTV cloud on SPV remoteness was seen to have raised SPV interest rates by a quarter of a point in the ensuing months. Kenneth Ayotte & Stav Gaon, *Asset–Backed Securities: Costs and Benefits of 'Bankruptcy Remoteness'*, 24 Review of Financial Studies 1299 (2010).

In a large 2009 real estate bankruptcy, the originator's bankruptcy petition included its SPVs, whose lenders had thought were "bankruptcy remote." The SPV creditors challenged the joint filing, but the judge allowed it, *In re General Growth Properties Inc.*, 409 B.R. 43 (Bankr. S.D.N.Y. 2009) (Gropper), and during the proceedings approved shifting some value out of some SPVs into other parts of the aggregated business, making members of a "corporate family" (the court's phrase) help one another. (The General Growth SPVs had operating assets, not passive financial assets, perhaps making those SPVs qualitatively different from many purely financial SPVs.) The judge did not question the legal separateness of the SPVs and signaled that he was not amenable to substantively consolidating the SPVs with the originator. The debtor's plan of reorganization largely fully paid all SPV creditors or reinstated them under §1124(2), and there was widespread creditor consent. The ultimate question of the SPV's bankruptcy remoteness (i.e., will the SPV's remoteness from the core company be compromised such that compensation in the plan changes?) has not been sharply tested.

The Enron SPV-based scandal loomed large in business and finance at the beginning of the last decade. Enron was a large natural gas and energy producer that collapsed in 2001 as the underlying fraud in its financial reporting came to light. It extensively used special purpose vehicles not just for straight-forward financing transactions outlined in the prior paragraphs in ¶ 815 but to obscure its true financial condition, moving debt off its balance sheet as a matter of form, even though Enron was still fully liable on the debt, and booking transfers to the SPVs as profitable sales, even though it had not really sold anything to an independent buyer. At the time of its collapse, Enron's market value made it one of the largest companies in the United States and its apparent (but fraudulent) rapid growth had made it a Wall Street darling. Many Enron transactions were the kind that are usually accompanied by lawyers' opinions attesting that the assets moving from the originator to the SPV were truly sold to the free-standing SPV and the resulting bankruptcy ensnared Enron's outside counsel. Public outrage at the Enron collapse and its underlying fraud contributed to the passage of the Sarbanes–Oxley Act of 2002, a major overhaul to corporate governance.

¶ 817: Asset Securitization

The asset securitization industry—of which Enron's effort was only a part—grew to multi-billion dollar size in only a short time.[7] A securitization transaction looks very much like the SPV transactions depicted in the figures above. The major difference is that instead of relying on bank lenders to finance the SPV's purchase of assets from the originator (like the accounts receivable in ¶ 815), the SPV sells debt securities to investors in public securities markets. The SPV uses the proceeds from the sale of securities to buy the assets from the originator, and public debt investors enjoy interest payments paid from the cash flow generated by the assets now owned by the SPV. The bond market has an investment with a predictable cash flow; the originator gets the cash. Everyone is happy.

[7] See Steven L. Schwarcz, Bruce A. Markell & Lissa Lamkin Broome, Securitization, Structured Finance and Capital Markets (2004), from which this section draws.

Maybe not everyone. The transferred assets are no longer available to the originator's other creditors. By the time the originator goes bankrupt the cash is presumably gone, so those unhappy creditors might try to get to the transferred assets by attacking the transfer as not really being a sale of the assets, or by seeking consolidation of the SPV with the originator. Lawyers are usually involved in assuring the creditors of the SPV that this—recharacterization as a non-sale or consolidation—won't happen. More about that below.

What made the originator, the SPV, and the investors happy, and what drives the burgeoning asset securitization market is the following. First off, it gives the company another source of financing. Instead of borrowing directly from a bank, the originator can segment the assets and get the lender to focus on those assets and not the rest of the originator's business. The lender to the SPV might charge less, partly because its loan is less risky and partly because the bond market can evaluate the SPV with a single type of asset more easily than it can evaluate the originator's overall business.[8] Second, the transaction gets cash into the originator (much like a secured borrowing would). Third, the originator gets the loan and the assets off of its balance sheet. Cosmetics sometimes are important.

While the securitization industry is big and many students reading this section are likely to be involved with it, the underlying legal structure is not rock solid. There's no definitive bankruptcy court opinion right on point guiding the players as to when the sale will be thought a non-sale, or when the SPV will be consolidated with the originator. Part of the reason is that few originators have thus far failed. Enron is exceptional and its structure, with multiple guarantees and buyback agreements with the originator (Enron) itself, went beyond industry practice.

Consider this interpretive conclusion as to whether a transfer to an SPV is a sale or a de facto loan:

> [R]ecourse is the most important aspect of risk allocation. . . . If the parties had intended a sale, then the buyer would have retained the risk of default, not the seller. The greater the recourse the SPV has against the Originator, . . . the more the transfer resembles a disguised loan rather than a sale. . . . Some courts view the presence of such a provision as nearly conclusive of the parties' intent to create a security interest [and not a true sale], while other view recourse as only one of a number of factors.

Kenneth Klee and Brendt Butler, *Asset-backed securitization, special purpose vehicles and other securitizations issues*, 35 Uniform Commercial Code Law Journal 23, 52 (2002).

In the proposed Bankruptcy Reform Act of 2001, some in Congress would have helped out the asset securitization industry by creating a

[8] The first possibility—that the loan is less risky—doesn't necessarily mean that the risk has disappeared. It may just mean that the risk is transferred to someone else's shoulders—either other creditors or the stockholders. They might charge for that extra risk if they understand it and, to the extent they do, this purported advantage disappears. Risk transfer is at the heart of finance theory, as discussed in Chapter 21's section on the Modigliani–Miller hypothesis.

safe harbor. The bill sought to bar bankruptcy courts from recharacterizing qualifying asset securitizations as loans to the originator, regardless of the true economics of the transaction. It would have overridden most of the preference and fraudulent conveyance avoidance powers in the Bankruptcy Code as applied to securitization transactions. The Act didn't pass, and perhaps Enron's collapse will stop anyone from trying again anytime soon.

Delaware—the home of most large American corporate charters—stepped in to try to protect asset securitizations: In 2002, it passed the Asset-Backed Securities Facilitation Act: "Any property, assets or right purported to be transferred . . . in the securitization transaction shall be deemed to no longer be the property, assets or rights of the transferor." And: "A transferor in the securitization transaction . . . or, in any insolvency proceeding with respect to the transferor or the transferor's property, a bankruptcy trustee, . . . shall have no rights, legal or equitable, . . . to reacquire . . . as property of the transferor any property, assets or rights purported to be transferred . . . by the transferor."

Delaware's law here hasn't yet been tested. It raises two fundamental aspects of bankruptcy: states usually define property rights, and Delaware purports to define those rights; but state law can't define how far the Bankruptcy Code's avoidance powers go, while Delaware purports to do this too. On the latter, consider Section 541 of the Bankruptcy Code:

§ 541. Property of the estate

(c)(1) . . . [A]n interest of the debtor in property becomes property of the estate . . . notwithstanding any provision in an agreement . . . or applicable non-bankruptcy law—

* * *

(B) that is conditioned on the insolvency or financial condition of the debtor, on the commencement of a case under this title, or on the appointment of or taking possession by a trustee in a case under this title . . . and that effects . . . a forfeiture, modification, or termination of the debtor's interest in the property.

Lawyers bump up against the bankruptcy securitization issues in two major ways. One way is when the bankrupt has securitized assets and their status in the chapter 11 is contested. Another is when lawyers are asked to give a true sale opinion when the assets move from the originator to the SPV. The bond buyers and the bond rating agencies want to be assured that the assets backing up their securities won't be pulled into a future bankruptcy of the originator. So the bond market wants an opinion of counsel that the SPV is indeed bankruptcy remote, that it won't be consolidated. This—issuing the "non-con" opinion—is where many lawyers nowadays review the bankruptcy consolidation cases and doctrines. The opinions are typically long on doctrine and detailed on the facts, typically concluding with something like:

> Based on the foregoing, and subject to the assumptions, qualifications and discussions contained herein and the reasoned analysis of analogous case law, it is our opinion that in the event that the [Originator] were to become a debtor in a case under the Bankruptcy Code, in a properly presented and argued case, a court of competent jurisdiction *would* recognize the separate existence of the [SPV] and the [Originator], and accordingly *would* not order the substantive consolidation of the assets and liabilities of the two.

Notice the italicized "would." Lawyers don't usually like to give such opinions as to what a court *would* do. They'd usually prefer to opine as to what a court *should* do and then, if the court doesn't, shrug their shoulders at the court's misunderstanding of the issues. Would is stronger, and that's what the bond market wants.

CHAPTER 9

RERANKING: PREFERENCES

A. PREFERENCES

¶ 901: Introduction to Preferences

To hold the bankrupt estate together, the Bankruptcy Code stays all creditors from collecting on their debts from the bankrupt. Before the bankruptcy ensues though, creditors could rush to twist the debtor's arm for repayment and the debtor may prefer to pay a stronger or more diligent creditor. To reduce the incentives for such a race, the Bankruptcy Code allows the bankrupt estate to recover these eve-of-bankruptcy payments that would otherwise frustrate the stay and the bankruptcy distribution scheme. Even payments to innocent creditors are not immune. The elements of a preference are stated in § 547(b), defenses are in § 547(c). From whom the preference can be recovered is delineated in § 550.

The basic elements of a preference are:

1. debtor makes a payment
2. within 90 days of the bankruptcy petition
3. on an antecedent debt
4. when the debtor is insolvent
5. that allows the recipient to collect more than otherwise (i.e., to be preferred).

Several defenses are listed in subsection (c); the key defense is that the trustee cannot recover payments made in the ordinary course of business.[1]

If there's a preference, the creditor returns the preference to the debtor. Its original claim is then left unsatisfied. Section 502, on the allowance of claims, says:

> (h) A claim arising from the recovery of property under section . . . 550 . . . shall be determined, and shall be allowed . . . or disallowed . . . as if such claim had arisen before the date of the filing of the petition.

¶ 902: Preference Problems

Preference basics can be seen better by reading the statute and then working through each of these problems:

> Example #0: Creditor lends $1000 to the debtor. Months pass. Creditor hears that the debtor's product is doing poorly, that it's laying off employees, and that it has hired bankruptcy counsel. The creditor begins collection proceedings against the debtor and obtains repayment one day before the debtor's bankruptcy. Is the repayment a preference?
>
> Example #1: Creditor is secured with good security and is paid off in full one day before bankruptcy, after the creditor made several collection calls. Is the repayment a preference?
>
> Example #2: Creditor has no security. It lent last year. Worried, it asks for payment. Debtor says "don't have the cash, but please take the security to make you comfortable with your antecedent debt." Creditor takes security. Next day the debtor goes bankrupt. Is the creditor's taking of security a preference?
>
> Example #3: Creditor has no security. Creditor also has made no loan prior to today. Today creditor lends to the debtor and takes full security, consisting of all the property of the debtor. Tomorrow the company goes bankrupt. Is the creditor's taking of security a preference?
>
> Example #4: The following events occur. Is the April payment a preference?

March 1:	Creditor ships goods to debtor, payable in 30 days.
April 1:	No payment comes. (Prior shipments were paid on time, and the industry practice is usually on-time payment.)
April 5:	Creditor's bookkeeper calls debtor, asks for payment.
April 5–10:	No payment.
April 10:	Bookkeeper calls, asks for payment.
April 15:	Debtor writes a check to pay for half of the goods.
April 20:	Check clears.
April 25:	Debtor files for bankruptcy.

---

[1] In 2005, Congress added what might be thought of as a "small transfer" exception, stopping the debtor from recovering a transfer of less than $5000.

Creditor is innocent and knows nothing of the debtor's insolvency and impending bankruptcy. The creditor has no influence on debtor. The creditor's bookkeeper was just making a credit collection call.

Example #5: Director lends $20,000 to her own company, when it has assets of $100,000 and other creditors are owed $20,000. Later, after the company's value has declined to $20,000, director pesters the bookkeeper and gets repaid. Is the repayment to the director a preference in the bankruptcy filed ***six*** months later?

¶ 903: Priority Equalizations Across Time Via Preference Rules: Lynn M. Lopucki & Christopher R. Mirick, Strategies for Creditors in Bankruptcy Proceedings 38–43 (6th ed. 2015)

§ 2.04 Avoidable preferences

Nonbankruptcy collection law encourages creditors to take action against a defaulting debtor. It does this by allowing priority in the distribution of the debtor's assets to unsecured creditors in . . . the order in which they . . . seize or encumber the debtor's property. In the absence of bankruptcy, the policy for distributing assets among previously unsecured creditors is essentially first in time, first in right.

Bankruptcy law, however, honors the maxim that "equality is equity" by favoring a distribution to unsecured creditors pro rata, in proportion to their claims. Asserting its supremacy over nonbankruptcy law, bankruptcy law seeks to impose its policy not only during bankruptcy cases, but also retroactively for a period of 90 days[2] before the filing of the bankruptcy petitions. It does this by giving the debtor in possession or the bankruptcy trustee the power to "avoid" transactions that took place during that period and that, if not set aside, would enable the creditors involved to fare better than others who simply waited to share pro rata in the bankruptcy case. Such transactions are "avoidable" as "preferences."

Some examples will help to illustrate that preference law is trying to prevent exactly what collection lawyers are trying to accomplish in the period before bankruptcy. In each of these examples it will be assumed that the debtor is insolvent at the time of the transaction[3] and that the debtor's bankruptcy estate is sufficient to pay unsecured creditors only a portion of what is owing:[4]

> **Example 1: Payment.** The debtor owes $10,000 to unsecured creditor C. C brings collection pressure, and as a result the debtor makes a partial payment of $6,000. Less than 90 days

[2] The period is one year if the recipient of the preferential transfer is an "insider." See Bankruptcy Code § 547(b)(4)(B).

[3] A transfer can be avoided as a preference only if the debtor was insolvent at the time it was made. See Bankruptcy Code §§ 547(b)(3) and 101[(32)]. There is a presumption of insolvency for purposes of Bankruptcy Code § 547. See Bankruptcy Code § 547(f).

[4] Full payment to an unsecured creditor in the period before bankruptcy would not be an avoidable preference if all unsecured creditors were paid in full in the bankruptcy case. See Bankruptcy Code § 547(b)(5). What is objectionable about the avoidable transfer is that it permits the creditor who received it to recover a greater portion of its debt than other creditors will recover of their debts.

later, the debtor files bankruptcy. The payment is probably an avoidable preference.[5]

Example 2: Grant of a security interest. The debtor owes $10,000 to unsecured creditor C. C brings collection pressure, and as a result the debtor grants C a mortgage or security interest against some of the debtor's property. C immediately perfects the interest by recording it in the appropriate public records. Less than 90 days after the recording, the debtor files bankruptcy. The grant is an avoidable preference.[6]

Example 3: Additional collateral. The debtor, D, owes $10,000 to C. C has a perfected security interest in the inventory of D's business. The inventory has a value of $6,000. D uses unencumbered cash to purchase $3,000 of additional inventory. The additional inventory automatically becomes additional collateral for the $10,000 debt as a result of an after acquired property clause in the security agreement. There is now $9,000 of collateral securing the debt to C. Less than 90 days after D acquired the additional inventory, D files bankruptcy. The addition of collateral to the security for this debt is an avoidable preference.

Example 4: Execution. The debtor, D, owes $10,000 to unsecured creditor C. C obtains a judgment against D and levies against D's property. The property is sold at a sheriff's sale and C is paid in full from the proceeds of sale. Less than 90 days after C acquired the execution lien against D's property, D files bankruptcy. The acquisition of the execution lien and the later payment to C are an avoidable preference.[7] Even if the debt had not been paid, the acquisition of the execution lien itself would have been an avoidable preference.

Notice that in each of these examples the transaction entered into, if not avoided, would have had the effect of enabling C to collect a greater portion of the debt owing to C than other unsecured creditors would collect of the debts owing to them. It is that improvement in position, as against other creditors, which preference law seeks to prevent. While the above examples included only payments and liens, virtually any kind of advantage that a creditor obtains from a debtor during the preference period is vulnerable to attack.

Over-secured creditors who acquired their liens prior to the preference period need not fear preference attack. The liens cannot be avoided because they are outside the preference period. Payments to such creditors cannot be avoided because they do not improve the creditors' positions. . . .

---

[5] See Bankruptcy Code § 547(b). However, some transfers which admittedly have a preferential effect are made unavoidable for policy reasons. The payment described here would not be an avoidable preference if the creditor could show that it was "made in the ordinary course of business." Bankruptcy Code § 547(c)(2). . . .

[6] "Transfer" includes the granting of a security interest. See Bankruptcy Code § 101[(54)].

[7] "Transfer" includes involuntary parting with an interest in property. See Bankruptcy Code § 101[(54)]. . . .

It is neither illegal nor improper for a debtor to make a preferential transfer or for a creditor to exact one. However, once the bankruptcy case has been filed, the trustee or the debtor in possession can sue to "avoid" the transfer and recover either the property transferred or its value.[8]

[A] Preference Avoidance: Strategic Implications

Unsecured creditors who extract a preferential payment or other transfer from a debtor should attempt to structure the transaction in such a way that the transfer will not be avoidable in a later bankruptcy. . . .

* * *

[Try to use the] ordinary course of business exception. Because payments made in the ordinary course of business on debts incurred in the ordinary course of business are excepted from preference recovery, the more "ordinary" the circumstances in which payments are made, the more likely they are to survive a preference attack. Some courts have held payments made under a "workout" agreement to have been made in the ordinary course of business, but others are less tolerant.[9] . . . The trend in the case law seems to be to focus on how often debts are paid in the manner in question in the particular industry.

* * *

Second, most improvements in the position of an unsecured creditor, whether by obtaining payment or security from the debtor, must be regarded as tentative until the preference period has expired. For example, a debtor who wishes to "buy time" from an unsecured creditor can enter into a settlement agreement with the creditor, make a substantial payment under the settlement agreement, take advantage of the forbearance thus purchased, then file a chapter 11 case, and, acting as debtor in possession, avoid the settlement and recover the payment.

Third, the tentative nature of payments or other benefits extracted from a debtor in financial difficulty must be taken into account in determining whether it will be cost effective to extract them. To illustrate: If a creditor estimates that it will take four months to file suit, obtain a judgment, and obtain a lien by levying on the debtor's property, the collection action can be expected to be futile if the debtor refuses to settle and files bankruptcy within seven months.[10] If an attempt at collection was considered marginal before the avoidability of preferences was taken into account, this additional period of exposure to risk may tip the balance against making the attempt.

Fourth, since many of the debtor's transactions with creditors only become unavoidable 91 days after they are made, other creditors have

[8] See Bankruptcy Code § 550(a).

[9] In re Xonics Imaging, Inc., 837 F.2d 763 (7th Cir. 1988) (the mere fact that payments are late may take them outside the "ordinary course" exception). . . .

[10] It will take four months for the collection to be completed. . . . [I]t will be avoidable in a bankruptcy proceeding field within three months thereafter, making a total of seven months.

the opportunity to discover, interpret, and respond to these transactions before they become irreversible. In particular, by observing the pattern of transfers that a debtor makes in the period before bankruptcy, an unsecured creditor may be able to reliably predict the date on which the debtor will file its voluntary petition and adjust its own strategy accordingly. For example, if the debtor has given a mortgage or security interest to secure a debt owing to a friendly creditor, the debtor probably will not file a bankruptcy case until the preference period on that transfer has expired. On the other hand, if an unfriendly creditor has exacted a substantial preference from a debtor, perhaps by obtaining a judgment lien, there will be a tendency for that debtor to file bankruptcy before the end of the preference period for that transfer. A creditor who discovers that its debtor has made preferential transfers of substantial size should consider filing an involuntary bankruptcy[11] petition against the debtor or demanding a share of the preferential transfers from the recipient for not doing so.

Fifth, until the preference period has expired, a creditor that has received a transfer that may be avoidable should be less willing to take aggressive action that might precipitate the debtor's bankruptcy. Debtors sometimes make preferential transfers to aggressive creditors specifically for the purpose of mollifying them.

The Code's legislative history explains basic preference policy:

> The purpose of the preference section is two-fold. First, by permitting the trustee to avoid prebankruptcy transfers that occur within a short period before bankruptcy, creditors are discouraged from racing to the courthouse to dismember the debtor during the slide into bankruptcy. The protection thus afforded the debtor often enables him to work his way out of a difficult financial situation through cooperation with all of his creditors. Second, and more important, the preference provisions facilitate the prime bankruptcy policy of equality of distribution among creditors of the debtor. Any creditor that received a greater payment than other of his class is required to disgorge so that all may share equally.

House Report No. 595, 95th Cong., 1st Sess. 117–18 (1977).

¶ 904: Preference Exceptions

Section 547(c) enumerates the preference exceptions, which offer a "safe harbor" for some preferences.

1. *Ordinary Course Exception*. The most important preference exception is the ordinary course of business exception (§ 547(c)(2)):

> (c) The trustee may not avoid under this section a transfer—
>
> (2) to the extent that such transfer was in payment of a debt incurred by the debtor in the ordinary course of business or fi-

[11] [See Bankruptcy Code, §303. – Roe.]

nancial affairs of the debtor and the transferee, and such transfer was—

(A) made in the ordinary course of business or financial affairs of the debtor and the transferee; or

(B) made according to ordinary business terms.

2. *Floating Lien Exception*. Section 547(c)(5) contains a special exception for "floating liens" on inventory and accounts receivable. A business that sells goods, say lumber, will regularly receive shipments of inventory for resale. It may take the goods on credit, giving a security interest to the lender. The Uniform Commercial Code allows "floating" liens, in which a secured creditor takes a lien in the "pool" of lumber, although the contents of the "pool" might change daily. From the bankruptcy perspective, each new receipt of lumber by the debtor is a transfer of a new security interest that benefits the secured creditor, even though the parties would have executed their security agreement and the creditor would have perfected its security interest at an earlier point. Section 547(e)(3) explains that for preference purposes, "a transfer is not made until the debtor has acquired rights in the property transferred." So the debtor can transfer security interests in the lumber only as it acquires rights in each lumber shipment. All the lumber shipped to the debtor in the 90 days before bankruptcy benefits the secured creditor, setting up a preference situation.

Ninety days before the bankruptcy, the lumber may be worth, say, $100,000. The total value may stay more or less constant for the 90 days, but the actual physical lumber on the day of bankruptcy may differ completely from the lumber in the lumberyard 90 days before because lumber was sold to customers and new lumber came in from the suppliers. Is each new shipment from a supplier a potential preference?

Assuming each transfer of lumber satisfies the § 547(b) requirements for a preference, § 547(c)(5) excepts some portion of the floating lien from preference attack. Preferential liens on inventory and accounts receivable are avoidable only to the extent the creditor improves its aggregate position during the 90 day period before bankruptcy (one year for insiders). "Improvement" here is measured by comparing the insufficiency of the secured creditor's security, if any, on the first day of the preference period with its deficiency on the petition date. To the extent any deficiency in its collateral coverage is smaller on the petition date than it was on the first day of the preference period (i.e., to the extent the secured creditor's collateral coverage improved during the preference period), security interests must be avoided to wipe out that improvement. If there is no improvement—that is, if the secured creditor's deficiency is at least as large on the petition date as it was on the first day of the preference period—then there is no avoidance.

3. *Delayed Perfection and the PMSI Exception*. With a typical secured loan, the loan agreement and its associated security agreement are executed at the same time. One might think the security interest in this scenario would therefore never raise an antecedent debt issue

for preference purposes. However, in general, the transfer of a security interest dates from its *perfection* date (§ 547(e)(2)(B)), not the date the agreement is created between the parties. Perfection normally entails a public filing. Section 547 does offer a 30-day grace period for that public filing to happen.

In addition to this grace period, there is a separate exception for certain purchase money security interests in § 547(c)(3). A purchase money loan is a loan to the debtor that enables it to buy new property. The lender's lien on the newly acquired property securing the purchase money loan is called a purchase money security interest (or PMSI). Ordinarily, when a secured lender files its financing statement with the public entities (or otherwise perfects) after expiration of the § 547(e)(2)(A) 30-day grace period, the security interest is deemed to have been given on an antecedent debt, subjecting the lien to the possibility of preference avoidance, assuming the other § 547(b) requirements are met.

Section 547(c)(3) rescues such late-filed purchase money security interests from preference attack, as long as the security interest is given at the time the loan is made and the secured lender gets its act together and files within 30 days of the debtor's receiving possession of the property:

§ 547. Preferences

(c) The trustee *may not* avoid under this section a transfer—

* * *

(3) that creates a security interest in property acquired by the debtor

(A) to the extent such security interest secures new value that was

(i) given at or after the signing of a security agreement that contains a description of such property as collateral;

* * *

(iii) given to enable the debtor to acquire such property; and

(iv) in fact used by the debtor to acquire such property; and

(B) that is perfected on or before 30 days after the debtor receives possession of such property[.]

---

4. *Postpetition Perfection?* Could a lender obtain (and "perfect," in the secured transaction vocabulary) its security interest *after* the debtor filed for bankruptcy, as long as the 30–day period hasn't run out? The creditor faces a steep problem, namely the bankruptcy stay in § 362, which bars all collection activities after the petition is filed.

In addition, § 544(a) creates the trustee's "strong-arm" avoidance power. It gives the trustee the rights of a judgment creditor on the date of bankruptcy. Judgment creditors (usually) beat unfiled, unperfected security interests. Hence, as of the date of the petition in bankruptcy, § 544(a) would enable the trustee or DIP to avoid all unperfected security interests. (This section is a bankruptcy aficionado's favorite because it creates intricacies in statutory construction.)

§ 544. Trustee as lien creditor . . .

(a) The trustee shall have, as of the commencement of the case . . . the rights and powers of, or may avoid any transfer of property of the debtor or any obligation incurred by the debtor that is voidable by

(1) a creditor that extends credit to the debtor at the time of the commencement of the case, and that obtains, at such time and with respect to such credit, a judicial lien on all property on which a creditor on a simple contract could have obtained such a judicial lien, whether or not such a creditor exists;

(2) a creditor that extends credit to the debtor at the time of the commencement of the case, and obtains, at such time and with respect to such credit, an execution against the debtor that is returned unsatisfied at such time, whether or not such a creditor exists; . . .

Thus the Bankruptcy Code as a general rule both bars the postpetition filing of the prepetition security interest (§ 362) and gives the trustee authority to avoid unperfected security interests (§ 544). (The debt exists, but the trustee need not respect the unfiled security interest.)

However, the creditor can surmount these two barriers in some states, because there's an interplay between state law and the Bankruptcy Code here.

Section 546 denies the trustee power to avoid some transfers that it could otherwise avoid under § 544. Recall that the general state law rule regarding conflicting security interests in the same collateral is a first-in-time rule—the first creditor to perfect its security interest, usually by filing notice, enjoys first priority in the collateral.

Section 546 says that the trustee *cannot* set aside an unperfected security interest *if* state law allows subsequent perfection to completion of the security interest to beat creditors that lent before the security interest was completed. So if the secured creditor is lending in a *state* that gives the secured creditor a 30–day grace period for filing, then § 546(b) says the trustee *can't* use § 544 to set aside the security interest.

(States that have adopted the updated, 2010 Uniform Commercial Code give a 20–day grace period, via U.C.C. § 317(e).)

§ 546. Limitations on avoiding powers

(b) (1) The rights and powers of a trustee under section[ ] 544 . . . are subject to any generally applicable [state] law that

(A) permits perfection of an interest in property *to be effective against an entity that acquires rights in such property before* the date of perfection. . . .

This exception would get the trustee past § 544 *if* the trustee were free to file the security interest after the bankruptcy petition were filed. But so far we haven't gotten the creditor past the § 362 stay. Section 546 only says that the secured creditor wins under § 544 *if* state law gives a grace period, but neither § 544 nor § 546 lifts the stay. So far, it works for creditors who are late, but who perfect their security interest before the debtor files for bankruptcy.

But another exception lifts the stay if the creditor's priority would be shielded by § 546:

§ 362. Automatic stay

(b) The filing of a petition . . . does *not* operate as a stay—

* * *

(3) . . . of any act to perfect . . . an interest in property to the extent that the trustee's rights and powers are subject to such perfection under section 546(b). . . .

So, if underlying state law gives a 30–day grace period, then the trustee can't set aside the subsequently perfected incomplete security interest under § 544 (because of the § 546(b) exception to the trustee's avoiding powers) and the stay is lifted (via the § 362(b)(3) exception to the stay), allowing the creditor to rush to file within the 30 days even if there's an intervening bankruptcy.

¶ 905: Indirect Preferences

Example #6: Senior secured is, and has always been, fully secured, and is owed $10,000. There's a junior secured due $10,000. (The junior secured does not have a subordination arrangement on the debt but on the security. It can claim out of the security after the senior secured is paid in full, with the senior secured getting first crack at the security.) On February 23rd, when the security is worth $15,000, the debtor gets a collection call from the senior's bookkeeper, who says the debtor is late in paying the loan off. The debtor then writes a check for $10,000 to the senior.

Is the payment on February 23rd a preference in the bankruptcy filed on March 1?

(1) Debtor, before payment:

$15,000 security	Senior secured	$10,000
$10,000 cash	Junior secured	$10,000
	Unsecured	$20,000

(2) Debtor pays senior with cash, then goes bankrupt. Debtor, after payment:

$15,000 security	Junior secured	$10,000
Preference claim?	Unsecured	$20,000

B. INTERCORPORATE PREFERENCES

Do creditors of a subsidiary have special reason to fear mistreatment in the year before the subsidiary's filing for bankruptcy? Consider the *Deprizio* decision below, which although not a corporate group setting is instructive, and the 1994 amendments to § 550 in ¶ 908, which overturned the *Deprizio* holding but didn't eliminate the "*Deprizio* problem." It just changed who wins and who loses.

¶ 906: Deprizio Construction Co. v. Ingersoll Rand Financial Corp., 874 F.2d 1186 (7th Cir. 1989)

EASTERBROOK, Circuit Judge.

We must decide a question no other appellate court has addressed: whether payments to creditors who dealt at arms' length with a debtor are subject to the yearlong preference-recovery period that 11 U.S.C. § 547(b)(4)(B) provides for "inside" creditors, when the payments are "for the benefit of" insiders, § 547(b)(1). The bankruptcy court in this case answered "no," and the district court "yes." We agree with the district court. . . .

I

In 1980 V.N. Deprizio Construction Co. was awarded contracts to do $13.4 million of work on the extension of Chicago's subway system to O'Hare Airport. By 1982 the company was in financial trouble. Because Mayor Byrne wanted the line open before the primary election for that office in February 1983, the City made the firm extraordinary loans of $2.5 million; the firm in turn donated $3,000 to the Mayor's campaign fund. Neither outlay achieved its purpose. The line wasn't finished on time, and Byrne lost. These and other dealings by Richard N. Deprizio, the firm's president, including suspicions of affiliation with organized crime, led the United States Attorney to open an investigation. In April 1983, Deprizio Co. filed a petition under the Bankruptcy Code of 1978. Other firms finished the subway, which opened in 1984.

As the investigation continued and Deprizio's indictment was imminent, word circulated that he might "sing." So in January 1986 Deprizio was lured to a vacant parking lot, where an assassin's gun and the obligations of a life-time were discharged together. Corporations are not so easily liquidated.

Deprizio Co. had borrowed money from many sources other than the City of Chicago, including [several banks]. Richard Deprizio and his brothers . . . , all insiders of the firm, also guaranteed its debts to other lenders. ("Insider," a term to which we return, includes officers of the debtor and the officers' relatives.)

As the district court observed "the record is devoid of detail" concerning these guarantees. Details are potentially important. . . .

Payments out of the ordinary course in the 90 days before filing a bankruptcy petition may be recovered for the estate under §§ 547 and 550. Creditors then receive shares determined by statutory priorities and contractual entitlements rather than by their ability to sneak in under the wire. Payments to or for the benefit of an insider during a full year, not just 90 days, may be recovered [for the bankrupt] by virtue of § 547(b)(4)(B). The Trustee filed adversary proceedings against the lenders . . . —none of them insiders—seeking to recover payments made more than 90 days but within the year before the filing. The Trustee reasoned that the payments made to these outside creditors were "for the benefit" of inside co-signers and guarantors, because every dollar paid to the outside creditor reduced the insider's exposure by the same amount.

The district court concluded that payment is only one transfer, although a transfer may create benefits for many persons. If the insider receives a benefit, then the transfer is avoidable under § 547(b)(4)(B) if made within a year of the bankruptcy and does not qualify for the exclusions in § 547(c). (These include payments in the ordinary course of business, payments for equivalent value received, and so on.) Section 550(a), as Judge Plunkett read it, allows the Trustee to recover the transfer from either the recipient or the indirect beneficiary, at the Trustee's option. The district court remanded the case so that the bankruptcy court could determine whether the payments identified by the Trustee occurred, whether an insider received a benefit from any particular payment, and whether any of them was protected by § 547(c). . . . [W]e granted leave to appeal.

II

Many bankruptcy and district judges have addressed the question we confront, as have commentators. A majority of judges have concluded that insiders' guarantees do not expose outside lenders to an extended preference-recovery period, frequently because they believe that recovery would be inequitable when ordinarily outside creditors need restore only preferences received within the 90 days before bankruptcy. The commentators are evenly divided.

A

Six sections of the Bankruptcy Code supply the texts. Section 547(b) says:

> . . . [T]he trustee may avoid any transfer of an interest of the debtor in property -
>
> (1) to or for the benefit of a creditor;
>
> (2) for or on account of an antecedent debt owed by the debtor before such transfer was made;
>
> (3) made while the debtor was insolvent;
>
> (4) made --
>
> (A) on or within 90 days before the date of the filing of the petition; or
>
> (B) between ninety days and one year before the date of the filing of the petition, if such creditor at the time of such transfer was an insider; and
>
> (5) that enables such creditor to receive more than such creditor would receive if --
>
> (A) the case were a case under Chapter 7 of this title;
>
> (B) the transfer had not been made; and
>
> (C) such creditor received payment of such debt to the extent provided by the provisions of this title.

This is § 547(b) as amended in 1984. . . .

Section 547(b) uses three terms of art: "creditor," "insider," and "transfer," and the definition of "creditor" brings in a fourth: "claim." Section 101 defines each.

> [5] "claim" means --
>
> (A) right to payment, whether or not such right is reduced to judgment, liquidated, unliquidated, fixed, contingent, matured, unmatured, disputed, undisputed, legal, equitable, secured, or unsecured; . . .
>
> [10] "creditor" means --
>
> (A) entity that has a claim against the debtor that arose at the time of or before the order for relief concerning the debtor; . . .
>
> [31] "insider" includes --
>
> . . .
>
> (B) if the debtor is a corporation --
>
> (i) director of the debtor;
>
> (ii) officer of the debtor;

(iii) person[12] in control of the debtor;

. . .

(vi) relative of a general partner, director, officer, or person in control of the debtor;

. . .

[54] "transfer" means every mode, direct or indirect, absolute or conditional, voluntary or involuntary, of disposing of or parting with property or with an interest in property, including retention of title as a security interest . . .

Finally there is § 550, which specifies who is liable for a transfer avoided under § 547:

(a) Except as otherwise provided in this section, to the extent that a transfer is avoided under section . . . 547, . . . the trustee may recover, for the benefit of the estate, the property transferred, or, if the court so orders, the value of such property, from

(1) the initial transferee of such transfer or the entity for whose benefit such transfer was made; or

(2) any immediate or mediate transferee of such initial transferee.

(b) The trustee may not recover under section (a)(2) of this section from

(1) a transferee that takes for value, including satisfaction or securing of a present or antecedent debt, in good faith, and without knowledge of the voidability of the transfer avoided; or

(2) any immediate or mediate good faith transferee of such transferee.

[(d)] The trustee is entitled to only a single satisfaction under subsection (a) of this section.[13]

The Trustee's argument for extended recovery from outside creditors flows directly from these interlocked provisions.

Suppose Firm borrows money from Lender, with payment guaranteed by Firm's officer (Guarantor). Section 101[(31)](B)(ii) renders Guarantor an "insider." Guarantor is not Firm's creditor in the colloquial sense, but under § 101[(10)] of the Code any person with a "claim" against Firm is a "creditor," and anyone with a contingent right to payment holds a "claim" under § 101[(5)](A). A guarantor has a contingent right to payment from the debtor: if Lender collects from

[12] [Section 101(41) says " 'person' includes individual, partnership, and corporation, but does not include [a] governmental unit." Hence a holding company would be a "person."—Roe & Tung.]

[13] [In 1994, several years after *Deprizio*, Congress amended § 550, by adding § 550(c):

If a transfer made between 90 days and one year before the filing of the petition

(1) is avoided under section 547(b) of this title; and

(2) was made for the benefit of a creditor that at the time of such transfer was an insider;

the trustee may not recover under subsection (a) from a transferee that is not an insider.

See notes after the case.—Roe & Tung.]

Guarantor, Guarantor succeeds to Lender's entitlements and can collect from Firm. So Guarantor is a "creditor" in Firm's bankruptcy. A payment ("transfer") by Firm to Lender is "for the benefit of" Guarantor under § 547(b)(1) because every reduction in the debt to Lender reduces Guarantor's exposure. Because the payment to Lender assists Guarantor, it is avoidable under § 547(b)(4)(B) unless one of the exemptions in § 547(c) applies. Once the transfer is avoided under § 547, the Trustee turns to § 550 for authority to recover. Section 547(b)(4) distinguishes according to [whether Guarantor is an "insider"], but [at the time we are deciding this appeal] § 550 does not.[14] It says that if a transfer is recoverable by the trustee, it may be recovered from either the "initial transferee" (Lender) or the "entity for whose benefit such transfer was made" (Guarantor). So Lender may have to repay transfers received during the year before filing, even though Lender is not an insider.

Judge Plunkett accepted this chain of reasoning. The creditors seek to break it. . . .

III

Now for the principal question: whether the Trustee may recover from an outside creditor under § 550(a)(1) a transfer more than 90 days before the filing that is avoided under § 547(b) because of a benefit for an inside creditor. The textual argument, which we have already given, is simple. Section 547(b) defines which transfers are "avoidable." No one doubts that a transfer to Lender produces a "benefit" for Guarantor. After § 547 defines which transfers may be avoided, § 550(a) identifies who is responsible for payment: "the initial transferee of such transfer or the entity for whose benefit such transfer was made." This gives the trustee the option to collect from Lender, Guarantor, or both, subject only to the proviso in § 550([d]) that there can be but one satisfaction.

More than language lies behind this approach. The trustee's power to avoid preferences (the "avoiding power") is essential to make the bankruptcy case a collective proceeding for the determination and payment of debts. Any individual creditor has a strong incentive to make off with the assets of a troubled firm, saving itself at potential damage to the value of the enterprise. Many a firm is worth more together than in pieces, and a spate of asset grabbing by creditors could dissipate whatever firm-specific value the assets have. Like fishers in a common pool, creditors logically disregard the fact that their self-protection may diminish aggregate value—for if Creditor A does not lay claim to the assets, Creditor B will, and A will suffer for inaction. All creditors gain from a rule of law that induces each to hold back. The trustee's avoiding powers serve this end in two ways: first, they eliminate the benefit of attaching assets out of the ordinary course in the last 90 days before the filing, so that the rush to dismember a firm is not profitable from a creditor's perspective; second, the avoiding

[14] [Section 550 did not so distinguish at the time *Deprizio* was decided. In 1994, subsequent to the decision, Congress amended § 550 to so distinguish. See notes after the case.—Roe & Tung.]

powers assure each creditor that if it refrains from acting, the pickings of anyone less civil will be fetched back into the pool. See Thomas H. Jackson, Avoiding Powers in Bankruptcy, 36 Stan. L. Rev. 725, 727–31, 756–68 (1984).

How long should this preference-recovery period be? If one outside creditor knows that the firm is in trouble, others will too. Each major lender monitors both the firm and fellow lenders. If it perceives that some other lender is being paid preferentially, a major lender can propel Firm into bankruptcy. Reasonably alert lenders can act with sufficient dispatch to ensure that the perceived preference is recoverable even when the preference period is short. Section 547(b) makes 90 days the rule, time enough (Congress concluded) for careful creditors to protect themselves (and when one does, small unsecured trade creditors get the benefits too).

Insiders pose special problems. Insiders will be the first to recognize that the firm is in a downward spiral. If insiders and outsiders had the same preference-recovery period, insiders who lent money to the firm could use their knowledge to advantage by paying their own loans preferentially, then putting off filing the petition in bankruptcy until the preference period had passed. Outside creditors, aware of this risk, would monitor more closely, or grab assets themselves (fearing that the reciprocity that is important to the pooling scheme has been destroyed), or precipitate bankruptcy at the smallest sign of trouble, hoping to "catch" inside preferences before it is too late. All of these devices could be costly. An alternative device is to make the preference-recovery period for insiders longer than that for outsiders. With a long period for insiders, even the prescient managers who first see the end coming are unlikely to be able to prefer themselves in distribution.

Loans from insiders to their firms are not the only, or even the most important, concern of outside creditors. Insiders frequently guarantee other loans. If the firm folds while these loans are outstanding, the insiders are personally liable. So insiders bent on serving their own interests (few managers hold outside lenders' interests of equal weight with their own!) could do so by inducing the firm to pay the guaranteed loans preferentially. If the preference-recovery period for such payments were identical to the one for outside debts, this would be an attractive device for insiders. While concealing the firm's true financial state, they would pay off (at least pay down) the debts they had guaranteed, while neglecting others. To the extent they could use private information to do this more than 90 days ahead of the filing in bankruptcy, they would come out like bandits. The guaranteed loans would be extinguished, and with them the guarantees. True, it is logically possible to recover from the insider the value of the released guarantee, even if the trustee could not reach the proceeds in the hands of the outside lender. But it is hard to determine the value of a released guarantee, and anyway insiders might think that they would be more successful resisting the claims of the trustee than the hounds of the outside creditors. So an extended recovery period for payments to outside creditors that benefit insiders could contribute to the ability of the bankruptcy process to deter last-minute grabs of assets. The outsiders who must kick into the pool when the trustee uses the avoiding powers retain their contractual entitlements; all the trustee's recovery does is ensure that those entitlements (as modified by any statutory priorities)—rather than the efforts of insiders to protect their own interests, or the cleverness of outsiders in beating the 90–day deadline—determine the ultimate distribution of the debtor's net assets.

A

* * *

The parties agree that there is no helpful legislative history. . . .

. . . An extended recovery period is consistent with the structure of the Code and does not subvert any of its functions. A longer period when insiders reap benefits by preferring one outside creditor over another facilitates the operation of bankruptcy as a collective process and ensures that each creditor will receive payment according to the Code's priorities and non-bankruptcy entitlements. Silence in the legislative history therefore does not require or authorize a court to depart from the text and structure of the Code.

B

The creditors do not argue that even if the Code extends the preference period, the extension should not be enforced because [it is] "inequitable." Perhaps our rebuff to "equity" arguments in other bankruptcy cases is responsible. . . .

Nonetheless, "equity" arguments have captivated a majority of the bankruptcy judges and several of the commentators who have spoken on this subject. . . . So it is worth pointing out that even if equity arguments were admissible, they would not help the creditors' cause. Rules of law affecting parties to voluntary arrangements do not operate "inequitably" in the business world—at least not once the rule is understood. Prices adjust. If the extended preference period facilitates the operation of bankruptcy as a collective debt-adjustment process, then credit will become available on slightly better terms. If a longer period has the opposite effect, creditors will charge slightly higher rates of interest and monitor debtors more closely. In either case creditors will receive the competitive rate of return in financial markets—the same risk-adjusted rate they would have received with a 90–day preference-recovery period. A rule may injure debtors and creditors by foreclosing efficient business arrangements and increasing the rate of interest low-risk borrowers must pay, . . . but inefficiency is not inequity. At all events, in what sense is it "inequitable" to recapture payments to creditors that may have been favored only because payment reduced insiders' exposure (recall that the insiders select which debts to pay first), then distribute these monies according to statutory priorities and contractual entitlements? In what sense is it "inequitable" to require the outside lenders to pursue the inside guarantors for any shortfall, when they bargained for exactly that recourse?

Our creditors press a cousin to "equity" arguments: "policy" arguments. According to the creditors, an extended preference period will force lenders to precipitate bankruptcy filings at the slightest sign of trouble in order to prevent erosion of their positions. The lenders paint a bleak picture of firms driven under when the problems could have been worked out—if only the lenders knew that they would keep what they receive in the "workout." Workouts often involve guarantees, and if these mean longer preference periods, then workouts may become less common (and formal bankruptcy more common). . . .

For what it may be worth, we doubt that an extended preference-recovery period will cause a stampede from workouts to bankruptcies. Unless there is a "preference," there is nothing for the trustee to avoid. Most of the tales of woe presented by the creditors do not involve preferences in light of § 547(b)(5), which says that a transfer is a preference only to the extent the creditor got more than it would have received in a liquidation, and § 547(c), which specifies situations that do not create avoidable preferences.

* * *

Consider some of the transactions the lenders use to illustrate what they view as pernicious consequences of an extended preference-recovery period:

- A fully-secured creditor with an insider's guarantee to boot is paid off nine months before bankruptcy and releases its security interest. The debtor uses the property as security for a new loan. The trustee recovers the payment as a preference, and the creditor has been stripped of its security.

- The trustee confronts two obstacles in such a case. First, if the creditor was fully secured, then payment does not produce a benefit for the inside guarantor, whose exposure was zero. The preference-recovery period therefore would be only 90 days. Second, under § 547(b)(5) a transfer is avoidable only to the extent the creditor received more than it would have in a Chapter 7 liquidation. A fully-secured creditor will be paid in full under Chapter 7, so there is no avoidable preference in this case with or without a guarantee by an insider. If, on the other hand, the security covered only 90% of the debt, then only the remaining 10% of the payment is avoidable as a preference.

* * *

- A creditor makes an unsecured loan guaranteed by an insider and requires monthly payments over a number of years. The trustee seeks to recover all of the payments during the year before the filing. To the extent the debtor paid on time, the creditor is protected by . . . § 547(c)(2), the "ordinary course rule." . . .

* * *

In light of these exclusions, there is no reason to use ambulatory arguments of "equity" or "policy" to defeat the Trustee's claims in this case. Congress has considered and addressed specifically the situations that most concern lenders. If these exclusions and exemptions are not "enough," creditors should complain to Congress.

IV

To sum up: . . . We hold in Part III that the preference-recovery period for outside creditors is one year when the payment produces a benefit for an inside creditor, including a guarantor.

The judgments of the district court are affirmed in part and reversed in part. The cases are remanded for further proceedings consistent with this opinion.

¶ 907: *Deprizio* Exercise

The following problem is best resolved after fully understanding *Deprizio*.

> At Time (1), Subsidiary, a chemical company, borrows $10,000 from Chemical Bank, which understands the chemical business. The bank seeks a tight dividend covenant, but the holding company managers, who want to be able to pull cash up from subsidiaries with a bad future and invest that cash in subsidiaries with a good future, like its computer subsidiary, resist the tight dividend covenant. The debtor and the bank strike a deal to use a slack (but not trivial) dividend covenant in the loan agreement and for the holding company to guarantee Chemical Bank that the holding company will pay up if the chemical subsidiary doesn't. The chemical subsidiary has $50,000 in assets and owes $5,000 to other creditors.
>
> Later, at time (2), the chemical subsidiary declines in value. When its operations are worthless and it only has $10,000 left in its own bank account, the loan officer seeks repayment. He threatens lawsuit, he calls up the holding company's CFO, and the CFO tells the subsidiary's bookkeeper to pay off the bank. Finally, at time (3) the bookkeeper writes the check out to the bank.
>
> Six months later, the subsidiary files for bankruptcy. The other creditors of the subsidiary are unhappy. Was the $10,000 payment to Chemical Bank preferential under § 547(b)?

(1)

Holding company

Assets	Guarantee to Chemical Bank
C/S of Chemical Subsidiary	
C/S of Computer Subsidiary	

Chemical Subsidiary

$50,000	$10,000 Chemical Bank
	$ 5,000 Creditor X

Computer Subsidiary

(2)

Holding company	
Assets C/S of Chemical Subsidiary C/S of Computer Subsidiary	Guarantee to Chemical Bank

Chemical Subsidiary	
$10,000	$10,000 Chemical Bank $ 5,000 Creditor X

Computer Subsidiary	

(3) Subsidiary pays the bank the $10,000 cash, then files for bankruptcy six months later:

Holding company	
Assets C/S of Chemical Subsidiary C/S of Computer Subsidiary	[Guarantee to Chemical Bank]

Chemical Subsidiary	
0	$5,000 Creditor X

Computer Subsidiary	

¶ 908: *Deprizio* Issues

1. How is a preference to an insider treated differently from a preference to an outsider? Why is an insider preference treated differently than an ordinary preference?
2. Were the financial creditors of the Deprizio Corporation insiders? If they weren't, was Richard Deprizio, the principal guarantor, an insider? Must he be a creditor for the insider provisions to be triggered? Did Mr. Deprizio hold a *contingent* claim against the company? Did that make him a creditor of the subsidiary? See the Code's definitions of claim and creditor in § 101. Is the holding company in ¶ 907 an insider? Is it a person in control of the debtor?
3. If the lender is not an insider, what's the point of making it "pay" for the insider's guarantee by subjecting it to the more severe preference period? Was the statute badly drafted? Or is there a plausible policy basis behind the court's reading of the statute? What did the Seventh Circuit say in *Deprizio*?
4. Is a guarantor always a creditor? Normally a guarantor is subrogated to the loans she pays off. That is, she takes over the loan she has paid off for the debtor, and she can assert the original creditor's claim against the debtor. Is she therefore a creditor, holding a contingent claim against the underlying debtor even before she takes over the loan? Are payments to the creditor payments for the benefit of an insider?
5. Ordinary course payments are excepted from the bite of § 547(c)(2). As a company slides to bankruptcy, it's not unusual for the firm and its creditors to recapitalize, to have a "work-out" of its debts.

The debtor may agree to close one unprofitable factory and use the proceeds to pay off some portion of a major creditor's loan, in return for the major creditor's promise not to accelerate and demand repayment in full. That kind of payment will usually be out of the ordinary course of business.

How about regular payments of interest under a long-term loan? Do they come under the "ordinary course" exception? Appellate Circuits split, with the Ninth Circuit (for a time) concluding that long-term creditors could not use the ordinary course exception, which the court apparently limited to the debtor's ordinary purchases that gave rise to a short-term debt, which, if paid in a timely manner, would get the ordinary course exception. In re CHG Int'l, Inc. 897 F.2d 1479 (9th Cir. 1990). The Supreme Court took certiorari, read the words of the statute, and concluded that there was no reason why payments on long-term debt were necessarily out-of-the-ordinary, or necessarily ordinary. Facts and circumstances need to be examined. Union Bank v. Herbert Wolas, 502 U.S. 151 (1991).

Judge Scalia concurred in a single paragraph opinion that stated: "It is regrettable that we have a legal culture in which such arguments [from legislative history and policy] have to be addressed (and are indeed credited by a Court of Appeals), with respect to a statute utterly devoid of language that could remotely be thought to distinguish between long-term and short-term debt."

The Supreme Court did not say that the creditor, who would otherwise have been preferred, must win. The *Union Bank* decision stopped the bank from being a sure loser. If the bank loan was not made in the ordinary course or if the actual payment to the bank was not in the ordinary course—e.g., if made during protracted negotiations or with accompanying unusual terms or facts—then the interest payment could be a preference.

6. Four circuits followed *Deprizio*. Bankers with insiders' guarantees were unhappy. Proposals, many originating with bankers and their representatives, arose to amend the Bankruptcy Code to overturn *Deprizio*. In 1994 Congress added a new subsection to § 550 (and renumbered the old sections). New § 550(c) reads:

> (c) If a transfer made between 90 days and one year before the filing of the petition
>
> (1) is avoided under section 547(b) of this title; and
>
> (2) was made for the benefit of a creditor that at the time of such transfer was an insider;
>
> the trustee may not recover under subsection (a) from a transferee that is not an insider.

7. After 1994, which creditor of the subsidiary needs advice about the "*Deprizio* problem"? What risks do the other creditors of the subsidiary run when the subsidiary borrows and the lender gets a parent-company (or owner-officer) guarantee? Anticipate the major contracting and strategic problems for deals involving holding company and controlling shareholder guarantees, after the amendment to § 550. What advice does Creditor X need in the ¶907 example?

8. Before Congress amended § 550, what transactional possibilities did the banks have? What if they got the guarantor to *renounce* all of its claims of subrogation? Who would have wanted the guarantor to renounce subrogation? Would the holding company have remained an insider if it renounced subrogation rights? Would it have persisted as a creditor of the debtor-borrower?

9. *Deprizio*-type problems persisted. In 2005, Congress added § 547(i), which states:

> If the trustee avoids under subsection (b) a transfer made between 90 days and 1 year before the date of the filing of the petition, by the debtor to an entity that is not an insider for the benefit of a creditor that is an insider, such transfer shall be considered to be avoided under this section only with respect to the creditor that is an insider.

The legislative history reports why Congress added sub-section (i):

> Section 547 of the Bankruptcy Code authorizes a trustee to avoid a preferential payment made to a creditor by a debtor within 90 days of filing, whether the creditor is an insider or an outsider. To address the concern that a corporate insider (such as an officer or director who is a creditor of his or her own corporation) has an unfair advantage over outside creditors, section 547 also authorizes a trustee to avoid a preferential payment made to an insider creditor between 90 days and one year before filing. Several recent cases, including *Deprizio*, allowed the trustee to "reach-back" and avoid a transfer to a noninsider creditor made within the 90–day to one-year time frame if an insider benefitted from the transfer in some way. This had the effect of discouraging lenders from obtaining loan guarantees, lest transfers to the lender be vulnerable to recapture by reason of the debtor's insider relationship with the loan guarantor. [In] 1994[, Congress] addressed the *Deprizio* problem by inserting a new section 550(c) into the Bankruptcy Code to prevent avoidance or recovery from a noninsider creditor during the 90–day to one-year period even though the transfer to the noninsider benefitted an insider creditor. The 1994 amendments, however, failed to make a corresponding amendment to section 547, which deals with the avoidance of preferential transfers. As a result, a trustee could still utilize section 547 to avoid a preferential lien given to a noninsider bank, more than 90 days but less than one year before bankruptcy, if the transfer benefitted an insider guarantor of the debtor's debt. Accordingly, [the new sub-section (i)] makes a perfecting amendment to section 547 to provide that if the trustee avoids a transfer given by the debtor to a noninsider for the benefit of an insider creditor between 90 days and one year before filing, that avoidance is valid only with respect to the insider creditor. Thus both the previous amendment to section 550 and the [new] perfecting amendment to section 547 protect the noninsider from the avoiding powers of the trustee exercised with respect to transfers made during the 90–day to one-year pre-filing period. . . .

House Report No. 109–31 (Part I), U.S. Code Cong. and Adm. News 143–44 (2005).

CHAPTER 10

EQUITABLE SUBORDINATION OF A STOCKHOLDER'S CLAIM

A. GENERAL

¶ 1001: Introduction to Equitable Subordination

In addition to the contract terms that control priority—subordination clauses, security, negative pledge clauses, and use of the holding company—the noncontractual actions of a party to the reorganization can affect the priority of the creditors or stockholders.

If a creditor also controls the debtor-subsidiary as its stockholder, other creditors of the subsidiary face problems. Since the controlling creditor could manipulate the debtor's business to its own advantage as creditor, to the detriment of other creditors, bankruptcy doctrine regulates the creditor's conduct. Insiders would normally, for example, prefer to repay themselves as the debtor slides toward bankruptcy. Accordingly, Congress set up a longer, one-year preference period for insiders under § 547. As an insider, the controlling stockholder might give itself beneficial terms when it sells product to (or buys product from) the subsidiary; these sales and purchases could be attacked as fraudulent transfers. And, as a controlling stockholder, it could be liable to the corporation or to other stockholders (preferred and minority common) for mismanagement under corporate law doctrines.

Shareholder suits against an unconflicted controlling stockholder will usually be judged under the low standard of the business judgment rule, but the controlling stockholder's loan would readily create a strong enough conflict to deny the stockholder use of the business judgment rule.

In *Taylor v. Standard Gas* (usually referred to as *"Deep Rock"*), we stay with the holding company setting and again examine the treatment of intra-holding company debts owed to a controlling stockholder. Does the court in *Deep Rock* simply conclude that the parent company mismanaged Deep Rock and is accordingly liable for that mismanagement? Does the court conclude that *all* debts due to a parent company are, because of the fact of the parent's control, subordinated to all other debts and all other stockholder claims? What is the creditor's conduct that led to the subordination of the creditor's claim in *Deep Rock?*

In *Oppenheimer* and related readings, we examine a different type of stockholder claim that could be subordinated: a security holder's claim arising from the debtor's fraud in the issuance of the security. The security holder could be a stockholder or a contractually subordinated creditor. Then, in the next chapter, we examine how outside creditors' too aggressive conduct may lead to subordination of their claims or even create independent liability.

B. EQUITABLE SUBORDINATION OF A STOCKHOLDER'S DEBT CLAIM

¶ 1002: Taylor v. Standard Gas & Electric Co., 306 U.S. 307 (1939)

MR. JUSTICE ROBERTS delivered the opinion of the Court.

The question presented is whether the District Court abused its discretion in approving the compromise of a claim by a parent against a subsidiary corporation and a plan of reorganization based upon the compromise. . . .

The petitioners are a committee for the protection of preferred stockholders. The respondents are the trustee of the debtor, Deep Rock Oil Corporation, . . . and Standard Gas and Electric Company, which owns practically all of the common stock of the debtor, claiming as a creditor.

The debtor was organized in 1919 to take over the properties then being operated by one C.B. Shaffer. Standard Gas & Electric Company . . . then had investments in various utility properties but had never been interested in oil. [Standard bought Deep Rock from Shaffer for] . . . $15,580,000 . . . of cash, a note, [new] preferred and [new] common stock of [Deep Rock]. . . .

. . . From its organization Deep Rock was, most of the time, "two jumps ahead of the wolf," as one of Standard's officers testified. . . .

Thenceforward the debtor was under the complete control and domination of Standard through ownership of the common stock. Standard's officers, directors, and agents always constituted a majority of the Board. The remaining directors were operating officers or employees of Deep Rock who had been employed on behalf of Deep Rock by Standard [or an affiliate] or were under the complete control of Standard. A majority of Deep Rock's officers were officers or directors of Standard or [an affiliate]. The officers of the debtor, who were chosen for their technical or business experience in the oil industry, although allowed some discretion in the matter of development and operation of the oil properties, reported to and were always subject to the direction of officers and directors of Standard. All of the fiscal affairs of the debtor were wholly controlled by Standard, which was its banker and its only source of financial aid.

Deep Rock was placed in the hands of a receiver in March 1933 and the present proceeding under . . . the Bankruptcy Act was instituted in June 1934. Standard filed a claim as a creditor . . . , which the receivers and the trustee resisted. . . . The basis of the claim was an open account which embraced transactions between Standard and Deep Rock from the latter's organization in 1919 to the receivership in 1933. The account consists of *thousands of items of debit and credit*. . . .

The account contains debits to Deep Rock in excess of $52,000,000 and credits of approximately $43,000,000 leaving a balance shown to be due Standard of $9,342,642.37, which was the amount of the claim presented. Cash payments by Standard to Deep Rock, or to others for its account, as shown by the books, total $31,804,145.04. Management and supervision fees paid or credited to [an affiliate of Standard] amount to $1,219,034.83. Interest charges by Standard to Deep Rock on open account balances total $4,819,222.07. Rental charges upon a lease to Deep Rock of oil properties owned by a Standard subsidiary but claimed by petitioners to belong, in equity, to Deep Rock, amount to $4,525,000. Debits by Standard to Deep Rock of the amounts of dividends declared by Deep Rock to Standard, but not paid, reached the sum of $3,502,653. In addition there are hundreds of debits and credits representing other intercompany items.

Two preferred stockholders were permitted to intervene in the proceedings and they joined in the trustee's objections to [Standard's] claim [on Deep Rock]. Many transactions entered in the account were attacked as fraudulent and it was asserted that as Standard had made Deep Rock its mere agent or instrumentality it could not transmute itself from the status of the proprietor of Deep Rock's business to that of creditor. . . . Standard proposed a compromise of its claim.

. . . The trustee . . . recommended the approval of the compromise, which involved the allowance of Standard's claim at $5,000,000 [not $9 million] . . . [and] Standard's claim to the extent of $3,500,000 was to stand on a parity with the debtor's notes [with the remainder of Standard's claim on Deep Rock presumably subordinated].

Months later the reorganization committee presented an amended plan which, as modified by the Court, contemplated the compromise of Standard's claim at $5,000,000, as before, and the organization of a new company [with more cash distributed to the noteholders and more stock to the old preferred stockholders]. The District Court permitted the petitioners to intervene and, over their objections, approved the compromise and the plan. A majority of the Circuit Court of Appeals examined the record only to the extent of determining that it was possible that Standard might establish its claim in whole or in part, and concluded that the District Court had not exceeded the bounds of reasonable discretion in granting its approval. One judge thought that the instrumentality rule was applicable; that, under the rule, Standard had no provable claim; and that it was an abuse of discretion to approve the compromise and the reorganization plan. We agree with the conclusion of the dissenting judge, *but for different reasons.*

* * *

Without going into the minutiae of the transactions between the two companies, enough may be stated to expose the reasons for our decision. As has been stated, Standard came into complete control of Deep Rock in 1921. From the outset Deep Rock was insufficiently capitalized, was top heavy with debt and was in parlous financial condition. Standard so managed its affairs as always to have a stranglehold upon it.

. . . *So inadequate was Deep Rock's capitalization* that, in the period from organization to 1926, the balance due on open account to Standard grew to more than $14,800,000. Standard determined to place some of this indebtedness of Deep Rock with the public. In order to do so it had to improve Deep Rock's balance sheet. This it did by purchasing 80,000 shares of preferred stock for which it credited Deep Rock $7,223,333.33. It then bought $7,500,000 face value two year six percent notes for $7,273,750, which were sold to the public. . . . Deep Rock's requirements of additional capital persisted and, by the spring of 1928, *the open account and a note which Deep Rock had given Standard for advances totaled over $11,000,000.* As the two-year notes held by the public were maturing, Standard found it necessary to make a new offering. There still remained nearly $2,000,000 of first mortgage bonds outstanding which had to be retired to make an unsecured note issue saleable. Standard, therefore, determined that Deep Rock's balance sheet must again be put in such shape that notes could be sold. *It accordingly purchased common stock from Deep Rock to the amount of the then open balance and commuted 90,000 shares of the preferred stock, which it held, into common.* It caused Deep Rock to issue $10,000,000 of six percent notes . . . and applied the proceeds to the redemption of the two-year notes and the outstanding mortgage bonds. . . . This $10,000,000 note issue is the one now outstanding. As before, Deep Rock's resources were wholly insufficient for its business and the open account began again to build up so that between February 1928 and February 1933, the date of receivership, the account had grown to $9,342,642.37.

No dividends were paid on preferred stock until 1926. In that and the following year existing arrearages were paid by Standard, for Deep Rock's account, in the amount of $1,435,813. Between 1928 and 1931 Standard advanced Deep Rock, for payment of preferred dividends, $1,106,706.

During the period between 1926 and 1929 Deep Rock declared dividends on its common stock in a total of $3,064,685.50. Of these dividends $1,946,672 was charged by Standard, as owner of common stock, against Deep Rock in the open account. Standard took new common stock for dividends to the amount of $1,015,437.50 and advanced Deep Rock cash to pay dividends to outside holders of common stock in the sum of $102,576. Against the total of $2,645,095 advanced by Standard to pay Deep Rock's dividends, Standard credited payments received from Deep Rock in the open account in the sum of $927,500.

These dividends were declared in the face of the fact that Deep Rock had not the cash available to pay them and was, at the time, borrowing in large amounts from or through Standard.

* * *

[Standard caused Deep Rock to buy various properties for Deep Rock's business. Many of the purchases were done by Standard employees. Some of the properties were held in the name of Standard employees.]

During the whole period from 1919 to the receivership, Standard charged Deep Rock interest at the [annual] rate of seven per cent . . . [on] the open account. During the entire period [Standard's affiliate] charged Deep Rock with round annual sums for management and supervision of Deep Rock's affairs which totaled $1,219,034.83, all of which Standard assumed and charged into the open account.

It is impossible within the compass of this opinion to detail the numerous other transactions evidenced by the books of the two companies many of which were to the benefit of Standard and to the detriment of Deep Rock. All of them were accomplished through the complete control and domination of Standard and without the participation of the preferred stockholders who had no voice or vote in the management of Deep Rock's affairs.

The suggested basis of compromise of Standard's claim needs comment. As has been said, when, in 1928, it became necessary to refinance Deep Rock's note obligations, Standard had to wipe out the enormous and threatening credit balance in its favor on Deep Rock's books. It, therefore, took common stock in payment of the balance. It is said that the compromise figure is reached by disregarding all transactions prior to February 24, 1928, when Standard commuted its then claim, starting fresh from that date, and considering only the items in the account thenceforward to the date of receivership. . . . It is said that this computation of the claim eliminates debits to Deep Rock made since 1928 for the fees of Management Corporation, for dividends on preferred and common stock held by Standard, and for every other questionable item; and that there can be no just criticism of the recognition of Standard's claim in the amount represented by the compromise offer.

Petitioners invoke the so-called instrumentality rule -- under which, they say, Deep Rock is to be regarded as a department or agent of Standard -- to preclude the allowance of Standard's claim in any amount. The rule was much discussed in the opinion below. It is not, properly speaking, a rule, but a convenient way of designating the application in particular circumstances of the broader equitable principle that the doctrine of corporate entity, recognized generally and for most purposes, will . . . be [dis]regarded when so to do would work fraud or injustice. This principle has been applied in appropriate circumstances to give minority stockholders redress against wrongful injury to their interests by a majority stockholder. It must be apparent that the preferred stockholders of Deep Rock assert such injury by

Standard as the basis of their attack on the decree below. We need not stop to discuss the remedy which would be available to them if . . . the Bankruptcy Act had not been adopted for we think that . . . the court, in approving a plan, was authorized and required, as a court of equity, to recognize the rights and the status of the preferred stockholders arising out of Standard's wrongful and injurious conduct in the mismanagement of Deep Rock's affairs.

. . . In the present case there remains an equity after satisfaction of the [outside] creditors. . . . Equity requires the award to preferred stockholders of a superior position [to Standard's loans] in the reorganized company. The District Judge, we think, properly exercised his discretion in refusing to approve the first offer of compromise and concomitant plan because it partly subordinated preferred stockholders to Standard['s loans]. The same considerations which moved him to reject that plan required the rejection of the new offer and the amended plan.

Deep Rock finds itself bankrupt not only because of the enormous sums it owes Standard but because of the abuses in management due to the paramount interest of interlocking officers and directors in the preservation of Standard's position[.] [It is] at once proprietor and creditor of Deep Rock. *It is impossible to recast Deep Rock's history and experience so as even to approximate what would be its financial condition at this day had it been adequately capitalized and independently managed and had its fiscal affairs been conducted with an eye single to its own interests.* In order to remain in undisturbed possession and to prevent the preferred stockholders having a vote and a voice in the management, Standard has caused Deep Rock to pay preferred dividends in large amounts. Whatever may be the fact as to the legality of such dividends judged by the balance sheets and earnings statements of Deep Rock, it is evident that they would not have been paid over a long course of years by a company on the precipice of bankruptcy and in dire need of cash working capital.[1] This is only one of the aspects in which Standard's management and control has operated to the detriment of Deep Rock's financial condition and ability to function. Others are apparent from what has been said and from a study of the record.

If a reorganization is effected the amount at which Standard's claim is allowed is not important if it is to be represented by stock in the new company, provided the stock to be awarded it is subordinated to that awarded preferred stockholders. No plan ought to be approved which does not accord the preferred stockholders a right of participation in the equity in the Company's assets *prior to that of Standard*, and at least equal voice with Standard in the management. Anything less would be to remand them to precisely the status which has inflicted serious detriment on them in the past.

Reversed.

---

[1] [Working capital is the excess of the company's short-term assets (cash, accounts receivable, and inventory) over its short-term liabilities, that is, not including its long-lived assets, like factory and machinery, and its long-term debt.—Roe.]

¶ 1003: *Deep Rock* Problems

1. Was the parent company's claim disallowed? Does it matter financially whether it was disallowed or subordinated?
2. Was the parent's claim affected only to the extent of the mismanagement and inadequate capitalization of the subsidiary?
3. Companies that fail will often in retrospect appear to have been undercapitalized. The problem of undercapitalization is one of judging the risks as perceived by reasonable business people at the time of the (under) investment. That's not a task easily done by a judge, or for that matter by anyone. See generally Robert Clark, *The Duties of the Corporate Debtor to Its Creditors*, 90 Harvard Law Review 505, 520 n.49 (1977), and sources cited therein.
4. Is there any difference between equitable subordination and recovery of a fraudulent transfer? Professor Clark suggests that the two doctrines deal with similar transactions and reach similar results. Why the two then? He speculates that equitable subordination arose because of the bankruptcy court's incomplete jurisdiction. To recover a fraudulent transfer, the bankruptcy trustee would have had to go into state or federal district court to sue for recovery under the general understanding of jurisdictional authority at the time. However, by subordinating a claim, the bankruptcy court could achieve the same financial result without going outside the bankruptcy court. See id. at 528–29.
5. Fraudulent transfer doctrine requires precise analysis of terms, evidence, and values transferred. Equitable subordination cut through the complexity and uncertainty to simply make the claimant wait until the others were paid. Id. at 530–31. But it'd be fortuitous that subordination measured fraudulent transfer liability accurately.
6. The Bankruptcy Code now authorizes bankruptcy courts to apply principles of equitable subordination. Bankruptcy Code § 510(c).
7. Is control via stock ownership crucial? If the creditor obtained control via contract (i.e., via loan covenants, a management contract, or a veto over strategy and action), could *Deep Rock* liability be triggered? Cf. infra *American Lumber*, *W.T. Grant*, *Farah Manufacturing*.

¶ 1004: From *Northern Pipeline* to Stern v. Marshall

As an aside to analyzing equitable subordination, the bankruptcy court's incomplete jurisdiction persists as a live issue into the twenty-first century's second decade. The blockbuster decision was Northern Pipeline v. Marathon, 458 U.S. 50 (1982), in which the Supreme Court held that the bankruptcy judge, as an Article I judge lacking the lifetime tenure of Article III judges, lacked the constitutional authority to decide a bankrupt's contract claim against a defendant that was not otherwise a party to the bankruptcy. Subsequent congressional efforts to elevate bankruptcy judges to Article III status failed, leading federal courts to adopt a reference system in which the basic jurisdiction rested in the district courts, with bankruptcy matters referred to the bankruptcy courts. Referred matters could, particularly upon challenge, be pulled back to the district court. Nearly three decades later, in Stern v. Marshall, 564 U.S. 2 (2011), the Court extended *Northern Pipeline*: a bankrupt debtor's counterclaim on a creditor, if the claim involved issues going beyond the creditor's claim itself, was not a case or controversy over which an Article I judge could exercise jurisdiction. Either the relevant state court or the federal district court needed to resolve the claim. Chapter 20 discusses the bankruptcy court's jurisdiction.

¶ 1005: *Deep Rock* and Corporate Planning

1. Subsidiary, an oil company, is worth $1000. Parent company owns all of Subsidiary's common stock. Subsidiary has $1000 (face amount) of preferred stock outstanding with the public. That is, in a liquidation, the preferred would get $1000 before common got anything. The dividend promised on the preferred was enough to make the income stream worth $1000—if the promised dividend were likely to be paid. The dividend rate is ordinary. There is no expectation that (absent the considerations noted below) the preferred will be redeemed soon.

Subsidiary	
$1000	$1000 Preferred
	Common stock

2. The oil company Subsidiary is drilling for oil. Its single oil well, its only business, will be fully evaluated in the next few months. The best guess now is that the well will be worth either $2000 (for which there is a 50% prospect) or nothing (for which there is also a 50% chance). How much should the preferred trade at in the marketplace? How much should the common stock trade at? (Ignore present value adjustments.)

(1)	Outcomes			Expected Values		
	Company	Preferred	Common	Company	Preferred	Common
.5 x 0	0	0	0	0	0	0
.5 x 2000	2000	1000	1000	1000	500	500
	Total expected value:			1000	500	500

3. Management of Parent company approaches you, as counsel to the corporate group. Management informs you that the oil engineers have said that with a $1000 investment by Parent company in Subsidiary, the expected value of Subsidiary can be increased by $1250. The investment will make certain at least a $1000 return (i.e., no dry well) and will increase the value of the good outcome (the "gusher") by more than $1000, to $3500.

4. Would management of Parent company, if properly representing the interests of their own stockholders, make the investment by buying $1000 of common stock of Subsidiary? What would the values be of the common stock and the preferred stock after the investment?

(2)	Outcomes			Expected Values		
	Company	Preferred	Common	Company	Preferred	Common
.5 x 1000						
.5 x 3500						
	Total expected value:					

5. Don't the economics of the drilling possibilities make a deal doable between the common stockholders and the preferred stockholders? Shouldn't the preferred be willing to accept payment of between $500 and $750 for the company to buy back the preferred? Shouldn't the common stockholders be willing to buy back the preferred for between $500 and $750?

6. Consider the company's alternatives if the preferred and the common cannot make a deal. Could Parent company lend the $1000 to Subsidiary? What are the respective values even if the capital structure is respected? What are the *Deep Rock* risks? If the top row ($1000) is the result, would the company appear in retrospect to have been badly managed and undercapitalized?

(3)	Outcomes				Expected Values			
	Company	Loan	Preferred	Common	Company	Loan	Preferred	Common
.5 x 1000								
.5 x 3500								
	Total expected value:							

7. This last table shows *Deep Rock* debilitating a worthwhile project. But these numbers are loaded to debilitate the investment in Subsidiary. Isn't the problem that parent companies will make such loans and take equity-like risks, because the equity risks redound to their benefit as stockholders? For instance, assume that the original profile for the $1000 company was $1800 or $200, each with equal likelihood:

(4)	Outcomes			Expected Values		
	Company	Preferred	Common	Company	Preferred	Common
.5 x 200	200	200	0	100	100	0
.5 x 1800	1800	1000	800	900	500	400
	Total expected value:					

The company could increase the value of the entire firm to $1975, with a $1000 investment, via a $1000 loan with an expected value of $975, but whose proceeds would be used to make a risky investment that redounds to the stockholders' benefit?

(5)	Outcomes				Expected Values			
	Company	Loan	Preferred	Common	Company	Loan	Preferred	Common
.5 x 950	950	950	0	0	475	475	0	0
.5 x 3000	3000	1000	1000	1000	1500	500	500	500
	Total expected value:							

What was the value of Parent company's investment before it lent to Subsidiary? What was the total value of Parent company's investment after it lent? Does the loan benefit the company as a whole? (No.) I.e., does the company's value go up by an amount equal to the amount loaned? If not, why would Parent company make the loan?

The loan is a slight loser from a company-wide perspective, but it enables the stockholder to take extra risk with the preferred, extra risk that lowers the preferred's expected value and shifts value down to the common. The lender-parent would make the risky loan because it gets the upside on the common; it maximizes the value of its common stock stick in the firm's bundle of sticks, at the price of a slightly bad loan. Its willingness to lend is due to its combining of the loan outcomes with the stock outcomes, making this scenario an excellent one for equitable subordination.

The problem in putting together an efficient and fair financial system is thus: Can a court distinguish the expected outcomes in [5] from those in [3]? The first set, [1]–[3], is a bad one for justifying equitable subordination; the second set, [4]–[5], is a good one for justifying it.

8. Can we extricate the holding company from the inefficiencies by using a third-party, arms-length lender? That is, if the third-party lender would make the loan, and doesn't benefit as stockholder, does that "prove" to the judge that the loan should not be equitably subordinated?[2] Third party lenders would not make the loan outlined above, but they would make the loan in the footnote. However, using a third-party loan standard is inadequate if the loan allows the controlling stockholder to shape the risk profile of the subsidiary.

---

[2] Actually, it shouldn't. The loan might just enable Parent company to shift value to itself. But properly understood, this would be attacked as Parent company mismanagement of Subsidiary.

	Outcomes			Expected Values		
	Company	Preferred	Common	Company	Preferred	Common
.5 x 200	200	200	0	100	100	0
.5 x 1800	1800	1000	800	900	500	400
	Total expected value:			1000	600	400

Expected value is $1000, with a new loan of $1000, the value will be $1950, but the risk-taking will be worthwhile for the stockholders:

	Outcomes				Expected Values			
	Company	Loan	Preferred	Common	Company	Loan	Preferred	Common
.5 x 1000	1000	1000	0	0	500	500	0	0
.5 x 2900	2900	1000	1000	900	1450	500	500	450
Total expected value:					1950	1000	500	450

The loan and its deployment lowers the company's total equity value by $50 and reduces the preferred expected value by $100, but increases equity's expected value by $50. The preferred lose $100, half to the common and the other half in a wasteful project.

9. And would a bank necessarily lend the $1000 in the first hypothetical? See the Posner excerpt, at ¶ 806. If Parent company has cash, the bank will be suspicious of even scenario [1]–[3]: If Parent company has the cash, the loan officer might think, why doesn't it make the loan itself? *Deep Rock* problems are one reason; lack of confidence in the project is another. Even if the bank lends, would the prospect of a claim against Parent company for mismanagement or undercapitalization be avoided? Is the damage claim (or state law veil piercing) less threatening to Parent company than *Deep Rock* subordination?

10. How do you remedy the bank's reluctance to lend? Can it be done in any way that presents no legal risks to Parent company? Consider the values that would be distributed if Subsidiary sold off the oil property *before* the investment. Would a guarantee from a solvent parent of the debt of a shaky subsidiary represent anything different than a loan to the parent by the bank and then a re-lending of the funds by the parent, as a conduit, to the subsidiary? If so, then does a guarantee fully shield the parent from *Deep Rock* damage?

    But if the bank were relying on the creditworthiness of the guaranteeing Parent company, shouldn't the same facts that would lead to subordination of Parent company's direct loan lead to subordination of the bank's loan and the Parent company's subrogation rights?

¶ 1006: Note re Washington Plate Glass Co., 27 B. R. 550 (D.D.C. 1982), 3 Bankruptcy News Letter (WGL), No. 6 (June 1986), at 1

Equitable Subordination Applied. In Washington Plate Glass Co., 27 B. R. 550 (D.D.C. 1982), one of two owners withdrew from the business and sold his stock to the corporation, receiving in return a note secured by the assets of the corporation. The transaction was not undertaken either with a fraudulent intent or in anticipation of bankruptcy. Three years later, the company defaulted on the note and, some months later, became insolvent.

In affirming the finding of the bankruptcy court, District Judge Gerhard A. Gesell did not apply Section 548[, the Bankruptcy Code's fraudulent transfer section,] but, rather, applied Section 510(c). He found that enforcement of the security interest held by the former shareholder as of the date of bankruptcy would be manifestly unfair to the general unsecured creditors of the debtor corporation and that, accordingly, the doctrine of equitable subordination should be applied.

Prejudice to Creditors Must Be Avoided. In the view of the court, the corporation did not acquire anything of a value equivalent to the depletion of its assets when it acquired the stock. Instead, the transaction was devised to achieve a distribution of the corporate assets to the stockholder. Since assets of a corporation are to be available first to creditors, the stockholders were not entitled to receive any part of the assets until the creditors were first paid in full. The court concluded that even in cases where no intent to defraud the creditors is present and the transaction is entered into in good faith, the transaction will not be upheld unless there is sufficient surplus available at the time that payment is made out of assets to retire the stock without prejudice to creditors.

[The issue of whether a court needed to see bad conduct in order to invoke equitable subordination has been litigated, with courts indicating generally that bad conduct isn't necessary. In many instances equitable subordination was invoked to favor the United States as a tax claimant (with the court equitably subordinating other creditors to the United States).]

¶ 1007: Partnership Liability and Debt Recharacterization

Two nonbankruptcy doctrines can bring about the same effect as equitable subordination—partnership liability and recharacterization.

Ordinary partners are liable for the partnership's debts. If the creditor has become a partner with the debtor, then the distributional results would resemble those obtained under equitable subordination doctrines. Without giving effect to equitable subordination, all creditors would claim on the enterprise and share pro rata. Then the non-partner creditors would claim against the creditor that is deemed to be a partner of the debtor.

J. William Callison, Partnership Law and Practice: General and Limited Partnership 5:1, 5:18 (2014)

* * *

[The] Uniform Partnership Act (UPA) [as revised in 2013] defines in [Section 102(11)] the term *partnership* as "an association of two or more persons to carry on as co-owners a business for profit."

* * *

[Profit Sharing in Creditor–Debtor Relationships]

Although profit sharing is prima facie evidence that a partnership exists, this is not the case if the profits are received in payment of "a debt by installments or otherwise."[3] It is clear under Uniform Partnership Act (UPA) § [202(c)(3)] that a person who loans money to a business and receives a profit share in consideration for the loan does not necessarily become a partner in the business.[4] When a creditor participates in business profits, the greatest legal risk lies in blurring the lines between investing in, and lending to, the debtor or the project being financed.[5] Creditors generally are entitled to repayment of the amount loaned regardless of whether profits exist. However, creditors may at times, particularly in the case of troubled businesses, agree that

---

[3] UPA § [202(c)(3)(a)].

[4] [Section 202(c)(3) of the UPA states: "A person who receives a share of the profits of a business is presumed to be a partner in a business, unless the profits were received in payment . . . of interest or other charge on a loan, even if the amount of payment varies with the profits of the business, including a direct or indirect present or future ownership of the collateral, or rights to income, proceeds, or increase in value derived from the collateral. . . . "—Roe.]

[5] See, e.g., In re Washington Communications Group, Inc., 18 B.R. 437 (Bankr. D.D.C. 1982); Cohen v. Orlove, 190 Md. 237, 57 A.2d 810 (1948).

principal payments will be required only if the business has profits. In such a case, the issue of whether a creditor has become a partner, and is thereby liable to other creditors who extend credit while he or she is a partner is important. For example, assume that Bank A makes a large loan to [XY], which subsequently encounters financial trouble and is unable to make principal payments as required by the note. If Bank A were to work out an arrangement with [XY] whereby note payments would equal 75 per cent of [XY's] net profits, it would be critical to Bank A that it not be considered a partner in [XY]. If Bank A were a partner, creditors of [XY] that extend credit while Bank A is a partner would be able to assert that Bank A is jointly liable for partnership obligations. . . .

The protected relationship under UPA § [202(c)] . . . extends to loans which will be repaid from business profits pursuant to their terms. If a debtor-creditor relationship can be shown, the person asserting the partnership's existence will have the burden of proving that all elements of the UPA § [102(11)] definition are met.[6] UPA § [202(c)(3)(a)] only eliminates the evidentiary inference arising from profit sharing and does not protect creditors from being considered partners if the elements of partnership can be proven. Although loan agreements often contain provisions describing the parties' intention to create a loan rather than a partnership,[7] the parties' characterization of their relationship is not controlling. . . .

If the normal formalities and terms of a loan transaction are absent, the courts are more likely to hold that the purported lender is a partner. For example, in *Minute Maid Corp. v. United Foods, Inc.*,[8] Minute Maid Corporation argued that United Foods, a direct purchaser from Minute Maid, was engaged in a partnership with Cold Storage Corporation, thereby making Cold Storage jointly liable for the unpaid purchase [orders of] commodities [that Minute Maid had] sold to United Foods. In concluding that a partnership existed, the court relied in part on the fact that the transaction between United Foods and Cold Storage did not take the form of a . . . loan. . . .

In addition, the courts have emphasized the degree of control exerted by the purported lender over the business in determining the existence of a partnership. For example, in *Minute Maid*, the court held [that the] borrower and the lender held and jointly exercised . . . control over the business enterprise:

> There can be no question but that the parties had joint control over this enterprise. This follows from the fact that United initially determined how much to buy but such determination was subject to Cold Storage's right to determine whether the proposed collateral would be "acceptable." Also it was provided that in case of pending price increases, which the court found would offer the opportunity to speculate on inventory, the parties would agree on the volume to be purchased. In point of fact the responsible officer for United testified that, "they

---

[6] [Section [102(11)] of the UPA says: "a partnership is an association of two or more persons to carry on as co-owners a business for profit."—Roe.]

[7] Careful drafters will include such provisions in their agreements if only to prevent the parties from arguing inter se that they entered into a partnership. . . .

[8] 291 F.2d 577 (5th Cir.), *cert. denied,* 368 U.S. 928 (1961).

> [Cold Storage] could have stepped in and written me [United] off pretty damned fast. . . . " [W]e think the operation heretofore outlined was clearly within the joint control of the parties.[9]

On the other hand, in *In re Washington Communications Group, Inc.*,[10] the court held that a passive creditor who did not participate in management was not a partner. Creditors are frequently given the power to approve or to disapprove significant transactions which might impair their ability to be repaid. Courts have held that lenders are permitted those controls which are necessary to protect the loan, and that the exercise of such controls does not create a partnership with the debtor.[11] To avoid partnership status, the lender should not participate in day-to-day management of the borrower's business, and the loan documentation should be drafted to avoid any implication that the lender has any power to participate in ordinary business management.

The case law indicates that courts allow extensive lender control in "salvage" or "distress" situations. In the landmark English case of *Cox v. Hickman*,[12] the creditors of a financially troubled ironworks exerted substantial, if not complete, control over the debtor's business. The court stated that the creditors ran the business strictly as creditors for the debtor's benefit and not as co-owners, and held that a partnership was not created. The *Cox* decision, and the American cases that have followed,[13] indicate that more control may be exercised by a creditor in a troubled business setting than would otherwise be permitted.

If the percentage of profits allocated to the purported creditor is abnormally high, or if there is no cap on the amount of profits which can be received by the purported creditor, courts have found a partnership between the creditor and the debtor. In *Minute Maid Corp. v. United Foods, Inc.*,[14] where a partnership was found to exist, the purported lender had a continuing interest in business profits beyond the amount required to repay its loan. Further, in *In re Kraus*,[15] the court held that there was a partnership where the purported creditor's share of profits would not end when its loan was recouped. Where the creditor's share of profits is limited to a specified dollar amount, courts have held that there is no partnership.[16]

If loan repayment is entirely contingent on the existence of profits, courts are more likely to hold that a partnership exists between the purported lender and the borrower. For example, in *Parker v. Northern Mixing Co.*[17] the court held that although "an agreement to share profits alone is not conclusive evidence of the existence of a

---

[9] Id. at 583.

[10] 18 Bankr. 437 (Bankr. D.D.C. 1982).

[11] See, e.g., Meechan v. Valentine, 145 U.S. 611 (1892); Spier v. Lang. 4 Cal. 2d 711, 53 P.2d 138 (1935); Martin v. Peyton, 246 N.Y. 213, 158 N.E. 77 (1927) (lender permitted to veto speculative ventures but not to initiate any transaction).

[12] 11 Eng. Rep. 431 (1860).

[13] See, e.g., Martin v. Peyton, 246 N.Y. 213, 158 N.E. 77 (1927).

[14] 291 F.2d 577 (5th Cir.), cert. denied, 368 U.S. 928 (1961).

[15] 37 Bankr. 726 (Bankr. E.D. Mich. 1984).

[16] See, e.g., Martin v. Peyton, 246 N.Y. 213, 158 N.E. 77 (1927); Cox v. Hickman, 11 Eng. Rep. 431 (1860).

[17] 756 P.2d 881, 887 (Alaska 1988).

partnership," a lender's receipt of profits is evidence of a partnership where repayment is contingent on profits:

> In general, an advance of funds is a loan (and thus does not indicate the creation of a partnership relation) if its repayment is not contingent on the profits of the enterprise; if repayment is contingent on profits, it tends to demonstrate the existence of a partnership because the funds are at risk in the business rather than being made the personal responsibility of the borrower.[18]

Debt recharacterization doctrine is related to equitable subordination. The latter recognizes that a debt existed, but the court lowers the creditor's priority. The former does not recognize the claim as a valid claim on the debtor.

Courts characterizing what formally looks to be debt as equity rely on a multiple factors test (about a dozen in the leading cases), such as whether the debt has a fixed maturity date and a fixed interest rate, whether the repayments come out of profits or similar pools of value. Whether the creditor and the stockholder are closely related, and whether the so-called debt is subordinated to other creditors' claims. "No one factor is controlling or decisive, and the court must look to the particular circumstances of each case." Roth Steel Tube Co. v. C.I.R., 800 F.2d 625 (6th Cir. 1986). For a similar list, but with thirteen factors, see In re Hedged-Investments Associates, Inc., 380 F.3d 1292 (10th Cir. 2004).

Some bankruptcy courts see the authority for recharacterization as coming from §105(a)—to administer a bankruptcy system, the bankruptcy court must have the authority to determine where claims fit on the priority ladder. Others see the authority coming from §502(b), under which bankruptcy courts allow or disallow claims, based presumably on whether the asserted claim would be enforceable as a debt under state law.

Proper characterization of debt (is it truly debt or is it equity?) is particularly important for tax purposes. Generally speaking, interest payments are deductible from a corporation's tax bill, but dividends are not.

C. SUBORDINATION OF SECURITIES LAW CLAIMS

¶ 1008: Oppenheimer v. Harriman Nat'l Bank & Trust Co., 301 U.S. 206 (1937)

For some years prior to the occurrences out of which this litigation arose the defendant bank was doing business in New York City. Being unable to meet current demands, it closed March 3, 1933. March 13 a conservator was appointed; October 16 the comptroller declared it

[18] Id. at 887.

insolvent and appointed a receiver . . . May 31, Oppenheimer brought this action in the federal court for the southern district of New York to recover damages upon an executed rescission of a sale to him of stock of the bank by means of fraudulent representations made by its president and vice president. . . . The Circuit Court of Appeals ordered that judgment for the amount demanded in the complaint be entered against the bank collectible out of assets of the receivership after payment in full of all who were creditors when the bank became insolvent. . . .

Plaintiff applied for a writ of certiorari, contending that the Circuit Court of Appeals erred in holding that his judgment is not entitled to rank with other unsecured creditors' claims and that its ruling conflicts with decisions of other Circuit Courts of Appeals. . . .

November 1, 1930, plaintiff purchased 10 shares of the bank's stock for $15,120. He was induced to buy the stock by false and fraudulent representations of the president and vice president of the bank. . . . Later, on May 6, 1933, he gave the bank notice of rescission [and] tendered it the certificate. . . . The bank rejected his demand; he brought this suit for $12,187 with interest and costs. . . .

[Is the] plaintiff's judgment . . . entitled to share equally in the receivership estate with other unsecured creditors' claims[?]

In 1930 when the bank by false representations sold him the stock and by that means obtained the price out of his deposit it immediately became bound to make restitution. The fraudulent sale was subject to rescission by the plaintiff at any time before the bank closed. Neither lapse of time while plaintiff remained ignorant of the fraud nor insolvency of the bank detracted from its liability. We assume that after March 3, 1933, the bank was without means sufficient to meet current demands and that its debts exceeded the value of its assets plus the statutory liability of its stockholders. After the appointment of a conservator, but some months before the comptroller declared the bank insolvent, the plaintiff rescinded and brought this suit. He claims no lien, preference, or priority but merely seeks to share in the estate as do other unsecured creditors.

* * *

[P]laintiff's judgment is entitled to rank on a parity with other unsecured creditors' claims.

¶ 1009: John Slain & Homer Kripke, *The Interface Between Securities Regulation and Bankruptcy—Allocating the Risk of Illegal Securities Issuance Between Securityholders and the Issuer's Creditors*, 48 New York University Law Review 261 (1973)*

Abstract

Securityholders who assert rescission claims against their issuer are presently afforded special treatment in bankruptcy [under *Oppenheimer* and subsequent cases]. Despite the fact that they are conscious risk-takers, these claimants are allowed to share equally with, or to take before, general creditors. Professors Slain and Kripke argue that this treatment gives inadequate recognition to interests which ought to be, and are in other contexts, protected in a bankruptcy distribution. Applying traditional concepts of reliance and laches, the authors propose a system which more nearly harmonizes securities law policies with those of the Bankruptcy Act.

Not many doctrines have passed more fully into the collective consciousness of the legal and commercial communities than the absolute priority rule, which states this prohibition: in bankruptcy, stockholders seeking to recover their investments cannot be paid before provable creditor claims have been satisfied in full. Nevertheless, there is a class of cases not subject to this rule under current practice. In these cases a dissatisfied investor may rescind his purchase of stock or subordinated debt by proving that the transaction violated federal or state securities laws. Under such circumstances, it is currently held that the investor's claim . . . shares pari passu with . . . claims of general creditors.

While rescission cases arise in a wide variety of factual contexts, they all have two characteristics in common: First, they disappoint the general creditor's expectation that in bankruptcy his claims will be paid out ahead of equity claims; secondly, they assume that the interests protected by federal and state securities regulation should take precedence over all other interests normally taken into account when dealing with claims against a distressed enterprise.

* * *

In this article, we question the basic wisdom of treating rescission claims any differently from equity claims in bankruptcy cases. It is our thesis that the present approach is wrong and that the problem should be reconceptualized as one of risk allocation. In our view, in any such allocation one interest should be weighted far more heavily than at present: the reliance interest of persons having the normal expectation that equity investment and junior debt will bear the first losses of the enterprise.

I

The Mis-en-Scene

The inequity of allowing rescinding shareholders to share equally in bankruptcy with general creditors can be demonstrated by use of a hypothetical. Assume XYZ, Inc., having just been organized to engage in the widget business, requires an additional $300,000 of capital to start up. XYZ's management, either directly or through investment bankers, searches for a group of substantial investors prepared to provide the $300,000 and accept equity risks. They locate one such investor, H, who has a personal investment portfolio of several million dollars. Prior to his retirement, H was employed as a portfolio manager for a financial business and is concededly a "sophisticated investor." H meets the principals in XYZ, investigates the affairs and prospects of the company to the extent he deems necessary, calls for and receives financial statements, and purchases 30,000 shares of XYZ's common stock for $180,000. Mr. H recognizes that the widget business provides both high risk and high return and is, in short, speculative. Another 20,000 shares are sold for $120,000 to others less sophisticated, who are impressed by the information that the sophisticated Mr. H is participating.

XYZ begins operations and for six months after H's stock purchase conducts an active business. The corporation quickly incurs $1,000,000 in liabilities to unsecured lenders and open-account vendors who have advanced money or credit in reliance on the general knowledge that XYZ has sold $300,000 of stock. XYZ does not prosper. Seven months after H's purchase, the corporation files a petition under Chapter XI of the Bankruptcy Act, and the reorganization quickly ripens into a straight bankruptcy proceeding. In this proceeding, H asserts a claim for rescission of his $180,000 stock purchase, alleging that the issuer violated § 5 of the Securities Act of 1933 [requiring registration of non-exempt securities with the Securities and Exchange Commission prior to their sale]. . . . XYZ's trustee in bankruptcy attempts to show that the issue was exempted as a nonpublic offering under § 4(2) of the [1933] Act, but fails when he is unable to demonstrate that all the persons to whom the $300,000 in stock had been offered were "sophisticated" and had access to the same information that would have been available had the stock been registered under the Securities Act.

. . . H has a claim entitled to share pari passu with the claims of general creditors. . . .

[True, t]he claim asserted by H in our hypothetical is unusual: a knowledgeable buyer does not often use an issuer's Securities Act violation to opt out of his investment if he has not actually been prejudiced by the violation. More commonly, a stockholder seeking to rescind will assert some claim of misrepresentation (or nondisclosure) of material information in connection with his purchase. Yet from the general creditor's point of view, the injustice of assigning to him a status merely equal to . . . that of a rescinding shareholder does not depend on the basis of the shareholder's claim. In extending credit, he has relied on the operation of the absolute priority rule in case of bankruptcy. Furthermore, in shifting his priority position, the courts impose upon him the burden of a risk he has never assumed and should not be made to assume—the possibility of a defective stock issue.

To avail himself of the present exception to the absolute priority rule,[19] the shareholder may base his rescission claim on one or more of several federal and state statutes and common law rules. A transaction may violate the Securities Act in two respects: it may be an unregistered nonexempt public offering of securities or it may be effected through the use of a deceptive prospectus. Section 12(1) of the Securities Act allows rescission by the purchaser in the first situation, and Section 12(2) allows rescission in the second. . . . An issuer's conduct may also violate other sections of federal securities law, most obviously the antifraud provisions of . . . rule 10b–5 under the

[19] [Is it truly an exception? Don't the defrauded and rescinding stockholders hold both an equity interest and a debt claim? The question is how to treat that debt claim in the debtor's bankruptcy.—Roe.]

Securities Exchange Act of 1934. . . . Each of these may be the predicate of a private action in which either rescission or damages are claimed by a continuing stockholder or damages are claimed by a former stockholder.

* * *

We are only incidentally concerned with the precise predicate of a disaffected stockholder's efforts to recapture his investment from the corporation. For present purposes it suffices to say that when the basis of the stockholder's disaffection is either the issuer's failure to comply with registration requirements or the issuer's material misrepresentations, one or more state or federal claims may be made. Our purpose is to consider the impact of such claims on the distribution of the corporation's assets in bankruptcy and the development of a plan of reorganization under Chapter X.

. . . Typically . . . two classes of investors benefit most dramatically from the availability of securities law remedies in bankruptcy: *stockholders and subordinated lenders such as the holders of [a] . . . subordinated debenture.*[20]

Some securityholders may not benefit from their securities law rights, since their contracts with the issuer often provide for equal or superior remedies. For example, the note evidencing a bank loan made to an issuer is a security, and if the loan has been obtained by misrepresentation, securities law remedies may be available to the bank. Since, however, the bank is already a creditor, these remedies will not ordinarily improve the bank's position vis-a-vis the issuer's general creditors. Assuming it holds documents in reasonably conventional form, the bank may demand its money by reason of an acceleration clause and may have a security interest in some assets of the issuer. . . . Except in a rare case, it is unlikely that the availability of securities law remedies will add significantly to the bank's bundle of rights.

By contrast, investors in stock or in subordinated debentures may be able to bootstrap their way to parity with . . . general creditors even in the absence of express contractual rights. This unexpected result is the product of the unthinking application of the policies underlying the securities laws at the expense of policies underlying bankruptcy distribution. Since this favored treatment is clearly outside the original contemplation of both the security holders and the general creditors affected, it is with securities of this type that we are concerned. Hereafter, the discussion is focused upon the rescinding stockholder. Mutatis mutandis, the discussion is equally applicable to holders of subordinated debentures and to other creditors whose debt securities are contractually subordinated. . . .

C. Classification of Creditors—Reliance

[A] distinction [ought to] be drawn between general creditors who have relied upon the stockholder's undertaking and those who have not.

---

[20] [How do subordinated debentureholders benefit?—Roe.]

The strongest reliance case would thus be made by parties who became creditors after the stockholder's investment and after viewing a financial statement which reflected the stockholder's investment in equity accounts.

* * *

If a contract law reliance test is applied between the rescinding stockholder and the post-investment general creditor, we suggest that the burden of proving nonreliance be placed on the stockholder. Creditor reliance may often be genuine but not susceptible of easy proof. Consider the case of the supplier who does not see a balance sheet and is unaware of a particular stock issue. Such a creditor may, in fact, rely derivatively on the stockholder's investment. Credit managers talk to one another. Any creditor who follows an issuer's affairs with any degree of regularity, by, for example, drawing Dun & Bradstreet reports or by reviewing financial statements, is likely to reveal his impressions to fellow credit suppliers. A stockholder's failure to seek rescission thus becomes an important part of a misleading picture seen vicariously. Reliance of this kind, while difficult to demonstrate, is nonetheless real.

. . . [W]hile subsequent creditors should be presumed to have relied on the rescinding stockholder's investment, prior creditors should be required to sustain the burden of proving their detrimental reliance. . . . [21]

VI
Conclusion

The absolute priority rule mandates the complete subordination of equity claims against a bankrupt to the claims of general creditors. Yet, under present law, a shareholder can escape the effects of the rule if he can prove a right to rescind his purchase. Establishment of such a claim will give him equality with or perhaps priority over general creditors. Although it is arguable that such treatment accords with policies of the securities acts, it takes no account of the rules and policies of bankruptcy distribution.

In particular, the present exception allocates to the general creditor risks of business insolvency and illegal stock offering which should be borne by the equity investor. The exception does not acknowledge the fact that the general creditor relies on the existence of an equity cushion in case of his debtor's bankruptcy. The exception allows a shareholder with a known rescission claim the option of retaining his interest if an enterprise prospers or reclaiming his investment if it fails. In sum, the exception gives full recognition to the interests of shareholders, but neglects the interests and expectations of laborers, lenders and trade creditors. We suggest that the exception be reconsidered in light of these interests.

* * *

---

[21] [As eventually enacted, § 510(b) makes no such reliance vs. no reliance distinction—Roe.]

The policies of state and federal securities regulation are important; they are not transcendental. In case of corporate bankruptcy, the public interest favoring private remedies for the violation of these laws must be balanced against other interests worthy of protection—notably the reliance interests of laborers, lenders and trade creditors. Adoption of the rules we have suggested would strike a more equitable balance among these interests.

In 1978, Congress responded to Slain & Kripke by enacting § 510, whose subsection (b) subordinates securities law claims against the bankrupt debtor. Section 510(b), as subsequently amended, reads:

> **§ 510. Subordination**
>
> (b) For the purpose of distribution under this title, a claim arising from rescission of a purchase or sale of a security of the debtor or of an affiliate of the debtor, for damages arising from the purchase or sale of such a security, or for reimbursement or contribution allowed under section 502 on account of such a claim, shall be subordinated to all claims or interests that are senior to or equal the claim or interest represented by such security, except that if such security is common stock, such claim has the same priority as common stock.

¶ 1010: *Oppenheimer,* Slain & Kripke, § 510, Rescission and Fraud

1. Does § 510(b) overturn *Oppenheimer*?
2. What is the policy basis for subordinating rescission and fraud claims? Is it the financial fact that creditors have knowledge of, and rely upon, bankruptcy law's absolute priority rule?

2a. What does such a relying creditor know about the securities laws? Can these creditors get legal advice on the consequences of bankruptcy law but be unable to find lawyers who can advise them about securities law?

3a. Is there a sound policy basis to disallow ranking a tort claim arising from a fraudulently-induced investment as a general creditor's claim? Where does the reliance interest lie? Why shouldn't the defrauded securityholder be allowed to rely on the integrity of the prospectus and financial statements he or she reviewed before buying the security?

3b. Does § 510(b) undermine the policies of the securities laws just at the moment in a company's life when those policies become critical, i.e., protecting securities claimants against deceit or irregularity in the issuance of stock of shaky companies?

4a. Who makes bankruptcy law? Institutional creditors, like banks, insurers, and finance companies, see the virtues of their claims being repaid. Debtors, managers, and employees see the virtues of rehabilitation and of the firm not being liable on securities law claims. These two groups—debtors and their managers, and institutional creditors (and lawyers for each)—are acutely interested in bankruptcy law. Securities issuers, underwriters, institutions holding public debt and equity bump into bankruptcy less often. Hence, they are less acutely concerned with bankruptcy results.

4b. XYZ Corp. sells a Magic Pill at $1,000 each to 1,000 customers, guaranteeing that it will cure baldness. A class action for fraud results in a judgment of $1 million against XYZ. In the subsequent bankruptcy, how does the class split up the $1 million in cash left in XYZ with XYZ's $1 million creditor?

4c. XYZ Corp. sells 1,000 shares of stock to new shareholders at $1,000 per share, under a prospectus that states, "Our new product, the Magic Pill, will cure baldness." A securities class action brings in a judgment of $1 million against XYZ and in favor of the defrauded stock purchasers. In the subsequent bankruptcy, how does the stock class split the $1 million in cash left in XYZ with XYZ's $1 million creditor?

4d. Distinguish ¶ 4b from ¶ 4c, if that is possible.

4e. On what did the creditor reasonably rely? For an informed institutional creditor could reliance depend on the bankruptcy rule? Or should the Bankruptcy Code depend, as § 510(b)'s content and Slain and Kripke's analysis suggest, on what creditors might think before they learned of the Bankruptcy Code's and the securities law's provisions?

5a. Company A sells stock to X for $50. A defrauded X. Had X known the true facts, he would have paid $20.

5b. A goes bankrupt before the proceeds of the stock sale are dissipated. A owed $50 to creditor C, but its only assets are from the stock sale. (I.e., A is insolvent.) If X were allowed to rescind, wouldn't X have avoided both the fraud loss and the business risk loss it would have willingly accepted for $20? What result under § 510(b)?

6a. Same numbers as in 5a. In addition, A, after the stock sale, is worth $100 and owes $50 to D. X sues in fraud and recovers $30, thereby reducing A's value to $70. A dissipates $40 in the next year or so, then goes bankrupt. Summarize the distributional results.

6b. Same numbers as 5a and 6a. However, while X is suing for fraud, A dissipates $40, defaults under a covenant in the loan agreement with D, and voluntarily files for bankruptcy. What distributional result?

6c. Same numbers. The stock sale by A to X was underwritten by Z, the investment banking firm, which distributes the stock for A to X, and which was aware of the fraud. A goes bankrupt. X asserts securities law fraud claims against A and Z. A has contract debt of $50 and the company had a value of $48 at the time of bankruptcy. What distributional result?

6d. Same numbers as 6c. A agreed to indemnify Z for any claims arising under securities laws. What distributional result, if such an agreement were fully enforceable? (Indemnification claims of this nature have been disfavored under securities law decisions such as *BarChris*, 283 F. Supp. 643 (S.D.N.Y. 1968)). What does § 510(b) say about claims for reimbursement and contribution relating to securities law claims? See generally Kenneth Davis, The Status of

Defrauded Security Holders in Corporate Bankruptcy, 1983 Duke Law Journal 1 (1983).

7a. Does § 510(b) always render a securities issuance claim valueless to the defrauded investor? Could it increase the *amount* of the claim, even if it could not affect the claim's priority? Cf. §§ 1124, 1129(b).

7b. Could it give cause for a separate class? What if some subordinated creditors were defrauded, but others not? Should there be a separate class for the fraud claims? Do they then get at least the nuisance value needed to purchase their consent? Cf. § 1129(a)(8).

8. Consider this last variation on the contrasting sales transaction results when there's fraud in a securities sale and when there's fraud in non-securities sale: Parent company has a factory, which it sells to the buyer. It defrauds the buyer. Buyer asserts a fraud claim in bankruptcy. Compare that version to this: Parent company has a subsidiary owning a factory. It sells its stock in the factory subsidiary, but does so fraudulently. What result under § 510(b) for the two scenarios? See Nicholas L. Georgakopoulos, *Strange Subordinations: Correcting Bankruptcy § 510(b)*, 16 Bankruptcy Developments Journal 91, 91–92 (1999).

¶ 1011: The Stockholders' Fraud Claim in the Modern Financial Scandals: SEC v. Worldcom, Inc., 273 F. Supp. 2d 431 (S.D.N.Y. 2003)

[The Sarbanes–Oxley Act of 2002, passed in reaction to major scandals at Enron and WorldCom, has a provision called "Fair Funds for Investors," which authorizes the SEC to seek that securities law violators disgorge funds from their wrong-doing to the SEC. The SEC can then use such funds "for the benefit of the victims of such violation[,]" says the statute. Consider the possibility that a company defrauds its stockholders, then goes bankrupt. The SEC obtains such fair funds for investors from the bankrupt for its wrongful actions. Can the SEC, consistently with § 510(b), then turn around and distribute those funds to the bankrupt's stockholders?]

RAKOFF, District Judge.

This case raises fundamental questions about how market regulators, and the courts, should respond when criminals use the vehicle of a public company to commit a massive fraud. While the persons who perpetrated the fraud can be criminally prosecuted, the exposure of the fraud . . . can drive the company into bankruptcy, leaving unsecured creditors with little *and shareholders with nothing*. . . .

In the case of WorldCom, Inc., we have perhaps the largest accounting fraud in history, with the company's income overstated by an estimated $11 billion, its balance sheet overstated by more than $75 billion, and the loss to shareholders estimated at as much as $200 billion. Those individuals who allegedly perpetrated the fraud are either under indictment or being criminally investigated by the Department of Justice; creditors are seeking recompense in the Bankruptcy Court . . . ; and shareholders and employees are seeking through private class actions . . . to recover what they can, if not from the company (which is in bankruptcy), then from other alleged participants in the effectuation of the fraud. These are the traditional responses.

In the instant lawsuit, however, the Securities and Exchange Commission (the "Commission") . . . has sought something different. . . .

* * *

[The Commission has sought a huge monetary penalty from WorldCom, which it plans to distribute to wronged security holders of WorldCom.] What, then, is the proper monetary penalty? From the Commission's standpoint, it must be one large enough to reflect the magnitude of the fraud and yet not so large as to force the company into liquidation and thereby undercut the Commission's own intensive efforts to reform the company through injunctive relief. The matter is further complicated by the bankruptcy laws and by section 308(a) of the Sarbanes–Oxley Act. Under the bankruptcy laws, the Commission's penalty claim is treated as simply another claim by one of many unsecured creditors, a group that, under the plan of reorganization . . . will generally recover about one-third of every dollar claimed. . . .

As for section 308(a), while it *gives the Commission the opportunity to pay any penalty it recovers to the shareholder victims* rather than to the U.S. Treasury, a penalty that was premised *primarily* on that basis might arguably run afoul of the provisions of the Bankruptcy Code that subordinate shareholder claims below all others. *As a general rule, defrauded shareholders can not expect to recover one penny in bankruptcy* [due to section 510(b)]; *and nothing in section 308(a) suggests that Congress intended to give shareholders a greater priority in bankruptcy than they previously enjoyed.*

This is not to say, however, that the Commission cannot give its penalty recovery to the shareholders, as section 308(a) [of the non-bankruptcy statute, Sarbanes–Oxley] so laudably prescribes, or that it cannot take some account of shareholder loss in formulating the size and nature of its penalty. . . . What the Commission may not do, at least in a case in which the company is in bankruptcy, is determine the size of the penalty *primarily* on the basis of how much shareholder loss will thereby be recompensed, for this would . . . be adverse to the priorities established under the bankruptcy laws [via section 510(b)]. . . .

. . . [T]he Commission has negotiated a settlement that results in a penalty dozens of times larger than any it previously imposed against a public company. . . . [T]he parties filed on July 2, 2003 a . . . proposed settlement . . . [netting out to] $750 million [after accounting for the one-third pro rata bankruptcy recovery for unsecured creditors]—or 75 times greater than any prior such penalty. . . .

* * *

Here, the Court is satisfied that the Commission has carefully reviewed all relevant considerations and has arrived at a penalty that, while taking adequate account of the magnitude of the fraud and the need for punishment and deterrence, fairly and reasonably reflects the realities of this complex situation. Undoubtedly the settlement will be criticized by, among others, those shareholders unfamiliar with the severe limits imposed on their recovery by the bankruptcy laws, . . . and those professed pundits and ideologues for whom anything less than a corporate death penalty constitutes an "outrage." But the Court is convinced, for the reasons already outlined above, that the proposed settlement is not only fair and reasonable but as good an outcome as anyone could reasonably expect in these difficult circumstances.

Accordingly, the settlement of the monetary penalty phase of this litigation is hereby approved, and the Court will enter today the Final Judgment as to Monetary Relief in the form submitted by the parties.

SO ORDERED.

¶ 1012: Questions on *Worldcom*

1. Is *WorldCom* inconsistent with § 510(b)?
2. If it is, what explains the inconsistency? Because § 510(b) wasn't such a good idea to begin with? Because creditors draft the Bankruptcy Code, while stockholders (or their representatives) draft the securities laws? That is, could it be that the SEC thinks the integrity of the stock market is more important than the potential surprise to creditors?
3. Who "pays" for the SEC's WorldCom fund? The "company"? Or WorldCom's creditors? Are they the players primarily culpable for WorldCom's management's fraud?

¶ 1013: Does Subordination Make the Rescission or Damages Claim Useless, Always?

Even a subordinated claim can have value, if the size of the subordinated securities claim is greater than that of the associated contract claim. For the subordinated securities claim to have value, the contract claim must be paid in full. Typically that would entail the damages for the fraud claim becoming nil. But consider the possibility, more as an exercise than as a matter of real transactional importance, if the securities law claim exceeds the size of the contract claim.

The bankrupt company is worth $2000, with $1000 of senior debt, $1000 of subordinated debt, and an issue of preferred stock. The subordinated debt has a low interest rate. If § 1124 were successfully invoked against them, the market value of their claim would be $500. The subordinated bondholders were defrauded in the issuance of their securities.

$2000	$1000 Senior
	$1000 Subordinated at 7%, worth $500 if § 1124(2) used
	Preferred stock
	Common stock

The 7% debentureholders would like to assert a fraud claim for $1000 as a general creditor of the bankrupt, but they can't because of § 510(b). And § 1124 hurts them further.

Is the following the balance sheet of the bankrupt company after invocation of § 1124 and subordination of the debentureholders' fraud claim under § 510(b)?

$2000	$1000 Senior
	$1000 [Contractually] Subordinated at 7%, worth $500 if § 1124(2) used
	$ 500 Fraud claim (subordinated due to § 510(b))
	Preferred stock
	Common stock

¶ 1014: Reranking

End of story? Can the damaged securities buyers who don't have access to a sympathetic agency's "fair fund for investors," as in WorldCom, turn around to sue the underwriter, the accountants, and management for their acts in the securities violations? Can *these* third parties then assert contractual claims for indemnification against the issuer? Will the indemnification claims be subordinated?

Rarely do courts stay proceedings against co-defendants of a bankrupt, even though § 362 stays proceedings against the bankrupt. So, while any proceeding against the debtor is stayed, the suits against co-defendants ordinarily are not. Melvyn Weiss, William Lerach & Jan Adler, *Obtaining Adequate Monetary Relief for Shareholders of Bankrupt Public Companies: The Nearly Impossible Dream, in* Complex Litigation in the Context of the Bankruptcy Laws 11, 16–24 (Michael Perlis ed. 1984) (Practising Law Institute) (collecting authorities).

Consider a suit against an investment bank for fraud in the issuance of a security. Outside of bankruptcy, the investment bank would usually have a claim, if the underlying plaintiff's suit for fraud is successful, for contribution or indemnity against the bankrupt corporation. Although some bankruptcy courts have decided that the claim for indemnity may only be asserted to the extent of the underlying claim (which would be subordinated under § 510(b)), does the statute explicitly cover indemnity claims?

In 1984 Congress amended the original form of § 510, adding the phrase "or for reimbursement or contribution . . . on account of such a claim [for rescission or damages in the purchase or sale of a security]." See § 510(b) in its entirety. In Christian Life Center Litigation Defense Comm. v. Silva, 821 F.2d 1370 (1987), a case that arose before the phrase "for reimbursement or contribution" was added in 1984, claims for contractual indemnity for litigation expenses—but not for liability—were reimbursable. Similarly-situated creditors failed after 1984. In re De Laurentis Entm't Grp., Inc. 124 B. R. 305 (C.D. Cal 1991) (claims for contractual indemnity for litigation expenses not reimbursable). See also In re Investors Funding Corp. of N.Y., 8 B. R. 260, 264 (S.D.N.Y 1980); In re Georgian Villa Inc., 9 Bankr. 969, 973 (N.D. Ga. 1981).

¶ 1015: Transition Problem

Bank lends to Corporation, a publicly-held firm. Corporation's fortunes then decline to an extent greater than is publicly known. Bank informs the management of Corporation that, absent an increase in their equity cushion, Bank will call its loan (or fail to renew the credit upon its maturity).

Thereafter Corporation issues common stock to the public under a prospectus that fails to disclose the full extent of its ill-fortune. In the subsequent bankruptcy the defrauded stock purchasers seek to assert a claim other than as stockholders. What result under § 510(b)? Under § 510(c)? Cf. *W.T. Grant* and *American Lumber,* next chapter.

CHAPTER 11

EQUITABLE SUBORDINATION OF THE CREDITOR'S CLAIM AND LENDER LIABILITY

Must the wrong-doing creditor have a stock interest to justify equitably subordinating the creditor? The legislative history to § 510(c) says:

> Section 510(c)(1) of the House amendment represents a compromise between similar provisions in the House bill and Senate amendment. After notice and a hearing, the court may, under principles of equitable subordination, subordinate for purposes of distribution all or part of an allowed claim to all or part of another allowed claim or all or part of an allowed interest to all or part of another allowed interest. . . . It is intended that the term "principles of equitable subordination" follow existing case law and leave to the courts development of this principle. To date, under existing law, a claim is generally subordinated only if the holder of such claim is guilty of inequitable conduct, or the claim itself is of a status susceptible to subordination, such as a penalty or a claim for damages arising from the purchase or sale of a security of the debtor. The fact that such a claim may be secured is of no consequence to the issue of subordination. However, it is inconceivable that the sta-

tus of a claim as a secured claim could ever be grounds for justifying equitable subordination.

Senate Report No. 95–989, 95th Cong., 2d Sess. 74 (1978). Section 510(c) says:

(c) Notwithstanding subsections (a) and (b) of this section, after notice and a hearing, the court may

(1) under principles of equitable subordination, subordinate for purposes of distribution all or part of an allowed claim to all or part of another allowed claim or all or part of an allowed interest to all or part of another allowed interest; or

(2) order that any lien securing such a subordinated claim be transferred to the estate.

A. EQUITABLE SUBORDINATION OF A CREDITOR'S CLAIM

¶ 1101: In re American Lumber Co., 7 B.R. 519 (Bankr. D. Minn. 1979)

[American Lumber was formed in January 1975. It obtained its financing largely from defendant bank.]

7. After January 17, 1975, ALC [American Lumber Company] commenced operation of a wholesale lumber business. It purchased lumber, held it in inventory and sold it to residential and commercial builders. The building and lumber business climate in the summer and fall of 1975 was unfavorable and ALC suffered losses in the following amounts:

May	1975	$27,144.00
June	1975	$31,380.00
July	1975	$102,360.00
August	1975	$42,380.00

* * *

9. On September 19, 1975, defendant loaned ALC $100,000.00, evidenced by a demand promissory note. The loan was made because ALC was short of cash.

* * *

11. On October 17, 1975, the three principals of ALC met with . . . officers of defendant, and advised them that the loan was in default and ALC was acutely short of cash, and proposed a "cut-back" plan designed to improve the financial stability of ALC.

* * *

13. On October 21, 1975, a meeting was held at the office of defendant-bank. It was attended by bank officers Shepley and Dingman, two of its counsel, Jerome Simon, Esq. and Charles Bans, Esq., ALC officers Lilja,

Kulas and Peterson, and ALC counsel Leo Stern. Shepley announced at the outset that defendant was calling all of the indebtedness of ALC. There was discussion concerning foreclosure of defendant's security interests in the assets of ALC. *Simon learned that defendant had no security interest in the inventory of ALC,* a discussion ensued between defendant's officers and its counsel, and Simon remarked in substance that he had an idea whereby a security interest could be taken on the inventory of ALC, *funds could be advanced by defendant to ALC to increase the value of certain accounts receivable on projects that were not completed and in which defendant had [a] security interest,* and the general creditors could be "screwed." No accommodation was reached during this meeting. Approximately $400,000.00 of unsecured creditors other than defendant existed at that time. Defendant considered placing ALC in bankruptcy.

14. On October 22, 1975, another meeting was held attended by Lilja, Kulas and Peterson of ALC and Shepley and Dingman of defendant. Discussion centered around the value of the interest of ALC in a housing project known as Lame Deer, Montana, in which ALC had made a substantial investment which would be seriously jeopardized if it were not completed. Again, no resolution of the situation occurred. *Plaintiff's officers refused to execute security agreements covering the inventory and equipment of ALC.*

15. On October 23, 1975, Shepley and Dingman of defendant advised Lilja of plaintiff that no further funds would be advanced to ALC, that defendant was declaring ALC in default on its promissory notes and the demand promissory note of September 19, 1975, and that defendant was offsetting all funds in the accounts of ALC with defendant. Such offsets were then made.

16. On October 24, 1975, Dingman hand-delivered a letter from Shepley to Lilja of ALC. The letter recited all the existing defaults, including the failure to pay the ESOT installment due on October 15, 1975 [to the Employee Stock Ownership Trust] and detailed what the bank had done and proposed to do. *Security Agreements describing inventory and equipment of ALC and corresponding financing statements were executed and delivered to defendant.*

17. On October 24, 1975, the liquidation of the business of ALC under the supervision of defendant began.

18. All cash and amounts collected on accounts receivable were given by ALC to defendant, which deposited them into a "collateral" or "dominion" account which was opened at Mr. Dingman's instruction and on which he was the sole signatory. On October 24, 1975, defendant foreclosed upon its security interests in accounts receivable and contract rights and at no time thereafter relinquished its control over the collection of accounts receivable.

19. On October 24, 1975, ALC's obligation on its Guaranty of the $1,000,000.00 loan obligation of ESOT to defendant was unconditional. The only assets of ESOT on that date were 10,000 shares of common stock of ALC which had been pledged to defendant and $93.47 in its general checking account. The common stock of ALC had no value.

20. On October 24, 1975, the fair market value of the assets of ALC [was] approximately as follows [in thousands of dollars]:

Cash	___
A/R . . .	1,262
Inventories	771
Prepaid	20
Fixed Assets	512
	2,565

21. On October 24, 1975, the liabilities of ALC were [in thousands of dollars] as follows:

Accounts Payable	$570
Accrued Liabilities	50
Salaries	20
Long Term Debt	1,587
Mortgage	167
Indebtedness on Guaranty to ESOT	938
	3,332

22. On October 24, 1975, the liabilities of ALC substantially exceeded the fair and reasonable value of its assets, by $766,500.00 more or less, and ALC was insolvent.

23. Prior to October 24, 1975, ALC had employed Park Detective Agency, Inc. a security guard service, to guard its lumber yard in Minneapolis. On October 24, 1975, defendant contacted Mr. Pavey, President of Park Detective Agency, Inc., and informed him that defendant wished to contract with his firm to secure the premises of ALC. A contract was entered into between Park Detective Agency and defendant on October 25, 1975. Thereafter, defendant instructed Park as to whom could be admitted to the premises and in effect took control over access to said premises. Defendant instructed Park that [bank officers] were to be contacted in emergency situations and gave Park their home telephone numbers. Defendant advised Park it would pay all fees of Park. It paid fees for those services rendered from October 25, 1975, to March 1, 1976, at which time it discharged Park. Park during this time period received instructions either by telephone or notes from defendant when admitting individuals to the ALC lumber yard.

24. On October 24, 1975, all employees of ALC were terminated. On or about October 31, 1975, effective October 28, 1975, ALC rehired a skeleton crew for the yard and truck driver employees, an accounts receivable clerk, an accounts payable clerk, two city desk clerks, and a receptionist. Its entire sales force of approximately four employees was not rehired because further sales were not contemplated. Before rehiring those employees identified above, in accordance with instructions from defendant, ALC advised Dingman who in its view were necessary to conduct an orderly liquidation and defendant approved of their rehiring and agreed to honor payroll checks for them. . . . This conduct was only consistent with orderly liquidation of ALC.

25. On or about October 24, 1975, defendant, by and through Dingman, began receiving and opening the incoming mail at the office of ALC and at all material times thereafter continued doing so on nearly a daily basis. All checks and cash so received were taken by Dingman and deposited into the collateral (dominion) account described in paragraph 18. This conduct was consistent with orderly liquidation of ALC.

26. On and after October 24, 1975, defendant, by and through Dingman, reviewed ALC checks prepared by ALC which had not been delivered to payees and ALC checks presented for payment by payees, and determined whether they respectively would be released or paid. Defendant made such determinations based upon its understanding and belief as to whether or not such payment would likely enhance the value of one or more of the accounts receivables in which defendant had a perfected security interest. When defendant believed there would be such an increase, the check was released or paid; when it believed the contrary, the release or payment was not authorized. General unsecured creditors were not paid unless that test was satisfied. On and after October 24, 1975, defendant did not intend to pay general unsecured creditors. Sales taxes incurred were not approved for payment by defendant. This conduct was only consistent with orderly liquidation of ALC.

27. During the course of meetings between October 17, 1975, and October 24, 1975, much discussion between representatives of ALC and defendant centered on a project known as Lame Deer, Montana, which was a government-financed housing development for Indians on and around the Cheyenne Indian Reservation. Defendant was advised that ALC had been awarded a subcontract by G.R. Construction Co., dated July 1975, which had a contract price of $1,026,365.00 payable to ALC if entirely completed. The terms of payment were stated in the subcontract. Under the subcontract ALC had the duty to furnish construction supplies and materials, fabricate them into panels, furnish all of the labor related to fabrication and construction, and construct residences. Payment to be made as residences were completed and accepted. Prior to October 24, 1975, only one payment had been made to ALC by G.R. Construction Co. That payment was in an approximate sum of $34,000.00 and ALC anticipated receiving more funds as the project continued. Virtually all materials and supplies required for completion of the project had been delivered to the Lame Deer project site prior to October 24, 1975[.] [H]owever, some additional materials and substantial amounts of labor were necessary. ALC had contracted with Aetna Oak–Mak Construction Co. to furnish all labor on the project. Defendant was advised about the status of the subcontract and decided that the potential high value of the G.R. Construction account receivable of ALC would be in serious jeopardy if the project were not completed and that such jeopardy justified the infusion of more funds for materials, supplies, and labor. This decision was only consistent with an orderly liquidation of ALC.

* * *

37. [In October and November, the bank advanced about $440,000 to the debtor. The advances] were used to pay suppliers, materialmen and laborers in connection with the Lame Deer, Montana project, [as well as] other projects where failure to pay suppliers, materialmen or

laborers would jeopardize the value of an account receivable in which defendant had a security interest or for ALC payroll for personnel critical to the handling of the orderly liquidation of ALC. At least $127,000.00 of said advances were used on or about November 18, 1975, to pay materialmen and suppliers in connection with the Lame Deer project, and $33,783.78 of said advances were used to pay Aetna Oak–Mak laborers working on said Lame Deer project between October 17, 1975, and December 7, 1975.

* * *

39. On October 24, 1975, defendant decided to not pay general unsecured creditors and at all material times thereafter adhered to that decision.

* * *

45. On or about October 30, 1975, ALC was operating under the supervision of defendant. ALC referred a telephone inquiry made by R.J. Long of the American Lumbermen's Credit Association, a trade credit organization, to defendant's officer Dingman. Dingman told Long that the business of ALC was continuing to the extent of fulfilling current contracts where it was necessary to supply additional material in order to protect the investment already made. Dingman advised Long that ALC was not in a bankrupt situation. Dingman advised Long that it was defendant's intention to run the liquidation on a completely orderly basis and that defendant did not view it as a fire sale situation.

46. On or about November 19, 1975, Dingman again received a telephone inquiry from Long of the American Lumbermen's Credit Association. At that time, *Dingman said ALC was not insolvent on the books,* that ALC continued to operate[,] was still delivering material on uncompleted contracts, and that defendant was paying cash for a little material necessary to complete such contracts.

47. During this conversation, Dingman represented that defendant was doing everything possible to salvage something for the unsecured creditors, and that the best evidence of this was the fact that defendant was giving ALC enough support to liquidate slowly, rather than on a quick sacrifice basis.

48. *The American Lumbermen's Credit Association disseminated the information received from defendant to one creditor.*

49. On or about November 21, 1975, defendant gave written notice to ALC that it was foreclosing its security agreement obtained on October 24, 1975.

50. On November 3 and 4, 1975, Dingman of defendant-bank and Timothy Peterson of ALC visited Lame Deer, Montana, for the purpose of inspecting the project to determine whether defendant should advance additional funds to complete the project. Dingman determined that the value of the account receivable which could be recovered by completing the contract was substantially in excess of the financial investment it would require. Any value realized would under the then circumstances have redounded solely to the benefit of the defendant.

* * *

52. On or about December 1, 1975, defendant had employed James Haney, formerly construction superintendent with ALC in charge of the

Lame Deer project, to watch the inventory at the construction site. First National agreed to pay Haney for his services, employed him through January 8, 1976, and paid him according to its agreement.

* * *

58. On or about October 24, 1975, defendant advised Lilja, Kulas and Peterson that it was not prepared to finance the salaries which each had been receiving from ALC. . . . Those salaries had been established at [$300,000.00 in the aggregate.] . . . On or about October 24, 1975, defendant told them it was prepared to pay lesser annualized salaries of approximately $30,000.00, $20,000.00, and $20,000.00, respectively, for their services. This was accepted and was a part of the orderly liquidation of ALC.

59. Checks were drawn about December 1, 1975 on the general checking account of ALC payable to Lilja in the sum of $2,190.00, Kulas in the sum of $2,190.00, and Peterson in the sum of $2,190.00. At defendant's demand, each was endorsed to defendant and applied by it to reduce the personal loans of the three principals of ALC. Defendant approved the payment.

60. After October 23, 1975 neither ALC nor its officers or directors had control over the moneys of ALC or have any sources of funds with which to pay suppliers or general unsecured creditors. Defendant exercised absolute control over the use of the funds resulting from its advances to ALC as reflected by promissory notes given between October 24, 1975, and December 2, 1975.

61. Between October 24, 1975, and December 2, 1975, defendant advanced an aggregate of $442,810.74 to ALC. Between October 24, 1975, and December 10, 1975, defendant had received and credited to the indebtedness of ALC the aggregate sum of $410,092.34. By December 11, 1975, such credits totaled $466,187.81. Such credits reflected the collection of ALC accounts receivable.

62. An Involuntary Petition in Bankruptcy against ALC was filed on February 11, 1976, and ALC was subsequently adjudicated bankrupt.

63. Defendant filed its Proof of Claim No. 37 for $1,781,382.69 in the resulting bankruptcy case. The claim included claimed indebtedness of $937,500.00 of ALC resulting from Guaranty of the [Employee Stock Ownership Trust] indebtedness to defendant.

64. By receiving the proceeds of sales of inventory and equipment of ALC, defendant received proceeds which otherwise would have been available for payment of general unsecured creditors of ALC.

65. When the principals resigned on December 5, 1975, all the books and records of ALC were intact. Defendant changed locks and had sole and exclusive use of the offices of ALC and sole and exclusive access to and control over such records. To the extent any existent records of ALC were not available at trial, such resulted from defendant's failure to properly maintain custody of such books and records.

CONCLUSIONS OF LAW

1. On October 24, 1975, ALC transferred security interests in inventory and equipment to defendant.

2. Said transfers occurred within four (4) months [the pre–1978 ordinary preference period] of the filing of the Involuntary Petition in

Bankruptcy against ALC. [Ninety days is the preference period under § 547 of the subsequently-enacted 1978 Bankruptcy Code.]

3. Said transfers were made to secure an antecedent debt of ALC to defendant.

4. Said transfers allowed defendant to obtain a higher percentage of the obligation of ALC to it than other creditors of the same class.

5. Such transfers occurred at a time that ALC was insolvent within the meaning of the Bankruptcy Act.

6. Defendant knew and had reasonable grounds to know of such insolvency, [a preference requirement dropped for the initial transferee, via § 550 in the 1978 Bankruptcy Code].

7. Said transfers constituted voidable preferences under § 60 of the Bankruptcy Act[, the predecessor to § 547 of the 1978 Bankruptcy Code].

18. Plaintiff is entitled to judgment in the sum of $488,744.65; representing the aggregate of $346,753.88 received by defendant from the sale of ALC Minneapolis inventory, the $94,554.00 fair and reasonable value of Montana inventory which defendant took into possession on or about December 5, 1975, and the $47,436.77 received by defendant from the sale of equipment, together with interest thereon according to law from January 1, 1976, to the present.

19. On October 24, 1975, and at all material times thereafter, defendant had and exercised control over all aspects of the finances and operations of ALC including the following: payment of payables and wages, collection and use of accounts receivable and contract rights, purchase and use of supplies and materials, inventory sales, the lumber yard in Minneapolis, the salaries of the principals, the employment of employees, and receipt of payments for sales and accounts receivable.

* * *

21. By reason of its exercise of control over ALC and its operation defendant had a duty and an obligation to deal fairly and impartially with ALC and its other unsecured creditors.

22. Defendant breached its duty by undertaking a course of liquidation that was designed solely to preempt from general unsecured creditors any portion of the value of the inventory and equipment of ALC and to thereby enhance the value of defendant's previously existing security interest in the accounts receivable and contract rights of ALC.

23. By reason of said breach of fiduciary duty to the creditors of ALC, defendant's claim shall be subordinated to the claims of general unsecured creditors in the interest of equity.

ORDER FOR JUDGMENT

Let judgment be entered accordingly.

¶ 1102: Questions on *American Lumber*

1. Consider the Bank's business problems in dealing with the failing American Lumber. First, it didn't have a security interest in the company's inventory. Second, it faced a problem generally encountered by creditors of a declining firm. The value of accounts receivable deteriorates when a firm liquidates. When the firm liquidates

(as opposed to reorganizing but staying in business), customers have one less incentive to pay the bill on time or in full. One crucial incentive for a customer to pay on time is that the customer wants to deal with its supplier again; if the customer fails to pay on time in full, the supplier is less likely to ship the next batch of goods to the customer. But when it becomes known that the supplier is going out of business (i.e., not just in trouble and reorganizing, although sometimes even then, but closing up its shop), some customers find fault with the delivery, state that the supplier breached the contract, or in some cases just do not pay:

> While it is true that under the stress of financial difficulties ordinarily honest debtors do things to their creditors that they would not do in the absence of financial stress, it is also true that financially disabled debtors have things done to them by ordinarily honest persons which would not be attempted if they enjoyed apparently good financial health. When word of financial difficulty spreads, the debtor's own trade creditors often decline to pay as they would have in the ordinary course, suddenly reporting that the dresses were the wrong size, were the wrong color, or were not ordered. The more formal the recognition of the debtor's plight, the greater the pressure on it, and the greater the damages through the debtor, to its creditors.

Peter Coogan, Richard Broude & Herman Glatt, *Comments on Some Reorganization Provisions of the Pending Bankruptcy Bills*, 30 Business Lawyer 1149, 1155 (1974).

2. What did the Bank do wrong? Was its taking a security interest in the inventory a basis for equitably subordinating its entire claim? Why isn't that a preference on the eve of bankruptcy? The remedy for taking a preference would usually be the return of the seized security for the benefit of all unsecured creditors (including the Bank, to the extent unsecured). In fact, didn't the court invoke and apply preference law? (Incidentally, don't be confused by the four month preference period in the case, which arose under pre–1978 bankruptcy law. In 1978 Congress changed the basic preference period to 90 days.)

3. What then did the Bank do wrong? Did it "control" American Lumber? How? What implications are there to control? If control put the Bank in a position analogous to that of a controlling shareholder or board of directors, what analysis? Was the controlling shareholder engaged in an interested party transaction?

4. The Bank misrepresented American Lumber's condition to the trade creditors' credit association. Did that hurt trade creditors as represented on the October 24 balance sheet? Did it hurt new trade creditors? To whom should the Bank be equitably subordinated? To what extent?

5. On October 24 what distribution in bankruptcy to trade creditors and the Bank? Use the balance sheets the court provides.

6. Why the remedy in the final paragraph of the opinion? What did the Bank do wrong? Cf. § 510(c) ("under principles of equitable sub-

ordination, [the court may] subordinate . . . all or part of an allowed claim"). Administrative convenience? Punishment? Deterrence?

7. Does *American Lumber* follow directly from *Deep Rock*?

8. Consider a comment on an earlier batch of equitable subordination cases:

> The lure of equitable subordination doctrine [is] . . . the erroneous but understandable belief of judges that any imprecision in the corrective function of the doctrine typically bears down on and punishes a transferee who was . . . at fault. . . .

Robert C. Clark, *The Duties of the Corporate Debtor to Its Creditors*, 90 Harvard Law Review 505, 532 (1977).

9. In the district court affirmation, In re American Lumber Co., 5 Bankr. 470, 478 (D. Minn. 1980), the affirming court said:

> While defendant [bank] argues that subordination will cause members of the financial community to feel they cannot give financial assistance to failing companies, but must instead foreclose on their security interests and collect debts swiftly, not leaving any chance for survival, the Court is singularly unimpressed.

¶ 1103: The Collapse of W.T. Grant Company

The following case, Gosoff v. Rodman (In re W.T. Grant Co.), 699 F.2d 599 (2d Cir. 1983), is the circuit court's final opinion on the settlement of the complex litigation surrounding the collapse of W.T. Grant Co. Grant's bankruptcy was, at the time (October 1975), both the largest failure of a retailer and the largest bankruptcy under the Bankruptcy Act that reigned from 1938 through 1978.

Prior to July 1973, Grant relied on its finance subsidiary, W.T. Grant Financial Corporation, for the majority of its short-term cash financing needs. Grant Financial obtained financing by selling commercial paper. Commercial paper is a short-term I.O.U. running directly from the borrower to the lender, usually without a bank as the intermediary. There is no indenture, loan agreement, or trustee. The lender relies on the high creditworthiness of the borrower and the short duration of the loan.

Later, Grant converted a portion of its outstanding commercial paper to long-term debt. (This may have been because short-term interest rates were unusually high at the time; however, as Grant deteriorated it was going to lose access to the commercial paper market anyway.) Morgan Guaranty Trust Company became the "lead bank" in the structuring and financing of Grant's long-term debt. A summary of the complex financial transactions that preceded the bankruptcy filing follows:

1. January 31, 1973: Grant has $380,033,500 of outstanding commercial paper and $10,000,000 in outstanding bank debt.
2. July 5, 1973: The Term Loan, under which Grant Financial borrows $100,000,000 from eight banks as a five year term loan. The banks include Chase Manhattan, which also was the indenture trustee for Grant's $92,507,000 of 4¾% unsecured

subordinated debentures, and Citibank, which also was the indenture trustee for Grant's $834,000 of 4% unsecured subordinated debentures.

3. Late 1973 and early 1974: Grant's financial performance declines; the credit rating agencies lower their rating for Grant's commercial paper.
4. December 1973: Grant Financial has $400,000,000 in outstanding commercial paper.
5. March 5, 1974: Moody's, the bond and credit rating agency, withdraws Grant's commercial paper rating and further lowers its long-term debt rating.
6. March 12, 1974: Eight banks re-establish Grant's lines of credit and advance funds; total outstanding loans to Grant Financial reach $415,000,000; $132,000,000 used to pay off commercial paper.
7. June 1974: Outstanding commercial paper has been reduced to $1,000,000.
8. Early August 1974: Secured Demand Loan, under which Morgan, Chase, and Citibank advance $5,000,000 to Grant secured by accounts receivable.
9. Late August 1974: Interim Loan and Guaranty Agreement, under which Grant Financial becomes indebted to 11 banks for $44,000,000; Grant Financial assumes Grant's obligation to repay $15,000,000 of Secured Demand Loans and incurs $29,000,000 of new loans. Grant guarantees the $44,000,000 and secures the guaranty by granting a security interest in accounts receivable from sales of goods. Total outstanding borrowings from term loans and short term borrowings to 12 banks reach $517,000,000.
10. September 16, 1974 (effective October 8, 1974): Loan and Guaranty Agreement, under which Grant Financial and Grant as guarantor receive additional advance from banks of $66,587,500. Banks agree to extend maturity of $44,000,000 and all other short-term loans to June 2, 1975. Banks receive security for total outstanding loans of $600,000,000 and $100,000,000 term loan. Security is all of Grant's accounts receivable and a pledge of stock in a Grant Canadian subsidiary. Loan is to be junior to inventory liens to certain suppliers and senior to unsecured debentureholders.
11. April 1, 1975 (executed June 2, 1975): Loan Extension Agreement, under which Grant pays 116 banks (those owed less than $5,000,000 each) a total of $56,931,665 from sale of inventory. Remaining banks extend maturity of short-term loans to March 31, 1976. Short-term outstanding bank loans now total $540,916,978.
12. May 15, 1975: To obtain inventory to sell in stores, Grant gives certain vendors and suppliers a lien on inventory.
13. August 6, 1975 (effective September 15, 1975): Amended Loan Extension Agreement, under which the maturity of $540 million of short-term loans is extended to July 30, 1976. Under a Trade Subordination Agreement, $300 million of $540 million is

subordinated to certain trade obligations. Under an Intercorporate Subordination Agreement, Grant Financial's loans to its parent of $819,887,663 are subordinated to bank claims against Grant under the various guaranty and loan agreements of $640,916,978.

14. October 2, 1975: Grant files for bankruptcy.

15. During the settlement negotiations, the trustee argued that the banks dominated and controlled Grant. A director of Morgan Guaranty, the lead bank, sat on Grant's Board and was a member of Grant's Executive Committee and Audit Committee. The banks agreed to settle the debentureholders' equitable subordination suit, with the settlement reflecting the banks' expectation that they might fail to persuade the court that they did not control Grant or that, if they did, their priority should not be altered. The subordinated debentureholders get 19 cents on each dollar of their claim, although the banks aren't paid back in full. Dissenting subordinated debentureholders sued, and the appellate opinion for their suit appears next.

See Gosoff v. Rodman, 699 F.2d 599, 601–04 (2d Cir. 1983); In re W.T. Grant Co., 4 Bankr. 53 (Bankr. S.D.N.Y. 1981); *Investigating the Collapse of W.T. Grant,* Bus. Week, July 19, 1976, at 60–62; M. Douglas–Hamilton, *ALI–ABA Resource Materials: Banking and Commercial Lending Law—1980, in* Some Problems Associated with Creditor Control of Debtor Companies 330–57 (1980).

¶ 1104: In re W.T. Grant Co., 699 F.2d 599 (2d Cir. 1983)

Friendly, Circuit Judge:

These appeals arise from the mammoth bankruptcy proceedings of W.T. Grant Co. Grant filed under Chapter XI on October 2, 1975. . . . The present appeals concern the last of a series of compromises and settlements designed to avoid what would necessarily have been extremely protracted litigation with the various claimants.

* * *

The Proceedings in the Bankruptcy Court and the District Court

After Grant had been ordered into liquidation, the banks and Charles G. Rodman, as Trustee, asserted a multitude of claims against each other. . . . [S]ettlement negotiations were instituted. These resulted in an agreement which, in addition to settling the claims of the banks, encompassed what [the trial judge] termed a "global settlement," i.e., a "framework for the further administration of the bankrupt estate and the satisfaction of claims filed against such estate." 4 Bankr. Ct. Dec. at 602. . . . [T]he settlement provided that the bank claimants were to receive an initial cash distribution of $165,700,000, or approximately 25% of their allowed claims. More was to be paid when and if funds became available. The Trustee agreed not to sue the 116 banks whose loans of $56,931,665.59 were paid in June, 1975 [although these repayments might have been preferential]. Finally, the agreement created a fund of $95,378,373, the full amount of the claims of subordinated debentureholders, pending resolution of their dispute with the bank claimants as to whether the subordination clauses of their indentures should be given effect so as to subordinate the debenture holder's claims to the bank claims. The Bankruptcy Judge approved the banks' settlement on July 20, 1978. . . . There was no appeal of this "global settlement" to the district court.[1]

Having thus provided the necessary framework, the Trustee, the bank claimants, United States Trust Company (U.S. Trust) as indenture trustee replacing Chase under the Indenture for the 4¾% Subordinated Debentures, and representatives of these debentureholders entered into negotiations for the settlement of the latter's claims. The rights of the debentureholders depended on the interpretation and application of a clause in their indentures subordinating their claims to "Senior Indebtedness" of Grant. The Indenture under which the 4¾% Debentures were issued defined this as stated in the margin;[2] the Indenture [governing] the small amount of outstanding 4% Debentures was to the same effect. If the bank claims were and remained enforceable as Senior Indebtedness to which the debentureholders were subordinated, the latter would receive nothing. However, [the debentureholders' trustee] alleged that . . . the conduct of the banks might require that the contractual subordination provisions be disregarded and even that the subordinated debentureholders be accorded a status prior to that of the banks. These reasons, stated in detail in [the trial judge's] opinion approving the settlement, . . . were as follows:

> (a) At the time of the Initial Security Agreement of September 16, 1974, the bank claimants knew or had reasonable cause to believe that Grant was insolvent and that the granting of security interests would discourage further extensions of trade credit to Grant and substantially reduce the flow of merchandise into Grant stores, thereby impairing the prospects for a successful reorganization of Grant.
>
> (b) By forcing Grant into the Inventory Security Agreement and Trade Subordination Agreement the bank claimants increased the amount of Senior Indebtedness to which the junior debentureholders were subordinated.
>
> (c) In the summer of 1974, the bank claimants directed Grant not to proceed with a proposed sale of $100,000,000 of customer accounts receivable to Beneficial Finance Corporation and the use of some undetermined portion of the proceeds to purchase 4¾% debentures at 25 cents on the dollar.

---

[1] An Ad Hoc Protective Committee of 4¾% Convertible Subordinated Debentures of W.T. Grant Company . . . raised objections to the bank's settlement at the hearing. The [Ad Hoc Committee's] failure . . . to pursue its objections by appealing [all issues] forecloses some of the issues raised in the present appeal[, including whether there should be a] re-opening of the question whether the Trustee properly agreed not to question the [potentially preferential] June 1975, payments of $56,931,665.59 to the 116 other bank creditors of Grant.

[2] The term "Senior Indebtedness" shall mean the principal of and premium, if any, and interest on (a) indebtedness . . . of the Company for money borrowed from or guaranteed . . . evidenced by notes or similar obligations, (b) indebtedness of the Company evidenced by notes or debentures . . . issued under the provisions of an indenture or similar instrument between the Company and a bank or trust company . . . ; *unless, in each case, by the terms of the instrument by which the Company incurred, assumed or guaranteed such indebtedness . . . is not superior in right of payment to the Debentures. . . .*

(d) The bank claimants used their position of control over Grant's management to prevent Grant from promptly seeking relief under the Bankruptcy Act, feeding it just enough money to keep its head above water while strengthening their security position, allowing the passage of the four months period for avoiding preferences under [the predecessor to § 547] and hoping to allow the passage of the one year provision of [the predecessor to § 550] for the avoidance of liens and fraudulent transfers.

The bank claimants made a variety of responses. They denied having had any fiduciary relationship to Grant, asserted that they had made loans in the belief fostered by Grant's management that Grant remained viable, contended that Grant's management itself had abandoned the proposed sale of accounts receivable, and denied that they had prevented Grant from seeking rehabilitation under the Bankruptcy Act. They asserted, moreover, that as to many of U.S. Trust's [the indenture trustee's] claims, the remedy, even if the claim were made out, would be invalidation of the banks' security interests rather than subordination to the debentureholders. U.S. Trust also raised claims of conflict of interest and derelictions of duty against Chase, its predecessor trustee. . . .

The settlement originally provided for the payment of 14% of the claims of the accepting subordinated debentureholders. . . .

At a hearing before Judge Galgay objections were made by eleven debentureholders. . . . The [eleven] objectors asserted principally that the . . . bank claims should be equitably subordinated to the debentures because of the control and dominion over Grant allegedly exercised by the banks. . . . Judge Galgay . . . concluded that the original settlement represented a fair compromise, taking into account the strengths and weaknesses of the claims of both sides and the delay and expense incident to litigation, and approved. . . .

Timely appeals were taken. . . .

* * *

Before the appeals could be heard, negotiations looking toward an improvement of the offer were begun. . . . These resulted in an amended offer. The amount payable to the debentureholders was raised from a floor of 14 cents on the dollar to one of 19 cents on the dollar. . . .

* * *

In undertaking an examination of the settlement, we emphasize that this responsibility of the bankruptcy judge, and ours upon review, is not to decide the numerous questions of law and fact raised by appellants but rather to canvass the issues and see whether the settlement "fall[s] below the lowest point in the range of reasonableness." . . .

[The structure of the loans and substantive consolidation]

We start with appellants' argument that, quite apart from the banks' conduct, part or all of the banks' claims are not "Senior Indebtedness," see note [2], supra, to which alone the claims of debentureholders are subordinated. . . . Appellants . . . argue that until

Grant's guaranty of August 21, 1974, the banks' claims did not qualify as Senior Indebtedness of Grant since their loans were not to Grant but to Grant Financial. Judge Galgay thought a sufficient answer to be that Grant's indebtedness to Grant Financial was evidenced at the time of the filing of the Chapter XI petition by an Intercorporate Demand Note in the amount of $819,887,663, more than the amount of the banks' loans to Grant Financial, and that this would qualify as Senior Indebtedness if the corporate entities are respected; if they are not, as well might be proper, the loans to Grant Financial, all evidenced by notes, would qualify even more directly [as Senior Indebtedness].[3] . . .

[Grant's guarantee as a fraudulent conveyance?]

Finally, under the Loan and Guaranty Agreement all loans to Grant Financial were guaranteed by Grant. While this did not become effective until October 8, 1974, which fell 6 days short of a year of the Chapter XI petition, there is no showing that the trustee could have established lack of fair consideration for the guaranty under [the predecessor to § 548, governing fraudulent conveyances]; the legal standard in a situation such as this, which is governed by [the predecessor to § 548] of the Bankruptcy Act, is whether "the economic benefit . . . that accrued to [the] bankrupt as a result of the third person's indebtedness" was " 'disproportionately small' when compared to the size of the security that that bankrupt gave and the obligations that it incurred," Rubin v. Manufacturers Hanover Trust Co., 661 F.2d 979, 993 (2d Cir. 1981). Through its subsidiary, Grant received the full benefit of the extended maturity of some $490,000,000 in short-term loans and additional loans up to the total amount of $600,000,000 in return for its guaranty and for security interests, estimated by the Bankruptcy Judge to amount to $288,000,000. We thus conclude that while the subordinated debenture holders have some arguments that the larger part of the bank debt would not qualify as Senior Indebtedness because the loans . . . were made to Grant Financial rather than to Grant, these did not have much chance of prevailing.

[The defective prospectus]

Appellants contend that, however things might otherwise stand, the banks are estopped from claiming that Grant's indebtedness to Grant Financial constituted Senior Indebtedness because the prospectus under which the 4¾% Debentures were issued showed Senior Indebtedness of only $28,775,000 whereas Grant then owed Grant Financial $246,420,216. . . . *Appellants[ ] argu[e] . . . [that] Grant, allegedly with the banks' knowledge,* acted in such a way as to make it inequitable for the banks to rely on [anything more than what the prospectus showed as outstanding]. Yet even if this were upheld—and we find no proof of the banks' complicity in Grant's prospectus, the point remains that the prospectus goes on to define Senior Indebtedness

[3] [To see why they "would qualify even more directly" as Senior Indebtedness, read the italicized last clause of the subordinated debentures' designation clause in the previous footnote. Compare it to the designation clause in the Drum Financial indenture. See ¶ 703 at p. 149.—Roe.]

as, inter alia, "indebtedness . . . for money borrowed from or guaranteed to persons, firms or corporations evidenced by notes or similar obligations" (emphasis supplied). Grant's fresh guaranty of the indebtedness of Grant Financial to the banks in 1975 would itself therefore qualify as Senior Indebtedness even if some principle of estoppel were to prevent the banks from claiming that the . . . intercorporate loans from Grant Financial . . . in 1971 [were senior].

[Equitable subordination for collecting on a loan?]

Once it is concluded that there was a strong probability that all of the bank debt would be deemed Senior Indebtedness and a certainty that some of it would be, appellants' other claims lose much of their force. It is true, as appellants urge, that the contractual subordination of the debentures to the bank debt would not prevent the bankruptcy court, as a court of equity, from placing the debentures on a plane of equality with or even . . . of superiority to all or part of the Senior Indebtedness if the banks had engaged in inequitable conduct. *However, what appellants disregard is that in judging the equity of the banks' conduct their position as creditors prima facie senior to the debentureholders must be taken into account.* We see no reason to quarrel with the substance of Judge Galgay's summary of the law of equitable subordination, 4 [Bankr.] at 74–75, although every judge would probably state his own version differently. We entirely agree with his conclusion that "[a] creditor is under no fiduciary obligation to its debtor or to other creditors of the debtor in the collection of its claim," 4 [Bankr.] at 75. *The permissible parameters of a creditor's efforts to seek collection from a debtor are generally those with respect to voidable preferences and fraudulent conveyances proscribed by the Bankruptcy Act; apart from these there is generally no objection to a creditor's using his bargaining position, including his ability to refuse to make further loans needed by the debtor, to improve the status of his existing claims.*

. . . [T]he gravamen of [the next] charge is that Grant management, apparently in the summer of 1974, contemplated taking action to place Grant in a Chapter XI proceeding, which might have enabled Grant to survive as a reduced operation with lower administrative expenses, but that the banks prevented this, making specious explanations but acting in reality to improve their preferred position. For this appellants cited passages from two depositions neither of which supports the contention they advance. In the first of appellants' references, John P. Schroeder, Morgan Guaranty's officer in charge of the Grant credit, merely agreed with questions suggesting that in the late summer of 1974 the banks wished "to recoup the most amount of money as possible on the Grant loans," an understandable and permissible desire, and that for this reason they "did not opt for liquidation at that time." In the second passage cited, Robert Dannenbaum of the Bank of New York stated that *at some unspecified time the banks would have liked an "unofficial reorganization program," by which he meant not a Chapter XI proceeding but rather nothing more than "general monitoring of the Company's affairs by the banks."* No suggestion is found in any passage of these witnesses' testimony reproduced by appellants that Grant itself actively contemplated undergoing voluntary liquidation or reorganization under the Bankruptcy Act in the summer of 1974. We also note that after July 1974, the banks increased their loans [and] subordinated $300,000,000 on their debt to trade obligations. While a sinister interpretation is possible, this is not demanded; considering that the fresh money provided by the banks after July 1974, amounted to some $226,000,000 as against $95,378,373 principal amount of the debentures, the banks would have been paying a rather high price to obtain whatever legal advantages [they obtained when Grant] invok[ed] the Bankruptcy Act.

[Control, or influence as creditor?]

With respect to [the equitable subordination claim], the Bankruptcy Judge was warranted in attaching little importance to general statements by Grant officials that the banks were "running" Grant. There is no doubt that, at least from March of 1974, the banks kept careful watch on what was going on at Grant; they would have been derelict in their duty to their own creditors and stockholders if they had not. *It is not uncommon in such situations for officers whose companies have been brought to the verge of disaster to think that they still have better answers than do the outsiders.* In order to establish their claims *the appellants must show not simply that the banks proffered advice to Grant that was unpalatable to management, even advice gloved with an implicit threat that, unless it were taken, further loans would not be forthcoming.* They must show at least that the banks acted solely for their own benefit, taking into account their reasonable belief that their claims constituted Senior Indebtedness vis-a-vis the debentureholders, and adversely to the interest of others.

[Causation vis-a-vis the sale of accounts receivable]

The allegation most discussed by appellants is that . . . Harry Pierson, the acting president of Grant and Robert Luckett, the controller, made a report to a meeting of the Grant board of directors in June of 1974 proposing a transaction wherein $100,000,000 of customer accounts receivable would be sold to Beneficial Finance Company (Beneficial) at a discount of up to 27% and some undetermined portion of the proceeds would be used to purchase on the market 4¾% subordinated debentures which were then selling at about 25 cents on the dollar. Pierson reported that two of the major banks, Morgan Guaranty and Chase, were opposed to the transaction. . . . Their reasons were that proceeds of one of Grant's most valuable assets would be used to pay junior debt and that trade creditors would be upset. According to Luckett, Pierson had nevertheless determined to sign the contract with Beneficial and apparently persisted in that intention after a meeting at Morgan Guaranty where the banks' opposition was strongly conveyed. [Negotiations over the sale broke down, apparently for other business reasons.] . . .

. . . [I]t would have been surprising if the banks had not objected to the portion of the transaction which involved use of proceeds of quick assets to purchase long-term subordinated debt. The banks reasonably thought that their claims were senior to the debentures. True, the purchase of debentures at 25 cents on the dollar would have meant a saving of interest of some 19% on the purchase price. But Grant's immediate problem was short term; what it needed was to conserve resources and obtain short-term loans in order to stay afloat until the tide turned. Even if we should assume the evidence went so far, we see nothing inequitable in the banks taking the position that if Grant wished to use quick assets to redeem subordinated long-term debt, even on an advantageous basis, it could expect no further help from them.

* * *

We conclude by reemphasizing that the task of the bankruptcy judge was not to determine whether the settlement was the best that could have been obtained, something that neither he nor we can ever know, but whether it "fall[s] below the lowest point in the range of reasonableness." If we take the Trustee's estimated realization of $600,000,000, and deduct the estimated $143,000,000 of administration and [higher] priority claims, the $76,000,000 owing to secured suppliers, and the $24,000,000 owing to senior debentureholders, there would be a balance of $357,000,000 available for distribution among $650,000,000 of bank claims, $95,000,000 of Subordinated Debentures and $82,000,000 of general unsecured claims. If the banks could sustain their claims of subordination, let alone their claims of lien protection for $288,000,000 of their debt, the subordinated debentureholders would take nothing. Even if the banks' claims to secured creditor status and subordination of the debentures were rejected but the banks were not subordinated to them, all of which was highly problematical, the debentureholders would receive only 43 cents on the dollar, after much further expense. After considering the strengths and weaknesses of the claims of the debentureholders a settlement assuring them of 19 cents can hardly be regarded as below the lowest point in the range of reasonableness.

We therefore affirm the judgment of the district court on the merits.

¶ 1105: Questions on *W.T. Grant*

1. Do the best you can to construct a balance sheet for the parent company and the finance subsidiary.
2. Can you find four different ways that the financial structure of W.T. Grant and Grant Financial would lead to the banks coming first, ahead of the subordinated debentureholders? For the parent company and the finance subsidiary, specify which company owed what to whom. Who guaranteed what? Which loans and guarantees were senior? Would a bank creditor of Grant Financial want Grant's guarantee to be senior to debt running from Grant to Grant Financial? Are the guarantee and the intercorporate note identical financially?
3. Did the banks ever "control" Grant? Does that make any difference?
4. By what mechanism is debt designated as senior under Grant's subordinated debenture indenture? How is it designated as senior under the Drum Financial indenture? Does it make any difference which designation clause was used in the event of consolidation of Grant with its subsidiary? Would the debt be senior if the Drum

Financial clause had been used? Would the guarantee merge with the debt?

5. The court says that the debentureholders "must show at least that the banks acted solely for their own benefit, taking into account their reasonable belief that their claims constituted Senior Indebtedness vis-à-vis the debentureholders, and adversely to the interest of others." (At p. 283.) While surely this is correct (the court says the debentureholders must "at least" show), didn't the debentureholders make this showing? Isn't it that the court wants something more: enough control to create a fiduciary duty in running Grant's operations (as opposed to just influencing them) with authority going beyond that of the loan agreement, and with that control exercised to the detriment of the other creditors?

6. The Restatement (Second) of Agency (1958) states:

§ 14O. Security Holder Becoming a Principal

A creditor who assumes control of his debtor's business for the mutual benefit of himself and his debtor, may become a principal, with liability for the acts and transactions of the debtor in connection with the business.

Comment:

a. A security holder who merely exercises a veto power over the business acts of his debtor by preventing purchases or sales above specified amounts does not thereby become a principal. However, if he takes over the management of the debtor's business either in person or through an agent, and directs what contracts may or may not be made, he becomes a principal, liable as any principal for the obligations incurred thereafter in the normal course of business by the debtor who has now become his general agent. The point at which the creditor becomes a principal is that at which he assumes de facto control over the conduct of his debtor, whatever the terms of the formal contract with his debtor may be.

Language similar to §14O does not appear in the next restatement of agency, Restatement (Third) of Agency (2006), which says:

> ... A position of dominance or influence does not in itself mean that a person is a principal in a relationship of agency with the person over whom dominance or influence may be exercised. A relationship is one of agency only if the person susceptible to dominance or influence has consented to act on behalf of the other and the other has a right of control, not simply an ability to bring influence to bear.
>
> The right to veto another's decisions does not by itself create the right to give affirmative directives that action be taken, which is integral to the right of control within common-law agency. Thus, a debtor does not become a creditor's agent when a loan agreement gives the creditor veto rights over decisions the debtor may make. Moreover, typically a debtor does not consent to act on behalf of the creditor as opposed to acting in its own interests.

7. Why did Grant switch from commercial paper financing to bank financing? What could banks do that buyers of commercial paper couldn't? The banks might have eventually charged more in interest (adjusting for the term of their loan), but that couldn't by itself explain why Grant switched to them (or more properly, why the commercial paper buyers abandoned Grant). Surely, commercial paper buyers, when they saw that Grant was deteriorating and becoming riskier, could have raised their interest rate. But could the commercial paper buyers efficiently meet with Grant's officers, gather information, and monitor Grant's operations? In a reorganization, in or out of bankruptcy, could they organize easily to renegotiate the loans?
8. What does the subordinated noteholders' settlement (at $.19 for each dollar of obligation) suggest about the banks' fears of equitable subordination? How easy is it to look at the facts and determine whether they warrant equitable subordination? Hence, how easy is it to determine the settlement value of an equitable subordination claim? Where and when does a creditor cross the line from permissible protection of its contract position over to impermissible control and pursuit of its own interests? Consider the Fifth Circuit's difficulties in dealing with facts similar to those of *W. T. Grant* and *American Lumber* in the next two decisions.

¶ 1106: In re Clark Pipe & Supply Co., Inc., 870 F.2d 1022 (5th Cir. 1989)

Before POLITZ and JOLLY, Circuit Judges, and HUNTER, District Judge.

E. GRADY JOLLY, Circuit Judge:

. . . [W]e are presented with three issues arising out of the conduct of the bankrupt's lender during the ninety days prior to the bankrupt's filing for protection from creditors. The first is whether the lender . . . received a voidable transfer. If so, the second question is whether the lender engaged in inequitable conduct that would justify subordination of the lender's claims to the extent that the conduct harmed other creditors. If so, we must finally determine whether avoiding the transfer and equitable subordination are duplicative or complementary.

I

Clark Pipe and Supply Company, Inc., ("Clark") was in the business of buying and selling steel pipe used in the fabrication of offshore drilling platforms. . . . Associates Commercial Corp. ("Associates") [made a] revolving loan [to Clark,] secured by an assignment of [its] accounts receivable and an inventory mortgage. . . . The agreements provided that Associates could reduce the . . . advance[s] at any time at its discretion. When bad times hit the oil fields in late 1981, Clark's business slumped. In February 1982 Associates began reducing [its] percentage advance[s] so that Clark would have just enough cash to pay its direct operating expenses. Clark used the advances to keep its doors open and to sell inventory, the proceeds of which were used to pay off the past advances from

Associates. Associates did not expressly dictate to Clark which bills to pay. Neither did it direct Clark not to pay vendors or threaten Clark with a cut-off of advances if it did pay vendors. But Clark had no funds left over from the advances to pay vendors or other creditors whose services were not essential to keeping its doors open. [When Clark's unpaid vendors began foreclosure proceedings] and seized the pipe [they] had sold Clark ... Clark sought protection from creditors by filing for reorganization under Chapter 11 of the Bankruptcy Code.[4]

... The trustee sought the recovery of alleged preferences and equitable subordination of Associates' claims. ... The [bankruptcy] court required Associates to turn over $370,505 of payments found to be preferential and subordinated Associates' claim. The district court affirmed. ...

II

... Clark, by selling its inventory and thereby converting the inventory to accounts receivable that had been assigned to Associates, made a preferential transfer to Associates that [is avoidable] in accordance with sections 547(b) and (c)(5) of the Bankruptcy Code. It is undisputed that the reduction of pipe to accounts receivable was in effect a transfer of the pipe to Associates. ... [T]he bankruptcy court correctly determined the existence of a voidable preference and the amount of the preference.

III

The second issue before us is whether the bankruptcy court was justified in equitably subordinating Associates' claims. The Fifth Circuit has enunciated a three-pronged test to determine whether and to what extent a claim should be equitably subordinated: (1) the claimant must have engaged in some type of inequitable conduct, (2) the misconduct must have resulted in injury to the creditors of the bankrupt or conferred an unfair advantage on the claimant, and (3) equitable subordination of the claim must not be inconsistent with the provisions of the Bankruptcy Code.

A

The courts have recognized three general categories of conduct as sufficient to satisfy the first prong of the three-part test: (1) fraud, illegality or breach of fiduciary duties; (2) undercapitalization; and (3) a claimant's use of the debtor as a mere instrumentality or alter ego.

... [T]he bankruptcy court found that once Associates realized Clark's desperate financial condition, Associates asserted total control and used Clark as a mere instrumentality to liquidate Associates' unpaid loans ... , to the detriment of ... Clark's other creditors.

[4 While the lender, Associates, had a security interest in both accounts receivable and inventory, Clark's suppliers had competing liens in the inventory they sold Clark, but not in the accounts receivable. 870 F.2d at 1031.—Roe.]

Associates contends that its control over Clark was far from total. Associates says that it did no more than determine the percentage of advances as expressly permitted in the loan agreement; it never made or dictated decisions as to which creditors were paid. Thus, argues Associates, it never had the "actual, participatory, total control of the debtor" required to make Clark its instrumentality. . . .

* * *

. . . [W]e look to equitable subordination cases for the applicable law. The case most directly on point is In re American Lumber Co., 5 B.R. 470 (D. Minn. 1980). In that case the bank was a formerly unsecured creditor that took a security interest in the inventory and accounts receivable. It began liquidation of the debtor by commencing a foreclosure on its security interests. The debtor's employees were all fired and a new skeleton crew was subsequently hired. The bank instituted a depository system into which all the debtor's collections were deposited and it determined who would be paid. The bank refused to pay general unsecured creditors or sales taxes while seeing to it that accounts receivable were enhanced.

. . . [T]he court said:

> [I]t was the Bank's use of its control over [the debtor's] operations in a manner detrimental to the unsecured creditors which constitutes the inequitable conduct. The purposeful exercise of that control to implement its plan is amply demonstrated, not merely by [an attorney's] comments as to the plan he had to disadvantage the general creditors by taking security interests in inventory and equipment, but also by the Bank's actions in following through with conduct designed to obtain [for] the Bank a greater percentage of the debt owed to it by [the debtor] than owed to other general creditors.

. . . Associates used its control in a manner detrimental to the unsecured creditors. As a de facto insider, . . . Associates knew that Clark was headed for bankruptcy and sought to defer it as long as possible in order to recoup its investment at the expense of the suppliers. Knowing that Associates would be grossly undersecured if Clark went under immediately, Fred Slice, Associates' loan officer responsible for the Clark account, devised a plan that would allow Clark to keep its doors open to generate accounts receivable by liquidating as much inventory as possible. Slice testified as to what he had in mind:

> I just kept on trying to get out of the loan, you know. My attitude was bankruptcy is inevitable. I want to get in the best position I can prior to the bankruptcy; i.e., I want to get the absolute amount of dollars as low as I can by hook or crook. And, you know, worry [about] preferences and all of that at a later date which, you know, I was aware there was a danger, but I don't know all of the legal ramifications. . . . As long as they were selling my pipe, collecting my receivables and turning my inventory from something that was highly illiquid into something more liquid, yeah. As long as I could—it was in my interest for Clark to keep operating. And, yeah, I personally would have preferred that to bankruptcy. But it was inevitable. It was going to happen in my opinion. I was trying to get in—the ship was going down. I

just wanted to get myself on a life raft with a few provisions so we could cut our losses.

Associates used its loan agreement and advances not merely to protect its investment, as it claims, but to leverage its recovery at the expense of other creditors. Because of Associates' policy, suppliers were forced to bear the cost of Associates' liquidation of Clark. . . . The unfairness to inventory vendors was especially egregious. Every time Clark sold pipe, Associates improved its position to the detriment of the vendor of that pipe. . . . The moment the pipe was sold . . . Associates took priority by virtue of its security interest in receivables. Thus, Associates' strategy was apparently to convert inventory into receivables as fast as possible without alerting the vendors to what was happening. . . . Associates reduced advances so that Clark received only enough to keep selling its inventory; any income from the sales was sent directly to Associates in Dallas. Thus, Associates' reduction of advances forced Clark to defer payments to its vendors and trade creditors, sell inventory out from under the vendors' privileges, and send the cash to Associates. Associates' intent is demonstrated by the following testimony [from Fred Slice]:

> If he [the comptroller of Clark] had had the availability [of funds to pay a vendor or other trade creditor] that particular day, I would have said, "Are you sure you've got that much availability, Jim," because he shouldn't have that much. The way I had structured it, he wouldn't have any money to pay his suppliers.
>
> But you know, the possibility that—this is all hypothetical. I had it structured so that there was no—there was barely enough money—there was enough money, if I did it right, enough money to keep the doors open. Clark could continue to operate, sell the inventory, turn it into receivables, collect the cash, transfer that cash to me, and reduce my loans. And, if he had ever had availability for other things, that meant I had done something wrong, and I would have been surprised. To ask me what I would have done is purely hypothetical[;] I don't think it would happen. I think it's so unrealistic, I don't know.

. . . [T]he bankruptcy court and the district court correctly concluded that Clark was an instrumentality of Associates for the limited purpose of equitable subordination. Moreover, they correctly held that Associates used that control to engage in the type of overreaching and spoliation to the detriment of the rights of fellow creditors that amounts to inequitable conduct. . . .

* * *

IV

The final issue is whether, by setting aside the preference and equitably subordinating Associates' claim to the claims of the other creditors, the bankruptcy court has awarded duplicate remedies. We think not. . . .

AFFIRMED.

In re Clark Pipe & Supply Co., Inc., 893 F.2d 693 (5th Cir. 1990)

ON SUGGESTION FOR REHEARING EN BANC

Before POLITZ and JOLLY, Circuit Judges, and HUNTER, District Judge.

E. GRADY JOLLY, Circuit Judge:

Treating the suggestion for rehearing en banc filed in this case by Associates Commercial Corporation ("Associates"), as a petition for panel rehearing, we hereby grant the petition for rehearing. After re-examining the evidence in this case and the applicable law, we conclude that our prior opinion was in error. We therefore withdraw our prior opinion and substitute the following:

* * *

. . . [W]e decide that equitable subordination is an inappropriate remedy. . . . [W]e need not decide whether avoiding the transfer [as a preference] and equitable subordination are duplicative or complementary remedies.

III

[Was] the bankruptcy court . . . justified in equitably subordinating Associates' claims[?] . . .

. . . [T]he bankruptcy court found that once Associates realized Clark's desperate financial condition, Associates asserted total control and used Clark as a mere instrumentality to liquidate Associates' unpaid loans . . . to the detriment of the rights of Clark's other creditors. Associates contends that its control over Clark was far from total. Associates says that it did no more than determine the percentage of advances as expressly permitted in the loan agreement; it never made or dictated decisions as to which creditors were paid. Thus, argues Associates, it never had the "actual, participatory, total control of the debtor" required to make Clark its instrumentality. . . . If it did not use Clark as an instrumentality or engage in any other type of inequitable conduct . . . , argues Associates, then it cannot be equitably subordinated.

A

. . . In our prior opinion, we agreed with the district court and the bankruptcy court that, as a practical matter, Associates asserted total control over Clark's liquidation, and that it used its control in a manner detrimental to the unsecured creditors. Upon reconsideration, we have concluded that we cannot say that the sort of control Associates asserted over Clark's financial affairs rises to the level of unconscionable conduct necessary to justify the application of the doctrine of equitable subordination.

We . . . cannot [now] escape the salient fact that, pursuant to its loan agreement with Clark, Associates had the right to reduce funding, just as it did, as Clark's sales slowed. We now conclude that . . . Associates [did not] exceed[ ] its authority under the loan agreement,

[n]or [did] Associates act[ ] inequitably in exercising its rights under that agreement.

* * *

. . . The agreement provided that Associates could reduce the . . . advance rates at any time in its discretion. When Clark's business began to decline . . . Associates . . . reduce[d its] advance[s]. . . . Clark prepared a budget at Associates' request that indicated the disbursements necessary to keep the company operating. The budget did not include payment to vendors for previously shipped goods. Associates' former loan officer, Fred Slice, testified as to what he had in mind:

> If he [the comptroller of Clark] had had the availability [of funds to pay a vendor or other trade creditor] that particular day, I would have said, "Are you sure you've got that much availability, Jim," because he shouldn't have that much. The way I had structured it, he wouldn't have any money to pay his suppliers.
>
> But you know, the possibility that—this is all hypothetical. I had it structured so that there was no—there was barely enough money—there was enough money, if I did it right, enough money to keep the doors open. Clark could continue to operate, sell the inventory, turn it into receivables, collect the cash, transfer that cash to me, and reduce my loans. And, if he had ever had availability for other things, that meant I had done something wrong, and I would have been surprised. To ask me what I would have done is purely hypothetical[;] I don't think it would happen. I think it's so unrealistic, I don't know.

Despite Associates' motive, which was, according to Slice, "to get in the best position I can prior to the bankruptcy, i.e., I want to get the absolute amount of dollars as low as I can by hook or crook," the evidence shows that the amount of its advances continued to be based on the applicable funding formulas. Slice testified that the lender did not appreciably alter its original credit procedures when Clark fell into financial difficulty.

In our original opinion, we failed to focus sufficiently on the loan agreement, which gave Associates the right to conduct its affairs with Clark in the manner in which it did. In addition, we think that in our previous opinion we were overly influenced by the negative and inculpatory tone of Slice's testimony. Given the agreement he was working under, his testimony was hardly more than [boasting] about the power that the agreement afforded him over the financial affairs of Clark. Although his talk was crass (e.g., "I want to get the absolute dollars as low as I can, by hook or crook"), our careful examination of the record does not reveal any conduct on his part that was inconsistent with the loan agreement, irrespective of what his personal motive may have been.

Through its loan agreement, every lender effectively exercises "control" over its borrower to some degree. A lender in Associates' position will usually possess "control" in the sense that it can foreclose or drastically reduce the debtor's financing. The purpose of equitable subordination is to distinguish between the unilateral remedies that a creditor may properly enforce pursuant to its agreements with the debtor and other inequitable conduct such as fraud, misrepresentation, or the exercise of such *total control over the debtor as to have essentially replaced its decision-making capacity with that of the lender*. The crucial distinction between what is inequitable and what a lender can reasonably and legitimately do to protect its interests is the distinction between the existence of "control" and the exercise of that "control" to direct the activities of the debtor. . . .

In our prior opinion, we drew support from In re American Lumber Co., 5 B.R. 470 (D. Minn. 1980), to . . . equitably subordinate . . . [Associates' claim]. Upon reconsideration, however, we find that the facts of that case are significantly more egregious than we have here. . . .

Associates exercised significantly less "control" over the activities of Clark than did the lender in American Lumber. . . . Associates did not . . . interfere with the operations of the borrower to an extent even roughly commensurate with the degree of interference exercised by the bank in American Lumber. Associates made no management decisions for Clark, such as deciding which creditors to prefer with the diminishing amount of funds available. *At no time did Associates place any of its employees as either a director or officer of Clark.* Associates never influenced the removal from office of any Clark personnel. . . . Associates did not expressly dictate to Clark which bills to pay, nor did it direct Clark not to pay vendors or threaten a cut-off of advances if it did pay vendors. Clark handled its own daily operations. The same basic procedures with respect to the reporting of collateral, the calculation of availability of funds, and the procedures for the advancement of funds were followed throughout the relationship between Clark and Associates. Unlike the lender in American Lumber, Associates did not mislead creditors to continue supplying Clark. Cf. American Lumber, 5 B.R. at 474. Perhaps the most important fact that distinguishes this case from American Lumber is that Associates did not coerce Clark into executing the [preferential] security agreements after Clark became insolvent. Instead, the loan and security agreements between Clark and Associates were entered into at arm's length prior to Clark's insolvency, and all of Associates' activities were conducted pursuant to those agreements.

Associates' control over Clark's finances, admittedly powerful and ultimately severe, was based solely on the exercise of powers found in the loan agreement. Associates' close watch over Clark's affairs does not, by itself, however, amount to such control as would justify equitable subordination. In re W.T. Grant, 699 F.2d 599, 610 (2d Cir. 1983). "There is nothing inherently wrong with a creditor carefully monitoring his debtor's financial situation or with suggesting what course of action the debtor ought to follow." In re Teltronics Services, Inc., 29 B.R. 139, 172 (Bankr. E.D.N.Y. 1983). Although the terms of the agreement did give Associates potent leverage over Clark, that agreement did not give Associates total control over Clark's activities. At all material times Clark had the power to act autonomously and, if it chose, to disregard the advice of Associates; for example, Clark was free to shut its doors at any time it chose to do so and to file for bankruptcy.

Finally, on reconsideration, we are persuaded that the rationale of In re W.T. Grant Co., 699 F.2d 599 (2d Cir. 1983), should control the case before us. In that case, the Second Circuit recognized that

> a creditor is under no fiduciary obligation to its debtor or to other creditors of the debtor in the collection of its claim. The permissible parameters of a creditor's efforts to seek collection from a debtor are generally those with respect to voidable preferences and fraudulent conveyances proscribed by the Bankruptcy Act; apart from these there is generally no objection to a creditor's using his bargaining position, including his ability to refuse to make further loans needed by the debtor, to improve the status of his existing claims.

699 F.2d at 609–10. Associates was not a fiduciary of Clark, it did not exert improper control over Clark's financial affairs, and it did not act inequitably in exercising its rights under its loan agreement with Clark.

B

. . . We therefore conclude that the district court erred in affirming the bankruptcy court's decision to subordinate Associates' claims.

IV

. . . Because we have held that equitable subordination is inapplicable in this case, we do not address the question whether avoiding the transfer and equitable subordination are duplicative or complementary remedies.

* * *

¶ 1107: Cross–Collateralization

Similar to creditors' conduct in *W.T. Grant* and *American Lumber* are the efforts by lenders advancing funds in bankruptcy to request or insist upon collateral not only for the new loan but for the prebankruptcy loans as well. In effect, the creditor, as a price for the new funds, insists upon enhanced repayment terms (seniority) on the old loans. Cross-collateralization of new lending made during the chapter 11 proceeding is discussed in ¶ 1608.

B. LENDER LIABILITY

¶ 1108: Sources of Lender Liability

There are other sources of lender liability in circumstances substantially similar to equitable subordination. Recall from *Deprizio* that an insider must return to the estate preferential payments or preferential increases in collateral obtained within one year of the debtor's filing of the bankruptcy petition. Insiders include any person in control of the bankrupt. Bankruptcy Code, §§ 101(31), 547(b)(4). An aggressive lender who squeezes out a preferential payment will have to return it.

And, apart from § 510 of the Bankruptcy Code, controlling persons can be held more directly liable for violations of the securities laws. Securities Act of 1933, § 15, 15 U.S.C. § 77o; Securities Exchange Act of 1934, § 20, 15 U.S.C. § 78t. Lenders face liability issues when handling their loan outside of bankruptcy. The next decision is one such liability problem for creditors.

¶ 1109: State National Bank of El Paso v. Farah Mfg. Co., 678 S.W.2d 661 (Tex. Ct. App. 1984)

[William Farah was the chief executive officer of Farah Manufacturing Company, Inc. ("FMC"). After a bitter labor dispute, during which the company lost much money, Farah left as CEO. The labor dispute was settled. FMC's banks agreed to extend new loans of about $22 million to FMC only on condition that Farah not return to FMC. Farah attempted to return to FMC; the banks blocked him. FMC's losses continued. Eventually Farah did succeed and returned as CEO. The company prospered, and Farah had the company sue the banks, resulting in a jury verdict of $19 million against the banks. The decision on appeal follows.]

CHARLES R. SCHULTE, Associate Justice

This case centers around a management change clause contained in a $22,000,00.00 loan agreement [between FMC] and the banks. The jury found Appellant bank, acting alone or in conspiracy with any of the other lenders, committed acts of fraud, duress and interference, proximately resulting in damages to Appellee, and set damages at $18,947,348.77. We reform and affirm.

[The creditors had implied that they would declare an Event of Default under the loan agreement, accelerate the maturity of the principal amount, and demand repayment in full if Farah, the debtor's former CEO, returned to manage the company; in fact, the trial court concluded, the creditors were uncertain about their intentions if he returned, and they may not have called the loan.]

[The management clause]

The management change clause set forth in Section 6.1(g) of the February 14, 1977, loan agreement made it an event of default if there occurred:

> Any change in the office of President and Chief Executive Officer of Farah [Manufacturing Company, Inc.] or any other change in the executive management of Farah [Manufacturing Company, Inc.] which any two Banks shall consider, for any reason whatsoever, to be adverse to the interests of the Banks.

* * *

. . . FMC began in 1919 as a family owned apparel manufacturer. Farah became CEO in 1964. In 1967 FMC went public. By 1970, the company had plants in Texas and overseas with annual sales of $136,000,000.00. Beginning in 1972, the firm suffered a strike and a nationwide boycott. The strike was settled in 1974. During the period 1972–1976 FMC experienced a pre-tax loss of $43,965,000.00. On July 9, 1976, the FMC Board named one of its members, Leone, as CEO of FMC replacing Farah. On February 14, 1977, a preexisting loan agreement between FMC [and the banks] was amended and included the management change clause previously set forth. [As the following paragraphs detail, over the opposition of the banks, several of whom had directors on the FMC board, Farah eventually returned to FMC as CEO.]

[The banks] characteriz[e] the case as one arising out of warnings issued to FMC in March, 1977, by [the banks] in reliance on the management change clause above set forth. Appellant's position is that when Farah attempted to persuade FMC's board to elect him CEO, the banks stated their intent to enforce their right under the loan agreement to treat Farah's election as a default and call their loan. Appellant insists that the warnings of the banks did not exceed their legal rights under the change clause (and otherwise). . . . [The banks] maintai[n] that the banks made the loan to FMC in reliance upon FMC's assurances in 1976 that the company was under new management and that the banks would be protected by the management change clause against any future change in management. . . . [The banks also maintain] that the covenant was a provision freely given by FMC, that it was undisputedly lawful, and that the subsequently strengthened and amended clause was approved by the entire FMC board with the clear understanding that the covenant could be used [by the banks] to resist an effort by Farah to return as CEO.

On the other hand, FMC, plaintiff below and Appellee here, asserts the general position that under the management change clause, when it became apparent that Farah was about to regain control of FMC, which was unacceptable to the banks, that the banks had two legitimate options. . . . They could attempt to call the loan or . . . live with Farah as CEO. Instead, Appellee maintains, the banks chose a third option and unlawfully prevented Farah's election and installed directors and officers to keep Farah out of management. The claim is made that the "hand picked minions" mismanaged the company and stripped it of valuable assets for unnecessary loan prepayments. Further, Appellee asserts, when the banks defrauded and coerced FMC's directors to prevent Farah's return to management, they defrauded and coerced FMC itself. When they installed their own choice of management, stacked the FMC board and undertook the actions to exclude Farah from management, the banks interfered with FMC's management and corporate governance rights through an unlawful course of conduct marked with deception and coercion. These alleged wrongful acts are stated to have proximately caused damages to FMC in two respects. First, the incompetent management installed and perpetuated by the banks resulted in losses. . . . Second, their preventing the election of competent management caused losses and lost profits. Appellee finally contends Farah fought his way back into control, saved the company from bankruptcy and restored it to profitability.

* * *

Following the [earlier] strike and boycott of 1972–1974, and substantial losses, on March 3, 1976, the FMC Board unanimously elected Leone, an FMC director since 1973 and chosen by Farah to succeed him, as president and COO. Farah retained [only] his positions as board chairman and CEO. . . . The lenders had no input in Leone's election. On the same day, Farah's son, J. Farah, was elected as a director. The board then consisted of Farah, J. Farah, Conroy, Leone, Gordon Foster, Frost, Kozmetsky and Lerner.

At its meeting on July 9, 1976, the board demanded that Farah resign as CEO [as well] . . . on the basis that he was the cause of FMC's management problems and poor financial condition. [He resigned.]

Farah later deemed Leone incapable of properly managing the company and unable to quickly adjust to changes in market demand for fashions. Under Leone, FMC's sales and profits declined. Farah urged Leone to change his practices. Both Leone and the board viewed this as unwarranted interference.

In the spring of 1976, FMC had begun to seek a $30,000,000.00 loan to survive losses. . . . On February 14, 1977, a restructured collateralized loan agreement was reached. . . . [It] had the strengthened management change clause earlier set forth in this opinion.

At a shareholders' meeting on March 7, 1977, Farah sought to have a new board of directors elected to insure his return to management. . . . Several factors induced him to change his mind and to vote for the incumbent board which he believed would elect him CEO anyway. Because of the management change clause, the board declined absent a statement of position from the lenders. The lenders initially refused to assert a position. The board suggested Farah personally present his management proposal to the lenders. He did so at [one of the bank's offices] in Dallas on March 14, 1977, stressing his return as CEO was the only way to save FMC. After his presentation, Farah was asked to leave the meeting so the lenders could discuss the matter. [One bank] voiced opposition to Farah. No decision was reached. Farah was informed of their indecision and that a change in CEO could constitute a violation of the management change clause. . . .

The lenders analyzed the ramifications of FMC's bankruptcy, should a default be declared, and their exposure to liability for changes in FMC management. According to the testimony of Daugherty, President of State National, the lenders felt that their only legitimate options, should Farah become CEO, were to either call the loan [i.e., to declare it in default—Roe] or let Farah hold office unmolested. Daugherty testified that neither choice was acceptable to the banks. . . . State National was unwilling to put El Paso's largest private employer into bankruptcy.

* * *

Then on March 22, Donohoe drafted a letter conveying the lenders' position to the board. The letter [was] approved by all the lenders. . . . [It] read in part:

> The Banks wish to advise the Board that a change of executive management which includes the election of Mr. William Farah as chief executive of the Company or results in his being the power to generally supervise and control the operations and affairs of the Company is unacceptable to the Banks, and the Banks will not grant any waiver of default based thereon. The Banks are, however, willing to consider a waiver of the default clause . . . if the Board decides that a change in the office of the Chief Executive of the Company (involving others than Mr. Farah) is in the best interests of the Company. The Banks do not intend hereby and do not waive any default based on the developments in the Company constituting a material adverse change of circumstances. . . . The Banks are still considering their position regarding the events which have and are coming to their attention.

Tom Foster testified that the lenders did not want to call the loan and create a default which would result in FMC's bankruptcy. He admitted that, if Farah were elected, the lenders had a choice of either doing nothing or attempting to call the loan. Although the interpretation of the letter was left to the board, he conceded that the statement of the lenders, that they would not waive a default, could have created an impression that there would be a default if Farah were elected. . . .

[At the board meeting at which Farah expected to be named CEO, the letter was presented to the board. Some directors were concerned that electing Farah CEO would put FMC in default, the loan would be accelerated, and the company would then be closed or bankrupt.] The meeting was recessed without an election of new directors or CEO.

[Thereafter, the bankers continued to oppose the return of Farah as CEO. T]he lenders then met with [FMC directors early in the day of the next board meeting, on March 23. One director,] Azar described Donohoe as the spokesman for the lender group and said Donohoe opened the meeting by saying that "Willie [Farah] was not acceptable as a chief executive officer and president." Azar said he told Donohoe that Farah was the only one who could turn the company around. When asked what else Donohoe had said, Azar responded, "[w]ell, it got to the point where if Willie Farah was elected president of the company, why, he would automatically bankrupt the company and he would padlock it the next day." Azar said that after talking to [the company's] attorney . . . on the phone he came back and told Donohoe that "he could take his loan agreement and shove it up his ass." Azar explained he did that "trying to determine how serious they were about bankrupting and closing the company, what was his intent. I intended to push him to the very brink and very edge and find out." Azar said Donohoe's response was "[w]e will." Azar said he then believed Donohoe would bankrupt and padlock the company if the board elected Farah. He said as a result of the meeting, "I was fearful of putting the company in bankruptcy. So I agreed to talk to Mr. Farah and ask him to stand down and not stand for election." . . .

Also, at the Azar meeting, J. Farah[, a director,] criticized his father's views on management of FMC and indicated he could not support him for CEO, expressing emotional pressure and danger from the management change clause. . . . Azar also testified that the lenders never told him that they would not, in fact, bankrupt FMC if Farah were elected. Several of those in attendance at the Azar meeting testified that Donohoe did not make any statement regarding bankrupting and padlocking the company. Tom Foster admitted that Azar was not informed of the lenders' meeting of March 21 [at which lenders tentatively concluded] that a default would be declared only after Farah's election or that a default might never be declared.

* * *

In accordance with his representation that he would talk to Farah, Azar met with Farah prior to the board meeting [scheduled for later that day]. Azar testified he told Farah that the lenders wanted Farah to resign as board chairman and to elect in his stead Gordon Foster (an employee of El Paso National Bank) and Conroy (a director of State National) as CEO. Azar asked Farah to stand down and told him of assurances by the lenders that they would bankrupt and padlock the company. Azar said he (Azar) believed there was no other way to save FMC and that the election of Gordon Foster and Conroy was the only way to prevent FMC's bankruptcy. Farah testified he believed what Azar and Donohoe had told him and that after talking to Azar, "I went to the board meeting, nominated Mr. Conroy to be chief executive officer and Mr. Gordon Foster to be Chairman."

Gordon Foster and Conroy were unanimously elected as nominated. Azar testified that his feelings for Conroy [as not being capable of running FMC] had not changed. Gordon Foster testified that in his opinion, in spite of reservations, Conroy was the only one available who could assume the position. The lenders agreed not to deem Conroy's election as an event of default.

* * *

[FMC continued to decline financially. Conroy was replaced as CEO by Galef, who had] proposed to the lenders in June that he replace Conroy as CEO. *He indicated to them his plan to make sizable loan prepayments during the next several months by selling company assets.* The lenders approved of his becoming CEO. Galef presented his proposal to the board and expressed that he could have FMC "in the black in 90 days." . . . Galef's projection for profitability never materialized. . . .

* * *

FMC also maintains that the evidence shows Galef was inexperienced in the men's apparel business. Galef failed to make improvements in the 1977 fall line and was responsible for introducing the 1978 spring line which was too expensive, poorly priced and contrary to market demand. The spring line, although heavily advertised, received poor public response. As a result thereof, many orders were canceled and excess inventory accumulated. With FMC losing much of its market to competitors by early 1978, Farah testified that Galef introduced the 1978 fall line with the dominant theme the same as that in the previously unsuccessful spring line.

FMC presented evidence showing that [FMC's condition deteriorated while Galef was CEO].

While Galef was CEO, assets of FMC were sold at internationally publicized auctions. The net proceeds from the sales were used to make prepayments on FMC's loan. FMC points to the evidence that the auctions stripped it of valuable assets and that its competitors purchased much of the machinery and equipment for use in competition with FMC and that State National financed the purchase of certain auctioned assets by one of FMC's competitors. . . . It is State National's position that the machinery and equipment sold were in excess of FMC's operating needs. The lenders requested FMC to sell the assets pursuant to a promise made by FMC in June, 1976, that it would do so. Such promise had been an inducement for the lenders to make the loan.

* * *

. . . In January, 1978, Farah gave notice of a proxy fight that he was preparing in order to elect a slate of directors at the March board meeting whereby he could be reinstated as CEO. Clifford and Virginia Farah responded with a suit to remove Farah as trustee under the trust holding their stock. This was viewed by Farah as a measure to force his vote for the incumbent board.

There is evidence that the lenders took an active interest to oppose Farah in his proxy fight and in his suit with Clifford and Virginia. Farah prevailed in the suit. This ultimately meant success for him in his proxy fight.

In January, 1978, FMC's financial condition was critical. At this time, the lenders determined that they were no longer willing to finance FMC's day-to-day operations although they did want to maintain some type of a long-term loan. FMC's short-term debts were soon to be due. Prior to Farah's return, the lenders had decided that the loan would be restructured whereby the management change clause would be deleted if: (1) FMC repaid the short-term debt by the middle of February, 1978; and (2) the long-term debts were substantially reduced and prepaid through third party accounts receivable financing. These conditions were met and the way was paved for Farah's return as CEO. The restructuring document originally contained a release for lender liability. When discovered by FMC, it was deleted.

* * *

On April 4, 1978, the FMC board approved the restructured loan agreement. Although FMC failed to make several payments that were due in the spring of 1978, those payments were made in July. *By July of 1979, FMC had refinanced and* then repaid the loan in full.

FMC cites to considerable testimony regarding Farah's abilities and the high regard in which he is now held by others in the apparel industry for his success in turning FMC around after his return. After his return, he reduced selling and administrative costs, disposed of unusable inventory to generate working capital, expanded international sales and regenerated employee, supplier and retailer confidence in FMC and its products. Since Farah's return to management, FMC has consistently experienced an increase in sales and profits and has regained its position as an effective competitor with other manufacturers of apparel.

[Fraud]

FMC's cause of action for fraud focuses upon the March 22 letter and the statements made by Donohoe to Farah and other board members on March 23 of bankruptcy and padlocking if Farah were elected as CEO. The evidence is legally and factually sufficient, albeit conflicting, that on March 21 the lenders had either decided not to declare a default which would result in FMC's bankruptcy or reached no decision on the matter. Neither position was conveyed to the board. Regardless of the position taken, the "warnings" (representations) made in the letter and by Donohoe are characterized by FMC as false threats constituting fraud.

Fraud may be effected by a misrepresentation. . . . A representation consists of words or other conduct manifesting to another the existence of a fact, including a state of mind. It may be made directly to the other or by a manifestation to third persons intended to reach the other. A misrepresentation is a representation which, under the circumstances, amounts to an assertion not in accordance with the facts. . . . A representation literally true is actionable if used to create an impression substantially false. . . .

[Good faith]

FMC maintains that the lenders were required to exercise good faith in their representations made to FMC on March 22 and 23. . . . In regard to good faith, the Texas Business and Commerce Code (Vernon 1968) provides:

> Sec. 1.203. Every contract or duty within this title implies an obligation of good faith in its performance or enforcement.
>
> Sec. 1.201(19). "Good faith" means honesty in fact in the conduct or transaction concerned.

FMC also maintains that once the lenders voluntarily conveyed information which was false or misleading (the March 22 letter and the representations attributed to Donohoe) and which would influence Farah and other board members, then the lenders were under a duty to disclose the whole truth regarding any decision on default. . . .

[The bank] maintains that fraud cannot arise from a warning of an intention to enforce legal rights. It argues that the issue is not whether the lenders had yet to commit to do what they had warned. Rather, the issue is whether they had a legal right to do it.

. . . The representations that a default would be declared and the company bankrupted and padlocked if Farah were elected as CEO concern a material fact and amount to more than a mere opinion, judgment, probability or expectation on the part of the lenders. . . . The March 22 letter and representations created a false impression regarding the lenders' decision (or lack of decision) to declare a default.

As a matter of law, FMC has established a cause of action for fraud. The evidence is legally and factually sufficient to support the jury's finding thereon. . . .

[Duress]

[Next is the question of] the legal and factual sufficiency of the evidence to support the jury's finding of duress. . . . Dale v. Simon, 267 S.W. 467, 470 (Tex. Comm'n App. 1924, judgment adopted) is the leading case as to the elements of and the limitations upon a cause of action for duress. It was there held:

> There can be no duress unless [1] there is a threat to do some act which the party threatening has no legal right to do. [2] Such threat must be of such character as to destroy the free agency of the party to whom it is directed. It must overcome his will and cause him to do that which he would not otherwise do, and which he was not legally bound to do. [3] The restraint caused by such threat must be imminent. [4] It must be such that the person to whom it is directed has no present means of protection.

* * *

Even where an insecurity clause is drafted in the broadest possible terms, the primary question is whether the creditor's attempt to accelerate stemmed from a reasonable, good-faith belief that its security was about to become impaired. Acceleration clauses are not to be used offensively such as for the commercial advantage of the creditor. They do not permit acceleration when the facts make its use unjust or oppressive.

* * *

Economic duress (business coercion) may be evidenced by forcing a victim to choose between distasteful and costly situations, i.e., bow to duress or face bankruptcy, loss of credit rating, or loss of profits from a venture.

There is evidence that the loan to FMC was not in default at the time the warnings were given by the lenders on March 22 and 23. There was then no impaired prospect of repayment but for the perpetuation of FMC's alleged poor financial condition or perhaps for the possibility of Farah's election as CEO (in view of his past performance). Admittedly, his election could have constituted a default under the management change clause thereby enabling the lenders to legitimately enforce their legal rights.

However, there was no circumstance to authorize the manner in which the warnings to declare default were made. This is particularly true when given the evidence that the lenders previously had either decided not to declare a default which would result in FMC's bankruptcy or reached no decision on the matter. . . .

FMC did undertake a new obligation to the lenders under duress. By virtue of the warnings made on March 22 and 23, it became specifically and absolutely obligated not to have Farah elected as CEO. Under the management change clause, however, Farah could have been elected. The board had been under no obligation to see that such would not occur. In the "event" that it did, then it was the legitimate option of the lenders to determine whether or not it should be viewed as a default. Instead, they chose to issue warnings designed to force the board to elect someone other than Farah.

It is argued that the management change clause was approved by the entire FMC board with the clear understanding that the clause could be used to resist an effort by Farah to return as CEO. It is true that use of the management change clause had been perceived by the board in context with the legitimate options available to the lenders. However, the evidence reflects that there was no anticipation of the manner in which it was ultimately used.

* * *

As a matter of law, FMC has established a cause of action for duress. The evidence is legally and factually sufficient to support the jury's finding thereon. . . .

* * *

[Damages]

Actual losses were awarded in the amount of $2,668,000.00. Generally, State National contends that there is no evidence that it caused such damages to be incurred or that the losses were attributable to the alleged mistakes of FMC's management during the year in controversy (April, 1977, through March, 1978) or to any lender action as distinguished from circumstances existing or events occurring prior to that time.

* * *

The evidence is legally sufficient to support the jury's finding of $2,668,000.00. Cases cited by [the banks] pertain to situations wherein there was no evidence to support a recovery of damages. The evidence is also factually sufficient to support the finding. . . .

[Next is the question of] the legal and factual sufficiency of the evidence to support the jury's finding of lost profits. . . . [The banks allege] that the trial court erroneously rendered judgment on such finding because as a matter of law FMC is not entitled to a recovery [and] that the evidence is factually insufficient to support the finding.

In contrast to the jury's finding of $15,482,500.00, [FMC's expert] testified that FMC lost profits totaling $51,232,000.00 (by use of the base period of 1959 through 1971). His calculations derived from the base period of 1959 through 1975 reflect lost profits totaling $24,377,000.00.

Numerous reasons are advanced by State National in support of its position that FMC has no legal basis for recovery. First, it is argued that the evidence does not distinguish between the effects of the lenders' alleged conduct and other known factors affecting FMC's profits. . . .

Numerous reasons are raised which, when construed together, allege that FMC's lost profits cannot be intelligently estimated. [FMC's expert used a base period of 1959 through 1975, not the most recent period of staggering losses.] . . .

* * *

FMC was an established business despite the fact that it had sustained these losses in the several years preceding the damage period. The omission of the year 1976 from either base period would not affect its ability to recover lost profits. . . .

State National argues that . . . [unpredictable] market fluctuations in the men's apparel business . . . render the projection of lost profits conjectural. Admittedly, the men's apparel business is volatile in nature due to the changes in market demand. . . .

* * *

[However, FMC's expert nevertheless] utilized a satisfactory methodology to calculate lost profits.

* * *

As a matter of law, FMC is entitled to the recovery of lost profits. The evidence is legally and factually sufficient to support the jury's finding thereon. . . .

. . . [T]he trial court's judgment is reformed to award Appellee judgment in the total sum of $18,647,243.77. . . .

. . . [A]ffirmed.

¶ 1110: Questions on Lender Liability in *Farah*

1. During 1972–1976, when Farah was CEO, the company lost $44 million. The company had poor labor relations. Farah resigned in July 1976. The banks put the management clause into the loan agreement in February 1977. Presumably the FMC board agreed to the management clause to assure lenders that the company was not about to return to the 1972–1976 labor tensions.
2. Is it surprising that the lenders were uncertain whether they would declare a default if Farah returned? As a business matter and apart from any legal obligation, one could expect that the lenders would bluff, threatening a default, but wait until Farah actually returned before finally deciding whether to declare one. Was the bank statement an inelegantly stated form of notice of probable intention to declare a default if Farah returned?
3. Shouldn't the lenders have been more circumspect in their letter to the Board and their other conversations? What result before the court would have been likely if they had instead written: "Under the loan agreement, a return of Farah as CEO could constitute an event of default, which could lead to FMC's bankruptcy and the padlocking of the company's factories. While the lenders have not yet reached any decision on whether a default will be declared, we point out that the clause was inserted for the purpose of preventing the return of Mr. Farah as CEO, that the banks have consistently opposed the return of Mr. Farah as CEO, and that the banks now oppose the return of Mr. Farah as CEO." Does the letter they actually wrote explicitly state that Farah's return would induce them to declare a default, accelerate, and call the loan?
4. On the duress theory, what did the bankers get from FMC beyond that which they were entitled to get under the management clause? That is, did the bankers threaten to invoke the management clause and thereby extract from FMC a higher interest rate, better securi-

ty, or other benefits? Or did the bankers threaten to invoke the management change clause so as to prevent a change in management?

5. Did the bankers threaten to invoke the management change clause to get more than a veto over the return of Farah? Did they use it to get particular people they wanted as managers? Divide the duress analysis into three parts: (1) keeping Farah out, (2) getting the bankers' preferred managers, associated with the banks, in, and (3) selling FMC assets.

   Banks usually get interest for their loan. What if a debtor doesn't pay and the banks threaten to sue under the loan agreement? Does the debtor have a claim for duress if the debtor under threat of suit pays up?

6. Creditors often impose strategic conditions on the debtor when waiving a covenant violation. Consider this corporate disclosure statement, made following the firm's default and negotiation with its creditor:

   > As of September 30, 2005, the Company was not in compliance with the covenant related to its leverage ratio. On November 9, 2005, the Company received a waiver from its lender. . . . In connection with securing this waiver, certain other changes were made in the credit facility which, among other things, reduced the amount that can be borrowed . . . from \$15.0 million to \$4.5 million.

   Greg Nini, David Smith & Amir Sufi, *Creditor Control Rights, Corporate Governance, and Firm Value*, 25 Review of Financial Studies 1713 (2012). They go on: "Beyond the \$10.5 million reduction in the company's line of credit, the 'other things' [the lender] required . . . included a[n] . . . increase in the interest rate . . . , stronger restrictions on dividend and intercompany payments, a 50 percent reduction in allowed capital expenditures, and a requirement that the company comply with its capital expenditures restrictions on a quarterly, rather than annual, basis." In other words, the lender required that the company slow any expansion and keep much of its cash and earnings in the debtor entity.

7. Damages in *Farah* were based on losses of \$2.6 million and lost profits of \$15.5 million. These damages were caused, concluded the court, by lenders that had loaned FMC \$22 million, a sum not much larger than the damages found. Again, if Farah and FMC thought that the banks were causing such damage to FMC, were they under any duty to mitigate? That is, should they have found another lender who (at a higher interest rate) would have lent money to FMC with Farah as CEO? Would the company's damage claim then have been the difference between the interest rate on the El Paso loan and the higher rate on the new loan, presumably 2% or 3% on \$22 million for a few years until FMC's profits stabilized at the (FMC–expected) high level?

8. Subsequent history: The losers appealed to the Texas Supreme Court, which granted a hearing, suggesting some possibility of revision or reversal. The parties settled, reportedly for about \$12 million, before the court reached a decision.

9. Had the lenders been directors, would the business judgment rule have protected their actions in a suit by the shareholders? Which actions? Sale of the machinery? Mistakes in running the business?

10. To the extent that Farah did (or could) control the company's Board of Directors, could Farah Manufacturing have obtained a loan from another bank, without the management clause and presumably at a higher rate of interest? Could he then have repaid the first loan with the proceeds of the new loan without the control clause?

11. To the extent that Farah could not control a majority of stock before January 1978, was it his family and not the banks who really kept him out of management?

12. Would or should the analysis of the banks' actions differ if the banks owned stock in FMC? Realistically, most banks would not want to own stock, but one could imagine that a "lead" creditor would own some stock in the company, with the other creditors not owning stock. For example, imagine this as FMC's balance sheet when the loans were first made:

$50M	$40 M loans, of which	$ 8M is held by El Paso Nat'l $42M is held by other banks
	$10 M stock, of which	$ 2M held by El Paso Nat'l $ 3M held by Farah family $ 5M publicly-held or held by other banks

This is imaginary historically for American banks, which were generally not allowed to own any stock in industrial firms. So use your imagination here.[5] Or imagine a nonbank creditor.

Were this financial scenario in play, should El Paso be entitled to business judgment deference? Would this kind of structure indeed undermine much of the justification for the automatic stay and chapter 11? Would it be distinguishable from *Deep Rock*? If the lead bank foreclosed and sold some of the firm's assets (as FMC did), would the financial structure support a court's deference to the business judgment of the lead bank?

¶ 1111: A Comparative Note

These doctrines and incentives are not the only ones imaginable. Consider how Japanese banks were said to have acted when a client was in trouble during the main banks' 1970s and 1980s heyday:

> The bank will send a director to an ailing firm. If the director succeeds in revitalizing the firm, he or she is a hero and is guaranteed a top position in the bank. If one bank pulls out its person before the company is rejuvenated, another bank will step in. If this director concludes that changes are necessary for the corporation's management practices, he or she will recommend

[5] The ban on bank ownership of stock originates in the 19th century National Bank Act and was re-confirmed in the more famous Glass–Steagall Act in 1933. In 1999, Congress repealed the Glass–Steagall Act in general but not the ban on direct stock ownership.

> them. The perspective as an objective third party who is not involved in daily affairs of the company lets this director perceive necessary changes better. The bank might also recommend that a supplier make certain changes that are necessary to revitalize the company. . . .

William Ouchi, The M–Form Society 88 (1984). Mainstream scholarship here saw the main bank as a crisis epicenter, making managerial, strategic, and financial changes when the first-line team failed.[6] This practice might have succeeded often when corporate failures were isolated, and their causes clear (such as poor management of a known technology). But when crises are economy-wide (as they became in Japan in recent years), and when the information needed to transform the firm is not likely to be within the bank's knowledge, then the system would presumably work less well (as it seems to have in recent years).

Practices like lender liability and equitable subordination played a role in Japan but in inducing bank involvement, not deterring it. Anecdotes say Japanese practice had the "main" bank—the largest stockholder with 5% of the firm's stock and a big chunk of the bank lending—subordinating its loan to the other financiers' loans. The bank could not avoid subordination by forsaking involvement, as the American bank can. Rather, the bank could improve its position by improving the value of the failing firm. It became the residual claimant, both formally through its stock holding and informally through the expectation of "voluntary" subordination.

[6] Masahiko Aoki, Ex Post Monitoring by the Main Bank (1992); Masahiko Aoki & Paul Sheard, The Role of the Japanese Main Bank in the Corporate Governance Structure in Japan (1991); Robert Reich and John Donahue, New Deals: The Chrysler Revival and the American System 81–85 (1985) (Mazda rescue).

CHAPTER 12

REJECTING PRE–BANKRUPTCY CONTRACTS AND REGULATORY OBLIGATIONS

A bankrupt company has contracts on which it owes performance. The type of contract we have examined thus far has been the financial contract: the bankrupt company is obligated to repay money it has borrowed, and bankruptcy adjusts the rights of those on the other side of a bankrupt's financial contracts. In this chapter, we consider other types of contractual and regulatory obligations of the debtor.

A. THE TRUSTEE'S RIGHT TO REJECT OR ASSUME

¶ 1201: The Debtor's Contracts

How should bankruptcy address the debtor's non-financial contracts, such as its prebankruptcy orders for goods and services? Are those left unadjusted? The Bankruptcy Code allows the bankrupt to either affirm or reject executory contracts—those contracts for which neither side has substantially performed its obligation under the contract. Upon the bankrupt's rejection, the nonbankrupt party obtains a claim in bankruptcy and shares with the bankrupt's other creditors.

§ 365. Executory contracts and unexpired leases

(a) . . . the trustee, subject to the court's approval, may assume or reject any executory contract or unexpired lease of the debtor.

(b) (1) If there has been a default in an executory contract or unexpired lease of the debtor, the trustee may not assume such contract or lease unless . . . the trustee

(A) cures . . . ;

(B) compensates . . . ; and

(C) provides adequate assurance of future performance. . . .

(2) Paragraph (1) of this subsection does not apply to a default that is a breach of a provision relating to

(A) the insolvency or financial condition of the debtor at any time before the closing of the case;

(B) the commencement of a case under this title;

(C) the appointment of . . . a trustee . . . ; or

(D) the satisfaction of any penalty rate or penalty provision relating to a default arising from any failure by the debtor to perform nonmonetary obligations under the executory contract or unexpired lease.

§ 502. Allowance of claims or interests

(g)(1) A claim arising from the rejection, under section 365 of this title or under a plan under chapter . . . 11 . . . of an executory contract . . . of the debtor that has not been assumed shall be determined, and shall be allowed . . . or disallowed . . . , the same as if such claim had arisen before the date of the filing of the petition.

The bankrupt's "right" to assume or reject an uncompleted contract is no different than the "right" of any contracting party to perform or to default. The consequence of default is often a lawsuit from the offended party. But because the contracting party's claim for damages is treated as a *prebankruptcy* default of the bankrupt, this power of the bankrupt gives it a heads-the-bankrupt-wins, tails-the-other-party loses quality: the bankrupt contracting party can assume profitable contracts and reject unprofitable ones, paying damages in discounted "bankruptcy dollars." If the bankrupt contracts before bankruptcy with A, for A to deliver 100 widgets at $10 each, and the market price rises to $15 each by the time of the bankruptcy, then the bankrupt assumes the contract and pockets the $500 gain (to be shared ultimately by all of the bankrupt's creditors). But if the market price declines to $5, then the bankrupt would reject the contract. A has a claim in bankruptcy for $500, which ordinarily would be paid (in essence by the unsecured creditors or the stockholders) at less than $500.

For spot transactions, the analysis is easy. For more complex, relational contracts, the analysis is only a little harder. If the bankrupt's and A's contract for the widgets is part of a larger deal, of say, a requirements contract, or a contract for A to build a factory for the bankrupt, part of which requires that the bankrupt deliver widgets to A, then the Bankruptcy Code takes an all-or-nothing approach: the bankrupt must assume the burdens of the contract along with its benefits. Once it affirms the entire contract, it must pay any of the missed partial installments.

Section 365 has three main exceptions to the all-or-nothing approach: First, the nonbankrupt cannot take advantage of an ipso facto clause, i.e., a clause that allows it, the nonbankrupt, to opt out of a contract just because the bankrupt has filed for bankruptcy. Once the debtor assumes the contract, it need not cure its own breach of an ipso facto clause. Second, if the contract has penalty rates that arise from a bankrupt's failure to perform, the penalty is not enforceable against the bankrupt. Third, the bankrupt can assign contracts and leases, notwithstanding that the contract or lease bars assignment. This allows the bankrupt to profit from contracts or leases that it cannot itself use as it shrinks its operations. It can profit from these otherwise unusable contracts and leases if they have better-than-market rates, by assigning them to those who can use them.

A large bankruptcy can take a year or more until the court confirms a plan of reorganization. When must the bankrupt decide whether to reject or assume its contracts and leases?

The bankrupt generally gets until the confirmation of the plan to assume or reject. Once assumed, the bankrupt's obligation becomes an administrative expense of the estate; once rejected, the contract claim is an ordinary creditor's claim, usually unsecured. (One exception to the debtor's authority to wait is for commercial real estate leases, which the bankrupt must decide on within 120 days of filing the petition.)

But as a business matter, the bankrupt might not be able to wait to decide. Imagine that an irate, unpaid supplier shipped goods before bankruptcy under a long-term supply contract. The bankrupt needs another delivery, but the supplier won't ship until it's paid on the old shipment. The bankrupt assumes the entire contract, so that the supplier knows that it has a long-term deal with the debtor.

Could the bankrupt "force" delivery—i.e., get specific performance—before it decides whether to assume or reject? Case law is mixed. On the one hand, some courts look at the supplier's refusal to deliver as contrary to the automatic stay. On the other hand, some courts see the supplier's refusal to ship as ordinary business prudence, with the supplier waiting for the debtor's adequate assurance that it will perform. As a practical matter when dealing with suppliers, the bankrupt may have to assume the contract to get satisfactory deliveries from the supplier under the contract. (The bankrupt can always reject the contract and buy elsewhere, if the goods are available—and will usually do so if the contract price has become unfavorable to the bankrupt.)

One delivery the bankrupt cannot force: it cannot make a lender honor a loan commitment:

§ 365. Executory contracts and unexpired leases

(c) The trustee may not assume or assign any executory contract . . . of the debtor . . . if—

* * *

(2) such contract is a contract to make a loan, or extend other debt financing . . . to or for the benefit of the debtor, or to issue a security of the debtor. . . .

What is an executory contract of the kind that gives the debtor the right to reject or assume under § 365? The standard notion is that each side has not finished performance, said the court in Lubrizol v. Richmond Metal Finishers, Inc., 756 F.2d 1043 (4th Cir. 1985), a leading case: "This court has recently adopted Professor Countryman's more specific test for determining whether a contract is 'executory' in the required [bankruptcy] sense. By that test, a contract is executory if the obligations of both the bankrupt and the other party to the contract are so far unperformed that the failure of either to complete the performance would constitute a material breach excusing the performance of the other.' . . . Countryman, *Executory Contracts in Bankruptcy: Part I*, 57 Minn. L. Rev. 439, 460 (1973)."

¶ 1202: Administrative Priority for Assumed and Postpetition Contracts

What about contractual commitments the debtor makes in bankruptcy? The debtor needs to buy supplies and services to recover in chapter 11. Its ongoing operations need to make and sell product. But if there is serious risk that post-petition suppliers' claims won't be paid, suppliers will be reluctant to sell to the debtor in bankruptcy. If the post-petition suppliers were treated like prepetition creditors, potential suppliers would be reluctant to ship and sell. Typically, on the first day of bankruptcy the trustee gets an order from the judge to be allowed to buy goods and operate the business, with the resulting expenses getting administrative priority under §§ 503 and 507:[1]

§ 507. Priorities

(a) The following expenses and claims have priority in the following order:

(1) First, [claims only relevant in personal bankruptcy] . . . ;

(2) Second, administrative expenses allowed under section 503(b). . . .

---

[1] Note also that even in the absence of a court order, § 364(a) authorizes the debtor to incur ordinary course unsecured debt, which enjoys administrative priority under § 503.

§ 503. Allowance of administrative expenses

(a) . . .

(b) After notice and a hearing, there shall be allowed administrative expenses . . . including

(1)(A) the actual, necessary costs and expenses of preserving the estate including . . . wages. . . .

(9) the value of any goods received by the debtor within 20 days before the date of commencement of [the bankruptcy] . . . [if] the goods have been sold to the debtor in the ordinary course of the debtor's business.

§ 1129. Confirmation of plan

(a) The court shall confirm a plan only if all of the following requirements are met:

(1) . . .

(9) . . . the plan provides that . . . [the holder of any] claim . . . specified in section 507(a)(2) . . . on the effective date of the plan . . . will receive . . . cash equal to the allowed amount of such claim . . .

Note the bankruptcy difference between a long-term supply contract, with multiple delivery dates, and a series of spot contracts. Contrast (1) a supplier who has a contract to deliver the bankrupt retailer 100 pairs of jeans weekly for the next year with (2) a dress manufacturer that has two separate, discrete prepetition orders from the bankrupt. In case (1), the bankrupt must assume or reject the entire contract. If assumed, the bankrupt must pay for everything; if rejected, the jean-maker has a claim for damages as a general, prebankruptcy creditor. In case (2), the dress manufacturer might ship the first order to the debtor a month before the debtor's eventual bankruptcy. Say the dress manufacturer is unpaid when the petition is filed. As to that first order, the dress manufacturer is merely a creditor with an unsecured prepetition claim. No executory contract exists because one party—the dress manufacturer in this example—has already performed. Section 502(g) will make the dress manufacturer wait until plan confirmation to be paid on this shipment, and the manufacturer will typically not be paid in full for that shipment. The same dress manufacturer who ships to the retailer *after* it has filed for bankruptcy and assumed the second contract will typically be paid in full and on time as an administrative expense entitled to priority. And if the dress manufacturer gets a third order for dresses *after* the debtor files its petition in bankruptcy, payment for that order will also be an administrative expense. If the debtor later rejects that contract, the dress manufacturer would then have a claim for damages, a claim usually paid in full as an administrative expense. The same is true for a prepetition contract that is assumed and then later breached or rejected.

The before-and-after filing break is not 100% clean: § 503(b)(9) gives prebankruptcy trade creditors an administrative expense priority for the value of goods delivered to the debtor in the ordinary course of business within 20 days of the bankruptcy filing.

¶ 1203: Efficiency Considerations

Consider a firm that contracts to buy widgets at $100 (the then-market price for widgets). The seller will produce these at a cost of $60. Before the seller delivers, the buyer files for bankruptcy. During the bankruptcy proceedings the debtor-in-possession can assume or reject the delivery contract.

What will the debtor's calculations be on whether to reject or assume? Let's assume that after the contract was signed, the market price for widgets dropped to $80 (but still cost the seller $60 to make). The bankrupt in retrospect regrets promising to pay $100 for the widgets; the contract is a $20 burden. Outside bankruptcy, if it rejected or breached the contract, it would be liable for $40 in damages (the seller's lost profit), so it would take delivery, accepting to pay the $20 above the market price, because it is obligated to do so. But if the trustee rejects the contract under § 365, then it is obliged under § 502(g) to pay up on the $40 damage claim, but *only as if* the supplier's claim had arisen *before* bankruptcy. The $40 will be paid in "bankruptcy dollars" at the rate of distribution to the unsecured creditors. If that rate is only 10%, the trustee will pay only four actual dollar bills in damages to get out of a contract that the bankrupt regrets.

The trustee has an incentive to reject in this hypothetical as long as the payout ratio on unsecured claims is 50% or less.

As shown in detail in Jesse Fried, *Executory Contracts and Performance Decisions in Bankruptcy,* 46 Duke Law Journal 517 (1996), and summarily in George G. Triantis, *The Effects of Insolvency and Bankruptcy on Contract Performance and Adjustment,* 43 University of Toronto Law Journal 679 (1993), this scenario is potentially inefficient. The social cost of producing the widgets is $60 and the reduced market value of the widgets is $80, yielding a social gain of $20 from the trade going forward. But because the bankrupt unburdens itself of $20 (the decrease in market value) at a private cost of only $4, the bankrupt will reject the contract, and accordingly $20 of social value, of gross national product, of valuable production, could be lost.

Some of this lost value can be recovered. After the trustee rejects the contract, it could place a new order for widgets at $80, which the calculating seller would presumably still fulfill because the widgets would cost it only $60 to make and the new widget order would be entitled to administrative priority under § 507. The seller loses $16 from its nonbankruptcy entitlement (a $40 loss from the original contract, a $4 bankruptcy damage payment, and a $20 profit on the second contract). But the social loss is avoided.

Similarly, it's possible that the bankrupt and the seller could renegotiate after the bankrupt rejects the contract, so as to make the deal still happen; they'd renegotiate the price, but the widgets would still change hands. The social loss then is the sum of the transaction costs of the renegotiation and the lost production when these renegotiations fail.

The bankrupt's power to reject contracts during bankruptcy and pay damages as if on a prebankruptcy claim is one of the disruptions that induces suppliers and customers to be wary of dealing with a near bankrupt.

¶ 1204: Critical Vendor Payments

Critical vendor payments are something of a flip side to contract rejection. It has become common practice in the bankruptcy courts to approve payment of prebankruptcy claims of so-called "critical vendors" early on in a bankruptcy case. These are not executory contracts, but merely claims for payment for goods or services provided to the debtor prepetition. The debtor designates as "critical" those prebankruptcy suppliers whose continuing supply during reorganization the debtor deems critical to reorganization, and whose good will the debtor wishes to preserve by favoring the supplier with postpetition payment in full of its outstanding debt. Code authority for these payments to favored claimants is murky at best.

Consider a related possibility. The failing debtor contemplating bankruptcy cannot pay its bills to its prime supplier. The prime supplier cuts off further shipments of the critical good. (Think: the engines to be supplied to a troubled automaker; the chips for a failing computer manufacturer; the skilled employee due back wages; the fuel for the factory; the best-seller for a retailer, etc.) The debtor, knowing it is insolvent, considers making the payment, but decides not to.

Would the payment if made have been a preference under § 547? Is it a payment that the Code authorizes the debtor to make? If the debtor pays prebankruptcy vendors but wasn't authorized to do so, a later-appointed trustee could recover those payments. And the court presumably would not authorize those payments unless the Code gave the court that authority.

The company then files for bankruptcy. The vendor still refuses to ship more of the critical good.

§ 549. Postpetition transactions

(a) . . . [T]he trustee may avoid a transfer of property of the estate—

(1) that occurs after the commencement of the case; and

(2) . . . that is not authorized under this title or by the court.

The debtor petitions the court to allow it to pay the critical vendor, which the court allows, saying that it must be pragmatic and allow payment if the new supplies were "essential to the survival of the debtor during the chapter 11 reorganization." In re Just for Feet Inc., 242 B.R. 821, 826 (D. Del. Nov. 17, 1999). Section 105 of the Bankruptcy Code provides for the general power of the bankruptcy court: "the court may issue any order, process, or judgment that is necessary or appropriate to carry out the provisions of this title. . . . "

Is the critical vendor doctrine consistent with preference policy? Is it consistent with § 1129(b)?

The following law firm memo summarizes the critical vendor doctrine and how it was faring in the lower courts in a leading critical vender case. The subsequent opinion is the appellate disposition.

Wachtell, Lipton, Rosen & Katz

May 7, 2003

Kmart Critical Vendor Payment Order Reversed

In a number of jurisdictions, it has become accepted practice for bankruptcy courts to grant "first day" motions by large chapter 11 debtors for authority to make payments to certain prepetition creditors, typically referred to as "critical vendors," based on contentions that (a) those vendors are an irreplaceable source of goods or services required for the debtors' continued operations and (b) such vendors would be unwilling or unable to continue to provide such goods or services postpetition if they were not promptly paid the amounts owing to them by the debtors. Although this practice originally involved relatively small payments to a few vendors in exceptional circumstances, over time it has expanded in a number of cases to involve larger payments to more creditors. In a recent decision arising out of the Kmart Corporation chapter 11 case, the United States District Court for the Northern District of Illinois has cast substantial doubt on the continued viability of that practice, at least for cases filed in the Chicago area.

Capital Factors, Inc. v. Kmart Corporation, No. 02C 1264 (N.D. Ill. April 8, 2003) (Grady, J.), involved a consolidated appeal of four "first day orders" entered by the Bankruptcy Court in the chapter 11 cases of Kmart Corporation. Those orders authorized the payment of the prepetition obligations of certain "critical vendors," foreign vendors, liquor vendors and letter of credit issuers. Kmart had contended that payment of these prepetition obligations was necessary to maintain relationships that were critical to the success of its efforts to reorganize. This argument, known as the "doctrine of necessity," relied upon the general conferral of power contained in section 105(a) of the Bankruptcy Code for its statutory basis. See 11 U.S.C. § 105(a) ("The court may issue any order, process, or judgment that is necessary or appropriate to carry out the provisions of this title.") Not surprisingly, critical vendor orders are often criticized by non-critical trade creditors, lenders and bondholders.

In *Capital Factors*, the District Court noted that there is a split among the courts whether section 105 authorizes the payment of prepetition unsecured claims outside of a plan of reorganization. Slip op. at 7. The Court held that section 105 does not authorize the bankruptcy court to override the statutory scheme of creditor priority outlined in the Bankruptcy Code to permit the making of otherwise unauthorized payments of prepetition debts, even if such payments might enhance the prospects for reorganization. *Id.* at 8. . . .

Amy R. Wolf

¶ 1205: In re Kmart Corp., 359 F.3d 866 (7th Cir. 2004)

EASTERBROOK, *Circuit Judge*. On the first day of its bankruptcy, Kmart sought permission to pay immediately, and in full, the prepetition claims of all "critical vendors." . . . The theory behind the request is that some suppliers may be unwilling to do business with a customer that is behind in payment, and, if it cannot obtain the merchandise that its own customers have come to expect, a firm such as Kmart may be unable to carry on, injuring all of its creditors. Full payment to critical-vendors thus could in principle make even the disfavored creditors better off: they may not be paid in full, but they will receive a greater portion of their claims than they would if the critical-vendors cut off supplies and the business shut down. Putting the proposition in this way implies, however, that the debtor must *prove,* and not just allege, two things: that, but for immediate full payment, vendors *would* cease dealing; and that the business will gain enough from continued transactions with the favored vendors to provide some residual benefit to the remaining, disfavored creditors, or at least leave them no worse off.

Bankruptcy Judge Sonderby entered a critical-vendors order just as Kmart proposed it, without notifying any disfavored creditors, without receiving any pertinent evidence (the record contains only some sketchy representations by counsel plus unhelpful testimony by Kmart's CEO, who could not speak for the vendors), and without making any finding of fact that the disfavored creditors would gain or come out even. The bankruptcy court's order declared that the relief Kmart requested—open-ended permission to pay any debt to any vendor it deemed "critical" in the exercise of unilateral discretion, provided that the vendor agreed to furnish goods on "customary trade terms" for the next two years—was "in the best interests of the Debtors, their estates and their creditors". The order did not explain why, nor did it contain any legal analysis. . . .

Kmart used its authority to pay in full the prepetition debts to 2,330 suppliers, which collectively received about $300 million. . . . Another 2,000 or so vendors were not deemed "critical" and were not paid. They and 43,000 additional unsecured creditors eventually received about 10 [cents] on the dollar, mostly in stock of the reorganized Kmart. Capital Factors, Inc., appealed the critical-vendors order immediately after its entry on January 25, 2002. A little more than 14 months later, after all of the critical-vendors had been paid and as Kmart's plan of reorganization was on the verge of approval, District Judge Grady reversed the order authorizing payment. . . .

Appellants insist that, by the time Judge Grady acted, it was too late. Money had changed hands and, we are told, cannot be refunded. But why not? Reversing preferential transfers is an ordinary feature of bankruptcy practice, often continuing under a confirmed plan of reorganization. If the orders in question are invalid, then the critical-vendors have received preferences that Kmart is entitled to recoup for the benefit of all creditors. . . .

* * *

Thus we arrive at the merits. *Section 105(a)* allows a bankruptcy court to "issue any order, process, or judgment that is necessary or appropriate to carry out the provisions of" the Code. This does not create discretion to set aside the Code's rules about priority and distribution; the power conferred by *§ 105(a)* is one to implement rather than override. . . . Every circuit that has considered the question has held that this statute does not allow a bankruptcy judge to authorize full payment of any unsecured debt, unless all unsecured creditors in the class are paid in full. We agree with this view of *§ 105*. "The fact that a [bankruptcy] proceeding is equitable does not give the judge a free-floating discretion to redistribute rights in accordance with his personal views of justice and fairness, however enlightened those views may be." *In re Chicago, Milwaukee, St. Paul & Pacific R.R., 791 F.2d 524, 528 (7th Cir. 1986).*

A "doctrine of necessity" [that has grown to justify these kinds of critical vendor payments] is just a fancy name for a power to depart from the Code. Although courts in the days before bankruptcy law was codified wielded power to reorder priorities and pay particular creditors in the name of "necessity" . . . today it is the Code rather than the norms of nineteenth century railroad reorganizations that must prevail. . . . Today the *Bankruptcy Code of 1978* supplies the rules. . . . Answers to contemporary issues must be found within the Code (or legislative halls). Older doctrines may survive as glosses on ambiguous language enacted in 1978 or later, but not as freestanding entitlements to trump the text. . . .

So does the Code contain any grant of authority for debtors to prefer some vendors over others? Many sections require equal treatment or specify the details of priority when assets are insufficient to satisfy all claims. E.g., *11 U.S.C. §§ 507, 1122(a), 1123(a)(4)*. Appellants rely on *11 U.S.C. §§ 363(b), 364(b), and 503* as sources of authority for unequal treatment. . . . *Section 503*, which deals with administrative expenses, . . . is irrelevant. Pre-filing debts are not administrative expenses; they are the antithesis of administrative expenses. Filing a petition for bankruptcy effectively creates two firms: the debts of the pre-filing entity may be written down so that the post-filing entity may reorganize and continue in business if it has a positive cash flow. . . . Treating pre-filing debts as "administrative" claims against the post-filing entity would impair the ability of bankruptcy law to prevent old debts from sinking a viable firm.

That leaves *§ 363(b)(1)*: "The trustee [or debtor in possession], after notice and a hearing, may use, sell, or lease, other than in the ordinary course of business, property of the estate." This is more promising, for satisfaction of a prepetition debt in order to keep "critical" supplies flowing is a use of property other than in the ordinary course of administering an estate in bankruptcy. Capital Factors insists that *§ 363(b)(1)* should be limited to the commencement of capital projects, such as building a new plant, rather than payment of old debts—as paying vendors would be "in the ordinary course" but for the intervening bankruptcy petition. To read *§ 363(b)(1)* broadly, Capital Factors observes, would be to allow a judge to rearrange priorities among creditors (which is what a critical-vendors order effectively does). . . . If the language [of *§ 363(b)(1)*] is too open-ended, that is a problem for the legislature. Nonetheless, it is prudent to read, and use, *§ 363(b)(1)* to do the least damage possible to priorities established by contract and by other parts of the Bankruptcy Code. We need not decide whether *§ 363(b)(1)* could support payment of some prepetition debts, because *this* order was unsound no matter how one reads *§ 363(b)(1)*.

The foundation of a critical-vendors order is the belief that vendors not paid for prior deliveries will refuse to make new ones. Without merchandise to sell, a retailer such as Kmart will fold. If paying the critical vendors would enable a successful reorganization and make even the disfavored creditors better off, then all creditors favor payment whether or not they are designated as "critical." This suggests a use of *§ 363(b)(1)* similar to the theory underlying a plan crammed down the throats of an impaired class of creditors: if the impaired class does at least as well as it would have under [an absolute priority plan], then it has no legitimate objection and cannot block the reorganization. . . . For the premise to hold true, however, it is necessary to show not only that the disfavored creditors *will* be as well off with reorganization as with liquidation—a demonstration never attempted in this proceeding—but also that the supposedly critical vendors would have ceased deliveries if old debts were left unpaid while the litigation continued. If vendors will deliver against a promise of current payment, then a reorganization can be achieved, and all unsecured creditors will obtain its benefit, without preferring any of the unsecured creditors.

Some supposedly critical vendors will continue to do business with the debtor because they must. They may, for example, have . . . contracts, and the automatic stay prevents these vendors from walking away as long as the debtor [assumes the relevant contracts and] pays for new deliveries. See *11 U.S.C. § 362*. Fleming Companies, which received the largest critical-vendors payment because it sold Kmart between $70 million and $100 million of groceries and related goods weekly, was one of these. No matter how much Fleming would have liked to dump Kmart, it had no right to do so [on any assumed contracts]. It was unnecessary to compensate Fleming for continuing to make deliveries that it was legally required to make. Nor was Fleming likely to walk away even if it had a legal right to do so. Each new delivery produced a profit; as long as Kmart continued to pay for new product, why would any vendor drop the account? That would be a self-inflicted wound. . . . Firms that disdain current profits because of old losses . . . might as well burn money or drop it into the ocean. . . .

Doubtless many suppliers fear the prospect of throwing good money after bad. It therefore may be vital to assure them that a debtor will pay for new deliveries on a current basis. Providing that assurance need not, however, entail payment for prepetition transactions. Kmart could have paid cash or its equivalent. (Kmart's CEO told the bankruptcy judge that cash on delivery arrangements were not part of Kmart's business plan, as if a litigant's druthers could override the rights of third parties.) Cash on the barrelhead was not the most convenient way, however. Kmart secured a $2 billion line of credit [with administrative priority] when it entered bankruptcy. Some of that credit could have been used to assure vendors that payment would be forthcoming for all post-petition transactions. The easiest way to do that would have been to put some of the $2 billion behind a standby letter of credit on which the bankruptcy judge could authorize unpaid vendors to draw. . . .

Yet the bankruptcy court did not explore the possibility of using a letter of credit to assure vendors of payment. The court did not find that any firm would have ceased doing business with Kmart if not paid for prepetition deliveries. . . . The court did not find that discrimination among unsecured creditors was the only way to facilitate a reorganization. It did not find that the disfavored creditors were at least as well off as they would have been had the critical-vendors order not been entered. For all the millions at stake, this proceeding looks much like [an effort to favor some creditors over others, and no more]. . . . Even if *§ 363(b)(1)* allows critical-vendors orders in principle, preferential payments to a class of creditors are proper only if the record shows the prospect of benefit to the other creditors. This record does not, so the critical-vendors order cannot stand.

AFFIRMED

¶ 1206: Reclamation and Other Rights of Suppliers re Eve-of-Bankruptcy Shipments

The Code offers some protection for the unfortunate supplier who sells goods to the debtor on credit on the eve of bankruptcy. Without such protection, the hapless supplier would have to wait for the conclusion of the case only to be paid a fraction of its claim. First, § 503(b)(9) gives suppliers an administrative priority for shipments to the debtor in the 20 days before bankruptcy. Second, § 546(c) protects suppliers' reclamation rights by reducing the susceptibility of reclamation to preference and other avoidance actions. For an eve-of-bankruptcy shipment of merchandise on credit, the supplier may enjoy a state law right to reclaim the goods—to simply take them back from the debtor. Such a reclamation would ordinarily be avoidable as a preference, since it would be a transfer relating to an antecedent debt. Section 546(c) protects many such reclamations from avoidance, and may even extend the reclamation period into the early part of the case:

§ 546. Limitations on Avoiding Powers.

(c) (1) . . . [S]ubject to the prior rights of a holder of a security interest in such goods or the proceeds thereof, the rights and powers of the trustee under sections 544(a), 545, 547, and 549 are subject to the right of a seller of goods that has sold goods to the debtor, in the ordinary course of such seller's business, to reclaim such goods if the debtor has received such goods while insolvent, within 45 days before the date of the commencement of a case under this title. . . .

¶ 1207: Specific Performance

Thus far we've been looking at basic contracts for the delivery of goods. Contracts are of course more complex, and § 365 has special rules for technology licensing contracts, real estate, and (via § 1113) labor. Case law confronts more unusual business deals that debtors wish to avoid under § 365.

In one bankruptcy, a Burger King franchisee that had being doing poorly filed for chapter 11 and rejected the franchise contract. As to the franchisee's obligation to pay royalties to Burger King, the analysis and case were unexceptionable. Controversy arose over the franchisee's non-competition obligation under the franchise agreement. After it filed, it rejected the franchise agreement under § 365, then pursued a hamburger business at the same location, but not as a Burger King franchisee. Burger King Corp. v. Rovine Corp., 6 Bankr. 661 (Bankr. W.D. Tenn. 1980).

How could the court deal with the franchisee's obligation not to compete, which the franchisee breached by competing anyway? Should it have given Burger King specific performance? If it did, would it be effectively making Burger King a priority creditor over the franchisee's other creditors?

§ 502. Allowance of claims or interests

(c) There shall be estimated for purposes of allowance under this section [502]—

(1) any contingent or unliquidated claim, the fixing or liquidation of which . . . would unduly delay the administration of the case; or

(2) any right to payment arising from a right to an equitable remedy for breach of performance.

The legislative history to § 502 is more specific:

> Subsection (c) requires the estimation of any claim liquidation of which would unduly delay the closing of the estate, such as . . . any claim for which applicable law provides only an equitable remedy, such as specific performance. This subsection requires that all claims against the debtor be converted into dollar amounts.

Thus, claims that state law judges find so speculative that they award specific performance are susceptible to estimation by the (more skillful?!) bankruptcy judges. So the bankrupt Burger King franchisee in *Rovine* rejected the franchise agreement and its non-competition clause under § 365. The bankruptcy court then had to estimate the value of Burger King's claim against the franchisee for specific performance under § 502(c), with the resulting damage claim coming in as a "pennies for dollars" prebankruptcy claim under § 502(g).

Rovine is carefully analyzed in Jay Westbrook, *A Functional Analysis of Executory Contracts,* 74 Minnesota Law Review 227 (1989).

¶ 1208: Assignment

The bankrupt may assign a contract, even if the contract itself bars assignment:

§ 365. Executory contracts and unexpired leases

(f)(1) . . . [N]otwithstanding a provision in an executory contract or unexpired lease of the debtor . . . that prohibits, restricts, or conditions the assignment of such contract or lease, the trustee may assign such contract or lease. . . .

(2) The trustee may assign an executory contract or unexpired lease of the debtor only if

(A) . . .

(B) adequate assurance of future performance by the assignee of such contract or lease is provided. . . .

The section allows the debtor to assign an executory contract to a third party even if the contract bars assignment; however, if state law, and not the contract itself, bars assignment, then the bankrupt cannot assign the contract. Bankruptcy Code § 365(c)(1) makes this explicit. (The same concept is applicable for the bankrupt assuming the contract: local law must allow it.)

Sections 1124(2), 365(a), and 365(f) all have similar financial effects: They give the bankrupt debtor "heads the debtor wins, tails the other party loses" powers in financial and executory contracts. If the contract's terms are, taken altogether, favorable to the bankrupt because of, say, interim changes in interest rates or prices of the underlying commodity, then the bankrupt reinstates, assumes, or assigns the contract. But if the underlying interest rate or product price has moved unfavorably to the bankrupt debtor, the debtor doesn't have to live with the unfavorable contracts and declines to reinstate or rejects them.

To reiterate, when the bankrupt rejects an executory contract under § 365, the contract creditor then has a damage claim under § 502(g). The contract is not null and void when rejected; the contract party has a claim that shares pro rata with other unsecured claims.

¶ 1209: Technology Licenses

In Lubrizol Enterprises, Inc. v. Richmond Metal Finishers, Inc., 756 F.2d 1043 (4th Cir. 1985); cert. denied, 475 U.S. 1057 (1986), the debtor Richmond Metal Finishers (RMF) had, prior to the bankruptcy filing, licensed a metal coating process technology to Lubrizol. When RMF filed for bankruptcy, it rejected the technology license to Lubrizol in order to facilitate sale or relicensing of the technology free of the constraints contained in Lubrizol's licensing agreement. The court held that the debtor's rejection left Lubrizol with only a claim for damages. Lubrizol could not retain any rights in the technology, as that would effectively give Lubrizol a specific performance remedy to which it was not entitled. The court recognized the "serious burdens" placed on nondebtor contracting parties from its approach.

In 1988, Congress reacted, adding § 365(n) to the Code's executory contract section via the Intellectual Property Bankruptcy Protection Act of 1988:

§ 365. Executory contracts and unexpired leases

* * *

(n)(1) If the trustee rejects an executory contract under which the debtor is a licensor of a right to intellectual property, the licensee under such contract may elect—

(A) to treat such contract as terminated . . . ; or

(B) to retain its rights (including a right to enforce any exclusivity provision of such contract, but excluding any other right . . . to specific performance . . .) . . . to such intellectual property . . . as such rights existed immediately before the case commenced, for . . . the duration of such contract. . . .

Trademarks. Section 365(n) covers technology licenses and other intellectual property, but somewhat surprisingly, trademarks are omitted from the definition of intellectual property in Code § 101(35A): Intellectual property "means" (not "includes") trade secrets, inventions, patents, plant varieties, and copyrighted writings and mask works.

What happens, then, when the debtor cartoon company licenses the exclusive right to use a trademarked logo from a popular cartoon to the licensee? The debtor has continuing obligations to notify the licensee of infringements. The licensee has built up a thriving business using the logo on T-shirts, coffee mugs, shoes, and so on. Can the bankrupt licensor reject the contract, pull back the logo, and then re-license the logo to someone else for more money?

A number of lower courts have reasoned by negative inference that Congress intended that the protections of § 365(n) not extend to trademark licensees. However, despite the definitional omission, courts of appeals in two circuits have offered two different paths to protecting trademark licensees in the face of debtors' attempts to terminate licensees' rights via contract rejection.

In *In re Exide Technologies*, 607 F.3d 957 (2010), the Third Circuit held that the contract at issue was no longer executory—and so could not be rejected—thereby allowing the trademark licensee to retain its rights. In a concurring opinion, Judge Ambro argued that the omission of trademarks from § 365(n) creates no negative inference, citing legislative history explaining that Congress left to the bankruptcy courts the development of equitable treatment of trademark licensees in rejection situations. Judge Ambro concluded that courts should use their equitable powers to "give [the debtor] a fresh start without stripping [the trademark licensee] of its fairly procured trademark rights." *Id.* at 967. Rejection should free debtor-licensors from burdensome duties under their licensing contracts, but it should not enable debtors to take back trademark rights bargained away to licensees.

Judge Easterbrook penned a different approach for the Seventh Circuit in *Sunbeam Products v. Chicago American Manufacturing*, 686 F.3d 372 (2012). Rejecting Judge Ambro's equitable approach in *Exide*, Judge Easterbrook found instead that rejection merely relieves the debtor from having to perform; it does not rescind the contract in order to put the parties back to their pre-contract positions.

Note that Judges Ambro and Easterbrook both reject the *Lubrizol* rescission approach.

B. LABOR

Union contracts are typically executory contracts, in substance covered by the trustee's power to reject. Debtors facing high labor costs might well be tempted to reject their labor contracts and then take the suit for damages. But, said a leading bankruptcy lawyer for debtors in the mid–1980s, union power had been so strong that no debtor would reject. To reject would mean that the union would strike, rendering the rejection an "exercise[ ] in futility. The [bankrupt] businesses . . . could not obtain substitute labor and could not sustain themselves during the course of a strike; thus, while the statutory power existed, in practical terms it was illusory." Harvey R. Miller, *The Rejection of Collective Bargaining Agreements Under the Bankruptcy Code—An Abuse or Proper Exercise of the Congressional Bankruptcy Power?,* 52 Fordham Law Review 1120, 1123 (1984). But union power declined, and in the 1980s, some bankrupts tried their hand at rejecting their union contracts.

Courts—including the Supreme Court in *Bildiscso*—approved the rejection of union contracts, and Congress then reacted, limiting but not barring the bankrupt's authority to reject labor union contracts.

For ordinary executory agreements, the debtor exercises its business judgment on whether to reject or assume, and the court approves (or doesn't). For labor contracts, the bankrupt must first negotiate with the union, by proposing "those necessary modifications . . . [to the employees'] benefits and protections that are *necessary* to permit the reorganization of the debtor and assure that all creditors, the debtor and all of the affected parties are treated fairly and equitably." Section 1113(b)(1) (emphasis supplied). The debtor must provide the union with the information needed for the union to evaluate whether the debtor's proposal meets § 1113's standards. If the union rejects the proposal from debtor's management, the court may nevertheless allow the debtor to reject the union contract, if it concludes that the union rejected the debtor's proposed modification without good cause and "the balance of the equities clearly favors rejection. . . ."

Congress put § 1113 in the Code in 1984 as a pro-labor measure, to modify prior court decisions allowing the bankrupt to unilaterally reject a collective bargaining agreement without getting a court to approve the rejection and without complying with labor law's standards for modifying or rejecting a union contract. The National Labor Relations Act governs labor contracts, and the question originally was in essence whether the NLRA was subservient to the Bankruptcy Code. In effect, the Supreme Court said "yes" in NLRB v. Bildisco & Bildisco, 465 U.S. 513 (1984), and then Congress, importing some key NLRA standards into the Bankruptcy Code, via § 1113, reversed the Court.

¶ 1210: Truck Drivers Local 807, Int'l Brotherhood of Teamsters v. Carey Trans. Inc., 816 F.2d 82 (2d Cir. 1987)

Plaintiff, a union representing bus drivers and service station attendants, to reject a collective bargaining agreement pursuant to the Bankruptcy Code, 11 U.S.C.S. § 1113. . . . [P]laintiff's members rejected debtor's prepetition efforts to lower debtor's operating costs. Debtor filed a Chapter 11 petition, then successfully applied to the bankruptcy court to reject the bargaining agreement. The district court affirmed. On appeal, the court held that under 11 U.S.C.S. § 1113, modifications to the collective bargaining agreement were necessary to rehabilitate debtor and to provide for a feasible reorganization plan. . . .

MESKILL, KEARSE, and ALTIMARI, Circuit Judges.

ALTIMARI, Circuit Judge:

This appeal involves the showing a debtor-employer must make in order to obtain Bankruptcy Court approval of the employer's application to reject a collective bargaining agreement in accordance with 11 U.S.C. § 1113. We . . . uphold[ ] Judge Lifland's approval of Carey Transportation's application to reject two collective bargaining agreements with Truck Drivers Local 807. . . .

Facts and Proceedings Below

Carey [Transportation] . . . fil[ed] a voluntary reorganization petition under Chapter 11 of the Bankruptcy Code in April 1985. Carey, both prior to and since that filing, has been engaged in the business of providing commuter bus service between New York City and Kennedy and LaGuardia Airports.

. . . Local 807 and Carey entered into collective bargaining agreements . . . on August 20, 1982, thereby settling a sixty-four day strike by union members. These . . . agreements were scheduled to expire on February 28, 1986.

Carey officials have blamed the strike for a subsequent 30% drop in ridership and the yearly revenue losses that preceded its filing for reorganization. Carey has operated at a loss since at least December 31, 1981, reporting annual losses of $750,000 for fiscal year 1983, $1,500,000 for fiscal year 1984, and $2,500,000 for fiscal year 1985.

* * *

. . . Carey proposed several modifications in its agreements with Local 807 . . . [and the union] rejected [them] by an 82–7 vote. According to Local 807's business agent, the union members were particularly adamant about not accepting the two-year contract extension and the freeze on wages and benefits.

Carey filed its Chapter 11 petition with the Bankruptcy Court on April 4, 1985, and one day later, delivered to Local 807 a proposal to modify its collective bargaining agreements pursuant to 11 U.S.C. § 1113(b)(1)(A). This post-petition proposal was designed to achieve annual savings of $1.8 million for each of the next three fiscal years.

* * *

When Carey presented this proposal to Local 807, company officers were projecting fiscal year 1986 losses of approximately $950,000. . . . [But i]n a cover letter accompanying this proposal, Carey [also] asserted that it needed to slash costs by considerably more than its projected losses in order to improve its long-term financial health by updating and expanding its bus fleet, operations, and maintenance facilities. Without savings of this magnitude, Carey explained, it would be unable to propose a feasible reorganization plan to creditors and resolve its indebtedness to them. Carey requested a meeting with Local 807 representatives "to discuss the proposals and to attempt to reach mutually satisfactory modifications of the agreement[s]."

Shortly after the Company submitted its post-petition proposal, dissension within Local 807 became obvious; in fact, virtually all union members formed a "Drivers Committee" and hired an attorney to represent them separately from Local 807 officials. The Drivers Committee then refused to participate in most post-petition negotiations, despite union officials' pleas that they reconsider that decision to "stonewall" these sessions.

In the meantime, Carey filed its section 1113 application to reject its bargaining agreements. . . . After the third day of hearings, a Local 807 officer presented to Carey a counter-proposal designed to achieve annual cost savings of $776,000. . . . Carey found the counter-proposal unacceptable, and the hearings continued.

The central issues at the hearing, as on this appeal, were whether the post-petition proposal contained only necessary modifications of the existing agreements, *see* 11 U.S.C. § 1113(b)(1)(A), whether that proposal treated all parties fairly and equitably, *see id.,* whether Local 807 lacked good cause for rejecting that proposal, *see* § 1113(c)(2), and whether the balancing of the equities clearly favored rejection of the bargaining agreements, see § 1113(c)(3).

On June 14, 1985, the bankruptcy court issued its decision approving Carey's application to reject the collective bargaining agreements. . . .

Discussion

Congress enacted section 1113 of the Bankruptcy Code, 11 U.S.C. § 1113,[2] in response to *NLRB v. Bildisco & Bildisco,* 465 U.S. 513

[2] Section 1113 provides in pertinent part:

(b)(1) Subsequent to filing a petition and prior to filing an application seeking rejection of a collective bargaining agreement, the debtor in possession or trustee (hereinafter in this section 'trustee' shall include a debtor in possession), shall

(A) make a proposal to the authorized representative of the employees covered by such agreement, based on the most complete and reliable information available at the time of such proposal, which provides for those necessary modifications in the employees benefits and protections that are necessary to permit the reorganization of the debtor and assures that all creditors, the debtor and all of the affected parties are treated fairly and equitably. . . .

(c) The court shall approve an application for rejection of a collective bargaining agreement only if the court finds that

(1984), where the Court concluded that a debtor-in-possession could reject a collective bargaining agreement, subject to certain constraints.

* * *

II. Merits of the Decision Below

* * *

. . . The statute permits the bankruptcy court to approve a rejection application only if the debtor . . . makes three substantive showings. The first is that its post-petition proposal for modifications satisfies § 1113(b)(1), which in turn limits the debtor to proposing only "those necessary modifications in . . . benefits and protections that are necessary to permit the reorganization of the debtor," and obliges the debtor to assure the court that "all creditors, the debtor and all affected parties are treated fairly and equitably." Second, the debtor must show that the union has rejected this proposal without good cause. Bankr. Code § 1113(c)(2). Third, the debtor must prove that "the balance of the equities clearly favors rejection of [the bargaining] agreement." Code § 1113(c)(3). . . .

* * *

1. Compliance with § 1113(b)(1)

(a) Necessity of the modifications

. . . [A] judicial controversy has arisen over two . . . related questions raised by [§ 1113]: (1) how necessary must the proposed modifications be, and (2) to what goal must those alterations be necessary? *See Wheeling–Pittsburgh Steel,* 791 F.2d at 1088. . . .

In answer to the first of these questions, the Third Circuit concluded that "necessary" as used in subsection (b)(1)(A) is synonymous with "essential" in subsection (e), which authorizes the court to approve certain non-negotiated interim changes while the rejection application is pending. . . . *Wheeling–Pittsburgh Steel,* 791 F.2d at 1088. As to the second question, the Third Circuit concluded that the statute requires the bankruptcy court to focus its attention on "the somewhat shorter term goal of preventing . . . liquidation . . . rather than the longer term issue of the debtor's ultimate future." *Id.* at 1089.

Local 807 asks us to adopt the Third Circuit's reasoning, arguing that the post-petition proposal must fail because it sought more than break-even cost reductions, because the proposed three year term was too long in relation to the eight months remaining under the existing agreement, and because it did not provide for wages and benefits to "snap-back" in the event that Carey's financial performance improved.

---

(1) the trustee has, prior to the hearing, made a proposal that fulfills the requirements of subsection (b)(1);

(2) the authorized representative of the employees has refused to accept such proposal without good cause; and

(3) the balance of the equities clearly favors rejection of such agreement.

11 U.S.C. § 1113(b), (c).

See Wheeling–Pittsburgh Steel, 791 F.2d at 1089–90. We decline to do so.

First of all, the legislative history strongly suggests that "necessary" should not be equated with "essential" or bare minimum. Although the Third Circuit may be correct that the "necessary" language was viewed as a victory for organized labor because it approximated the "minimum modifications" language urged by Senator Packwood, *see id.* at 1088, Congress obviously did not adopt Senator Packwood's proposal. Instead, as the *Wheeling–Pittsburgh Steel* panel acknowledged, Congress settled on "a substitute for this clause." *Id.* at 1087. Congress' ultimate choice of this substitute clause suggests that it was uncomfortable with language suggesting that a debtor must prove that its initial post-petition proposal contained only bare-minimum changes.

* * *

The Third Circuit's answer to the "necessary to what" question is also troubling. In our view, the *Wheeling-Pittsburgh* court did not adequately consider [that a] final reorganization plan . . . can be confirmed only if the court determines that neither liquidation nor a need for further reorganization is likely to follow. *Id.* at 417 (quoting Bankr. Code § 1129(a)(11)). Thus, in virtually every case, it becomes impossible to weigh necessity as to reorganization without looking into the debtor's ultimate future and estimating what the debtor needs to attain financial health. . . . [W]e conclude that the necessity requirement places on the debtor the burden of proving that its proposal . . . contains necessary, but not absolutely minimal, changes that will enable the debtor to complete the reorganization process successfully. . . . Judge Lifland [found the] modifications necessary to rehabilitate Carey and to provide for successful reorganization. . . . [He neither] misread [nor] misapplied the "necessary modifications" requirement as a matter of law.

. . . Carey was losing large sums of money, . . . its Local 807 labor costs (in contrast to other employees' salaries and benefits) were well above industry averages, and . . . Carey lacked sufficient assets to meet its current expenses. . . . Moreover, . . . Carey needed to upgrade its facilities and its vehicles in order to complete reorganization successfully. . . . Carey needed to obtain modifications of the magnitude requested, and not merely break-even cost reductions. . . .

(b) Fairness as to all parties

The requirement that the debtor assure the court that "all creditors, the debtor and all affected parties are treated fairly and equitably," Code § 1113(b)(1)(A), is a relatively straightforward one. The purpose of this provision, according to *Century Brass,* 795 F.2d at 273, "is to spread the burden of saving the company to every constituency while ensuring that all sacrifice to a similar degree." Local 807 argues that the bankruptcy court erred as a matter of both law and fact in assessing the burdens imposed on management, non-union employees, the parent company, and Carey's creditors. We disagree.

The debtor is not required to prove, in all instances, that managers and non-union employees will have their salaries and benefits cut to the same degree that union workers' benefits are to be reduced. To be sure, such a showing would assure the court that these affected parties are being asked to shoulder a proportionate share of the burden, but we decline to hold that this showing must be made in every case.

. . . Particularly where, as here, the court finds that only the employees covered by the pertinent bargaining agreements are receiving pay and benefits above industry standards, it is not unfair or inequitable to exempt the other employees from pay and benefit reductions.

* * *

The lower court also correctly looked to prepetition concessions obtained from the mechanics' union and two of Carey's principal creditors—the M[etropolitan] T[ransit] A[uthority] and the Port Authority—as proof that these parties were contributing fairly and equitably to the effort to keep Carey afloat. . . .

In light of this evidence, we affirm the bankruptcy court's ruling that all parties were participating "fairly and equitably" in the attempt to save Carey from liquidation.

2. Good Cause

. . . The bankruptcy court here reasoned that because the proposed modifications were necessary, fair, and equitable, the union's refusal to accept them was without good cause. . . . This reasoning, of course, suggests that the good cause provision adds nothing to the other substantive requirements of the statute. . . .

We conclude, nonetheless, that this analysis is proper where, as here, the union has neither participated meaningfully in post-petition negotiations nor offered any reason for rejecting the proposal other than its view that the proposed modifications were excessive. . . . [The union] "stonewall[ed]" post-petition negotiations [while] hoping that the courts will find that the proposal does not comply with subsection (b)(1). This tactic is unacceptable and inconsistent with Congressional intent. . . .

. . . [T]he union must come forward with evidence of . . . its reason for declining to accept the debtor's proposal in whole or in part. . . .

2. Balancing the Equities

This requirement . . . is a codification of the *Bildisco* standard. . . . Therefore, the factors identified in *Bildisco* and other cases preceding section 1113's enactment remain applicable today. . . .

* * *

. . . [Carey's] unionized labor costs were approximately 60% above the industry average, . . . 66% of Carey's employees are unionized, . . . [and] managers, supervisors, and non-union workers were receiving less than average compensation while taking on increased workloads, and . . . Local 807, therefore, could fairly be expected to bear a substantial proportion of the needed cost-cutting measures. . . .

Conclusion

For these reasons, we affirm the judgment of the district court upholding the bankruptcy court's approval of Carey's section 1113 application to reject its bargaining agreements with Local 807.

¶ 1211: Wheeling–Pittsburgh Steel Corp. v. United Steelworkers of Am., AFLCIO–CLC, 791 F.2d 1074 (3d Cir. 1986)

SLOVITER, Circuit Judge.

I. Issue

. . . On May 31, 1985, Wheeling–Pittsburgh Steel Corp., a debtor-in-possession . . . , sought . . . to reject its collective bargaining agreements with the United Steelworkers of America, AFL–CIO–CLC. . . . [T]he bankruptcy court authorized Wheeling–Pittsburgh to do so, finding that it had satisfied the requirements of the statute. The district court affirmed that order, and the Union appeals. . . . [We reverse and decide for the Steelworkers' Union.]

II. Factual Background

Wheeling–Pittsburgh is the seventh largest steel manufacturing corporation in the United States. . . .

. . . Wheeling–Pittsburgh's average gross labor costs (including wages, benefits, current pension costs and other benefits for retirees, and payroll taxes) under [its] 1980 collective bargaining agreement were about $25 per hour. Because of its financial problem, Wheeling–Pittsburgh asked the Union for concessions twice in 1982. The April concession consisted of a $1.65 an hour reduction in labor costs in return for entitlement to preferred stock which each employee could redeem when s/he quit, died or retired.

[Wheeling–Pittsburgh thereafter sought and received further concessions from the Union.] In mid-January 1985, Wheeling–Pittsburgh asked the Union for a fourth reduction in labor cost. The Union, however, refused to make further concessions until Wheeling–Pittsburgh gained concessions from its lenders, who had made none to that date.

After mediation efforts, Wheeling–Pittsburgh issued a restructuring proposal on March 8, 1985, which sought concessions from the Union, the lenders, and shareholders. . . . [When the negotiations for concessions failed in April, Wheeling–Pittsburgh filed for reorganization in chapter 11.]

The Union hired Lazard Freres & Co. and Arthur Young & Co. to assist it in evaluating the Wheeling–Pittsburgh proposal and formulating a response. The financial advisors sought certain financial information from Wheeling–Pittsburgh, which provided some. . . . On May 24, Wheeling–Pittsburgh announced it would provide no additional information, demanded the Union's response by May 30, and threatened to seek authorization to reject the agreement. When the Union replied that it could not respond until it had all the requested information, Wheeling–Pittsburgh filed its application with the bankruptcy court for authorization to reject the collective bargaining agreement on May 31, 1985.

The bankruptcy court . . . authoriz[ed] . . . Wheeling–Pittsburgh to reject the agreement. Wheeling–Pittsburgh did so, and announced that it would institute a $17.50 labor cost, effective immediately, and make various other changes. In response, the Union commenced a strike on July 21, 1985. It also appealed the decision of the bankruptcy court. . . .

* * *

IV. The Proceedings Below

The issue before the bankruptcy court was whether Wheeling–Pittsburgh established by a preponderance of the evidence the necessary prerequisites for rejection of its collective bargaining agreement under section 1113. . . . On the hotly contested issue of . . . whether Wheeling–Pittsburgh's proposed modification was necessary for reorganization, the Union had argued that neither the proposed $15.20 per hour labor cost nor the five-year agreement was necessary for reorganization. . . .

* * *

V. Background of 11 U.S.C. § 1113

* * *

In *Bildisco,* the Supreme Court held that a collective bargaining agreement is an executory contract subject to rejection by a debtor-in-possession under section 365(a) of the Bankruptcy Code. . . .

Labor groups mounted an immediate and intense lobbying effort in Congress to change the law. . . .

In the fall of 1983, even before the *Bildisco* decision, several members of Congress had expressed concern that some companies were using the bankruptcy law as a "new collective bargaining weapon." At hearings of the Labor Management Relations and Labor Standards Subcommittees of House Education and Labor Committee, "six airline unions testified that employers were improperly using federal bankruptcy law." . . . The *Bildisco* decision was announced on February 22, 1984. . . .

On February 22, 1984, Congressman Rodino introduced H.R. 4908 to "clarify the circumstances under which collective bargaining agreements may be rejected." 130 Cong. Rec. H809 (daily ed. February 22, 1984). . . .

As enacted, the new section on collective bargaining agreements, section 1113, provides that a debtor-in-possession may assume or reject a collective bargaining agreement only by following the provisions of the statute. *See* 11 U.S.C. § 1113(a). The subsections at issue in this appeal read as follows:

> (b) (1) Subsequent to filing a petition and prior to filing an application seeking rejection of a collective bargaining agreement, the debtor in possession or trustee . . . shall—
>
> > (A) make a proposal to the authorized representative of the employees covered by such agreement . . . , which pro-

vides for those necessary modifications in the employees benefits and protection that are necessary to permit the reorganization of the debtor and assures that all creditors, the debtor and all of the affected parties are treated fairly and equitably; and

(B) provide . . . the representative of the employees with such relevant information as is necessary to evaluate the proposal.

(2) During the period beginning on the date of the making of a proposal provided for in paragraph (1) and ending on the date of the hearing provided for in subsection (d)(1), the trustee shall meet, at reasonable times, with the authorized representative to confer in good faith in attempting to reach mutually satisfactory modifications of such agreement.

(c) The court shall approve an application for rejection of a collective bargaining agreement only if the court finds that

(1) the trustee has, prior to the hearing, made a proposal that fulfills the requirements of subsection (b)(1);

(2) the authorized representative of the employees has refused to accept such proposal without good cause; and

(3) the balance of the equities clearly favors rejection of such agreement.

11 U.S.C. § 1113(b) & (c) (Supp. II 1984). . . .

VI. Discussion

A. Whether Consideration of the Proposal Can Be Pretermitted

. . . The Union asserts that undisputed evidence showed that Wheeling–Pittsburgh could have adhered to that agreement for its remaining 13 months and still have had sufficient cash to operate for both the short and long term. It further asserts that even if assets were reduced by some $80 million as a result of the adherence to the labor contract, creditors could not rationally have preferred liquidation to reorganization. *Accordingly, the Union contends that no modification could be "necessary", and that the bankruptcy court erred in even evaluating Wheeling–Pittsburgh's proposal under section 1113.*

* * *

. . . [Even if the status quo would have resulted in liquidation, the] ultimate issue of the debtor's application for rejection is different. In section 1113(c), the statute directs the court to determine whether the "proposal" meets the substantive standard of section 1113(b)(1). The bankruptcy court correctly recognized, "[T]he question is *not* simply whether Wheeling–Pittsburgh can continue to pay the $21.40 rate required by the current *collective bargaining agreement* and still emerge with enough cash in hand at the expiration of the contract term to meet current operational expenses," but instead is "whether it is necessary for Wheeling–Pittsburgh to pay the $15.20 rate found in its *proposal* in order to successfully reorganize." *In re Wheeling Pittsburgh,* 50 B.R. at 978 (emphasis in original).

* * *

B. Whether the Proposed Modifications Were "Necessary" and Treated All Parties "Fairly and Equitably"

* * *

The parties offer widely varying interpretations of "necessary". Because the statute contains no definition, we must turn to the legislative history for enlightenment. . . .

In *Bildisco,* the Supreme Court opted for a lenient test which permitted rejection if "the equities balance in favor of rejecting the labor contract." *Bildisco,* 465 U.S. at 526.

It was this lenient standard that caused the labor forces to mobilize on Congress. . . . Representative Rodino, Chairman of the House Judiciary Committee with jurisdiction over bankruptcy legislation . . . decried "[t]he balancing-of-the-equities standard adopted by the Supreme Court" because it would give "no special weight to collective bargaining interests and the significant concerns underlying the national labor policy." [130 Cong. Rec. H809, at] H780 [(daily ed. February 22, 1984)].

The February bill . . . passed the House on March 21. When it reached the Senate, Senator Thurmond offered an amendment which would have "preserve[d] the balancing of the equities standard for rejection of such contracts." *Id.* at S6082 (May 1984). Senator Packwood offered a substitute amendment which required the trustee's proposal to make the "minimum modifications in [the] employees' benefits and protections that would permit the reorganization," *id.* at S6181–82 (daily ed. May 1984), and was recognized to represent the position of organized labor on this issue[,] . . . *id.* at S8898 (daily ed. June 29, 1984) (remarks of Sen. Kennedy). Senator Packwood based his proposal on the approach suggested by Professor Vern Countryman of the Harvard Law School. . . . This approach argues for a strong presumption against rejection of labor contracts on the ground that rejection seriously undercuts fundamental aspects of federal labor policy which should be permitted "only in extraordinary cases." *See* 130 Cong. Rec. S6185 (daily ed. May 22, 1984) (quoting Bordewieck & Countryman, [*The Rejection of Collective Bargaining Agreements by Chapter 11 Debtors,* 57 Am. Bankr. L.J. 293], at 299–300 [(1983)]).

* * *

The Packwood amendment, supported by labor, provided that the debtor's proposal should contain "the minimum modifications in such employees' benefits and protections that would permit the reorganization." 130 Cong. Rec. S6181–82 (daily ed. May 22, 1984). As a substitute for this clause, the Conference Committee proposed, and section 1113 provides, that the debtor's proposal provide "for those necessary modifications in the employees' benefits and protections that are necessary to permit the reorganization of the debtor." § 1113(b)(1)(A). This was seen as a victory for labor.

* * *

The "necessary" standard cannot be satisfied by a mere showing that it would be desirable for the trustee to reject a prevailing labor contract so that the debtor can lower its costs. Such an indulgent standard would inadequately differentiate between labor contracts, which Congress sought to protect, and other commercial contracts, which the trustee can disavow at will. The congressional [history] . . . requires that "necessity" be construed strictly to signify only modifications that the trustee is constrained to accept because they are directly related to the Company's financial condition and its reorganization. . . .

The question of " 'necessary' to what" is not easily answered by reference to the statutory language which merely provides "necessary to permit the reorganization of the debtor." It is significant that the Thurmond amendment, which the conferees did not accept, and *Bildisco,* which they clearly sought to modify, seemed directed to the successful rehabilitation of the debtor, which suggests focus on the long-term economic health of the debtor. While we do not suggest that the general long-term viability of the Company is not a goal of the debtor's reorganization, *it appears from the legislators' remarks that they placed the emphasis in determining whether and what modifications should be made to a negotiated collective bargaining agreement on the somewhat shorter term goal of preventing the debtor's liquidation,* the mirror image of what is "necessary to permit the reorganization of the debtor." This construction finds additional support in the conferees' choice of the words "*permit* the reorganization," which places the emphasis on the reorganization, rather than the longer term issue of the debtor's ultimate future.

It is also important to note that the requirement that the proposal provide only for "necessary" modifications in the labor contract is conjunctive with the requirement that the proposal treat "all of the affected parties . . . fairly and equitably." The language as well as the legislative history makes plain that a bankruptcy court may not authorize rejection of a labor contract merely because it deems such a course to be equitable to the other affected parties, particularly creditors. Such a construction would nullify the insistent congressional effort to replace the *Bildisco* standard with one that was more sensitive to the national policy favoring collective bargaining agreements, which was accomplished by inserting the "necessary" clause as one of the two prongs of the standard that the trustee's proposal for modifications must meet.

* * *

Congressional intent with regard to the meaning of "fair and equitable" is reflected in the comments of . . . Senator Packwood . . . :

> The second requirement of the proposal—that it assure fair and equitable treatment for all creditors, the debtor and other affected parties . . . guarantees that the focus for cost cutting

> must not be directed exclusively at unionized workers. Rather the burden of sacrifices in the reorganization process will be spread among all affected parties. This consideration is desirable since experience shows that when workers know that they alone are not bearing the sole brunt of the sacrifices, they will agree to shoulder their fair share and in some instances without the necessity for a formal contract rejection.

130 Cong. Rec. S8898 (daily ed. June 29, 1984).

The bankruptcy court recognized that the focus of inquiry as to "fair and equitable" treatment should be whether the Company's proposal would impose a disproportionate burden on the employees.[3] . . .

* * *

. . . [T]he proposal's failure to provide workers a share in a possible recovery, is particularly significant [on the fair and equitable issue] in this case since the proposal asked workers to take substantial reductions over a five-year period based on extremely pessimistic forecasts. . . . [T]he bankruptcy court's failure to recognize the need for some parity in this regard flaws the court's conclusion that the proposal was "fair and equitable." Therefore, we cannot affirm the district court's order approving the debtor's rejection of the collective bargaining agreement.

* * *

---

1. Can § 1113 be seen as a statutorily-explicit critical vendor exception?
2. What's the difference between the *Wheeling–Pittsburgh* court's notion of "necessity" and the *Teamsters* court's view?
3. If the union contract isn't rejected, is the result "like" making the wage claim under the contract a priority claim in bankruptcy?
4. If management of a debtor thinks rejection of a collective bargaining agreement is critical to success in chapter 11, would it prefer that proceedings occur in the Second Circuit or the Third? The debtor has considerable choice on where to file. See Chapter 20.
5. If a solvent firm got past § 1113 and rejected a labor contract, what would the financial result be? Consider § 502(g)'s effect on § 365. How much would the rejected claim be worth? Cf. §§ 1129(a)(8), 1129(b)(2)(B)?
6. If the contract is rejected under § 1113, the debtor would presumably pay labor less than the higher union contract rate anticipated under the rejected collective bargaining agreement.

---

[3] Although there is "fair and equitable" language in other sections of the bankruptcy statute, the construction of these words in § 1113 is not aided by reference to the other sections. For example, "fair and equitable" is specifically defined in 11 U.S.C. § 1129(b)(2) in terms of priority of claims, patently inapplicable here.

What is the formal status under the Code of any labor claim for the difference between new wage rate and the contract rate? True, the parties may make a new deal, with an agreed-to wage rate between the higher contract rate and the lower market rate, and they may subsume all their formal bankruptcy claims to the new contract.

But if they cannot agree to a new contract, what ought to be the status structurally, given what we know of §§ 507, 365 and 502(g)? Three logical possibilities seem in play: (i) administrative priority for the claim; (ii) no claim for contract breach, with the contract not just rejected, but null and void; or (iii) a general unsecured § 502(g) claim as if that claim had arisen before the bankruptcy.

And what do the words of the statute say precisely?

Section 1113(a) says that a collective bargaining contract can be rejected or assumed under the Code "only in accordance with this section." Once the contract is rejected "in accordance with" § 1113, there's potentially a claim for damages. If the debtor incurs an expense to preserve the estate (such as by rejecting an otherwise binding contract), that normally creates a prioritized administrative expense. §§ 507, 503(b)(1). But § 502(g) says that "[a] claim arising from the rejection, under section 365" comes in "as if such claim had arisen before the date of the filing of the petition." Since the collective bargaining agreement was rejected under § 1113, is § 365 therefore inapplicable? If it's inapplicable, does that raise the status of the union's claim under the rejected collective bargaining agreement above that of rejected non-labor contracts? Does the labor claim become an administrative expense?

Odd result, if the labor claim became an administrative expense? Statutory glitch? How could that claim obtain administrative priority, a result that would in effect make the collective bargaining agreement effectively non-rejected? Can't be.

Or does the § 1113 rejection mean that the union employees lose their claim for contract damages, because there's not even a § 502(g) prebankruptcy claim for a § 1113 rejection? Section § 502(g) gives prebankruptcy damage claims to contracts rejected under § 365. It does not explicitly refer to § 1113.

Isn't that an equally odd result? And could that result even make contextual sense, since § 1113 was *labor*-induced to improve labor's position over what it got under *Bildisco* via § 365. Odd, because interpreting § 502(g) as inapplicable would get labor *less* than it got under § 365, prior to § 1113?

Odd or not, that's the result the court reached in *In re* Northwest Airlines Corp. v. Ass'n of Flight Attendants, AFL–CIO, 483 F.3d 160 (2d Cir. 2007), holding that § 365 did not apply to a collective bargaining agreement rejected under § 1113.

True, a null and void claim might not make a major bottom line difference to the union's post-rejection pay. If the employees will not show up for work the day after contract rejection or, more tellingly, if the union with a rejected contract strikes, then the practical §§ 1113/502(g) issue is minor, because the result from a rejected contract is that labor and management go back to the negotiating room to come up with a global new deal between them, with each side having substantial leverage, one to hire new workers and the other to strike.

A third potential construction of the statute: To reject a collective bargaining agreement, the debtor must satisfy *both* § 365 *and* § 1113. Section 1113 is a subset of § 365, requiring that the debtor show more to support contract rejection than is required under § 365, but only if the contract is a collective bargaining agreement. But it's still an executory contract requiring rejection under § 365, under this interpretation. All rejected contracts, under this statutory construction, are rejected under § 365, which is an easy section for the debtor to satisfy. (The debtor pretty much just has to tell the bankruptcy judge that in the debtor's management's judgment, the contract should be rejected.) But to successfully reject a collective bargaining agreement, in this third interpretation, the debtor must *also* clear the § 1113 hurdles, not just the low § 365 hurdle. Hence, a rejected collective bargaining agreement is rejected under both § 365 and § 1113. As such, § 502(g) would apply and the employees would have an unsecured claim for contractual damages. (This interpretation takes force from the logic of § 365, as a general section, and that interpretation gets some added force from the language in § 502(g), that leads by saying § 502(g) applies to "[a] claim arising from the rejection under section 365 . . . or under a plan under chapter . . . 11".) The overall statutory structure for debtor rejection of prebankruptcy contracts would remain intact under this interpretation even for § 1113 rejections.

Regardless of whether such a construction fits better with the statute's general framework than the other two, it's not the interpretation that prevails in the Second Circuit, since the 2007 *Northwest* decision. *But see* In re Pinnacle, 483 B.R. 381, 417 n.238 (Bankr. S.D.N.Y. 2012), where the court mused:

> If the Court were writing on a clean slate, it would construe "rejection" in section 1113 and "rejection" under section 365 consistently and as a unified whole—to the end that the rejection of a collective bargaining agreement after compliance with section 1113 results in the same consequences as the rejection of any other executory contract, and that section 1113 merely imposes additional requirements that must be satisfied before rejection can be invoked.

7. The National Labor Relations Act bars courts from issuing injunctions against ordinary strikes. But § 362(a)(3) seems to enjoin strikes, as it stays "any act . . . to exercise control over the property of the estate" and (a)(6) stays "any act to . . . recover a claim against the debtor that arose before the commencement of the case." The bankruptcy stay thus seems to conflict with the NLRA. If a bankrupt's union goes on strike, which policy wins? Appellate courts last reached the issue in the 1980s, deciding that the National Labor Relations Act anti-injunction rule trumped the bankruptcy stay. E.g., Briggs Trans. Co. v. Int'l Brotherhood of Teamsters, 739 F.2d 341 (8th Cir. 1984), cert. denied, 469 U.S. 917 (1984).

8. Northwest Airline's unions were covered by the Railway Act, which bars strikes on public carriers. That labor structure could have affected the bargaining dynamic and importance of whether rejection under § 1113 (and § 365?) rendered the contract null and void or gave the union and its members a claim for contractual damages.

C. MASS TORT CLAIMS

Not all of the debtor's pre-bankruptcy obligations are contractual.

The firm releases a toxin; thousands of people are injured. They sue, their damages render the firm insolvent, and the firm files for bankruptcy. The injured tort claimants are general creditors of the company.

Mass torts aren't easy to resolve. Beneath the complexities are priority issues: Should tort claimants do better than financial creditors, or should they be treated the same? Would massive tort liability lead firms to act strategically to off-load the tort liability by divesting themselves of tort-heavy operations, liquidating the firm or subsidiaries, moving clean operations to special purpose vehicles, and borrowing more with secured credit than previously? How can fair tort compensation be reconciled with smooth financing arrangements?

The actual mass torts thus far also raise key issues of compensation of the tort victims among themselves. That is, the toxin is released, many are injured, but many of those who've been exposed won't come down with disease for years; this problem of delay in manifestation of the disease has been fundamental to the asbestos crisis. Yet the firm's financial crisis from both the current claims and the overhanging future claims demands bankruptcy attention. A central institutional problem thus far has been to compensate future claimants—people at risk, but without disease yet. Some of those people will be sick sometime in the future. If the bankruptcy compensates all the currently visible claimants—both those who are now sick and the firm's financial and other usual creditors—then nothing will be left for the future claimants when they get sick. But if nothing is done to resolve the overhanging potential liability to the future claimants, then the firm cannot operate well.

Moreover, the problems of judicial administration are not small. Should tort victims have their day in court with an individualized but expensive trial, or should they be paid under a schedule, similar to worker's compensation claims? Would the latter systematically under-compensate the victims? Would the former be so expensive that masses of tort claimants would go under- or un-compensated? And how much of the contest can be seen as a struggle between different groups of lawyers, such as trial lawyers who represent the plaintiffs and financial lawyers (and their clients) who represent the lenders?

¶ 1212: The Problem of Mass Compensation

First consider a mass of contracts: the bankrupt owes many creditors modest amounts of money. It owes 10,000 creditors $10,000 each, making the total obligation $100 million. Each creditor when making the loan knows that the transactions costs of suing would eat up $5,000 easily for each claim. It's hardly worthwhile to sue.

What institutional solution for the creditors? Review the discussion in Chapter 7 of the bond indenture, if you don't see an immediate solution.

Consider the tort analogue: a firm commits a tortious act, harming 10,000 tort claimants, each with claims on the debtor worth $10,000. For each tort claimant, the cost of bringing suit would easily chew up $5,000. (Or for each tort claimant, the cost to the tortfeasor of defending each lawsuit would be $5,000.)

An institutional solution would build a collective mechanism similar to that of the bond indenture, which collects the bondholders into one contractual mechanism.

Next consider this variation. A firm has committed the core of a tort, exposing 10,000 people to possible harm. Each has a probabilistic claim worth $10,000, but their claims are more complicated than the prior ones: Although 10,000 people have been exposed to harm, only 100 of them will eventually be hurt. Those 100 though will develop mesothelioma (a deadly lung disease) and have a claim for $1 million.

What institutional solution?

Our last variation grafts an insolvent debtor onto the prior mass tort claim. Again, the firm has exposed 10,000 people to harm, and 100 of those people will develop mesothelioma, which would yield 100 claims for $1 million each, but we don't know now which 100 will succumb. On top of this, the firm is insolvent: although the firm's operations are worth $100 million, the firm also owes another $100 million to its contract creditors.

What institutional solution? The bankruptcy apparatus can put the $100 million aside for the future tort claimants and pay the $1 million out to each tort victim as the disease manifests itself.

Lastly, consider the possibility that we don't know the level of harm with certainty. In the prior paragraphs, we knew that 100 people will come down with mesothelioma. This time the epidemiologists say that there's a 50% chance that another 100 people will come down with mesothelioma. But we won't know for a few years.

Each of these probabilistic uncertainties is embedded in the mass tort problems thus far. Presumably the ideal institutional result would have some collective vehicle for the tort claimants to prosecute their claims (and for the company to defend against those claims), something analogous to the bond indenture and its trustee. The process would need some means to estimate and resolve claims, perhaps paying the claimants proportionately. From an operating perspective, the firm would want to eliminate the debt overhang costs of the tort claims. Overhanging debt (see the discussion following *Deep Rock* if this term and its relevance here aren't immediately clear), from whatever source, whether massive tort claims or huge financial debt, diminishes the insolvent firm's ability to operate or get new financing.

¶ 1213: The Results Thus Far

The early court decisions: (1) refused to acknowledge that future claimants had claims cognizable in bankruptcy, but (2) appointed a special representative for the future claimants, to press their financial interests in the mass tort bankruptcies. In the early asbestos bankruptcies, the courts set up trusts for the tort claimants, pouring over some cash from the bankrupt, its insurance policies, and some securities of the operating firm. (Similar results could be achieved outside of bankruptcy if a functional and effective class action could be constructed. Thus far, none has. In *Ortiz v. Fibreboard Corp,* 527 U.S. 815 (1999), the Supreme Court refused to certify a mass tort class under Rule 23 of the Federal Rules of Civil Procedure.)

In the Manville reorganization, an early and major mass tort bankruptcy, the trust for the tort claimants effectively controlled Manville, the firm that exposed the victims to asbestos, with the trust owning about 80% of the reorganized Manville's stock. Tort victims thereby ironically became the company's principal owners. The bankruptcy court issued a channeling order—an injunction—directing all future tort claimants to sue the trust, not the operating company.

Congress partly codified this result by adding § 524(g) to the Bankruptcy Code in 1994. It still didn't make the future asbestos victims claimants under the Code, but it validated the trust-and-channeling order. The bankrupt (and typically its insurers) would turn assets over to a trust. Those assets would include cash, perhaps some physical assets, and stock or other obligations of the debtor. The § 524(g) trust solution would only be available if the trust controlled a majority of the debtor's voting stock. Presumably the idea was to signal to debtor's management that the problem was serious—they wouldn't typically give up a majority of the firm's stock to the tort victims unless the problem was serious. See generally Mark J. Roe, *Bankruptcy and Mass Tort,* 84 Columbia Law Review 846 (1984).

Section 524(g) gives current asbestos claimants and their attorneys considerable authority. The judge may only issue the channeling injunction if 75% of the asbestos claimants voting vote in favor of the proposed plan of reorganization. Section § 524(g) has no equivalent to a § 1129(b) cram-down. The statute thus formally pits current claimants against future claimants. If future claimants had claims then they'd presumably be able to vote, perhaps through a court-appointed representative who would decline to support a plan that seriously short-changed the future claimants. But they don't have Code-cognizable claims.

§ 524. Effect of discharge

(g)(1)(A) After notice and hearing, a court that enters an order confirming a plan of reorganization . . . may issue . . . an injunction in accordance with this subsection to supplement the injunctive effect of a discharge. . . .

(B) An injunction may . . . enjoin entities from taking legal action for the purpose of . . . recovering . . . [on] any claim . . .

that . . . is to be paid . . . by a trust described in paragraph (2)(B)(i) . . .

(2)(A) . . .

(B) The requirements of this subparagraph are that—

(i) the injunction is to be implemented in connection with a trust that . . .

(I) is to assume the liabilities of a debtor which . . . has been named as a defendant . . . for damages allegedly caused by the presence of, or exposure to, asbestos or asbestos-containing products;

(II) is to be funded in whole or part by the securities of 1 or more debtors involved in such plan and by the obligation of such debtor . . . to make future payments . . . ;

(III) is to own . . . a majority of the voting shares of . . . such debtor . . . ; and

(IV) is to use its assets or income to pay claims and demands; and

(ii) . . . the court determines that

(I) the debtor is likely to be subject to substantial future demands for payment arising out of the . . . conduct or events that gave rise to the claims . . . ;

(II) the actual amounts, numbers, and timing of such future demands cannot be determined;

(III) pursuit of such demands outside the procedures prescribed by such plan is likely to threaten the plan's purpose to deal equitably with claims and future demands;

(IV) as part of the process of seeking confirmation of such plan . . . a separate class . . . of the *claimants whose claims* are to be addressed by a trust described in clause (i) . . . votes, by at least 75 percent *of those voting*, in favor of the plan . . .

(V) . . . the trust will operate through mechanisms such as . . . pro rata distributions, matrices, or periodic review of estimates of the numbers and values of present claims and future demands, or other comparable mechanisms, that provide reasonable assurance that the trust will value, and be in a financial position to pay, present claims and future demands that involve similar claims in substantially the same manner.

(3)(A) If the requirements of paragraph (2)(B) are met and the order . . . was issued . . .

(i) the injunction shall be valid and enforceable . . . ;

(ii) no entity that . . . becomes a direct or indirect transferee of, or successor to any assets of, [such] a debtor or trust . . . shall be liable with respect to any claim or demand made against such entity by reason of its becoming a transferee or successor; and

(iii) no entity that . . . makes a loan to such a debtor or trust or to such a successor or transferee shall, by reason of making the loan, be liable with respect to any claim or demand made against such entity, nor shall any pledge of assets made in connection with such a loan be upset or impaired for that reason;

(B) Subparagraph (A) shall not be construed to . . . relieve any such entity of the duty to comply with . . . any Federal or State law regarding the making of a fraudulent conveyance . . . ;

(4) (A) . . .

(B) . . . if . . . a trust described in paragraph (2)(B)(i) [is established] . . . then such injunction shall be valid . . . if

(i) as part of the proceedings . . . the court appoints a legal representative for the purpose of protecting the rights of persons that might subsequently assert demands . . . ; and

(ii) the court determines, before entering the order confirming such plan, that . . . such injunction . . . is fair and equitable with respect to the persons that might subsequently assert such demands. . . .

Michelle White summarizes the number of people affected, the dollars involved, and the bankruptcies precipitated in the abstract to her Asbestos and the Future of Mass Torts, Nat'l Bureau of Economic Research Working Paper No. 10308, Feb. 2004 (later published at 18 Journal of Economic Perspectives 183 (2004), without the abstract):

> Asbestos was once referred to as a 'miracle mineral' for its ability to withstand heat and it was used in thousands of products. But exposure to asbestos causes cancer and other diseases. As of the beginning of 2001, 600,000 individuals had filed lawsuits for asbestos-related diseases against more than 6,000 defendants. 85 firms have filed for bankruptcy due to asbestos liabilities and several insurers have failed or are in financial distress. More than $54 billion has been spent on the litigation—higher than any other mass tort. Estimates of the eventual cost of asbestos litigation range from $200 to $265 billion. . . . [D]espite the disappearance of asbestos products from the marketplace [by the late 1970s], asbestos litigation continued to grow. Plaintiffs' lawyers used forum-shopping to select the most favorable state courts techniques for mass processing of claims, and substituted new defendants when old ones went bankrupt. Because representing asbestos victims was extremely profitable, lawyers had an incentive to seek out large numbers of additional plaintiffs, including many claimants who were not harmed by asbestos exposure. . . . [A]sbestos [litigation] was unique in a number of ways, so that future mass torts are unlikely to be as big. However new legal innovations developed for asbestos are likely to make future mass torts larger and more expensive. . . . Two mechanisms—bankruptcies and class action settlements—. . . devel-

oped to resolve mass torts [but] neither has worked [well]. . . . As a result, Congressional legislation is needed. . . .

Congressional efforts to pass legislation that would centralize the system to resolve asbestos claims failed repeatedly. In 2006, the Senate held hearings on the Fairness in Asbestos Injury Resolution Act of 2006. If it had been adopted, the FAIR Act of 2006 would have stayed any asbestos claim pending in a state or federal court. The Act would have set procedures for filing claims and the amount of compensation, established a fund to pay asbestos-related injury claims, and set up a commission to determine the amounts each insurer would pay into the fund. The bill did not come to a vote in Congress.

Thus far, the first trusts ran out of cash before all of the future claimants were paid. That they ran dry suggests that either not enough was poured into the trust (usually meaning that the financial creditors did better, getting a higher pay-out ratio than the tort claimants), or the early tort claimants got paid too much (with the trust not reserving enough for later claimants), or both. Current claimants vote on the trust plan, see § 524(g)(2)(B)(ii)(IV); future claimants, because they don't hold Code-recognized claims, do not.

Critics say that the trusts were set up poorly, and that their defects reflect a victory of the interests of the early claimants and their attorneys, who'd want to be paid as much as possible, over later-claiming tort victims. Some future claimants on the Manville trusts got only 10% of their claim paid, while Manville's general unsecured creditors were fully paid. See Manville Personal Injury Settlement Trust, History, at http://www.mantrust.org/history.htm. Subsequent trusts did better, but they still ran dry. By 2011, the Government Accounting Office reports there were sixty § 524(g) asbestos trusts with a total of $37 billion in assets, with the trusts having paid about $17 billion on 3.3 million claims from 1988 to 2010. GAO, Asbestos Injury Compensation, at cover, 3 (GAO Report 11–819, Sept. 20, 2011).

Since 75% of the claimants subject to the trust and channeling order must approve the plan, and since there's no cram-down method, these claimants—and their lawyers—wield significant power over the plan. It's 75% though not of all those affected, but of all those holding claims and actually voting. The plan thus pits currently identifiable claimants against future, not-yet-identified claimants. And we could thus expect payouts weighted toward compensating them well and undercompensating others. *Tort Lawyers: There They Go Again!*, Fortune, Sept. 6, 2004, at 186.

D. SETOFF

Imagine that the Debtor, D, owes $100 to A, and A in turn owes D $100. From the structure we've seen thus far, D would collect the $100 from A, but A would then have a $100 claim on D, which would be paid ratably with D's other creditors. However, for mutual claims A can invoke the setoff doctrine and net the two obligations, one running from D and the other running to D. D's other creditors will presumably be disappointed, particularly if A's setoff is large.

¶ 1214: Balancing Debtor and Creditor Interests

The obligations between a bankrupt debtor and its creditor do not always run in one direction, as the creditor may also owe sums *to* the debtor. From the debtor's perspective these monies due *from* the creditor are an asset of the debtor. But, through the setoff provision, the Bankruptcy Code allows the creditor to use its own obligation to the debtor to pay off the debtor's obligations to the creditor, provided that the mutual debts were incurred prior to the debtor's bankruptcy and state law allows for the set-off.

§ 553. Setoff

> [T]his title does not affect any right of a creditor to offset a mutual debt owing by such creditor to the debtor that arose before the commencement of the case under this title against a claim of such creditor against the debtor that arose before the commencement of the case. . . .

While setoff balances the interests of the debtor and the creditor, in doing so, it unbalances the interests between the creditor and other creditors with equal claims against the debtor. If some creditors can exercise setoff while other creditors lack a mutual debt for setoff, the favored creditors' ability to set-off affects the priority between otherwise equal creditors. Consider the following example. In the first set-up, the debtor owes \$100 to two creditors A_1 and B. It has a single asset worth \$100, its claim on Counterparty A_2:

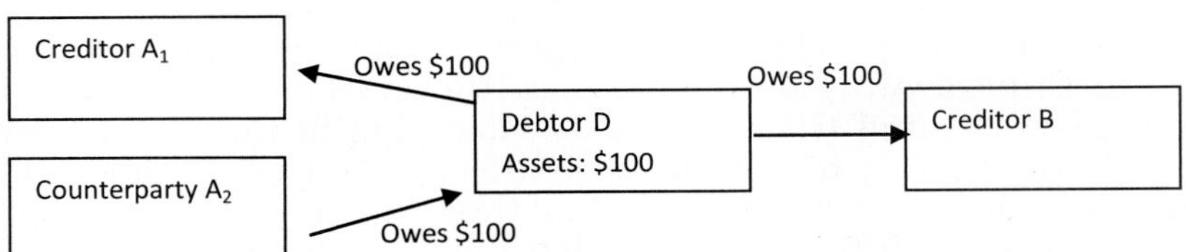

This set-up is unremarkable, differing little from what we've seen thus far in bankruptcy. The trustee in D's bankruptcy would obtain the \$100 from A_2 and then distribute it ratably to A_1 and B, each of whom would receive \$50.

Next, collapse A_1 and A_2 into a single creditor, A, with mutual obligations running from and to D:

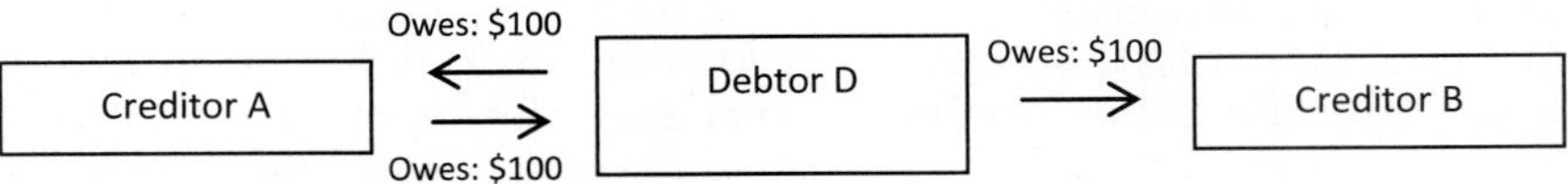

D's only asset is the obligation it has from A to pay over $100. Ordinarily A would be obligated to deliver $100 to D. Then, with D having $100 in assets, A and B would each receive $50, or 50 cents on each dollar owed. That is, A would pay over $100 to D but then receive back $50. B would also get $50 in the bankruptcy. But if A can setoff, then it nets its $100 obligation *to* D *against* D's $100 obligation back to A. A would pay over nothing, effectively obtaining $100 from the bankrupt D's estate. B would thus receive nothing in D's bankruptcy, because D would have no assets after A's setoff. Although A and B each had equal-sized unsecured claims, setoff allows A to gain priority over B.

¶ 1215: Setoff as Security

We could, and should, reconceptualize A's setoff rights away from those of an unsecured creditor to those of a creditor having a security interest, albeit one that doesn't flow through the filing and notice provisions of the Uniform Commercial Code, in its own obligation to pay $100 to the debtor.

The automatic stay applies to the creditor's setoff power, thwarting the creditor's capacity to immediately setoff mutual debts upon the debtor's filing of a bankruptcy petition. This resembles how the stay stymies a secured creditor from immediately seizing and selling its security. The secured creditor can eventually seize and sell, but not as soon as the debtor files for bankruptcy, and it must be adequately protected during the period when the debtor is trying to reorganize.

§ 362. Automatic stay

(a) . . . [A] petition filed under . . . this title . . . operates as a stay, applicable to all entities, of—

* * *

(7) the setoff of any debt owing to the debtor . . . against any claim against the debtor. . . .

Setoff opportunities are also confined by preference law. If the non-bankrupt creditor acquires the debtor's obligation within the preference period, it cannot exercise setoff.

§ 553. Setoff

(a) [T]his title does not affect any right of a creditor to offset a mutual debt except to the extent that—

(2) such claim was transferred . . . to such creditor—

(A) after the commencement of the case; or

(B) (I) after 90 days before. . . . ; and

(II) while the debtor was insolvent. . . .

¶ 1216: John C. McCoid, Setoff: Why Bankruptcy Priority?, 75 Virginia Law Review 15 (1989)

Between solvent parties, setoff makes perfect sense. If you owe me $10 and I owe you $7, it is certainly efficient for you simply to pay me $3; it also avoids the possibility of my default after you have paid what you owe me. Striking that balance affects no one else. If, however, one of us is insolvent and has other creditors, the sense of this solution is less obvious. . . . Those who created setoff thought that 'natural justice and equity' between the debtor and the indebted creditor required this result. . . .

[T]hree additional justifications for setoff have been offered. The first of these [is] that the creditor with a nonbankruptcy right of setoff should be viewed as a secured creditor. . . . It is quite modern, however, in its theoretical concern for the relative rights of the creditors of an insolvent.[4] In contrast, the other justifications are more practical. The older of these functional arguments is simply that setoff conforms to business understanding. A more recent proposition is that setoff should be preserved in order to encourage banks to carry debtors in times of trouble. . . .

If the creditors with the power to set off have come, because of that power, to feel secure against the prospect of bankruptcy, it is only because the preferential effect of setoff has so long been indulged. It is true that setoff has a bankruptcy history of long standing. Thus it might be argued that it has acquired a security-priority purpose. That ought not to be the case unless there are practical reasons for the priority. Absent such reasons, creditors with setoff power should be subject to the principle of equality that underlies preference recapture and bankruptcy distribution. . . .

[The argument that setoff conforms to business understanding] is a circular argument. If the ability to set off with impunity on the eve of bankruptcy or after the petition is filed is what is expected, that is so only because that is what the law has been. Should it be concluded that the law ought to be different—that there is no basis for granting priority to creditors just because they happen to have an obligation to the debtor—"business understanding" and "commercial expectation" would quickly reflect the change.

[P]roponents of the status quo might argue that the change would undermine an important policy served by setoff—the power encourages banks to keep troubled debtors afloat when the debtor is "sinking into financial difficulty." It is far from clear, however, that carrying financially troubled debtors is a good thing[, especially if t]he consequence of doing so is . . . to further deplete the estate available to creditors on ultimate failure [rather than to] sav[e] a struggling enterprise. . . . [And, if that policy is to be fostered, the creditor does not need setoff rights, as

---

[4] [Secured creditors typically must file a notice of their security interest with a state office, making their priority claim on those assets knowable to other creditors, who can then adjust the terms of their own loan as they see fit. Setoff rights typically are not filed and thereby noticed to the public.—Roe.]

it can make an ordinary, publicly-filed secured loan to the failing but salvageable debtor.]

Who wanted creditor setoff rights to be broad? Consider this description in David Skeel, Debt's Dominion 98 (2001) of the maneuvering to put together the 1938 Bankruptcy Act:

> An issue that banks cared deeply about was their common-law right of setoff—in particular, their right to use a debtor's deposit account at the bank to offset, or pay down, the amount that a debtor owed to the bank. James McLaughlin [a Harvard Law School bankruptcy professor of the time, who was active in drafting the 1938 statute] wanted [in the congressional negotiations] to treat setoffs effected prior to bankruptcy as preferential transfers, and he persuaded the [lawyers at the] National Bankruptcy Conference to include such a proposal in an early draft of [what became] the [1938] Chandler bill. Banks fiercely resisted this assault on their traditional setoff rights ... , however, and McLaughlin was forced to back down. 'I am not going to revisit [the setoff proposal] all over again,' he said in the 1937 Chandler Act hearings. "I think that would constitute breach of faith with my banker friends."

CHAPTER 13

GOVERNMENT ENTITIES

Though government entities often find themselves as simple creditors in bankruptcy proceedings—most typically relating to claims for unpaid taxes—government entities are also often involved in more complicated ways. State and federal authorities regulate numerous business activities. Regulation may prohibit or require specific behaviors by private firms that do not directly relate to any debt obligation of a firm to the government authority. For example, government entities often issue licenses or permits that allow private firms to carry on particular regulated activities. The Federal Aviation Administration allocates take off and landing rights (called "slots" in the industry) to airlines operating at the busiest U.S. airports.[1] The Federal Communications Commission allocates "spectrum" licenses to prospective radio and television broadcasters and cellular telephone companies in order to rationalize use of the limited bandwidth of airwaves in the U.S. What happens to those licenses when the licensee goes into bankruptcy?

---

[1] See Pension Benefit Guaranty Corp. v. Braniff Airways, Inc. (In re Braniff Airways, Inc.), 700 F.2d 935 (5th Cir. 1983) (finding that airport landing slots are not property).

Regulation may also conflict with key features of a debtor's restructuring plan. For instance, in certain sensitive industries, national security concerns or other public interest concerns may preclude the debtor's desired sale of assets to a specific purchaser. Can bankruptcy override state or federal regulation that impedes the debtor's rehabilitation? Finally, municipal entities—cities, counties, hospital districts, for example—may be debtors in bankruptcy. They may find themselves in financial distress and may resort to the Code's Chapter 9 for relief.

In this Chapter, we highlight several of the ways government entities can become involved in bankruptcy that go beyond the traditional creditor role.

A. GOVERNMENT REGULATION: ENVIRONMENTAL CLEAN–UP OBLIGATIONS

Environmental laws require firms to clean up some of the messes that they make. How are these obligations treated in bankruptcy? While not usually a contractual obligation, these prebankruptcy obligations are analogous to prebankruptcy contract obligations and, hence, we briefly discuss them here.

Suppose a firm spills toxins into the river and thereafter goes bankrupt. Downstream homeowners sue for damages the toxin inflicts on them and their property, or they seek a court order against the bankrupt to clean up the mess. Presumably though the court would estimate damages, and the homeowners would be paid in "bankruptcy dollars," thereby having to foot the unpaid part of the clean-up bill themselves or bear the costs of the pollution. (Post-bankruptcy spills would presumably be actionable and paid as an administrative expense.)

Now suppose that the toxin-spilling polluter violated an environmental law and the Environmental Protection Agency sued the bankrupt firm under one of Congress' environmental laws, to clean up the mess caused before the bankruptcy and to stop polluting in the future.

The Bankruptcy Code awards no special explicit priority here to the government. And, what's worse for the government, its suit for prebankruptcy pollution (at first) seems clearly stayed under § 362(a):

§ 362. Automatic stay

(a) . . . [A bankruptcy petition] operates as a stay . . . of

(1) the commencement or continuation, . . . of a judicial, administrative, or other action or proceeding against the debtor that was or could have been commenced before the commencement of [the bankruptcy];

(2) the enforcement, against the debtor or against property of the estate, of a judgment obtained before the commencement of the case under this title;

(3) any act to obtain possession of [the bankrupt's] property . . . or to exercise control over property of the estate;

(4) any act to create, perfect, or enforce any lien against property of the [bankrupt];

(5) any act to create, perfect, or enforce against property of the debtor any lien to the extent that such lien secures a claim that arose before the commencement of the [bankruptcy];

(6) any act to collect, assess, or recover a claim against the debtor that arose before the [bankruptcy];. . . .

Sections (1) and (2) clearly stop the government from pursuing the litigation for prebankruptcy pollution. Other sections also might. But, after October 1998, the government lawyer could turn to subsection (b), the exceptions to the stay provisions:

§ 362. Automatic stay

(b) The filing of a petition . . . does *not* operate as a stay—

* * *

(4) under paragraph (1), (2), (3), or (6) of subsection (a) . . . , of the commencement or continuation of an action or proceeding by a governmental unit . . . to enforce such governmental unit's . . . *police or regulatory power,* including the enforcement of a judgment other than a money judgment, obtained in an action . . . by the governmental unit to enforce such governmental unit's . . . police or regulatory power; . . .

This exception to the stay allows the EPA to pursue its lawsuit against the bankrupt firm to clean up the prebankruptcy pollution, despite (a)(1), (a)(2), (a)(3), (a)(6), and the equality policy behind the stay.

Consider the priority effects of the exception to the stay. Lifting the stay in effect makes the bankrupt's clean-up obligation prior to the bankrupt's other obligations. This de facto priority may be sensible from several policy perspectives. The de facto priority could help to induce the other players in the firm to monitor the debtor more carefully in making sure it's not a gross polluter. If policymakers want to privilege environmental improvement, then the de facto priority pushes failing and bankrupt firms in that direction.

Notice the policy basis for allowing the government to proceed. It isn't so much that when the debtor is in bankruptcy the only alternative would be more pollution: the government can clean it up (as it often does) and then bill the company. The government's bill would then come in as a general creditor's claim. When seen in this way, the post-filing stay issue is a priority issue: who will pay for the clean-up, the polluting debtor's creditors or the American taxpayer? (Once more, an order to stop *post*-bankruptcy pollution is different: post-bankruptcy pollution is an operation of administering the bankrupt estate and subject to any applicable regulation.)

The prebankruptcy policy issues are more difficult. If the government isn't stayed, and accordingly becomes de facto prior to the firm's other creditors, then imagine how the firm's other creditors will act prebankruptcy. If they conclude that the debtor is a high risk for bankruptcy and is a heavy polluter, the creditors either will not lend or will themselves insist on a clean-up. If the creditor won't lend, then a polluter has fewer assets and presumably the social good is usually improved by diminishing the debtor's assets, which should diminish its capacity to pollute. If the lender induces the debtor to clean up the toxins by, say, insisting on EPA-compliance certificates from an environmental engineer, then the result is that the creditor then enforces environmental policy. (This analysis assumes that the environmental policy is in fact correct and does not over- or under-enforce environmental clean-ups.)

Note three issues here: First, the same sort of analysis applies to typical tort claimants. If tort policy is correct, then priority for tort claimants would make creditors enforce tort policy. Second, priority comes at a price: some creditors want to lend without understanding the debtor in detail; de facto EPA priority means that creditors have to understand something (or accept the risk). Third, the only way for the government to get its *effective* priority under the statute is to sue the debtor to clean-up; it has no direct, formal priority, i.e., the government cannot do the clean-up and then bill the company. If it cleans up the toxins itself and sends the bankrupt a bill, it would be a mere general creditor, not a priority creditor.

Early cases concluded that because the environmental clean-up obligation under environmental law required the debtor to spend money, the obligation was a "claim" under § 101(5). Hence, the clean-up obligation could be discharged in bankruptcy. Ohio v. Kovacs, 469 U.S. 274 (1985). But later decisions integrated the prepetition pollution of the debtor's own properties with the post-petition situation. These later decisions rested on the idea that, for the debtor to operate its property, it would have to comply with the environmental laws. Hence, they reasoned, the debtor would have to clean up the site, and the court wouldn't parse the difference between prepetition pollution and post-petition waste. In re Chateaugay Corp., 944 F.2d 997, 1008 (2d Cir. 1997). A regulatory injunction wouldn't be turned into a dollar claim; but if the environmental agency cleaned up the mess and asserted a reimbursement claim for prepetition pollution, its claim would be that of a general creditor. Since 1998, as we saw, the EPA is exempt from the stay when employing its regulatory power but not when seeking to enforce a money judgment.

---

1. Is the (b)(4) exception to the stay "like" giving the government agency the power to get specific performance?

2. Is it "like" giving the government agency priority?

3. Creditor plans to lend to a company operating a factory with a history of EPA problems. It's a borderline business, and it's planning to borrow from the bank to clean up some of the toxic spills. The bank's lawyers brief the loan officer on § 362(b)(4)'s de facto priority for the

EPA. The loan officer asks the lawyers what can be done, and the talk turns to special purpose vehicles. The loan officer suggests that an SPV buy the operating company's accounts receivable. If there's a bankruptcy and an EPA clean-up order, that order will hit the operating company, not the "clean" accounts receivable. (a) Would the special purpose vehicle complement or undermine the EPA's environmental policy? (b) Would it reconcile lender uncertainty ("we don't understand this company and we don't want to take the time to understand it") with nonbankruptcy public policy? Or would the two conflict? (c) Would such a transfer to the SPV be a fraudulent transfer?

B. GOVERNMENT LICENSES

Consider the government's grant of a license to a firm outside of bankruptcy. The debtor violates the licensing rules and the agency could revoke the license, but then the debtor files for chapter 11, before the agency cancels the license.

Can the agency cancel without violating the automatic stay? The government's action—an effort to exercise control over the estate's property via an administrative action—comes within the general ambit of the stay, which we know is designed to prevent prebankruptcy creditors from dismembering the bankrupt. Little could more effectively dismember a bankrupt than the government revoking a license critical to the bankrupt's business. If the debtor needs the license to operate, the stay would seem particularly attuned to preventing a shut-down of the debtor.

What does the Code say about licenses? It would seem easy to view the license as property of the debtor under § 362(a)(3). And it's obvious that the administrative proceedings to cancel a license could often have been commenced (and maybe actually were commenced) before the petition was filed, making a stay under sub-section (1) apt.

Without more, under either § 362(a)(1) or (3), the agency's effort to revoke the license would be stayed.

But under the next subsection of the stay provision, § 362(b), the Code exempts from the automatic stay a government agency that's pursuing its police or regulatory power. Hence, if the bankrupt isn't complying with the government's regulatory terms, the agency could ordinarily revoke the license.

§ 362. Automatic stay

(a) . . . [A bankruptcy petition] operates as a stay . . . of

(1) the commencement or continuation, . . . of a judicial, administrative, or other action or proceeding against the debtor that was or could have been commenced before the commencement of [the bankruptcy]; . . .

(3) any act to obtain possession of [the bankrupt's] property . . . or to exercise control over property of the estate; . . .

(b) The filing of a petition . . . does not operate as a stay—. . .

(4) under paragraph (1), (2), (3), or (6) of subsection (a) of this section, of the commencement or continuation of an action or proceeding by a governmental unit . . . to enforce such governmental unit's . . . police and regulatory power, including the enforcement of a judgment other than a money judgment, obtained in an action . . . by the governmental unit to enforce such governmental unit's . . . police or regulatory power; . . . .

Note again the priority implications of the Code's exception to the stay here.

Next consider the possibility that the agency seeks to revoke the license (a) because the debtor is in chapter 11, and hence the agency feels insecure, or (b) because the debtor fails to pay for the license. Section 525(a) says:

§ 525. Protection against discriminatory treatment

(a) . . . [A] governmental unit may not deny, revoke, suspend, or refuse to renew a license, permit, charter, franchise, or other similar grant to . . . a person that is . . . a debtor under . . . the Bankruptcy Act . . . solely because such bankrupt or debtor is or has been a debtor under . . . the Bankruptcy Act, has been insolvent before the commencement . . . or has not paid a debt that is dischargeable in [chapter 11]. . . .

One of the most valuable licenses in recent years has been the Federal Communication Commission's license to use the wireless spectrum. The FCC auctioned off licenses for the wireless spectrum for cell-phones and the like, and, as a matter of public policy and congressional mandate, awarded some of the licenses to small firms that could only bid for the licenses if they could pay for them over time, in installments. But before a winning bidder gets its wireless network up and running profitably, and before it pays off the installment debt to the FCC, the buyer files for chapter 11. The FCC immediately cancels the license, stating that the debt payments were sufficiently tied up with government regulatory policy—those running the wireless spectrum should be financially sound—that it wants to re-award the licenses to another user. This is approximately what happened with NextWave.

Large telephone companies were the typically buyers. Congress sought to have the FCC sell parts of that spectrum to small businesses, so the FCC offered some licenses on substantial credit. NextWave, a qualifying small firm, won a bid for a slice of the wireless spectrum for about $4.7 billion in 1998, paying 10% down and promising to pay the rest in installments.

Cellular communication was not immediately profitable and NextWave filed for bankruptcy. But technology and the cellular market changed during NextWave's bankruptcy. The FCC canceled NextWave's licenses, put the wireless "space" up for bids, and got bids of about $16 billion from a consortium formed by Verizon and several others. The stakes were high when NextWave filed for bankruptcy: NextWave asserted that the FCC could not cancel the licenses, that these licenses were the bankrupt's property, and that it would re-sell its licenses privately to Verizon and the bidding group for that $16 billion. The dispute went to the Supreme Court.

¶ 1301: FCC v. Nextwave Personal Comm. Inc., 537 U.S. 293 (2003)

Justice SCALIA delivered the opinion of the Court.

In these cases, we decide whether § 525 of the Bankruptcy Code, 11 U.S.C. § 525, prohibits the Federal Communications Commission (FCC or Commission) from revoking licenses held by a debtor in bankruptcy upon the debtor's failure to make timely payments owed to the Commission for purchase of the licenses. [We hold that it does.]

I

In 1993, Congress amended the Communications Act of 1934 to authorize the FCC to award spectrum licenses "through a system of competitive bidding." ... 47 U.S.C. § 309(j)(1). It directed the Commission to ... "disseminat[e] licenses among a wide variety of applications, including small businesses [and] rural telephone companies." § 309(j)(3)(B). In order to achieve this goal, Congress directed the FCC to "consider [allowing small businesses to pay in installments]." § 309(j)(4)(A).

... [The FCC] in accordance with [the statute] restricted participation in two ... auction[s] ... to small businesses and other designated entities with total assets and revenues below certain levels, and it allowed the successful bidders in these two blocks to pay in installments over the term of the license.

Respondent NextWave ... participated ... in the FCC's [small business] auctions. NextWave was awarded ... licenses on winning bids totaling approximately $4.74 billion.... In accordance with FCC regulations, NextWave made a down payment on the purchase price, signed promissory notes for the balance, *and executed security agreements that the FCC perfected by filing under the Uniform Commercial Code. The security agreements gave the Commission a first "lien on and continuing security interest in all of the Debtor's rights and interest in [each] License."* Security Agreement between NextWave and FCC ¶ 1 (Jan. 3, 1997), 2 App. to Pet. for Cert. 402a. In addition, the licenses recited that they were "conditioned upon the full and timely payment of all monies due pursuant to ... the terms of the Commission's installment plan as set forth in the Note and Security Agreement executed by the licensee," and that "[f]ailure to comply with this condition will result in the automatic cancellation of this authorization." Radio Station Authorization for Broadband PCS (issued to NextWave Jan. 3, 1997), 2 App. to Pet. for Cert. 388a.

After the ... licenses were awarded [the wireless spectrum developed slowly.] ... NextWave [had] difficulty obtaining financing ... and petitioned the Commission to restructure their installment-payment obligations. The Commission suspended the installment payments, and adopted several options that allowed [NextWave] to surrender some or all ... licenses for full or partial forgiveness of their outstanding debt. It set a deadline of June 8, 1998 [for NextWave] to elect a restructuring option. . . .

On June 8, 1998, after failing to obtain stays of the election deadline from the Commission or the Court of Appeals for the District of Columbia Circuit, NextWave filed for Chapter 11 bankruptcy protection in New York. It suspended payments to all creditors, including the FCC, pending confirmation of a reorganization plan. . . .

... The FCC ... assert[ed] that NextWave's licenses had been canceled automatically when the company missed its first payment-deadline in October 1998. The Commission simultaneously announced that NextWave's licenses were "available for auction under the automatic cancellation provisions" of the FCC's regulations. NextWave sought emergency relief in the Bankruptcy Court, which declared the FCC's cancellation of respondent's licenses "null and void" as a violation of various provisions of the Bankruptcy Code. . . .

... The [D.C.] Court of Appeals ... [held] that the FCC's cancellation of NextWave's licenses violated 11 U.S.C. § 525: "Applying the fundamental principle that federal agencies must obey all federal laws, not just those they administer, we conclude that the Commission violated the provision of the Bankruptcy Code that prohibits governmental entities from revoking debtors' licenses solely for failure to pay debts dischargeable in bankruptcy." 254 F.3d 130, 133 (2001). We granted certiorari.

II

... Respondent contends, and the Court of Appeals for the D.C. Circuit held, that the FCC's revocation of its licenses was not in accordance with § 525 of the Bankruptcy Code.

Section 525(a) provides, in relevant part:

> "[A] governmental unit may not ... revoke ... a license ... to ... a person that is ... a debtor under this title ... solely because such ... debtor ... has not paid a debt that is dischargeable in the case under this title. . . . "

... Petitioners argue ... that the FCC did not revoke respondent's licenses "solely because" of nonpayment. . . . They also argue that a contrary interpretation would unnecessarily bring § 525 into conflict with the Communications Act. We find none of these contentions persuasive, and discuss them in turn.

A

The FCC has not denied that the proximate cause for its cancellation of the licenses was NextWave's failure to make the payments that were due. It contends, however, that § 525 does not apply because the FCC had a "valid regulatory motive" for the cancellation. In our view, that factor is irrelevant. When the statute refers to failure to pay a debt as the sole cause of cancellation ("solely because"), it cannot reasonably be understood to include, among the other causes whose presence can preclude application of the prohibition, the governmental unit's *motive* in effecting the cancellation. Such a reading would deprive § 525 of all force. It is hard to imagine a situation in which a governmental unit would not have some further motive behind the cancellation—assuring the financial solvency of the licensed entity . . . or punishing lawlessness, or even (quite simply) making itself financially whole. Section 525 means nothing more or less than that the failure to pay a dischargeable debt must alone be the proximate cause of the cancellation—the act or event that triggers the agency's decision to cancel, whatever the agency's ultimate motive in pulling the trigger may be.

Some may think (and the opponents of § 525 undoubtedly thought) that there *ought* to be an exception for cancellations that have a valid regulatory purpose. Besides the fact that such an exception would consume the rule, it flies in the face of the fact that, where Congress has intended to provide regulatory exceptions to provisions of the Bankruptcy Code, it has done so clearly and expressly, rather than by a device so subtle as denominating a motive a cause. There are, for example, regulatory exemptions from the Bankruptcy Code's automatic stay provisions. 11 U.S.C. § 362(b)(4). And even § 525(a) itself contains explicit exemptions for certain . . . [regulatory agricultural] programs. . . . These latter exceptions would be entirely superfluous if we were to read § 525 as the Commission proposes—which means, of course, that such a reading must be rejected.

B

. . . What petitioners describe as a conflict boils down to nothing more than a policy preference on the FCC's part for (1) selling licenses on credit and (2) canceling licenses rather than asserting security interests in licenses when there is a default. . . .

III

. . . [As to whether the FCC can] take and enforce a security interest in an FCC license, . . . [it is not clear] that the FCC *cannot.* ([T]he FCC purported to take such a security interest in the present case. What is at issue, however, is not the enforcement of that interest in the bankruptcy process, but rather elimination of the licenses through the regulatory step of "revoking" them—action that the statute specifically forbids.) . . .

For the reasons stated, the judgment of the Court of Appeals for the District of Columbia Circuit is

Affirmed.

Justice BREYER, dissenting.

The statute before us says that the Government may not revoke a license it has granted to a person who has entered bankruptcy "*solely because [the bankruptcy debtor] . . . has not paid a debt that is dischargeable in [bankruptcy].*" 11 U.S.C. § 525(a) (emphasis added). The question is whether the italicized words apply when a government creditor, having taken a security interest in a license sold on an installment plan, revokes the license not because the debtor has gone bankrupt, but simply because the debtor has failed to pay an installment as promised. The majority answers this question in the affirmative. It says that the italicized words mean

> *nothing more or less* than that the failure to pay a dischargeable debt must alone be the proximate cause of the cancellation—the act or event that triggers the agency's decision to cancel, whatever the agency's ultimate motive . . . may be. ([E]mphasis added).

Hence, if the debt is a dischargeable debt (as virtually all debts are), then once a debtor enters bankruptcy, the Government cannot revoke the license—irrespective of the Government's motive. That, the majority writes, is what the statute says. Just read it. End of the matter.

It is dangerous, however, in any actual case of interpretive difficulty to rely exclusively upon the literal meaning of a statute's words divorced from consideration of the statute's purpose. That is so for a linguistic reason. General terms as used on particular occasions often carry with them implied restrictions as to scope. "Tell all customers that . . . " does not refer to every customer of every business in the world. That is also so for a legal reason. Law as expressed in statutes seeks to regulate human activities in particular ways. Law is tied to life. And a failure to understand how a statutory rule is so tied can undermine the very human activity that the law seeks to benefit. "No vehicles in the park" does not refer to baby strollers or even to tanks used as part of a war memorial. See Fuller, *Positivism and Fidelity to Law—A Reply to Professor Hart,* 71 Harv. L. Rev. 630, 663 (1958).

I

In my view this statute's language is similarly restricted. . . . Where the fact of bankruptcy is totally irrelevant, where the government's action has no relation either through purpose or effect to bankruptcy or to dischargeability, where consequently the revocation cannot threaten the bankruptcy-related concerns that underlie the statute, then the revocation falls outside the statute's scope. Congress intended this kind of exception to its general language in order to avoid consequences which, if not "absurd," are at least at odds with the statute's basic objectives. . . .

The Court's literal interpretation of the statute threatens to create a serious anomaly. It seems to say that a government cannot *ever* enforce a lien on property that it has sold on the installment plan as long as (1) the property is a license, (2) the buyer has gone bankrupt, and (3) the government wants the license back solely because the buyer did not pay for it. After all, in such circumstances, it is virtually *always* the case that the buyer will not have paid a debt that is in fact "dischargeable," and that "event" alone will have "trigger[ed]" the government's "decision" to revoke the license. See *supra,* at 843.

Yet every private commercial seller, every car salesman, every residential home developer, every appliance company can threaten repossession of its product if a buyer does not pay—at least if the seller has taken a security interest in the product. Why should the government (state or federal), and the government alone, find it impossible to repossess a product, namely, a license, when the buyer fails to make installment payments?

The facts of this case illustrate the problem. NextWave bought broadcasting licenses from the Federal Communications Commission (FCC) for just under $5 billion. It promised to pay the money under an installment plan. It agreed that its possession of the licenses was "conditioned upon full and timely payment," that failure to pay would result in the licenses' "automatic cancellation," that the Government would maintain a "fi[r]st lien on and continuing security interest" in the licenses, and that it would "not dispute" the Government's "rights as a secured party." NextWave never made its installment payments. It entered bankruptcy. And the FCC declared the licenses void for nonpayment. In a word, the FCC sought to repossess the licenses so that it could auction the related spectrum space to other users. . . .

II

. . . Congress . . . sought to forbid discrimination against those who are, or were, in bankruptcy. . . . Where that kind of government activity is at issue, the statute forbids revocation. But where that kind of activity is not at issue, there is no reason to apply the statute's prohibition.

The statute's title, its language, and its history all support this description of its purpose. The title says, "Protection against discriminatory treatment." 11 U.S.C. § 525(a). The statute's text, read as a whole . . . strongly suggests that bankruptcy-related discrimination is the evil at which the statute aims. . . .

The statute's history demonstrates an antidiscriminatory objective. . . . The House Report says that its "purpose . . . is to prevent an automatic reaction against an individual for availing himself of the protection of the bankruptcy laws." In describing related provisions, the House Report refers to an intent to prevent the Government from punishing "bankruptcy per se" by denying "a license, grant, or entitlement" on the premise "that bankruptcy itself is sufficiently repre[h]ensible behavior to warrant . . . a sanction." . . .

* * *

IV

Finally, the majority points out that . . . this case is now not about "enforcement of [a security] interest in" the Bankruptcy Court. But the majority's interpretation certainly seems to cover that circumstance, and more. Under the majority's understanding, a government creditor who seeks to enforce a security interest in a broadcasting license (after the bankruptcy stay has been lifted or after bankruptcy proceedings terminate) would be seeking to repossess, and thereby to revoke, that license "solely because" of the debtor's failure to pay a "dischargeable" debt. After all, under such circumstances, "failure to pay" the debt that is *in fact* dischargeable would "alone be the proximate cause" of the government's action. It is "the act or event that triggers the agency's decision to cancel, whatever the agency's ultimate motive."

If I am right about this, the majority's interpretation means that private creditors, say, car dealers, can enforce security interests in the goods that they sell, namely cars, but governments cannot enforce security interests in items that they sell, namely licenses. . . .

* * *

V

. . . I would vacate the Court of Appeals' judgment and remand for further proceedings. I respectfully dissent.

---

1. Is the ban in § 525 an exception to the § 362(b) regulatory exception?
2. If the FCC licensed NextWave and made the license conditional on NextWave's operations (i.e., minimum transmission capacity, minimum subscriber base, etc. by various dates), could the FCC have used NextWave's failure to implement these conditions as a reason to cancel the license, even though its failure to implement was primarily due to NextWave's financial problems?
3. Stevens's concurrence stated: "The Senate Report explained that § 525(a) "does not prohibit consideration of other factors, such as future financial responsibility or ability, and does not prohibit imposition of requirements such as net capital rules, if applied nondiscriminatorily." S. Rep. No. 95–989, p. 81 (1978), U.S. Code Cong. & Admin. News 1978, pp. 5787, 5867.
4. The FCC took a security interest in the licenses. Does the Supreme Court bar the FCC from enforcing the security interest? Justice Scalia implies that the debtor could enforce it, but Breyer's dissent says that so barring the FCC would be the natural (but absurd) interpretation: if the government agency can't cancel the license to collect its debt, as the Court held, then it shouldn't be able to seize its security by foreclosing, if the underlying security is a government license.
5. Would the FCC have found it enough to be able to collect on its security, as the court opinion seems to leave open? Its claim from the auction would assuredly have been paid in full anyway. If the FCC had a security interest in the licenses, and indeed was oversecured, why would it want, or need, to cancel the licenses?
6. The value of the licenses shifted dramatically over time. When NextWave filed for bankruptcy, the licenses were worth much less than the $4.7 billion it bid for them. The cellular system was not developing as first envisioned. Indeed, the issues in the early bankruptcy litigation were whether NextWave could avoid paying fully for the licenses. But technology and markets change. As the bank-

ruptcy went on, the FCC sought to auction off the licenses. Verizon and a group of bidders were prepared to pay $16 billion for NextWave's licenses. See Yochi Dreasen, *NextWave Nears Deal to Sell Wireless Licenses*, Wall Street Journal, Sept. 21, 2001, at A3; Yochi Dreasen, *NextWave, FCC Are Closer to a Deal on Licenses*, Wall Street Journal, Sept. 24, 2001, at B7.

7. Does the change in value help to explain why the FCC didn't see its security interest as good enough?
8. Consider the stay on seizing security in § 362(a)(4)–(5). Does the regulatory exemption in § 362(b) exempt the government from the stay on seizing security? Relevance? The FCC had a security interest in the licenses. Was the FCC, by (trying to) cancel the licenses, trying a self-help seizure of its security?
9. If the statute's regulatory exceptions to the stay allowed the FCC to revoke NextWave's licenses, notwithstanding § 525, what would be left for § 525 to do? Justice Breyer says the statute would bar government agencies from, say, refusing licenses to someone just because they became bankrupt or refusing to employ bankrupts just because of their status as a bankrupt.

C. STATE REGULATORY POLICY

Does the bankruptcy power preempt contrary state regulation? That is, could the plan confirmation power override state regulation? Congress seemed to take a broad view in § 1123(a)(5), which asserts that "*notwithstanding any otherwise applicable nonbankruptcy law,* a plan shall . . . provide adequate means for the plan's implementation such as . . . the transfer of all or any part of the property of the estate to one or more entities. . . ."

California's Pacific Gas and Electric Company filed for chapter 11 and sought to divide itself into four companies. The California regulator objected, because the California Public Utilities Code barred a utility from disposing of any electrical generation facility before January 1, 2006. The state purpose was environmental: to be sure that the state could better control environmental emissions by keeping the facilities under existing ownership.

PG&E argued that § 1123, if used by the bankruptcy court, overrode state policy. The Ninth Circuit held to the contrary. It concluded that the simultaneously enacted § 1142(a), which explicitly limited the bankruptcy court's power to override nonbankruptcy law only to those nonbankruptcy laws relating to the financial condition of the debtor, reflected the extent of § 1123's preemption: it preempted contrary laws relating to the debtor's financial condition but not contrary general regulation. Congress does "not undertake lightly to preempt state law, particularly in areas of traditional state regulation" and "absent clear indications to the contrary. . . . Congress did not intend to change preexisting bankruptcy law or practice [which would not have preempted state law here] in adopting [§ 1123(a)(5)]." Pacific Gas and Electric Co. v. California, 350 F.3d 932 (2003).

D. MUNICIPAL BANKRUPTCY

Chapter 9 of the Bankruptcy Code offers a bankruptcy procedure for municipalities—cities, counties, and any other "political subdivision or public agency or instrumentality of a State." Bankruptcy Code § 101(40). This definition includes smaller special purpose local entities—school districts and hospital districts, for example—as well as cities and counties. While Chapter 9 filings are rare compared to Chapter 11s, a number of large and small municipal entities have taken advantage of Chapter 9 over the years to restructure their debts and contractual commitments. The largest cases in recent years include the following, each of which was at the time of its filing the largest in history in terms of liabilities:

> Orange County in 1994 ($1.7 billion of debt). Its financial distress arose from massive losses in a leveraged investment pool run by the county treasurer for the benefit of the county and a number of other local government entities.
>
> Jefferson County, Alabama in 2011 (over $4 billion of debt). This case was rife with scandal relating to a massive construction project to build a new county sewer system and a $3 billion municipal bond offering to fund the project.
>
> City of Detroit, Michigan in 2013 ($18-20 billion in debt). This was the largest municipal bankruptcy to date in terms of debt and also the largest filing by a city in terms of population. Detroit's financial woes were a product of long-term economic decay (particularly of the local auto industry), outsized pension and other retiree benefits, and an imprudent investment strategy involving interest-rate arbitrage intended to help manage the city's pension obligations.

While the basic purpose of Chapter 9 is similar to Chapter 11—to facilitate the debtor's formulation of a workable repayment plan for creditors—the structure of Chapter 9 and its relative balancing of power between debtors and creditors differs from Chapter 11.

While Chapter 9 specifically incorporates a number of Chapter 11's features, including many of its plan formulation and confirmation rules, 11 U.S.C. § 901, there are several more hurdles for a municipality trying to enter Chapter 9 than for a private firm filing for Chapter 11. For example, Constitutional constraints relating to state sovereignty require that a municipality be specifically authorized by its state to file for bankruptcy.[2]

Somewhat ironically, however, once a municipality has successfully entered Chapter 9, state sovereignty concerns also limit the bankruptcy court's power over the municipality's operations in bankruptcy as compared to the Chapter 11 debtor. For example, while the Chapter 11

---

[2] 11 U.S.C. § 109(c)(2). While entry into bankruptcy enables the municipality to impair contracts, a power specifically reserved to Congress and denied to the states, U.S. CONST., art. I, § 10, the Tenth Amendment preserves states' sovereignty, U.S. CONST. amend. X, which includes their power to govern the affairs of their political subdivisions. A municipality's entry into federal bankruptcy proceedings therefore requires its state's authorization. *See* Frederick Tung, *After Orange County: Reforming California Municipal Bankruptcy Law*, 53 Hastings Law Journal 885, 888 (2002).

debtor may use, sell, or lease estate property out of the ordinary course of business only after notice and a hearing, 11 U.S.C. § 363, Chapter 9 specifically forbids the court from interfering with any of the municipal debtor's government powers, its property and revenues, and its use of any income-producing property. 11 U.S.C. § 904.

The following excerpt elaborates.

¶ 1302: Omer Kimhi, *Chapter 9 of the Bankruptcy Code: A Solution in Search of a Problem*, 27 Yale Journal on Regulation 351 (2010)

Like a commercial debtor, a municipality that files for Chapter 9 enjoys an automatic stay. . . . Under the auspices of the stay, the locality can begin negotiations on debt readjustment. The locality may try to reach a consensual agreement with its creditors, but it may also attempt to cram down a debt readjustment plan notwithstanding its creditors' objections. If the debt readjustment plan meets certain conditions specified in sections 1129 and 943, the plan receives approval of the bankruptcy court, and the locality is discharged of all prepetition debts except for the debts that it assumed under the plan.

However, notwithstanding the similarities between Chapter 9 and Chapter 11, there are several major differences between the two chapters. First, in order to enjoy bankruptcy protection, a municipality must meet thresholds that are different from what corporations or individuals must meet. Whereas being a debtor under Chapter 11 or Chapter 7 requires only some sort of connection to the United States, being a debtor under Chapter 9 requires proving five substantive conditions. These conditions include, among other things, that the locality is insolvent, that the locality is expressly and directly authorized to file for bankruptcy by the state, and that the locality tried and failed to negotiate debt readjustment proceedings, or that such negotiations are impracticable. Entering the gates of municipal bankruptcy is, therefore, much harder than entering the gates of other types of bankruptcy, and in many instances a municipal bankruptcy filing is rejected because the municipality is unable to prove that it meets the threshold requirements.

However, once the bankruptcy filing is approved, the municipality has greater powers than a regular corporate debtor does. For constitutional reasons, the federal bankruptcy court has limited jurisdiction over a municipal debtor, and, as a result, localities enjoy greater latitude in the bankruptcy process. Thus, as opposed to Chapter 11, within Chapter 9 the locality has exclusive rights to submit debt readjustment plans for the court's confirmation. Creditors may not submit plans of their own, even if the locality fails to submit any plan for a long period of time. Likewise, a trustee cannot be appointed for the locality. The local leadership continues to run the municipality, even when the locality is mismanaged, and even if the local leadership's behavior harms the creditors' interests. But perhaps most importantly, the bankruptcy court itself is unable to interfere with or jeopardize the locality's political powers in any way. The court may not instruct local officials to take any action (such as a tax increase or an expenditures cut), and so it is incapable of steering the locality towards rehabilitation. The management of the distressed locality is left to local officials' absolute discretion.

Another major difference between corporate and municipal bankruptcies concerns the creditors protection rules against a cram down. Seemingly these protection rules are directly incorporated into Chapter 9 from Chapter 11, and so Chapter 9 creditors are supposed to have the same level of protection as Chapter 11 creditors do. Practically, however, the adoption of the "corporate" protection rules to municipal bankruptcy does not yield the same results, and creditors of municipalities are much less protected. Perhaps the best example is the application of the absolute priority rule. In the private context, the absolute priority rule provides a potent protection mechanism. If the shareholders, the creditors with the lowest priority, wish to keep their holdings in the company, all other creditors, and particularly the unsecured creditors, must be paid in full. In the municipal context, however, the same rule provides very weak protection. Municipalities have no shareholders, and the unsecured creditors are essentially the lowest priority creditors (the residents, the conceptual equivalents of the shareholders, are not considered creditors). Consequently, the absolute priority rule is met even when the unsecured creditors are impaired under the plan, and even when the locality gives extra funds to its residents at the expense of its creditors. Providing goods and services to the residents, even unreasonably expensive services, is not considered payment to low priority creditors, and so, as a result, the absolute priority rule is not violated. Chapter 9 thus enables municipalities to increase their costs, and to confirm plans that harm their creditors' basic interests.

An additional difference between Chapter 9 and Chapter 11 concerns the debtor's collective bargaining agreements (CBAs). Under Chapter 11, the rejection of a CBA is governed by section 1113. This section allows the debtor to reject a CBA only after the debtor's negotiations with the authorized representatives of employees, the unions, fail, and only if a court concludes that the modification to the agreement proposed by the debtor is no more than the modification necessary to permit the debtor's reorganization. Section 1113, however, is not incorporated into Chapter 9. There is no statutory instruction as to the rejection of CBAs in municipal bankruptcy, and courts have had to fill this statutory void. Some courts applied the standard of NLRB v. Bildisco & Bildisco, which was the CBA rejection standard prior to the enactment of section 1113. The Bildisco decision offers a relatively lenient standard for the rejection of CBAs, compared to section 1113. . . .

We can see, therefore, that Chapter 9 provides municipalities with relatively easy debt relief. The locality remains politically independent, while confirming a debt readjustment plan from a position of power. Due to these advantages, one could expect that financially distressed localities would use Chapter 9 to deal with a financial crisis. Filing for bankruptcy would enable the locality to get rid of at least part of its debts, and continue to operate with a decreased debt service. However, Chapter 9 statistics show a different story. The chapter has until recently in fact seldom been used . . . .

CHAPTER 14

INTEREST

A. THE STATUTE

¶ 1401: Interest Accruals and Nonaccruals in Bankruptcy for Unsecured Creditors

§ 502(b)(2). Allowance of claims or interest

[T]he court, after notice and a hearing, shall determine the amount of such *claim* . . . *as of the date of the filing of the petition*, and shall allow such claim in such amount, except to the extent that . . . *such claim is for unmatured interest*[.]

§ 362. Automatic stay

(a) . . . [A bankruptcy petition] operates as a stay . . . of

(1) the commencement or continuation, . . . of a judicial, administrative, or other action or proceeding against the debtor that was or

could have been commenced before the commencement of [the bankruptcy] . . .;

(2) the enforcement, against the debtor or against property of the estate, of a judgment obtained before the commencement of the [bankruptcy];

(3) any act to obtain possession of [the bankrupt's] property . . . ;

(4) any act to create, perfect, or enforce any lien against property of the [bankrupt];

(5) any act to create, perfect, or enforce against property of the debtor any lien to the extent that such lien secures a claim that arose before the commencement of the [bankruptcy];

(6) any act to collect, assess, or recover a claim against the debtor that arose before the commencement of the [bankruptcy];. . . .

§ 1129. Confirmation of plan

(b)(2) . . . [T]he condition that a plan be fair and equitable . . . includes the following requirements:

(B) With respect to a class of unsecured claims

(i) . . . each holder . . . receive[s] . . . property of a value, as of the effective date of the plan, *equal to the allowed amount of such claim*; or

(ii) [claims and interests junior to the dissenting class are eliminated.]

§ 726. Distribution of property of the estate [in chapter 7]

(a) . . . [P]roperty of the estate shall be distributed—

(1) first, in payment of claims of the kind specified in . . . Section 507 [such as administrative claims] . . .;

(2) second, in payment of any allowed unsecured claim . . . ;

(3) third, in payment of any allowed unsecured claim proof of which is tardily filed . . . ;

(4) fourth, in payment of [certain fines];

(5) fifth, *in payment of interest at the legal rate from the date of the filing of the petition,* on any claim paid under paragraph (1), (2), (3), or (4) of this subsection; and

(6) sixth, to the debtor.

¶ 1402: Interest Accruals

Time is money. The Bankruptcy Code stays the creditors' attempts to seize collateral or bring their unsecured claim to judgment and collect on the claim. While the stay is in place, the debtor tries to reorganize, and that reorganization takes time. Because creditors can't collect on their security or their debt, whether or not interest must be paid is a critical financial issue. Do the creditors get interest on their claims while their efforts to collect are stayed under § 362?

The answer is not a simple yes or no. The Bankruptcy Code's interest rate results come from a cross-current of policy issues, leading to overlapping and sometimes contradictory statutory provisions.

At least five interest payment contests are embedded in bankruptcy:

1. All creditors versus stockholders: do creditors of a solvent company get interest before the stockholders get anything?
2. Seniors versus juniors: do senior creditors get interest before juniors get principal?
3. Secured versus unsecured: do secured creditors get interest before unsecured get principal? Does it make a difference whether the secured creditor is over- or under-secured?
4. Guarantors versus the guaranteed: do guarantors have to make good on a creditor's claim for interest, even when the Code disallows the claim for interest?
5. High-interest creditors versus low-interest creditors: for insolvent bankrupts, do creditors with a high rate of interest in their contract do better than creditors with a low rate of interest?

To see these contests in a transactional, problem-based form, recall the Dieglom problem at ¶ 312. A summary balance sheet based on the firm's market value looks about like this when the petition in bankruptcy is filed:

Dieglom

$50M	Current liabilities:	$20M
	7% senior debentures:	20M
	3½% mortgage bonds:	20M
	14% subordinated debentures:	30M
		$90M

When the petition is filed what are the allowed amounts of the claims? While unpaid interest due from the bankrupt *before* the bankruptcy is an allowed claim, what about claims for post-petition interest? See § 502(b)(2). Do the allowed claims include interest that has not yet matured as of the date of the petition for reorganization?

Assume that reorganization takes five years or more, a longer than normal bankruptcy. During that time the firm has about $10 million income annually. After five years with some compounding, the firm will have retained about $60 million:

Dieglom

$110M	Current liabilities:	$20M+ interest
	7% senior debentures:	20M+$7M interest
	3½% mortgage bonds:	20M+$3.5M interest
	14% subordinated debentures:	30M+$21M interest
		$90M+31.5M interest

The stockholders propose that the creditors be paid their full principal amount, and that the stockholders get the $20 million excess beyond the $90M needed to pay the creditors their principal amount.

Stockholders' Plan of Reorganization for Dieglom

$110M	Current liabilities:	$20M
	7% senior debentures:	20M
	3½% mortgage bonds:	20M
	14% subordinated debentures:	30M
	Stockholders:	20M
		$110M

The financial creditors reject the shareholders' plan, which would not give any accumulated interest to the creditors. The trade creditors consent. The shareholders seek cramdown. (For now, ignore the fact that one of the creditors, the mortgagee, has security.) Who wins? See Bankruptcy Code §§ 502(b)(2) and 1129. Doesn't cramdown under § 1129(b)(2) tie to the *allowed amount* of the claim, an amount determined on the filing *date of the bankruptcy petition?* Isn't the statute constructed as if bankruptcy were nearly instantaneous, as if the debtor filed the petition in the morning, proposed the plan at lunch-time, and had the plan confirmed in the afternoon?

Do the creditors have room to maneuver and argue by using the predicate to § 1129(b)(2), that the requirement that the plan be fair and equitable *includes* payment of the allowed amount of the claim or wipe-out of the juniors?

If the creditors fail to convince the bankruptcy court that the concept of fair and equitable requires interest to be paid by bankrupt debtors that are solvent by the time a plan is confirmed, can they turn elsewhere in the Code for support? What result if the firm were liquidated? See Bankruptcy Code, § 726(a)(5). Does § 726(a) give the creditors an incentive to move the firm from chapter 11 to chapter 7? Could they import § 726 into chapter 11 via § 1129(a)(7)?

B. CREDITORS VERSUS STOCKHOLDERS

¶ 1403: Chaim Fortgang & Lawrence King, The 1978 Bankruptcy Code: Some Wrong Policy Decisions, 56 N.Y.U. L. Rev. 1148 (1981)*

Postpetition Interest

A routine principle that was developed under the case law construing the Bankruptcy Act of 1898 was that interest on claims ceased to accrue as of the date a bankruptcy petition was filed. . . . [T]here was no specific provision in the statute dealing with [any significant] postpetition interest. The courts, however, developed a policy that the accrual of interest should cease as a matter of convenience and efficiency in the administration of bankrupt estates; cessation avoided the necessity for recomputation of interest each time a distribution of dividends was made to creditors. In cases in which the assets of the debtor were insufficient to pay all of the claims of creditors, cessation did not change the actual amounts paid to creditors, since claims were paid on a pro rata basis. . . .

The drafters of the new Bankruptcy Code were not content to permit the judicially developed principle of convenience to continue. Instead, several sections of the Code explicitly deal with postpetition interest in technical detail. Specifically, § 502(b)(2) of the Code provides that a claim for unmatured interest is not allowable. The House and Senate committee reports accompanying the Code make clear that this provision requires disallowance of interest unmatured at the date of the filing of the petition, *including postpetition interest not yet due*. . . . Postpetition interest under the Code . . . explicitly is made a nonallowable part of a creditor's claim.

The nonallowability of such claims has important ramifications under the Bankruptcy Code. . . . Nonallowed claims are not entitled to any distribution in a case, whether it be a chapter 7 liquidation case or a chapter 11 reorganization case. Section 726 of the Code, which establishes the order of distribution of property of the estate for liquidation cases, includes as the second rung of the payment ladder "any allowed unsecured claim." . . . Pursuant to the "cramdown" provisions of § 1129(b)(2)(B), an unaccepting class of unsecured claims may be forced to accept a plan even if a class lower than it is to receive a distribution, as long as the unaccepting class receives property under the plan "equal to the allowed amount" of the claims of that class. . . .

Moreover, the concept of allowability is inflexible. Under the [old] Bankruptcy Act, courts would invoke the general principle that a creditor is entitled to full payment [even] if the convenience factor was not present. If an estate proved to be solvent, the notion that it would be inconvenient to recompute interest was not invoked. The rationale was that, in this instance, the nonpayment of postpetition interest would permit the return of property to the debtor while creditors were not being paid in full—a patently unjust result. Section 502(b)(2), on the other hand, appears absolute on its face. Section 502, read simply and applied exclusively, provides that postpetition interest is not an allowable part of a claim. This appears to be so even if the debtor's assets have a value in excess of all its liabilities including postpetition interest.

A. Chapter 7 Liquidation Cases

Under chapter 7, there is one exception, in section 726(a)(5), to the absolute rule of section 502(b)(2): If an estate is solvent, before the debtor is entitled to retain any property of the estate, creditors are required to receive postpetition interest in an amount computed at the "legal rate."

* * *

B. Reorganization Cases

Postpetition interest issues are of even greater significance and the problems created by the Code appear to be exacerbated in chapter 11 reorganization cases. A fundamental underpinning of new chapter 11 is that a successful arrangement should be the result of informed negotiations between the interested parties culminating in a consensually arrived-at chapter 11 plan. . . . Nevertheless, there are inevitably situations in which creditors cannot agree on a plan. This generally occurs when there are disparate views as to the enterprise value of the debtor or as to the type of plan that is in the best interests of the creditors. If a dissenting view is held by a creditor that is in a class by itself, in control of a class, or in a position to influence the voting of a class, acceptance of the plan may not be achievable on a voluntary basis. Thus, chapter 11 provides for the treatment of recalcitrant classes of creditors.

. . . [F]or a plan to be confirmed by the court, it must either be accepted by all "impaired" classes of creditors and equity security holders, or it must be capable of being crammed down pursuant to section 1129(b) of the code. This has serious implications for the recovery of postpetition interest.

1. [Best interests test under Section 1129(a)(7)]

* * *

[What about] section 1129(a)(7)(ii) . . . [?] Under that subsection, the confirming court must find that each holder of a claim or interest in a given class will receive or retain under the plan property having a value not less than that which such holder would have received or retained on account of such claim or interest had the case been administered under the liquidation provisions of chapter 7. This provision . . . bring[s] into play the distribution scheme set forth in section 726 as a minimum standard. That requirement needs to be satisfied, even if the class has accepted the plan, as long as there is a dissenting holder in the class. In other words, it cannot be waived by a class vote unless it is unanimous.[1]

* * *

2. Cramdown

Pursuant to section 1129(b) of the Code, when any impaired class of creditors or equity security holders does not accept the plan . . . the plan may nevertheless be confirmed by the court if (i) the proponent of the plan requests confirmation, and (ii) the court finds that the plan is "fair and equitable" as to the dissenting class. . . .

. . . [S]ection 1129(b)(2) provides that the phrase "fair and equitable . . . includes the following requirements" with respect to a class of unsecured claims: The court must find either that the plan provides the

---

[1] [Is there a better way to understand § 1129(a)(7) here? Is it that it cannot be waived by a class vote unless it is unanimous? Or is it that dissenters cannot be bound by the class vote? Those who assent are bound; the assenters though cannot bind the dissenters under § 1129(a)(7).—Roe.]

holders of a class of unsecured claims with property having a value at least equal to the allowed amount of their claims or that no class junior to the dissenting class will receive any distribution under the plan.

The operation of this provision can be seen in the following hypothetical case. Assume a situation in which a plan proposes to distribute to a class of unsecured creditors property having a value equal to the principal amount of their claims plus interest up to the date of the filing of the petition. Assume further that the plan provides for the equity holders to retain an interest in the debtor. May this plan be confirmed over the objection of the class of unsecured creditors on the ground that the dissenting class is receiving property equal to the full amount of its allowed claim? The allowed amount of the claim would not, by reference to section 502(b)(2), include postpetition interest. . . . Thus, the cramdown provisions of section 1129(b) may produce the same inequitable result that has been alluded to previously: . . . shareholders . . . may retain an interest in the debtor, while creditors of a concededly senior class are not receiving the full amount dictated by their contractual rights.

* * *

C. Significance of the Problem

It is not an adequate response to contend that because there will be few cases of solvency, the issue of postpetition interest has no practical significance. In the context of very large chapter 11 cases, depending on the length of the proceedings, solvency may not be terribly unlikely. Moreover, the way the new Code is written, the number of solvent debtors is likely to increase [because insolvency is not a prerequisite to filing for chapter 11]. . . . [T]here is a substantial potential for abuse by recalcitrant debtors in out-of-court workouts and by debtors going out of business who might seek to liquidate their businesses under the aegis of the Bankruptcy Code. Conceivably, solvent debtors could begin to use the Bankruptcy Code strictly for the purpose of reducing their debt service. This could be accomplished by extending a case over a protracted length of time, during which the debtor would obtain a direct subsidy from its creditors either through the complete forgiveness of postpetition interest or through a reduction in the rate of interest from the contractual rate to the statutory rate.

* * *

One solution may be for courts and creditors to exercise some control over the duration of cases. However, such control is impossible in most instances, particularly in large cases. Other possible remedies, such as allowing creditors to file their own plan after the lapse of the exclusivity period set forth in section 1121, allowing the appointment of a trustee to terminate the exclusivity period, or allowing interim distributions prior to a plan, are equally unrealistic. This is because of the historical predilection of bankruptcy courts to view debtors in a paternalistic manner—to routinely accept the positions propounded by frail debtors, especially when confronted with contested issues that may adversely affect the debtors' future viability. It is not at all unusual for a bankruptcy judge to permit delaying tactics so long as the debtor provides some reasonable justification. For example, debtors can easily stretch arguments about the amount of time and information they need to propose a plan and to negotiate with creditors. In short, there often is a built-in delay in the reorganization process that is compounded by the delays that ordinarily occur during all court proceedings. Because of the reduced postpetition interest rate, such delay could give solvent debtors the benefit of reduced debt service—a result that is not only unjust, but contrary to the aims of the Bankruptcy Code.

¶ 1404: Case Law, and Then Congress Acts

Fortgang and King note that "solvent debtors could begin to use the Bankruptcy Code strictly for the purpose of reducing their debt service." While that kind of problem did not seem to be common in the dozen years after their article came out, a similar one was: The bankruptcy occurs for legitimate operating reasons. For the year or two before bankruptcy, managers faced creditors who were trying to collect, managers felt harassed trying to come up with the cash to meet interest and principal payments, and dark clouds threatening foreclosure overhung managers' negotiations with creditors. Once the firm entered chapter 11, these clouds cleared and the managers saw sunshine: no creditor could harass the managers (due to the bankruptcy stay in § 362), managers did not usually have to scramble to come up with the cash to meet interest and principal payments, and interest did not need to be paid on basic claims. Life for the managers became much more comfortable.

Remember that § 502(b) does not include post-petition interest on the allowed claim and that § 1129(b)(2) uses the allowed amount of the claim as the value that must be given to a dissenting class (if lower ranking claims and interests are not wiped out). Congress in 1994 amended neither § 502(b)(2) nor § 1129(b). But it did say in the 1994 legislative history:

> If a plan proposed to pay a class of claims in cash in the full allowed amount of the claims, the class would be impaired [under § 1124, as we are now amending it] entitling creditors to vote for or against the plan of reorganization. [The plan] . . . can be confirmed [over] the vote of a dissenting class of creditors only if it complies with the "fair and equitable" test under section 1129(b)(2). . . .
>
> The words "fair and equitable" are terms of art that have a well established meaning under the case law of the Bankruptcy Act as well as under the Bankruptcy Code. Specifically, courts have held that where an estate is solvent, in order for a plan to be fair and equitable, unsecured and undersecured creditors' claims must be paid in full, including postpetition interest, before equity holders may participate in any recovery. [Citation to *Consolidated Rock*.]

Bankruptcy Reform Act of 1994, Section–By–Section Description, 140 Cong. Rec. H10752 (1994).

But if Congress wanted creditors to receive post-petition interest, why would it do so in such a convoluted way, by using legislative history to undermine the structure of the Code, and by referring to pre-Code cases? Wouldn't a simple addition to the Bankruptcy Code have resolved the issue definitively? What could explain why an easy-to-draft concept found its way into the legislative history, but not into the statute? Legislators' convenience? The possibility that an explicit provision would have more troubled getting passed? Moreover, a common mode for statutory interpretation is not to look to legislative history until one finds ambiguity or inconsistency in the statute itself. How unclear is § 502(b)(2)?

C. SENIORS VERSUS JUNIORS

¶ 1405: Subordination

Thus the creditors' strongest claim for post-petition interest against the debtor resides in the interpretation of the open-ended phrase, "fair and equitable," against the specific bar of a claim for "post-petition" interest in § 502(b)(2). More bankruptcy courts give post-petition interest to creditors of solvent bankrupts than not, but as of now no appellate court has definitively resolved the issue.

Most bankrupts are insolvent at the time a plan of reorganization is confirmed. So for now, put aside the question of whether the debtor must pay interest if the bankrupt turns out to be slightly solvent at the end of the bankruptcy proceeding. Consider now the contests for interest *between* creditor classes. The first contest that we shall examine is the contest between seniors and juniors.

What if the debtor's assets allow it to pay the seniors' principal in full, with a little more value spilling over to the juniors? Do the seniors get interest paid to them before the juniors get any principal repaid?

The second contest is in the setting of a guarantor of repayment: The creditor cannot get interest from the debtor (§ 502(b)). Does the guarantor have to pay the interest even though the Bankruptcy Code disallows the guaranteed's interest claim? The third contest is between the secured and the unsecured: does a secured creditor get interest during the period it is stayed from seizing its security?

To exemplify the first contest, the one between seniors and juniors, return to the Dieglom interest accrual problem, ¶ 1402. All creditor classes, except the senior debentureholders, now consent to forgoing their post-petition interest. The seniors dissent and turn to their bond indenture. See Drum Financial "Description of Debentures—Subordination of Debentures," ¶ 703. Under the Drum Financial indenture and the American Bar Foundation subordination provisions, can senior creditors obtain post-petition interest out of the subordinated creditors' principal? Isn't that the end of the senior vs. subordinate interest contest? See Bankruptcy Code § 510(a). Would the court's requiring that the juniors turn over their principal to make good on the seniors' claim for interest surprise the juniors? See *In re King Resources,* next.

¶ 1406: In re King Resources, Inc., 528 F.2d 789 (10th Cir. 1976)

The issue here to be resolved is whether the trial court erred in its determination that certain so-called senior lenders to King Resources Company, the debtor, were not entitled to interest from and after the date an involuntary petition was filed against the debtor under Chapter X of the Bankruptcy Act. Our study of the record leads us to conclude that the trial court did not err, and we therefore affirm.

* * *

The senior lenders in the present proceeding agree with the general proposition that in a bankruptcy proceeding an unsecured creditor, such as the senior lenders, cannot recover post-petition interest on a claim against the bankrupt. To escape the effect of this general rule the senior lenders emphasize that here they are not seeking post-petition interest from the debtor, and that should post-petition interest be allowed it would be at the expense of the debenture holders and not the debtor. Such result should obtain in the instant case, according to the senior lenders, because of certain subordinating language contained in the indenture agreement. The subordination provisions in the indentures in the present case read as follows:

> Upon any distribution of assets of the Company upon ... reorganization of the Company ... (a) The holders of all Senior Indebtedness shall first be entitled to receive payment in full of the principal thereof (and premium, if any) and interest due thereon before the holders of the Debentures are entitled to receive any payment on account of the principal of (or premium, of any) or interest on the Debentures. . . .

. . . [T]he subordination provisions make no specific reference to the question of post-petition interest. . . . [W]here the subordinating provisions are unclear or ambiguous as to whether post-petition interest is to be allowed a senior creditor, the general rule that interest stops on the date of filing of the petition in bankruptcy is to be followed. In [one prior case] appears the following pertinent comment:

> The district court's conclusion that the subordination provision contained in the debenture notes did not appropriately apprise the debenture note holders that their claims against the bankrupt would be subordinated to [the senior]'s demand for post-petition interest is not incorrect and, thus, is adequate to sustain its order denying [the senior]'s claim for post-petition interest. Certainly, in light of this conclusion of the district court, we cannot say that its refusal to allow post-petition interest constituted an abuse of the discretion it has with regard to the exercise of its equitable power.[10] If a creditor desires to establish a right to post-petition interest and a concomitant reduction in the dividends due to subordinated creditors, the agreement should clearly show that the general rule that interest stops on the date of the filing of the petition is to be suspended, at least vis-a-vis these parties. 491 F.2d at 844.

Footnote 10 in the above quotation from [a prior case] reads as follows:

[10] "It is manifest that the touchstone of each decision on allowance of interest in bankruptcy, receivership and reorganization has been a balance of equities between creditor and creditor or between creditors and the debtor." Vanston Bondholders Protective Committee v. Green, 329 U.S. 156, 165 (1946). *See* In re Magnus Harmonica Corp., 262 F.2d 515, 518 (3d Cir. 1959).

In the instant case the indentures do not "clearly show" that the senior lenders are entitled to post-petition interest at the expense of the debenture holders. Hence, . . . the trial court did not err or in any case abuse its discretionary powers in following the general rule that interest stops on the date of the filing of a petition in bankruptcy.

Judgment affirmed.

---

§ 510. Subordination

(a) A subordination agreement is enforceable in a case under this title to the same extent that such agreement is enforceable under applicable nonbankruptcy law.

Must the indenture "clearly show" that the seniors get *post-petition* interest from the juniors after 1978, when § 510(a) became law? For the first twenty years of § 510(a)'s life, bankruptcy courts continued the pre-Code rule of explicitness, looking for a clear statement in the indenture that the junior's principal was subordinated to the senior's post-petition interest, and several courts read the indenture at issue as not being sufficiently clear. In re Ionosphere, 134 B.R. 528 (Bankr. S.D.N.Y. 1991); In re Southeast Banking, 188 B.R. 452 (Bankr. S.D. Fla. 1995).

The 11th Circuit interpreted § 510(a) in 1998 as requiring that the subordination contract be enforced as it read. Nevertheless, it concluded that the required level of notice to juniors was an issue of state law, even as to post-petition matters. It thus certified the question of post-petition contract interpretation to the New York Court of Appeals. In re Southeast Banking Corp., 156 F.3d 1114 (11th Cir. 1998). The New York court answered that New York law "would require specific language in a subordination agreement to alert a junior creditor to its assumption of the risk and burden *of allowing the payment of a senior creditor's post-petition interest* demand." In re Southeast Banking Corp., 93 N.Y.2d 178 (N.Y. 1999). The state court seemed to feel itself a bit out-of-place as it was answering, as the court expressed it, an "unusually intermingled Federal State law question."

Perhaps the state court felt uncomfortable because it was in fact answering a federal bankruptcy question.

Here's why. If the 11th Circuit had run with its initially logical reading of § 510, would it have certified the question as to what New York law was *post-petition,* or, rather, what New York law was *in the absence* of a bankruptcy? Why might, or should, the source of governing law differ between pre-and post-petition interest?

Perhaps the courts were deferring to prior practice, as both the *Ionosphere* and *Southeast Banking* courts partly implied: financial parties expected post-petition explicitness, partly due to pre-Code decisions like *King Resources* and the no-interest rule of § 502(b)(2). Perhaps the courts were loath to upset financiers' expectations, regardless of what Congress said in § 510(a). But *King Resources* preceded the passage into law of § 510(a).

And the circuits have now split. The First Circuit ruled a half-dozen years later that § 510(a) abrogates the rule of explicitness in bankruptcy: the contract should be enforced in the same way in and out of bankruptcy. It criticized the 11th Circuit for certifying the question it had sent to the New York court.

> There is simply no reason to believe that the New York courts would apply the Rule of Explicitness outside the bankruptcy context. Accordingly, the Rule of Explicitness cannot hold sway. To find otherwise would do violence to the language of *section 510(a)* and set state and federal law on a collision course.

In re Bank of New England Corp., 364 F.3d 355 (1st Cir. 2004).

Then isn't the differing 11th Circuit result simply a trap for unwary senior creditors lacking up-to-date counsel on the bankruptcy decisions or a trap for creditors absent from the conference room where the debtor and the underwriters for the debentures draft the subordination clause? Consider this provision from the American Bar Association's Model Simplified Indenture:

> ***ARTICLE 11***
> ***SUBORDINATION***
>
> * * *
>
> **Section 11.03. *Liquidation; Dissolution; Bankruptcy.*** Upon any distribution to creditors of the Company in a liquidation or dissolution of the Company or in a bankruptcy, reorganization, insolvency, receivership or similar proceeding relating to the Company or its property:
>
> (1) holders of Senior Debt shall be entitled to receive payment in full in cash of the principal of and interest *(including interest accruing after the commencement of any such proceeding)* to the date of payment on the Senior Debt before [the Subordinated Debentureholders] shall be entitled to receive any payment of principal of or interest on [their Subordinated] Securities; and
>
> * * *

Or, consider how the alert senior creditor could make the post-petition interest accrual explicit when drafting the indenture's definitions. That's the way the ABA drafters handled the matter in the ABA's update to the indenture project, in Revised Model Simplified Indenture, 55 The Business Lawyer 1115, 1124–25 (2000):

> "*Senior Debt.*" Debt of the company whenever incurred, outstanding at any time except . . . Debt that by its terms is not senior in right of payment to the Securities. . . .

> "*Debt*" means . . . any obligation . . . to pay the principal of, premium of, if any, interest on (including interest accruing on or after the filing of any petition in bankruptcy or for reorganization relating to the company, whether or not a claim for such post-petition interest is allowed in such proceeding). . . .

Consider next this argument that the subordinated creditors might make: The seniors' claim for interest is *extinguished* by § 502(b)(2). The subordinated, hence, need *not* make the seniors whole on a claim that Congress has destroyed.

That is, could the juniors successfully argue that for them to be subordinated to something, that something, namely "Senior Indebtedness" of the debtor company, must exist? Since § 502(b)(2) *extinguished* the seniors' claim for post-petition interest, they argue, the claim doesn't exist. If it doesn't exist, it can't be Senior Indebtedness. The seniors have *no* claim for post-petition interest *against the debtor;* therefore, there's nothing left to which the juniors can be subordinate. The seniors' interest claim is gone and, hence, so is the juniors' obligation to subordinate themselves to it.

Could you reconceive the subordinated debentureholders as nonrecourse guarantors of the seniors' interest and use the guarantee cases, where similar arguments have been made? (A nonrecourse loan usually has the creditor obliged to claim against the pool of the debtor's assets, but leaves the creditor unable to claim against the debtor directly if that pool is insufficient to pay off the creditor.) That is, can we view the subordinated as having guaranteed the seniors' repayment, but with the guarantee payments limited to the proceeds that the subordinated get from the debtor?

With that analogy in mind (of the subordinated as a nonrecourse guarantor), we can better evaluate how the subordinated's extinguishment argument would fare, at least in the First Circuit. See *In re Bruno*, next.

D. GUARANTORS VERSUS GUARANTEED

¶ 1407: In re Bruno, 747 F.2d 53 (1st Cir. 1984)

Plaintiff United States . . . loaned a sum of money . . . to [the debtor]. Plaintiff received a note in the principal amount of the loan, with a stated rate of interest. It also, as consideration for making the loan, received personal guarantee agreements from defendants herein, the debtor's principal officers. In August 1981 the debtor filed a Chapter XI bankruptcy reorganization proceeding. Thereafter the fishing vessel, its principal asset, sank. The note, and accrued interest except for certain post filing interest, was ultimately paid from the hull insurance proceeds. Plaintiff sues defendants for the interest unpaid. The facts being agreed upon, both sides moved for summary judgment. The district court held for plaintiff, and defendants appeal. We affirm.

It might not surprise even a legally uninformed person who lent money on a note to learn that interest might no longer accrue after the debtor filed in bankruptcy, even though the note called for interest until the principal was paid. This is, in fact, the law. 11 U.S.C. § 502(b)(2). He might be surprised, however, to learn that one of the reasons given is that interest is a "penalty" for non-payment of the principal, and that there should not be a penalty when, by law, a bankrupt is forbidden to make payments. Vanston v. Green, 329 U.S. 156, 163 (1946). He would have wondered why interest was regarded as consideration for the loan, and did not become a penalty when the debtor's lack of assets prevented payment, but did become such when the lack of assets served as a basis for a petition in bankruptcy. He might wonder even more when, as here, guarantors used the penalty reasoning to assert that "it is unjust to make . . . guarantors pay a penalty for a detention of funds for which they are not to blame." Guarantors are never to "blame" for the debtor's lack of assets. Their liability is a matter of contract, not fault. Nor did the bankruptcy court forbid them to pay.

Apart from alleged "unjustness," defendants advance two arguments why they should not be liable. The first is that as the bankruptcy filing terminated the debtor's obligation for future interest, and the guarantors only undertook to guarantee the debtor's obligations, there had been no default. . . . But even if we accept defendants' contention that a simple guaranty is coextensive with the debtor's ultimate obligation, theirs was not a simple guaranty. Their agreement guaranteed payment in accordance with the note's original terms regardless of future events.

In addition to the general provision guaranteeing the obligor's performance (¶ 2), the guaranty contained further provisions.

> 3. The obligations, covenants, agreements and duties of the Guarantor under this Guaranty Agreement shall in no way be affected or impaired by . . .
>
> (f) the voluntary or involuntary . . . bankruptcy, assignment for the benefit of creditors, reorganization . . . or other similar proceedings affecting the Obligor or any of its assets; and
>
> (g) the release of the Obligor . . . from the performance or observance of any of the agreements, covenants, terms or conditions contained in . . . such instrument(s) by the operation of the law.

We have quoted more than is necessary in order to show the general breadth of defendants' undertaking. Nothing, however, could be more specific than the provisions of paragraph 3(g). One of the debtor's agreements was that interest was due until the principal was paid. While "the operation of law" relieved the debtor-obligor, the guaranty agreement expressly provided that it did not release the guarantors.

Defendants say that this undertaking, and the consequences, are, and would be, contrary to the provision of the bankruptcy act designed to prevent depletion of the funds available for other creditors by the payment of post-filing interest, for, if plaintiff recovers from defendants, defendants will claim over against the bankrupt estate. Thus there would be accomplished indirectly what cannot be accomplished directly. This contention is a perfect example of assuming the point. Nor does it wash. The debtor did not agree to repay the guarantors; it was not even a party to the guaranty agreement. A guarantor recovers from an obligor simply as a matter of being subrogated to the creditor's claim. In this case, quite apart from the fact that defendants' claim against the obligor would not arise until after bankruptcy, plaintiff, as defendants themselves vigorously assert, has no claim against the debtor for the post filing interest. Hence, when the guarantors paid such, there would be nothing for them to be subrogated to, and the bankruptcy proceedings could not be affected.

In sum, defendants promised that plaintiff would be paid in accordance with the terms of the note, "in no way . . . affected or impaired by . . . bankruptcy . . . [or] by the operation of law." They are liable on their contract, even though, because of bankruptcy, the debtor itself was relieved. Even if this were a matter of equity, which it is not, we see no reason why they should not be liable.

Affirmed.

¶ 1408: The Lawyers

Can lenders chart their way through the interest minefield without a lawyer?

E. SECURED VERSUS UNSECURED

¶ 1409: Adequate Protection for Secured Creditors

Does the Code entitle secured creditors to be better treated than unsecured creditors as to interest accruing during a reorganization?

§ 506. Determination of secured status

(b) To the extent that an allowed secured claim is *secured by property the value of which*, after any recovery under subsection (c) of this section, *is greater than the amount of such claim*, there shall be allowed to the holder of such claim, interest on such claim, and any reasonable fees, costs, or charges provided for under the agreement . . . under which such claim arose.

Section 506(b) benefits the oversecured creditor, giving it the claim in bankruptcy that other creditors, due to § 502(b)(2), lack. And what about the secured creditor who is not oversecured? Section 506(b) is unhelpful to the undersecured creditor.

Do other sections of the Bankruptcy Code protect the undersecured creditor? Does either the policy underlying these sections or their explicit wording demand that interest be paid to the secured creditor, even if the secured creditor is not oversecured?

Consider first the concept of adequate protection. For secured creditors who are stayed from seizing their security, § 362 of the Code entitles them to adequate protection:

§ 362. Automatic stay

(a) . . . [A bankruptcy petition] operates as a stay . . . of—

(3) any act to obtain possession of [the bankrupt's] property . . . ;

(4) any act to create, perfect, or enforce any lien against property of the [bankrupt];

(5) any act to create, perfect, or enforce against property of the debtor any lien to the extent that such lien secures a claim that arose before the commencement of the [bankruptcy];

(6) any act to collect, assess, or recover a claim against the debtor that arose before the commencement of the [bankruptcy]; . . .

(b) . . .

(c) . . .

(d) On request of a party in interest and after notice and a hearing, the court shall grant relief from the stay . . .

(1) for cause, including the lack of adequate protection of an interest in property of such party in interest; . . .

Section 362(d) requires the court to lift the stay if the stayed secured creditor is not adequately protected. And, if the secured creditor obtains "relief from the stay," then the secured creditor could seize the security, sell it, apply the proceeds to its loan, and then reinvest those proceeds, thereby obtaining a return on those funds.

But what protection is the secured creditor entitled to? Does a missed post-petition interest payment lead to the secured creditor being entitled to obtain adequate protection? Or is the creditor entitled only to protection from deterioration of the collateral? Is the secured creditor entitled to the time value of money, because the secured creditor could, were it not for the automatic stay, seize the collateral, sell it, and reinvest the proceeds at a market rate of interest?

In early cases under the Code, secured creditors argued that their bargain entitled them to seize their collateral and that they should be adequately protected from the business loss they would incur due to the Code's delaying them from realizing upon the security. They asserted that the court should order that the debtor compensate them for that delay, presumably by paying them what the undersecured creditor would otherwise get in interim interest payments.

§ 361. Adequate protection

When adequate protection is required under section 362 . . . , such adequate protection may be provided by—

> (1) requiring the trustee to make a cash payment or periodic cash payments . . . to the extent that the stay . . . results in a decrease in the value of [the protected entity's] interest in such property;
>
> . . .
>
> (3) granting such other relief . . . as will result in the realization by such entity of the indubitable equivalent of such [protected] entity's interest in such property.

In 1984, the Ninth Circuit held for the secured creditor, who sought to be paid interest under the adequate protection provisions, in In re American Mariner Indus., Inc., 734 F.2d 426 (9th Cir. 1984).

The holding faced doctrinal difficulties. In pre-Code cases, such as *Yale Express* and *Bermec,* the Second Circuit had held that the protection that must be afforded secured creditors who could seize their collateral was only against deterioration in the value of the collateral, not to make up for the lost time value of money. So consider the Ninth Circuit's statement:

> The secured creditor's right to take possession of and sell collateral on the debtor's default has substantial measurable value. The secured creditor bargains for this right when it agrees to extend credit to the debtor and both parties consider the right part of the creditor's bargain.

This argument has a surface-level, contractarian, benefit-of-the-bargain appeal. But putting contract together with the Bankruptcy Code makes the argument more complex: Does it make sense to consider the right a part of the creditor's bargain if Congress or the courts will not enforce that right? Does it make sense to think of the right to interest as part of the bargain if creditors know full well (under *Bermec* and *Yale Express* or interpretation of the Bankruptcy Code) that they *won't* get interest? If they know they won't, the creditors will adjust elsewhere: by not making loans to some supplicants or by charging a slightly higher interest rate to those to whom they do make the loans. That result may be inefficient, but is not intrinsically unfair.

The Ninth Circuit seemed to be making an expectations argument. But institutional creditors' expectations are formed in important part with reference to clear legal rules. If knowledgeable creditors understand that adequate protection means protection of the value of the collateral only (the pre-Code understanding from *Bermec* and *Yale Express*) then isn't *that* the bargain they get?

Presumably in the business world governed by *Bermec* and *Yale Express,* secured creditors took into account the inability to get interest in bankruptcy. So they either charged a premium to reflect that risk, ignored that inability as insignificant to their return, or swept businesses hovering near bankruptcy out from credit markets (because creditors did not want to take the bankruptcy risk in those deals where they could not readily be compensated with a prebankruptcy interest premium). A poorly functioning credit market for companies on the verge of bankruptcy may be a negative consequence of rules that mandate nonpayment of interest, but this is not an *expectations* argument.

Second, would § 506(b) add anything to the *over*-secured creditor's entitlement once the Ninth Circuit interpreted § 361 as it did in *American Mariner?*

The Circuits split, with some following *American Mariner* and giving interest as part of adequate protection under § 361, and others following the pre-Code cases, *Bermec* and *Yale Express.* The Supreme Court granted certiorari from the Fifth Circuit in *Timbers*, excerpted next.

Notice the (lack of) finance and policy arguments as to whether a decision one way or another would encourage delay in reorganization, help or hinder prebankruptcy reorganizations, facilitate prebankruptcy financing, or facilitate reorganizations that could not be financed with new investors.

Are those who drafted the Code really likely to have parsed the implications of the interplay between § 361, § 362 and § 506(b) as carefully as did the Supreme Court in *Timbers*?

¶ 1410: United Savings Ass'n v. Timbers of Inwood Forest, 484 U.S. 365 (1988)

SCALIA, J., delivered the opinion for a unanimous Court.

Petitioner United Savings Association of Texas seeks review of an en banc decision of the United States Court of Appeals for the Fifth Circuit, holding that petitioner was not entitled to receive from respondent debtor, which is undergoing reorganization in bankruptcy, monthly payments for the use value of the loan collateral which the bankruptcy stay prevented it from possessing. We granted certiorari to resolve a conflict in the Courts of Appeals regarding application of §§ 361 and 362(d)(1) of the Bankruptcy Code. . . .

I

On June 29, 1982, respondent Timbers of Inwood Forest Associates, Ltd., executed a note in the principal amount of $4,100,000. Petitioner is the holder of the note as well as of a security interest created the same day in an apartment project owned by respondent in Houston, Texas. . . . On March 4, 1985, respondent filed a voluntary petition under Chapter 11 of the Bankruptcy Code, in the United States Bankruptcy Court for the Southern District of Texas.

[Two weeks later], petitioner moved for relief from the automatic stay . . . on the ground that there was lack of "adequate protection" of its interest within the meaning of 11 U.S.C. § 362(d)(1). At a hearing before the Bankruptcy Court, it was established that respondent owed petitioner $4,366,388.77, and evidence was presented that the value of the collateral was somewhere between $2,650,000 and $4,250,000. . . . It was therefore undisputed that petitioner was an undersecured creditor. . . . The Bankruptcy Court . . . on April 19, 1985 . . . conditioned continuance of the stay on monthly payments by respondent, at the market rate of 12% per annum, on the estimated amount realizable on foreclosure, $4,250,000. . . . The District Court affirmed but the Fifth Circuit en banc reversed.

We granted certiorari to determine whether undersecured creditors are entitled to compensation under 11 U.S.C. § 362(d)(1) for the delay caused by the automatic stay in foreclosing on their collateral.

II

When a bankruptcy petition is filed, § 362(a) of the Bankruptcy Code provides an automatic stay of, among other things, actions taken to realize the value of collateral given by the debtor. The provision of the Code central to the decision of this case is § 362(d), which reads as follows:

> On request of a party in interest and after notice and a hearing, the court shall grant relief from the stay provided under subsection (a) of this section, such as by terminating, annulling, modifying, or conditioning such stay
>
> (1) for cause, including the lack of adequate protection of an interest in property of such party in interest; or
>
> (2) with respect to a stay of an act against property under subsection (a) of this section, if
>
> (A) the debtor does not have an equity in such property; and
>
> (B) such property is not necessary to an effective reorganization.

The phrase "adequate protection" in paragraph (1) of the foregoing provision is given further content by § 361 of the Code, which reads in relevant part as follows:

> When adequate protection is required under section 362 . . . of an interest of an entity in property, such adequate protection may be provided by—
>
> (1) requiring the trustee to make a cash payment or periodic cash payments to such entity, to the extent that the stay under section 362 of this title . . . results in a decrease in the value of such entity's interest in such property;
>
> (2) . . . ; or
>
> (3) granting such other relief . . . as will result in the realization by such entity of the indubitable equivalent of such entity's interest in such property.

It is common ground that the "interest in property" referred to by § 362(d)(1) includes the right of a secured creditor to have the security applied in payment of the debt upon completion of the reorganization; and that that interest is not adequately protected if the security is depreciating during the term of the stay. Thus, it is agreed that if the apartment project in this case had been declining in value petitioner would have been entitled, under § 362(d)(1), to cash payments or additional security in the amount of the decline, as § 361 describes. The crux of the present dispute is that petitioner asserts, and respondent denies, that the phrase "interest in property" also includes the secured party's right (suspended by the stay) to take immediate possession of the defaulted security, and apply it in payment of the debt. If that right is embraced by the term, it is obviously not adequately protected unless the secured party is reimbursed for the use of the proceeds he is deprived of during the term of the stay.

The term "interest in property" certainly summons up such concepts as "fee ownership," "life estate," "co-ownership," and "security interest" more readily than it does the notion of "right to immediate foreclosure." Nonetheless, viewed in the isolated context of § 362(d)(1), the phrase could reasonably be given the meaning petitioner asserts. Statutory construction, however, is a holistic endeavor. A provision that may seem ambiguous in isolation is often clarified by the remainder of the statutory scheme—because the same terminology is used elsewhere in a context that makes its meaning clear, or because only one of the permissible meanings produces a substantive effect that is compatible with the rest of the law. That is the case here. Section 362(d)(1) is only one of a series of provisions in the Bankruptcy Code dealing with the rights of secured creditors. The language in those other provisions, and the substantive dispositions that they effect, persuade us that the "interest in property" protected by § 362(d)(1) does not include a secured party's right to immediate foreclosure.

Section 506 of the Code defines the amount of the secured creditor's allowed secured claim and the conditions of his receiving postpetition interest. In relevant part it reads as follows:

> (a) An allowed claim of a creditor secured by a lien on property in which the estate has an interest . . . is a secured claim to the extent of the value of such creditor's interest in the estate's interest in such property, . . . and is an unsecured claim to the extent that the value of such creditor's interest . . . is less than the amount of such allowed claim. . . .
>
> (b) To the extent that an allowed secured claim is secured by property the value of which . . . is greater than the amount of such claim, there shall be allowed to the holder of such claim, interest on such claim, and any reasonable fees, costs, or charges provided for under the agreement under which such claim arose.

In subsection (a) of this provision the creditor's "interest in property" obviously means his security interest without taking account of his right to immediate possession of the collateral on default. If the latter were included, the "value of such creditor's interest" would increase, and the proportions of the claim that are secured and unsecured would alter, as the stay continues—since the value of the entitlement to use the collateral from the date of bankruptcy would rise with the passage of time. No one suggests this was intended. The phrase "value of such creditor's interest" in § 506(a) means "the value of the collateral." H.R. Rep. No. 95–595, pp. 181, 356 (1977); see also S. Rep. No. 95–989, p. 68 (1978). We think the phrase "value of such entity's interest" in § 361(1) and (2), when applied to secured creditors, means the same.

Even more important for our purposes than § 506's use of terminology is its substantive effect of denying undersecured creditors postpetition interest on their claims—just as it denies oversecured creditors postpetition interest to the extent that such interest, when added to the principal amount of the claim, will exceed the value of the collateral. Section 506(b) provides that "*[t]o the extent* that an allowed secured claim is secured by property the value of which . . . is greater than the amount of such claim, there shall be allowed to the holder of such claim, interest on such claim." (Emphasis added.) Since this provision permits postpetition interest to be paid only out of the "security cushion," the undersecured creditor, who has no such cushion, falls within the general rule disallowing postpetition interest. See 11 U.S.C. § 502(b)(2). If the Code had meant to give the undersecured creditor, who is thus denied interest on his claim, interest on the value of his collateral, surely this is where that disposition would have been set forth, and not obscured within the "adequate protection" provision of § 362(d)(1). Instead of the intricate phraseology set forth above, § 506(b) would simply have said that the secured creditor is entitled to interest "on his allowed claim, or on the value of the property securing his allowed claim, whichever is lesser." Petitioner's interpretation of § 362(d)(1) must be regarded as contradicting the carefully drawn disposition of § 506(b).

Petitioner seeks to avoid this conclusion by characterizing § 506(b) as merely an alternative method for compensating oversecured creditors, which does not imply that no compensation is available to undersecured creditors. This theory of duplicate protection for oversecured creditors is implausible even in the abstract, but even more so in light of the historical principles of bankruptcy law. Section 506(b)'s denial of postpetition interest to undersecured creditors merely codified pre-Code bankruptcy law, in which that denial was part of the conscious allocation of reorganization benefits and losses between undersecured and unsecured creditors. "To allow a secured creditor interest where his security was worth less than the value of his debt was thought to be inequitable to unsecured creditors." Vanston Bondholders Protective Committee v. Green, 329 U.S. 156, 164 (1946). It was considered unfair to allow an undersecured creditor to recover interest from the estate's unencumbered assets before unsecured creditors had recovered any principal. See id. at 164, 166. We think it unlikely that § 506(b) codified the pre-Code rule with the intent, not of achieving the principal purpose and function of that rule, but of providing over secured creditors an alternative method of compensation. Moreover, it is incomprehensible why Congress would want to favor undersecured creditors with interest if they move for it under § 362(d)(1) at the inception of the reorganization process—thereby probably pushing the estate into liquidation—but not if they forbear and seek it only at the completion of the reorganization.

* * *

Section 362(d)(2) . . . belies petitioner's contention that undersecured creditors will face inordinate and extortionate delay if they are denied compensation for interest lost during the stay as part of "adequate protection" under § 362(d)(1). Once the movant under § 362(d)(2) establishes that he is an undersecured creditor, it is the burden of the debtor to establish that the collateral at issue is "necessary to an effective reorganization." See § 362(g). What this requires is not merely a showing that if there is conceivably to be an effective reorganization, this property will be needed for it; but that the property is essential for an effective reorganization that is in prospect. This means, as many lower courts, including the en banc court in this case, have properly said, that there must be "a reasonable possibility of a successful reorganization within a reasonable time." 808 F.2d, at 370–371, and nn.12–13, and cases cited therein. The cases are numerous in which § 362(d)(2) relief has been provided within less than a year from the filing of the bankruptcy petition.

III

A

* * *

[P]etitioner contends that failure to interpret § 362(d)(1) to require compensation of undersecured creditors for delay will create an inconsistency in the Code . . . when the debtor proves solvent. When that occurs, 11 U.S.C. § 726(a)(5) provides that postpetition interest is allowed on unsecured claims. Petitioner contends it would be absurd to allow postpetition interest on unsecured claims but not on the secured portion of undersecured creditors' claims. It would be disingenuous to deny that this is an apparent anomaly, but it will occur so rarely that it is more likely the product of inadvertence than are the blatant inconsistencies petitioner's interpretation would produce. Its inequitable effects, moreover, are entirely avoidable, since an undersecured creditor is entitled to "surrender or waive his security and prove his entire claim as an unsecured one." United States Nat. Bank v. Chase Nat. Bank, 331 U.S. 28, 34 (1947). Section 726(a)(5) therefore requires no more than that undersecured creditors receive postpetition interest from a solvent debtor on equal terms with unsecured creditors rather than ahead of them—which, where the debtor is solvent, involves no hardship.

B

Petitioner contends that its interpretation is supported by the legislative history of §§ 361 and 362(d)(1), relying almost entirely on statements that "[s]ecured creditors should not be deprived of the benefit of their bargain." H.R. Rep. No. 95–595, at 339; S. Rep. No. 95–989, at 53. Such generalizations are inadequate to overcome the plain textual indication in §§ 506 and 362(d)(2) of the Code that Congress did not wish the undersecured creditor to receive interest on his collateral during the term of the stay. If it is at all relevant, the legislative history tends to subvert rather than support petitioner's thesis, since it contains not a hint that § 362(d)(1) entitles the undersecured creditor to postpetition interest. Such a major change in the existing rules would not likely have been made without specific provision in the text of the statute; it is most improbable that it would have been made without even any mention in the legislative history.

* * *

The Fifth Circuit correctly held that the undersecured petitioner is not entitled to interest on its collateral during the stay to assure adequate protection under 11 U.S.C. § 362(d)(1). . . . Accordingly, the judgment of the Fifth Circuit is Affirmed.

F. ORIGINAL ISSUE DISCOUNT

If the debtor issues a new $1,000 bond for which the creditor pays only $900, what is the allowed amount of the claim in the bankruptcy that shortly follows on the day of issuance, $1,000 or $900?

§ 502. Allowance of claims or interests

(b) . . . [T]he court, after notice and a hearing, shall determine the amount of such [filed] claim . . . as of the date of the filing of the petition, and shall allow such claim in such amount, except to the extent that—

* * *

(2) such claim is for unmatured interest[.]

The legislative history of § 502(b)(2) answers the question clearly: If the new $1,000 is issued for $900 in cash, and the debtor quickly goes bankrupt, the allowed amount of the claim would be $900, not $1000:

> Interest disallowed under [Section 502(b)(2)] includes postpetition interest that is not yet due and payable, and any portion of . . . interest that represents an original [issue] discounting of the claim, yet that would not have been earned on the date of bankruptcy. For example, a claim on a $1,000 note issued the day before bankruptcy would only be allowed to the extent of the cash actually advanced. If the original discount was 10%, so that the cash advanced was only $900, then notwithstanding the face amount of the note, only $900 would be allowed. If $900 was advanced under the note some time before bankruptcy, the interest component of the note would have to be pro-rated and disallowed to the extent it was for interest after the commencement of the case.

1. What is original issue discount?
2. So a $1000 bond, maturing ten months from now, is issued for $900 in cash. If the debtor goes bankrupt later in the day, the legislative history tells us what the allowed amount of the claim would be. If the debtor goes bankrupt in five months, about how much is the allowed claim?

G. WHAT RATE?

¶ 1411: Unsecureds With High Interest Rates Versus Those With Low Rates

1. In a multi-year reorganization does value shift among claimants?
   a. Debtor owes the bank $10 million, at prime (5%) plus another 5% per annum. Debtor owes on longer-term debentures of $10 million, due 2015, at 5% per annum. At bankruptcy debtor has $12 million in value.
   b. What are the allowed amounts of the claims?
2. a. If post-petition interest accrued at the pre-default contract rate, what would happen to the distribution proportions in a plan confirmed two years after the filing of the petition?
   b. Would accrual at the contract rate systematically favor short-term creditors that renegotiate their interest rate shortly be fore the bankruptcy filing?

Fortgang and King, supra, after noting that § 726(a)(5) provides creditors in liquidations with interest at the "legal rate," discuss alternatives to the standard notion (the post-judgment rate of interest): contract rate and market rate:

> . . . [N]either the statute nor the legislative history defines "legal rate." Legal rate may mean (i) the rate set statutorily by each state to be paid on judgments of its courts; (ii) the rate agreed to contractually by the parties . . . ; or (iii) the market rate of interest at the particular time.
>
> [Using the judgment rate yields] inequitable results. For instance, assume that a creditor's claim is based on a loan agreement that provides for the payment of interest at the rate of 15% per annum, that the statutory rate applied to the payment of judgments in that particular state is 7%, and that the estate turns out to be solvent. If there were more than sufficient value to provide for the liabilities set forth in the first four levels of priority in section 726, then, under section 726(a)(5), the creditor's claim would be allotted 7% interest from the date of the filing of the petition until the date of payment, instead of the 15% interest for which the creditor has bargained. The allowed portion of the creditor's claim would also include the principal unpaid balance plus interest at the rate of 15% up to the date of the filing of the petition. But . . . the creditor would be entitled to recover interest of only 7% for the entire period after the date of filing.

Courts usually use the judgment rate as the legal rate, although some have noted the disparity between a judgment rate that lagged market interest rates; those courts often then turned to the contract rate. Does § 506(b) use the contract rate for oversecured creditors? (Careful readers will note that the (lack of) placement of a comma in § 506(b) creates some ambiguity, an ambiguity that some lawyers will exploit.[2])

---

[2] In U.S. v. Ron Pair Enterprises Inc., 489 U.S. 235 (1989), the Supreme Court held that the phrase "interest on such claim" in § 506(b) was independent of the statute's phrase allowing payment for fees "provided for under the agreement."

¶ 1412: What Rate for the Oversecured Creditor?

The oversecured creditor under § 506(b) gets "interest on such claim, and any reasonable fees, costs, or charges provided for under the agreement under which such claim arose." Is that interest the pre-default contract rate, the post-default penalty rate, or something else?

In re Terry Limited Partnership, 27 F.3d 241 (7th Cir. 1994)

BAUER, Circuit Judge.

Following the declared bankruptcy of Terry Limited Partnership ("Terry"), its chief asset, an office building, was sold at a public auction. The sale generated revenue sufficient to repay the first and second mortgage holders. Equitable Life Insurance ("Equitable") was the second mortgage holder. According to Equitable's agreement with Terry, if Terry defaulted, interest would begin to accrue at a higher rate. At issue in this case is whether Equitable is entitled to receive this higher rate of interest for the period following Terry's default. The bankruptcy court awarded Equitable post-default interest at the higher contract rate. Having received nothing and not liking it, Invex Holdings, holder of a third mortgage on Terry's building, contends that Equitable's postdefault interest should only have accrued at the lower predefault rate. The district court affirmed the bankruptcy court's decision. We also affirm.

I.

. . . Terry executed a promissory note to Equitable . . . secured by a mortgage on the building. The note was payable at an interest rate of 14¼% per annum and was first due to mature on February 1, 1990. . . . In the event of default, interest was to accrue at the rate of 17¼% per annum. Invex Holdings's note was payable at the rate of 17¼%. . . .

Terry failed to meet its obligations under either note. . . .

. . . [T]he court ordered that the Society Bank Building be sold at a public auction. Invex Holdings purchased the building for $4,005,001. . . . The interest on Equitable's claim, both before and after default, was calculated at the predefault rate of interest. Equitable objected, contending that interest accrued between the time of Terry's default and the sale of the property should have been calculated at the higher default rate contained in its agreement. Invex Holdings [which held the next-ranking mortgage, objected].

In ruling that it was reasonable for Equitable to be paid the higher default rate of interest, the bankruptcy court relied on several considerations. First and foremost, the court noted the testimony of Invex Holdings's own expert witness, Donald Schefmeyer, who testified that it was routine for lenders to insist upon a higher default rate of interest because of the unforeseeable costs involved with collecting from debtors in default. According to Schefmeyer, a default rate of interest which exceeds the contract rate of interest by three percent was customary. . . . Second, the court attached significance to the fact that Invex Holdings's contract rate was equivalent to Equitable's default rate. Finally, the court emphasized the importance of enforcing, as close as possible, the parties' bargained-for contract rights. When Invex Holdings entered its agreement with Terry, it did so fully aware of Roosevelt's and Equitable's superior interests in the property and the extent of those interests. In short, Invex Holdings bargained for the risky position in which it later found itself. . . .

II

* * *

Crucial to the outcome of this case is the significance of the contract default rate. Section 506 of the Bankruptcy Code provides that a holder of an oversecured claim is entitled to "interest on such claim, and any reasonable fees, costs, or charges provided for under the agreement under which such claim arose." 11 U.S.C. § 506(b). The Supreme Court, in *United States v. Ron Pair Enters, Inc.*, 489 U.S. 235, 242 (1989), held that while an award of "fees, costs, or charges" is dictated by the loan agreement, the award of interest is not. The Court did not elaborate, however, as to how the interest rate in the agreement should be treated.

Bankruptcy courts have construed *Ron Pair* to require analyzing default rates based on the facts and equities specific to each case. . . . This does not render the contracted-for default rate irrelevant. . . . What emerges from the post-*Ron Pair* decisions is a presumption in favor of the contract rate subject to rebuttal based upon equitable considerations. . . .

Courts have found the presumption to be sufficiently rebutted in cases where the contract rate was significantly higher than the predefault rate without any justification offered for the spread. . . . In [two bankruptcy cases], contract default rates of thirty-six percent and twenty-five percent respectively were rejected because no evidence was presented to show that these rates were common in the market at the time of the transactions.

* * *

III.

. . . The decisions of the bankruptcy court and the district court awarding Equitable postdefault interest at the rate provided for in its agreement are

AFFIRMED.

¶ 1413: What Rate in Cramdowns?

When the court crams down a reorganization plan on a non-accepting creditor class under § 1129(b), the plan must award property of a value equal to the allowed amount of the non-accepting claims if any lower-ranking claim or interest is not wiped out. If the plan pays the crammed down creditor class in cash, it is easy to figure out if creditors are receiving property with a value equal to the allowed amount of their claims. But if the cramdown consideration comes in the form of a new note—that is, a new promise of future payment—things become more complicated. What is the appropriate interest rate for the replacement note that pays the crammed down creditors the present value of their claims?

In *In re MPM Silicones, LLC*, No. 531 B.R. 321 (S.D.N.Y. 2015), which lawyers often refer to as the *Momentive* decision, from the "M" in "MPM", the bankruptcy court approved a cramdown of dissenting noteholders' claims under Section 1129(b)(2). The plan proposed to pay the dissenters with replacement notes, and the dissenters contested the propriety of the replacement notes' proposed interest rates. Presumably a good case can be made that property of a value equal to the allowed amount of the claim would require the market rate of interest for the debtor. However, the court, relying in part on language in the Supreme Court's *Till* opinion, *Till v. SCS Credit Corp.*, 541 U.S. 465 (2004), rejected a market-based approach in favor of a "formula" approach, which starts with a riskless rate reflecting the duration of the replacement note and then adds a premium to reflect risks of non-payment unique to the debtor. The creditors complained that the court's approved formula rates were noticeably lower than the best rates at which the debtor could have borrowed in an arms'-length transaction. The case is still active as of December 2015, with an appeal filed with the Second Circuit.

CHAPTER 15

THE NEW FINANCE IN BANKRUPTCY

The past decades have seen an explosive growth of new financial instruments, such as derivatives and repurchase agreements ("repos"). Here we look at how these instruments play out in bankruptcy. First, we look at what they are and what business problems they seek to handle. We see how they're exempt from core aspects of chapter 11: the automatic stay, preference law, fraudulent conveyance law, and the debtor's § 365 right to assume or reject. These safe harbors, as they're called, have proven controversial and played a role in the 2008–2009 financial crisis.

A. DERIVATIVES AND REPO 101

¶ 1501: Basic Definitions

A *derivative* is an agreement between two parties, whose value is determined by (i.e., derived from) the price of something else. An American firm may face currency risk, for example, when it commits to buy and pay for inventory in Europe under contracts denominated in euros if the American firm plans to resell the inventory in the United

States in dollar-based contracts. The firm may wish to protect itself against a rise in the euro before it pays for the inventory. So it buys a currency derivative from, say, a bank. Similarly, airlines whose operating income heavily depends on the price of jet fuel often buy protection from a spike in oil prices via an oil derivative.

The mechanics for the oil derivative might be as follows. Say oil costs $100/barrel, and the airline wants to hedge against the risk of oil prices rising too much. The airline may buy a contract for the option to get delivery of 100,000 barrels of oil at the end of the year at a price of, say, $110/barrel. It pays $5 per barrel for that right, or $5 x 100,000. If the price of oil rises above $110/barrel, the counterparty (the other side to the contract) delivers the oil or, more likely, buys itself out from the obligation to deliver the physical oil, by paying the airline the difference between the price of oil at the end of the year and the $110 per barrel contract price.

A *swap* is a derivative embodied in an agreement between two parties to exchange cash flows at specified times in the future according to a prearranged formula. The most common type of swap is a "plain vanilla" interest rate swap: two parties agree to swap interest rate risks on a specified principal amount (referred to as the notional amount) over a specified period. Party A agrees to pay Party B a specified fixed rate of interest on the notional amount (on say $1 million); Party B agrees to pay Party A a floating rate (e.g., a standardized interbank lending rate) with respect to the same notional amount of $1 million. The $1 million notional amount does not change hands, but the differences in the interest rates do. When one party is very sensitive to short-term changes in interest rates, while the other is more focused on long-term rates, an interest rate swap is the way they can exchange risks.[1]

These derivatives exchange risks. By contrast, a *repurchase agreement*, or *repo*, is in substance a contract for a short-term loan, which is structured as a combination of (1) a sale of an asset by the borrower-seller to the lender-purchaser, followed by (2) the borrower's repurchase of that same asset from the lender at a price slightly higher than the original sale price. Most typically, the asset in play is a financial instrument—say, an obligation issued by the U.S. Treasury. The borrower, who owns the Treasury bond, sells it today and promises to buy it back at a slightly higher price in the future, often the next day. This repo seller also obtains a promise from its counterparty, the lender buying the Treasury bond today, to sell it back in the future, again often the next day, at an agreed-upon (slightly higher) price.

In loan terms, we can think of (1) the original sale price as the loan principal; (2) the Treasury bond as collateral; and (3) the spread between the original sale price and the slightly higher repurchase price as interest. The repo buyer is in substance lending to the repo seller. The buyer earns interest from the difference between the sale price and the higher repurchase price. The buyer-lender gets a near-cash deposit

[1] The definitions paraphrase those in Robert L. McDonald, Derivatives Market 1 (2d ed. 2006); René M. Stulz, *Should We Fear Derivatives?*, 18 Journal of Economics Perspectives 173 (2004); and John C. Hull, Options, Futures, and Other Derivatives 1 (8th ed. 2010).

of money that earns some interest but still gives the buyer quick, liquid access to the money.

REPURCHASE AGREEMENT

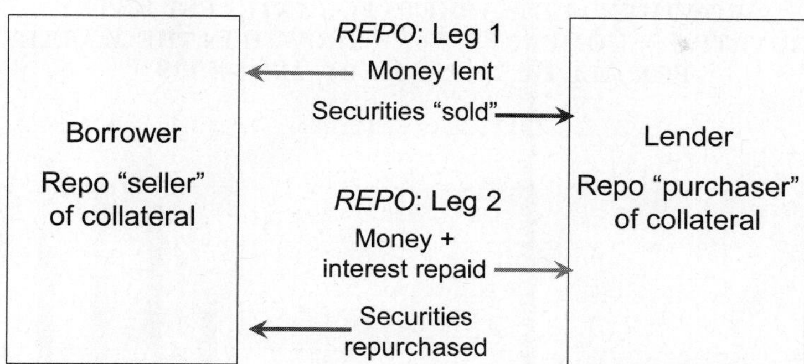

The mechanics of a repo deal might resemble the following: Say a corporation has $100 million in cash that will be used to expand the firm, but the operating people don't know when they will start using the cash. They're examining plans day-to-day. The chief financial officer wants to get the best return possible on the $100 million, but still have it ready, in cash, to invest tomorrow if that's what the operating people want to do. She might deposit the $100 million in a bank. But the size of the deposit would be much larger than the amount that the government insures (which tops out at $250,000). Worse, the deposit might have a low interest yield, and the CFO wants to get as much interest as possible while still preserving the ability to access the cash quickly. The corporation might buy a security with the appropriate maturity; for example it could buy a short-term, $100 million obligation of the United States, due in a week. Or the CFO might, if the return is better, have the firm do a repo with a bank that owns $100 million in U.S. Treasury securities that mature in several months. The corporation doesn't want to tie up its cash for those several months, so it isn't interested in an outright purchase of the securities, and the counterparty wants cash for at least a day. The corporation might get a higher interest rate with the repo transaction than by depositing the $100 million with the bank or by buying a short-term obligation of the U.S. Treasury, coming due in the next few days. That's because the corporation is taking a slice (in time) of a longer-term investment, of, say, a 30-year Treasury bond, and longer term investments usually pay higher returns than shorter-term investments. So, if the appropriate interest rate is 2% annually, the corporation could buy the longer-term U.S. Treasury securities for $100 million, with the other party agreeing to buy them back the next day for approximately $100,005,555 (which is the $100 million principal + a one-day slice or 1/360th of the $2 million annual interest).

¶ 1502: Economic Significance

The derivatives market has exploded in size over the past few decades. In December 2009, the notional value or the value of the underlying assets in derivatives contracts neared $700 trillion and the gross market value of all over-the-counter contracts outstanding was around $22 trillion. Figure 1 shows the growth in the interest rate swap market alone over the years compared to the growth in traditional debt.

GROWTH IN THE MARKETS FOR INTEREST RATE DERIVATIVES, COMPARED WITH GROWTH IN THE MARKET FOR ALL BUSINESS DEBT, 1994-2009

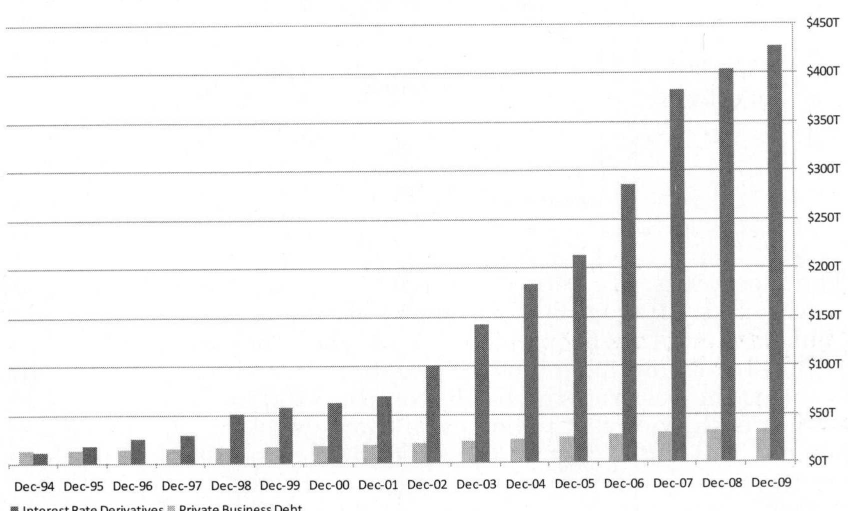

Repo also plays an integral part in the functioning of the financial system. The Federal Reserve uses repos extensively to implement monetary supply open market operations, and financial institutions rely on repos as a significant source of funding. On the eve of its collapse in 2007, at the beginning of the recent financial crisis, a quarter of Bear Stearns' capital came from overnight repo borrowing. Lehman Brothers, which failed later, had a third of its total assets coming in short-term repo debt.

As noted above, nonfinancial corporations also use derivatives to hedge market volatility, transferring risks to the parties most capable of bearing it.

Deep derivatives markets can reduce bankruptcy risk. Consider the following hypothesized mine owner and steelmaker. The mine owner can produce iron, which the steelmaker needs for its steel mill. The future market price of iron, however, is hard to predict. It could (say) either be $100/ton or $500/ton, each with equal likelihood. The steelmaker can run the steel mill profitably if iron costs $250/ton, but is bankrupt (given its general financing constraints) if the price of iron is $500/ton over the life of its mill. Conversely, the mine owner can run the mine satisfactorily if it can sell its iron for $250/ton, but is bankrupt (given its other constraints) if the price of iron is only $100/ton. Assume further that the chances are equally likely that iron will end up costing $100/ton as $500/ton over the lives of the mill and the mine. As such, either the mine or the mill will go bankrupt. Their own bankruptcy would be something they'd find unpleasant, but they'd also find that the other's bankruptcy would likely disrupt their sales or supply chain. (True, they could solve their pricing problem here by merging, but that's for another course in the curriculum; suffice it to say here that mergers don't always work nicely. Similarly, they could solve their pricing problem with a long-term contract for the miner to deliver iron to the mill at $250/ton; but such long-term contracts can't always be hammered out between parties, particularly parties that don't fully trust one another.)

Derivatives trading can ameliorate the mine owner's and the mill owner's risks. Each buys or sells rights to iron at $250/ton with derivatives traders in the commodity market. Each is confident that its counterparty will perform, because the counterparty is a big bank, indeed often a bank that the authorities deem to be "too-big-to-fail." The derivatives traders can absorb or diversify the risk of sharp moves in the price of iron better than either the mill or the mine. The mill and the mine can then run nicely, without fear of bankruptcy disrupting their operations.

B. SAFE HARBORS FOR DERIVATIVES AND REPOS

The Bankruptcy Code exempts derivatives and repos from core features of bankruptcy: preference law, fraudulent conveyance law, and the automatic stay. The favored creditors here also get strong setoff opportunities.

---

§ 101. Definitions

(47) The term "repurchase agreement" . . .

(A) means—

(i) . . . an agreement . . . for the transfer of [specified types of securities and loans, such as mortgages and obligations of the United States] . . . with a simultaneous agreement by [the] transferee to transfer [back] to the transferor . . . at a date certain not later than 1 year after such transfer or on demand, against the transfer of funds;

(53b) The term "swap agreement"—

(A) means—

(i) any agreement, including the terms and conditions incorporated by reference in such agreement, which is—

(I) an interest rate swap. . . ;

(II) a spot, same day-tomorrow, tomorrow-next, forward, or other foreign exchange, precious metals, or other commodity agreement;

(III) a currency swap, option, future, or forward agreement;

* * *

(VI) a total return, credit spread or credit swap. . . ;

* * *

(VIII) a weather swap, option, future, or forward agreement;

. . .

(ii) any agreement or transaction that is similar to any other agreement or transaction referred to in this paragraph and that—

(I) is of a type that has been, is presently, or in the future becomes, the subject of recurrent dealings in the swap or other derivatives markets (including terms and conditions incorporated by reference therein); and

(II) is a forward, swap, future, option, or spot transaction on one or more rates, currencies, commodities, equity securities, . . .

* * *

(v) a master agreement that provides for an agreement or transaction referred to in clause (i), [or] (ii). . . .

§ 362. Automatic stay

(b) The filing of a petition . . . does *not* operate as a stay—

(6) under subsection (a) of this section, of the exercise by a . . . financial institution . . . of any contractual right . . . to offset or net out any termination value, payment amount, or other transfer obligation arising under or in connection with 1 or more such contracts, including any master agreement for such contracts;

(7) under subsection (a) of this section, of the exercise by a repo participant or financial participant of any contractual right . . . under any security agreement or arrangement or other credit enhancement forming a part of or related to any repurchase agreement, or of any contractual right . . . to offset or net out any termination value, payment amount, or other transfer obligation arising under or in connection with 1 or more such agreements, including any master agreement for such agreements. . . ;

* * *

(17) under subsection (a) of this section, of the exercise by a swap participant . . . of any contractual right . . . under any security agreement . . . related to any swap agreement. . . .

§ 365. Executory contracts and unexpired leases

(e)(1) Notwithstanding a provision in an executory contract . . . an executory contract . . . of the debtor may not be terminated . . . at any time after the commencement of the case solely because of a provision in such contract . . . that is conditioned on ---

(A) . . . insolvency . . . ;

(B) the commencement of a case under this title. . . .

§ 559. Contractual right to liquidate, terminate, or accelerate a repurchase agreement

The exercise of a contractual right of a repo participant . . . to cause the liquidation, termination, or acceleration of a repurchase agreement because of a condition of the kind specified in section 365(e)(1) . . . shall not be stayed, avoided, or otherwise limited by operation of any provision of this title . . . .

---

1. Section 559 similarly safe harbors swap agreements. Note the scope of the exception from baseline bankruptcy practice: "shall not be stayed, avoided, or otherwise limited . . . ."
2. Note the differing application of the automatic stay to ordinary loans and to financings via repo. Note the differing application of the automatic stay to a supply contract for, say, oil and a derivatives contract keyed to changes in the price of oil.
3. We can think of the special treatment for derivatives and repos as similar to the treatment parties seek for special purpose vehicles. See ¶¶ 815–816. It's a super-charged variety of separating out risks and liabilities.
4. Consider an investment-grade company that does derivatives deals. Counterparties do not ask the company to post collateral to back up its derivatives trades because the company is of such high financial quality. But they have in their derivatives agreement an obligation from the company to post collateral if it loses its investment grade rating. The derivatives contracts move against the investment grade company. In derivatives language, the company is out-of-the-money. Later, it loses its investment grade rating and posts collateral. Within 90 days of the posts, it files for bankruptcy.

   Are the posts preferential? If you're uncertain, re-read § 547. But even if the posts are preferential, are they exempt from preference law? See § 546(f)–(g). Is there a safe harbor from ordinary preferences and fraudulent conveyances?

---

§ 546. Limitations on Avoiding Powers

(f) Notwithstanding sections . . . 547, 548(a)(1)(B), and 548(b) of this title, the trustee may not avoid a transfer made by or to (or for the benefit of) a repo participant . . . in connection with a repurchase agreement and that is made before the commencement of the case . . . .

> (g) Notwithstanding sections . . . 547, 548(a)(1)(B), and 548(b) of this title, the trustee may not avoid a transfer made by or to (or for the benefit of) a swap participant . . . in connection with any swap agreement and that is made before the commencement of the case . . . .

C. DEVELOPMENT OF THE SAFE HARBORS

¶ 1503: Early Treatment

In the early 1980s, a bankruptcy court treated a repo as a simple secured loan, whose characteristics it resembles (and indeed, repo parties still call the security sold the "collateral"). In the bankruptcy of Lombard-Wall, a securities dealer, the judge said that "[s]ince Lombard[, the bankrupt,] requires immediate turnover of all of the Securities in order to accomplish a reorganization, turnover [to Lombard] of the Securities is required." 23 B.R. 165, 166 (Bankr. S.D.N.Y. 1982). He stopped Lombard-Wall's counterparties from seizing and liquidating the securities, effectively applying the automatic stay to the repo transaction. Perhaps because it seemed obvious to him that a repo was a secured transaction and no more than that (i.e., not a true sale), he did not articulate his rationale, but by freezing the securities held by Lombard-Wall's repo counterparties, he treated repos as secured loans, not straight sales. As the counterparties to repo agreements were usually large banks and, often enough, the Federal Reserve, this early attempt to characterize them as secured loans ran into strong opposition. The derivatives industry turned to Congress.

¶ 1504: Legislative History and Justification for the Safe Harbors

The legislative history to the safe harbors indicates a concern with contagion: one derivatives- or repo-heavy institution might fail and, if unable to make good on its own derivatives and repo contracts, induce the failure of its counterparties:

> It is essential that stockbrokers and securities clearing agencies be protected from the issuance of a court or administrative agency order which would stay the prompt liquidation of an insolvent's positions, because market fluctuations in the securities markets create an inordinate risk that the insolvency of one party could trigger a chain reaction of insolvencies of the others who carry accounts for that party and undermine the integrity of those markets.[2]

And, in later expansions of the derivatives and repo safe harbors, Congress again emphasized the rationale that it was protecting counterparties:

> [C]ounterparties could be faced with substantial losses if forced to await bankruptcy court decision on assumption or rejection of financial transaction agreements. Unlike ordinary leases or executory contracts, where the markets change only gradually, the financial markets can

---

[2] 128 Cong. Rec. S15981 (daily ed. July 13, 1982) (statement of Senator Dole).

> move significantly in a manner of minutes. The markets will not wait for a court decision. . . . There is a clear need for Congress to assure counterparties that they will be able to terminate these agreements and exercise contractual liquidation and netting rights if a party to the agreement files for bankruptcy relief.[3]

The main "micro" rationale for the special treatment is that repos and derivatives cannot handle the risk of delay and, to accommodate worthwhile transactions, they deserve exception from core bankruptcy rules, as they cannot operate smoothly, derivatives and repo market supporters state, if subject to the bankruptcy basics of §§ 362, 365, 547, 548—the automatic stay, the debtor's right to assume or reject, preference law, and fraudulent conveyance law. The main "macro" rationale for the special treatment is the management of systemic risk: without the safe harbors, the thinking goes, failure in one financial firm will spread to another firm, leaving the entire financial system tottering. Allowing derivative counterparties to quickly liquidate their contracts with the bankrupt firm thereby restrains the losses to one firm and prevents contagion. The 1980s safe harbor principally applied to U.S. Treasury securities. By 2009, about half of the repo'd securities were of mortgage pools.

Consider practical and political realities. Professor Kettering argues that the legislative developments of the safe harbor provisions show that the products became "too big to fail," with strong interests protecting and expanding the safe harbors:

> The repo experience . . . suggests that if a financial product with shaky legal underpinnings becomes sufficiently well established, those who are invested in the success of the product may find powerful allies in the financial regulators, who may lobby both judges (by intervening as amici curiae in support of the product) and legislatures (by supporting legislation to validate the product). The Federal Reserve . . . intervened in both of these ways to make the world safe for repos. It is true that the Federal Reserve had a direct interest in supporting the liquidity of the repo markets in U.S. government and federal agency securities, in which markets it regularly deals for the purpose of implementing monetary policy. But, beyond that, its reasons for intervening included a desire to preserve a product that, in its eyes, had grown too big to fail. . . .
>
> What motivates financial regulators to support a widely-used financial product that has shaky legal underpinnings? A possible answer would invoke the theory of agency capture, which posits that regulatory agencies tend to become pawns of the firms they regulate. . . .
>
> An alternative answer would take the financial regulators at their word when they say that their actions are motivated by a desire to minimize systemic risk to the financial markets. . . .

Kenneth C. Kettering, *Securitization and Its Discontents: The Dynamics of Financial Product Development*, 29 Cardozo Law Review 1553, 1645–47 (2008).

---

[3] 135 Cong. Rec. S1414 (daily ed. Feb. 9, 1989) (statement of Senator DeConcini).

¶ 1505: Policy Skepticism

Could the safe harbors exacerbate the systemic risks that they are intended to reduce? First off, the safe harbors could cause the very runs on the institutions that the safe harbors are extolled as slowing down. If the stronger parties aren't subject to the automatic stay or preference law, they could seize and liquidate their cash and near-cash collateral, sapping a failing financial institution of the liquidity it needs to survive. Bear Stearns faced a run on its repo financing before it was forced to merge with a stronger bank. AIG, the giant insurer that was a big player in the derivatives market, faced a run of required collateral posts when it lost its investment grade rating.

Second, the safe harbors may simply transfer risk elsewhere in the weakened firm's capital structure. Many of the safe harbors work like setoff does, as described at the end of Chapter 12. The parties that set off do better, but others face losses. For major financial institutions, the missing creditor is effectively the United States, which backs up too-big-to-fail institutions and too-big-to-fail financial markets, like the repo market.

Third, the safe harbors may incentivize inefficient activity by weakening market discipline. Repo and derivatives participants need not assess the riskiness of their counterparties to the extent that the safe harbors protect them. Weak financial institutions can therefore continue to find willing counterparties. With the safe harbors, stronger institutions need not be overly concerned that their weaker counterparties will fail. As one example, when Bear Stearns failed at the beginning of the financial crisis, it had a quarter of its total liabilities in short-term repos, an amount about eight times its equity capital at risk.

Ed Morrison, Mark Roe, and Christopher Sontchi argue, in *Rolling Back the Repo Safe Harbor*, 69 Business Lawyer 1015 (2014), that whatever the theoretical pluses and minuses of the safe harbors promoting systemic safety, they were unable to arrest the run on repo during the 2008–2009 financial crisis:

> The repo safe harbors exacerbated the financial crisis of 2007-2009 by encouraging the use of short-term repo financing by major American financial firms. The bulk of repo volume is overnight and the vast majority has a maturity of less than three months. This expansion of repo led that market to use securities that could not, and did not, retain their value in the crisis, thereby worsening the crisis and weakening financial firms and markets. The broad expansion of short-term repo, particularly repos of mortgage-backed securities, made major American financial firms more sensitive to financial shocks, more sensitive to disruption in the housing market, and more likely to propagate those shocks through the financial system via rapid close-outs, such as those that induced massive government backing of the financial system in 2007-2009. That government backing included a guarantee of the money market industry after the Reserve Primary Fund broke the buck in the wake of Lehman's failure, the rescue of AIG after the Lehman failure, the bailout of government agencies—Fannie Mae and Freddie Mae—that issue widely-repo'ed securities, and the Federal Reserve's Primary Dealer Credit Facility—sized in the tens of bil-

lions of dollars—to support the repo market. This wide and deep governmental support makes clear that, although it is often mistakenly thought (particularly by industry representatives) that the safe harbors *mitigate* systemic risk, the reality is that the safe harbors both (1) make too many core financial institutions more fragile, by facilitating their relying on short-term debt that is unstable in a crisis and (2) shift the epicenter of systemic risk to other sectors of the financial market, particularly after the government buttresses the safe-harbored market.

Roe and Adams point out that the safe harbors did not prevent a chaotic close-out of Lehman Brothers derivatives portfolio when the investment bank failed and by allowing immediate termination seems to have contributed to further losses to Lehman and disruption in the world-wide derivatives market. Mark Roe & Stephen Adams, *Restructuring Failed Financial Firms in Bankruptcy*, 32 Yale Journal on Regulation 363 (2015).

On policy skepticism generally, see Franklin Edwards & Edward Morrison, *Derivatives and the Bankruptcy Code: Why the Special Treatment?,* 22 Yale Journal on Regulation 91 (2005); Frank Partnoy & David A. Skeel, *The Promise and Perils of Credit Derivatives,* 75 University of Cincinnati Law Review 1019 (2007); Richard Squire, *Shareholder Opportunism in a World of Risky Debt,* 123 Harvard Law Review 1151 (2010); Stephen Lubben, *Repeal the Safe Harbors,* 18 American Bankruptcy Institute Law Review 319 (2010).

¶ 1506: Mark J. Roe, The Derivatives Market's Payment Priorities as Financial Crisis Accelerator, 63 Stanford Law Review 539, 541–43 (2011)

[B]ankruptcy priority [for derivatives and repo players] perniciously weakens market discipline in the derivatives and repo markets because the stronger counterparties know that they often enough will be paid even if their derivatives or repo counterparty fails. Were the Bankruptcy Code superpriorities not so broad, [AIG, Bear Stearns, and Lehman Brothers'] financial trading partners would have anticipated that they might not be paid if they had weak counterparties that failed. Understanding this, they would have been further incentivized to lower their exposure to a potential failure of Lehman, AIG, or Bear. . . . [E]ach failed firm would itself have been incentivized [much earlier] to substitute away from [its] own risky, often overnight financing and toward a stronger balance sheet to better attract trading partners. . . .

. . . Th[e weakened market incentives are] the downside of favoring the derivatives and repo markets in bankruptcy. But risk-free investments with a very high bankruptcy priority have major efficiency potential. Superpriority investment channels can lower information and negotiation costs for lenders and borrowers, facilitating financing flows that otherwise would not occur. Such efficient flows, if they could proceed without imposing costs on other parties or on the financial system and the economy, deserve a supportive legal framework. The problem, though, is that the major superpriority [safe harbor] vehicles come packaged with systemically dangerous consequences, because systemically central institutions disproportionately use the bankruptcy-safe package. And, while a low-risk channel is supported, some major part of that risk ends up borne by the United States as backer of major, too-big-to-fail financial institutions. If we could separate efficient flows from systemically dangerous flows—and then allow the first, while restricting the second—we could strengthen finance in two dimensions. But if we cannot separate the efficient from the dangerous, we need to choose.

[When the early exceptions were accorded to derivatives and repos, it would have been hard to predict the derivatives and repo markets' explosive growth, such that the size of those markets could overwhelm vital financial institutions.]

D. CONGRESSIONAL REACTION AFTER THE 2007–2008 FINANCIAL CRISIS

In 2009, Congress passed the Dodd-Frank Wall Street financial reform act in response to the financial crisis. It did not amend the Bankruptcy Code's safe harbors. However, financial institutions that might have been subject to the Code's derivatives and repo rules are now subject to resolution by regulators, if the regulators deem the institution to be systemically vital. (Banks aren't eligible for chapter 11, for example, but their holding companies and affiliates are. Dodd-Frank made it possible for regulators to take the bank holding company and affiliates out from the bankruptcy orbit and into the bank regulatory orbit.)

However, the treatment of derivatives and repos will be essentially the same as before 2009 for such financial institutions that are moved from chapter 11 to bank-type resolution. Dodd-Frank reintroduces a stay, but it is short. Regulators can stay the non-bankrupt counterparties of the failing financial institution, but only for 24 hours. During that time, they can transfer the derivatives book to a new institution, but they must do so by transferring all the transactions between the bankrupt institution and the counterparty, effectively still netting out the counterparty's losses with its gains. The similarities between the Dodd-Frank resolution and the Code are discussed in Douglas G. Baird & Edward R. Morrison, *Dodd-Frank for Bankruptcy Lawyers*, 19 American Bankruptcy Institute Law Review 287 (2011). However, because neither Dodd-Frank nor the Code allows for the derivatives portfolio of a major derivatives dealer to be broken up, because the act preserves the full range of setoff rights, the possibility of a government bailout does loom large.

E. THE EMPTY CREDITOR

Derivatives can affect the incentives and bona fides of out-of-bankruptcy workouts and in-bankruptcy voting. If a creditor owed $1,000 has also purchased derivative securities under which it would profit more if the firm failed, then it has reason to vote against the restructuring. Consider this description of the workout and eventual bankruptcy of CIT, a major consumer financial firm:

> [O]ver-hedged creditors are rumored to have prevented the out-of-bankruptcy restructuring of CIT Group, Inc., a major financial services company. In the fall of 2009, CIT launched a debt exchange offer to reduce its debt and stave off bankruptcy. The transaction would have reduced the face value of creditors' claims but promised higher actual payments by preventing bankruptcy and thereby preserving value in CIT. At the time, it was widely believed that a bankruptcy filing would greatly harm a financial services company like CIT, as customers would withdraw deposits and draw down credit lines. Some creditors, however, allegedly possessed credit insurance for amounts higher than their debt claims against CIT. One major creditor, Goldman Sachs was said to be over-insured to the extent that it would gain $1 billion if CIT filed for bankruptcy. If true, these over-insured creditors rank not only had nothing to gain from the proposed exchange offer, but would lose the benefit of their over-insurance if the proposed transaction successfully averted bankruptcy. CIT's creditors rejected the exchange offer, and the company filed for bankruptcy.

Holger Spamann, Derivatives and Corporate Governance: Over–Hedging, Negative Voting, and Counterparty Incentives 6–7 (Harv. Law School working paper, Jan. 18, 2011).

Inside bankruptcy, § 1126(e) authorizes bankruptcy courts to designate votes as not having been cast in good faith, which then excludes the votes. And in In re DBSD North America, Inc., 421 B.R. 133, 143 n.44 (Bankr. S.D.N.Y. 2009), *aff'd*, 634 F.3d 79 (2d Cir. 2011), the court designated votes of one bankruptcy player because it had a strategic interest in preventing a buyout in chapter 11. (Dish Network, the satellite company, had obtained the votes of the First Lien Debt after DBSD filed for bankruptcy, seeking to obtain control over DBSD as a strategic asset.) In re DBSD N.A., Inc., 634 F.3d 79, 87–88 (2d Cir. 2011). But for parties to complain about a bad-faith, conflicted vote to the judge, the parties must know that some of their peer creditors are conflicted. Without adequate disclosure mechanisms in place, they cannot readily find out.

Both the in-bankruptcy and out-of-bankruptcy derivatives-induced conflicts have some natural tendency to a contractual self-correction: the financiers selling the credit insurance to the conflicted creditor do not want an inefficient bankruptcy. Hence, over time one might expect that they could insist on contractual correctives, such as that they automatically re-acquire voting power in specified conflict situations.

CHAPTER 16

DEBTOR-IN-POSSESSION FINANCING

¶ 1601: Operating the Business in General

Business continues after the company enters chapter 11. It'll often be a year or more before the bankruptcy is over, with a confirmed reorganization plan in place. During that time the debtor-in-possession runs the business and typically needs fresh cash to run it well.

¶ 1602: Operating the Business, Getting Inventory

Most businesses need to buy something, transform that something, and sell that something at a profit. A retailer needs to buy merchandise to sell; an airline needs to buy fuel for the planes and food for the passengers. Vendors usually ship such goods in on credit, expecting to be paid in a few days or a few weeks. Vendors frequently insist that weak customers pay cash on delivery. But the bankrupt is usually cash-strapped. The Code strengthens the bankrupt company's ability to buy.

Sections 503(b) and 507(a)(1) make an expense of administering the bankruptcy a priority claim, coming before prebankruptcy nonsecured creditors. Credit obtained in the ordinary course of business, such as when a vendor ships goods to the bankrupt and expects to be paid within a few weeks, is entitled to this administrative expense priority (§ 364(a)). This priority usually makes it safe for vendors to ship goods to a bankrupt customer.

Why isn't the administrative priority absolutely safe for the vendor, absolutely assuring that the vendor will be repaid in full? First off, the reorganization might fail: the firm may do so badly and lose so much value during the bankruptcy that it can't even pay off its administrative expenses, such that the bankrupt is administratively insolvent. The judge isn't a guarantor. Second, if secured creditors obtained "adequate" protection (when they were stopped from seizing their security) and that "adequate" protection turns out to be inadequate, then the inadequately protected secured creditor's "administrative" expense claim comes ahead of the ordinary vendor's administrative expense claim. Third, the vendor's shipment must be an ordinary course business event. Fancy terms may deny the vendor administrative expense treatment (and the court may let the claim sink to a run-of-the-mill prepetition unsecured claim). Fourth, some creditors, usually those providing new financing to the debtor-in-possession, can get a superpriority claim that must be paid before other administrative expenses.

¶ 1603: Credit Outside the Ordinary Course of Business

These administrative priority provisions for buying new goods help the debtor operate, but many bankrupts still lack cash and, if they are to survive, need to raise fresh cash immediately after going bankrupt. They might have to borrow money in a new, special loan facility. The credits will be outside the ordinary course of business—and hence not entitled to regular § 364(a) administrative priority obtained for debts incurred when running the business in the ordinary course. But the bankrupt needs those funds to operate. Without the court giving those new loans an administrative priority, it will not get them.

The creditor can get administrative expense priority for its new loan, but only after notice and a hearing (§ 364(b)). The notice provisions allow the affected creditors to object and try to convince the court not to allow the bankrupt to take the out-of-ordinary-course action if they think the new, prioritized DIP loan would hurt their claims.

What if the debtor's potential DIP lender says that the debtor is in such sad shape that the creditor won't lend unless it gets a superpriority above *all* other administrative expenses. It wants assurance that it will come ahead of the amounts due vendors who shipped ordinary course merchandise into the stores, and that it will be prior to the amounts due to any other creditors who (after court order) made out-of-the-ordinary-course extensions of credit. Section 364(c) allows the court to give a creditor a superpriority over any or all administrative expenses. Section 364(d) goes further.

---

§ 364. Obtaining credit

(a) If the trustee is authorized to operate the business of the debtor under [chapter 11], the trustee may obtain unsecured credit and incur unsecured debt in the ordinary course of business allowable under section 503(b)(1) of this title as an administrative expense.

(b) The court, after notice and a hearing, may authorize the trustee to obtain unsecured credit or to incur unsecured debt other than under subsection (a) of this section, allowable under section 503(b)(1) of this title as an administrative expense.

(c) If the trustee is unable to obtain unsecured credit allowable under section 503(b)(1) of this title as an administrative expense, the court, after notice and a hearing, may authorize the obtaining of credit or the incurring of debt—

(1) with priority over any or all administrative expenses of the kind specified in section 503(b) or 507(b) of this title;

(2) secured by a lien on property of the estate that is not otherwise subject to a lien; or

(3) secured by a junior lien on property of the estate that is subject to a lien.

(d) (1) The court, after notice and a hearing, may authorize the obtaining of credit or the incurring of debt secured by a senior or equal lien on property of the estate that is subject to a lien only if

(A) the trustee is unable to obtain such credit otherwise; and

(B) there is adequate protection of [the previously-secured creditor].

§ 503. Allowance of administrative expenses

(b) After notice and a hearing, there shall be allowed, administrative expenses . . . including

(1)(A) the actual, necessary costs and expenses of preserving the estate, including . . . wages, salaries, and commissions for services rendered after the commencement of the case . . . .

§ 507. Priorities

(a) The following expenses and claims have priority in the following order:

(1) First, [some claims relevant only in individual bankruptcies];

(2) Second, administrative expenses allowed under section 503(b) . . . .

§ 1129. Confirmation of plan

(a) The court shall confirm a plan only if all of the following requirements are met:

* * *

(9) Except to the extent that the holder of a particular claim has agreed to a different treatment of such claim, the plan provides that

(A) with respect to a claim of a kind specified in section 507(a)(2) . . . on the effective date of the plan, the holder of such claim will receive on account of such claim cash equal to the allowed amount of such claim;. . . .

¶ 1604: Debtor-in-Possession Financing

Many Chapter 11 debtors now ask the court to approve debtor-in-possession financing under § 364(b)–(d) soon after filing for bankruptcy, often on the first day of bankruptcy. The usual catalyst for a filing in chapter 11 is that the debtor runs out of cash, can't borrow, and soon would be unable to pay suppliers or meet its payroll. The automatic stay stops the outflow of cash from the debtor, but many debtors need new cash to flow in as well. Indeed, the need for DIP financing is often the proximate cause of the bankruptcy filing. Drafts of the motion papers and loan documents could be ready as the petition is filed, and the firm would move the court to approve debtor-in-possession financing minutes after petitioning for bankruptcy.

Consider § 364(b)–(d) in light of (1) the company's deterioration and apparently poor prospects, (2) the debt overhang effect as analyzed for Chrysler abstractly in Chapter 19, in ¶1923 in particular, and that was at the base of the Chrysler restructuring deal documents in ¶707, and (3) the kind of financial covenants found in the Drum Financial indenture in ¶703 (Limitation on Senior and Pari Passu Funded Debt, at p.152).

Prebankruptcy creditors sometimes want to prevent the debtor from taking on new debt that would dilute their own claims, because they fear that the debtor will take on the debt, lose the proceeds in operations, and then have to pay more creditors out of a diminishing pool of value or, worse, pay creditors with newly-obtained priorities first. So such creditors obtain covenants restricting their debtors from taking on the new debt. The DIP financing provisions in § 364 can resolve a debt overhang problem for the debtor; they can create a dilution problem for the prebankruptcy creditors.

What would § 364(d) do for the debtor-in-possession financier that § 364(c) doesn't? But how easy should it be for the debtor to meet both of (d)'s prerequisites simultaneously?

The § 364(d) requirements should not be rare to find met, separately. Sometimes the debtor cannot obtain credit; sometimes the debtor can adequately protect a preexisting secured creditor while the debtor offers security to a new creditor. But how often are both conditions likely to exist simultaneously?

Assume that a secured lender, A, lent $100 on $200 of security before the bankruptcy. During the bankruptcy, the debtor-in-possession offers a new DIP lender a § 364(c) junior position on the $200 of security, but doesn't reach agreement with the lender, who does not want to lend on the junior security. The new lender seeks priority over the old secured lender. Could the judge, without self-contradiction, approve priority for the new lender by accepting the debtor's assertion that it's unable to obtain credit otherwise *and* conclude that the prebankruptcy lender, A, is adequately protected?

If the preexisting secured creditor is adequately protected after taking second place behind the new secured creditor, could the debtor have obtained new credit otherwise, i.e., by giving the new creditor that second place?

¶ 1605: Statutory Principles Limiting DIP Financing; Contractual Over–Rides of Prebankruptcy Debt Covenants

1. *Judicial discretion in DIP financing*. Is there any limit to the judge's discretion in granting DIP financing? Should the approval be automatic? Consider the general standard for administrative expenses:

---

§ 503. Allowance of administrative expenses

(b) After notice and a hearing, there shall be allowed administrative expenses, . . . including

(1)(A) the actual, necessary costs and expenses of preserving the estate, including . . . wages, salaries, and commissions for services rendered after the commencement of the case[.]

The § 503(b) standard—actual, necessary costs of preserving the estate—would in principle not be a trivial hurdle to surmount: After all, many bankrupts are deteriorating in value. If the court allows them to borrow, and if they use up the funds, losing the money in operations, don't the loans thereby fail to preserve the estate? Such borrowings would not be necessary to preserve the estate.

However, that kind of fine parsing isn't available in the first few days of bankruptcy, when the bankrupt is trying to gather its resources, steady the ship, and see what can be done to survive and recover. To get through that period, it typically needs cash and a court isn't likely to deny the debtor that cash, if a lender is prepared to lend.

2. *Risk of dilution*. Keep in mind why creditors in ordinary financings outside chapter 11 don't want debtors to borrow without limit: An early creditor fears that the later creditor will lend, that the company will at the moment of the loan be equally well off (assets and liabilities increase equally), but that thereafter the debtor wastes the new funds, losing money, but remains burdened with higher liabilities. When the day of reckoning arrives, the early creditor is claiming alongside a larger number of creditors against a diminished pool of value. The creditor has been diluted. Hence, creditors sometimes limit the debtor's ability to borrow with debt limitation covenants, such as those in the Drum Financial indenture.

   So the judge should have to determine that the new § 364 DIP loan is not likely to lead to the debtor having diminished net assets: the estate would be preserved, the debtor will make more than the cost of funds with the new loan. But, given the weak opportunities that most bankrupts have, this result—that it ends up making more money than the cost of new lending—should not be a foregone conclusion.

3. *Overriding*. Consider the interplay between prebankruptcy debt limitation covenants and debtor-in-possession loans. The debtor has, say, reached the limit of a debt incurrence covenant, such as

the one in the Drum Financial indenture. The debtor could not, without the consent of the lender, incur new senior debt. But then the debtor files for bankruptcy. As such, a DIP loan under § 364(b)–(c) *is* entitled to priority as an administrative expense, over the prepetition loans. The new § 364 debt is de facto senior indebtedness. Creditors with the debt limitation covenant are disappointed.

4. *Solving the debt overhang*. The result though need not be inefficient: if the debtor's value will increase (the § 503(b)(1)(A) standard), then the old creditor has not much to complain about substantively. (It's primarily worried about new lending that leads to a decrease in the debtor's value.) And given the debt overhang impediments to new lending outside of bankruptcy, it's logically plausible that loans, even value-enhancing loans, wouldn't have been made before bankruptcy but would be made inside chapter 11.

   Notice that creditors with loan covenants preventing priority lending, and creditors with negative pledge clauses as well, could be disappointed to see DIP loans made under § 364(c), by which the creditor gets security, notwithstanding the debt incurrence limits and the negative pledge clauses. Again, if the debt overhang effect is large and if the judge reaches the "enhance-the-estate" determination, the § 364(c) result can be justified by more than just sympathy for the debtor and a generalized desire to rehabilitate bankrupts.

¶ 1606: Chapter 11 Melt–Downs and Administrative Insolvency

1. *Adequate protection claims*. The stay stops a secured creditor from seizing its secured assets. But the secured creditor need not (at first) worry about the insufficiency of value to pay off the administrative expenses. At the end of the bankruptcy, the secured creditor beats even administrative expenses (or, as we shall see, most administrative expenses). The security is the creditor's property, just "temporarily" under the debtor's administration.

   Let's say that the secured party obtained a judicial order for "adequate protection." Usually adequate protection protects the secured party successfully. This time, in this particular bankruptcy, the adequate protection fails, and there's not enough value in the bankrupt estate to protect the creditor (adequately).

   What does the frustrated secured creditor do? The claim for adequate protection is an administrative claim, as a cost of running the estate. So in the ordinary, successful chapter 11, the secured creditor will get paid, even if the judge had miscalculated and the promised adequate protection fails.

2. *Superpriority for inadequate protection*. But let's say there's been a financial melt-down in the proceeding. The debtor deteriorated so rapidly that it wasn't able to pay the adequate protection claim and, indeed, the debtor lacks enough value to pay all administrative claims off. Big problem. Do the angry administrative expense claimants all share pro rata, or can one jump to the head of the line?

Most share pro rata. Some can jump the line.

The first jump to the head of the line comes from the inadequately-protected secured creditor:

---

§ 507. Priorities

(b) If the trustee, under section 362, 363, or 364 . . . provides adequate protection . . . [to] a [secured] claim . . . and if, notwithstanding such protection, such creditor has [an administrative expense] under subsection (a)(2) of this section arising from the stay of action against such property . . . then such creditor's claim . . . shall have priority over every *other* . . . [administrative] claim allowable under such subsection [(a)(2)]].

This superpriority lets the inadequately protected secured creditor breathe easier: it automatically beats other administrative expenses.

3. *DIP loan superpriority under §364(c)*. But some creditors can jump farther: consider the DIP lender. Can it get the court to allow it to come in ahead of any § 507(b) adequate protection claims? For a § 364(b) DIP lender: no, there's nothing in the Code that helps. But the Code says yes, if that kind of superpriority had been written into the DIP financing arrangement for a § 364(c) DIP lender:

---

§ 364. Obtaining credit

(c) If the trustee is unable to obtain unsecured credit allowable . . . as an [ordinary] administrative expense, the court, after notice and a hearing, may authorize the obtaining of credit or the incurring of debt

(1) with priority over any or all administrative expenses of the kind specified in section 503(b) *or 507(b)* of this title. . . .

Thus the § 364(c) lender is superior to other administrative claims, including the secured creditor's § 507(b) inadequate protection claim. (The statute does get caught in a bit of a circle, however, as § 507(b) gives the claim for inadequate protection priority over all other administrative claims. Presumably the specificity in § 364(c) makes the DIP lender the winner.)

4. *First day order for the DIP loan*. Consider the speed with which the judge must make the §§ 364 and 507 determinations. The debtor, running out of cash before bankruptcy, lines up a prospective DIP lender and files for chapter 11 when it runs out of cash. On the first day of the bankruptcy, it moves that the court approve the DIP loan, telling the court that the business will fail without the DIP loan in place immediately. The judge needs to make valuation and liquidation vs. reorganization decisions on the fly under these sec-

tions. Typically, the judge's first-day decision on the DIP loan will be an interim order, approving some portion of the requested loan amount sufficient to maintain the debtor's operations until a more thorough consideration can be had. The subsequent hearing on a final DIP order will have noticed all the important parties, some of whom may raise objections to particular aspects of terms of the DIP loan.

6. *Paying administrative claims in full in cash at confirmation*. For completeness, recall the plan confirmation consequences of an administrative melt-down. I.e., posit that at the end of the chapter 11 proceeding there's not enough to pay all of the administrative claims. Presumably the debtor is then a candidate for liquidation. Section 1129(a)(9) gives the disappointed administrative claims veto power over the reorganization:

---

§ 1129. Confirmation of plan

(a) The court shall confirm a plan only if all of the following requirements are met:

(9) Except to the extent that the holder of a particular claim has agreed to a different treatment of such claim, the plan provides that—

(A) with respect to a claim of a kind specified in section 507(a)(2) [for administrative expenses] . . . on the effective date of the plan, the holder of such claim will receive on account of such claim cash equal to the allowed amount of such claim. . . .

The firm thereby becomes a candidate for conversion to chapter 7 (because it's plausible that no reorganization plan can be made to happen, and there's no longer value in rehabilitating a firm that can't even pay off its administrative expenses). Notice the requirement in § 1129(a)(9) that the administrative claimant that gets cash can't (or at least shouldn't) stymie reorganization of an otherwise viable firm that's seen in lending markets to be viable: the firm can borrow from a new lender (so-called "exit financing"), using that cash to fund the administrative expense as well as post-reorganization operations. The problem is more that if there's not enough to go around for even administrative expenses, the firm is really a candidate for liquidation, and each administrative expense claimant can scuttle the plan unless paid in full.

¶ 1607: George W. Kuney, Hijacking Chapter 11, 21 Emory Bankruptcy Developments Journal 19 (2004)

II. Secured Creditor DIP Financing Provisions and Techniques

Secured creditors may acquire substantial control of a chapter 11 case by providing postpetition financing—also known as DIP financing—and consent to use of their cash collateral by the debtor-in-possession. As debtors typically require financing to reorganize, secured creditors willing to allow use of their cash collateral—which may encompass all of the debtor's liquid assets—or offering additional financing possess substantial bargaining power. Lenders may secure preferential treatment of both their prepetition and postpetition debts, while collecting high rates of interest and large fees and effectively gaining control over the debtor, its management, and the chapter 11 case itself. What follows is an examination of the methods used by DIP lenders to benefit their interests.

B. The Structure of DIP Financing

In addition to any protections or priority received under the Bankruptcy Code, DIP lenders generally require greater consideration for any amount loaned to the debtor because of the perceived, or advertised, risks of lending to a chapter 11 debtor. Therefore, a DIP loan is generally a relatively short-term, restrictive loan that contains more stringent covenants and features higher interest rates and fees.

* * *

2. Covenants in DIP Financing

As additional protection, DIP lenders include stringent affirmative and negative covenants in their loans. The affirmative covenants normally require the debtor to periodically disclose financial records and information so that the DIP lender can easily monitor the debtor's performance. The DIP lender may require the debtor to submit operating budget proposals to the lender for approval prior to making expenditures, as well as proposals for any significant transactions outside the debtor's ordinary course of business. The financing agreement may require that the debtor collect all of its accounts receivable through a lock box or deposit account controlled by the DIP lender. Finally, these financing agreements also include standard non-DIP loan provisions such as terms requiring the debtor to pay any applicable taxes, insurance premiums, or other obligations during the loan term.

DIP financing agreements usually include a number of negative covenants as well, including:

- Restrictions on operating activities;
- Restrictions on capital expenditures;
- Restrictions on disposition of assets;
- Restrictions on financing activities;
- Maintenance of specific financial ratios;
- Restrictions on cash payouts;
- Preservation of DIP lender's collateral and seniority;
- Prohibitions on changes in management, control, or ownership (including appointment of a bankruptcy trustee or conversion of the case to chapter 7); and
- Restrictions on parent-subsidiary transactions.

These negative covenants greatly restrict the debtor's operating decisions, providing the DIP lender with both control and protection in the transaction. A violation of these covenants is typically an event of default under the DIP loan documents entitling the lender to relief from the stay and the ability to immediately realize upon its security, begin assessing default interest rates and penalty fees, and terminate any further financing. The overall effect of these covenants is to give the DIP lender almost complete control over the debtor's reorganization.

3. Pricing and Fees Associated with DIP Financing

The one feature that almost all forms of DIP financing share is an interest rate significantly higher than that of similar loans provided to non-debtors. A study of 106 DIP loans and 186 similar, non-DIP loans found that the DIP loans had a median interest rate of approximately two hundred basis points [i.e., 2% per year] higher than "matching" non-DIP loans. Additionally, DIP loans include provisions demanding significantly higher default rate interest, fees, and other monetary penalties for defaults and late payment. DIP lenders justify these increased rates and harsh default penalties because of the additional "risk" of nonpayment by a chapter 11 debtor. In reality, however, this increased rate appears to be a windfall for banks willing to provide DIP financing based on the additional protections and benefits the bankruptcy court grants DIP lenders. The "risk" cited by lending institutions appears to be nonexistent as the principal of nearly every DIP loan is paid back in full, regardless of whether the chapter 11 debtor reorganizes or liquidates.

C. Controversial DIP Lender Protections

In addition to the DIP lender protections codified in § 364 of the Bankruptcy Code and the somewhat standard loan document provisions discussed above, insolvency professionals have fashioned a number of other, not-so-standard incentives to induce and protect DIP financing and have convinced bankruptcy judges to approve them. These provisions include waivers of claims against the DIP lender, grants of superpriority claims in cases later converted to chapter 7, limitations on carve-outs for professional fees, enhanced default provisions coupled with automatic relief from the stay, prohibitions on changes controlled by the debtor, prohibitions on plans not approved by the lender, enhancement fees for lenders when a debtor's business attains certain performance levels, cross-collateralization, rollups of pre- and post-petition debts, and grants of liens on avoidance actions and their proceeds. Although often deferring to the debtor's business judgment when obtaining postpetition financing, bankruptcy courts assert that they carefully scrutinize DIP loans containing these controversial incentives, recognizing that debtors are in a weak bargaining position. Thus, some courts require as a matter of course that any proposed order specifically and conspicuously request these types of relief. Nonetheless, bankruptcy judges will order these additional incentives and protections upon a showing that they are "necessary" to attract DIP lenders. Given the protections authorized by § 364 and high interest rates typical of DIP loans, however, these additional protections and incentives appear unnecessary and, in conjunction with the less controversial loan document terms discussed earlier, more likely have the effect of giving DIP lenders explicit and perhaps unnecessary control over much of the chapter 11 case. As discussed earlier, the Bankruptcy Code removed bankruptcy judges from most of the job of administering the estate. This set the stage for domination and control of the chapter 11 process by the monied interests—in the large chapter 11 cases, the secured creditors and DIP lenders—regardless of how much process, how many duties, and how many powers were granted or thrust upon unsecured creditors [and] their committees. . . .

* * *

. . . DIP lenders and their counsel have taken the sparse authorizing language of Bankruptcy Code § 364 and used it to perfect a transaction that garners them high fees, good return on investment, substantial control over the debtor's management and operations, and enhanced prospects for repayment of their prepetition debt. All these effects come at the expense of lower priority unsecured creditors and equity holders.

¶ 1608: DIP Lender With Control

The DIP lender with control could be excessively risk-averse. As such, its incentives could be to liquidate too quickly. See *Atlas Pipeline* analysis.

¶ 1609: Cross–Collateralization and Roll-Ups

A prebankruptcy creditor might be ready to extend credit *if* the court will grant it security not only on the new, § 364 debtor-in-possession loan, but also on its prepetition loan. That is, it might want to cross-collateralize, getting security for the new debt and its old prepetition debt at the same time. What should the court do? What do they do?

1. *Cross-collateralization*. The bankrupt debtor and the new creditor argue that cross-collateralization gives the debtor its only chance to survive and escape liquidation. The potential lender says it needs not just statutory superpriority for the new money but it needs to have its other prepetition loans to the bankrupt secured by the bankrupt's remaining free assets. The debtor has approached other creditors and they won't make even a superpriority loan. The judge finds the evidence of creditor refusal to be credible: no one will lend with just administrative superpriority, and without new financing the enterprise is doomed to switch over to chapter 7 for liquidation. Only superpriority with cross-collateralization has a chance. Should the judge permit cross-collateralization?

2. *Skepticism in Texlon*. The DIP creditor and the debtor made such a request in In re Texlon Corp., 596 F.2d 1092 (2d Cir. 1979). There, the debtor and creditor requested cross-collateralization ex parte; that is, they made the request without a hearing where other creditors could object. While cross-collateralization was not prohibited, the appellate court held the ex parte hearing to be inadequate. Judge Friendly noted that the debtor-in-possession was hardly neutral; the debtor was giving away not its own money but the bankruptcy claims of the unsecured creditors. Accordingly, a hearing

was required to "determine [whether] other sources of financing are available; [whether] other creditors would like to share in the financing if similarly favorable terms are accorded them; or [whether] the creditors do not want the business continued at the price of preferring a particular lender." Although the procedural requirement would be onerous if the debtor needed the loan immediately, the judge saw no obvious alternative. Of course, the extent of the burden would depend on the differential capacity of the prebankruptcy creditor to act quickly and cheaply. If third-party lenders (i.e., without prebankruptcy loans) would be just as good, there would be no reason for the debtor to go to the prebankruptcy lender and offer cross-collateralization. (Management presumably wants to "buy" the money as cheaply as possible when the "purchase" will be made with the bankrupt enterprise's funds. But when the payment will be made with the pre-existing creditors' funds, it is less concerned with keeping the loan cheap.)

3. Saybrook says no. The 11th Circuit struck down cross-collateralization as barred by § 364, § 507 and, indirectly, the preference provisions. In re Saybrook Mfg. Co., 963 F.2d 1490 (11th Cir. 1992). Prepetition, the bank lent the debtor $34 million, secured by only $10 million of collateral. Post-petition, the bank lent an additional $3 million. The bankruptcy court had then allowed the debtor to offer all of its assets to secure the total $37 million in bank loans.

   Section 364 allows a court to "authorize the obtaining of credit or the incurring of debt." The 11th Circuit said this section allowed collateralization only of the new debt, not the old debt. The bank argued the bankruptcy court's inherent and wide equitable powers authorized cross-collateralization. The court believed that such a wide grab of equitable powers would violate § 507, which fixes priorities and contemplates equal treatment among the priorities. Cross-collateralization would create super-priorities not allowed by § 507, making the previously unsecured (but now cross-collateralized) claim superior to other unsecured claims. If undertaken by an insolvent company before bankruptcy, cross-collateralization would be a preference. A court that sanctioned cross-collateralization would violate central principles of bankruptcy.

   However, bankruptcy courts in other Circuits have allowed cross-collateralization. And, because some courts are reluctant to approve cross-collateralization directly, lenders have "improve[d] their position by 'rolling' their prepetition debt into the postpetition facility." Marcia L. Goldstein, Michele J. Meises and Timothy Graulich, Current Issues in Debtor in Possession Financing, SJ082 ALI–ABA 29, 40 (2004); Craig R. Bucki, Cracking the Code: The Legal Authority Behind Extrastatutory Debtor–In–Possession Financing Mechanisms and Their Prospects for Survival, 2005 Columbia Business Law Review 357, 372.

4. Roll-up. The roll-up works like this: the prospective DIP lender had lent to the debtor before bankruptcy. The lender conditions its willingness to make the DIP loan on the debtor using part of the DIP proceeds to pay off the old, prebankruptcy loan. I.e., the lender had

lent $100 million. The DIP loan will be for $200 million, but the DIP lender conditions that new loan on the debtor using $100 million of the proceeds to pay the prebankruptcy loan off. When the debtor pays off the prebankruptcy loan with DIP funds, the old loan thereby rolls into the DIP facility. If the prebankruptcy loan was fully secured, without infirmities, the roll-up doesn't alter priorities. The soft spot for bankruptcy policy is that no one other than the lender may look carefully at whether the security fully covered the prebankruptcy loan. To the extent the roll-up strengthens the prebankruptcy loan, it's effectively increasing the interest rate of the DIP facility.

5. *One court's criteria for cross-collateralization*. "In seeking to grant cross-collateralization, the debtor-in-possession must demonstrate that: (1) Absent the proposed financing, its business operations will not survive; (2) It is unable to obtain alternative financing on acceptable terms; (3) The proposed lender will not accede to less preferential terms; and (4) The proposed financing is in the best interests of the general creditor body." In re Vanguard Diversified, Inc., 31 B.R. 364, 366 (Bankr. E.D.N.Y. 1983).

6. *Hidden interest?* Cross-collateralization's impact resembles a § 364(c) DIP loan with a high rate of interest: The DIP lender lends $30 million at 10% and gets full security. Its prebankruptcy loan of $12 million had no security and would, without cross-collateralization, be paid 50 cents on the dollar. If it's cross-collateralized and the bankruptcy lasts one year, the effective rate of interest on the DIP loan is about 30%, isn't it? That's the real rate of interest because the cross-collateralization lets the lender get an extra $6 million that it would not otherwise have obtained. Perhaps 30% is the right rate for this kind of loan to this particular business. That 30% rate, though, is not vividly visible to the court and the non-calculating parties. Were it more visible, the court might reevaluate whether reorganization is viable; the unsecured may see value flowing from them to the DIP lender; perhaps other potential DIP lenders might lend at a lower rate of, say, 20% to this company, if only they could see that the real rate is 30%, not 10%. The rate is easily obscured if the prebankruptcy loan was secured, but the security's value is uncertain. Worse for others, it's the existing secured creditor and the debtor that are often best positioned to evaluate the viability of the security.

7. *Mootness of appeal*. Consider the limited usefulness of an appeal for creditors upset with a DIP facility's terms:

§ 364. Obtaining credit

(e) The reversal or modification on appeal of an authorization under this section to obtain credit or incur debt, or of a grant under this section of a priority or a lien, does not affect the validity of any debt so incurred, or any priority or lien so granted, to an entity that extended such credit in good faith, whether or not such entity knew of the pendency of the appeal, unless such authorization and the incurring of such debt, or the granting of such priority or lien, were stayed pending appeal.

In *Saybrook*, the district court found that § 364(e) rendered the appeal moot. The Eleventh Circuit, however, said that:

> Cross-collateralization is directly inconsistent with the priority scheme of the Bankruptcy Code. Accordingly, the practice may not be approved by the bankruptcy court under its equitable authority. . . . Cross-collateralization is not authorized by section 364. Section 364(e), therefore, is not applicable and this appeal is not moot.

But, again, the Eleventh Circuit decision stands alone, with many bankruptcy courts not following it. Perhaps even the Eleventh Circuit would have invoked § 364(e) to support the validity of the DIP loan if the DIP loan had merely unwise terms that, say, kept a dying business going for too long, as opposed to self-interested cross-collateralization terms.

8. <u>Contract override in bankruptcy</u>. Note that § 364 allows the court to over-ride a negative pledge clause in a bond. That is, a firm outside of bankruptcy might be unable to get new financing without giving the new financiers priority. Negative pledge clauses in preexisting debt could preclude new priority debt. Section 364 substitutes the court's judgment for the contractual limitation of a negative pledge clause.
9. <u>*Kinship with critical vendor payments*</u>. Note the similarity between cross-collateralization and critical vendor status, in that both contemplate priority jumps that would not be compliant with the specifics of the Code. Easterbrook's *Kmart* opinion, supra at ¶ 1205, could provide a structure for analyzing cross-collateralization requests. And what would that conceptual structure be?
10. <u>*Whose money is at stake?*</u> Should the judge be wary if creditors won't make loans even with superpriority? With whose money are the bankrupt and the cross-collateralizing creditor gambling?

¶ 1610: Loan-to-Own DIP Lending—David A. Skeel, *The Story of Saybrook: Defining the Limits of Debtor-in-Possession Financing, in* Bankruptcy Law Stories 177, 197–98 (Robert Rasmussen ed., 2007)

Since the mid 1990s, post-petition financing has become the principal governance lever in Chapter 11 cases. . . . On the whole, the increasing influence of the debtor-in-possession financer has improved the Chapter 11 process. To the extent they limit managers' ability to entrench themselves or to dissipate assets, DIP financers are in effect protecting the interests of all of the company's creditors. . . .

But in one category of cases, the DIP financer's influence is worrisome: cases where the lender not only serves as financer, but also as a potential buyer of the debtor's assets. The problem . . . stems from the fact that the DIP lender, often referred to as a loan-to-own or loan-and-control financier—has an interest in paying as little as possible for the debtor's assets. . . . One possible response would be to hold an open auction, and thus subject the DIP lender's bid to a market test. [But the DIP lender] is likely to have better information than any outside bidder, since [it] will have thoroughly investigated the debtor as a precondition to making its loan, and will be monitoring the company's financial condition on a continuous basis. The information asymmetry between the [lender] and other potential bidders creates a classic winner's curse dilemma: other bidders know that, if they outbid the better informed [DIP lender], this probably means that they bid too much. . . . As a result, outside bidders will either underbid or stay home; and the DIP lender may walk away with the assets at a bargain price.

¶ 1611: Using Cash to Operate the Business

Sometimes the bankrupt is healthy enough to generate some cash from its operations because it no longer has to pay back creditors.

When a company issues secured debt covering, say, its inventory and accounts receivable, it will sell inventory. When it collects from its customer, it will have cash. Typically outside of bankruptcy it will have to pay some or all of that cash over to its financing creditor.

The bankrupt company doesn't as a general rule have to pay over that cash to its creditor. The general rule comes from the bankruptcy stay in § 362, barring all creditors from collecting on their debts. When the cash is generated from a secured asset, by the debtor, say, selling off the inventory that had been given as security, the cash proceeds of the sale are called "cash collateral."

The Code doesn't allow the bankrupt to spend this "cash collateral" automatically. The bankrupt must either get the consent of the affected secured creditor or must apply to the court under § 363(c). The court would normally allow the bankrupt to spend the cash collateral only if the court believes that the secured creditor is otherwise adequately protected (usually because the other secured property is more than enough to be sure that the secured creditor will be paid back).

CHAPTER 17

CORPORATE GOVERNANCE AND CHAPTER 11

The normal means of corporate governance—shareholder elections, boards of director decisions, shareholder proxy solicitations, and so on—must change in a chapter 11 proceeding. It's not the shareholders' company anymore usually, and so they—or their board—usually shouldn't run it alone anymore. But who does run it?

If reorganization were instantaneous, we could (once again) easily keep to our basics of shareholder-oriented corporate governance: the creditors would force a bankruptcy petition and quickly become the debtor's owning shareholders. For only a brief instant, the firm would be in a state of suspended animation with shareholdings and loans in flux. When it came out of the trance, it would find itself with new stockholders (drawn from the old creditors), and those new stockholders would go through the normal routines of shareholder-based corporate governance.

But once again, that transformation-by-reorganization takes time. And during that time the bankrupt company must be run. And someone must run it.

Not just the incumbent management, but also an official creditors' committee, a bankruptcy trustee, the U.S. trustee, an examiner, and, of course, the judge, can all play key roles.

A. WHO RUNS THE BANKRUPT DEBTOR?

¶ 1701: Displacing Management With a Trustee

While lawyers consider formally replacing the debtor-in-possession management with a trustee to be an unusual remedy, informal managerial replacement isn't unusual. Nearly half of the directors of public bankrupts are gone by the end of the proceeding and common stock ownership becomes more concentrated. Stuart C. Gilson, *Bankruptcy, boards, banks, and blockholders: Evidence on changes in corporate ownership and control when firms default,* 27 Journal of Financial Economics 355 (1990). The turnover of CEOs of public firms going into chapter 11 is even higher. Lynn M. LoPucki & William C. Whitford, *Corporate Governance in the Bankruptcy Reorganization of Large, Publicly Held Companies,* 141 University of Pennsylvania Law Review 669, 750 (1993). Multiple explanations are available: the directors may be disgusted with failure, they may find a better company to work at, etc. But creditor pressure is also a key part of the reason for managerial turnover.

¶ 1702: The Creditors Committee, the U.S. Trustee, and the Examiner

The official creditors' committee plays a role akin to that of a shadow board of directors. Soon after the filing, the U.S. Trustee appoints the creditors' committee, usually by appointing the seven largest creditors. Bankruptcy Code § 1102(b)(1). The U.S. Trustee is an administrative official, coming out of the Justice Department. The next reading briefly summarizes the U.S. Trustee's tasks.

Another key player in the governance of the large (and sometimes not-so-large) chapter 11 is the examiner. The examiner is appointed ad hoc by the bankruptcy judge, often to examine questionable prebankruptcy transactions of the debtor, such as those that might give the debtor a fraudulent transfer or preference claim against a creditor, or transactions that might give the debtor a claim against its prebankruptcy management. The second reading is excerpted from the examiner's report in the WorldCom bankruptcy.

¶ 1703: Dep't of Justice, About the U.S. Trustee Program & Bankruptcy[1]

The United States Trustee Program is a component of the Department of Justice that seeks to promote the efficiency and protect the integrity of the Federal bankruptcy system. . . . [The U.S. Trustee

---

[1] From DOJ website, as of Jan. 2004.

(not to be confused with a bankruptcy trustee or a bond indenture trustee)] monitors the conduct of bankruptcy parties and . . . trustees, oversees related administrative functions, and acts to ensure compliance with applicable laws and procedures. It also identifies and helps investigate bankruptcy fraud and abuse in coordination with United States Attorneys, the Federal Bureau of Investigation, and other law enforcement agencies.

Background of the U.S. Trustee Program

The Program was established by the Bankruptcy Reform Act of 1978. . . . The primary role of the U.S. Trustee Program is to serve as the "watchdog over the bankruptcy process."[2] As stated in the USTP Mission Statement:

> The United States Trustee Program acts in the public interest to promote the efficiency and to protect and preserve the integrity of the bankruptcy system. It works to secure the just, speedy, and economical resolution of bankruptcy cases; monitors the conduct of parties and takes action to ensure compliance with applicable laws and procedures; identifies and investigates bankruptcy fraud and abuse; and oversees administrative functions in bankruptcy cases.

The Attorney General . . . appoint[s] . . . [the] United States Trustees. . . .

* * *

Specific responsibilities of the United States Trustees include:

- Appointing and supervising [the bankruptcy] trustee[ ] . . . ;
- Taking legal action to enforce the requirements of the Bankruptcy Code and to prevent fraud and abuse;
- Referring matters for investigation and criminal prosecution when appropriate;
- Ensuring that bankruptcy estates are administered promptly and efficiently, and that professional fees are reasonable;
- Appointing and convening creditors' committees . . . ;
- Reviewing disclosure statements and applications for the retention of professionals; and
- Advocating matters relating to the Bankruptcy Code and rules of procedure in court.

¶ 1704: The Examiner

Under § 1104(c), most larger chapter 11 reorganizations have an examiner. The examiner investigates whether there are fraudulent transfers, preferences, and similar claims available to the trustee, who is usually the player who brings such actions. One justification for having an examiner is that usually the incumbent managers take over

[2] House Report No. 989, 95th Cong., 2d Sess. at 88. . . .

the company as debtor-in-possession, at least initially. They may be unwilling to sue themselves and their friends, so the examiner alerts the court (and the other parties) as to the possibilities and plausibility of lawsuits.

§ 1104. Appointment of trustee or examiner

(c) If the court does not order the appointment of a trustee . . . then . . . on request of a party in interest or the United States trustee . . . the court shall order the appointment of an examiner to conduct . . . an investigation . . . of any allegations of fraud, dishonesty, incompetence, misconduct, mismanagement, or irregularity in the management of the affairs of the debtor of or by current or former management of the debtor, if

(1) such appointment is in the interests of creditors . . . ; or

(2) the debtor's . . . debts . . . exceed $5,000,000.

¶ 1705: The WorldCom Examiner's Report

IN THE UNITED STATES BANKRUPTCY COURT

SOUTHERN DISTRICT OF NEW YORK

In re:	§	Chapter 11
WORLDCOM, INC., et al.,	§	Case No. 02–13533 (AJG)
Debtors.	§	Jointly Administered

THIRD AND FINAL REPORT OF DICK THORNBURGH,

BANKRUPTCY COURT EXAMINER January 26, 2004

Kirkpatrick & Lockhart LLP
Counsel to Dick Thornburgh,
Bankruptcy Court Examiner

* * *

I. INTRODUCTION

On July 21, 2002, roughly five weeks after WorldCom, Inc. ("WorldCom" or the "Company") publicly announced significant accounting irregularities that would require initial adjustments to its financial statements totaling approximately $3.8 billion, the Company filed petitions for protection under Chapter 11 of the United States Bankruptcy Code. It was the largest bankruptcy proceeding in U.S. history.

On August 6, 2002, the Honorable Arthur J. Gonzalez, Chief Judge of the United States Bankruptcy Court for the Southern District of New York, approved the appointment of Dick Thornburgh as Bankruptcy Court Examiner. The Court prescribed a broad mandate for the Examiner's investigation, directing that the Examiner "shall investigate any allegations of fraud, dishonesty, incompetence, misconduct, mismanagement or irregularity in the arrangement of the affairs of [WorldCom] by current or former management, including but not limited to issues of accounting irregularities."

* * *

The Examiner believes that WorldCom has causes of action against a number of persons and entities that bear responsibility for WorldCom's injuries. The potential claims identified by the Examiner are briefly summarized as follows:

* * *

> • Claims for breaches of the fiduciary duties of loyalty and good faith against Mr. Ebbers [WorldCom's former CEO] for awarding investment banking business to Salomon . . . in return for lucrative financial favors, including extraordinary allocations of shares in initial public offerings ("IPO's") from 1996 until August 2000 and extraordinary loan assistance in 2000–2002. The Examiner also believes that the Company has claims against Salomon . . . for aiding and abetting Mr. Ebbers' breaches of his fiduciary duties.
>
> • Claims for breaches of the fiduciary duties of loyalty and good faith against Mr. Ebbers for accepting more than $400 million in loans from WorldCom at noncommercial interest rates and for accepting loans without disclosing his inability to repay them. The Examiner also believes that WorldCom has claims against the remaining former Directors for their breaches of their duties of care and loyalty in connection with such loans. WorldCom also has a claim against Mr. Ebbers for breach of his April 30, 2002 Severance Agreement.
>
> • Claims for fraud and breaches of the fiduciary duties of loyalty and good faith against former Chief Financial Officer ("CFO") Scott Sullivan and those other former WorldCom employees who have pled guilty to crimes related to the Company's accounting irregularities. In addition, claims related to the accounting irregularities may exist against other former WorldCom personnel, including Mr. Ebbers.
>
> • Claims for accounting malpractice or negligence and breach of contract against Arthur Andersen [WorldCom's accountants] and certain of its former personnel based upon their failure to satisfy professional standards in their audits of WorldCom's financial statements for audit years 1999 through 2001.

* * *

The Examiner recognizes that the WorldCom plan of reorganization assigns any such claims to WorldCom and that the Company may have valid reasons, in exercising its business judgment, not to pursue particular potential claims, such as the inability to pay by certain defendants, the costs of litigation weighed against potential recovery, the presence of shareholder suits, or the strength of a particular claim. The Examiner expresses no opinion whether any of the claims actually should be pursued. Rather, the Examiner views it as his responsibility to identify potential claims and to leave it to the Company to decide which, if any, of the claims to pursue. . . .

II. PROCESS OF EXAMINATION

Upon his appointment, the Examiner engaged Kirkpatrick & Lockhart LLP as his legal counsel and J.H. Cohn LLP as his forensic accountants and set out to marshal the massive factual data related to the conduct of WorldCom's Management, Board of Directors and [accountants]. . . . This examination process has been described by the Examiner in [earlier] . . . Interim Reports. . . .

Since the filing of the Second Interim Report on June 9, 2003, the Examiner has continued the review and analysis of millions of pages of documents and the interviews of dozens of persons knowledgeable about the issues under investigation.[3]

* * *

X. CONCLUSION

. . . WorldCom's corporate governance lapses were part and parcel of the Company environment that permitted not only a massive accounting fraud but also multiple other lapses, such as . . . poorly managed and unchecked debit and credit management, and lack of due diligence pertaining to loans to Mr. Ebbers. The Examiner's further investigation has confirmed the breadth of these lapses in proper corporate governance, including the unprecedented financial favors that Mr. Ebbers traded for WorldCom's investment banking work. . . . The further investigation also has identified contributions to the failures by certain outside service providers to WorldCom, including [its accountants], Arthur Andersen. . . . These findings have served to underscore that the failures surrounding WorldCom went far beyond the early reports of accounting fraud by a few persons and have reconfirmed the Examiner's earlier observations that virtually every level of gatekeeper and advisor, both within and outside WorldCom, was to some degree derelict in his/her/its responsibilities.

The Examiner has now completed his investigation with his Third and Final Report. The Examiner recognizes that this does not mean that the past lapses pertaining to WorldCom are no longer of current relevance. To the contrary, the Examiner recognizes that there are ongoing government investigations and prosecutions and lawsuits by former WorldCom shareholders, and the Company must decide whether to pursue certain claims pertaining to past lapses.

The Examiner's mandate from this Court was to examine allegations of fraud, etc., "by current or former management. . . ".

. . . [T]he Examiner . . . observes that notwithstanding the corporate governance lapses recited in his three Reports, there were many persons within WorldCom, at all levels, who appear admirably to have performed their duties to the best of the Examiner's knowledge. Accordingly, the Examiner does not want his criticism of many formerly in WorldCom management inadvertently to tarnish the reputations of the many faithful WorldCom employees who were just as much victims of the corporate governance lapses as were shareholders and creditors.

---

[3] Altogether, the Examiner interviewed 49 present and former Company employees and Directors, 11 present and former Salomon . . . personnel, 6 former Arthur Andersen personnel, 5 present and former KPMG personnel and 9 other persons with knowledge of relevant matters. Many of these persons were interviewed several times. In addition, the Examiner was present at and participated in 62 interviews conducted by counsel for the Special Investigative Committee of WorldCom's Board of Directors.

* * *

Respectfully submitted
Dick Thornburgh Examiner
January 26, 2004

By Examiner's Counsel:

* * *

KIRKPATRICK & LOCKHART LLP
1800 Massachusetts Avenue, NW
Washington, DC 20036

B. WHO SUES?

Section 550 refers to the trustee as the party that seeks to recover preferences and fraudulent transfers. Section 1107 says that the debtor-in-possession—essentially the bankrupt's management—takes on the powers of the trustee.

What if a creditor sees a fraudulent transfer to another creditor, say a friend of incumbent management, but the trustee—i.e., the debtor-in-possession's—management doesn't seek to avoid the transfer or the obligation? As one court said:

> This situation immediately gives rise to the proverbial problem of the fox guarding the henhouse. If no trustee is appointed, the debtor—really, the debtor's management—bears a fiduciary duty to avoid fraudulent transfers that it itself made. One suspects that if managers can devise any opportunity to avoid bringing a claim that would amount to reputational self-immolation, they will seize it. . . . [And] a debtor may be unwilling to pursue claims against individuals or business, such as critical suppliers, with whom it has an ongoing relationship that it fears damaging.

In re Cybergenics, 330 F.3d 548, 573 (3d Cir. 2003). The Code doesn't explicitly allow the unhappy creditor to sue directly. True, the unhappy creditor can petition the court under § 1104 to have the court appoint a suit-friendly trustee. Appointing a trustee is usually seen to be an extraordinary remedy, although a debtor-in-possession's failure to sue on a clear fraudulent transfer could motivate a court to appoint a trustee. Section 1104 authorizes the court to appoint a trustee "for cause" or if appointing one would be "in the interests of creditors." (Even if incumbent management is lax in pursuing the fraudulent transfer claim, those managers might be the best bet to turn around the debtor's business; hence, displacing those managers might still not be in the interests of creditors.)

Cybergenics held that the creditors' committee could bring the fraudulent transfer action derivatively. The court looked to § 1109(b), which empowers a creditors' committee to "raise and [to] appear and be heard on any issue in a case under [chapter 11]." Conceptually, it's still the trustee who is suing, with the creditors' committee bringing an action requesting that the court order the trustee to sue to recover the fraudulent transfer.

Two interpretive issues get raised thereby: First, § 1109 was typically seen as giving the party the right to be heard, not the right to initiate suit, as the dissent pointed out. *Cybergenics* 330 F.3d at 581. The majority opinion argued, however, that other sections of the Code contemplate reimbursing creditors for their expenses in recovering assets for the estate (§ 503(b)(3)(B)) and that implied the right to initiate a suit. Moreover, the overriding equity power of the bankruptcy courts could be deployed here.

The second interpretive issue is that § 1109 refers to any creditor as having the right to be heard. If § 1109 is the basis for a creditors' committee's power to begin a derivative suit, its text would therefore seem to empower any creditor to do the same. That authority—if it goes that far—would seem particularly useful to a complaining creditor when the purported fraudulent transfer had gone to a member of the creditors' committee.

C. SQUELCHING PRE–BANKRUPTCY LAWSUITS?

¶ 1706: The Status of Corporate Lawsuits

Companies that go bankrupt are often sued. Shareholders, upset about corporate performance, might sue the directors, either directly or derivatively. The derivative suits are an asset of the bankrupt company. The direct suits that shareholders or creditors have against directors or third parties would seem to have little conceptual contact with the bankrupt estate, since they are suits between non-parties to the bankruptcy. Consider the following decision in the *Texaco* bankruptcy.

In re Texaco, 84 B.R. 893 (Bankr. S.D.N.Y. 1988)

HOWARD SCHWARTZBERG, Bankruptcy Judge

After less than one year from the filing . . . on April 12, 1987, the debtor, Texaco Inc. . . . scheduled hearings commencing March 22, 1988 for the confirmation of their Second Amended Joint Plan of Reorganization (the "Plan"). The Plan was proposed by the debtors and Pennzoil Company ("Pennzoil"). Pennzoil is the largest unsecured creditor of Texaco Inc. as a result of a jury verdict entered in its favor against Texaco in the state court in Harris County, Texas, on November 19, 1985 in the amount of . . . $11.12 billion. . . . The Pennzoil judgment against Texaco Inc. is the largest civil judgment in history. Similarly, these Chapter 11 cases are the largest bankruptcy cases ever filed in this country.

. . . Texaco Inc. and Pennzoil agreed to propose a Joint Plan of Reorganization pursuant to which Pennzoil would agree to accept from Texaco Inc. the sum of $3 billion in settlement of its state court judgment. . . . This settlement followed on the heels of this court's rulings on December 2 and 8, 1987 that Texaco's plan exclusivity under

11 U.S.C. § 1121 could be modified on motion with 48 hours notice if the General Committee of Unsecured Creditors, the Equity Committee and Pennzoil could agree upon a plan, with input from Texaco.

. . . [T]he Plan in general provides for the payment in full of all allowed claims of creditors against the debtors, together with interest to the date of payment or, in the case of certain debt obligations, the reinstatement of such debt obligations by curing all arrears in payment of principal and interest (including interest on any past due interest payments) and by the continued payment of all such obligations in accordance with their original terms and maturities. Under the Plan, Texaco shareholders will retain their equity interests. . . . [T]he shareholders are deemed impaired and, therefore, they may vote to accept or reject the plan.

[The court next listed in this paragraph all claims besides Pennzoil's. The listed claims would either be paid in full or left unimpaired.]

10. Pennzoil Judgment Claim. The Plan provides [that] . . . Texaco will pay Pennzoil $3 billion in cash, [to settle] . . . Pennzoil's claims against Texaco arising out of the Pennzoil $10 billion Judgment. The settlement also resolves all controversies and disputes between Texaco and Pennzoil relating to . . . [Pennzoil's] attempted acquisition of . . . Getty Oil Company . . . [in the Getty Oil Transaction] including . . . the tender offer and merger by which Texaco acquired such Getty Oil shares[;] . . . the Merger Agreement . . . between Texaco and Getty Oil . . . [; and] any disclosures, representations or failures to disclose or represent facts and materials relating to . . . [the] above. . . .

11. Releases, Indemnifications and Discontinuances of Derivative Actions. . . . Texaco and Pennzoil will release each other, and the other's predecessors, successors, assigns, *present and former officers, directors*, employees, agents, attorneys, accountants, investment bankers, receivers, parents, trustees, subsidiaries and affiliates, from all Claims arising out of, relating to or in connection with the Getty Oil Transaction. . . . Texaco . . . will discontinue and dismiss 16 Shareholder Derivative actions brought by certain Texaco shareholders on behalf of Texaco arising out of the Pennzoil judgment against Texaco.

12. Interests of Texaco Stockholders. Under the Plan, Texaco Stockholders will retain their equity interests in Texaco. Nevertheless, Texaco Stockholders are deemed impaired for purposes of the Plan and, therefore, may vote to accept or reject the Plan.[4]

* * *

. . . [T]hirteen shareholders of Texaco Inc., identified as the Delaware Group . . . who[ ] are the plaintiffs . . . in sixteen shareholder derivative actions[,] brought in the right of and for the benefit of Texaco Inc. which are pending in Delaware, Texas and New York, . . . object[ed] to the confirmation of the Plan.

---

[4] [Is it ¶ 11 that primarily leads to the shareholders being impaired under the Plan?—Roe.]

The derivative plaintiffs . . . support the $3 billion settlement. . . . However, they objected to the . . . abandonment and dismissal of the plaintiffs' derivative actions and the grant of releases and indemnifications to the defendants in such actions, including officers, directors and other representatives of Texaco, as well as the Getty Oil Company . . . , First Boston Corporation and Goldman Sachs & Co., investment bankers for Texaco and Getty, respectively. The derivative plaintiffs maintained that the derivative actions constitute an asset of the debtor's worth at least as much as Texaco must pay to Pennzoil if the settlement is approved. . . .

The objectants pointed to *11 U.S.C. § 1129*(a)(1) and argued that the Plan is not confirmable in that it allegedly violates *11 U.S.C. § 554* because it contemplates the abandonment of the derivative actions which are of value and not burdensome to the estate.

The objectants contended that *11 U.S.C. § 1129*(a)(2) is not satisfied because applicable provisions of the Bankruptcy Code were not complied with because the Plan is the product of alleged gross breaches of fiduciary duty by Texaco's self-interested officers and directors who are among the parties directly benefited by the grant of releases. . . .

Section 1129(a)(3) . . . requires that a plan shall be proposed in good faith and not by any means forbidden by law. . . . [T]he objectants alleged that the Plan was not proposed in good faith because it allegedly stripped the shareholders and Texaco of the value of significant causes of action in order to protect insider management and . . . that the Plan failed to comply with applicable state law because independent investigation and evaluation by a special committee or other similar independent person . . . are alleged as necessary [for] dismiss[ing the] derivative actions and . . . granting of releases and indemnifications. . . .

. . . The Icahn Group purchased approximately 14.8% of Texaco's common stock after the commencement of the chapter 11 cases and represents the largest single ownership of Texaco's equity interest. The Icahn Group joined the derivative plaintiffs in objecting that the indemnifications, releases and discontinuances of derivative actions should not be approved because the derivative actions are intended to retrieve for Texaco valuable causes of action which should not be dismissed or confirmed. The Icahn Group suggests that the provisions in the plan dealing with indemnifications, releases and discontinuances of derivative actions should be severed from . . . the $3 billion settlement with Pennzoil.

* * *

Texaco states that the Pennzoil [original] complaint was without merit. . . . However, Texaco believes that . . . catastrophic results for Texaco's shareholders will result if the case is not settled. . . . Nonetheless, in order for Texaco or any of the derivative plaintiffs which sued on its behalf, to recover against any defendant on the claims asserted by the derivative plaintiffs, they would probably have had to assert and prove some or all of the elements of Pennzoil's case against Texaco. In such case, Texaco, or anyone suing on its behalf, might be confronted with Texaco's own repeated assertions that, as a matter of law, there was no binding contract among Pennzoil and the Getty Oil entities. Texaco believes there is little merit to any derivative action because the Getty Oil defendants and others covered by the releases and indemnifications might succeed in establishing as Texaco has consistently asserted, that there was no binding contract with Pennzoil. Thus, Texaco asserts that it has been advised by outside counsel that there would be substantial difficulties in achieving any recovery on Texaco's potential claims against the Board of Directors and other third parties. Texaco, therefore, reasons that the releases and indemnifications, with respect to actions of questionable value, should be given and the derivative actions discontinued in order to achieve a settlement of the Pennzoil litigation.

* * *

On March 22, 1988, in the morning just before the confirmation hearing was about to commence, the derivative plaintiffs entered into a settlement with Texaco whereby they withdrew their objections to the issuance of releases, indemnifications and discontinuances of the derivative actions.

The derivative plaintiffs withdrew their objections to the Plan with the understanding that their attorneys would be permitted to file applications for prepetition and postpetition legal services not to exceed a total of $10 million for all of the twenty-one law firms representing the derivative plaintiffs. Half of the legal fees would be paid by Texaco's liability carriers and the other half would be paid on behalf of the J. Paul Getty Trust. Thus, Texaco would not be required to bear the direct cost of the derivative plaintiffs' legal fees.

The Icahn Group continues to object to the inclusion in the Plan of releases and indemnifications in favor of Texaco's own officers and directors as well as the issuances of releases and indemnifications to the Getty interests, lawyers, accountants and investment bankers.

* * *

. . . [T]his court finds that the releases and indemnifications to be issued by Texaco under the Plan are in the best interests of Texaco in obtaining an integrated settlement of the Pennzoil judgment and do not amount to the relinquishment or abandonment by Texaco of valuable causes of action.

DISCUSSION

. . . The plan must . . . have been proposed in good faith and not by any means forbidden by law, as mandated under *11 U.S.C. § 1129*(a)(3). . . . This is so even if Texaco's shareholders, who are deemed under the Plan as the only impaired class for purposes of voting, have overwhelmingly voted to accept the plan, which they have done by a majority vote of approximately 96 percent. . . . The objectants . . . argue[ ] that . . . the Texaco shareholders were compelled to vote for an entire package, which . . . include[d both the advantageous settlement with Pennzoil and the] releases and indemnities which Texaco will issue to its own officers and directors and to third parties including attorneys, accountants, [and] investment bankers . . . who [participated in the sale of] the Getty Oil stock to Texaco which precipitated the Pennzoil suit and judgment against Texaco.

. . . The objecting Icahn Group contends that Pennzoil and the creditors of Texaco have no legitimate interest in discouraging the derivative shareholder plaintiffs from attempting to recover against the Texaco officers, directors, third parties, and their insurance carriers, so long as Pennzoil is paid $3 billion and is given indemnities and releases under the Plan. The Icahn Group reasons that the derivative suits seek to recover assets for Texaco to compensate for what Texaco has to pay to Pennzoil under the Plan . . .

The net effect of the indemnities and releases of non-Pennzoil interests and the discontinuances of the objectants' derivative actions is to erase the potential liabilities of these third parties to Texaco. . . . The Plan proposes to release any claims that the debtors may have against Texaco's officers and directors and against the non-Pennzoil third parties arising out of Texaco's acquisition of the Getty Oil stock. . . .

* * *

INDEMNIFICATIONS, RELEASES AND DISCONTINUANCES OF DERIVATIVE ACTIONS

The provisions in the Plan which propose to dismiss with prejudice the derivative actions commenced by certain shareholders on behalf of Texaco with respect to the Getty Oil Transaction and to grant releases and indemnifications to the defendants in such actions was viewed by the objectants as the relinquishment of valuable property rights. This position is tenable only if Texaco has a meritorious claim against the defendants in the derivative actions. However, the derivative claims are premised on the Pennzoil judgment, which reflects the Texas jury's conclusion that Texaco had knowledge of the contract existing between Getty Oil Company and Pennzoil and that Texaco nevertheless willfully induced a breach of that contract. Hence, Texaco was found liable to Pennzoil for compensatory and punitive damages. . . .

* * *

The . . . release[ ] . . . [of] Texaco's own officers and directors and the discontinuances of the derivative actions against the Texaco defendants . . . does not amount to the relinquishment of a valuable property right of the Texaco estate. The fact that Texaco has been found to have tortiously interfered with an existing agreement between Pennzoil and the Getty interests, does not mean that Texaco's officers and directors are estopped from denying that they breached their fiduciary duties to Texaco or were guilty of mismanagement. These issues were not litigated in the Texas action brought by Pennzoil against Texaco. Indeed, Chief Judge Charles L. Brieant, in affirming this court's approval of Texaco's disclosure statement . . . [said]:

> . . . While Texaco may itself be estopped by the Texas judgment after it becomes final, the corporate directors and other fiduciaries were not parties to that action and . . . so they probably are not bound by principles of collateral estoppel.

C. J. Kirk et al. v. Texaco Inc. et al., 82 Bankr. 678 (S.D.N.Y. 1988).

. . . Texaco officers and directors [would] be free to demonstrate that they . . . were not in breach of their fiduciary responsibilities or guilty of mismanagement. . . .

[Moreover, t]he court may not selectively reform the comprehensive Plan because it represents a consensus arrived at by Pennzoil and Texaco, with the full support of the statutory committees and has been accepted by approximately 96 percent of Texaco's voting shareholders. Modifications of this Plan cannot be imposed upon Texaco, Pennzoil, Texaco's creditors and Texaco's shareholders without their consent.

The value of the derivative actions against Texaco's own officers and directors is further diminished by the fact that under Texaco's By-laws, its officers and directors are indemnified for liabilities incurred while acting on behalf of Texaco. Hence, the claims asserted by the derivative plaintiffs would be offset pursuant to the Bylaw indemnifications. The issuance of releases and indemnifications under the Plan to Texaco's officers and directors would represent no additional relinquishment of causes of action by Texaco.[5]

* * *

CONCLUSIONS OF LAW

. . . The debtors have satisfied all of the requirements for confirmation imposed under 11 U.S.C. § 1129(a), and are entitled to an order from this court confirming the Second Amended Joint Plan of Reorganization.

¶ 1707: Robert H. Mnookin & Robert B. Wilson, Rational Bargaining and Market Efficiency: Understanding Pennzoil v. Texaco, 75 Virginia Law Review 295 (1989)

* * *

The bargaining game between Pennzoil and Texaco illustrates the classic dilemma of negotiation: the efforts of each party to get as large a share of the pie as possible may shrink the size of the whole pie. Negotiations involve both an efficiency element, because agreements create mutual benefits for the parties and thus increase the size of the pie, and a distributive element, because bargainers strive to advance their own interests when the pie is being carved up. . . .

Let us first consider the distributive element: How did judicial actions during the course of the litigation affect expectations about the distribution of wealth between the parties? . . . [Even w]hen the jury awarded $11 billion, the expected transfer from Texaco to Pennzoil . . . was . . . only a fraction of the verdict. Texaco initially had the opportunity to have the verdict overturned by four different courts: (1) the trial court could have set aside the verdict; (2) the Texas Court of Appeals could have reversed; (3) the Texas Supreme Court could have granted review and reversed; or (4) the United States Supreme Court could have granted certiorari and reversed. As each of the first three courts ruled against Texaco, the odds that Texaco would succeed in overturning the judgment went down, and the expected value of the transfer went up. This is the obvious explanation for the fact that when

[5] [Note though that in some key suits, the plaintiffs sought to have the indemnification agreements declared void or inapplicable.—Roe.]

each of these events occurred the value of Texaco shares declined and the value of Pennzoil shares increased.

While the two companies were wrangling over what transfer, if any, would be made, there were important efficiency costs being incurred. Both companies were running up substantial legal, accounting, and investment banking bills. As a result, any transfer from Texaco to Pennzoil would actually have cost Texaco significantly more than the net benefits to Pennzoil. . . .

One plausible explanation for this loss [is] . . . the distraction of both firms' managements from managing current operations and positioning their firms for the future. These expected efficiency costs were probably far greater for Texaco than for Pennzoil. The dispute posed for Texaco a genuine threat of insolvency and protracted bankruptcy proceedings. Bankruptcy and reorganization can involve enormous efficiency costs in addition to the professional fees involved. . . .

. . . [A] vast number of contractual relationships must be changed. The scope of this task is enormous; indeed, the entire firm can be viewed as nothing more than a cluster of implicit and explicit contracts, each of which may be affected. The interests of different claimants often conflict, and within each class of claimants there are often multiple parties. A reorganization . . . involves a very complicated bargaining game in which many claimants try to maximize their own self-interest. The fear that a firm is or may soon become insolvent causes various claimants on the firm to engage in behavior that is not joint wealth maximizing. . . . [D]uring this period, the current operations of a company can be severely hampered. Relations with customers, suppliers, and bankers can all be disrupted. Attention may be diverted and the quality of service may decline. Key employees may leave, and a vast amount of firm-specific capital may be lost because of uncertainty about the structure or needs of the reorganized firm. . . .

The management talents needed to orchestrate a reorganization may be very different from the skills needed to operate a firm in normal times. For a large corporation, management should be well qualified to deploy assets profitably in peacetime—that is, when the firm is operating in a reasonably normal economic environment and has sufficient assets. A firm that is insolvent, however, may need a wartime general—a person prepared to set aside normal bureaucratic routines, to be less concerned about long-run considerations than winning battles in the short run. . . . It is unlikely that these are the same skills that are required to manage and develop a firm during peacetime. . . .

* * *

. . . Given the substantial efficiency costs of protracted appellate proceedings and especially of the risks of bankruptcy proceedings, why didn't the case settle earlier, and why did Texaco management file for bankruptcy?

Delay in Settlement: The Agency Problem

* * *

... [T]he litigation was controlled by the directors, officers, and lawyers for each company, whose interests differed [from shareholders] in important respects. . . .

The directors and officers of Texaco were themselves defendants in fourteen lawsuits brought after the Pennzoil verdict. These suits asked that the defendants ... account to the Texaco corporation for the damages suffered by reason of the Pennzoil litigation.[6] ... [T]hese lawsuits ... claimed that Texaco's directors and officers had violated their duty of care to the corporation by causing Texaco to acquire Getty Oil in a manner that led to the multi-billion dollar Texas judgment.

... [T]he duty of care ... has two aspects. First, there is ... the basic obligation, which is usually couched in traditional negligence terms: a director or officer must 'perform his functions ... with the care that an ordinarily prudent person would reasonably be expected to exercise in a like position and under similar circumstances.'[7] The second aspect is the so-called 'business judgment rule,' which describes the standard by which courts evaluate whether a director or officer has discharged his obligation. . . . The business judgment rule ... [insulates] an officer or director ... from liability if in good faith he makes a business judgment that he reasonably believes is an appropriately informed decision and that he rationally believes is in the best interests of the corporation.

The purpose of the business judgment rule is to protect officers and directors 'from the risks inherent in hindsight reviews of their unsuccessful decisions, and to avoid the risk of stifling innovation and venturesome business activity.'[8] It serves 'to prevent courts ... from exercising regulatory powers over the activities of corporate managers.'[9] ...

In light of the fact that the Texas trial court found that Texaco had tortiously interfered with Pennzoil's contract with Getty, thus subjecting Texaco to enormous damages, how likely was it that, under Delaware law, the business judgment rule would not have insulated these corporate officials from personal liability for their decisions?

Before 1985, most commentators would have advised corporate officers and directors that because of the business judgment rule they faced no real risk of personal liability for decisions made in good faith. Views changed drastically, however, after the Delaware Supreme Court

---

[6] These suits also asked for judicial declarations that various indemnification agreements between the corporation and its officers and directors were void.

[7] Principles of Corporate Governance: Analysis and Recommendations § 4.01(a) (Tent. Draft No. 4, 1985). . . .

[8] Id.

[9] Manne, *Our Two Corporation Systems: Law and Economics*, 53 Va. L. Rev. 259, 271 (1967); see Gilson, *A Structural Approach to Corporations: The Case Against Defensive Tactics in Tender Offers*, 33 Stan. L. Rev. 819, 822–24 (1981).

decided Smith v. Van Gorkom.[10] *Van Gorkom* [created] uncertainty in predicting how [a] . . . court [would] evaluate corporate decisions.

In *Van Gorkom,* the Delaware Supreme Court held outside directors . . . personally liable for approving a proposed all-cash merger in which a publicly traded company was acquired for a substantial premium above market price. . . . The Delaware Supreme Court reversed, . . . [and held] that the directors were not entitled to the protection of the business judgment rule because they had failed to inform themselves of 'all information reasonably available to them and relevant to their decision.'[11] . . .

. . . [T]he *Van Gorkom* decision must have been very troubling indeed to the Texaco officers and directors. Their greatest concern may have been that a court would conclude that they had failed to make 'appropriately informed decisions' (1) to acquire Getty in the face of Getty's prior dealings with Pennzoil, (2) to indemnify the various Getty interests as part of the transaction, and (3) to allow the Pennzoil litigation ever to reach a Texas jury. Van Gorkom created uncertainty about whether the business judgment rule would offer protection from personal liability.

* * *

Assume that the Texaco directors are faced with a choice of either settling the case for $3 billion or continuing to litigate the case, in which event there are two possible outcomes for Texaco shareholders: (1) a reversal of the judgment below, meaning that Texaco must pay nothing, or (2) an affirmance, causing the shareholders to lose their entire equity. . . . Assume further that there is a fifty percent chance for each outcome on appeal.

From the shareholders' perspective, a $3 billion settlement would surely be preferred over a continuation of the litigation, which would have an expected cost of $5.5 billion, plus whatever extra transaction costs were involved in litigating rather than settling. But from a director's point of view, the continuation of the litigation would be preferable.

This can be seen by examining the alternatives from a director's perspective. If the litigation is won on appeal, the director faces no risk of duty of care liability. If the appeal is lost [or if the director settles], the director must then face a derivative suit. . . . [A]ssume that the odds of the director winning the derivative suit are ninety percent, with a ten percent chance of a loss. . . . [12] Under the tort damages rule, the personal liability of Texaco's directors would be equal to the amount Texaco would pay Pennzoil—either $3 billion or $11 billion. From the directors' point of view, a $3 billion liability is no better than an $11 billion liability.[13] Either judgment surely would far exceed the limits of

---

[10] 488 A.2d 858 (Del. 1985). . . .

[11] Id. at 893.

[12] [T]he odds of the director being held liable in a derivative suit are not much affected by whether the case is resolved by settlement or by a courtroom loss. . . . [T]he basic claims against the directors would [still] arise from the acquisition of Getty Oil.

[13] [Even with a 90% chance of winning the derivative suit following a $3 billion settlement, directors' expected loss would equal $300,000,000.—Tung.]

Texaco's insurance for its directors.[14] . . . [T]he entire net worth of every Texaco director would be wiped out by his share of a $3 billion liability. So long as the amount of potential liability through settlement exceeds the director's net worth, a settling director essentially gives up a fifty percent chance of exoneration [i.e., the 50% chance of winning on appeal]. . . . [A] . . . loss of the duty of care litigation is a 'wipeout' for the directors . . . . As a consequence, a director would rationally prefer to litigate the Pennzoil judgment, because half the time the director will then never have to face the risk of duty of care litigation.

* * *

We cannot be certain that this conflict of interest motivated the Texaco directors and officers, but the facts are certainly consistent with this view. . . .

[But if *Van Gorkom* liability fears explain why the directors initially litigated instead of settled, why did Texaco in the end settle anyway?]

Two unexpected events [induced] settlement. . . . First, Carl Icahn began to purchase Texaco stock. By March 1988, he owned almost fifteen percent of the outstanding shares. He soon made it clear that he thought the case should settle [and] that he would play a role. . . . Second, the bankruptcy judge also intervened. On December 2, 1987, . . . Texaco [sought] to extend the exclusivity period for filing a plan of reorganization. . . . The creditors' committee sought . . . to file a settlement plan [separate from management's plan]. . . . Bankruptcy Judge Schwartzberg granted Texaco [only] a short, forty-day extension to its exclusivity period [and] stated that it would terminate this period sooner and consider some other plan of reorganization . . . *if the creditors' committee and the shareholders' committee . . . could agree to a settlement with Pennzoil.*[15] Thus, the court might well have forced Texaco's management to accept a bargain struck by Pennzoil and the committees.

* * *

Finally, . . . the reorganization plan itself . . . releas[ed] all of Texaco's present and former directors, officers, investment bankers, and attorneys from all claims arising out of the Getty transactions. The plan also . . . dismiss[ed] . . . the derivative stockholder actions. . . . It is not clear why these provisions of the reorganization were in the interests of Texaco shareholders, unless the directors would not settle without them.[16]

---

[14] Although statutes in every state recognize the power of a corporation to indemnify directors and officers within specified limits against expenses and liabilities incurred while carrying out their duties, most statutes expressly deny indemnification for amounts paid in settlement of derivative actions. . . .

[15] In re Texaco, Inc., 84 Bankr. 893, 894 (Bankr. S.D.N.Y. 1988).

[16] Although . . . an overwhelming majority of the Texaco shares were voted to approve the reorganization, which included the provisions dismissing the derivative actions, the shareholders [did] not . . . vote separately on whether to let management off the hook for the duty of care claims. Instead, in order to get the benefit of the $3 billion settlement, the whole package had to be accepted. . . .

---

1. Was Texaco slow to settle because the firm's directors were concerned about personal liability? Once the firm was hit with the $10 billion verdict, the directors feared that a successful suit for negligence liability could bankrupt them personally *even if* they settled the suit for $3 billion; hence, they were gambling at overturning the suit completely. The then-recent decision of the Delaware Supreme Court in *Van Gorkom* might have frightened Texaco's directors: a Delaware court might find them liable for negligence, as it had found the *Van Gorkom* directors. But when (i) a takeover entrepreneur, Carl Icahn, acquired a block of stock while announcing that he intended to force a settlement, (ii) the bankruptcy judge aggressively pushed for settlement, announcing that he might terminate management's period of exclusivity to file a plan, and (iii) creditors agreed with Pennzoil that a $3 billion settlement was about right, then management settled.
2. The Delaware legislature later effectively tightly limited *Van Gorkom*, by adding § 102(b)(7) to its corporations code. That section allowed shareholders to vote in advance to lift *Van Gorkom*-type negligence liability from their boards.

D. MANAGERIAL COMPENSATION IN CHAPTER 11

Bankrupt debtors use key employee retention plans (KERPs) to tie top executives to the debtor during its bankruptcy. These plans incentivize executives with bonuses and stock options to stay with the debtor.

KERPs can also affect the direction of senior management's loyalty and incentives. After the Code's passage in 1978, the early view was that the Code was management- and debtor-friendly, as the debtor-in-possession was typically run by incumbent management. But in the early 1990s "executive flight following retail bankruptcies . . . (hitherto not seen in the 1980s bankruptcies) led creditors to propose pay to stay plans for key employees to preserve the value of the business . . .). Creditor and court-approved KERPs promise key executives bonuses that are often explicitly tied to the speed of the reorganization process, thus counteracting the tendency for managers to draw out Chapter 11 reorganizations." Sreedhar T. Bharath et al., *The Changing Nature of Chapter 11*, at 3 (Indian Inst. of Mgmt. Bangalore, Working Paper No. 461, 2014), available at http:/ssrn/ abstract=2443248. If creditors have a say in setting the KERP's structure, then they can shape managers' incentives away from those of stockholders and closer to those of creditors, with incentives to keep the chapter 11 proceeding short. David A. Skeel, Jr., *Creditors' Ball: The "New" New Corporate Governance in Chapter 11*, 152 University of Pennsylvania Law Review 917, 919 (2003).

But because managers also have a hand in structuring the KERPs, managers may overcompensate themselves, and thereby fail to increase managers' loyalty to the debtor, its creditors, or its shareholder:

> First, corporate executives in bankruptcy are usually the same group that managed the corporation into its financial crisis. Second, compensation to key executives takes money away from creditors, shareholders, and wage-level employees. Third, as executives receive larger salaries, the corporation has less money to operate the struggling business and pay its creditors.

Dorothy Hubbard Cornwell, *To Catch a Kerp: Devising a More Effective Regulation Than S 503(c)*, 25 Emory Bankruptcy Developments Journal 485, 488 (2009).

Congress, reacting in 2005 to highly publicized instances of likely managerial over-compensation, enacted § 503(c), which requires that the court approve a range of KERPs as a condition for the KERP compensation getting administrative priority. Section 503(c) thereby gives creditors a wedge to affect KERP terms, because the creditors could oppose the KERP proposal at a § 503(c) hearing, and managers may well want creditors to support their KERP approval motion.

Section 503(c) provides that:

> (c) Notwithstanding subsection (b) [pertaining to administrative expenses], there shall neither be allowed, nor paid—
>
> (1) a transfer made to, or an obligation incurred for the benefit of, an insider of the debtor for the purpose of inducing such person to remain with the debtor's business, absent a finding by the court based on evidence in the record that—
>
> (A) the transfer or obligation is essential to retention of the person because the individual has a bona fide job offer from another business at the same or greater rate of compensation;
>
> (B) the services provided by the person are essential to the survival of the business; and
>
> (C) either—
>
> (i) the amount of the transfer made to, or obligation incurred for the benefit of, the person is not greater than an amount equal to 10 times the amount of the mean transfer or obligation of a similar kind given to nonmanagement employees for any purpose during the calendar year in which the transfer is made or the obligation is incurred; or
>
> (ii) if no such similar transfers were made to, or obligations were incurred for the benefit of, such nonmanagement employees during such calendar year, the amount of the transfer or obligation is not greater than an amount equal to 25 percent of the amount of any similar transfer or obligation made to or incurred for the benefit of such insider for any purpose during the calendar year before the year in which such transfer is made or obligation is incurred;
>
> (2) a severance payment to an insider of the debtor, unless—
>
> (A) the payment is part of a program that is generally applicable to all full-time employees; and
>
> (B) the amount of the payment is not greater than 10 times the amount of the mean severance pay given to nonmanagement

employees during the calendar year in which the payment is made; or

(3) other transfers or obligations that are outside the ordinary course of business and not justified by the facts and circumstances of the case, including transfers made to, or obligations incurred for the benefit of, officers, managers, or consultants hired after the date of the filing of the petition.

In enforcing § 503(c), courts distinguish plans that aim to retain as their primary goal—and therefore must meet the high bar imposed by § 503(c)(1)—from plans that serve to incentivize employees.[17] Key employee incentive programs (KEIPs)—the latter—need only be "justified under the facts and circumstances of the case" under § 503(c)(3). *In re Dana Corp.*, 358 B.R. 567 (Bankr. S.D.N.Y. 2006).

Courts applying § 503(c) to KEIPs have largely held that the requirement that a plan be "justified by the facts and circumstances of the case" is identical to the business judgment standard of § 363. Some courts have held that KEIPs proposed within the ordinary course of business are not subject to § 503(c) at all.[18]

KEIPs may also present an opportunity for increased influence by creditors. A 2012 study shows that while KERPs have no noticeable effect on the outcome of bankruptcy proceedings, "incentive plans *significantly* improve outcomes for creditors." Scott A. Wolfson & Valerie R. Jackson, *Key Employee Incentive Programs Make "Cents" for Creditors*, 31 American Bankruptcy Institute Journal, Nov. 2012, 22, 23, 31. And "the amount of creditor control is predictive of whether a company will adopt retention and/or incentive bonuses" and that "[b]oth retention and incentive bonuses are more common in cases with a large amount of creditor control." Id. at 91.

Senior management may pay itself a large bonus prebankruptcy, to avoid § 503(c) approval. That bonus though can be a fraudulent conveyance.

> Six months before filing for bankruptcy, Hostess [Brands, the maker of Twinkies] raised the salary of its then-CEO by 300 percent (from approximately $750,000 to $2,550,000), and gave sizable raises to at least nine other top executives. When that news became public, Hostess's creditors were furious. They ran to the bankruptcy court demanding a formal investigation into the pre-bankruptcy raises. They also alerted the press, which ran stories decrying the 'payday before mayday' raises. For its part, Hostess claimed that the raises were approved long before it decided to file for bankruptcy. But in the face of creditor pressure and public embarrassment, Hostess ultimately agreed to rollback the raises. Thus, while the idea of rewarding man-

---

[17] *See, e.g.*, *In re Hawker Beechcraft, Inc.*, 479 B.R. 308 (Bankr. S.D.N.Y. 2012); *In re Velo Holdings Inc.*, 472 B.R. 201 (Bankr. S.D.N.Y. 2012); *In re Global Home Products, LLC*, 369 B.R. 778 (Bankr. D. Del. 2007).

[18] *See In re Nellson Nutraceutical, Inc.*, 369 B.R. 787 (Bankr. D. Del. 2007); *In re Global Home Products, LLC*, 369 B.R. 778 (Bankr. D. Del. 2007).

> agement prior to a public bankruptcy filing can be alluring, companies must think carefully about the risks involved.

James Sprayregen, Christopher Greco & Neal Donnelly, *Recent lessons on management compensation at various stages of the Chapter 11 process*, Financier Worldwide Magazine, March 2013, at 1, 2.

CHAPTER 18

DUTIES TO CREDITORS?

A. DUTIES OF THE TRUSTEE

¶ 1801: Trustees Under the Trust Indenture Act

The Trust Indenture Act governs the standards for trustee behavior for publicly-sold bonds. Trust indentures have several justifications. For secured bonds, any mechanism giving each bondholder a security interest directly in the debtor's property would be prohibitively complex, because each bondholder would have to write, file, and police an individualized mortgage or its own Uniform Commercial Code filing. Moreover, the company could be annoyed by small lawsuits, some without merit. Instead, a single trustee takes the security interest on behalf of all bondholders.

In addition to the transaction costs of the individual bondholders taking security, the bondholders were distant from the enterprise and, at least early on, until holdings concentrated in recent decades, were scattered as well. Thus there would be extensive free-riding among bondholders, who would collectively fail to monitor the debtor well. A single trustee operating under a bond indenture would in theory police the debtor, be sure that it was complying with the bond indenture's covenants, and if need be sue the debtor company. (In addition, the bondholders' original underwriters sometimes took on the "policing" function, at least after a default. The Morgan bank did so for bondholders of the many railroads that defaulted at the end of the 19th century.)

Problems arose in implementation. As documented in a massive 1930s study begun by William O. Douglas, the bondholders' collective action problem extended back to the negotiation of the bonds. Frequently the bond issue had clauses that exculpated the indenture trustee, usually a bank, from wrong-doing and watered down the trustee's obligation to actively check the debtor. Few bondholders read through the indenture to see the extent of the exculpation and adjust their bond price accordingly. (Since few did so, it's possible that the exculpatory clauses were not a fundamental economic problem, but a secondary one.) Douglas and the SEC proposed the Trust Indenture Act to reduce these bondholder problems.

The Trust Indenture Act's structure was (and is) unusual, differing from that of the other securities laws. Rather than establishing statutory standards (or, via SEC regulation, regulatory standards), the TIA established *contractual* requirements for judicial enforcement. It requires that before a debtor issues bonds in the United States, the debtor must have the bond indenture "qualified." The company's lawyers qualify the bond indenture by inserting into the indenture the terms that the TIA requires and by assuring that the terms that the TIA bars are not in the indenture. The SEC declares that the bond indenture qualifies under the TIA, the underwriters sell the bonds, and thereafter the SEC disappears from the TIA enforcement. (This disappearance was formal until 1990 because the SEC lacked statutory authority to act after the bond indenture was qualified; after the 1990 amendments to the TIA, the SEC has more authority, but it has other tasks keeping it busy.) Congress also amended the TIA in 1990 to require that the TIA's standards govern the relationship, even if the lawyers forget to put them into the bond indenture. 15 U.S.C. § 77rrr(c).

The TIA seeks to control the trustee's conflicts and duties: it says whether the indenture can allow the debtor to control the trustee (it can't); whether the indenture can exculpate the trustee from investigating possible defaults or can conclusively rely on the company's certificates (it can rely, if the indenture so provides, TIA § 315(a), 15 U.S.C. § 77ooo(a)); the minimum capital required of a qualifying trustee; whether the trustee shall have access to any lists of bondholders that the company maintains; whether the trustee must examine certificates from the debtor about the debtor's compliance with the indenture; whether the trustee must notify the bondholders if it learns of the debtor's default; whether the indenture can relieve the trustee of liability to the bondholders for the trustee's own willful misconduct; whether the trustee who is simultaneously a lender must return payments it receives within 90 days of the debtor's default (it must), in a return analogous to the Bankruptcy Code's preference provisions. Collectively, it yields one of the most boring statutes conceivable.

Can the trustee, which is usually a bank, also simultaneously lend to the debtor company? One might have thought that this setting was so fraught with danger that Congress would have barred a trustee from simultaneously being a lender. Congress, however, did not. The *Morris* case, the Fleischman memo, and the 1990 TIA amendments show the history of the problem.

¶ 1802: The Depression–Era SEC Investigation Into Trustees

During the 1930s, under William O. Douglas's leadership, the SEC conducted a multi-year investigation into corporate reorganizations and produced a massive report, some of which touched on the conflicts of interest facing bond trustees.

Its results are summarized in Securities and Exchange Commission, Report on the Study and Investigation of the Work, Activities, Personnel and Functions of Protective and Reorganization Committees—Part VI, at 2–6 (1936):

> Under modern trust indentures securing issues of corporate bonds, debentures and notes, important powers are vested in the trustee. The security holders themselves are generally widely scattered and their individual interest in the issue is likely to be small. The trustee, on the other hand, is usually a single bank. By virtue of the broad discretionary powers vested in it under the typical trust indenture it is in a position to take immediate action in a variety of ways to protect or enforce the security underlying the bonds, debentures and notes. . . . Theoretically, the result should be beneficial to all concerned: to the security holder because of increased efficiency, expedition and economy; to the issuer because a trustee is a convenient legal device for conveying title, and because the presence of the trustee relieves the issuer of possible suits and supervision by many individual security holders.
>
> * * *
>
> . . . [A]n examination of the provisions of modern trust indentures and their administration by trustees will show that this reliance [on the trustee] is unfounded. . . . [T]ypically the trustees do not exercise the elaborate powers which are the bondholders' only protection; that they have taken virtually all of the powers designed to protect the bondholders, but have rejected any duty to exercise them; and that they have shorn themselves of all responsibilities which normally trusteeship imports. The "so-called trustee" which is left is merely a clerical agency and a formal instrument which can be used by the bondholders when and if enough of them combine as specified in the indenture.
>
> * * *
>
> The basic problem is to refashion the trust indenture for the purpose of according greater protection to investors. That entails prescribing certain minimum standard specifications for the conduct of trustee and issuer thereunder. As in the case of the other contracts involving persons not capable nor in a position to protect themselves, the contents of the trust indenture can no longer be left to the conventions of the issuer, the trustee or the underwriter.

The SEC report's image is of thousands of bondholders, ignorant of the indenture and perhaps of finance and corporate events as well. In today's financial markets, the bondholders are overwhelmingly institutional investors—banks, pension funds, mutual funds, and insurance companies—institutions that make these investments for a living. (Nor is it altogether clear how different the ownership structure was for bonds back in the 1930s. It seems to have already been overwhelmingly institutional then.) However, Douglas and the framers at the SEC may have picked up the image of scattered stockholder-owners from Berle & Means, The Modern Corporation and Private Property (1932), which described the scattered owners of the corporation, who typically then were in fact individuals, often distant from the firm and ill-informed about it.

¶ 1803: The Notion of Trustee: Fiduciary or Contracted—For Agent? (From Brudney & Chirelstein, Corporate Finance 148–49 (3d ed. 1987))

Notwithstanding the title, "trustee," the norms determining the care and fidelity to which indenture trustees were held prior to enactment of the Trust Indenture Act of 1939 derived more from the terms of the indenture (and its exculpatory clauses) than from any legally imposed fiduciary obligations. The breadth and effectiveness of the exculpatory language of the indenture in relieving the trustee of fiduciary obligations was demonstrated in Hazzard v. Chase National Bank of the City of New York, 159 Misc. 57 (Sup. Ct. N.Y.C., 1936), aff'd, 257 App. Div. 950, (1st Dept.1939), aff'd, 282 N.Y. 652 (1940), which raised the question whether the bank serving as trustee for an issue of debentures of a public utility holding company was to be liable for permitting withdrawal of valuable collateral securing the issue and accepting, in substitution thereof, worthless collateral at a time when the obligor was also a direct borrower from the bank. The plaintiffs predicated their claim upon the propositions that (1) the bank's tolerance of withdrawal and substitution of collateral breached its fiduciary duty because it enabled the obligor to obtain the wherewithal to continue to pay interest on the outstanding debentures and thus to stave off inevitable default, and during the time thus "bought," to repay the outstanding bank loan, and (2) the bank was guilty of the "gross negligence" [that] the indenture established as the trustee's norm, in appraising the adequacy of the new collateral. In rejecting the suggestion that the trustee should be held "to [a] fiduciary's duty in spite of the various verbal devices used to free it from such responsibility . . . " the Court said: "Irrespective of holdings or tendencies in other jurisdictions, it is now the well-settled doctrine of this state that so long as the trustee does not step beyond the provisions of the indenture itself, its liability is measured, not by the ordinary relationship of trustee . . . , but by the expressed agreement between the trustee and the obligor of the trust mortgage. Where the terms of the indenture are clear, no obligations or duties in conflict with them will be implied. . . . The question is, therefore, whether gross negligence . . . has been committed under the terms of the indenture." The Court answered the question in the negative.

The dominance of the "contract" over the "trust" aspects of the indenture trustee's duties at common law, which is reflected in the *Hazzard* case, has not been uniformly accepted.

¶ 1804: Passage of the Trust Indenture Act

From Joel Seligman, The Transformation of Wall Street 196 (1982):

> Enactment of the Trust Indenture Act of 1939 was facilitated by policy differences between the two principal bank lobby organizations, which Douglas skillfully exploited. Soon after [the SEC's study,] 'Trustees Under Indentures[,]' was published, [the chair] of an ad hoc committee of the American Bankers Association, the commercial bankers' lobbying organization, wrote his fellow commercial bankers that the report was 'most drastic' and 'astonishingly unfair to corporate trustees as a class.' . . . Douglas and the American Bankers Association [then] negotiated the provisions of what ultimately became the Trust Indenture Act. Because commercial bankers' concern with the bill was for the most part limited to preserving the power of trustee banks to lend money to a corporate debt issuer and to limiting trustees' exposure to negligence liability, the SEC won pledges that the commercial banks would not oppose the trust indenture bill, with relatively few concessions. This isolated the Investment Bankers Association in opposition and undermined many of their arguments against the bill, because they no longer could claim that most bankers found the bill impractical.

¶ 1805: Broad v. Rockwell Int'l Corp., 642 F.2d 929–30 (5th Cir. 1981)

The first significant activities of the Trust Company [vis-à-vis Rockwell] . . . came in the fall of 1973 when the Trust Company was called upon to consider whether the terms of a proposed supplemental indenture to be executed by Rockwell, as successor by merger to the obligations of Collins under the Indenture, complied with the terms of the Indenture. Under that supplemental indenture, Rockwell would assume in full all of the obligations of Collins under the Indenture, including the obligation to pay interest, and eventually to repay the principal, on the outstanding Debentures until they either were redeemed or matured in 1987. With regard to the conversion feature of the Debentures, the proposed supplemental indenture provided that each holder of a Debenture would have the right to convert his Debenture into the amount of cash that would have been payable to him under the Merger Plan had he converted his Debenture into Collins Common Stock immediately prior to the merger. In other words, a holder of Debentures could, at any time while his Debentures were outstanding, choose to convert them into exactly that which he would have received had he converted immediately before the merger and participated therein as a holder of Collins Common Stock. Because the holders of Collins Common Stock received no common stock in the merger, the holders of Debentures would have no right to convert into common stock either of Collins (who would have no more common stock) or of Rockwell after the merger. Rockwell's view of its post-merger obligations under the Indenture was shared by its counsel (the New York firm of Chadbourne, Parke, Whiteside & Wolff), and by Collins and Collins' counsel (the Los Angeles firm of Gibson, Dunn & Crutcher).

In order to determine whether the proposed terms of the supplemental indenture complied with the terms of the Indenture, the

Trust Company engaged the New York law firm of Curtis, Mallet–Prevost, Colt & Mosle. Two partners in that firm—John P. Campbell and John N. Marden—. . . took the position in September 1973 that a court might in the future find that the intent of the parties at the time the Indenture was executed was that the right to convert into common stock would survive a merger of Collins into another company, and that every holder of Debentures would have the right to convert his Debentures into common stock of the surviving company as long as the Debentures remained outstanding. . . . Campbell and Marden contended that Rockwell would be bound to agree in a supplemental indenture with terms providing for a conversion right of the Debentures into the common stock of Rockwell ("Rockwell Common Stock"). . . . Furthermore, they contended, Rockwell's voting control of Collins prior to the merger imposed upon Rockwell and the directors of Collins a fiduciary obligation to the holders of Debentures.

The record indicates that discussions and exchanges of memoranda and drafts of opinions between counsel for Rockwell and Collins on the one hand, and counsel for the Trust Company on the other hand, continued for several weeks, and their disagreement was heated. . . . Rockwell exerted considerable pressure on the Trust Company to change its position, threatening the withdrawal of certain other business from the Trust Company and possible litigation if the Trust Company blocked the merger by refusing to execute a supplemental indenture. At something of an impasse with counsel for Rockwell, Campbell advised the Trust Company on September 18, 1973, that it could follow any of four alternative courses of action: (1) the Trust Company could decline to execute a supplemental indenture (thus blocking the Collins–Rockwell merger) unless the supplemental indenture provided for a right to convert into Rockwell Common Stock; (2) the Trust Company, as a policy decision, could refuse to take a position as to the rights of the holders of the Debentures after the merger, relying on the provisions in the Indenture and in the supplemental indenture by which Rockwell would indemnify the Trust Company from liability in any lawsuits that might later be brought; (3) the Trust Company could resign as Trustee under the Indenture; or (4) the Trust Company could seek a declaratory judgment with respect to the conversion rights of the holders of Debentures after the merger. Campbell recommended alternative (2), and the Trust Company ultimately followed that recommendation.

¶ 1806: Questions on *Rockwell*

1. Since Rockwell was willing to assume Collins's obligations under the indenture and was willing to offer the debentureholders the right to convert into the consideration offered to all Collins's stockholders (cash), what explains the reluctance of the debentureholders?
2. If Collins's stock disappeared, into what would the convertible debentureholders be convertible?
3. If the trustee's choices outlined by Campbell, counsel to the Trust Company, were always available to trustees, how would the trustee serve as centralized protector of the debentureholders, as the agency through which the debentureholders' free-rider problems are

overcome? Does the trustee's having that range of choices facilitate the purposes of the Trust Indenture Act?

4. Is the case a hard one in business terms? Could the merger transaction have still been overall good for the bondholders?

¶ 1807: Edward Fleischman, Proposed Amendments to the Trust Indenture Act of 1939 (SEC Memorandum Aug. 10, 1987)[1]

The Trust Indenture Act of 1939 . . . regulates terms of most non-governmental debt securities offered and sold in interstate commerce. . . . [A]spects of the Trust Indenture Act have become obsolete, and [the SEC] . . . authorized its staff to draft specific proposals designed to modernize the TIA. . . .

What follows is an analysis and a description of the several legislative proposals, as presented to and approved by the Commission in its open meeting. . . .

I. Qualification Procedures

A. The present requirements for qualification of debt securities [include] . . . conformity to sections 310 through 318 of the TIA (the "mandatory provisions"), description of the terms of the debt, and eligibility of the indenture trustee. . . .

B. Qualification under the Trust Indenture Act . . . [:] Under section 305(b) of the TIA, the SEC is directed to issue an order prior to the effective date of a registration statement refusing to permit the registration statement to become effective if it finds that the requirements of the TIA have not been met. . . . The Commission's authority ends abruptly at that moment.[2] See section 309(e) of the TIA (forbidding "an investigation or other proceeding for the purpose of determining whether the provisions of [a qualified] indenture . . . are being complied with, or to enforce such provisions"). . . .

C. The Trust Indenture Act assumes, therefore, that the terms of the debt will be fixed at the moment of effectiveness and qualification. . . .

D. . . .

E. . . . [T]he best way to ensure compliance with the Trust Indenture Act is to make the mandatory provisions self-executing. . . . What is required, essentially, is a new provision in the TIA to the effect that those provisions of sections 310 to 318, inclusive, that are required to be included in an indenture are a part of and govern every qualified indenture, whether or not they are physically contained therein, while those provisions of such sections that may be included at the option of the obligor are not a part of such an indenture unless they are specifically included. (. . . [C]ertain of the provisions in sections 310 through 318 are optional.) Obviously, this approach would eliminate the

---

[1] Commissioner, Securities and Exchange Commission; member New York bar. . . .

[2] [The SEC's authority "ended abruptly" at that moment for the first fifty years of the statute but then was extended when the Fleischman proposals led to Congress amending the TIA.—Roe.]

need for any lawyer, either inside or outside the SEC, at whatever time of day or night, to review indentures for compliance with the mandatory provisions. . . .

* * *

III. Conflicts of Interest

A. Conflict as Disqualification Only at Time of Default

1. Despite the SEC's [contrary] urging . . . , Congress enacted section 315(a) of the TIA in a form that permits indentures to limit the trustee's liability to duties "specifically set out" in the indenture and to permit well-nigh "conclusive" reliance on certificates and opinions of compliance. As a result, trustees are not bound to perform real duties of guardianship prior to default.

a. The statute requires the trustee, prior to default, to preserve lists of debt holders, act as a medium for communications among them, and receive reports and certificates from the obligor. While these functions are important, they are also ministerial.

b. In addition, the section 315(a) "option" is always elected, with the uniform result that the trustee, unless directed by debt holders, is under no duty to investigate the existence of an event of default. The trustee does not follow the obligor closely; its knowledge of the obligor's operations and condition, and of the obligor's compliance with financial covenants, is ordinarily limited to what the obligor reports. A contrary position was considered by the Reporter for the Federal Securities Code, who concluded: "It has been persuasively urged that extension of the 'prudent man' test for purposes of ascertaining the occurrence of a default . . . would be impracticable and prohibitively expensive in terms of increased trustees' fees."

> [Louis Loss, ALI Federal Securities Code, Introduction, at xl (1978). If the trustee had such a duty it would be a lightning rod for lawsuits when problems arose. Anticipating this, the trustee would raise its fees.]

c. On the other hand, section 315(d) forbids exculpatory terms as to trustee negligence or willful misconduct. The trustee is thus held to a general standard of due care in the performance of its administrative duties.

d. A conflict of interest cognizable under section 310(b) should not cause a trustee, with limited pre-default duties and a minimal standard of care, to withhold performance or to perform unfaithfully. To insist on an absolute standard of independence prior to default appears unnecessary under the circumstances.

2. Adoption of a post-default conflict provision [is sought by the banker-trustees].

* * *

c. Bearing in mind the ministerial quality of a trustee's duties prior to default, it therefore appears to the author that nothing would be lost, and something would be gained, by moving to a post-default conflicts standard. Under that standard, a trustee would not be prohibited by the Trust Indenture Act from engaging or having engaged in underwriting activities except in the case of a default. At the time of default, any underwriting or other present "conflict" by the trustee or any of its affiliates within the preceding twelve months would constitute a disqualifying conflict of interest. . . .

3. Moving to a post-default standard might trigger concerns about untimely trustee resignations. Trustees will resign, it may be said, just when they are really needed. Yet, that has *always* been the case. The obligor's customary debtor-creditor relationship with its trustee bank has not heretofore been treated *by the TIA* as a prohibited conflict of interest. . . . Trustees themselves, however, have been rather more practical. They routinely resign upon a default, or even earlier when default is anticipated, . . . passing the trustee's hat to another eligible institution that has no lending relationship with the obligor. . . . Revising the law should not be expected to affect these bankers' decisions.

B. Debtor–Creditor Relationship as a Proscribed Conflict

1. Strange as it may seem to the uninitiated, the Trust Indenture Act does *not* treat a debtor-creditor relationship between the obligor and the trustee as a disqualifying conflict of interest. The SEC recommended that treatment when the Act was written, see [VI Securities and Exchange Commission, Report on the Study and Investigation of the Work, Activities, Personnel and Functions of Protective and Reorganization Committees 107 (1936)], but Congress decided the issue in favor of the banks.

2. That decision has been subject to vehement criticism on the ground that no conflict of interest possibly could be clearer. . . . The proposed amendment, accordingly, would require creditor-trustees, at the time of a default, to do what they have always done anyway—resign. Since conflicts of interest would matter only once a default occurs . . . , [t]he banks should not be troubled by this particular development.

* * *

¶ 1808: Amendments to the Trust Indenture Act

At the end of 1990, Congress adopted most of Commissioner Fleischman's proposals. The SEC can grant exemptions from the TIA, either by exempting an individual transaction or a class of transactions. 15 U.S.C. § 77ddd(d).

As Commissioner Fleischman pointed out, trustees who had lent to the debtor typically had resigned when the debtor defaulted, as the trustees understood that lending made the trustee highly conflicted. The SEC's and Congress's reaction in 1990 was to formalize the practice, by requiring resignation. As Fleischman then points out, an alternative would have been to bar the trustee from lending to the debtor.

The 1990 reform made the Act's required contractual provisions statutory standards as well.

¶ 1809: The Trust Indenture Act's New Conflicts Provision

Section 310, as amended in 1990 and codified at 15 U.S.C. § 77jjj, provides:

(b) Disqualification of trustee

If any indenture trustee has or shall acquire any conflicting interest as hereinafter defined—

(i) then, within 90 days after ascertaining that it has such conflicting interest, and if the default . . . to which such conflicting interest relates has not been cured or duly waived or otherwise eliminated before the end of such 90–day period, such trustee shall either eliminate such conflicting interest or . . . resign . . . ;

* * *

(iii) . . . any security holder who has been a bona fide holder of indenture securities for at least six months may, on behalf of himself and all others similarly situated, petition any court of competent jurisdiction for the removal of such trustee . . .

. . . [A]n indenture trustee shall be deemed to have a conflicting interest if the indenture securities are in default (as such term is defined in such indenture . . .) and—

(1) such trustee is trustee under another indenture . . . of an obligor upon the indenture securities . . .

* * *

(10) . . . the trustee shall be or shall become a creditor of the obligor.

B. DUTIES OF THE COMPANY

¶ 1810: Metlife v. RJR Nabisco

UNITED STATES DISTRICT COURT
SOUTHERN DISTRICT OF NEW YORK

METROPOLITAN LIFE INSURANCE COMPANY	X	
and JEFFERSON–PILOT LIFE INSURANCE COMPANY,	:	
Plaintiffs,	:	88 Civ. 8266
-against-	:	(JMW)
RJR NABISCO, INC. and F. ROSS JOHNSON,	:	FIRST AMENDED
Defendants.	X	COMPLAINT

Plaintiff[ ] Metropolitan Life Insurance Company ("MetLife") . . . allege[s] . . . :

1. MetLife . . . bring[s] this action for a declaratory judgment and permanent injunction to protect [its] rights as holder[ ] of long-term debt securities of Defendant RJR Nabisco, Inc. ("RJR Nabisco" and the "Company"). These rights are threatened by the proposed "buy-out" of the Company's shareholders that has been agreed to between the Company and Kohlberg Kravis Roberts & Co. ("Kohlberg Kravis").

2. The "buy-out" was initiated by RJR Nabisco's top management, and will . . . strip[ ] the Company of substantially all the value of its assets and distribut[e] it to the Company's shareholders. To finance the "buy-out," RJR Nabisco will be burdened by $19 billion of additional debt, without one new product or asset added to its balance sheet.

3. RJR Nabisco sold the bonds [now] held by MetLife . . . expressly on the basis that the bonds represented investment grade debt of one of America's strongest companies. In the "buyout," the Company intends not to redeem the existing $5 billion of blue chip bonds but instead to misappropriate their value by using this investment grade debt to help finance the high risk "buy-out." The public bond market immediately recognized this impact by reducing the value of RJR Nabisco's outstanding long-term debt, on the day following management's "buy-out" proposal, by almost $1 billion.

4. This action seeks relief before the Company incurs substantial liabilities . . . and thereby irreparably injures Plaintiffs' investments. The transaction is imminent. . . .

The Parties

5. Plaintiff MetLife is a life insurance company organized . . . under the laws of the State of New York. . . .

* * *

7. Defendant RJR Nabisco is one of America's premier companies, and the owner of such diverse businesses and product lines as Del Monte canned fruits and vegetables, LifeSavers candy, Shredded Wheat cereal, Nabisco cookies and Winston cigarettes. In the diversity of its products and the strength of its balance sheet, RJR Nabisco stands at the highest tier of corporate America. . . .

8. Defendant F. Ross Johnson is [RJR's] Chief Executive Officer. . . .

* * *

Plaintiffs' Purchase of the Company's Investment Grade Debt

* * *

12. MetLife . . . own[s] $340,542,000 in principal amount of the notes and debentures of Defendant RJR Nabisco. . . . MetLife also owns approximately 186,000 shares of RJR Nabisco common stock.

13. RJR Nabisco actively solicited "investment grade" ratings for its debt, which are forecasts of the future creditworthiness of the Company. As a result, RJR Nabisco and its shareholders received the benefits of fixed rate, long-term debt with interest rates at only a modest spread above comparable maturity United States Treasury obligations. . . .

14. Plaintiffs agreed to invest in RJR Nabisco based upon the Company's blue chip business; upon its descriptions of a strong capital structure and earnings

record that include prominent display of its ability to pay the interest obligations on its long-term debt several times over; upon express and implied representations of the Company concerning its future creditworthiness; and upon implied representations that it would not deliberately deplete or dissipate its assets. Plaintiffs also relied upon the good faith of RJR Nabisco and its management. . . .

15. The Company's long-term bonds were issued in a market environment *in which "leveraged buy-outs" of $25 billion were not expected.* RJR Nabisco's investment grade rating did not reflect the possibility that management of one of America's leading companies would, in order to amass personal fortunes, put the Company's future at risk and strip the Company of substantially all the value of its assets in a "leveraged buy-out," and, as part of the scheme, would deliberately misappropriate the investment grade value of the long-term debt. Such a transaction is contrary to RJR Nabisco's express and implied representations, and undermine[s] the foundation of the investment grade debt market which the Company knowingly availed itself of and upon which the Company and Plaintiffs have relied for decades.

16. The indentures under which the securities were issued are typical of indentures used by blue chip issuers at the times of issuance of the securities. The indentures include covenants protecting the first priority position of bondholders. . . . As is common with blue chip debt of America's largest companies, however, the indentures do not purport to limit dividends or debt; nor do they contain other express covenants, found in indentures for weaker companies, that are intended to guard against financial deterioration. Such covenants were believed unnecessary with blue chip companies. Such covenants would have also unnecessarily added to transaction costs and could have unduly restricted the management of blue chip companies acting in good faith during the long term of blue chip debt. The prospect of a blue chip company deliberately stripping the value of its assets through a "buy-out" of all its shareholders was not contemplated.

The Events Leading to the "Buy-out" Agreement

17. On October 20, 1988, the Company announced that its Chief Executive Officer, F. Ross Johnson, had proposed to "buy-out" all of the Company's shareholders at $75 per share. Subsequent disclosures indicated that, for more than a year before this announcement, Johnson and other members of management were . . . developing a "buy-out" proposal. . . .

18. While top management pursued the possibility of a "buyout" of the shareholders, RJR Nabisco continued to issue its investment grade debt securities. In 1988 alone, the Company issued $1.4 billion in blue chip debt. The Company solicited an investment grade rating for this debt, which projects creditworthiness and low risk into the future, and confirms the appropriateness of investment by insurance companies, pension funds and other institutional savers.

The "Buy–Out" Proposals

19. Johnson initially offered to purchase all of the outstanding shares of RJR Nabisco for $75 per share, for a total price of $17 billion. A key motive was huge personal profit: if successful in his bid, Johnson expected to make at least $100,000,000. . . .

20. Kohlberg Kravis . . . countered Johnson's bid with a $90 per share proposal, and Johnson thereafter increased his offer to the shareholders by $3.8 bil-

lion, to $92 per share. A special committee of the directors of RJR Nabisco announced that it would put the Company on the auction block.

21. All of the proposals were premised upon replacing the shareholders' equity with high-interest, high-risk debt. Rather than redeeming and refinancing the existing blue chip debt to reflect the deliberate depletion of the value of the Company's assets, the Company permitted the proposals to assume that the existing blue chip debt, with low-risk interest rates, could be used to help finance the "buy-out." The investment grade debt previously issued by RJR Nabisco would be transformed into "junk bonds," but with investment grade interest rates.

22. On December 1, 1988, the special committee recommended Kohlberg Kravis's bid, nominally valued at $109 per share, and the Company and Kohlberg Kravis signed a merger agreement.

Outline of the Proposed Transaction

23. Under the agreement, Kohlberg Kravis states that it is paying $25 billion for the Company. . . . The cash payment to shareholders totals $18.4 billion. Another $700 million will be paid in fees and "transaction costs."

24. To raise the necessary funds, Kohlberg Kravis entities will borrow, and the Company will guarantee, about $19 billion in addition to the $5 billion of existing debt. As a result, the Company, which currently earns about $2 billion before taxes and interest, and is obligated on $5 billion of debt, will be required to service or repay an additional $19 billion of debt. . . .

25. The new debt by itself exceeds the total assets of the Company before the "buy-out." . . . [T]he Company [will sell several] divisions[, t]he proceeds from [which] will be used primarily to repay new debt, which has a shorter maturity than the original investment grade debt.

26. . . . The plan . . . subjects existing debtholders to dramatically greater risk of non-payment, and the Company to a significant risk of insolvency.

27. If successful, the participants in the "buy-out," having achieved private ownership of the common stock of RJR Nabisco, have the potential for tremendous profits.

28. If the plan is unsuccessful, even to a minor degree, RJR Nabisco will face default on its debt obligations and possible bankruptcy.

29. . . . The lenders of the $19 billion of additional debt will also receive either a high interest rate or a chance to participate in future profits, or both.

30. A major portion of the risk will be borne by parties who will have no share of the reward and who will be irreparably damaged: the holders of RJR Nabisco's existing blue chip debt. The $1 billion decline in value on the day following the announcement of the initial "buy-out" proposal . . . reflects the market's understanding that, under the proposals considered, RJR Nabisco would deliberately convert its investment grade debt into "junk." . . .

Nature of the Complaint

31. This complaint is based upon . . . (i) the contractual obligations that RJR Nabisco undertook when it sold its longterm debt; (ii) fraud; (iii) violations of securities laws; . . . and (vi) . . . state fraudulent conveyance . . . laws. . . .

Count I
Breach of Implied Covenant of Good Faith
and Fair Dealing
(Against RJR Nabisco)

33. At the time MetLife and [its affiliate,] Jefferson–Pilot[,] acquired these securities, each rated issue of the Company had an "A" credit rating or better. The Company actively solicited these ratings, which project the future financial security of the Company, in order to induce their purchase by MetLife. . . . The liquidations of substantially all the value for the Company's assets—more than quadrupling the debt and distributing the proceeds to the shareholders—is not an event that was contemplated at the time MetLife . . . invested in RJR Nabisco's investment grade debt. The transaction contradicts the premise of the investment grade market and invalidates the blue chip rating that the Company solicited and took the benefit from.

34. . . . Defendant RJR Nabisco owes a continuing duty of good faith and fair dealing in connection with the contracts through which it borrowed money from MetLife . . . , including a duty not to frustrate the purpose of the contract to the debtholders or to deprive the debt-holders of the intended object of the contracts—purchase of investment-grade securities.

35. In the "buy-out," the Company breaches the duty of good faith and fair dealing by . . . destroying the investment grade quality of the debt and transferring that value to the "buyout" proponents and to the shareholders.

Count II
Fraud

37. The proposed "buy-out" of RJR Nabisco wrongfully and fraudulently seeks to expropriate the investment grade value of Plaintiffs' securities. The deliberate effort to use the blue chip bonds to finance a high-risk "buy-out" is contrary to the express and implied representations made by RJR Nabisco when offering the securities.

38. The conduct of the Defendants in connection with the proposed acquisition of RJR Nabisco is knowing, intentional and fraudulent. . . .

Count III
Violations of Section 10(b) of the 1934 Act

40. In documents and statements disseminated to the public (including annual reports and statements to securities analysts), and in statements made to the entities responsible for rating the quality of its debt securities, Defendants made or caused to be made untrue statements of material facts, or omitted to state material facts required to be stated or necessary to make its statements not misleading, in connection with RJR Nabisco's offering of its long-term debt to the public. For example, the RJR Nabisco Annual Report, issued in February 1988, states that one of the Company's "strategies for growth is to continu[e] to maximize our balance sheet strength[ ]". . . . In an address on November 12, 1987 to the New York Society of Security Analysts, Johnson emphasized the same point:

> Our strong balance sheet is a cornerstone of our strategies. It gives us the resources to modernize facilities, develop new technologies, bring on new products, and support our leading brands around the world.

The prospectuses for debt securities issued by the Company contain or incorporate similar statements and representations.

41. Defendants acted willfully or recklessly in making these untrue statements of material facts, and omitting to state material facts regarding the "buy-out."

42. . . . Defendants [thereby] violated Section 10(b) of the 1934 Act . . . and Rule 10b–5 promulgated thereunder. . . .

43. MetLife . . . relied on Defendants' misrepresentations and misleading statements, and upon the credit ratings for RJR Nabisco debt, in deciding whether to purchase the Company's long-term debt securities.

44. As a result of Defendants' misrepresentations and omissions to state material facts, MetLife and Jefferson–Pilot have been damaged.

* * *

Count IX
Fraudulent Conveyance Act
(Against RJR Nabisco)

63. [T]he "buy-out" will be a fraudulent conveyance because: (a) it will be a conveyance made or obligation incurred without fair consideration . . . by a person that: (i) is or will thereby be rendered insolvent; (ii) is engaged or is about to engage in a business or transaction for which the property remaining in its hands after the conveyance constitutes an unreasonably small capital; or (iii) intends or believes that it will incur debt beyond its ability to pay as they mature; or (b) it will be a conveyance made or obligation incurred with actual intent to injure present creditors.

64. The "buy-out" constitutes a fraudulent conveyance . . . because the post "buy-out" equity in the Company will consist mainly of overstated goodwill created by the transaction, because transfers will be made out of, and obligations will be incurred on behalf of, the stockholders without any consideration benefiting the Company, and because the solvency appraisal upon which the transaction is conditioned will not involve an appraisal of the Company's largest contingent liability—tobacco-related diseases.

WHEREFORE, MetLife and Jefferson–Pilot demand judgment as follows:

(i) A declaration that the "buy-out" constitutes a breach of the implied covenant of good faith and fair dealing owed to Plaintiffs;

(ii) A declaration that the "buy-out" constitutes fraud upon Plaintiffs;

* * *

(iv) A declaration that Defendants violated the securities laws by their misstatements and omissions;

* * *

(vii) A declaration that the transfers made and debt incurred in the "buy-out" may be avoided by Plaintiffs under applicable fraudulent conveyance statutes;

OR, if Defendant RJR Nabisco seeks to consummate the "buyout" before a final judgment declaring the rights of the parties, MetLife . . . demand[s] judgment as follows:

(viii) For restitution or damages for violations of the rights and duties set forth in the above First Amended Complaint;

* * *

(xi) For preliminary and permanent injunctions requiring RJR Nabisco to hold in trust for MetLife . . . an amount sufficient to ensure that restitution or damages can be paid as demanded above.

AND FURTHER, awarding Plaintiffs pre-judgment and post-judgment interest, and the costs and expenses of the action, including attorney's fees, together with such further relief as the Court deems just and proper.

Plaintiffs demand a trial by jury.

New York, New York — HOWARD, DARBY & LEVIN

Dated: December 8, 1988

By: ______________________________

A Member of the Firm
10 East 53rd Street
New York, New York 10022
(212) 751–8000

Attorneys for Plaintiffs
Metropolitan Life Insurance Company . . .

The MetLife complaint was disposed of in Metropolitan Life Ins. Co. v. RJR Nabisco, Inc., 716 F. Supp. 1504 (S.D.N.Y. 1989): The parol evidence rule barred the bondholders from trying to include Ross Johnson's speeches as part of the contract; the court refused to imply a financial ratio covenant into the bond indenture, thereby disposing of the good faith claim; 10b–5 securities fraud requires a purchase or sale, not refraining from purchasing or selling. The fraudulent conveyance claim was dismissed for lack of particularity, as required by F.R.C.P. Rule 9(b).

However, MetLife and RJR later settled, before any appellate resolution, on terms favorable to MetLife. Richard D. Hylton, *Metropolitan Life Settles Its Bond Dispute with RJR*, N.Y. Times, Jan. 25, 1991, at D1.

What exactly was MetLife's financial complaint? Its priority wasn't altered, its covenants weren't stripped. Nothing was done to its indenture. It had the same obligation from the same company as it had before the transaction.

But after the transaction, the obligation to repay MetLife comes from a financially different company. Before the buyout of the stock, which was financed with new debt, RJR Nabisco's balance sheet in very round numbers looked like this:

RJR Nabisco	
$20 billion [$10B or $30B]	$5 billion [due to MetLife and others at 8% interest per annum]
	$15 billion common stock

Although RJR Nabisco, a company in the tobacco business, faced risks (of, say, being worth either $10 billion or $30 billion, depending on how cigarette tort exposure or overall smoking habits developed), in all normally foreseeable circumstances the company could repay MetLife and the other lenders. Even if the company declined in value to $10 billion, it would be able to pay off MetLife and the other creditors.

Then, the buyout organizers buyback a large portion of RJR's common stock, financing the buy-back with new debt. The company's overall operations are made more valuable. But look at what happens to the preexisting bondholders.

RJR Nabisco	
$22 billion [$12B or $32B]	$5 billion [due to MetLife and others, at 8% interest per annum, with a market value now of about $4.5B]
	$10 billion new debt at 12% interest [with $10B market value; 50% chance of default compensated for by high, 12% interest rates]
	$7.5 billion common stock

The new debt could have a market value equal to its face value because it carries an interest rate commensurate with its riskiness. The old MetLife debt, however, carries an interest rate meant for a low-risk borrower that can in all foreseeable circumstances pay back the debt. But after the buyout transaction, if the low-end results come about, $15 billion of debts will seek satisfaction from a company worth $12 billion, and the MetLife bondholders will get only about 80 cents on the dollar. And because the new debt matures earlier than the old, previously-investment grade debt, there's some chance that a noticeable portion of the new debt would be paid back in full, and then, if the company went bankrupt afterward, the old bondholders would be paid from an even further shrunken pie.

Financial alchemy? The company has stock worth $15 billion before the transaction. It borrows $10 billion to buyback the stock, and the residual common stockholders (the buyout organizers) put in $5 billion of pre-transaction stock, but end up with stock worth $7.5 billion. How could the organizers subtract $15 billion in stock, then add $15 billion in new financing, and have $2.5 billion extra?

Well, $500 million of the value should be clear now: it came from the preexisting bondholders. But $2 billion is still to be accounted for. The best explanations come from taxes and operations. The new capital structure is taxed more favorably than the old one. (See Chapter 21.) And the new capital structure could make managers run RJR more effectively: Managers usually want to ward off bankruptcy. With bankruptcy a more serious risk after the RJR recapitalization, they could be motivated to work harder, or smarter. And with a large portion of the company's cash flow dedicated to debt repayment, the managers have less discretion to expand the company. So, if this company were one for which expansion was unwarranted (but managers wanted to expand anyway), the new capital structure would impede managers from ill-advisedly expanding the company.

That then is the bondholders' financial complaint and the core motivations of organizers and managers for the transaction.

If you were the judge, how would you handle MetLife's contractual complaint, knowing, as you do, about the terms of the Drum Financial indenture?

¶ 1811: Bondholder reaction

The RJR bondholder problem—which had RJR's bondholders in the aggregate losing $1 billion in value overnight due to the buyout—was not unique. "Between 1984 and 1988 there were 254 downgrades of industrial debt by Moody's Investors Service as a result of takeovers, buyouts, or defensive maneuvers by companies borrowing heavily to avoid a raid." Gary Hector, *The Bondholders' Cold World*, Fortune, Feb. 27, 1989. Rating agencies estimated that bondholders lost $13 billion overall in these kinds of transactions, with "these creditors . . . talking about 'theft.'"

But because the typical bondholder is an institutional investor with professional experience, journalists wondered why these professionals were "mouthing off instead of [acting]." While bondholders' representatives urged that bondholders be treated fairly with expanded fiduciary duties, other public figures in the business regulatory world thought differently about the needed for expanded fiduciary duties. Said SEC Chair David Ruder: "I am of the school of thought that the fiduciary obligations of the board of directors and the officers of the corporation run to the shareholders and not to the bondholders. Most of the holders of corporate bonds in today's markets are sophisticated institutional investors. They are quite able to take care of themselves." The obvious way for bondholders to protect themselves would be through tougher covenants that made transactions such as the RJR transaction an event of default. Another way would be to charge for the risk. A third would be to lend for a shorter period, during which a damaging transaction was less likely to occur. Id.

Over time, that kind of contractual reaction happened. "[P]oison puts were included in over half of our sample debt issues in 2012, compared to a range of 8.1%–27.4% of debt issues in our sample in the 1990s." Frederick L. Berskin & Helen Bowers, Poison Puts: Corporate Governance Structure or Mechanism for Shifting Risk? (working paper, Sept. 8, 2015), available at http://irrcinstitute.org/reports/more-than-half-of-bond-agreements-include-poison-puts/.

"A poison put . . . gives the bondholder the option of redeeming the bond before maturity if a specified event occurs, such as a change in control." Poison puts could be motivated by executives' desire to ward off outsiders from seeking to displace the executives' control—similar to the impact of a corporate poison pill—and not a desire to protect bondholders. But the authors find that the poison puts are more driven by bondholders seeking protection than executives seeking entrenchment, as their presence tends to be associated with other bondholder protection mechanisms: shorter maturities, higher interest rates, and more protective covenants. Id.

¶ 1812: Credit Lyonnais Bank Nederland, N.V. v. Pathe Commc'ns Corp., 1991 Del.Ch. LEXIS 215 at N.55 (Dec. 30, 1991)

[In evaluating the actions of the controlling stockholder and the board of directors of an LBO company, Judge Allen said: "At least where a corporation is operating in the vicinity of insolvency, a board of directors is not merely the agent of the residual risk bearers, but owes its duty to the corporate enterprise."]

ALLEN, Ch.: The possibility of insolvency can do curious things to incentives, exposing creditors to risks of opportunistic behavior and creating complexities for directors. Consider, for example, a solvent corporation having a single asset, a judgment for $51 million against a solvent debtor. The judgment is on appeal and thus subject to modification or reversal. Assume that the only liabilities of the company are to bondholders in the amount of $12 million. Assume that the array of probable outcomes of the appeal is as follows:

[Outcome] Expected Value	
25% chance of affirmance ($51mm)	$12.75 million
70% chance of modification ($4mm)	$2.8 million
5% chance of reversal ($0)	$0
Expected Value of Judgment on Appeal	$15.55 million

Thus, the best evaluation is that the current value of the equity is $3.55 million.[3] ($15.55 million expected value of judgment on appeal [minus] $12 million liability to bondholders.) Now assume an offer to settle at . . . $17.5 million. By what standard do the directors of the company evaluate [whether to accept this settlement offer]?

The creditors of this solvent company would . . . favor . . . accepting . . . [the offer, because accepting it would] avoid the 75% risk of insolvency and default. The stockholders, however, . . . very well may be opposed to acceptance of the $17.5 million offer [even though] the residual value *of the corporation* would increase from $3.5 to $5.5 million.[4] This is so because the litigation alternative, with its 25%

[3] [Actually, because the debt is only paid off if the judgment is affirmed, the value of the equity is much higher, as Allen recognizes in the next paragraph. A better way to analyze the situation is to conclude that the operational value of an appeal is $15.55 million and that the operational value of a settlement is $17.5 million, but, due to risk, the stockholders prefer an appeal.—Roe.]

[4] [Actually again, the residual value to the stockholders is higher. It would be better to think of the total value of corporation increasing from $15.55 million to $17.5 million if the

probability of a $39 million outcome to them ($51 million [minus] $12 million = $39 million) has an expected value *to the residual risk bearer* of $9.75 million ($39 million x 25% chance of affirmance), substantially greater than the $5.5 million available to them in the settlement.[5]

. . . [I]t seems apparent that one should in this hypothetical accept the best settlement offer available providing it is greater than $15.55 million, and one below that amount should be rejected. *But that result will not be reached by a director who thinks he owes duties directly to shareholders only. It will be reached by directors who are capable of conceiving of the corporation as a legal and economic entity.* Such directors will recognize that in managing the business affairs of a solvent corporation in the vicinity of insolvency, circumstances may arise when the right (both the efficient and the fair) course to follow for the corporation may diverge from the choice that the stockholders (or the creditors, or the employees, or any single group interested in the corporation) would make if given the opportunity to act.

¶ 1813: Questions on *Credit Lyonnais*

1. What standard for the board does Allen articulate? When does it apply?
2. Courts have usually said that the board's duties shift to creditors when the company becomes insolvent. Was the company in Judge Allen's hypothetical insolvent? If the company takes an appeal, what are the chances that the firm will be insolvent? 75%?
3. Is the judge's standard that in the vicinity of bankruptcy, the company must maximize the value of its creditors' claims? The stockholders' value? The value of the corporation? Or must the board of directors balance stockholders against creditors? Or is the standard something else?
4. The last paragraph begins with directors thinking of the firm as a whole. In Judge Allen's hypothetical, for a firm in the vicinity of bankruptcy, is there any operational difference between the directors owing their duty to the firm or owing it to the creditors? Or are they functionally the same?
5. Reconcile a duty to creditors and to the firm with the following possibility.

---

board accepts the settlement offer. The offer is worth $1.95 million to the corporation as a whole.—Roe.]

[5] [To use Allen's chart from above, deduct the $12 million due to the bondholders before the expected values are summed up:

[Outcome] Expected Value to Stockholders	
25% chance of affirmance ($51mm minus $12mm)	$9.75 million
70% chance of modification ($4mm minus $12mm)	$0
5% chance of reversal ($0)	$0
Expected Value to Shareholders of Judgment on Appeal	$9.75 million

—Roe.]

[Outcome] Expected Value on Firm	
25% chance of affirmance ($80mm)	$20.00 million
70% chance of modification ($4mm)	$2.80 million
5% chance of reversal ($0)	$0
Expected Value of Judgment on Appeal	$22.80 million

Should the directors take a settlement at $17.5 million, which would yield creditors $12 million and shareholders $5.5 million? Doesn't the formulation of the duty (to shareholders, to creditors, to the corporation as a whole) make a difference here? Is the firm here in the vicinity of bankruptcy? Doesn't an appeal put it in the same vicinity as Allen's hypothetical (75%)? If the board's duties here are to creditors, what should the board do: appeal or settle? If the board's duty is to maximize the value of the firm, what should the board do: appeal or settle?

[Outcome] Expected Value on Debt	
25% chance of affirmance ($80mm)	$3.00 million
70% chance of modification ($4mm)	$2.80 million
5% chance of reversal ($0)	$0
Expected Value to Creditors of an Appeal	$5.80 million

6. When the expectations and probabilities are unclear, does Allen's standard face difficulties? Are they the kind of difficulties that support corporate law's business judgment rule? And if the business judgment rule were applied to a new standard (of, presumably, maximizing the corporation's value), then would the board's work continue to be unreviewable?
7. The tough case under Allen's standard: The expected value of the appeal is $15.55 million, just as it is in Allen's opinion. The settlement offer though is also for $15.55 million.[6] Does Allen's standard tell us what to do? Or, if in the problem in paragraph 5, the settlement offer was at a risk-adjusted $22.8 million, would Judge Allen's opinion guide the board of directors?

   (The setting here resembles that in one of the hypotheticals following *Atlas Pipeline,* in which the judge, listening to the First's and the Second's valuation and views on whether to liquidate or keep the firm going, cannot readily rely on either party.)
8. *Credit Lyonnais* caused much discussion. In the following decades, the Delaware courts distanced themselves from *Credit Lyonnais.* The Delaware court concluded recently that boards adopting risky strategies that favor shareholders are protected by the business

[6] Ignore risk for this problem, or if one cannot ignore risk, assume that the settlement offer is at the certainty equivalent of the appeal's expected value. That is, you can assume that the certainty equivalent is $15.55 million and that's the settlement offer.

judgment rule, even if the company is insolvent, if the strategy seems to maximize overall company value. Quadrant Structured Prods. Co. v. Vertin, 102 A.3d 155. 187–88 (Del. Ch. 2014); Quadrant Structured Prods. Co. v. Vertin, C.A. no. 6990-VCL (Del. Ch. Oct. 20, 2015).

If the company is insolvent, can the strategy be viewed as a fraudulent conveyance?

9. The conventional view is that creditors are "outside" the corporation and they get the contractual covenants that they bargain for but usually no more. Occasionally contractual gaps have to be filled in, and the debtor does owe a duty of good faith. See generally Steven L. Schwarcz, *Rethinking a Corporation's Obligations to Creditors,* 17 Cardozo L. Rev. 647 (1996). A reason for the conventional view is that financial creditors could bargain for lower risk, and then pay for it. A reason not to imply terms is that if the court implies a term, then if later parties find a better way to deal with the problem, they may not use that better way, because the court has already decided how the parties will deal with the problem.

10. Perhaps a potential justification for a fiduciary duty (or aggressive contract gap-filling) might come from the feedback effects of chapter 11: The creditors *would* in this or that setting have bargained for a covenant that would have allowed them to quickly seize the firm if the debtor defaulted. The firm would default in the morning, but by the afternoon the creditors would have seized and sold their collateral, or taken over the board of directors, installed their own people, and displaced the old stockholders with themselves. The new board's duties would continue to run to stockholders, but the stockholders would, by the afternoon, be the old creditors. The corporation's duties could then *always* run to shareholders; upon default the identity of the shareholders would (nearly) instantaneously change. Chapter 11, however, the argument would run, disallows this kind of contractual seizure and instantaneous shift in shareholder identity; in its place (advocates of fiduciary duties to creditors might argue) should be fiduciary duties to creditors.

11. Commentary on *Credit Lyonnais,* such as that from former Delaware Chief Justice Norman Veasey, emphasized that the board ought not to owe special fiduciary duties to creditors in the "vicinity of bankruptcy." The board's obligation in the vicinity should, he indicated, be to exercise their sound business judgment and do what is in "the best interests of the corporate entity."[7]

12. Consider ¶ 7 again. Does a simple board duty to act the "best interests of the corporate entity" give a trial court any standard to review a board's decision when the directors choose to appeal rather than settle in ¶ 7 (or vice versa).

---

[7] E. Norman Veasey & Christine T. di Guglielmo, *What Happened in Delaware Corporate Law and Governance From 1992–2004? A Retrospective on Some Key Developments,* 153 University of Pennsylvania Law Review 1399, 1431 (2005). See also Stephen M. Bainbridge, *Much Ado about Little? Directors' Duties in the Vicinity of Insolvency,* 1 Journal of Business and Technology Law 607 (2007), and Frederick Tung, *Gap Filling in the Zone of Insolvency,* 1 Journal of Business and Technology Law 335 (2007).

13. Vice Chancellor Strine emphasized considerations similar to Veasey's. In Production Resources Group v. NCT Group, 863 A.2d 772 (Del. Ch. 2004), he said:

> The obligation of directors in that context of high risk and uncertainty . . . was not "merely [to be] the agent of the residu[al] risk bearers" but rather to remember their fiduciary duties to "the corporate enterprise" itself, in the sense that the directors have an obligation "to the community of interest that sustained the corporation . . . " and to preserve and, if prudently possible, to maximize the corporation's value to best satisfy the legitimate claims of all its constituents, and not simply to pursue the course of action that stockholders might favor as best for them.[8]

But does this obligation create any new causes of action for the creditors? Vice Chancellor Strine continued:

> Creditors are typically better positioned than stockholders to protect themselves by the simple tool of contracting. . . . The reality that creditors become the residual claimants of a corporation when the equity of the corporation has no value does not justify expanding the types of claims that the corporation itself has against its directors. It simply justifies enabling creditors to exercise standing to ensure that any valuable claims the corporation possesses against its directors are prosecuted.

14. During the financial crisis in 2008, Bear Stearns failed and was merged into J.P. Morgan, with the Bear shareholders' initial consideration being nominal, at $2 per share. The Bear Stearns board of directors approved the deal after their attorneys briefed them on their duties:

> The moment had come to seal the fate of Bear Stearns, the fifth-largest Wall Street securities firm. The lawyers walked the board through its fiduciary duties under Delaware law, which required them to consider their duty to creditors if they turned down the JP Morgan deal and opted for bankruptcy. Given that the choice was between nominal consideration for shareholders and 100 cents on the dollar for creditors or nothing for shareholders and pennies for creditors, Sullivan & Cromwell's advice for the board was that its fiduciary duties had shifted from shareholder to all other stakeholders of Bear Stearns, among them creditors, employees, and retirees.

William D. Cohan, House of Cards: A Tale of Hubris and Wretched Excess on Wall Street 108–09 (2009).

¶ 1814: *Credit Lyonnais*, Vicinity of Bankruptcy

Financial economists detect a small but significant financial impact from *Credit Lyonnais* for companies close to default. If managers took fewer unwise risks in the firm or otherwise avoided unwisely favoring equity over debt, then these firms' riskiness should decrease, creditors should be more willing to lend, and covenants would be less deeply used (because directors could be expected more than previously to "do the

---

[8] The quotations inside the excerpt are from *Credit Lyonnais*.

right thing" for the firm and its creditors). Such effects, albeit narrow, were found following *Credit Lyonnais*. Bo Becker & Per Stromberg, *Fiduciary Duties and Equity–Debtholder Conflicts*, 25 Review of Financial Studies 1931 (2012).

¶ 1815: N. Am. Catholic Educ. Programming Found. v. Gheewalla, 930 A.2d 92, 103 (Del. 2007)

Recognizing that directors of an insolvent corporation owe direct fiduciary duties to creditors, would create uncertainty for directors who have a fiduciary duty to exercise their business judgment in the best interest of the insolvent corporation. To recognize a new right for creditors to bring direct fiduciary claims against those directors would create a conflict between those directors' duty to maximize the value of the insolvent corporation for the benefit of all those having an interest in it, and the newly recognized direct fiduciary duty to individual creditors. Directors of insolvent corporations must retain the freedom to engage in vigorous, good faith negotiations with individual creditors for the benefit of the corporation.

Accordingly, we hold that individual creditors of an insolvent corporation have no right to assert direct claims for breach of fiduciary duty against corporate directors. Creditors may nonetheless protect their interest by bringing derivative claims on behalf of the insolvent corporation or any other direct nonfiduciary claim, as discussed earlier in this opinion, that may be available for individual creditors.

¶ 1816: E. Norman Veasey, *Counseling the Board of Directors of a Delaware Corporation in Distress*, American Bankruptcy Institute Journal, No. 1, at 64 (2008)

In *Trenwick America Litigation Trust v. Ernst [&] Young LLP,* Vice Chancellor Strine clarified further the import of the Credit Lyonnais language. He stated in *Trenwick*, as he had in *Production Resources*, that the language in *Credit Lyonnais* was not intended as a sword hanging over the heads of directors. Rather, it was more in the nature of a shield. That is, to the extent that directors of a corporation in the zone of insolvency may consider the rights of creditors in the context of their duties in serving the corporate entity, they may not be breaching their duty to stockholders.

C. CONTRACT THEORY

¶ 1817: Allan Farnsworth, *Disputes Over Omission in Contracts*, 68 Columbia Law Review 860, 891 (1968)*

Introduction

... [A]bsent some overriding public policy, courts are to enforce contracts in accordance with the "expectations of the parties." Usually the parties will have aided the court by expressing at least some of their expectations in contract language, oral or written. Even so, disputes will arise. . . . Sometimes . . . the parties will disagree over what they did not say, over the effect of their contract on a situation for which they have failed to provide. . . . What should a court do when a party had expectations that he failed to reduce to contract language? . . . What should a court do when a party failed to foresee the situation and so had no expectation as to it? . . .

... [C]ommon law courts . . . purport[ ] to determine what the parties would have said if they had said something about it. What the court decides they would have said is then called an "implied term" and is "read into" the contract.

* * *

Th[is] . . . approach . . . disguise[s] the role played by the courts. It . . . refer[s] to a fictional "intention" of the parties which is in turn supposed to take the form of fictional "terms" of the contract. . . . [But] it is more realistic to assume that the parties form their expectations in connection with a limited number of significant situations, selected from a much larger number of foreseeable ones. . . . When they reduce their expectations to contract language, a . . . process of selection takes place, and they use their language only in connection with a limited number of the significant situations with respect to which they formed their expectations. As to the rest, there is an understatement of expectation.

... The process of determining whether there is [an omission] is that of interpretation. The process of resolving [such a case] is that of inference, based either on actual expectations or on general principles of fairness and justice. So where a dispute over omission concerns the qualification of a duty that has been expressed without qualification, a court must first determine by the process of interpretation whether the case at hand was one of the significant situations with respect to which the language was used. If it was not, then . . . the court should recognize that it is within its power to extend the duty by analogy to the case at hand, to refuse to extend it, or to reach an adjustment that lies between these extremes.

---

* This article originally appeared at 68 Colum L. Rev. 860 (1968). Reprinted by permission.

CHAPTER 19

WORKOUTS TO AVOID A BANKRUPTCY

A. GENERAL

¶ 1901: Workouts to Avoid Bankruptcy

Bankruptcies are costly. Lawyers and advisors must be paid. The persistent proceedings divert the attention of the firm's managers to dealing with financial and legal matters at a time when their firms' operations badly need sustained attention. Customers, suppliers, and employees frequently become uneasy and abandon the firm.

If bankruptcy is costly, why don't the creditors and the debtor recapitalize the firm outside of bankruptcy and split up these saved costs?

Some firms try to recapitalize outside of bankruptcy and succeed. Some try and fail. Some try and fail because of the rules and incentives we shall examine in this chapter.

¶ 1902: Arthur S. Dewing, The Financial Policy of Corporations (5th Ed. 1953)[1]

[The contents of the bond indenture can be summarized:]

This rather elaborate document has, ordinarily, [five] important sets of provisions, some of which are mere recapitulations or elaborations of statements made in the primary contract, the bond, and some provisions only indirectly referred to in the bond. There is, first, the set of provisions summarizing the amounts [and] future dates of payment, the interest rate and the time of interest payment-provisions which acknowledge that the bondholder is a creditor of the corporation entitled to the payment of his loan with interest. Furthermore, if the payment of the debt may be anticipated by the corporation, the fact will be clearly stated, together with the specific mechanism of prepayment which shall insure fairness to all the scattered bondholders. . . . *Fourthly, there is a set of provisions which defines with a high degree of precision the exact course the bondholders, acting individually or together, must pursue in order to levy on the corporation, as general creditors,* or to levy on the specific property, if any, set aside for the security of the bonds issued under the indenture. Again, fifthly, there are provisions describing the duties and the obligations of the trustee. These clauses define with precision what he can and what he cannot do, on behalf both of the corporation and of the individual and collective bondholders. . . .

B. MODIFICATION OF THE INDENTURE

¶ 1903: Aladdin Hotel Co. v. Bloom, 200 F.2d 627 (8th Cir. 1953)

GARDNER, Chief Judge.

. . . Josephine Loeb Bloom as plaintiff sought for herself and other minority bondholders of the Aladdin Hotel Company similarly situated equitable relief. She named as defendants Aladdin Hotel Company, a corporation, Charles O. Jones, Inez M. Jones, Charles R. Jones, Kathryn Dorothea Jones, Barbara Ann Jones and Mississippi Valley Trust Company, a corporation. She alleged that the class whom she purported to represent consisted of approximately 130 members who were the owners of a minority in value of certain bonds issued by the Aladdin Hotel Company . . . ; that on September 1, 1938, the Aladdin Hotel Company executed and delivered a series of 647 bonds aggregating in principal amount the sum of $250,000.00. The bonds on their face were made payable September 1, 1948, with interest to that date at 5 per cent per annum . . . ; *that the bonds and deed of trust contained provision[s] empowering the bondholders of not less than two-thirds principal amount of the bonds, by agreement with the Hotel Company, to modify and extend the date of payment of said bonds*

---

[1] As reproduced in Victor Brudney and Marvin Chirelstein, Corporate Finance (3d ed., 1987).

provided such extension affected all bonds alike. She then alleged that . . . the defendants, other than the Hotel Company . . . were all members of the so-called Jones family and during the period from May 1, 1948 to the time of the commencement of this action they were the owners of a majority of the stock of the Hotel Company and controlling members of its Board of Directors and dominated and controlled all acts and policies of the Hotel Company; that they were also the owners and holders of more than two-thirds of the principal amount of said bonds, being the owners of more than 72 per cent thereof; that they entered into an agreement with the Hotel Company June 1, 1948 to extend the maturity date of said bonds from September 1, 1948 to September 1, 1958. . . . It was alleged that . . . the purported changes were made on application of the Hotel Company and with the consent of the holders of two-thirds in principal value of the outstanding bonds; that no notice of said application for change in the due date of the bonds was given to the mortgage bondholders and that plaintiff did not consent nor agree to the modification. She then alleged that the modifications were invalid because [they were] not made in good faith and were not for the equal benefit of all bondholders but were made corruptly for the benefit of the defendants and such modification deprived plaintiff and the other mortgage bondholders of their rights and property. . . . Plaintiff prayed for a declaratory judgment declaring and holding that the purported modifications, waivers and certifications are illegal, inequitable and void; that she and all other bondholders of the defendant Aladdin Hotel Company have judgment against defendant Aladdin Hotel Company for the principal amount of the bonds held by each of them with interest thereon . . . .

* * *

. . . [T]he Hotel Company . . . contends: (1) that the modification . . . extending the time of maturity of the bonds was effected in strict compliance with the provisions of the contract of the parties and hence was binding on all the bondholders; . . . (4) that if a cause of action resulted from the acts of the parties to the contract it could be prosecuted only by the Mississippi Valley Trust Company, named as trustee in the trust deed.

[Modification clauses in the bond and indenture]

The trust deed contained [a] provision that,

> In the event the Company shall propose any change, modification, alteration or extension of the bonds issued hereunder or of this Indenture, such change, if approved by the holders of not less than two-thirds in face amount of the bonds at the time outstanding, shall be binding and effective upon all of the holders of the then outstanding bonds, provided, however, that such modification, change, alteration or extension shall affect all of the outstanding bonds similarly.

The bonds, including those held by plaintiff, contained the following:

> The terms of this bond or of the Indenture securing the same may be modified, extended, changed or altered by agree-

> ment between the Company and the holders of two-thirds or more in face amount of bonds of this issue at the time outstanding. Any default under the Indenture may be waived by the holders of two-thirds or more in face amount of the bonds at the time outstanding.
>
> The bonds also contained the following provision:
>
> For a more particular description of the covenants of the Company as well as a description of the mortgaged property, of the nature and extent of the security, of the rights of the holders of the bonds and of the terms and conditions upon which the bonds are issued and secured, reference is made to said General Mortgage Deed of Trust.

[Joneses have no fiduciary duty to bondholders]

It appears without dispute that the modification here under consideration was made in strict compliance with the provisions contained in the trust deed and by reference embodied in the bonds. The Hotel Company made the application to the trustee and it was approved by the holders of more than two-thirds in face amount of the bonds at the time outstanding. . . . It required that such application have the approval of those holding two-thirds or more in face value of the bonds. The only other limitation contained in the contract with reference to the power to modify its terms was to the effect that "such modification, change, alteration or extension shall affect all of the outstanding bonds similarly." The modification did affect all outstanding bonds similarly and it is important, we think, to observe that the contract does not require that such modification affect all bondholders similarly. What effect this change might have on various bondholders might depend upon various circumstances and conditions with which the trustee was not required to concern itself. The so-called Joneses were the controlling stockholders of the Hotel Company and were its officers and the court found that the alteration was advantageous to the Hotel Company. *It was doubtless effected primarily to benefit the financial standing and operating efficiency of the hotel.* It does not follow, however, that such modification was prejudicial to the bondholders. Their security was greatly improved in value by the management and *it is inconceivable that the Joneses should deliberately act to the prejudice or detriment of the bondholders when* they held and owned some 72 per cent of the entire outstanding bond issue. It is urged that because the Joneses were acting in a dual capacity they became trustees for the other bondholders and that as such it was incumbent upon them to do no act detrimental to the rights of the bondholders. The rights of the bondholders, however, are to be determined by their contract[,] and courts will not make or remake a contract merely because one of the parties thereto may become dissatisfied with its provisions, but if legal will interpret and enforce it. There is no question that the provision in the trust deed and bonds was a legal provision which violated no principle of public policy nor private right. . . .

We have searched the record with great care and find no substantial evidence warranting a finding of bad faith, fraud, corruption or conspiracy of the Joneses. When Charles O. Jones became manager of the hotel properties in 1944 no interest had been paid on the bonds prior to that date. The Hotel Company paid the interest to all bondholders in 1944 and the interest has been paid each year since. Numerous improvements were made in the hotel property at an expense of over $300,000. At the time the Joneses took over the management in 1944 the Company had a deficit of $70,000 and a balance due of $24,000 on the first mortgage of $50,000, all of which has been paid off, and the gross income of the hotel has increased from $219,000 in 1944 to $600,000 in 1951, and the book value of the stock has increased from $384,000 in 1944 to $916,000 in 1951. The properties covered by the trust deed were at the time of the trial of the proximate value of $1,000,000.

* * *

[No-action clause in the bond indenture]

It remains to consider the contention that plaintiff in her individual capacity could not maintain this action. The deed of trust provides that,

> No holder of any bond hereby secured shall have any right to institute any suit or other action hereunder unless the Trustee shall refuse to proceed within thirty (30) days after written request thereto of the holders of not less than twenty per cent (20%) in face value of the bonds then outstanding and after tender to it of indemnity satisfactory to the Trustee.

More than 20 per cent of the bonds were in the hands of the minority bondholders but no written request was made upon the trustee to bring this suit. The court has held that the trustee at all times acted in good faith and no reason appears why he was not requested to bring this suit. Plaintiff is the owner of only $3500 face value of a bond issue of $250,000. According to her complaint there are 130 other minority bondholders and if she can maintain this action individually then the defendant may be subjected to 130 other similar lawsuits. As stated by this court in Central States Life Ins. Co. v. Koplar, 80 F.2d 754, 758:

> The reason for the rule is not far to seek. If in a mortgage securing thousands of bonds every holder of a bond or bonds were free to sue at will for himself and for others similarly situated, the resulting harassment and litigation would be not only burdensome but intolerable.

We think plaintiff could not maintain this action in her individual capacity without first having complied with the provisions of the deed of trust which vests in the trustee the right to maintain such an action.

The judgment appealed from is therefore reversed and the cause is remanded to the trial court with directions to dismiss plaintiff's complaint.

¶ 1904: Questions on *Aladdin*

1. When representing Ms. Bloom in a future bond issuance, what clauses might you seek? Would you seek a rigid clause, such as one that barred any modification of the payment terms over the, say, 20–year life of the bond issue? If you did, how might the company

respond? Might you seek a super-majority modification clause, requiring that at least, say, two-thirds or three-quarters of all non-insider bondholders, or of all voting non-insider bondholders, consent to any modification, compromise, extension, or change of interest rates?

2. Could the transactions in the *Aladdin* case have been accomplished under the Drum Financial indenture? See "Description of Debentures—Modification of Indenture," at ¶ 703.

3. Why is the Modification of Indenture provision in the Drum Financial indenture? Cf. Trust Indenture Act of 1939, § 316(b):

   § 316(b) Prohibition of impairment of holder's right to payment

   Notwithstanding any other provision of the indenture to be qualified, the right of any holder of any indenture security to receive payment of the principal of and interest on such indenture security, on or after the respective due dates expressed in such indenture security, or to institute suit for the enforcement of any such payment on or after such respective dates, shall not be impaired or affected *without the consent of such holder. . . .*

4. In the event of reorganization in chapter 11, what is the effect of the Drum Financial's (and § 316(b)'s) Modification of Indenture provision? Cf. §§ 1126(c), 1129(a)(8).

5. Consider § 1126(e):

   > On request of a party in interest, and after a notice and a hearing, the court may designate any entity whose acceptance or rejection of such plan was not in good faith, or was not solicited or procured in good faith or in accordance with the provisions of this title.

6. Modifying an indenture is more complex than modifying a loan from a single bank. The conventional wisdom as to renegotiation of public debentures used to be:

   > In a private borrowing from an institutional lender, the debtor may be less concerned with the scope of restrictions on additional debt in the loan agreement than in the case of a public borrowing from scattered debenture holders. In the former case, not only is obtaining the lender's waiver, or consent to alteration, mechanically feasible, but the creditor is likely to be responsive to changes which it perceives will enhance the borrower's economic well being. In the latter case, the mechanics of consent to change are more cumbersome, and the scattered debenture holders are less likely to be able or willing to make the judgment that concessions are advantageous to themselves as well as to the debtor.

   Victor Brudney & Marvin Chirelstein, Corporate Finance 175 note h (3d ed. 1987). But institutional changes in recent decades make modification institutionally possible and plausible. See the Chrysler consent solicitation at ¶ 707; when Chrysler sought to renegotiate key provisions of its negative pledge clause, it discovered that a large portion of the bonds was owned by two or three junk bond mutual funds. Does the institutionalized debt market give reason to think that successful consent solicitation would be mechanically easier in the 1980s than in the 1920s, if it were legally facilitated? Cf. Katz, ¶ 1910, n.12.

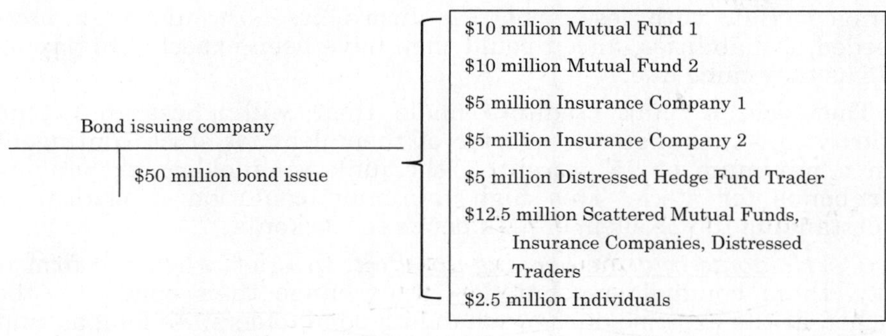

C. HOLDING OUT AND BUOYING-UP

¶ 1905: Collapse of a Workout

A. The MGF Oil Story

In the 1970s, MGF Oil Corporation explored for, developed, and produced oil, principally in west Texas and nearby states. As the price of oil soared in the 1970s, its business expanded. It financed much of its expansion with bank and other debt. In 1981, it sold $75 million of junk bonds.[2]

In the early 1980s, MGF's business declined. As the world price for oil fell, the demand for drilling activity declined and the value of finding oil decreased. Losing money, MGF stopped much of its drilling. By then, it owed several hundred million dollars to old junk bondholders, but it was worth much less than the face value of its debt. MGF was insolvent and headed for bankruptcy.

B. The Attempted MGF Workout

1. Why are there bankruptcies? If bankruptcy is costly, why don't the owners and creditors of the firm negotiate a deal to avoid its cost? They make a deal to split the gains from improved efficiency of the firm, or from the avoided bankruptcy costs. The creditors could take a large stock position, or they could reduce their demand for current cash payments in return for a greater deferred return. In the workout, they could then split among themselves (and perhaps with stockholders) any gains and savings. Creditors and stockholders often make that attempt. Sometimes they succeed.

That's what MGF tried to do in August 1984.

[2] Recall from chapter 7: Junk bonds lack an investment grade rating, because the issuers have more than a trivial chance of defaulting. By the mid–1980s junk bonds made up one-quarter of the corporate bond market. Issuers and their bankers prefer to call the bonds "high yield securities."

2. *The MGF exchange offer*. MGF tried to eliminate two-thirds of its debt by getting the creditors to exchange their debt for stock. The maturity of the remaining debt would be extended for five years. Had the exchange offer succeeded, MGF still would have been highly leveraged. But, with less debt, the firm's assets would then have exceeded its liabilities, and it could then have been expected to pay its debts as they came due.

The secured bank creditors made their willingness to extend maturity and exchange one-quarter of their debt for stock contingent upon a minimum of 95 percent of the junk bondholders exchanging their bonds for stock. This high minimum condition is critical to understanding the problem of junk bonds in workouts.

3. *Holdouts and the buoying-up effect*. In brief: when the firm is shaky, those bondholders that do not exchange their bonds will be enriched at the expense of the exchanging bondholders. As long as that subsidy to the nonexchanging, overhanging bondholders is greater than the savings in avoided bankruptcy costs accruing to potentially exchanging bondholders, the potentially exchanging bondholders are better off holding fast, frustrating the workout. Recognizing this, those that want to exchange condition their willingness to participate on others also exchanging. The exchanging bondholders face a type of debt overhang problem, which disincentivizes them to exchange.

We can use another metaphor: Think of ice cubes jammed in a cylinder partly filled with water. Vis-à-vis other substances in the cylinder, each substance is entitled to a pay-off dependent on its height in the cylinder. Vis-à-vis other ice cubes, each cube is entitled to a pay-off commensurate with its size. Most of the cubes voluntarily melt to free up the cylinder. The remaining few cubes then float to the top. Since pay-off vis-à-vis other substances depends on the position in the cylinder, the icy holdouts profit from others' melt-down. The holdouts see their pay-off increase. They are buoyed up.

Same goes for exchange offers. If only some of the creditors exchange, the exchanging creditors give up their priority compared to the nonexchangers, thereby benefiting the nonexchangers, who then share among themselves the priority amount. The nonexchangers thereby get more than the exchangers.

Now with numbers. Simplify the MGF scenario by positing a firm worth $150 million, with a single bond issue that was worth $200 million when issued. Five creditors hold the debt in equal-sized portions. Stockholders, we assume for some realism, cannot be eliminated outside of bankruptcy. Let's give stockholders a hold-up value of $25 million; the debt is worth the remaining $125 million.

So MGF's simplified, market-oriented balance sheet looks like this:

MGF Balance Sheet 1

$150M	$125M	Market value of debt ($200M face value)
	$ 25M	Common stock[3]

Arithmetic tells us that the bonds are worth $.625 on the dollar. Would four of the five bondholders agree to exchange their $.625–per–dollar debt for common stock? Before the exchange, their debt is worth $100 million (4/5 of the debt's $125 million market value). They hope to put the firm on a sound footing and obtain some of the enhanced value for themselves. Let's tentatively say they'd all be willing to exchange their bonds for X amount of stock, if they expect that stock to be worth $100 million, and they tentatively work out an allocation with the common stockholder on the percentage of the stock the four exchanging bondholders would take.

What would happen to the residual $40 million bondholder, whose claim was worth only $25 million before the proposed exchange?

Her bond would increase in real value from $25 million to $40 million. Because after the four other bondholders exchange their bonds for stock, a further workout becomes unnecessary and the last remaining creditor could then be paid according to her bond's original terms. That is, after the exchange the company would have the wherewithal to pay the $40 million. The holdout bondholder's gains would come at the expense of the four exchanging bondholders (and the stockholder). The subsidy would cost them $15 million.

To see the subsidy, imagine MGF's balance sheet after the hypothetical exchange:

MGF Balance Sheet 2

$150M + Y*	$40M	Nonexchanging bondholders
	X+4/5Y	Four exchanging bondholders
	$25M+1/5Y	Old stockholders

(*Y is the increase in MGF's operational value if the exchange offer succeeds)

The exchanging bondholders and the old stockholders have $110 million (plus Y) among them. ($150 million in firm value, minus $40 million in debt going to the nonexchanger equals $110 million.) Imagine that the first deal offered is for each exchanging bondholder to get 100 shares of common stock, the same number of shares outstanding before the deal. If *all five* bondholders took the deal, each would get $25 million in stock, plus a share of Y, the efficiency gains, for their $25 million bond.

But if only four of the bondholders took the exchange, the exchange would cost the exchanging bondholders (and the stockholders) $15 million overall, which would have to be offset by a $15 million Y for the

[3] The $25 million could come from the stockholders' hold-up value or from the possibility the firm's oil prospects give it a .5 chance of being worth $250 million and a .5 chance of being worth $50 million.

deal to be worthwhile to them. See supra MGF Balance Sheets 1 and 2, in which the four exchanging bondholders had 4/5 of $125 million before the exchange but only 4/5 of $110 million after the exchange. The holdout bondholder was "buoyed up" by $15 million.

If we ignore Y for the moment, then we see that the exchanging bondholders would have exchanged their $100 million of debt for $88 million of stock. The stockholders would have done a deal that lowered the value of their stock by $3 million. Charity of that kind is not big on Wall Street. Unless Y, the enhancement in the firm's operational value, is expected to be greater than $15 million, the deal-preferring bondholders' incentives are not to do the deal.

Because of the buoying-up effect, a successful reorganization requires that all five bondholders go along with the proposed exchange of bonds for stock. Even an overwhelming majority of an 80 percent potential acceptance can fail to get a deal done, because too much value would be shifted from the exchanging bondholders to the nonexchanging bondholders.

These problems are succinctly captured in the lawyers' maxims that a creditor should not lightly "give up its priority" and that the "principle of equality of sacrifice" ought to govern a workout. Creditor and bondholder self-protection will induce adherence to these maxims in serial form (i.e., do not give up your priority unless there's equality of sacrifice among creditors). Serial adherence will put the firm in the MGF bind: without (near) unanimity, a workout of a seriously troubled firm fails.

4. *Failure: MGF files for bankruptcy*. Eighty percent of MGF's bondholders tendered their bonds into the exchange offer. If MGF could have used (and chose to use) a majority action clause that bound all bondholders to a majority vote, a choice not open to it or its bondholders due to the Trust Indenture Act prohibition, the workout would have succeeded. But some creditors had conditioned their agreement to exchange and extend maturity on 95 percent bondholder acceptance. Overwhelming bondholder acceptance is a usual and necessary condition to effectiveness of a distressed company recapitalization, Wall Street bond traders report.[4] The offer failed and MGF filed for bankruptcy.

One peculiarity to which we will return: MGF stated repeatedly in its exchange offer prospectus, starting with a boldface statement on the prospectus cover page, that if the exchange offer failed, it would file for bankruptcy and expected to "present as its plan of reorganization a plan substantially identical to the restructuring plan set forth in the [Exchange Offer] Prospectus." MGF did eventually present such a plan.[5]

Ironic? What procedure is needed to bind the class in bankruptcy? A vote? What happens to the holdouts? See Bankruptcy Code

[4] Fritz Wahl, A New Technique for Evaluating Exchange Offers (1986) (Morgan Stanley & Co. memorandum).

[5] MGF Exchange Offer Prospectus, at 1, 4, 9; Disclosure Statement Accompanying First Amended Plan of Reorganization of MGF Oil Corp., No. 7–84–02160–E–11, at 1 (Bankr. W.D. Tex. filed June 11, 1985).

§§ 1125(b), 1126(b). Why was resort to bankruptcy necessary? Did TIA § 316(b) drive MGF into bankruptcy?

¶ 1906: The Economics of Holding Out

Why are there holdouts? And why do recapitalizations sometimes fail? If there is a gain to split—the avoided bankruptcy costs—then money can be made by having a deal. But some good deals don't get done.

1. Single creditor bargains. Even if MGF had had a single creditor, it is possible although unlikely that a deal might have failed. Disparate expectations, mutual mistrust, and strategic action could still thwart a deal.

Disparate expectations. Disparate expectations can thwart the deal: The creditor thinks the firm is worth enough to pay the creditor off, so it won't renegotiate. Moreover, if the stockholder thinks there is some chance that the firm will be worth more than it owes (e.g., if the oil market turns up), he or she will often find it worthwhile to take the gamble and wait it out, hoping that the firm will pull through without a recapitalization.

More subtle variations may thwart a deal. Creditor and stockholder may both believe the firm is worth $150 million. But if their dispersion estimates are different, a deal could be thwarted.

Mutual mistrust. On what informational base does the creditor assess the firm's value? True, most of the crucial information comes from outside the firm. MGF's value was critically dependent on the future price of oil. To form an estimate of future oil prices, the creditor could go to oil consultants or just read the newspaper.

But how does the creditor estimate the size of the company's Permian Basin oil reserves? Again, a third party—an independent oil engineer—might be employed by the creditor (or by the firm itself). But some information is in the control of the firm. The creditor may fear receiving misleadingly pessimistic information from the firm's managers and shareholders; the misleading information could induce the creditor to accept a disadvantageous deal.

The managers may never provide erroneous information, but the creditor will not know whether the information is slanted to the creditor's detriment. When that mistrust is present, completing the deal will be harder than otherwise.[6]

---

[6] Offering stock for debt can reduce the mutual mistrust problem. Bondholders might fear that the insider-owner would tell the bondholders the firm is on the brink of bankruptcy and only an exchange offer will avoid the firm's destruction, when the firm is in fact much healthier than that. But to the extent the stockholders paint an excessively grim picture to the bondholders to justify the exchange, they are saying that the firm is not worth much. Hence, they must offer a large portion of the common stock to the bondholders. The grim picture gets painted into the bonds and new common stock that the firm is trying to "sell" to the bondholders: the bondholders would undervalue both. Bondholders might mistakenly exchange undervalued bonds, but the exchange would be for undervalued stock. Furthermore, when the stockholders obtain a small percentage of the restructured common stock, the room for effective misrepresentation is reduced. For example, MGF stockholders planned to take only 7 percent of the stock of the recapitalized firm. Disclosure Statement Accompanying First Amended Plan of Reorganization of MGF Oil Corp., No. 7–8402160E–11, at 22 (Bankr. W.D.

Strategic action. The parties have a gain to split—the avoided costs of bankruptcy and continuing financial stress—but they have no ready-made guide on where to cut that bargain. The parties are not truly in a marketplace setting, where a single acceptance from one out of many offerees will suffice. The debtor and creditor are mutually dependent. In an economist's terms, they are bilateral monopolists. The operational gain—avoidance of bankruptcy costs—cannot be obtained unless both sides consent. But what if the other side asks for 90 percent of the gain as a precondition to consent? The parties may waste time thrashing out the bargain.

* * *

Disparate expectations, mutual mistrust, and strategic action are reasons why a single creditor and the firm might fail to reach a bargain that would avoid bankruptcy.

2. Multi-creditor bargains. Multi-creditor bargains present more obstacles. The buoying-up effect is crucial to understanding why. Holdout creditors that do not agree to a recapitalization will be buoyed up; value will flow from agreeing creditors to the holdouts. Agreeing creditors cannot just strike their own deal and ignore those that do not go along.

The buoying-up effect in combination with any of the single creditor debilities can be deadly. If enough creditors have optimistic expectations, mistrust managerial or stockholder representations, or seek for themselves a greater portion of the gains of recapitalization, then the deal could well be unmarketable. And then other creditors—willing to go along if their fellow creditors do so—may recognize the buoying-up effect and defend their own interests by also holding back their consent.

Unresponsive creditors. Although few individuals today hold bonds directly (instead of through mutual funds and pension funds), just getting individual bondholders to act could be hard. Some may be hard to find or fail to respond. When a bondholder's holding is small in relation to her wealth, she sees the request for action as a nuisance. If the recapitalization is complex, the investment in time may not be worthwhile. If the bondholder is a doctor, not a lawyer or financial analyst, professional help may be necessary but expensive. A busy professional has other responsibilities. She could leave the mail unopened, the proxy solicitor's phone calls unreturned.

Lack of authority. Occasionally, some bondholders' authority to act on the recapitalization may be in flux. The bond may have been transferred; the new owner will get it in a week or two. Or some bonds

---

Tex. filed June 11, 1985). The prospect that a stock-for-debt exchange would reduce cheating is important, because the rationale behind the Trust Indenture Act's § 316 ban on majority action was a belief that bondholders would be cheated. A stock-for-debt exchange reduces one form of potential mulcting.

Institutional bondholders presumably sense the information problem and, when inside information seems possibly crucial, will evaluate proposals to exchange bonds for stock differently from stretch-out and reduction proposals. Cf. Robert Reich & John Donahue, New Deals: The Chrysler Revival and the American System 178, 253–55 (1985) (bank creditors insist upon receiving warrants in Chrysler recapitalization; warrants later become very valuable).

may be tied up in a decedent's estate for which letters testamentary have yet to be issued by the court.

Strategic action against other bondholders: seeking to be buoyed up. Some bondholders will seek to use the buoying-up effect offensively. They see themselves as small holders who are unlikely to influence the outcome of the recapitalization effort. In a multi-million dollar recapitalization, their refusal to exchange their $25,000 face value of defaulted bonds will not in itself hold the deal up. But by withholding consent, they may see the economic value of their bonds go from $10,000 to $20,000. In the right circumstances, that would look like a good bet to play. But if enough bondholders think the same way and act offensively, the deal cannot go through. Furthermore, even if only a few act offensively, their holdout combined with the unresponsive bondholders, the optimistic bondholders, and the mistrusting bondholders may induce others to act defensively to protect themselves. Again, the deal collapses.

(A question worth pursuing is why so many of MGF's bondholders did not hold out. One explanation lies in the plausible size of each holding: because of the 95 percent minimum for effectiveness, anyone with 5 percent or more of a bond issue could never have been a buoyed-up holdout since by not tendering their entire holding, each large holder would have destroyed the deal. The holdout problem, however, could not regularly be solved though by increasing the minimum needed percentage to, say, 98 percent. Although the increase will reduce the buoying-up problem (because more bondholders will know that their refusal to tender will kill the deal), the increase also will increase the chance that a single errant bondholder who thinks the deal is a bad one will kill the deal. Balancing these chances is part of the dilemma that investment bankers face when advising firms in workouts.)

The MGF failure and the general issues here are discussed in excruciating detail in Mark J. Roe, *The Voting Prohibition in Bond Workouts*, 97 Yale L.J. 232 (1987).

* * *

The Trust Indenture Act was part of a unified recapitalization framework that emerged at the end of the 1930s. The Los Angeles Lumber decision shows some of the thinking behind the hostility to recapitalization deal-making.

¶ 1907: Case v. Los Angeles Lumber Prods. Co., 308 U.S. 106 (1939) (again)

MR. JUSTICE DOUGLAS delivered the opinion of the Court.

These cases present the question of the conditions under which stockholders may participate in a plan of reorganization . . . where the debtor corporation is insolvent.

. . . The debtor's principal asset consists of the stock of Los Angeles Shipbuilding and Drydock Corporation which is engaged in shipbuilding and ship repair work in California. [The debtor] has fixed assets of $430,000 and current assets of approximately $400,000 [and] current debts of a small amount, not affected by the plan. . . .

The debtor's liabilities consist of principal and interest of $3,807,071.88 on first lien mortgage bonds issued in 1924 and maturing in 1944, secured by a trust indenture covering [its] fixed assets. . . .

In 1937 the management prepared a plan of reorganization to which over 80% of the bondholders and over 90% of the stock assented. This plan of reorganization, as we shall discuss hereafter, *provided for its consummation either on the basis of contract or in a [bankruptcy] proceeding, such election to be made by the board of directors.* In January 1938 the directors chose the latter course . . . with the [reorganization] plan . . . reciting, inter alia, that the required percentage of security holders had consented to it. This plan . . . provides for . . . a capital structure of 1,000,000 shares of authorized $1 par value voting stock. . . .

. . . 641,375 shares . . . are to be issued to the bondholders. . . . The . . . stockholders will receive the 188,625 shares of common stock . . .

The plan was assented to by approximately 92.81% of the face amount of the bonds, 99.75% of the . . . stock. . . . Petitioners own $18,500 face amount of the bonds. They . . . objected that the plan was not fair and equitable to bondholders.

The District Court found that . . . the total value of all assets of Los Angeles Shipbuilding and Drydock Corporation was $830,000. . . . Yet in spite of this finding, the court, in the orders now under review, confirmed the plan. And the court approved it despite the fact that the old stockholders, who have no equity in the assets of the enterprise, are given 23% of the assets and voting power in the new company. . . .

[The lower court noted that] companies are unwilling to assume the risk of becoming surety for the debtor or its principal subsidiary "because of the outstanding bond issue." The government's construction program will provide "valuable opportunities" to the debtor if it is prepared to handle the business. Hence, the value to the bondholders of maintaining the debtor "as a going concern, and of avoiding litigation, is in excess of the value of the stock being issued" to the old stockholders.

* * *

[A]s a matter of law the plan was not fair and equitable.

[W]here a plan is not fair and equitable as a matter of law it cannot be approved by the court even though the percentage of the various classes of security holders required by [bankruptcy law] for confirmation of the plan has consented. It is clear from a reading of § 77B(f)[7] that the Congress has required *both* that the required percentages of each class of security holders approve the plan and that the plan be found to be "fair and equitable." The former is not a substitute for the latter.[8] *The court is not merely a ministerial register of the vote of the several classes of security holders.* All those interested in the estate are entitled to the court's protection. Accordingly the fact

---

[7] It provides in part: "After hearing such objections as may be made to the plan, the judge shall confirm the plan if satisfied that (1) it is fair and equitable and does not discriminate unfairly in favor of any class of creditors or stockholders, and is feasible; . . . [and] (3) it has been accepted as required by the provisions of subdivision (e), clause (1) of this section;. . . . "

[8] [Is it a substitute in the 1978 Bankruptcy Code?—Roe.]

that the vast majority of the security holders have approved the plan is not the test of whether the plan is a fair and equitable one. . . . The contrary conclusion in such cases would make the judicial determination on the issue of fairness a mere formality and would effectively destroy the function and the duty imposed by the Congress on the district courts under § 77B. . . .

Hence, in this case the fact that 92.81% in amount of the bonds . . . have approved the plan *is* as *immaterial* on the basic issue of its fairness as is the fact that petitioners own only $18,500 face amount of a large bond issue.

* * *

. . . [Is] the plan here in issue . . . fair and equitable . . . ?

We do not believe it is. . . . Admittedly there are assets not in excess of $900,000, while the claims of the bondholders for principal and interest are approximately $3,800,000. Hence even if all of the assets were turned over to the bondholders they would realize less than 25 per cent on their claims. Yet in spite of this fact they will be required under the plan to surrender to the stockholders 23 per cent of the value of the enterprise.

* * *

And there is a further reason why this result necessarily follows, if the will of the Congress as expressed in § 77B is not to be thwarted and if the integrity of such proceedings is to be maintained. As we have said, this plan had its origin in an endeavor on the part of the debtor in 1937 to effect a voluntary reorganization. A plan was proposed by the debtor which was the same as that here involved except for the amount and nature of the stock to be received by the bondholders. That plan contained two methods for its consummation. *The first was by means of an amendment to the trust indenture and a recapitalization of the debtor, a method to be followed if the board felt that sufficient approvals had been obtained.* The second was by means of § 77B. Over 80% of the bondholders and over 90% of the stock approved the original plan. Thereupon the debtor filed its petition in § 77B. . . . Thus respondent argues that since the plan of reorganization was entered into between the bondholders and the stockholders before institution of the reorganization proceedings under § 77B, the consideration flowing from the stockholders had been furnished and the interests of the bondholders and stockholders in the assets of the debtor had been fixed prior to the filing of the petition. In fact, respondent frankly insists that the stockholders' "right of [participation] was secured by contract before, and as a condition precedent to, the institution of the 77B proceedings."

But the mere statement of this proposition is its own refutation. If the reorganization court were bound by such conventions of the parties, it would be effectively ousted of important duties which the Act places on it. Federal courts acting under § 77B would be required to place their imprimatur on plans of reorganization which disposed of the assets of a company not in accord with the standards of "fair and equitable" but in compliance with agreements which the required percentages of security holders had previously made. Such procedure would deprive scattered and unorganized security holders of the protection which the Congress had provided them under § 77B. The scope of the duties and powers of the Court would be delimited by the bargain which reorganizers had been able to make with security holders before they asked the intercession of the court in effectuating their plan. Minorities would have their fate decided not by the court in application of the law of the land as prescribed in § 77B, but by the forces utilized by reorganizers in prescribing the conditions precedent on which the benefits of the statute could be obtained. No conditions precedent to enjoyment of the benefits of § 77B can be provided except by the Congress. To hold otherwise would be to allow reorganizers to rewrite it so as to best serve their own ends.

* * *

We therefore hold that the plan is not fair and equitable and that the judgment below must be and is

Reversed.

¶ 1908: Notes on Los Angeles Lumber

1. While not all elements of *Los Angeles Lumber's* bankruptcy doctrine survive today in the Bankruptcy Code, more elements survive in the Trust Indenture Act, an act whose structure Douglas strongly influenced. I.e., individualized consent doesn't survive in the Code's § 1129(a)(8), but it does survive in the less intrusive § 1129(a)(7). Individualized consent survives, however, in § 316(b) of the Trust Indenture Act.
2. Recall the fair and equitable standard, which is the statutory basis for the *Los Angeles Lumber* doctrinal result. Would it be relevant in determining whether the result was fair and equitable to note, as the lower court had, that the creditors took the bonds under a bond indenture that allowed a majority vote to compromise the claim of the bonds and that the bondholders had given an approving vote prior to the reorganization of Los Angeles Lumber? See In re Los Angeles Lumber Prods., 24 F. Supp. 501, 504 (S.D. Cal. 1938), rev'd sub. nom. Case v. Los Angeles Lumber Prods. Co., 308 U.S. 106 (1939).
3. Presumably a strong basis for strict priority is that priority is what the parties bargained for. See Chapter 7 supra, Drum Financial Prospectus: "Description of Debentures—Events of Default and Notice Thereof." Is that strong basis vitiated if the parties also bargained to allow a majority vote of the bondholders to recapitalize the bonds and the majority vote is obtained?
4. Is the hindrance value of the claim a persuasive reason to prohibit the creditors from giving the stockholders something? 308 U.S. at 129. A partnership agrees to take most actions by a 2/3 vote. A customer of the partnership defaults in payment for $1000 of goods sold and delivered. The partnership votes to accept $900 because the litigation process is slow, uncertain, and expensive. Could similar considerations have motivated the bondholders in *Los Angeles Lumber*?

5. *Los Angeles Lumber* was decided toward the end of the depression; markets were distrusted, administrators trusted. At the heart of the decision (and its later companion, *Consolidated Rock*) was a faith in the valuation process. Courts could quickly and accurately value the firm. Claims could then be compensated. That faith in the valuation process seems to have been misplaced. Congress sought to avoid the valuation hearing in 1978. See infra Bankruptcy Code § 1129. How much of *Los Angeles Lumber* survives the new Bankruptcy Code? Compare § 1129(a)(7) with § 1126 & § 1129(a)(8).
6. Does a nonwaivable rule give the bondholders a negotiating advantage? That is, by being available to negotiate, which § 316(b) prevents, they might have to give up something in the negotiation. Lack of availability can sometimes be advantageous in a negotiation.
7. The Los Angeles Lumber bond indenture, a pre–1939, non-TIA indenture, apparently allowed a majority of the bondholders to amend the payment terms of the indenture. Yet although the company got a super-majority to consent, it (i) had asked in its consent solicitation for bondholder consent also to use the bankruptcy law to confirm the plan, and (ii) did in fact use bankruptcy law to confirm the plan. The explanation for this action probably lies in the 1930s negotiability rules. In the 1930s, for a bond to be negotiable (i.e., for a bond-buyer to take the debt free and clear of the company's defenses), it had to have a sum certain due on a date certain. Some of Los Angeles Lumber's bonds may well have been negotiated to holders who had no notice of the recapitalization proceeding. As holders in due course (i.e., holders who took free of the company's defenses), they could usually demand payment in full when the bond came due. They would have been buoyed up.
8. If holdouts cannot be bound by a vote to change in payment terms, could the company induce a majority of the bondholders to change their bonds' nonpayment terms in a nonbankruptcy workout? Could the change in terms affect the calculations of the holdout? See the next paragraph, which deals with exit consents, and *Katz*.

D. EXIT CONSENTS

¶ 1909: Exit Consents

1. Reconsider the MGF hypothetical. One holdout destroys the plan to recapitalize into all common stock, because the four bondholders who were willing to exchange their bonds for stock anticipate the shift in value from them to the nonexchanging bondholder. Anticipating the shift, they refuse to exchange without the fifth bondholder also exchanging.

   The company now comes up with a more complex plan. The company's and its investment banker's lawyers read the bond indenture to find what terms the bondholders *can* modify by a vote. They find dividend, debt incurrence, and other covenants, all of which can be modified by a vote. These covenants are similar to those that we've seen when looking at the Drum Financial indenture in ¶ 703, at p.152. These covenants aren't covered by the individualized-consent requirement of § 316(b), and Drum Financial's indenture allows bondholders to modify them by vote, see p. 154.

The company and its investment bankers set up the following as the deal: Moments before the four exchanging bondholders would exchange their bonds into stock, the four bondholders would vote to modify the indenture by eliminating the covenants. After the vote and modification, the four would exchange the bonds into stock.

2. What are the effects and purpose of the vote? With the bond stripped of covenants, the bond is worth less than its face value. If the buoying-up effect is so strong as to alleviate the risk of default after the exchange, then the nonexchanging bond's value would still increase substantially. But if the risk of default is, although reduced, still substantial, and the covenants protected bondholders well, then the vote stripping the bond indenture of covenants would noticeably damage the nonexchanging bondholder. In principle, this covenant-stripping alone could induce the holdout bondholder to go along with the deal. But because junk bond indentures tend not to be filled with valuable covenants and because the positive buoying-up effect can be much stronger than a smaller negative effect of stripping the covenants, voting to reduce the covenants would often not be enough to change incentives. (The validity of such a vote and exchange is at issue in *Katz*, below. For now though we are focusing on incentives, not validity.)

So, if covenant-stripping doesn't get a deal done, the company and its investment bankers come up with a more complex plan, one targeted to make the holdout bondholder even more fearful of not participating in the exchange. They seek a post-exchange structure that would eliminate the buoying-up effect and, if possible, even *reduce* the value of any nonexchanging bondholder's bond. If they could reduce the value of the nonexchanging bondholder's bond, then they could induce unanimity and make the exchange work.

The investment bankers come up with a new, complex deal for the company. The company offers the holders of the bonds a package of new bonds and new stock. Each one of the five holders is offered a bond, with a face value of a little over $26 million. The bond will be due next year. (The original MGF bonds are due, say, the year after that.) The bonds will be secured and be senior to the old bonds.

If four bondholders take the deal, and one doesn't, what would the balance sheet look like?

MGF Balance Sheet 3

$150M	$105M Market value of debt, due next year, senior, secured
	$ 40M Face value of old debt (now subordinated)
	$ 25M Common stock

Analyze the incentives of the holdout bondholder. If the holdout refuses to exchange and a bankruptcy ensues (when the firm declines in value below, say, $105 million), then the *exchanging* bondholders will get all of the value of the firm, because they will be made senior and they will have security. If there's a fifty-fifty chance of a decline in value of the firm below $105 million, then the holdout's value is $20 million (50% of $40 million + 50% of zero), plus whatever value the frictions of bankruptcy could give the holdout. If the frictions are insufficient to make up for the holdout's lost value, then the holdout would be made *worse off* by refusing to exchange.

3. But the company and the stockholders have a problem in offering this plan. The bond indenture for these old bonds has a negative pledge clause and has no subordination clause. To remedy this problem, the company asks the old bondholders (before the exchange of new bonds for old) to vote to delete the negative pledge clause from the indenture and to add a subordination clause into the old indenture.
4. The company next realizes that with the debt so high, Y will be low. So it modifies the recapitalization plan to use a little less debt, by offering the bondholders a package of debt and stock in a more complex plan. Before the recapitalization, the firm is worth $150 million, from equal chances of being worth $80 million or $220 million.

MGF Balance Sheet 4

$150M+Y [$80M or 240M]	$80M	Senior debt (face value) maturing next year, a year earlier than original maturity
Y=$10M (by increasing upside from	$20M	Real value of old debt (now subordinated), market value is $20M, although face is $40M
$220M to $240M)	$25M	Stock issued to the four exchanging bondholders + 1/2Y
	$25M	Common stock + 1/2Y

Y, the increase in operational value from avoiding a bankruptcy, is $10 million because, although some debt is eliminated, not enough is. If the recapitalization succeeds, the company will have a 50% chance of being worth $80 million and a 50% chance of being worth $240 million, for an expected value of $160 million.

5. The company asks the bondholders to vote for the amendment and to send their old bonds in to the company at the same time. Again, analyze the incentives of the holdout bondholder.
6. Four of the bondholders vote to amend the bond indenture and send their old bonds in for new ones. The holdout sues to enjoin the vote and the exchange offer, as in *Katz*. What result?

¶ 1910: Katz v. Oak Industries, Inc., 508 A.2d 873 (Del. Ch. 1986)

[Chancellor Allen rendered the decision:]

* * *

Plaintiff is the owner of long-term debt securities issued by Oak Industries, Inc. ("Oak"), a Delaware corporation; in this class action he seeks to enjoin the consummation of an exchange offer and consent solicitation made by Oak to holders of various classes of its long-term debt. As detailed below that offer is an integral part of a series of transactions that together would effect a major reorganization and recapitalization of Oak. The [nonexchanging bondholder, the plaintiff, asserts] that the exchange offer is a coercive device and, in the circumstances, constitutes a breach of contract. This is the Court's opinion on plaintiff's pending application for a preliminary injunction.

I.

The background facts are involved. . . .

[Oak] has now entered into an agreement with Allied-Signal, Inc. for the sale of the Materials Segment of its business and is currently seeking a buyer for its Communications Segment.

. . . [Oak is] . . . a company in deep trouble[, with] unremitting losses from operations; on net sales of approximately $1.26 billion during that period it has lost over $335 million. . . . [T]otal stockholders' equity has . . . disappeared completely (. . . [and] there was a $62 million deficit in its stockholders' equity accounts). Financial markets, of course, reflected this gloomy history.[9] Unless Oak can be made profitable within some reasonably short time it will not continue as an operating company.

. . . Allied-Signal, Inc. [agreed to buy] for $15 million cash . . . 10 million shares of the Company's common stock together with warrants to purchase additional common stock. The Stock Purchase Agreement provides as a condition to Allied-Signal's obligation that at least 85% of the aggregate principal amount of all of the Company's debt securities shall have tendered and accepted the exchange offers that are the subject of this lawsuit. Oak has six classes of such long term debt.

If less than 85% of the aggregate principal amount of such debt accepts the offer, Allied-Signal has an option, but no obligation, to purchase the common stock and warrants contemplated by the Stock Purchase Agreement. . . . Thus, as part of the restructuring and recapitalization contemplated by the Acquisition Agreement and the Stock Purchase Agreement, the Company has extended an exchange offer to each of the holders of the six classes of its long-term debt securities. These pending exchange offers include a Common Stock Exchange Offer (available only to holders of the 9 5/8% convertible notes) and the Payment Certificate Exchange Offers (available to holders of all six classes of Oak's long-term debt securities). The Common Stock Exchange Offer currently provides for the payment to each tendering noteholder of 407 shares of the Company's common stock in exchange for each $1,000 9 5/8% note accepted. . . .

---

[9] The price of the company's common stock has fallen from over $30 per share on December 31, 1981 to approximately $2 per share recently. The debt securities that are the subject of the exchange offer here involved . . . have traded at substantial discounts.

The Payment Certificate Exchange Offer is an any and all offer. Under its terms, a payment certificate, payable in cash five days after the closing of the sale of the Materials Segment to Allied-Signal, is offered in exchange for debt securities. The cash value of the Payment Certificate will vary depending upon the particular security tendered. In each instance, however, that payment will be less than the face amount of the obligation. The cash payments range in amount, per $1,000 of principal, from $918 to $655. These cash values however appear to represent a premium over the market prices for the Company's debentures as of the time the terms of the transaction were set.

The Payment Certificate Exchange Offer is subject to certain important conditions before Oak has an obligation to accept tenders under it. First, it is necessary that a minimum amount . . . of each class of debt securities be tendered, together with consents to amendments to the underlying indentures.[10] Indeed, under the offer *one may not tender securities unless at the same time one consents to the proposed amendments to the relevant indentures.*

The condition of the offer that tendering security holders must consent to amendments in the indentures governing the securities gives rise to plaintiff's claim of breach of contract in this case. *Those amendments would . . . remov[e] significant negotiated protections to holders of the Company's long-term debt including . . . all financial covenants. Such modification may have adverse consequences to debt holders who elect not to tender pursuant to either exchange offer.*

Allied-Signal apparently was unwilling to commit to the $15 million cash infusion contemplated by the Stock Purchase Agreement, unless Oak's long-term debt is reduced by 85% (at least that is a condition of their obligation to close on that contract). . . . But existing indenture covenants . . . prohibit the Company, so long as any of its long-term notes are outstanding, from [buying] the debentures. . . . Thus, in this respect, amendment to the indentures is required in order to close the Stock Purchase Agreement as presently structured.

Restrictive covenants in the indentures would appear to interfere with effectuation of the recapitalization in another way. Section 4.07 of the 13.50% Indenture provides that the Company may not "acquire" for value any of the 9⁵/8% Notes or 11⁵/8% Notes unless it concurrently "redeems" a proportionate amount of the 13.50% Notes.[11] This covenant, if unamended, would prohibit the disproportionate acquisition of the 9⁵/8% Notes that may well occur as a result of the Exchange Offers; in addition, it would appear to require the payment of the "redemption" price for the 13.50% Notes rather than the lower, market price offered in the exchange offer.

In sum, the failure to obtain the requisite consents to the proposed amendments would permit Allied-Signal to decline to consummate both the Acquisition Agreement and the Stock Purchase Agreement.

---

[10] The holders of more than 50% of the principal amount of each [class of notes and debentures] must validly tender such securities and consent to certain proposed amendments to the indentures governing those securities.

[11] [Why would the 13.50% noteholders want this proportionate buyout?—Roe.]

* * *

The Exchange Offers are dated February 14, 1986. This suit seeking to enjoin consummation of those offers was filed on February 27. Argument on the current application was held on March 7.

II.

Plaintiff's claim that the Exchange Offers and Consent Solicitation constitutes a threatened wrong to him and other holders of Oak's debt securities[12] appear[s] to be summarized in paragraph 16 of his Complaint:

> The purpose and effect of the Exchange Offers is [1] to benefit Oak's common stockholders at the expense of the Holders of its debt securities, [2] to force the exchange of its debt instruments at an unfair price and at less than face value of the debt instruments [3] pursuant to a rigged vote in which debt Holders who exchange, and who therefore have no interest in the vote, must consent to the elimination of protective covenants for debt holders who do not wish to exchange.

... [P]laintiff's claim is that no free choice is provided to bondholders by the exchange offer and consent solicitation. Under its terms, a rational bondholder is "forced" to tender and consent. Failure to do so would face a bondholder *with the risk of owning a security stripped of all financial covenant protections and for which it is likely that there would be no ready market.* A reasonable bondholder, it is suggested, cannot possibly accept those risks and thus such a bondholder is coerced to tender and thus to consent to the proposed indenture amendments.

It is urged this linking of the offer and the consent solicitation constitutes a breach of a contractual obligation that Oak owes to its bondholders to act in good faith. Specifically, plaintiff points to [two] contractual provisions from which it can be seen that the structuring of the current offer constitutes a breach of good faith. Those provisions (1) establish a requirement that no modification in the term of the various indentures may be effectuated without the consent of a stated percentage of bondholders; [and] (2) restrict Oak from exercising the power to grant such consent with respect to any securities it may hold in its treasury[.]

III.

* * *

---

12 ... [A] high percentage of the principal value of Oak's debt securities are owned ... by a handful of large financial institutions. Almost 85% of the value of the 13.50% Notes is owned by four such institutions (one investment banker owns 55% of that issue); 69.1% of the 9⅝% Notes are owned by four financial institutions (the same investment banker owning 25% of that issue) and 85% of the 11⅝% Notes are owned by five such institutions. Of the debentures, 89% of the 13.65% debentures are owned by four large banks; and approximately 45% of the two remaining issues is owned by two banks. [Could these bondholders alone have killed the deal? Could these larger bondholders have been coerced?—Roe.]

. . . This case does not involve the measurement of corporate or directorial conduct against that high standard of fidelity required of fiduciaries when they act with respect to the interests of the beneficiaries of their trust. Under our law—and the law generally—the relationship between a corporation and the holders of its debt securities . . . is contractual in nature. Arrangements among a corporation, the underwriters of its debt, trustees under its indentures and sometimes ultimate investors are typically *thoroughly negotiated and massively documented.* The rights and obligations of the various parties are or should be spelled out in that documentation. The terms of the contractual relationship agreed to and not broad concepts such as fairness define the corporation's obligation to its bondholders.[13]

Thus, the first aspect of the pending Exchange Offers about which plaintiff complains—that "the purpose and effect of the Exchange Offers is to benefit Oak's common stockholders at the expense of the Holders of its debt"—does not itself appear to allege a cognizable legal wrong. It is the obligation of directors to attempt, within the law, to maximize the long-run interests of the corporation's stockholders; that they may sometimes do so "at the expense" of others (even assuming that a transaction which one may refuse to enter into can meaningfully be said to be at his expense) does not for that reason constitute a breach of duty. It seems likely that corporate restructurings designed to maximize shareholder values may in some instances have the effect of requiring bondholders to bear greater risk of loss and thus in effect transfer economic value from bondholders to stockholders. . . . But if courts are to provide protection against such enhanced risk, they will require either legislative direction to do so or the negotiation of indenture provisions designed to afford such protection. The second preliminary point concerns the limited analytical utility, at least in this context, of the word "coercive" which is central to plaintiff's own articulation of his theory of recovery. If, pro arguendo, we are to extend the meaning of the word coercion beyond its core meaning—dealing with the utilization of physical force to overcome the will of another—to reach instances in which the claimed coercion arises from an act designed to affect the will of another party by offering inducements to the act sought to be encouraged or by arranging unpleasant consequences for an alternative sought to be discouraged, then . . . further refinement is essential. Clearly some "coercion" of this kind is legally unproblematic. Parents may "coerce" a child to study with the threat of withholding an allowance; employers may "coerce" regular attendance at work by either docking wages for time absent or by rewarding with a bonus such regular attendance. Other "coercion" so defined clearly would be legally relevant (to encourage regular attendance by corporal punishment, for example). Thus, for purposes of legal analysis, the term "coercion" itself—covering a multitude of

[13] To say that the broad duty of loyalty that a director owes to his corporation and ultimately its shareholders is not implicated in this case is not to say, as the discussion below reflects, that as a matter of contract law a corporation owes no duty to bondholders of good faith and fair dealing. See, Restatement of Law, Contracts 2d, § 205 (1979). Such a duty, however, is quite different from the congeries of duties that are assumed by a fiduciary. See generally, Bratton, The Economics and Jurisprudence of Convertible Bonds, 1984 Wis. L. Rev. 667.

situations—is not very meaningful. For the word to have much meaning for purposes of legal analysis, it is necessary in each case that a normative judgment be attached to the concept ("inappropriately coercive" or "wrongfully coercive", etc.). But, it is then readily seen that what is legally relevant is not the conclusory term "coercion" itself but rather the norm that leads to the adjective modifying it.

In this instance, assuming that the Exchange Offers and Consent Solicitation can meaningfully be regarded as "coercive" (in the sense that Oak has structured it in a way designed—and I assume effectively so—to "force" rational bondholders to tender), *the relevant legal norm that will support the judgment whether such "coercion" is wrongful or not will, for the reasons mentioned above, be derived from the law of contracts.* I turn then to that subject to determine the appropriate legal test or rule.

Modern contract law has generally recognized an implied covenant to the effect that each party to a contract will act with good faith towards the other with respect to the subject matter of the contract. See, Restatement of Law, Contracts 2d, § 205 (1981).... The contractual theory for this implied obligation is well stated in a leading treatise:

> If the purpose of contract law is to enforce the reasonable expectations of parties induced by promises, then at some point it becomes necessary for courts to look to the substance rather than to the form of the agreement, and to hold that substance controls over form. What courts are doing here, whether calling the process "implication" of promises, or interpreting the requirements of "good faith", as the current fashion may be, is but a recognition that the parties occasionally have understandings or expectations that were so fundamental that they did not need to negotiate about those expectations. When the court "implies a promise" or holds that "good faith" requires a party not to violate those expectations, it is recognizing that sometimes silence says more than words, and it is understanding its duty to the spirit of the bargain is higher than its duty to the technicalities of the language. Corbin on Contracts (Kaufman Supp. 1984), § 570.

It is this obligation to act in good faith and to deal fairly that plaintiff claims is breached by the structure of Oak's coercive exchange offer. Because it is an implied contractual obligation that is asserted as the basis for the relief sought, the appropriate legal test is not difficult to deduce. It is this: *is it clear from what was expressly agreed upon that the parties who negotiated the express terms of the contract would have agreed to proscribe the act later complained of as a breach of the implied covenant of good faith—had they thought to negotiate with respect to that matter[?]* If the answer to this question is yes, then, in my opinion, a court is justified in concluding that such act constitutes a breach of the implied covenant of good faith.[14]

With this test in mind, I turn now to a review of the specific provisions of the various indentures from which one may be best able to infer whether it is apparent that the contracting parties—*had they negotiated with the exchange offer and consent solicitation in mind—*

---

[14] [Emphasis supplied, as usual. Who wrote the relevant contract terms?—Roe.]

would have expressly agreed to prohibit contractually the linking of the giving of consent with the purchase and sale of the security.

IV.

Applying the foregoing standard to the exchange offer and consent solicitation, I find first that there is nothing in the indenture provisions granting bondholders power to veto proposed modifications in the relevant indenture that implies that Oak may not offer an inducement to bondholders to consent to such amendments. Such an implication, at least where, as here, the inducement is offered on the same terms to each holder of an affected security, would be wholly inconsistent with the strictly commercial nature of the relationship.

Nor does the second pertinent contractual provision supply a ground to conclude that defendant's conduct violates the reasonable expectations of those who negotiated the indentures on behalf of the bondholders. *Under that provision Oak may not vote debt securities held in its treasury.* Plaintiff urges that Oak's conditioning of its offer to purchase debt on the giving of consents has the effect of subverting the purpose of that provision; it permits Oak to "dictate" the vote on securities which it could not itself vote.

The evident purpose of the restriction on the voting of treasury securities is to afford protection against the issuer voting as a bondholder in favor of modifications that would benefit it as issuer, even though such changes would be detrimental to bondholders. But the linking of the exchange offer and the consent solicitation does not involve the risk that bondholder interests will be affected by a vote involving anyone with a financial interest in the subject of the vote other than a bondholder's interest. *That the consent is to be given concurrently with the transfer of the bond to the issuer does not in any sense create the kind of conflict of interest that the indenture's prohibition on voting treasury securities contemplates.* Not only will the proposed consents be granted or withheld only by those with a financial interest to maximize the return on their investment in Oak's bonds, but the incentive to consent is equally available to all members of each class of bondholders. Thus the "vote" implied by the consent solicitation is not affected in any sense by those with a financial conflict of interest.

In these circumstances, while it is clear that Oak has fashioned the exchange offer and consent solicitation in a way designed to encourage consents, I cannot conclude that the offer violates the intendment of any of the express contractual provisions considered or, applying the test set out above, that its structure and timing breaches an implied obligation of good faith and fair dealing.

* * *

Accordingly, I conclude that plaintiff has failed to demonstrate a probability of ultimate success on the theory of liability asserted.

V.

An independent ground for the decision to deny the pending motion is supplied by the requirement that a court of equity will not issue the extraordinary remedy of preliminary injunction where to do so threatens the party sought to be enjoined with irreparable injury that, in the circumstances, seems greater than the injury that plaintiff seeks to avoid.

Oak is in a weak state financially. Its board, comprised of persons of experience and, in some instances, distinction, have approved the complex and interrelated transactions outlined above. It is not unreasonable to accord weight to the claims of Oak that the reorganization and recapitalization of which the exchange offer is a part may present the last good chance to regain vitality for this enterprise. I have not discussed plaintiff's claim of irreparable injury, although I have considered it. I am satisfied simply to note my conclusion that it is far outweighed by the harm that an improvidently granted injunction would threaten to Oak.

For the foregoing reasons plaintiff's application for a preliminary injunction shall be denied.

IT IS SO ORDERED.

¶ 1911: *Katz* and the Trust Indenture Act

1. The type of transaction outlined in *Katz* is frequently used, although not always successfully.
2. Does the nature of the consent given in *Los Angeles Lumber Products* differ from that given in *Katz*? Is one judge more solicitous of individualized consent than the other? Do both judges have the same view of bankruptcy and of the judicial review of a reorganization plan inside bankruptcy as desirable or undesirable?
3. What does "intent of the parties" mean for a contractual provision that a statute required the parties to place in their contract?
4. Is § 316 of the Trust Indenture Act relevant to the *Katz* decision and the underlying transaction? Is it relevant as a matter of doctrine? Is it relevant to understanding why the *Katz* transaction ever took place? If § 316 didn't exist what might the bond indenture's modification clause have looked like? Could you imagine a different transaction than that used by Oak Industries, if § 316 didn't exist? That is, wouldn't the debentureholders simply have voted? Trust Indenture Act of 1939, § 316 (15 U.S.C. § 77ppp).

15 U.S.C. §77ppp . . . [P]rohibition of impairment of holder's right to payment.

(a) Directions and waivers by bondholders

The indenture to be qualified

(1) shall automatically be deemed (unless it is expressly provided therein that any such provision is excluded) to contain provisions authorizing the holders of not less than a majority in principal amount of the indenture securities . . . at the time outstanding . . . on behalf of the holders of all such indenture securities, to consent to the waiver of any past default and its consequences; . . .

(2) may contain provisions authorizing the holders of not less than 75 per centum in principal amount of the indenture securi-

> ties . . . at the time outstanding to consent on behalf of the holders of all such indenture securities to the postponement of any interest payment for a period not exceeding three years from its due date.

For the purposes of this subsection . . . , in determining whether the holders of the required principal amount of indenture securities have concurred in any such direction or consent, *indenture securities owned by any obligor upon the indenture securities, or by any person directly or indirectly controlling or controlled by or under direct or indirect common control with any such obligor, shall be disregarded. . . .*

5. Financial institutions, such as mutual funds, pension funds, and insurance companies, owned most of the Oak Industries' bonds. That ownership structure militates toward a view on whether the bondholders *as a group* could have been meaningfully coerced. (Individual bondholders maybe could have been coerced, if one took a more expansive view of coercion than the court did. But could the overall group have been pushed into a bad deal?)

   First, how much coercion can the company bring to bear on a bondholder owning 55 percent of the bonds? On an owner of 15 percent of the bonds? Of 2 percent? Isn't it relevant that the offering company has conditioned the offer on getting 85 percent of the bondholders to exchange and some bondholders owned more than 15 percent by themselves? Second, does this concentrated ownership structure indicate who might get hurt in the exit-consent recapitalization used in *Katz?* Small, uninformed bondholders or larger institutional bondholders? Whom was Douglas trying to protect in *Los Angeles Lumber* and in § 316?

6. Did § 316(b) of the Trust Indenture Act induce the company to use exit consents in *Katz*? Ironic?

7. Could an issuing company give bondholders $35 for every $1000 face amount of bonds that the holders voted in favor of giving up an important protective financial covenant? The payment, although available to every assenting bondholder, would not go to bondholders voting against the indenture amendment or to those that did nothing. Eastern Airlines did just that during its merger with Texas Air. Held (by the same court that wrote the *Katz* opinion): no violation of the Eastern Airlines indenture or of any implied contractual terms. Kass v. Eastern Air Lines, Civ. No. 8700, slip op. at 11–14 (Del. Ch. Nov. 14, 1986); accord, Pisik v. BCI Holdings Corp., No. 14593, slip op. (N.Y. Sup. Ct. June 25, 1987).

8. *Katz* was decided in 1986 in the midst of a merger boom. In the mid–1980s, two-tiered tender offers for a target company's stock became a serious issue for the Delaware courts. In a two-tiered tender offer, the offering company offers to pay, say, $75 for the first 51 percent of the shares tendered. With a majority of the stock in hand, the offering company will force a merger of the target with itself, and pay the dissenters, say, $60. These terms were seen to be coercive because shareholders that feared being on the back end of the offer rushed to tender. Arguably they would rush to tender even if they thought the blended, average price ($67.50) was too low. They'd rush because they feared that if everyone else tendered and

they held out, they'd get only $60. Managers at targets sought to deter takeovers and their counsel justified tactics such as poison pills as deterring the coercive effects of a two-tiered tender offer. Relevance to *Katz*?

9. The "coercion" of exit consents could reduce the value of the bonds if they don't participate in sharing any gains. The buoying-up effect might induce some issuers to give bondholders their "due." Which effect is greater? In the abstract, one can't know whether buoying up is more important than the "coercive," value-reducing elements of an exit consent. Research suggests that bondholder returns around the time of an exit consent solicitation are, on average, positive. Marcel Kahan & Bruce Tuckman, *Do Bondholders Lose from Junk Bond Covenant Changes?,* 66 Journal of Business 499 (1993); Lewis S. Peterson, *Who's Being Greedy? A Theoretical and Empirical Examination of Holdouts and Coercion in Debt and Exchange Offers,* 103 Yale Law Journal 505 (1993). Thus, on average, buoying up and efficiency are more important than coercion. Moreover, half of the $40 billion bond restructurings attempted in the period examined failed; failed restructurings have no one, in the end, being coerced.

10. Could Oak Industries have used a "prepackaged" bankruptcy? That is, could it have used the consents obtained outside of bankruptcy to bind all of the bondholders *inside* bankruptcy? Bankruptcy Code § 1126(b) says:

> . . . [A] holder of a claim or interest that has accepted or rejected the plan before the commencement of the case under this title is deemed to have accepted or rejected such plan, as the case may be, if—
>
> (1) the solicitation of such acceptance or rejection was in compliance with any applicable nonbankruptcy law, rule, or regulation governing the adequacy of disclosure in connection with such solicitation; or
>
> (2) if there is not any such law, rule, or regulation, such acceptance or rejection was solicited after disclosure to such holder of adequate information. . . .

11. Although before 1986 these prepackaged bankruptcies were unpopular and apparently nonexistent, after the 1980s proliferation of junk bonds, prepackaged bankruptcies (sometimes engineered with exit consents) became more popular. By the first half of 1993, prepackaged bankruptcies made up just under half of the bankruptcy filings of publicly-traded firms having assets of more than $100 million. They took an average of three months to complete after filing (but needed 18 months to negotiate before the filing). Elizabeth Tashjian, Ronald C. Lease & John J. McConnell, *Prepacks: An Empirical Analysis of Prepackaged Bankruptcies,* 40 Journal of Financial Economics 135 (1996).

12. As an aside, compare the court's attitude toward fiduciary duties to creditors in *Katz* to the court's attitude on the same issue in *Credit Lyonnais*.

13. The individualized consent required under the Trust Indenture Act parallels a recurrent problem in restructuring sovereign debt. Na-

tions historically issued their debt via bond issues that did not allow votes to reposition the bonds, adjust their principal amount, lower their interest rate, or extend their maturity date. When a financial crisis hit, the modification clause made it hard to renegotiate the bonds terms. Argentina, for example, suffered a serious financial crisis at the beginning of the 21st century and could not readily obtain new external financing while its old bonds were outstanding on their original terms. But due to the individualized consent clauses, those bondholders otherwise willing to adjust their bonds' terms and allow new, higher-ranking financing to go forward would not consent to do so if the holdouts were too many. Newly-issued sovereign debt in the 21st century has tended to use majority action clauses to govern future modifications. This tendency in the sovereign debt market suggests that if domestically-issued bonds were freed from the Trust Indenture Act ban on majority action clauses, issuers and buyers might not continue to muddle through (with exit consents and pre-packaged bankruptcies) but would use carefully-drafted, protective majority action clauses.

¶1912: Section 316(b) Litigation

Sporadic decisions have explicitly addressed the interplay between the voting prohibition in § 316(b) and exit consents, without definitive appellate resolution. The recent run of district court decisions have interpreted § 316(b) as barring exit consent deals.

In December 2014, plaintiffs sought to enjoin a transaction that would have left them with claims on a debtor unable to pay, as assets (and the liabilities to the agreeing bondholders) would be transferred to a related company. The Southern District of New York refused to enjoin the transaction, because any harm to the plaintiff would not be irreparable, as money damages paid later would be good enough. But the court then stated its serious doubts that the defendants could prevail on the merits. The judge concluded that the transaction effectively ousted the plaintiffs' of their effective right to payment at the maturity date of the original principal amount, as no rational bondholder would stay as a claimant on an empty company if it had no effective lawsuit against the defendants. Marblegate Asset Mgmt. v. Educ. Mgmt. Corp., 75 F. Supp. 3d 592 (S.D.N.Y. 2014) (Failla, J.). The litigation is ongoing as of this writing in January 2016.

The *Marblegate* court viewed the intercompany sale as "precisely the type of debt reorganization that the Trust Indenture Act is designed to preclude." Although the court recognized that it would make a successful out-of-bankruptcy restructuring harder to achieve, it felt bound by its view that "the Trust Indenture Act simply does not allow the company to precipitate a debt reorganization outside the bankruptcy process to effectively eliminate the rights of nonconsenting bondholders."

Two other decisions reached similar interpretations of § 316(b), in transactions in which the restructuring required a vote to amend the indenture agreement. The vote would have amended the bond indenture to eliminate restrictive covenants. With the restrictive covenants eliminated, the debtor could have transferred all of its assets to another entity. Nonconsenting bondholders who stayed behind with the original debtor would have seen the value of their bond substantially diminished. MeehanCombs Global Credit Opportunities Funds, LP v. Caesars Entm't Corp., 80 F. Supp. 3d 507 (S.D.N.Y. 2015); Federated Strategic Income Fund v. Mechala Grp. Jamaica Ltd., No. 99 CIV 10517 HB, 1999 WL 993648 (S.D.N.Y. Nov. 2, 1999).

Other courts have not reached similar conclusions on the scope of § 316(b), with some seeing § 316(b) as protecting only the formal right to receive payment from the debtor, without protecting the economic interest of the bondholder to actually be paid. In re Northwestern Corp., 313 B.R. 595 (Bankr. D. Del. 2004), concluded that § 316(b) "applies to the holder's *legal* rights and not the holder's *practical* rights to the principal and interest itself. Plaintiffs' legal rights were not impaired. Again, there is no guarantee against default." The court did not halt a transfer that left the debtor unable to pay its creditors. See also YRC Worldwide Inc. v. Deutsche Bank Trust Co. Americas, No. 10-2106-JWL, 2010 WL 2680336 (D. Kan. July 1, 2010); Upic & Co. v. Kinder-Care Learning Centers, Inc., 793 F. Supp. 448 (S.D.N.Y. 1992).

¶ 1913: Assénagon Asset Management v. Irish Bank Resolution Corp., No. HC11C01320 (British High Court of Justice, Chancery, July 27, 2012) (Mr. Justice Briggs)

1. This [case] test[s], for the first time, the legality under English law of a technique used by the issuers of corporate bonds which has acquired the label "exit consent". The technique may be summarised thus. The issuer wishes to persuade all the holders of a particular bond issue to accept an exchange of their bonds for replacement bonds on different terms. The holders are all invited to offer their bonds for exchange, but . . . are required to commit themselves irrevocably to vote at a bondholders' meeting for a resolution amending the terms of the existing bonds so as seriously to damage or, as in the present case substantially destroy, the value of the rights arising from those existing bonds. The resolution is what has become labelled the exit consent.

2. The exit consent has no adverse effect in itself upon a holder who both offers his bonds for exchange and votes for the resolution. . . . By contrast, a holder who fails to offer his bonds for exchange and either votes against the resolution or abstains takes the risk, if the resolution is passed, that his bonds will be either devalued by the resolution or, as in this case, destroyed by being redeemed for a nominal consideration. This is in part because the efficacy of the technique depends upon the deadline for exchange being set before the bondholders' meeting so that, if the resolution is then passed, the dissenting holder gets no [opportunity] to exchange his bonds on the terms offered, and accepted in time, by the majority.

3. It is readily apparent, and not seriously in dispute, that the purpose of the attachment of the exit consent to the exchange proposal is to impose a dissuasive constraint upon bondholders from opposing the exchange, even if they take the view that the proffered new bonds are (ignoring the exit consent) less attractive than the existing bonds.

The constraint arises from the risk facing any individual bondholder that a sufficient majority of his fellow holders will participate in the exchange and therefore (as required to do) vote for the resolution. The constraint is variously described in textbooks on both sides of the Atlantic as encouraging, inducing, coercing or even forcing the bondholders to accept the exchange.

4. The technique depends for its persuasive effect upon the difficulties faced by bondholders in organising themselves within the time allowed by the issuer in such a way as to find out before the deadline for accepting the exchange whether there is a sufficient number (usually more than 25% by value) determined to prevent the exchange going ahead by voting against the resolution. They were described in argument as facing a variant of the well-known prisoner's dilemma.

5. Exit consents of this type (but falling short of expropriation) have survived judicial scrutiny in the USA, in the face of challenge by minority bondholders. In *Katz v. Oak Industries Inc.* (1986) 508 A.2d 873 the attachment of an exit consent designed to devalue the existing bonds in the hands of dissenting holders who declined an associated exchange offer was challenged in the Delaware Chancery Court as amounting to a breach of the contractual obligation of good faith by the issuer, as against the bondholders. . . . Chancellor Allen concluded that the particular exit consent in that case, (which included the removal of significant negotiated protections to the bondholders, and the deletion of all financial covenants), did not despite its coercive effect amount to a breach of the contractual obligation of good faith between issuer and bondholders in what he evidently regarded as an ordinary commercial arms-length contract.

6. . . . . [T]his technique has been put into significant, if not yet widespread, use within the context of bonds structured under English law, in particular in connection with the affairs of banks and other lending institutions requiring to be re-structured as a result of the 2008 credit crunch, so that a decision on this point of principle may be of much wider consequence than merely the amount at issue between the parties to this claim, which relates to subordinated notes in the company then known as Anglo Irish Bank Corporation Limited ("the Bank") acquired by the claimant Assenagon Asset Management S.A. . . .

7.–8. . . .

The Facts

9. The bond issue to which this dispute relates consists of the Bank's subordinated floating rate notes due 2017 ("the 2017 Notes") issued by the Bank. . . .

10. . . . [H]olders of the 2017 Notes were, at the time of the exchange offer, sophisticated professional investors.

12–15. . . .

16. Paragraph 13 of Schedule 3 contained provision as to who might attend or speak at Noteholders' meetings, but continued:

> "Neither the Issuer nor any Subsidiary shall be entitled to vote at any meeting in respect of Notes beneficially held by it or for its account."

17. Paragraph 18 of Schedule 3 set out in detail the powers capable of being exercised by a majority of Noteholders by Extraordinary Resolution. They included:

> "(a) Power to sanction any compromise or arrangement proposed to be made between the Issuer and the Noteholders. . . .
>
> . . .
>
> Power to assent to any modification of the provisions contained in these presents which shall be proposed by the Issuer or the Trustee."

18. . . . Paragraph 19 provided that a resolution duly passed at a Noteholders' meeting would be binding upon all Noteholders whether present or absent, voting or abstaining.

19. By September 2008 the Bank had become the third largest bank in the Irish domestic market with €101 billion of gross assets on its balance-sheet, representing about 50% of Irish GDP. It had a particular focus on commercial property lending, and as a result of the 2008 financial crisis, with a linked rapid decline in commercial property values, the Bank faced a liquidity crisis which, unless it was rescued by the Irish Government, would have forced it into insolvent liquidation. Nonetheless, being regarded as of systemic importance to the maintenance of the stability of the Irish financial system, it was indeed rescued by the Irish government. . . .

20. . . .

21. On 21 January 2009 the Bank was nationalised, because of its systemic importance to the maintenance of the stability of the Irish financial system, pursuant to the Anglo Irish Bank Corporation Act 2009.

22–25. . . .

26. It was during the staged rescue of the Bank which I have summarised, and the currency of the October 2008 guarantee of (inter alia) the 2017 Notes, that the claimant acquired its holding of 2017 Notes in the market. . . . It may safely be inferred that it did so on behalf of sophisticated investors.

27. On 30 September 2010 . . . , the Minister of Finance made a statement on the banking system in Ireland which, while stating an intention to respect all senior debt obligations in the Bank, continued:

> "The principle of appropriate burden sharing by holders of subordinated debt, however, is one with which I agree. As can be seen from the figures outlined above, the losses in the bank are substantial and it is right that the holders of Anglo's subordinated debt should share the costs which have arisen.
>
> * * *
>
> I expect the subordinated debt holders to make a significant contribution towards meeting the costs of Anglo."

28. This announcement contemplated a . . . voluntary re-structuring of subordinated debt, if possible, by agreement with Noteholders (or a qualifying majority of them). . . . The exchange proposal to the 2017 Notes [commenced].

The 2010 Exchange Offer

29. On 21 October 2010 the Bank announced exchange offers in respect of certain series of its Notes, including the 2017 Notes. . . .

30. The Announcement . . . propos[ed] to Noteholders an exchange of . . . the 2017 Notes for new Notes ("the New Notes") in the exchange ratio 0.20, i.e. an offer of a holding of 20 cents New Notes for every one Euro of 2017 Notes. The New Notes were not to be subordinated. They were to carry a coupon of three month Euribor[15] plus 3.75 per cent, to be guaranteed by the Irish government and to mature in December 2011. The Announcement continued as follows:

> "In connection with the Exchange Offers, the Bank is also convening . . . [a bondholder's] meeting[ ] inviting the Holders of . . . the 2017 Notes[ ] to approve, . . . proposed amendments to the terms and conditions . . . including giving the Bank the right to redeem all, but not some only, of the Existing Notes of each Series at an amount equal to €0.01 per €1000 in principal amount of Existing Notes at any time after the relevant Settlement Date. . .

* * *

32. . . . By contrast with the exchange ratio of 0.20 in the Exchange Offer this amounted to a payment ratio of 0.00001.

33. [The Bank went on:]

> "By offering to exchange its Existing Notes, a holder will be deemed to have given instructions for the appointment of the exchange and tabulation agent (or its agent) as its proxy to vote in favour of the relevant Extraordinary Resolution in respect of all Existing Notes of the relevant series offered for exchange by such holder and which are accepted by the Bank at the . . . 2017 Notes Meeting. . . .
>
> "It will not be possible for Holders . . . to validly offer to exchange Existing Notes pursuant to the Exchange Offer without at the same time appointing the Exchange Tabulation Agent (or its agent) as their proxy to vote in favour of the Extraordinary Resolution in respect of the relevant Series as described above. . . . "

34. Under the heading Risk Factors and Other Considerations, the Memorandum provided (inter alia) as follows:

> "If an Extraordinary Resolution is passed in respect of [the] Notes and the approved amendments are implemented . . . , the amendments shall be binding on all Holders of Existing Notes . . . , whether or not those Holders attended or were otherwise represented at the relevant Meeting and/or voted in favour of the relevant Proposal.
>
> (heavy type) If the Bank chooses to exercise such call right (which the Bank currently intends to do . . .), the redemption amounts payable to a Holder of Existing Notes (being €0.01 per €1000 in principle amount of Existing Notes) will be significantly less than the principal amount of the New Notes such Holder would have received had such Existing Notes been exchanged pursuant to the relevant Exchange Offer.

---

[15] [A standard reference interest rate for euro-denominated loans.—Roe.]

* * *

35–36. . . .

37. The Bank notified acceptance of all notes offered for exchange on 22 November and the Resolution was therefore duly passed by at least the same majority at the 2017 Noteholders' meeting held on the following day. Settlement of the exchange of Existing Notes for New Notes duly then occurred in accordance with the advertised timetable and, on 30 November 2010, the Bank exercised its newly acquired right to redeem the remaining 2017 Notes at the nominal price of €0.01 per €1000 face value pursuant to which the claimant received €170 for its €17 million face value of 2017 Notes.

38. . . .

The Claimant's Case

39. In their skeleton argument and in oral submissions, [counsel for the claimant] put the claimant's case for a declaration that the resolution purportedly passed at the 2017 Noteholders' meeting on 24 November 2010 was invalid . . . :

. . .

(2) At the time of the Noteholders' meeting on 23 November, all those noteholders whose votes were counted in support of the Resolution held their Notes beneficially, or for the account of, the Bank. Accordingly, all those votes are to be disregarded pursuant to paragraph 13 of Schedule 3 to the Trust Deed.

(3) . . . the Resolution constituted an abuse of the power of the voting majority because:

   (i) It conferred no conceivable benefit or advantage upon the 2017 Noteholders as a class; and,

   (ii) It affected, and could by then only have affected, the Notes of that minority which had not coupled an offer of their Notes for exchange with a commitment to vote in favour of the resolution. Accordingly it was both oppressive and unfair as against that minority.

* * *

40–48. . . .

49. . . . [S]tatute may also intervene. There is in England and Wales the statutory remedy for unfairly prejudicial conduct now to be found in Part 30 of the Companies Act 2006. In the USA, the US Trust Indenture Act of 1939 provides at s.316 (b) a general prohibition against the modification of payment terms without the unanimous consent of all the holders of securities issued and registered with the SEC under the US Securities Act of 1933. There are however no statutory safeguards against abuse of power by a majority of the 2017 Noteholders in the present context.

* * *

Disenfranchisement under paragraph 13 of Schedule 3

56. It was, as I have said, common ground that the purpose of the disentitlement to vote in respect of Notes beneficially held by the Bank

or for its account was to prevent a vote designed to serve the interests of the Noteholders from being undermined by the exercise of votes cast in the interests of the Bank. . . . It was also common ground that, although the language of the prohibition speaks in terms of the Issuer or its Subsidiary being disentitled to vote, *it applies equally to any other person who or which holds his or its Notes for the benefit or for the account of the Bank.*

* * *

61. [Counsel for the Bank] gained considerable support from the analysis of a similar point by Chancellor Allen in the *Oak Industries* case (*supra*). . . . The terms of the bonds in that case prohibited the Issuer (Oak) from voting debt securities held in its treasury, and it was submitted that by linking its exchange offer with the giving by the bondholders of consent to the amendment to the terms of the bonds, Oak had been permitted to "dictate" the vote on securities which it could not itself vote. He continued:

> "The evident purpose of the restriction on the voting of treasury securities is to afford protection against the issuer voting as a bondholder in favour of modifications that would benefit it as an issuer, even though such changes would be detrimental to bondholders. But the linking of the exchange offer and the consent solicitation does not involve the risk that bondholder interests will be affected by a vote involving anyone with a financial interest in the subject of the vote other than a bondholder's interest. That the consent is to be given concurrently with the transfer of the bond to the issuer does not in any sense create the kind of conflict of interest that the indenture's prohibition on voting treasury securities contemplates. Not only will the proposed consents be granted or withheld only by those with a financial interest to maximize the return on their investment in Oak's bond, but the incentive to consent is equally available to all members of each class of bondholders. Thus the "vote" implied by the consent solicitation is not affected in any sense by those with a financial conflict of interest."

62–63. . . .

64. I have nonetheless concluded that [the claimant's view] that . . . Notes . . . offered and accepted for exchange were held for the benefit of the Bank by the time of the meeting, is correct. All those Notes were by that time held under contracts for sale between the relevant majority Noteholders and the Bank. . . .

65–68. . . .

Abuse of Power

69–83. . . .

84. . . . I have concluded that . . . [counsel for the claimants] arrived eventually at the correct question, which is whether it can be lawful for the majority to lend its aid to the coercion of a minority by voting for a resolution which expropriates the minority's rights under their bonds for a nominal consideration. In my judgment the correct answer to it is in the negative. My reasons derive essentially from my understanding of the purpose of the exit consent technique, as described at the beginning of this judgment. It is not that the issuer positively wishes to obtain securities by expropriation, rather than by the contractual exchange for value which it invites the bondholders to agree. On the

contrary, the higher percentage of those accepting, generally the happier the issuer will be. Furthermore, the operation of the exit consent (here the Bank's new right to redeem for a nominal consideration) is not the method by which the issuer seeks to achieve the reconstruction constituted by the replacement of existing securities with new. *The exit consent is, quite simply, a coercive threat which the issuer invites the majority to levy against the minority, nothing more or less. Its only function is the intimidation of a potential minority*, based upon the fear of any individual member of the class that, by rejecting the exchange and voting against the resolution, he (or it) will be left out in the cold.

85. This form of coercion is in my judgment entirely at variance with the purposes for which majorities in a class are given power to bind minorities, and it is no answer for them to say that it is the issuer which has required or invited them to do so. True it is that, at the moment when any individual member of the class is required (by the imposition of the pre-meeting deadline) to make up his mind, there is at that point in time no defined minority against which the exit consent is aimed. But it is inevitable that there will be a defined . . . minority by the time when the exit consent is implemented by being voted upon, and its only purpose is to prey upon the apprehension of each member of the class (aggravated by his relative inability to find out the views of his fellow class members in advance) that he will, if he decides to vote against, be part of that expropriated minority if the scheme goes ahead.

86. Putting it as succinctly as I can, oppression of a minority is of the essence of exit consents of this kind, and it is precisely that at which the principles restraining the abusive exercise of powers to bind minorities are aimed.

Conclusions

87. The claimant therefore . . . succeeds. . . .

---

1. Which underlying transaction is more coercive, that in *Katz* or that in *Assénagon*?
2. Compare the two courts' views on whether the bondholders' vote is effectively a vote of the issuers of treasury bonds.
3. The appeal from *Assénagon* was withdrawn before the higher court rendered a decision.
4. "Bond documentation generally includes disenfranchisement provisions, which prevent bonds beneficially held by the issuer from counting in a vote. In *Assénagon*, a quirk in the timing of the exchange meant that the Bank had notified acceptance of the Existing Bonds offered for exchange the day *before* the bondholders' meeting. Because the issuer had agreed to buy these Existing Bonds (and the holders had agreed to sell), the issuer entered into a specifically enforceable contract to acquire the Existing Bonds, meaning that it had acquired a beneficial interest in the Existing Bonds. So the disenfranchisement provisions prevented them from voting at the meeting. . . . The standard approach in such exchanges (where the acceptance of bonds for exchange is conditional on the passing of the resolutions, with results only announced after the relevant meeting is complete) would prevent any such issues [from]

arising. . . . " Cleary Gottlieb Alert Memo, Exit Consents in Restructurings—Still a Viable Option?, May 1, 2013.

5. Presumably some, or all, of the coercive aspects of the exchange could be ameliorated by "dragging along" the dissenting bondholders, such that they received the same new security (or other consideration) as the approving bondholders, or were given the opportunity to do so after the exchange was approved. Id. See also the Fidelity application, at ¶ 1914, next.

¶ 1914: Fidelity Investments Petition to the SEC

Robert C. Pozen
General Counsel
Managing Director
November 16, 1990

FMR Corp.
82 Devonshire Street
Boston MA 02109
617–570–7703

Mr. Jonathan G. Katz
Secretary
United States Securities and Exchange Commission
450 Fifth Street, N.W., Mail Stop 6–9
Washington, D.C. 20549

Dear Mr. Katz:

FMR Corp., the parent of Fidelity Management & Research Company ("FMR"), respectfully petitions the Securities and Exchange Commission (the "Commission") . . . to revise Securities Exchange Act Rule 14e–1 (the "Rule"). We are joined in this petition by [many financial] . . . institutions listed under Exhibit A to this petition. The Petitioners are proposing the Rule amendment in response to a manipulative and deceptive practice used by bidders in connection with tender offers for debt securities. Specifically, the proposal would address simultaneous tender offers/consent solicitations and would require the results of the consent solicitation to be disclosed before the tender offer could be closed.

<u>Background</u>

* * *

Some of the high-yield debt obligations which the Petitioners hold on behalf of their clients have been the subject of issuer tender offers, coupled with the threat that investor protections in the indenture will be removed at the completion of the tender offer. If these protections are removed at the completion of the tender offer, the market value of any debt still outstanding will decline sharply. Thus, the holders of these debt obligations are effectively forced to tender before they know whether the indenture protections will remain after the tender offer.

Issuers have begun using this strategy with alarming frequency since the market for high-yield securities has weakened. Recent examples have included . . .

. . . [M]any issuers of high-yield debt want to eliminate certain restrictive provisions pursuant to which the debt was issued. During the 1980s, many of these issuers restructured through leveraged buyouts, acquisitions by third parties, or the assumption of massive debt as a takeover defense. As part of that restructuring, the companies agreed to incorporate certain debtholder protections (the "Protections") into their indentures in order to sell their debt to investors.

The Protections exist to help assure repayment of the debt, generally by prohibiting the issuer from taking any of a number of specified corporate actions. Protective covenants may prohibit an issuer from inter alia, incurring additional debt; declaring dividends to stockholders or affiliated companies; granting liens upon assets of the company; selling or otherwise disposing of assets of the company; or taking actions which would affect the seniority of the security holders. Other typical Protections might include providing collateral for the debt or a guarantee of the debt by a third party.

Issuers are obviously entitled to bargain with investors, and to persuade their security holders to part with value for fair value received. Collectively, the Petitioners have participated in hundreds of issuer tender offers on behalf of their clients.

However, issuers which couple a tender offer with a consent solicitation often do so to force security holders to tender. Realistically, investors are coerced into tendering their debt because they do not know the outcome of the consent solicitation. As is discussed in greater detail below, if the consent solicitation is successful, the value of the security may plummet.

Accordingly, without knowing the results of the consent solicitation, debt holders have no economic alternative to tendering their securities in these dual offers, regardless of the fairness of the price offered by the issuer. The Petitioners believe that this strategy is a deceptive and manipulative practice in violation of the policies underlying Section 14(e) of the Securities Exchange Act of 1934. Under that Section, the Commission is given the responsibility to promulgate rules reasonably designed to prevent such practices. Therefore, we request that the Commission adopt a new section (e) to Rule 14e–1 as set forth below.

Structure of the Tender Offer

A dual tender offer/consent solicitation is generally structured as follows. A tender offer is made by the issuer (or an affiliate of the issuer) to purchase all or part of an outstanding class of debt obligations at a fixed price. However, in addition to the normal preconditions to consummation of the tender offer, the offer is made contingent on either or both of two unusual conditions. First, the bidder will not accept tendered securities from any security holder which does not also give its consent in the accompanying consent solicitation. Second, the bidder will not accept any securities at all unless a specified majority approves the accompanying consent solicitation.

The accompanying consent solicitation seeks security holder approval of one or more changes to the terms of the debt. Generally, approval is sought to strip all or some of the Protections from the debt's governing indenture. In some of these offers, the bidder provides a separate payment for a consent, in addition to the tender offer price. For example, an issuer might bid $600 to purchase a $1,000 face amount bond in the tender offer, and offer an additional $50 per $1,000 face amount as a payment for the consent. Alternatively, a single price might be offered for both consent and tender by a security holder. For example, in exchange for both a consent and tender, an issuer might offer $650 for each $1,000 face amount security. However, in either alternative the two offers are integrated, in that no tenders will be accepted unless the consent solicitation is successful.

A key feature of these offers is that debt holders do not know whether the consent solicitation will succeed before they must accept or reject the tender offer. Bidders are not required to disclose this information to security holders before completing the tender offer. Accordingly, investors do not know the ultimate terms of the security they are being asked to tender.

* * *

Manipulative and Deceptive Nature of the Tender Offer

In our view, a simultaneous tender offer/consent solicitation is usually designed to coerce debt holders into both tendering and consenting, regardless of whether the total compensation to be paid reflects the true value of the target security. Several aspects of these offers support our view.

First, unlike traditional consent solicitations, simultaneous tender offer/consent solicitations are inherently more likely to obtain consents to proposals which disadvantage security holders. Obviously, if the solicitation is successful, security holders who both tender and consent will no longer own the security and accordingly will have no interest left to protect. In contrast, investors who consent in traditional solicitations affect the terms of a security they will continue to hold. Because investors who consent will continue to bear the costs of the changed terms of a security, these investors have an interest in disapproving unfair or disadvantageous proposals. Second, the issuer's offer invariably ties together the two decisions of security holders. As noted above, some issuers offer one price for both decisions. However, even if the prices are technically separate, it makes no economic sense for a security holder to tender and not consent, or consent and not tender.

For example, assume the price is $600 for tenders and $50 for consents per $1,000 face amount. A security holder which tenders for $600 would also consent: the gain would be an additional $50 and, because the holder would no longer own the debt, the holder would be unconcerned about the elimination of Protections on the debt. Conversely, a security holder would not consent without tendering, because the consent price would almost never compensate the holder for the decline in price attributable to the elimination of the Protections.

Accordingly, a security holder has no choice but to tender and consent, because the holder will not know whether the consent solicitation has been successful until it is too late to tender. If the holder does not tender and the consent solicitation is successful, the Protections will be eliminated and the holder's debt security will fall significantly in market value.

The adverse effect of a successful consent solicitation upon the market value of an investor's holding can be dramatic. Once the Protections have been stripped from the target securities, the issuer becomes free to take actions which may make repayment of the debt less likely, e.g., paying dividends, selling assets which once supported the debt, or incurring additional debt senior to the target securities. Obviously, the market revalues the stripped securities at a much lower price.

Simultaneous offers are not justified by the legitimate rights of an issuer to repurchase or renegotiate outstanding debt. If an issuer's board of directors determines in good faith that it is in the best interests of the company and its security holders to commence a tender offer for its own securities, the company may do so without simultaneously mounting a consent solicitation. If the company offers a fair price for the securities, security holders will tender, and the tender offer will be successful. If the company offers an unrealistically low price instead, security holders will be free to retain their debt.

Similarly, we understand that, from time to time, it may be in the best interest of an issuer and its security holders to amend the terms of the company's outstanding debt. Most indentures provide that the terms of the debt may be amended by the consent of the holders of either a majority or two-thirds in principal amount of the outstanding debt. The issuer is free to propose a restructuring of the terms of the debt, and to offer debt holders some incentive to consent to the restructuring. Debt holders can be provided the opportunity to decide for themselves whether to accept the new terms or retain the old terms.

Individually, a consent solicitation or a tender offer each can be structured to provide the security holder with a fair choice. However, when a tender offer is structured so that material information—i.e., whether the securities will retain their Protections—is withheld until the tender offer ends, it is clear to us that the offer is designed to foreclose any rational choice that security holders might exercise regarding the tender offer.

<u>The Proposed Rule</u>

We respectfully submit that the Commission adopt the following amendment to the Rule. New language is underlined:

> Rule 14e–1. Unlawful Tender Offer Practices As a means reasonably designed to prevent fraudulent, deceptive or manipulative acts or practices within the meaning of section 14(e) of the Act, no person who makes a tender offer shall:
>
> . . . (e) <u>During the course of a tender offer for any security, solicit the holders of such security to approve, by proxy, consent or otherwise, a material change in the terms of such security, or a material change in the terms of such security's governing instrument, unless such tender offer . . . remains open until the expiration of ten business days after the results of the concluded solicitation of approval have been publicly disclosed. . . .</u>

The proposed Rule amendment would require bidders to disclose whether a security's protections have been stripped before security holders decide whether or not to tender. It would apply to changes in the terms of the security itself, or to changes in the security's governing instrument, such as an indenture. It would impose a period of ten business days after disclosure of the results of the consent solicitation for the market to digest the information and possibly revalue the target security. . . .

* * *

The Petitioners believe that this amendment to the Rule is the least burdensome means of preventing issuers from using consent solicitations to force security holders to tender. Under the Rule as amended, issuers would still have the ability to solicit tenders. Security holders would determine for themselves whether the price offered for the security was fair, and would tender or not on that basis. Similarly, issuers would remain free to bargain with their investors for a change in the terms of the debt. The proposed Rule would only restrict the ability of issuers to coerce their debt holders into accepting an unfair price by withholding a decisive piece of material information.

* * *

Sincerely,
Robert C. Pozen

cc: Richard C. Breeden, Chairman
Edward H. Fleischman, Commissioner
Philip R. Lochner, Jr., Commissioner
Richard Y. Roberts, Commissioner
Mary L. Schapiro, Commissioner . . .

¶ 1915: Questions on Fidelity Application

1. How can the Fidelity application be reconciled with the *Katz* result? The court says no coercion in the exit consent exchange offer; Fidelity says there's regular financial coercion.
2. Analyze exit consent offers in three settings: (i) institutions own big blocks of bonds of a deeply insolvent company, (ii) institutions own small blocks of bonds of a deeply insolvent company, (iii) the company is in good shape, or only slightly insolvent, but the company seeks exit consents to modify the bond indenture and restructure the core terms of the bonds. If the company is in good shape financially, then the bonds should not be highly discounted in the marketplace. If not highly discounted, then the buoying-up or debt overhang effect should be minimal. Thus for exit consent exchange offers for diffusely distributed bonds of healthy firms or weak but not deeply insolvent firms (setting iii, but not settings i or ii), the buoying-up effect could easily be less than the coercive effect.
3. Keep in mind that there are two trigger points. The first is the portion needed to amend the bond indenture's nonpayment terms, typically a simple majority or two-thirds. The second is the amount

needed to effectuate an exchange offer, which for a deeply distressed company is typically 80 percent or 90 percent. An institution holding a large block, but less than one-third, might be able to veto the second, but not the first.

4. Coordination among bondholders costs something. If the bonds are in ten blocks of 10 percent each, two bondholders can veto the exchange and five can veto the amendments. But to succeed, the two (and the five) must talk and coordinate their actions.

¶ 1916: The Fidelity Hypothetical

The Fidelity problem can be seen by working off of the MGF exchange offer. Posit a firm worth $150 million, from a 50% chance of being worth $100 million and a 50% chance of being worth $200 million. Absolute priority is expected this time (to keep the facts tractable), so the bonds (originally issued for $200 million) are worth $150 million, with each of the five having an expected value of $30 million. The stockholders then make a simple offer: $25 million in senior bonds to each bondholder, upon (a) tender of the old bond, and (b) a valid amendment subordinating the old bonds (if any remain) to the new bonds.

If a single non-exchanging bond is left, it'd be worth $20 million. If four exchange, each exchanging bondholder would get $25 million, and if all 5 exchange, each would end up with $22.5 million. In each case, the bondholders do worse than the status quo, but they each might be stampeded if they fear being stuck with a non-exchanged bond worth only $20 million.

What are the legal, financial, transactional, and policy consequences here?

1. Prior to the exchange offer, the company's operations are worth $150 million. In an absolute priority bankruptcy, the 5 bondholders split the $150 million. Shareholders offer $25 million in senior bonds to each bondholder. Each bondholder concludes the deal is overall a bad one.

2. However, each bondholder fears being on the "back-end." If the other four tender, but one doesn't, the non-tendering bondholder ends up with $20 million in expected value.

3. If four tender and one doesn't, then the shareholders end up with $30 million in expected value. (If the firm is worth $200 million, the firm pays the exchangers $100 million and the non-exchanger $40 million, leaving $60 million for the stockholder; if the firm turns out to be worth $100 million, the senior bondholders take everything.) $10 million of value shifts from the non-exchanger to the stockholders; $5 million in value shifts from each of the exchanging bondholders.

4. A plausible strategy for each bondholder is to tender and hope that the other bondholders don't tender, killing the deal. But if all five tender, because they're all scared of being left behind, then the bondholders are owed $125 million, but the bond issue would then be worth only $112.5 million (because the firm has a 50% chance of being worth $100 million). Each bondholder gets $22.5 million for tendering (but still tenders because each fears getting $20 million if he or she is

the single holdout). The stockholder gets $37.5 million in expected value.

5. If the bondholders could coordinate, they'd agree not to tender. If they had to vote to reposition the bonds, they'd all vote against the amendment to the bond indenture.

This example has four relevant features: i) it's close to the example we've been using all along (showing how hard it is to distinguish efficient exchanges from manipulative ones), ii) it illustrates the 2–tiered motivations in a realistic setting, iii) it shows how and why the stockholders would want to engineer this exchange, *and* iv) it shows that Douglas's perspective was incomplete: the bondholders here would be *better* off if their principal amount, interest rate, and maturity date could *only* be affected by a vote. They are here, under today's rules, made worse off *because* a non-voting mechanism is used and it can force them all into a bad exchange. Moreover, the bondholder who does nothing—the distant individual bondholder whom Douglas was trying to protect from being bound by a bondholder vote—is made worst off, if it fails to get the positive part of the transaction: the consideration given in exchange for the consents or the tendered bonds.

Consider the Fidelity application in ¶1914: We can see why Fidelity wanted to split the vote from the prior type of exchange. If the bondholders vote first and *then* decide whether to tender, they vote *against* the amendment that would allow, say, subordination of the target bond issue. Normally they would defeat it, because no bondholder has reason to vote for it (other than by mistake). Only if the amendment goes through over their dissent do they tender; if the amendment fails, they hold their bonds. But if they must tender *and* vote simultaneously, they could be stampeded.

The SEC did not act on the Fidelity application.

¶ 1917: The Allowed Amount of the Claim: Before and After an Exchange

Let's work with a modified version of the exchange offer problems we were using earlier in this chapter. Let's say that in the 1990s, Debtor borrowed $200 million in a junk bond offering, with each of five bond investors holding $40 million in face value of bonds. The bonds initially traded at face value, $200 million overall. The questions to be alert to here are: If the Debtor later deteriorates and resorts to an exchange offer to recapitalize, might the exchange offer affect the amounts of bondholders' allowed claims in a subsequent bankruptcy? Will exchanging and nonexchanging bondholders have the *same* allowed claim or not?

Original bond issuance. Here's the company's balance sheet when the bonds are issued and everyone is anticipating good business results.

XYZ Balance Sheet (when bonds are issued)

$250M	$200M bond issue
	Common stock

Deterioriation. Years later, XYZ's asset value falls to $150 million.

XYZ Balance Sheet (just before exchange)

$150M	$200M bond issued Common stock

At that moment, each of the five bondholders would hold a $40 million claim against the company. In an absolute priority bankruptcy, each would be paid $30 million, equal to 75% (or 150/200) of their claim. Not surprisingly, they'd each wind up with 1/5 of the value of the company.

If the company deteriorated further in value to $120 million, inducing a bankruptcy, each of the five bondholders would still get 1/5 of the company, though now that 1/5 of the company would be worth only $24 million and only a 60% payout (120/200) on their $40 million claims.

Parallel universe: exchange offer. So far so good. Now consider what happens with respect to claim allowance when the bankruptcy is preceded by an exchange offer. Say that at the time the Debtor's asset value drops to $150 million, the Debtor offers its bondholders a mix of senior debt and common stock in exchange for their existing bonds, and that each tendering bondholder is required to consent to the stripping of covenants from the old indenture. Four of the five bondholders exchange, and one holds out. The post-exchange balance sheet looks like this:

XYZ Balance Sheet (after exchange)

$150M	$80M Senior debt (taken in the exchange offer) $40M Unexchanged bond (trading at $20 million because of the stripped covenants and because there's a significant chance that the company's value declines to, say, $80 million) Common stock (held by the old stockholder and the exchanging bondholders)

The exchange makes the company borderline solvent (with $120 million face amount of debt owed by a company worth $150 million operationally). Each of the five creditors has a claim worth about $20 million. The exchangers each now hold a $20 million senior debt claim (along with stock); the nonexchanger refused to budge, and its newly junior position plus the covenant stripping have left its $40 million face value of bonds on the wrong end of the exchange offer. For now.

The exchange succeeds in restructuring the company's debt, but the company is still iffy operationally, because it's only borderline solvent and might decline in value.

And indeed, a few months after the exchange, the company declines in value to $120 million and goes bankrupt. What does each creditor get?

XYZ Balance Sheet (after exchange, further decline in value and bankruptcy)

$120M	$80M Exchanged senior debt
	$40M Unexchanged bond
	Common stock

The total allowed claims are now, post-exchange, $120 million, with $80 million owned by the exchangers and $40 million owned by the nonexchanger. In an absolute priority bankruptcy of the $120 million debtor, the 4 exchanging bondholders together get their $80 million in claims paid in full, but it amounts to only 80/120 of the firm's value, or 66⅔%. The nonexchanging bondholder gets the remaining $40 million of the firm's value, amounting to 33⅓% (40/120).

What if the 4 exchangers had not exchanged (and the exchange had not gone through)? The exchangers would collectively have enjoyed 160/200 or 80% of the firm's value, or 20% individually, the same percentage that the holdout would have received. That is, the 5 original bondholders would have divided the firm's value equally. Instead, having exchanged their original $160 million face amount of bonds for $80 million (albeit senior), the exchangers halved the allowed amount of their claims in the subsequent bankruptcy, which on these numbers left them with only 66⅔% of the firm's value. The exchange divests them of 13⅓% of the company's value.

Consequently, when deciding whether to exchange, the bondholders should consider the possibility that (1) the company doesn't recover, but instead deteriorates and files for bankruptcy anyway, (2) that the size of their claims will be smaller (although ranked higher), and (3) that the diminished size of the claim will mean that in plausible value configurations (such as a $120 million value in our hypothetical), the exchanging bondholders will do less well after the exchange than if they had stayed put and had not exchanged.

On these numbers, going from a bankruptcy "take" of 80% down to one of 66⅔% means the four exchanging bondholders go from getting $96 million down to $80 million. The exit consent exchange offer backfires for them, losing them $16 million compared to doing nothing. (And, conversely, the nonexchanger would have received $24 million had there been no exchange and, due to the exchange, gets $40 million.)

This possibility of losing their bigger claim size in bankruptcy doesn't mean that the exchangers will necessarily refuse to exchange. It's just a factor that they need to take into account. They might conclude that the exchange will put the company on a sound enough footing such that the bankruptcy scenario is sufficiently unlikely that potentially suffering from a shift in the size of the bankruptcy claim isn't important to them. They may consider the advantage of getting some of their claims bumped up in seniority (in the particular hypothetical deal we've been working with) to be even more valuable. If the firm goes bankrupt anyway and it's worth only $80 million, for example, the exchange into senior debt would put them ahead of where they'd have been without the exchange. That is, the claim size warp is a negative but not necessarily determinative factor that bankruptcy lawyers, conscious of the importance of the size of the allowed amount of a claim, will see and will alert the potential exchangers accordingly.

Summary: An exchange offer can alter the relative size of the exchangers' and the nonexchangers' claims. The shift in relative claim size will affect the value of the exchange. In the specific exchange exemplified above, the exchange alters the allowed amount of the claims of the exchangers (moving down from $160 million to $80 million), while the nonexchanging holdout's allowed amount of claim stays at $40 million. The holdout gets 1/3 of the $120 million firm instead of 1/5 of the firm; the exchangers get 2/3 of that firm instead of 4/5.

* * *

The problem of the size of the claim in a bankruptcy is yet more complex when discounted bonds are used in the exchange. To see this, we must recall how discounted bonds are treated in bankruptcy when there's been no exchange.

Suppose a firm issues a $1000 bond, which carries no interest. It'll mature in ten months. The creditor though turns over only $900 to the company. Obviously the difference between the price at which the bond is sold ($900) and is scheduled for repayment ($1000) represents the interest to the creditor. This difference is called "original issue discount."

If the issuer goes bankrupt in the afternoon of the day the $1000 bond was issued (or is it a $900 bond that day?), what should the allowed amount of the claim be in the bankruptcy? If the issuer goes bankrupt five months later, what should the allowed amount of the claim be?

The legislative history of the Bankruptcy Code says (at H.R. Rep. No. 595, 95th Cong., 1st Sess. 352–53, reprinted in 1978 U.S. Code Cong. & Admin. News 5963, 6307–08):

> Interest disallowed under [§ 502(b)(2)] includes postpetition interest that is not yet due and payable, and any portion of . . . interest that represents an original [issue] discounting of the claim, yet that would not have been earned on the date of bankruptcy. For example, a claim on a $1,000 note issued the day before bankruptcy would only be allowed to the extent of the cash actually advanced. If the original discount was 10%, so that the cash advanced was only $900, then notwithstanding the face amount of the note, only $900 would be allowed. If $900 was advanced under the note some time before bankruptcy, the interest component of the note would have to be pro-rated and disallowed to the extent it was for interest after the commencement of the case.

Consider this sequence:

1. Issuer issues a $1000 bond in the morning and is paid $900 in cash. It files for bankruptcy in the afternoon. What is the allowed amount of the claim in bankruptcy?
2. Issuer issues a $1000 bond in the morning for $900 worth of gold. It files in the afternoon. What is the allowed amount of the claim?
3. Issuer issues a $1000 bond in the morning for $900 worth of IBM's bonds. It files in the afternoon. What is the allowed amount of the claim?

4. Issuer issues a $1000 bond in the morning *for $900 worth of its own bonds. The bondholder bought those old bonds from a broker for $900 earlier that morning.* The old bonds were originally issued for $900 and were worth $900 on the morning of the exchange. Brokers would have bought or sold the bonds for $900 that day. The issuer files in the afternoon. What is the allowed amount of the bondholder's claim?
5. Issuer issues a $1000 bond in the morning *for $900 worth of its own bonds, which an old bondholder turns in for the new bonds.* The old bonds were originally issued to the bondholder some time ago for $900 and were worth $900 on the morning of the exchange. The issuer files in the afternoon. Brokers and other investors would have bought or sold the bonds for $900 that day. What is the allowed amount of the bondholder's claim?
6. Issuer issues a $1000 bond in the morning *for $900 worth of its own bonds, which an old bondholder turns in for the new bonds.* The old bonds were originally issued years ago for $1000, but are worth only $900 on the morning of the exchange. The issuer files in the afternoon. What is the allowed amount of the bondholder's claim?

¶ 1918: Exchange Offer Prospectus (The *Chateaugay* Problem)

Prospectus and Consent Solicitation

The Date of this Prospectus and Consent Solicitation is November 8, 1990

Burlington Northern Railroad Company . . . hereby offers . . . to exchange the following new securities of [Burlington] to be issued . . . for the following publicly held outstanding securities of [Burlington] (the "Old Debt Securities") as set forth below:

* * *

. . . If a holder of [targeted] Securities wishes not to consent to one or more of the Proposed Amendments, such holder must not tender or otherwise deliver a consent.

Each of the Exchange Offers is subject to certain conditions as specified herein, including, in the case of the Exchange Offers to holders of [the targeted Old Debt] Securities, that there have been received on or prior to the applicable Expiration Date (as defined herein) valid and unrevoked consents to the Proposed Amendments by the holders of at least $66^2/_3$% of the outstanding aggregate principal amount of the [targeted] Bonds and . . . Debentures, respectively.

Certain Effect of the Exchange Offers on Non–Tendering Holders of Old Debt Securities

Holders of All Old Debt Securities

To the extent that other holders of each issue of Old Debt Securities exchange for New Bonds, holders of the same issue who do not so exchange [may suffer].

The market price for untendered Old Debt Securities may be affected adversely to the extent that the principal amount of Old Debt Securities tendered pursuant to the Exchange Offers reduces the principal amount available for trading. A debt security with a smaller outstanding principal amount available for trading (a smaller "float") may command a lower price than would a comparable debt security with a greater float. The reduced float may also tend to make the market price of untendered Old Debt Securities more volatile.

In addition, if after the expiration of the Exchange Offers the aggregate principal amount or market value of each issue of Old Debt Securities publicly held is less than $1,000,000, the NYSE under its current published guidelines may delist such issue of Old Debt Securities. The Company intends to have the Old Debt Securities delisted from the NYSE and deregistered under the Exchange Act upon successful completion of the Exchange Offers, if the conditions for such delisting and deregistration are satisfied.

* * *

In the event of delisting of any Old Debt Securities there might be no viable market for such Old Debt Securities or, if publicly traded, such Old Debt Securities would likely be traded in the over-the-counter market. Trading in an issue of Old Debt Securities in the over-the-counter market may be subject to higher commission rates for executing trades and greater uncertainty with respect to such matters as eligibility for margin borrowing and the probable execution price of trades than is currently the case for Old Debt Securities listed on the NYSE.

If, after the expiration of the Exchange Offers, any issue of Old Debt Securities is delisted from the NYSE and deregistered under the Exchange Act, any further solicitations of consents from holders of such Old Debt Securities would not be subject to the provisions of the Exchange Act.

* * *

<u>Holders of [targeted] Bonds and . . . Debentures</u>

If the Requisite Consents are obtained, supplemental indentures amending both the . . . Mortgage and the . . . Debenture Indenture will be executed upon the completion of the Exchange Offers. . . . [H]olders of [the targeted] Bonds and . . . Debentures who do not tender such securities in the Exchange Offers will [be subject to the amended indentures] whether or not such non-tendering holders have consented to the Proposed Amendments. . . .

. . . [T]he rights of non-exchanging holders of [the targeted] Securities will be adversely affected. The Proposed Amendments . . . would (i) eliminate the requirement that the Company maintain a Special Reserve Fund, with the effect of reducing the collateral securing the . . . Bonds by approximately $5.5 millions, the amount in the Special Reserve Fund, (ii) eliminate the prohibition against the Company's paying dividends on common stock or purchasing its common stock for purposes of retirement while the amount in the Special Reserve Fund is less than $500,000, and (iii) [otherwise reduce the] collateral securing the . . . Bonds. . . .

The Proposed Amendment . . . would [also] (i) eliminate a provision permitting the . . . Indenture Trustee to declare a default on the [targeted] Debentures simply because of a default of the Company under any other debt instrument to which it is a party, (ii) eliminate a [negative pledge] provision prohibiting the Company . . . from creating or permitting any new mortgage or lien to be created on the property or assets then owned by or leased to the Company . . . unless the [targeted] Debentures are secured by such mortgage or lien equally or ratably with the bonds or other obligations issued under or secured by such new mortgage or lien. . . .

Amount of Claim in Bankruptcy

In general, a bond or debenture represents a potential bankruptcy claim equal to its face amount plus accrued and unpaid interest as of the date a bankruptcy is commenced. Unmatured interest, including original issue discount, generally is not allowable as a claim under the Bankruptcy Code. Therefore, if a bond or debenture is issued with original issue discount, a holder's claim in respect of such bond or debenture will be reduced by the amount of unamortized original issue discount at the date a bankruptcy is commenced. A claim in respect of the New Bonds in a bankruptcy of the Company (unlike a claim outside of bankruptcy) could be reduced below the stated principal amount of such New Bonds by the amount of unamortized original issue discount, if any, with respect thereto at the date such bankruptcy is commenced. It is unclear whether and to what extent the issuance of bonds in an exchange transaction should be determined to involve original issue discount for the purpose of fixing the claim of a holder of such bonds in a subsequent bankruptcy, although it is likely that a bankruptcy court would compare the face amount of the New Bonds to the value of the consideration received by the Company in the Exchange Offers to make such a determination. Under one possible formula, the value of the consideration received by the Company would be equal to the principal amount of the Old Debt Securities less any unamortized original issue discount of such securities plus accrued interest relating thereto. A bankruptcy court adopting this view would likely determine that there was no additional original issue discount on the New Bonds and allow a bankruptcy claim for their full face amount, less any unamortized original issue discount attributable to the Old Debt Securities.

In contrast, a bankruptcy court that chose to follow the recent bankruptcy court decision in In re Chateaugay Corporation, 109 Bankr. 51 (Bankr. S.D.N.Y. 1990) ("Chateaugay"), might reach a contrary result. Under Chateaugay, a bankruptcy court would likely determine that the value of the consideration received by the Company would be equal to the fair market value of the Old Debt Securities on the date the exchange occurred. In Chateaugay, the court determined that holders of old unsecured debentures of LTV Corporation ("LTV") who elected to accept in exchange therefor an equal face amount of new unsecured debentures and shares of common stock of LTV were not entitled to a claim for unamortized original issue discount under the applicable provisions of the Bankruptcy Code, and the amount of such unamortized original issue discount was equal to the face amount of the new unsecured debentures less the fair market value of the old debt securities on the exchange date, calculated under the constant interest method . . . , thereby limiting the claims of the holders of unsecured [claims] to the fair market value of the old debt securities on the exchange date plus that amount of original issue discount which is amortized prior to the date of bankruptcy.

¶ 1919: Original Issue Discount

If a $40 million bond is exchanged for a $20 million bond and the company then goes bankrupt, is the allowed claim in bankruptcy $40 million or $20 million?

Begin first with the problem of original issue discount. If the debtor *issues* a new $40 million bond and the creditor pays only $20 million for the bond (presumably because the interest rate is low), what is the allowed amount of the claim in the bankruptcy that shortly follows, $40 million or $20 million?

Again, the legislative history to § 502(b)(2) (see Chapter 14, Part F) answers one question clearly: if the new $40 million bond were issued for $20 million in cash, and the debtor quickly went bankrupt, the allowed amount of the claim would be $20 million.

> Interest disallowed under [Section 502(b)(2)] includes postpetition interest that is not yet due and payable, and any portion of . . . interest that represents an original [issue] discounting of the claim, yet that would not have been earned on the date of bankruptcy. For example, a claim on a $1,000 note issued the day before bankruptcy would only be allowed to the extent of the cash actually advanced. If the original discount was 10%, so that the cash advanced was only $900, then notwithstanding the face amount of the note, only $900 would be allowed. If $900 was advanced under the note some time before bankruptcy, the interest component of the note would have to be pro-rated and disallowed to the extent it was for interest after the commencement of the case.

The next issue, one that the exchanging bondholders in Burlington and Chateaugay would worry about, is whether the amount of the claim would similarly be $20 million if the creditor paid for that very same bond not with a check for $20 million but with property worth $20 million. The property is, however, not gold or real estate or securities of other companies, but an *old* bond of the debtor company, a bond originally issued for $40 million and whose value had declined to $20 million.

Same answer? $20 million? Or should the old $40 million amount be carried over to the new bond as the claim allowed under § 502(b)(2)? The bankruptcy court in *Chateaugay,* to which the Burlington prospectus referred, clearly concluded that the fair market value of the bonds tendered was the amount from which the discounted interest should start accreting.

The *Chateaugay* bankruptcy court opinion was controversial, with critics claiming in the finance media that the result would induce more bankruptcies and fewer out-of-court workouts. The bondholders appealed, and the appellate decision follows.

¶ 1920: Subsequent Developments (*Chateaugay* on Appeal)

In re Chateaugay Corp., 961 F.2d 378 (2d Cir. 1992)

Opinion: OAKES, Chief Judge:

[The indenture trustee] and intervenors appeal from a judgment of the United States District Court for the Southern District of New York, Shirley Wohl Kram, Judge, affirming a judgment of the United States Bankruptcy Court for the Southern District of New York, Burton R. Lifland, Chief Judge. The bankruptcy court granted partial summary judgment in favor of the debtor, the LTV Corporation ("LTV"), disallowing [the indenture trustee's] claims to the extent they included unamortized original issue discount ("OID"). On this appeal, [the indenture trustee] argues that the bankruptcy court and district court erred by holding . . . that new OID arose on an exchange of debt securities performed as part of LTV's failed attempt to avoid bankruptcy through a consensual workout. . . . We hold . . . that while claims must be disallowed to the extent of unamortized OID, no new OID arose on LTV's debt-for-debt exchange. . . .

FACTS

In July 1986, LTV, a steel company that makes defense and industrial products, filed for Chapter 11 reorganization. . . . LTV filed objections in September 1989 to two proofs of claim [that had been] filed in November 1987 by [the Trustee] on behalf of the holders of two securities, the "Old Debentures" and the "New Notes." . . .

The Old Debentures are 13⅞% Sinking Fund Debentures due December 1, 2002, of which LTV had by December 1, 1982 issued a total face amount of $150,000,000 [for $133,000,000]. The proceeds received for the Old Debentures thus amounted to 88.67% of their face value.

The New Notes are LTV 15% Senior Notes due January 15, 2000. In May 1986, LTV offered to exchange $1,000 face amount of New Notes and 15 shares of LTV common stock for each $1,000 face amount of Old Debentures. As of June 1, 1986, $116,035,000 face amount of Old Debentures had been exchanged for the same face amount of New Notes and LTV Common Stock.

In its proofs of claim, [the Indenture Trustee] did not deduct any amount for unamortized OID. LTV objected to the claims and moved for partial summary judgment, seeking an order disallowing unamortized OID. LTV argued that unamortized OID is unmatured interest which is not allowable by virtue of section 502(b)(2) of the Bankruptcy Code, 11 U.S.C. § 502(b)(2) (1988), and that therefore the claims must be reduced by the amount of unamortized OID. . . .

The bankruptcy court granted partial summary judgment for LTV. . . . The court held that unamortized OID is not allowable under section 502(b)(2). . . .

. . . The district court affirmed the bankruptcy court's decision in its entirety.

DISCUSSION

I. Original Issue Discount and Section 502(b)(2)

A

Original issue discount results when a bond is issued for less than its face value. The discount, which compensates for a stated interest rate that the market deems too low, equals the difference between a bond's face amount (stated principal amount) and the proceeds . . . received by the issuer. OID is amortized, for accounting and tax purposes, over the life of the bond, with the face value generally paid back to the bondholders on the maturity date. If the debtor meets with financial trouble and turns to the bankruptcy court for protection, as in the present case, then OID comes into play as one of the factors determining the amount of the bondholder's allowable claim in bankruptcy.

Section 502 of the Bankruptcy Code, the framework for Chapter 11 claim allowance, provides that a claim shall be allowed "except to the extent that . . . such claim is for unmatured interest." The first question we face is whether unamortized OID is "unmatured interest" within the meaning of section 502(b)(2). We conclude that it is. As a matter of economic definition, OID constitutes interest. Moreover, the Bankruptcy Code's legislative history makes inescapable the conclusion that OID is interest within the meaning of section 502(b)(2). The House committee report on that section explains:

> Interest disallowed under this paragraph includes postpetition interest that is not yet due and payable, and any portion of prepaid interest that represents an original discounting of the claim, yet that would not have been earned on the date of bankruptcy. For example, a claim on a $1,000 note issued the day before bankruptcy would only be allowed to the extent of the cash actually advanced. If the original issue discount was 10% so that the cash advanced was only $900, then notwithstanding the face amount of [the] note, only $900 would be allowed. If $900 was advanced under the note some time before bankruptcy, the interest component of the note would have to be pro-rated and disallowed to the extent it was for interest after the commencement of the case.

H. Rep. No. 595, 95th Cong., 1st Sess. 352–53 (1977), reprinted in 1978 U.S.C.C.A.N. 5963, 6308–09.

. . . [U]nder section 502(b)(2) . . . unamortized OID is unmatured interest and therefore unallowable as part of a bankruptcy claim.

. . . We now turn to the main issue in dispute: the applicability of section 502(b)(2) to the New Notes, which were issued in a debt-for-debt exchange offer as part of a consensual workout.

B

A debtor in financial trouble may seek to avoid bankruptcy through a consensual out-of-court workout. Such a recapitalization, when it involves publicly traded debt, often takes the form of a debt-for-debt exchange, whereby bondholders exchange their old bonds for new bonds. The debtor hopes that the exchange, by changing the terms of the debt, will enable the debtor to avoid default. The bondholders hope that by increasing the likelihood of payment on their bonds, the exchange will benefit them as well. The debtor and its creditors share an interest in achieving a successful restructuring of the debtor's financial obligations in order to avoid the uncertainties and daunting transaction costs of bankruptcy.

An exchange offer made by a financially troubled company can be either a "fair market value exchange" or a "face value exchange." . . . In a fair market value exchange, an existing debt instrument is exchanged for a new one with a reduced principal amount, determined by the market value at which the existing instrument is trading. By offering a fair market value exchange, an issuer seeks to reduce its overall debt obligations. . . . A face value exchange, by contrast, involves the substitution of new indebtedness for an existing debenture, modifying terms or conditions but not reducing the principal amount of the debt. . . .

The question is whether a face value exchange generates new OID. The bankruptcy court, in an opinion endorsed by the district court, held that it does. The court reasoned that, by definition, OID arises whenever a bond is issued for less than its face amount, and that in LTV's debt-for-debt exchange, the issue price of the New Notes was the fair market value of the Old Debentures. The court therefore concluded that the New Notes were issued at a discount equaling the difference between their face value and the fair market value of the Old Debentures.

The bankruptcy court's reasoning leaves us unpersuaded. *While its application of the definition of OID to exchange offers may seem irrefutable at first glance, we believe the bankruptcy court's logic ignores the importance of context, and does not make sense if one takes into account the strong bankruptcy policy in favor of the speedy, inexpensive, negotiated resolution of disputes, that is an out-of-court or common law composition.* See H.R. Rep. No. 95–595, 95th Cong., 1st Sess. 220 (1977), reprinted in 1978 U.S.C.C.A.N. 5963, 6179–80; see also In re Colonial Ford, Inc., 24 B.R. 1014, 1015–17 (Bankr. D. Utah 1982) ("Congress designed the Code, in large measure, to encourage workouts in the first instance, with refuge in bankruptcy as a last resort."). If unamortized OID is unallowable in bankruptcy, and if exchanging debt increases the amount of OID, *then creditors will be disinclined to cooperate in a consensual workout* that might otherwise have rescued a borrower from the precipice of bankruptcy. We must consider the ramifications of a rule that places a creditor in the position of choosing whether to cooperate with a struggling debtor, when such cooperation might make the creditor's claims in the event of bankruptcy smaller than they would have been had the creditor refused to cooperate. The bankruptcy court's ruling places creditors in just such a position, and unreversed would likely result in fewer out-of-court debt exchanges and more Chapter 11 filings. Just as that ruling creates a disincentive for creditors to cooperate with a troubled debtor, it grants a corresponding windfall both to holdouts who refuse to cooperate and to an issuer that files for bankruptcy subsequent to a debt exchange.

The bankruptcy court's decision might make sense in the context of a fair market value exchange, where the corporation's overall debt obligations are reduced. In a face value exchange such as LTV's, however, it is unsupportable. LTV's liability to the holders of the New Notes was no less than its liability to them had been when they held the Old Debentures. The bankruptcy court, by finding that the exchange created new OID, reduced LTV's liabilities based on an exchange which, because it was a face value exchange, caused no such reduction on LTV's balance sheet.

We hold that a *face value* exchange of debt obligations in a consensual workout does not, for purposes of section 502(b)(2), generate new OID. Such an exchange does not change the character of the underlying debt, but reaffirms and modifies it.

In the absence of unambiguous statutory guidance, we will not attribute to Congress an intent to place a stumbling block in front of debtors seeking to avoid bankruptcy with the cooperation of their creditors. Rather, given Congress's intent to encourage consensual workouts and the obvious desirability of minimizing bankruptcy filings, we conclude that for purposes of section 502(b)(2), no new OID is created in a face value debt-for-debt exchange in the context of a consensual workout. Thus, OID on the new debt consists only of the discount carried over from the old debt, that is, the unamortized OID remaining on the old debt at the time of the exchange.

* * *

Accordingly, the judgment of the district court is affirmed in part and reversed in part, and the matter remanded to the district court for remand to the bankruptcy court for further proceedings consistent with this opinion.

¶ 1921: Exchange Offers and Original Issue Discount

1. Original issue discount was discussed in Chapter 14. Review your understanding of the following situation: if a $1000 bond, maturing ten months from now, is issued for $900 in cash and the debtor goes bankrupt later in the day, what is the allowed claim in bankruptcy? If the debtor goes bankrupt in five months, about how much is the allowed claim?
2. If instead of bankruptcy, the $1000 bond is exchanged five months from now for a new bond worth $500 and having a face value of $500 (because the firm deteriorated badly in the intervening five months and the original bond fell to $500 in value), what is the allowed claim in a subsequent bankruptcy later in the day of the exchange?
3. If the bond is exchanged five months from the issuance date for a $1000 face value bond with different terms, at a time when the trading value of the bond was $500 (and when the new bond is worth $500) what is the allowed claim in the bankruptcy that is filed later in the day of the exchange? If the firm issues brand new $1000 face value bonds five months from now, for $500, what is the allowed amount of the new issue claim in the bankruptcy?
4. If zero coupon and interest bearing securities can be made financially equivalent, which one will exchanging bondholders prefer after the Second Circuit decision? After the *Chateaugay* holding on

appeal do some exchanging bondholders and companies have an incentive to use a face value exchange?

The court thought that the face value exchange was usually an exchange of one bond for another approximately equal bond. And in fact the LTV exchange did involve roughly the same interest rate, roughly the same maturity date, and exactly the same face value. But face value exchanges do not have to fit this mold. A face value exchange could radically alter the other terms of the bond.

The court concludes: "We hold that a face value exchange of debt obligations . . . does not generate new OID." That would seem to apply to bonds that gave up all their interest and covenants, and grossly altered the maturity date. If the face value rule is followed scrupulously—that rule is, after all, the formal holding—would it then apply to exchanges where the exchanged bonds differ radically from the bonds that were traded in?

5. How faithful is the Second Circuit's opinion to the text of the Bankruptcy Code? If the core rationale of the Second Circuit's opinion is that the carryover of the allowed amount of the claim facilitates exchange offers that allow the company to avoid bankruptcy, then why not allow the same carryover for market value exchanges that do not retain the same face value?

¶ 1922: Exchange Offers and Original Issue Discount, OID Chart

The verbal questions in paragraphs 2 and 3 can be charted:

Original (5 months ago)	Today	Claim in Ch. 11, later today
	<u>Exchanged for original bond:</u>	
2. $1000 bond → face = FMV, when issued	$500 face = FMV	[ ]
	<u>Exchanged for original bond</u>:	
3a. $1000 bond → face = FMV, when issued	$1000 face, but $500 FMV	[ ]
	<u>New issue of new discounted bond</u>:	
3b.	$1000 face, but $500 FMV	[ ]

¶ 1923: Debt Overhang Again: Chrysler on the Verge of Shut–Down, 1978–1979

Could a firm in financial stress but with a profitable project be denied the capital for that project by an otherwise efficient capital market? Could good operational bets not be taken because the preexisting creditors would take too much of the winning outcome? (Usually we have seen stockholders get the upside of the winning bets.

In this chapter, we have been examining such bets when the firm is insolvent. The payoffs have been different: *creditor* gains, not stockholder gains, distort the operational decision.) These distortions from overhanging debt affect the heavily-indebted firm's ability to recapitalize, to raise new capital, and to merge.

Consider XYZ Corp., a large manufacturing company that borrowed several billion dollars to finance production of a product that, due to massive shifts in consumer preferences, no longer is profitable. It verges on bankruptcy, although its book value indicates solvency:

(1)

XYZ Corp.	
$6.4 billion	$3.4 billion bank, trade, and other debt
	$1 billion junk bonds
	$2 billion common stock

In market terms the company's balance sheet is gruesome. Creditors are no longer sure of fully being paid back. The publicly-traded debt is valued at 50 cents on the dollar. The bank and other debt is similarly discounted.

(2)

XYZ Corp. (Market-oriented balance sheet)	
$2.6 billion	$2.2 billion debt ($4.4 billion face value)
	$400 million common stock

(As a realistic matter, the common stock will have a positive value even if the firm is insolvent. The stock will have hold-up value for two major reasons: First, deals cannot commence without their consent. And second, they get value from the prospect of an unusually good outcome, because the $2.6 billion comes from a bell curve of expected values, some exceeding $4.4 billion. These have been considered earlier; let's put these problems aside for now to isolate the new capital problem for insolvent firms.)

Let's suppose the firm has a unique opportunity to sell a new product that people expect will have good marketplace acceptance. However, it needs $1.6 billion to tool-up its factories, to advertise, and to pay employees until the cash starts flowing in. The expected value of the project is $2.8 billion, making it clearly worth pursuing.

<u>Common stock offering</u>?

Could the firm raise the money via a common stock offering?

Clearly not. Imagine new stockholders pay $1.6 billion for new stock and the company's operating value increases by $2.8 billion. But $2.2 of that $2.8 billion increase would go to the preexisting creditors. Of the newly enhanced $5.4 billion in total asset value, the first $4.4 billion goes to the creditors, leaving the total common worth only $1 billion. So the cash from the $1.6 billion stock offering would enhance the stock value by only $600 million. Anticipating immediate enhancement to the creditor layers, Wall Street investors could be expected not to make the investment *even if they believed the project was a billion-dollar-plus winner.*

New borrowing?

Could the firm raise the money via new debt?

The answer is also no, but getting to the answer for debt is more complicated than getting there for stock. If the debt came in at the same level as the preexisting debt, what resultant distribution of value?

(3)

XYZ Corp.
Market balance sheet (assets), with book value of liabilities after $1.6 billion debt infusion

$5.4 billion	$4.4 billion face value old debt
	$1.6 billion face value new debt
	$400 million common stock

Obviously the firm would still be insolvent. The expected value of the debt will be about 5/6 of its face value. The new $1.6 billion creditor would not have a liability worth the amount it would have pumped into the company. The new creditor's liability would be worth about $1.4 billion, although the creditor provided $1.6 billion. The deal cannot go through, despite that it would produce extraordinary operational value. The problem again is that a disproportionate amount of the value is not produced for the investor.

Other priority techniques?

What must be done? One of the priority techniques *might* work: if the firm could offer the new project (or preexisting assets) as security, or if the preexisting overhanging creditors allow themselves to be subordinated, or if the firm could develop the new project in a subsidiary *and* insulate the subsidiary from the claim of the preexisting overhanging debt, then the capital could flow in for the project.

Many times, these separation techniques will work. It's the lawyers' job, as transaction cost engineers, to find the technique that will work. But when the priority techniques still fail (or often in order to make them succeed), the preexisting creditors must be dealt with. That is, the creditors must, in the simplest separation scenario, agree to subordinate themselves to the new debt. The difficulty with this is that we now have a multi-party workout, subject to the chancy prospects of deadlock and delay. The new funding is not impossible, but requires renegotiation.

How real can this hypothetical be?

In 1979 Chrysler had a project it wanted to pursue: tooling of automotive plants to produce the K-car, a fuel-efficient, front-wheel drive car that the American public seemed to demand. It had factories to produce large rear-wheel drive, inefficient cars that the consumer did not want. It also had a lot of debt, incurred to produce the large cars made unmarketable by an unexpected shift in consumer preferences due to the rise in oil prices. That old debt did not permit its subordination. That debt had negative pledge clauses, prohibiting security that would make a new creditor senior (see supra ¶¶706-708, discussing Chrysler's negative pledge clause).

At the end of 1979, Chrysler had a book value of $6.6 billion. Obviously the market value of its factories and inventory was much lower. Consider the liabilities shown on Chrysler's balance sheet, reproduced next:

CHRYSLER CORPORATION
(In millions of dollars)

	1979
LIABILITIES AND SHAREHOLDERS' INVESTMENT:	
Current Liabilities:	
Accounts payable	$1,530.4
Accrued expenses	807.9
Short-term debt (Notes 3 and 4)	600.9
Payments due within one year on long-term debt (Notes 3 and 11)	275.6
Taxes on income	16.8
TOTAL CURRENT LIABILITIES	**3,231.6**
Other Liabilities and Deferred Credits:	
Deferred employee benefit plan accruals	301.4
Deferred taxes on income	83.0
Unrealized profits on sales to unconsolidated subsidiaries	47.7
Other noncurrent liabilities	134.9
TOTAL OTHER LIABILITIES AND DEFERRED CREDITS	**567.0**
Long-Term Debt (Notes 3 and 11):	
Notes and debentures payable	880.7
Convertible sinking fund debentures	96.0
TOTAL LONG–TERM DEBT	**976.7**
Obligations Under Capital Leases (Note 9)	**15.4**
Minority Interest in Net Assets of Consolidated Subsidiaries	**38.3**
Preferred Stock—no par value (Note 12)	218.7
Common Stock—par value $6.25 a share (Note 13)	416.9
Additional Paid–In Capital (Note 15)	692.2
Net Earnings Retained (Note 16)	496.3
TOTAL LIABILITIES AND SHAREHOLDERS' INVESTMENT	**$6,653.1**

See notes to financial statements.

Vastly simplifying Chrysler's balance sheet (and ignoring that Chrysler had an unconsolidated finance subsidiary), we come up with a balance sheet of:

(4)

Chrysler	
Book value	$3.4 billion bank, trade, and other debt $1 billion junk bonds Common stock

The bonds traded at *34* cents on the dollar. Using a higher 50% figure for simplicity, we can reconstruct a simple market-oriented balance sheet. Since the debt was not subject to intercreditor priorities, we can apply the 50% discount to all of the debt. A market value of the common stock—presumably a result of its holdout value and the prospect of government funding—comes from taking the stock's trading price at the time and multiplying the price by the shares outstanding. Chrysler's market-oriented balance sheet looks quite a bit like this:

(5)

Chrysler	
$2.6 billion	$2.2 billion debt ($4.4 billion face value) $400 million common stock

New debt or equity would have had to provide an unusually good return. Even if the project would yield a good risk-adjusted return on a $1.6 billion inflow, buoying up would require that it provide a value of at least *$3.8* billion. (If the old creditors refuse to subordinate themselves, and if the old stockholders insist on getting stock that after the transaction would be worth at least $400 million, then the total value of the company would have to be $4.4 billion + $1.6 billion + $400 million, or $6.4 billion, after the transaction. To be worth $6.4 billion, the project would have to be a $3.8 billion winner. Anything less and a priority technique would be needed but might fail.)

The intuition behind this is simple: the new money would have buoyed up the preexisting debt. When the buoying-up effect is small, or when the previously-negotiated covenants allow senior debt (and the interim outflow of interest to preexisting creditors does not stymie the deal), or a transactional alternative, such as separate incorporation or sale of the new opportunity exists, then such deals can be worked out. But these techniques are not always available. Often they are barred by preexisting financial arrangements (loan agreements with negative pledge clauses or clauses requiring the buyer to assume the seller's debts, for example) that would have to be renegotiated.

To be sure, Chrysler's position was so complex—and perhaps operationally untenable without informal import quotas on cars—that even if the risky debt effects were absent, the financial market might well still have viewed the investment as not worthwhile. Buoying up was sufficient but not necessary to thwart financing of the K-car; operational debilities were *also* sufficient to thwart the project.

Keep in mind that firms in financial stress do not usually have worthwhile new opportunities. Oftentimes they should be shrinking, not expanding. But when they do have good opportunities that require new cash, a merger, or sale of most of their assets, they cannot readily take them. When the lawyers' separation techniques are exhausted, only a renegotiation with preexisting creditors—a workout or a bankruptcy—will do.

Atlas Pipeline again. This analysis of Chrysler helps us understand a central point in *Atlas Pipeline*. Recall that the SEC thought that Atlas could not be renewed. Once its facilities wore out, it would not have access to new financing, assumed the SEC. This led to a double count, as the SEC seemed to increase the discount rate for the years *before* new financing was needed. A critique of the SEC's view could also revolve around the potential efficiency of the marketplace: *if* Atlas had a good project, why shouldn't it be able to raise money to finance it? Companies with too much overhanging debt might not be able to finance worthwhile projects, because of the buoying-up effect.

The bankruptcy apparatus can help the bankrupt firm get future access to capital markets: the court can help the firm avoid the Chrysler scenario by making sure that the firm is not top-heavy with debt when it emerges from bankruptcy.

¶ 1924: Mergers

"[Donald Dewey] has argued [in Dewey, *Mergers and Cartels: Some Reservations about Policy,* 51 Market Economy Review 257 (1961)] that most mergers [at that time were] . . . merely a civilized [early] alternative to bankruptcy or the voluntary liquidation that transfers assets from falling to rising firms. . . . If, as Dewey suggests, mergers are superior to bankruptcy as a method of 'shifting assets from falling to rising firms,' and if mergers were completely legal, we should anticipate relatively few actual bankruptcy proceedings in any industry which was not itself contracting. The function so wastefully performed by bankruptcies and liquidations would be economically performed by mergers at a much earlier stage of the firm's life." Henry Manne, *Mergers and the Market for Corporate Control*, 73 Journal of Political Economy 110, 111–12 (1965).

A vexing question asked in the merger and tender offer literature is why failing firms are so infrequently the subject of hostile tender offers. The answer is important because a central purpose for the hostile tender offer has been to discipline unimaginative target firm management. Why, it was sometimes asked, wasn't Chrysler in the late 1970s the target of a hostile offer? While the firm's problems were not of management's doing—demand shifts, an oil crisis, and a depressed economy did the company in—incumbent managers were criticized as unimaginative in responding to the deteriorating environment. Substantial changes in management eventually were made, but they were made through internal governance mechanisms, not through a tender offer or the explicit threat of one.

Several good explanations are available: Offering firm managers do not want to take on the burden of a near-bankrupt. The target firm was too far gone; money could not be expected to be made by managing the target firm any better. Antitrust barriers would have thwarted those most interested in the acquisition. Chrysler was unique.

The buoying-up effect is another (sufficient but not necessary) explanation: the offering firm would have seen a disproportionate share of the returns from superior management going to the preexisting, overhanging creditors. For the offer to be worth pursuing, a deal with creditors (as well as stockholders and managers) would have been necessary. And, with reorganizations of public firms requiring two years or more, that might have been too complex to pursue and succeed quickly.

Although the inability to merge was less important to Chrysler than its inability to get private financing for the K-car, the inability to merge probably is more important for the ordinary bankrupt firm. Why?

It's plausible that bankrupt firms are drawn disproportionately from industries that are contracting. As technologies and markets change, some industries just have to contract, because the demand for their product isn't there or because competitors can make the same product more cheaply with new technology. As these technologies and markets change, the incumbent firms lose money, either because they sell less product, sell it at a lower price, or face high costs on their old technologies (or all of these). If they lose enough money, they become candidates for bankruptcy.

In fact, bankruptcies sometimes come in industry waves—oil firms in the 1980s, retailers in the 1990s, maybe telecommunications in the first decade of the 21st century, airlines several times that oil prices spiked, and the auto industry in 2009. The policy consequence here is that often the best disposition for some firms in a contracting industry is to merge. The merged entity can preserve the strong parts of each constituent firm and close down the weak parts. The cost then of the buoying-up effect, of recapitalizations, of deadlocks, and of slow, multi-year chapter 11 proceedings is that American society cannot get the benefit of quick, low-cost mergers in these kinds of industries. Note that after a long delay, Chrysler was eventually acquired by a foreign automaker, a result discussed during 1979 and 1980 as an alternative to a government loan or a bankruptcy.

CHAPTER 20

JURISDICTION AND VENUE

Bankruptcy courts lack the general jurisdiction of federal district courts and therefore lack the power to render final decisions on some claims and disputes that arise in a bankruptcy. In recent decades two major Supreme Court decisions sought to explicate the scope of the bankruptcy courts' jurisdiction, but the lines of what the bankruptcy courts can and cannot decide are still uncertain.

Debtors filing for bankruptcy have a wide choice of the bankruptcy court where they will file and, with rare exceptions, their selection becomes the court that will hear their case. On some issues, bankruptcy and appellate courts disagree on how the Code should be interpreted. The wide choice of venue gives some strategic leverage in filing choice.

A. THE LIMITED JURISDICTION OF THE BANKRUPTCY COURT

¶ 2001: Constitutional background: Article III courts and Article I courts

Bankruptcy courts lack the full jurisdictional authority of federal district courts. Article III of the Constitution vests judicial power in the Supreme Court and "such inferior Courts as the Congress may from time to time ordain and establish." Section 1 of Article III provides that the judges of such courts "shall hold their Offices during good Behavior, and shall, at stated Times, receive for their Services a Compensation for which shall not be diminished during their Continuance in Office." This clause is interpreted as requiring that Article III judges have lifetime tenure. Thus, the core federal judicial system in the United States consists of district court judges, whose decisions can be appealed to the Circuit Courts of Appeal. The Supreme Court of the United States sits atop these two federal levels. All of these federal judges—at the Supreme Court, at the Circuit Court level, and the District Court level—have lifetime appointments.

The Constitution also deals with judicial power outside Article III. Article I empowers Congress to "constitute tribunals inferior to the Supreme Court." These courts are often specialized, with a targeted jurisdiction. For instance, Congress established, pursuant to Article I, the United States Tax Court to decide federal tax issues. Tax court judges serve for 15 years.[1] The bankruptcy courts are Article I courts. Bankruptcy judges are appointed to 14-year terms.[2] Because they lack lifetime tenure, they cannot be Article III judges.

¶ 2002. The Broad Jurisdiction that Congress Wanted

Congress, in the 1978 Code, sought to give bankruptcy courts broad jurisdiction, one that would cover: all "civil proceedings arising under title 11 or arising in or related to cases under title 11." However, the bankruptcy judges, although granted broad jurisdiction, would be appointed for limited, 14-year terms by the Court of Appeals in the circuit in which its district is located, after considering the recommendations of a judicial conference.[3]

The scope of bankruptcy courts' jurisdiction was quickly tested, with the Supreme Court ruling in 1982 that the bankruptcy courts' jurisdiction could not be as wide as Congress provided because bankruptcy judges, lacking lifetime tenure, were not Article III judges with plenary jurisdiction. They were "only" Article I judges, with limited jurisdiction. Northern Pipeline v. Marathon, 450 U.S. 50 (1982).

The federal courts consequently faced an emergency. The Supreme Court had declared the bankruptcy court system unconstitutional and, because Congress did not react quickly, there was the practical problem of what to do with the pending bankruptcies. The federal courts then promulgated an emergency interim rule, requiring that thenceforth bankruptcy proceedings would be heard in United States District Courts. District Courts could refer the bankruptcy proceedings to bankruptcy judges, who could enter final orders in core matters but not for related proceedings. The courts awaited a congressional solution.

Congress passed the Bankruptcy Amendments and Federal Judgeship Act in 1984. Rather than giving the bankruptcy judges

---

[1] 26 U.S.C. § 7443(e).

[2] 28 U.S.C. § 152(a)(1).

[3] 28 U.S.C. § 152(a)(1).

lifetime tenure, as some proposed,[4] Congress largely enacted the courts' stopgap emergency system. Bankruptcy courts, Congress said, "shall constitute a unit of the district court" and each bankruptcy judge was made an officer of the district court in which he or she served. 28 U.S.C. § 151. District courts have subject matter jurisdiction over bankruptcy cases pursuant to 28 U.S.C. § 1334, but may refer their bankruptcy cases and matters to the bankruptcy court.[5] After the district court refers a case to a bankruptcy court, the bankruptcy court can hear the case. But whether or not the bankruptcy court may issue a final judgment turns on whether the matter is "core" to the bankruptcy proceeding or "non-core."

¶ 2003: The Supreme Court Narrows Jurisdiction: Core vs. Noncore Proceedings

Bankruptcy judges may enter final orders on core proceedings. For noncore proceedings, bankruptcy courts may only enter proposed findings of fact and proposed conclusions of law. The district court then reviews the bankruptcy courts' proposals and the proceeding de novo. It enters the final judgment, not the bankruptcy court.

Congress listed examples of core proceedings in 28 U.S.C. § 157(b). The proceedings on the list generally involved the direct administration of bankruptcy proceedings or key functions that the bankruptcy court must undertake if it is to efficiently facilitate the reorganization of companies. Core proceedings include:

> (A) matters concerning the administration of the estate;
>
> (B) allowance or disallowance of claims against the estate or exemptions from property of the estate, and estimation of claims or interests for the purposes of confirming a plan of reorganization but not the liquidation or estimation of contingent or unliquidated personal injury tort or wrongful death claims against the estate for purposes of distribution in a bankruptcy case;
>
> . . .
>
> (D) orders in respect to obtaining credit;
>
> (E) orders to turn over property of the estate;
>
> (F) proceedings to determine, avoid or recover preferences; motions to terminate, annul or modify the automatic stay;
>
> . . .
>
> (I) determinations as to the dischargeability of particular debts;
>
> (J) objections to discharges;

[4] "After two calamitous years of living under emergency rules[,] Congress passed the [1984 Act]. Congress again was faced with the choice of making bankruptcy judges Article III judges or playing another game of let's pretend. The debate was furious. The district judges opposed creating a specialized Article III court. . . . In addition, the plaintiff's personal injury bar, [which] was just getting into lucrative asbestos litigation, did not want bankruptcy judges hearing their proofs of claims when juries likely would be much more generous. Finally, bankruptcy judges themselves didn't make a compelling case for Article III status." Ronald R. Peterson, Stern v. Marshall: Bleak House Revisited, NABTalk, Fall 2011, at 10, 13.

[5] Reference can also be withdrawn—an abnormal occurrence—under 28 U.S.C. §157(d).

(K) determinations of the validity, extent, or priority of liens.

(L) confirmations of plans; . . . [and]

(M) orders approving the use or lease of property, including the use of cash collateral.

But the congressional list is not the last word on core vs. non-core here. While Congress listed what it thought could be core to bankruptcy, the question persisted after 1984 whether Congress could make that determination. In 2011, the Court spoke again, in Stern v. Marshall, 564 U.S. 2 (2011), with the Court holding that § 157(b)'s list of core proceedings exceeded congressional authority.

The question before the Court in *Stern* was whether a bankruptcy court could hear, and enter a final order on, a debtor's state law counterclaim of tortious interference. The Court found that while § 157(b)(2)(C) afforded the court a *statutory* basis to enter a final judgment on the state law counterclaim,[6] the bankruptcy court lacked the requisite *constitutional* authority to do so. An Article III judge, with lifetime tenure, could hear and decide such claims, not an Article I judge. Claims that Congress listed as "core" in § 157 but that are constitutionally "non-core" came to be dubbed "*Stern* claims."

Because the dividing line between constitutionally core and constitutionally non-core is not bright and precise—not well-defined by the Court—post-*Stern* litigation has been substantial, with some of it expanding beyond whether the claim could be finally adjudicated by the bankruptcy court to whether the bankruptcy court had authority even to hear the *Stern* claim at all, since it lacked ultimate authority to decide the claim. The Supreme Court in 2014 conclusively resolved that second issue, unanimously holding that for *Stern* claims, "the bankruptcy court simply treats the claims as a statutory non-core claim: The bankruptcy court should hear the proceeding and submit proposed findings of fact and conclusions of law to the district court for de novo review and entry of judgment."[7]

The next broad jurisdictional issue moving through the courts is whether the parties to a *Stern* claim proceeding can consent to have the court hear the case and enter a final judgment, as the judge can with standard non-core claims under § 157(c)(2). Congress sought to allow the parties to consent to jurisdiction: "with the consent of all the parties to the proceeding" the bankruptcy court may "hear and determine" non-core matters "and . . . enter appropriate orders and judgments" as though the matter were core.[8] The Supreme Court held in *Wellness International Network v. Sharif*[9] that the parties can consent to having the bankruptcy court hear *Stern* claims.[10]

---

[6] Section 157(b)(2)(C) lists "counterclaims by the estate against persons filing claims against the estate" among the nonexhaustive list of core proceedings.

[7] Executive Benefits Ins. Agency v. Arkison, 134 S. Ct. 2165, 2173 (2014).

[8] 11 U.S.C. § 157(c)(2).

[9] 575 U.S. __ (2015).

[10] Thus far the consent issue has been whether the parties can consent during the proceeding. Presumably one party or another will typically have a strategic advantage in not consenting, so the Court's actual decision may not much affect practice. But if parties to a loan agreement or a simple contract can consent in advance, and if such a consent practice became widespread, then perhaps consent jurisdiction will become important.

B. THE WIDE VENUE POSSIBILITIES IN BANKRUPTCY

¶ 2004: The Venue Statute and Forum Shopping

Bankruptcy cases may be filed in any district in which the debtor has its "domicile, residence, principal place of business . . . or principal assets" during the 180 days prior to the commencement of the case. 28 U.S.C. § 1408(1). A company's domicile is its state of incorporation. To this extent, the venue statute is unexceptional.

But the statute goes on in its second section to state that venue is also proper in any district in which the debtor's "affiliate, partner, or general partner" has a pending case under chapter 11. 28 U.S.C. § 1408(2). So if a company operates in Chicago and is incorporated in Illinois, but has a subsidiary in New York, the New York subsidiary could file for bankruptcy in New York's bankruptcy court and the Chicago-based parent company could file shortly thereafter, appending its bankruptcy to that of its New York subsidiary.

Thus, a large firm with multiple subsidiaries across the country has a wide choice for venue. In recent years, the typical forum sought has been either the bankruptcy court in the District of Delaware or that in the Southern District of New York. Since a majority of public firms and many private firms are incorporated in Delaware, the venue statute's first section, which confers jurisdiction on the corporation's domicile, suffices for venue. The subsequent affiliate section, which broadens the venue choice, is not needed for those who want to be heard in the Delaware bankruptcy court, if the firm is already incorporated in Delaware.

The overall value of broad venue has been sharply debated, with some seeing the court competition as encouraging speedy reorganizations and others seeing wide venue choice as degrading the bankruptcy process. Those in the first camp see a value to experience and, with many of the large firm chapter 11 proceedings going to Delaware or the Southern District of New York, the bankruptcy judges there have strong experience in moving large firms through chapter 11. Those in the second camp emphasize that those who place the case—typically the debtor's senior management and its lawyers, and sometimes an influential creditor—will seek venue in jurisdictions whose rulings they find favorable.[11] The Seventh Circuit, for example, was said to have been a place for management to avoid after the *Kmart* decision made critical vendor payments harder to effectuate. Others saw the differences in the standards for rejecting labor contracts in *Carey* (in the Second Circuit) and *Wheeling-Pittsburgh* (in the Third Circuit, where the Delaware court lies) as affecting venue filing choices. In *In re Caesars Entertainment Operating Co. Inc.*,[12] the debtors acknowledged that the Seventh Circuit's "favorable legal precedents" concerning another issue—"the assumption of executory contracts and

[11] LYNN M. LOPUCKI, COURTING FAILURE: HOW COMPETITION FOR BIG CASES IS CORRUPTING THE BANKRUPTCY COURTS 137–82 (2005).

[12] 2015 WL 495259, Case No. 15–10047 (KG) (Bankr. D. Del. Feb. 2, 2015).

third-party releases (as they relate to a plan of reorganization)"—were meaningful considerations in their decision to file for Chapter 11 in the Northern District of Illinois.[13]

¶ 2005: *Patriot Coal* and Limits to Forum Shopping

The venue statute does not require that a subsidiary or affiliate hold a threshold level of assets or a minimum percentage of the parent's assets, and there are no explicit statutory limits on how long the subsidiary must have been in existence. A corporate debtor could in principle create an affiliate shell company and incorporate the affiliate in a district in which the parent wishes to file and have its bankruptcy heard. After an affiliate files a chapter 11 petition in its district, the parent can then bootstrap into that district.

However, bankruptcy courts have recently pushed back against the forum shopping that § 1408(2) makes possible. Courts may transfer venue in chapter 11 cases when doing so is "in the interest of justice" or "for the convenience of the parties." 28 U.S.C. § 1411. Historically, judges tended to defer to the debtor's choice of venue. In large-scale bankruptcies such as Enron (whose operations were based in Texas) and General Motors (much of whose operations are based in Michigan), for instance, the debtor firms filed chapter 11 in the Southern District of New York, and in neither case did the court transfer venue.

But in *Patriot Coal*, Judge Shelley Chapman transferred the Patriot Coal Corporation's bankruptcy case from the Southern District of New York to the Eastern District of Missouri. In the six weeks prior to filing, Patriot Coal created two entities in New York, neither of which had any employees or operations. Patriot Coal stipulated that the sole purpose of creating these entities was to comply with § 1408(1) so that the firm could file chapter 11 in the Southern District of New York. The company, headquartered in St. Louis, Missouri, principally operated in West Virginia and held no significant assets in New York. The United Mine Workers of America moved to transfer venue, arguing that New York venue was improper, and alleging that the debtors chose to file in New York in part "due to the perceived ease of rejecting collective bargaining agreements in New York as compared to other districts."[14] Judge Chapman rejected this line of argument but nonetheless ruled that allowing "purposeful creation of the venue-predicate affiliates in New York on the eve of filing must be considered in the 'interest of justice' analysis" in § 1411, and that technical compliance with §1408 does not suffice for establishing proper venue. Accordingly, the court held that allowing Patriot Coal's case to proceed in New York would "elevate form over substance in a way that would be an affront to the

[13] *Id.* at *3.

[14] Sharon J. Richardson, David E. Kronenberg & Thomas Curtin, *Because Of Winn-Dixie? SDNY Bankruptcy Court Looks Beyond Literal Compliance With Venue Statute and Transfers Patriot Coal Cases to Eastern District Of Missouri*, MONDAQ.COM (Dec. 12, 2012), http://www.mondaq.com/unitedstates/x/211102/Insolvency+Bankruptcy/Because+Of+WinnDixie+SDNY+Bankruptcy+Court+Looks+Beyond+Literal+Compliance+With+Venue+Statute+And+Transfers+Patriot+Coal+Cases+To+Eastern+District+Of+Missouri.

purpose of the bankruptcy statute and the integrity of the bankruptcy system."[15]

¶ 2006: Venue in Congress: Michael L. Cook & Jessica L. Fainman,[16] *No Time for Bankruptcy Venue Hypocrisy*, Law Journal Newsletters, June 2005

Senator John Cornyn of Texas introduced the "Fairness in Bankruptcy Litigation Act of 2005" (S. 314) on Feb. 8, [2005,] calling it the "end to judge shopping. . . ." According to the Senator, "[F]orum shopping is wrong. It distorts and corrupts our justice system."

* * *

There may be merit to Sen. Cornyn's bill, but not in his rhetoric, driven, as the facts show, by a desire to increase his home state's market share in the competition for big bankruptcy reorganizations.

Federal bankruptcy law is theoretically uniform around the country. What varies, of course, is who administers the law. Just as baseball pitchers have quirks, so do judges, regardless of their location. Effective baseball managers and hitters work around pitchers' quirks, just as lawyers do with judges. . . . Effective litigators always consider legal venue options. . . . Sen. Cornyn's bill would . . . require a corporation to file a bankruptcy petition in the venue of its principal place of business or its principal assets. No longer would a company's state of incorporation (e.g., Delaware) or its affiliate's location be a proper basis for venue.

* * *

'Coryn's Crusade'

Sen. Cornyn's moral crusade, in our view, is contrived, hiding a more cynical objective: enhancing his constituents' financial interests. The Senator's attempt to disguise a valid legislative debate as a moral issue is political grandstanding.

The Senator apparently first encountered the Code's venue provision during his term as Texas Attorney General from 1999 through 2002. When Enron filed its 2001 Chapter 11 petition in New York, then-Attorney General Cornyn unsuccessfully "tried to steer th[e] case toward federal court in Houston," where it was headquartered. According to the Senator, his experience with Enron "opened [his] eyes to a very real abuse in our current bankruptcy system and the need to end the current practice of judge shopping." [Citation omitted]. Cornyn's moral justifications for his bill mask a less heroic objective, however: protecting Texas's market share in the contest for big reorganizations, and making sure that another Enron does not get away. A city's

[15] 482 B.R. 718, 743 (Bankr. S.D.N.Y. 2012).

[16] Michael L. Cook is a partner and Jessica L. Fainman is an associate at Schulte Roth & Zabel LLP in New York.

lawyers, accountants, financial advisers and hotels profit when a large company seeks refuge in the local bankruptcy court.

Texas

The Texas legal community, in fact, was working to position itself as a player in the competition for large bankruptcy cases prior to Enron's filing its reorganization petition in New York. In 2000, lawyers and judges in the Southern District of Texas (i.e., Houston) formed the "Advisory Committee on Chapter 11 Issues" to make the courts' administration of complex Chapter 11 cases "more responsive, more predictable, and more accessible." [Citation omitted.] It came up with uniform procedures that eliminated limits on professional fees. At the luncheon to unveil the new rules to the Houston bar, then—Judge William R. Greendyke proclaimed, "The war on fees is over." . . .

Sen. Cornyn cites WorldCom, Enron, Polaroid and Kmart as examples of the troubling "migration." But he fails to mention the forum shoppers that chose Texas as the venue for their reorganizations after Texas courts got religion. For example, Mirant Corporation, an Atlanta-based company incorporated in Delaware, filed its 2003 Chapter 11 petition in . . . Texas. Avado Brands, Inc., incorporated and headquartered in Georgia, also filed in . . . Texas in 2004. Logix Communications Enterprises Inc., incorporated and headquartered in Oklahoma; Pentacon, Inc., incorporated in Delaware and headquartered in California; and Erly Industries Inc. incorporated and headquartered in California, also went to debtor-friendly Texas for Chapter 11 relief.

* * *

¶ 2007: Subsequent Venue Efforts in Congress

In July 2011, Rep. Lamar Smith (R-Tex.) and Rep. John Conyers (D-Mich.) co-sponsored a bill entitled the "Chapter 11 Bankruptcy Venue Reform Act of 2011" (H.R. 2533). Under their proposed bill, a corporate debtor could "file its [chapter 11] case only in the district that encompasses its principal place of business or where its principal assets are located for the year preceding commencement of the bankruptcy case or for the longer portion of such year." By so requiring, the statute would have curtailed filings in Delaware by eliminating the ability of the debtor to file in its domicile (i.e., state of incorporation). In contrast to § 1408, the proposed bill would have permitted affiliates and subsidiaries to file in the district in which the parent or controlling affiliate files, but not the other way around. In this way, the proposed bill also seeks to curtail filings in New York by disallowing parent companies from bootstrapping into its affiliates' districts.

These venue issues are said to be important to Delaware officials, who are often well positioned to be influential. Joe Biden, when Senator from Delaware, blocked Texas Senator John Cornyn's 2005 venue legislation, described in the prior section.[17] Chris Coons, who succeeded Joe Biden as Senator from Delaware, became chairman of the Senate Judiciary Subcommittee on Bankruptcy and the Courts.[18]

¶2008. U.S. Jurisdiction Over Foreign Firms

The contact with the United States required to file for bankruptcy in U.S. courts is minimal. Property in the United States—say an American bank account—can suffice:

Section 109. Who may be a debtor

. . . [O]nly a person that resides or has a domicile, a place of business, or property in the United States . . . may be a debtor under this title.

However, for the foreign debtor to maintain the bankruptcy proceeding in the United Sates is harder. Section 1112(b) allows the court to dismiss a chapter 11 case if the debtor lacks the "[]ability to effectuate . . . a confirmed plan." If the government of the nation in which the foreign firm's principal assets are located is not expected to respect the American bankruptcy court's plan of reorganization, then the American court is unable to effectuate the plan and, under § 1112(b), the court will dismiss the filing.

[17] *See* Mark Curriden, *Playing on Home Court: New York and Delaware May Lose Their Grip on Bankruptcy Cases*, ABA JOURNAL (Mar. 1, 2012), *available at* http://www.abajournal.com/magazine/article/playing_on_home_court_new_york_and_delaware_may_lose_their_grip_on_bankrupt/.

[18] Steven Church, *Delaware Democrat Takes Over Senate Bankruptcy Panel*, BLOOMBERG NEWS (Jan. 31, 2013), http://www.bloomberg.com/news/articles/2013-01-31/delaware-senator-coons-to-take-over-panel-on-bankruptcy.

CHAPTER 21

MODIGLIANI–MILLER, BANKRUPTCY COSTS, AND TAXES

¶ 2101: Why Then Debt?

Debt causes intractable problems. Reorganizations work poorly. Risks, stress, and foregone opportunities afflict the firm with too much overhanging debt. Negotiating and enforcing debt covenants in the loan agreement or the bond indenture is not always an easy task. Some financial economists suggest that in the aggregate these costs to the economy are quite high. Highly leveraged firms lose market share and shrink more rapidly than their competitors during industry-wide downturns.[1]

If debt presents problems, what offsetting advantages induce its use?

Risk aversion. One's first instinct is to turn to debt's relative safety as the main reason for its wide use. Debt is safer for the creditor, so one might think that it must be cheaper for the borrower. Investors who prefer to avoid risk take debt; those who can handle risk take common stock. That answer—risk packaging, with debt as a cheaper source of capital—was the conventional wisdom for quite some time. But in a series of deductive proofs, Franco Modigliani and Merton Miller

[1] Roger Gordon & Burton Malkiel, *Corporation Finance, in* How Taxes Affect Economic Behavior 161, 171 (Henry Aaron & Joseph Pechman eds., 1981); Tim C. Opler and Sheridan Titman, *Financial Distress and Corporate Performance,* 49 Journal of Finance 1015 (1994).

demonstrated that perspective's fallacies. Safer for the creditor doesn't necessarily mean cheaper for the borrower.

Their work has been central to modern financial thinking. When awarding Modigliani the Nobel Prize in 1985, the Nobel committee cited his contribution as helping to lay the foundation for the field of corporate finance. Miller shared the Nobel Prize in 1990. Much of the remaining material of this section outlines the Modigliani–Miller Hypothesis, its necessary assumptions, and its ramifications.

Two economic features render risk packaging unconvincing as an explanation for corporate debt: First, investors can replicate its advantages on their own. Individual investors, for example, can use personal leveraging as a substitute for corporate leveraging. The examples in the following paragraphs demonstrate this replication. Second, competition among issuing corporations should have eroded risk packaging's big advantages, if it had any, long ago.

The problem then, after one understands that risk packaging can't explain debt, is to explain its advantages otherwise. Since there's lots of debt out there, if risk-packaging doesn't explain its widespread incidence, something else must.

Taxes. Taxes might explain debt. The borrower can deduct interest from taxable income but can't deduct dividend payments. That can make debt a cheaper source of capital.

The deductibility of interest is indeed a core component of the story.

Information. Information disparities might help explain debt. Insiders know more about the firm than the outsiders. Investors might more precisely evaluate a loan's value than a stock's value; because the $1 million loan from the $3 million or $4 million firm returns the first $1 million of the firm's value to the creditor, the creditor need not assess the probabilities of the firm being worth $3 million or $4 million. In contrast, a prospective stockholder would worry whether the firm is worth $3 million or $4 million.

The experience in raising new capital supports the information rationale: stock is the least preferred method, new debt the next preferred, and retained earnings the most preferred.

Agency costs. Managers might not manage well. Passive investors understand that they will bear some of the costs of managerial shirking. Investing via debt means that the less-skilled managers will eat through the common equity account first. Creditors incur less in the way of managerial agency costs; sometimes they need not monitor the firm as much as common stockholders.

Control. The original entrepreneur may wish to maintain working control of the enterprise and expand the scope of the enterprise's operations. To issue new stock might cause the entrepreneur to lose his or her majority (or working) control of the enterprise. Debt could solve the ambitious entrepreneur's dilemma. The creditors' influence is substantially limited to the effects of the covenants they negotiate for the loan agreement or bond indenture.

Bonding advantages. Managers of public firms with diffuse stockholding could shirk. Or they may take on low-value projects that enhance managerial prestige and perhaps salary but at the cost of shareholder profitability. The value of shares may decline. Debt, however, may bond managers to the firm's own capital-providers, making the managers more motivated to work well.

How could debt motivate managers? Unlike equity, debt includes contractual obligations to pay periodic interest and eventually to pay off principal. While equity holders could sometimes eventually force out bad management, debt holders have more direct and immediate remedies. Missed payments to creditors allow debt holders to sue to be repaid and, outside of bankruptcy, to seize the borrower firm's assets to satisfy the debt. Debt therefore increases the risk of turmoil in which the managers could be thrown out, making managers work harder to avoid that turmoil. Managers who use debt "bind" themselves to work hard to avoid the turmoil, not to shirk. Debt could be a pre-commitment by managers to work hard or to refuse to take low-value (but easy to handle) projects (because the low-return projects won't throw off enough cash to pay down the debt).

An example might illustrate. In the mid–1980s, several oil firms were takeover targets. Offerors said that the target firms were spending too much money on oil exploration when the stock market consensus was that the oil wouldn't sell for enough to make back the finding and production costs. These expenditures may have resulted from mistake, differing assessments of the future price of oil, an inability of engineer-managers to fire their friends in the exploration department, or a sense among the engineer-managers that exploration was the task of oil companies. Some firms beat back takeover attempts by recapitalizing with debt. The firm bought much of its common stock with the proceeds of newly-issued debt. By promising such a high cash payout to its new "owners"—the new creditors—the firm had to cut current expenditures, such as oil exploration, to the bone. Debt "bound" the firm to a low-exploration operating strategy.[2]

This analysis looks at the agency cost problem from the perspective of motivating the managers. Debt can also bring new players into the firm, some of whom can provide specialized information to management, and some of whom have skills in monitoring managers and reducing the chances that the firm, their debtor, would make egregious mistakes.

Signaling costs. The firm's managers and insiders know best how much the firm is worth, note the signaling theorists. The managers (if they also own some stock) will be reluctant to issue new stock if they think that capital markets are under-valuing the stock. They turn to debt. But if the managers think the stock is over-priced, they would use debt. Buyers, aware of managers' incentives and superior information, would be wary of buying the stock.

Moreover, more debt will also signal that managers believe their firm's value is higher than if they use more equity. Why? The greater

---

[2] Michael C. Jensen, *Agency Costs of Free Cash Flow, Corporate Finance, and Takeovers*, 76 American Economic Review 323 (1986).

the debt, the greater the chance of turmoil and bankruptcy. Since that's so costly to managers (and maybe stockholders), the market believes that managers won't issue a lot of debt unless they believe the chances of bankruptcy are low. A low chance of bankruptcy ought to go along with profitable future projects. Lots of debt thus means managers think the firm is worth a lot.

* * *

Gregor Andrade and Steven Kaplan summarize: "The qualitative costs [of financial distress due to too much debt] include evidence of (1) irrevocable and costly reductions in capital expenditures; (2) asset sales at depressed prices; (3) undesired losses of key customers; (4) undesired losses of suppliers; (5) asset substitution; and (6) delay. . . . [The operational benefits of debt include] (1) the removal of poor management, (2) operating improvements, and (3) the sale or discontinuation of poorly performing assets." Gregor Andrade and Steven N. Kaplan, *How Costly is Financial (Not Economic) Distress? Evidence from Highly Leveraged Transactions that Became Distressed*, 53 Journal of Finance 1443 (1998).

No single factor may explain debt. Each factor may explain one firm's use of debt but not another's.

The next reading describes Modigliani and Miller's famous arbitrage proof, which showed how under basic restrictions (a business world without taxation, without bankruptcy costs, but with perfect investor information about the firm's business), the risk-splitting rationale for choosing between debt and equity was false.

¶ 2102: Richard Brealey, Stewart Myers and Franklin Allen, Principles of Corporate Finance 427–31, 440, 442-43 (11th Ed. 2014)*

Does Debt Policy Matter?

A firm's basic resource is the stream of cash flows produced by its assets. When the firm is financed entirely by common stock, all those cash flows belong to the stockholders. When it issues both debt and equity securities, it splits the cash flows into two streams, a relatively safe stream that goes to the debtholders and a riskier stream that goes to the stockholders.

The firm's mix of debt and equity financing is called its **capital structure**. Of course capital structure is not just "debt versus equity." There are many different flavors of debt, at least two flavors of equity (common versus preferred), plus hybrids. . . . The firm can issue dozens of distinct securities in countless combinations. It attempts to find the particular combination that maximizes the overall market value of the firm.

Are such attempts worthwhile? We must consider the possibility that *no* combination has any greater appeal than any other. Perhaps the really important decisions concern the company's assets, and decisions about capital structure are mere details—matters to be attended to but not worried about.

Modigliani and Miller (MM) . . . showed that financing decisions don't matter in perfect markets. Their famous "proposition 1" states that a firm cannot change the total value of its securities just by splitting its cash flows into different streams: The firm's value is determined by its real assets, not by the securities it issues. Thus capital structure is irrelevant as long as the firm's investment decisions are taken as given.

MM's proposition 1 allows complete separation of investment and financing decisions. It implies that any firm could [invest, manufacture, and build] . . . without worrying about where the money for capital expenditures comes from. . . .

We believe that in practice capital structure does matter, but . . . [i]f you don't fully understand the conditions under which MM's theory holds, you won't fully understand why one capital structure is better than another. The financial manager needs to know what kinds of market imperfection to look for.

. . . [T]he imperfections that are most likely to make a difference [are] taxes, the costs of bankruptcy and financial distress, the costs of writing and enforcing complicated debt contracts, differences created by imperfect information, and the effects of debt on incentives for management. . . .

The Effect of Leverage in a Competitive Tax-free Economy

Financial managers try to find the combination of securities that has the greatest overall appeal to investors—the combination that maximizes the market value of the firm. . . .

Let D and E denote the market values of the outstanding debt and equity of the Wapshot Mining Company. Wapshot's 1000 shares sell for $50 apiece. Thus

$$E = 1000 \times 50 = \$50{,}000$$

Wapshot has also borrowed $25,000, and so V, the aggregate market value of all Wapshot's outstanding securities, is

$$V = D + E = \$75{,}000$$

Wapshot's stock is known as *levered equity*. Its stockholders face the benefits and costs of **financial leverage**, or *gearing*. Suppose that Wapshot "levers up" still further by borrowing an additional $10,000 and paying the proceeds out to shareholders as a special dividend of $10 per share. This substitutes debt for equity capital with no impact on Wapshot's assets.

What will Wapshot's equity be worth after the special dividend is paid? We have two unknowns, E and V:

Old debt	\$25,000 }	\$35,000	= D [Value of Total Debt]
New debt	\$10,000 }		
Equity		?	= E [Value of Equity]
Firm value		?	= V [Total value of the firm]

If V is \$75,000 as before, then E must be $V - D$ = 75,000 – 35,000 = \$40,000. Stockholders have suffered a capital loss that exactly offsets the \$10,000 special dividend. But if V *increases* to, say, \$80,000 as a result of the change in capital structure, then E = \$45,000 and the stockholders are \$5,000 ahead. In general, any increase or decrease in V caused by a shift in capital structure accrues to the firm's stockholders. . . . [Can Wapshot increase its value to \$80,000 just by borrowing and declaring a dividend to stockholders?]

* * *

Enter Modigliani and Miller

. . . [T]he financial manager would like to find the combination of securities that maximizes the value of the firm. How is this done? MM's answer is that the financial manager should stop worrying: In a perfect market any combination of securities is as good as another. The value of the firm is unaffected by its choice of capital structure.[3]

You can see this by imagining two firms that generate the same stream of operating income and differ only in their capital structure. Firm U is unlevered. Therefore the total value of its equity E_U is the same as the total value of the firm V_U. Firm L, on the other hand, is levered. The value of its stock is, therefore, equal to the value of the firm less the value of the debt: $E_L = V_L - D_L$.

Now think which of these firms you would prefer to invest in. If you don't want to take much risk, you can buy common stock in the unlevered firm U. For example, if you buy 1% of firm U's shares, your investment is $.01V_U$ and you are entitled to 1% of the gross profits:

Dollar Investment	Dollar Return
$.01V_U$	.01 x Profits

Now compare this with an alternative strategy. This is to purchase the same fraction of *both* the debt and the equity of firm L. Your investment and return would then be as follows:

[3] [MM's paper is] F. Modigliani and M. H. Miller, "The Cost of Capital, Corporation Finance, and the Theory of Investment," American Economic Review 48 (June 1958), pp. 261–297[.]

Dollar Investment		Dollar Return
Debt	$.01D_L$	.01 x Interest
Equity	$.01E_L$	.01 x (Profits-interest)
Total	$.01(D_L+E_L)$ $= .01V_L$	.01 x Profits

Both strategies offer the same payoff: 1% of the firm's profits. . . . [I]n well-functioning markets two investments that offer the same payoff must have the same price. Therefore, $.01V_U$ must equal $.01V_L$: The value of the unlevered firm must equal the value of the levered firm.

Suppose that you are willing to run a little more risk. You decide to buy 1% of the outstanding shares in the *levered* firm. Your investment and return are now as follows:

Dollar Investment	Dollar Return
$.01E_L$ $= .01\ (V_L–D_L)$	.01 x (Profits-interest)

But there is an alternative strategy[— personal leveraging.] This is to borrow $.01D_L$ on your own account and purchase 1% of the stock of the unlevered firm. In this case, your strategy gives you 1% of the profits from V_U, but you have to pay interest on your loan equal to 1% of the interest that is paid by firm L. Your total investment and return are as follows:

Dollar Investment		Dollar Return
Borrowing	$–.01D_L$	–.01 x Interest
Equity	$.01\ V_U$	.01 x Profits
Total	$.01\ (V_U–D_L)$	.01 x (Profits–interest)

Again both strategies offer the same payoff: 1% of profits after interest. Therefore, both investments must have the same cost. The investment $.01(V_U – D_L)$ must equal $.01(V_L – D_L)$ and V_U must equal V_L.

It does not matter whether the world is full of risk-averse chickens or venturesome lions. All would agree that the value of the unlevered firm U must be equal to the value of the levered firm L. As long as investors can borrow or lend on their own account on the same terms as the firm, they can "undo" the effect of any changes in the firm's capital structure. This is the basis for MM's famous proposition 1: "The market value of any firm is independent of its capital structure."

The Law of the Conservation of Value

MM's argument that debt policy is irrelevant is an application of an astonishingly simple idea. . . .

. . . We can slice a cash flow into as many parts as we like; the values of the parts will always sum back to the value of the unsliced stream. . . .

This is really a *law of conservation of value.* The value of an asset is preserved regardless of the nature of the claims against it. Thus proposition 1: Firm value is determined on the *left-hand* side of the balance sheet by real assets—not by the proportions of debt and equity securities issued to buy the assets.

* * *

The law also applies to the *mix* of debt securities issued by the firm. The choices of long-term versus short-term, secured versus unsecured, senior versus subordinated, and convertible versus nonconvertible debt all should have no effect on the overall value of the firm.

. . . When we showed that capital structure does not affect choice, we implicitly assumed that both companies and individuals can borrow and lend at the same risk-free rate of interest. As long as this is so, individuals can undo the effect of any changes in the firm's capital structure.

In practice corporate debt is not risk-free. . . . Some people's initial reaction is that this alone invalidates MM's proposition. It is a natural mistake, but capital structure can be irrelevant even when debt is risky.

If a company borrows money, it does not *guarantee* repayment: It repays the debt in full only if its assets are worth more than the debt obligation. The shareholders in the company, therefore, have limited liability.

Many individuals would like to borrow with limited liability. They might, therefore, be prepared to pay a small premium for levered shares *if the supply of levered shares was insufficient to meet their needs.*[4] But there are literally thousands of common stocks of companies that borrow. Therefore it is unlikely that an issue of debt would induce them to pay a premium for *your* shares.[5]

* * *

Is corporate borrowing . . . cheaper [than an individual's borrowing]? It's hard to say. Interest rates on home mortgages are not too different from rates on high-grade corporate bonds.[6] Rates on margin debt (borrowing from a stockbroker with the investor's shares tendered as security) are not too different from the rates firms pay banks for short-term loans.

---

[4] Of course, individuals could *create* limited liability if they chose. In other words, the lender could agree that borrowers need repay their debt in full only if the assets of company X are worth more than a certain amount. . . . [These are called non-recourse loans: the lender agrees not to take recourse against the debtor's other assets.—Roe.]

[5] Capital structure is also irrelevant if each investor holds a fully diversified portfolio. In that case he or she owns *all* the risky securities offered by a company (both debt and equity). But anybody who owns *all* the risky securities doesn't care about how the cash flows are divided between different securities.

[6] One of the authors once obtained a home mortgage at a rate 1/2 percentage point *less* than the contemporaneous yield on long-term AAA bonds.

* * *

[But even if corporate borrowing is cheaper,] [m]aybe the market for corporate leverage is like the market for automobiles. Americans need millions of automobiles and are willing to pay thousands of dollars apiece for them. But that doesn't mean that you could strike it rich by going into the automobile business. You're at least 90 years too late.

* * *

Summary

Think of the financial manager as taking all of the firm's real assets and selling them to investors as a package of securities. Some financial managers choose the simplest package possible: all-equity financing. Some end up issuing dozens of debt and equity securities. The problem is to find the particular combination that maximizes the market value of the firm.

Modigliani and Miller's (MM's) famous proposition 1 states that no combination is better than any other—that the firm's overall market value (the value of all its securities) is independent of capital structure. Firms that borrow do offer investors a more complex menu of securities, but investors yawn in response. The menu is redundant. Any shift in capital structure can be duplicated or "undone" by investors. Why should they pay extra for borrowing indirectly (by holding shares in a levered firm) when they can borrow just as easily and cheaply on their own accounts?

MM agree that borrowing increases the expected rate of return on shareholders' investments. But it also increases the risk of the firm's shares. MM show that the higher risk exactly offsets the increase in expected return, leaving stockholders no better or worse off.

Proposition 1 is an extremely general result. It applies not just to the debt-equity trade-off but to *any* choice of financing instruments. For example, MM would say that the choice between long-term and short-term debt has no effect on firm value.

The formal proofs of proposition 1 all depend on the assumption of perfect capital markets. MM's opponents, the "traditionalists," argue that market imperfections make personal borrowing excessively costly, risky, and inconvenient for some investors. This creates a natural clientele willing to pay a premium for shares of levered firms. The traditionalists say that firms should borrow to realize the premium.

But this argument is incomplete. There may be a clientele for levered equity, but that is not enough; the clientele has to be *unsatisfied*. There are already thousands of levered firms available for investment. Is there still an unsatiated clientele for garden-variety debt and equity? We doubt it.

Proposition 1 is violated when financial managers find an untapped demand and satisfy it by issuing something new and different. The argument between MM and the traditionalists finally boils down to whether this is difficult or easy. We lean toward MM's view: Finding unsatisfied clienteles and designing exotic securities to meet their needs is a game that's fun to play but hard to win. . . .

¶ 2103: Leverage, Value, and Modigliani–Miller

The prior reading illustrates the "irrelevance" proposition with text and simple algebra. This section illustrates the proposition with two simple balance sheets and an income statement.

Two companies, XYZ and TUV, are operational clones of one another, operating in a world of perfect markets, no taxes, and no bankruptcy costs. The expected annual income of each is $100,000 if they can put their project onstream. The project will cost $1 million to set up. Each project is identical.

Mr. A is the promoter of XYZ. He finances the project by selling its common stock to the public for $1 million. Buyers of XYZ's stock demand an expected return of 10% on their investment (that is, they demand a 10x capitalization rate).

XYZ

$1 million project (cost)	Common stock: $1 million
Expected income: $100,000/yr.	

Ms. B is the promoter of TUV. She finances the project by seeking to sell common stock to risk-preferring potential stockholders. She gets a loan commitment for TUV of $500,000 from the Bank at 5% interest. The Bank commits to provide these funds to TUV upon TUV's having received at least $500,000 in common equity for the Project. Ms. B states to her prospective investors that because the Project's operations are expected to yield $100,000 per year and, because the first $25,000 of income will be devoted to debt service, the investors could expect $75,000 per year. If the investors demand the same 10x capitalization rate (i.e., they expect a 10% return, on average), they should be willing to pay $750,000 in total for the stock. If Ms. B succeeds in promoting TUV, she will have made the value of TUV's securities total up to $1,250,000, more than the total value of XYZ's securities. (Before Modigliani and Miller came along, financiers believed they could package securities to create this extra value.)

Ms. B though concedes that the increased risk associated with that income stream might not justify using the same 10x earnings capitalization rate of XYZ. But, she says, the risk-return trade-off leads to a suggested 8x earnings capitalization rate. That capitalization rate, she says, leads to a stock price of $600,000.

TUV

$1 million project (cost)	Bank debt $500,000 at 5%
Expected income: $100,000/yr.	Common Stock $600,000 (8x capitalization rate)

TUV's expected earnings from operations:	$100,000
Debt service	(25,000)
Net	75,000

Advise the prospective buyers of TUV stock on a cheaper way to achieve Ms. B's offered return, by building upon the capital structure of XYZ.

In perfect, untaxed capital markets where many projects have an expected return close to that of these two projects, what should the value of the aggregate capital of XYZ be? And that of TUV? Should or could "packaging" the operational income enhance the firm's value?

¶ 2104: With Risk

Does risk make a difference? Assume that both XYZ's and TUV's operations have an expected return of $100,000, based on a 1/3 chance of earning $25,000, a 1/3 chance of earning $100,000, and a 1/3 chance of earning $175,000.

Earnings from operations:	.33 x $25,000
	.33 x 100,000
	.33 x 175,000

For TUV, $25,000 of interest must be paid each year. After paying the interest to the creditor, this is what is left for the owners:

.33 x [$25,000 — $25,000]	=	.33 x	0 =	0
.33 x [$100,000 — $25,000]	=	.33 x	$75,000 =	$25,000
.33 x [$175,000 — $25,000]	=	.33 x	$150,000 =	$50,000

The expected value is $75,000. Can't the same return with the same riskiness be achieved by buying XYZ with money borrowed personally? If it can, shouldn't the total value of securities issued by TUV equal the total value of securities issued by XYZ?

¶ 2105: With Corporate Taxes

Do corporate taxes make a difference? Assume that both XYZ's and TUV's operations are expected to earn $100,000 annually and that corporate income is taxed at a 33 1/3% tax rate. Doesn't the corporate tax and the deductibility of the interest expense increase the total return to TUV's owners over the total return to XYZ's owners?

TUV, the levered firm, returns nearly $8,000 more to its owners, because TUV's debt partially shields its income stream from corporate taxation. More income, all other things being equal, should create more value. The value of TUV's stock and debt should, again all other things being equal, exceed that of XYZ, if the corporate tax story is the only missing piece here.

This result led to the standard modern synthesis of the M–M Hypothesis and its real world application: capital structure counts, but not due to risk packaging as the prior view had it, but due to a trade-off of the tax benefits of debt, in shielding corporate income from the IRS, against its disadvantages. In its simplest form, capital structure optimization is a trade-off of the tax benefits of debt (interest being deductible from corporate taxes and dividends not being deductible) against the costs of bankruptcy and recapitalization.

XYZ:	
Earnings from operations:	100,000
Corporate income tax:	(33,333)
After-tax income to SH of XYZ:	66,667
Income to creditors of XYZ:	0
Total income to XYZ's investors:	66,667

TUV:	
Earnings from operations:	100,000
Deductible interest:	(25,000)
Net income before corp. taxes:	75,000
Corporate income tax:	(25,000)
Income to SH of TUV:	50,000
Income to creditors of TUV:	25,000
Total income to TUV's investors:	75,000

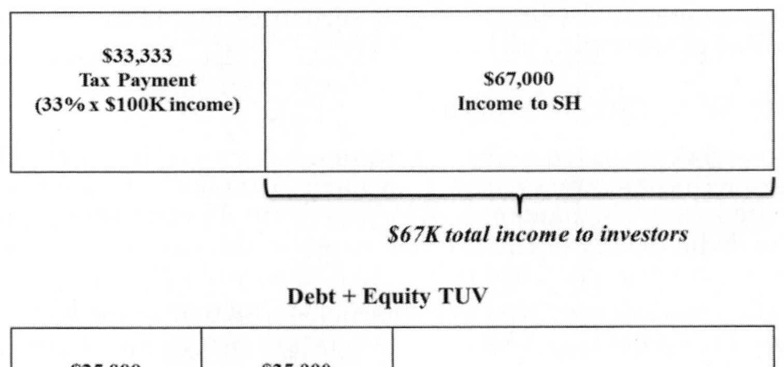

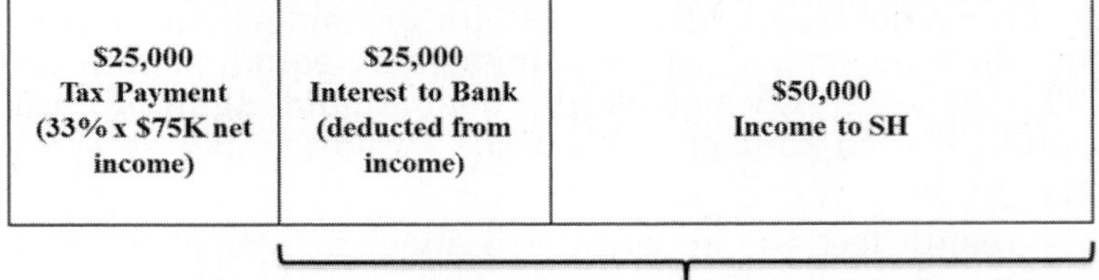

Isn't the leveraged company (TUV) worth more to its investor-owners than the non-leveraged company (XYZ)? How much is each worth to the economy overall? Once we add back the tax stream to the creditors' and equityholders' incomes, what number do we get for XYZ? For TUV? Would Modigliani and Miller feel vindicated?

¶ 2106: With Owner–Level Taxes

Could owner level taxes modify this synthesis? If owners are taxed favorably on equity, but unfavorably on debt, we have offsetting and contrary tilts—toward debt at the corporate level and toward equity at the ownership level.

Equity is indeed taxed favorably to owners, as compared to debt. Much of the return to equity is in the form of capital gains, which have historically been taxed favorably. In recent years, even the tax rate on dividends has been lowered, as compared to the tax rate on interest payments. Hence, while debt is tax favored at the corporate level, equity is tax favored at the owner level. The offset isn't one-for-one, because equity is weakly taxed at the owner level, while interest is fully deductible at the corporate level.

The owner-level tax status complicates further: some capital-owners, including pension plans, charitable institutions such as university endowments and foundations, and some insurance plans, are not taxed (or forever defer taxation). They are tax-favored regardless of whether they receive their income as interest or dividends.

What if these institutions dominate the market for provision of capital? Recent estimates indicate that half of all dividends are now paid to tax exempt entities. Karen C. Burke, I*s the Corporate Tax System Broken?*, 28 Virginia Tax Review 341, 348 (2008). Cf. Merton Miller & Myron Scholes, *Dividends and Taxes,* 6 Journal of Financial Economics 333 (1978). If the dominant owners are institutions that do not themselves pay taxes, then, all else equal, corporations will use corporate debt to shield more of their income from the IRS.

¶ 2107: Some Stages of the Trade-off Analysis

Finance theory on the trade-off of bankruptcy costs for debt's tax deduction has gone through several stages. In the first stage, the theorists ignored taxation. Only risk-packaging counted, and the individual could arbitrage risk to create whatever the corporation could create.

In the second stage, the theorists attended to taxes but only at the corporate level. At the corporate level, the interest deduction makes debt more valuable than equity, all other things being equal.

In the third stage, the theorists focused on owner-level taxes. This stage breaks down into subcategories, as tax rates and the institutional composition of ownership changed: If the shareholder obtains all of her equity returns in dividends, when dividends and interest payments were taxed at the same rate, the corporate tax shield via the interest deduction was valuable. But, if equity is taxed favorably at the individual level via capital gains or via tax-favored dividends (as is now the case), while interest income is taxed unfavorably, then the tax advantages of debt and equity tend to even up.

Institutional owners can modify the analysis to the extent that they are tax-favored, making both their receipts on debt holdings and on equity holdings untaxed. To the extent that institutional ownership is dominant, the corporate sector as a whole obtains a tax advantage from debt's tax deduction. But eventually competition leads firms to bid away the advantage of the deduction, as Brealey, Myers and Allen indicate, and then no particular corporation obtains much of an advantage.

¶ 2108: Tax Consequences of Recapitalizations in Bankruptcy

The bankruptcy lawyer should know of two transactional tax consequences of recapitalizing in bankruptcy.[7] Each can affect the restructuring deal, as the parties will try to avoid negative tax effects of their deal.

The first transactional tax issue is that the recapitalizing firm will usually incur a tax to the extent its creditors release the debtor from its debt obligation. A creditor "forgives" the debt by either accepting less than it is owed or by taking stock in exchange for the debt. The amount forgiven is income to the debtor. U.S. v. Kirby Lumber, 284 U.S. 1 (1931). Once a creditor no longer requires that the debtor repay the loan, the creditor suffers a loss and the debtor has income.

The second tax issue is that the firm could lose a tax "asset" because the I.R.C. requires that net operating loss carryforwards (NOLs, explained below) be reduced when ownership changes. If the firm's ownership changes during a recapitalization, the new owners cannot use the old NOLs at all.

What are the basic pitfalls and policy considerations in avoiding forgiveness of indebtedness income and preserving NOL carryforwards?

Forgiveness of indebtedness

As a general rule, a firm that exchanges its old debt for new stock whose fair market value is less than the original issuance value of the debt will produce taxable discharge-of-indebtedness income. Essentially, the debtor has gotten a break by being able to satisfy its debt obligation without paying it back in full. This generates taxable income equal to the difference between the old debt's original value and the new stock's market value. This tax liability hurts the debtor and discourages it from restructuring.

But when the firm is in bankruptcy, several exceptions are available. When a debtor exchanges old debt for new stock in Chapter 11, there is no discharge-of-indebtedness income.[8] The Chapter 11 debtor does better here than the non-debtor negotiating with its creditors: The solvent non-debtor gets taxable income. The insolvent non-debtor, also gets an exception to discharge of indebtedness income, limited though to the extent of the debtor's insolvency. Bankruptcy takes the lid off of the insolvency exception.

But the exceptions to discharge-of-indebtedness income don't come for free. The bankrupt or insolvent corporate taxpayer has to reduce

[7] This section reflects tax law as of August 2014. The tax rules here have been unstable, changing every few years, perhaps because of tension between those who set tax policy and those who wish to help bankrupt firms via favorable taxation.

[8] This exception has come and gone from the tax code several times. It's now in IRC § 108(a)(1).

beneficial tax attributes, such as net operating loss carryforwards. I.R.C. § 108(b). When a firm loses money, it can carry the loss back several years to offset recent past income. Once the firm exhausts recent earnings, it can carry the loss forward to offset future income. These are net operating loss carryforwards or NOLs. They are valuable to the debtor, because they allow it to pay less tax on its future income.[9]

But the tax rules essentially apply discharge-of-indebtedness income against the debtor's NOLs.

Because debtors often have large NOLs, the net effect equals that of the basic rule: Discharge of indebtedness creates income for the debtor. Only when the discharge income exceeds the NOLs does the exception have value for the debtor. In such cases the I.R.C. requires the debtor to reduce its other valuable tax attributes, such as the debtor's basis in property it owns.

The rules suggest a disheartening scenario: Before a possible bankruptcy, a firm and its creditors sense trouble. Public debt was issued for $200 million but trades at, say, 75 cents on each $1.00 of face value, because the debt is riskier than it was when the firm originally issued it, or because the implicit interest rate for the firm is higher than when the debt was issued. But if the firm and its creditors work out the problem immediately with a stock-for-debt exchange, through which the old creditors turn in their debt (face amount of $200 million but worth only $150 million) for about $150 million of stock, the firm will incur $50 million of taxable discharge-of-indebtedness income. That tax cost might induce the firm's managers to wait and not recapitalize.

Debt-for-debt?

Debt-for-debt exchanges are subject to an analogous rule. The 1990 Tax Reform Act provided that the company will have discharge-of-indebtedness income equal to the difference between the fair market value of the debt exchanged and the *original* issue price of the debt. So: (1) the company issues debt of $200 million, then a few years later (2) falls on hard times, with the debt trading at $150 million. The company exchanges the old debt for new debt with better terms (e.g., extended maturity, lower interest). The new debt is worth $160 million. The company realizes $40 million of discharge-of-indebtedness income.[10]

---

[9] Bankrupt corporations often have run losses for several years and have big NOLs. One might think that the value of the NOL is small, because the firm could be expected to have anemic earnings for some time. But several bankrupt firms have emerged and then acquired the earnings against which they could use their NOL. That is, the surviving bankrupt bought other companies with high current earnings, turning each $.66 of post-tax acquired earnings into $1.00 of post-tax earnings through use of the bankrupt's NOLs.

[10] I.R.C. § 108(e)(10). If the debt-for-debt exchange involves publicly-traded debt, then the prices in the public market become easy reference points for the value given in exchange for the old debt. If neither end of the debt involves publicly-traded debt, the values exchanged are harder to determine, and typically the IRS does not require that the company incur discharge-of-indebtedness income. For example, an insurance company loan of $200 million that has become riskier and leads to a change of terms (but no public quote in the bond market) would not lead to discharge-of-indebtedness income because the IRS would view the principal amount as unchanged. 26 C.F.R. 1.1273-2 (2012). If neither the old debt or new debt is

Net operating loss carryforwards and ownership changes

Again, a company that loses money can deduct some of its losses against its future income; hence, it can carry forward its net operating loss. These carried-forward deductions are valuable, because they lower the firm's future tax bill.

In general, a corporate debtor loses its net operating loss carryforwards if its ownership changes. However, if the firm's ownership changes in chapter 11, the NOL is less likely to be lost.[11]

How is ownership change measured for this tax rule? As long as prior shareholders and historic creditors continue to own 50% or more of the bankrupt's stock, the NOL carryforwards continue. Historic creditors include creditors who own more than 5% of the reorganized company and who owned their claim for 18 months or more before the bankruptcy began. Smaller creditors—who come to own less than 5% of the reorganized entity—count as continuing owners, even if they acquired their debt within the 18–month prebankruptcy window. I.R.C. § 382(l)(5).[12]

Hence, the debtor would like to keep these historic creditors in place as post-plan stockholders, to preserve the NOL carryforward. Bankruptcy courts have treated favorable tax attributes such as NOL carry forwards as property of the bankrupt firm's estate that, as such, can be protected via the automatic stay. See the General Motors NOL motion, ¶ 2109.

* * *

Because ownership changes imperil the NOL, the tax code gives an incentive for the parties to avoid a full house-cleaning by recapitalizing with stock-for-debt. The tax rule can discourage a sale of the firm in its entirety to a new management group, if the change in control imperils the NOLs, often a bankrupt firm's most valuable "asset."

Moreover, the NOL extinction rule's chapter 11 exception, which views the firm's ownership as not having been changed if long-term creditors become stockholders, can be lost if ownership changes after the bankruptcy is completed. Section 382 has a "look-back" provision that eliminates the post-chapter 11 carryforward if ownership changes during the two years after the plan is confirmed. Hence, plan proponents will seek to limit the potential for a change in control.

Overall, NOL carryforwards are important in chapter 11. In public firms that reorganized in the 1980s and early 1990s, NOLs averaged 25% of the reorganized firm's assets. Because the NOL is a deduction

---

publicly traded, then the issue price of the new debt is generally its face value, not market value. *Id.* § 1274.

[11] The "loss" of the NOL is not straightforward. It is more a "cap" than an elimination. If ownership changes, the debtor's annual use of the NOLs is capped at a percentage of the debtor's post-chapter 11 equity. The cap percentage is the "long-term tax exempt rate," an item defined in the Internal Revenue Code to approximate the return on long-term state and municipal bonds.

[12] Creditors that became creditors within the 18–month window can be counted as continuing owners if they became creditors in the ordinary course of trade or business with the debtor and the debt was held by these ordinary course creditors continuously until exchanged for stock.

from income (and not a dollar-for-dollar reduction of the firm's tax bill), and because firms typically cannot use all of their NOLs, as they expire eventually, the total value of the tax benefit is less than 25%, but was still estimated to amount to 10% of the bankrupt firms' value.[13] Not a small sum.

* * *

The convoluted institutional structure governing risky debt is ironic. The longstanding favored tax status of debt (interest is deductible, dividends are not) has encouraged widespread use of debt, such that some portion of the firm's cash flow is dedicated to the fixed charges on the debt. If the firm falls into trouble and attempts an early renegotiation to modify those fixed charges, the firm incurs tax penalties (increased taxable income, decreased tax benefits). But if it waits until the eve of bankruptcy, non-tax considerations become more difficult than they were well before a bankruptcy, due to the holdout and buoying-up problems discussed in Chapter 19. Moreover, because the firm would often lose its NOLs in a sale of its operations, tax policy discourages what often might be the best disposition of a failing firm, namely sale to another company.

¶ 2109: General Motors NOL Motion to Bar Claims Trading

IN THE UNITED STATES BANKRUPTCY COURT
SOUTHERN DISTRICT OF NEW YORK

In re General Motors Corp., *et al.*, Debtors.	Chapter 11 Case No. 09–______ (___) (Jointly Administered)

MOTION OF THE DEBTORS PURSUANT TO 11 U.S.C. §§ 105(a) AND 362 FOR ENTRY OF . . . ORDERS ESTABLISHING NOTIFICATION PROCEDURES REGARDING RESTRICTIONS ON CERTAIN TRANSFERS OF INTERESTS IN THE DEBTORS . . .

. . . General Motors Corporation ("GM") and certain of its subsidiaries, as debtors and debtors in possession in the above-captioned chapter 11 cases . . . respectfully represent:

1. The Debtors request entry of interim and final orders authorizing the Debtors to establish procedures to protect the potential value of the Debtors' net operating loss carryforwards ("NOLs") and certain other tax attributes, including foreign tax credit and other

[13] Stuart C. Gilson, Edith S. Hotchkiss & Richard S. Ruback, *Valuation of Bankrupt Firms,* Review of Financial Studies 43, 46, 57 (2000).

excess credit carryforwards (collectively with the NOLs, the "Tax Attributes"). . . .

* * *

32. The Debtors estimate that, as of the date hereof, the Debtors have incurred, for U.S. federal income tax purposes . . . consolidated NOLs in excess of $16 billion. . . .

33. The Debtors' Tax Attributes are valuable assets of the Debtors' estates because the Internal Revenue Code of 1986, as amended (the "Tax Code"), generally permits corporations to carry over their losses and tax credits to offset future income, thereby reducing the tax liability of the Debtors and, following the 363 Transaction, also New GM in future periods. . . . The Debtors' Tax Attributes potentially allow the Debtors and (as contemplated by the 363 Transaction) New GM to significantly reduce future U.S. federal income tax liability. . . . These savings could substantially enhance the Debtors' and New GM's cash position for the benefit of all parties in interest and contribute to the Debtors' and New GM's efforts toward a successful reorganization.

34. The ability of the Debtors and New GM to use the Debtors' Tax Attributes to reduce future tax liability is subject to certain statutory limitations. Sections 382 and 383 of the Tax Code limit a corporation's use of its NOLs, tax credits and certain other tax attributes to offset future income or tax after the corporation experiences an "ownership change." For purposes of section 382, an ownership change generally occurs when the percentage of a loss corporation's equity held by one or more "5% shareholders" (as such term is defined in section 382) increases by more than 50 percentage points over the lowest percentage of stock owned by such shareholder(s) at any time during the relevant testing period (usually three years). A section 382 ownership change *prior* to the effective date of a chapter 11 plan and, particularly, prior to the 363 Transaction, would effectively eliminate the ability of the Debtors and New GM to use the Debtors' Tax Attributes, thereby resulting in a significant loss of value. . . .

35. Accordingly, consistent with the automatic stay in these cases, the Debtors need the ability to preclude certain transfers of, and monitor and possibly object to other changes in the ownership of, GM Stock to ensure that a 50% change of ownership does not occur prior to the effective date of a chapter 11 plan.

Proposed Trading and Other Disposition Procedures

36. To preserve the potential value of the Tax Attributes and ensure that the Debtors receive the full benefits of the automatic stay, the Debtors propose [notification requirements and restrictions on trading of GM stock or options]:

* * *

Unauthorized Transactions in GM Stock or Options. Effective as of the date of the filing of this Motion and until further order of the Court to the contrary, any acquisition, disposition or other transfer of equity securities (including Options to acquire such securities) of the Debtors in violation of the procedures set forth herein shall be null and void ab initio as an act in violation of the automatic stay under sections 105(a) and 362 of the Bankruptcy Code.

The Tax Attributes Are Property of the Debtors' Estates; Thus, the Automatic Stay Bars Any Equity Transfers That Would Diminish or Limit the Debtors' Interest in the Tax Attributes

37. Section 362(a) of the Bankruptcy Code operates as a stay of, among other things, "any act to obtain possession of property of the estate or of property from the estate or to exercise control over property of the estate." 11 U.S.C. § 362(a)(3). Accordingly, "where a non-debtor's action with respect to an interest that is intertwined with that of a bankrupt debtor would have the legal effect of diminishing or eliminating property of the bankrupt estate, such action is barred by the automatic stay." *Official Committee of Unsecured Creditors v. PSS Steamship Co. (In re Prudential Lines Inc.)*, 928 F.2d 565 (2d Cir. 1991).

38. It is well established that a debtor's NOLs are property of the debtor's estate which is protected by section 362 of the Bankruptcy Code. *See Nisselson v. Drew Indus., Inc. (In re White Metal Rolling & Stamping Corp.)*, 222 B.R. 417, 424 (Bankr. S.D.N.Y. 1998) ("It is beyond peradventure that NOL carrybacks and carryovers are property of the estate of the loss corporation that generated them."). The United States Court of Appeals for the Second Circuit, in its seminal *Prudential Lines* decision, . . . stated:

> Including NOL carryforwards as property of a corporate debtor's estate is consistent with Congress' intention to "bring anything of value that the debtors have into the estate." Moreover, "[a] paramount and important goal of Chapter 11 is the rehabilitation of the debtor by offering breathing space and an opportunity to rehabilitate its business and eventually generate revenue." Including the right to a NOL carryforward as property of [the debtor's] bankruptcy estate furthers the purpose of facilitating the reorganization of [the debtor].

* * *

40. The Second Circuit also held that the permanent injunction was supported by the court's equitable powers pursuant to section 105(a) of the Bankruptcy Code, which authorizes the court to "issue any order, process, or judgment that is necessary or appropriate to carry out the provisions of" the Bankruptcy Code. Because the NOLs were valuable assets of the debtor, the Second Circuit refused to disturb the bankruptcy court's determination that elimination of the right to apply its NOLs to offset income on future tax returns would impede the debtor's reorganization. *Prudential Lines*, 928 F.2d at 574.

42. In short, it is well established by courts . . . that the automatic stay under section 362(a)(3) of the Bankruptcy Code enjoins actions that would adversely affect a debtor's NOLs and other tax attributes. These actions, including the trading of stock in and claims against a debtor, may be determined to be null and void *ab initio*.

* * *

WHEREFORE the Debtors respectfully request entry of an order granting the relief requested herein and such other and further relief as is just.

Dated: New York, New York
June 1, 2009

/s/ Stephen Karotkin
Harvey R. Miller
Stephen Karotkin
Joseph H. Smolinsky

WEIL, GOTSHAL & MANGES LLP
767 Fifth Avenue
New York, New York 10153
Telephone: (212 310–8000
Facsimile: (212) 310–8007
Attorneys for Debtors
and Debtors in Possession

---

1. Not all courts agree that the NOL is an asset of the estate that the bankruptcy court can act upon. The Seventh Circuit viewed § 362 as requiring more for the stay than an asset of the estate that needed protection. Section 362(a)(3) bars "any act to obtain possession of property of the estate . . . or to exercise control over property of the estate." The trading of a claim on the debtor adversely affects the debtor's value and may destroy the debtor's asset, i.e., the NOL carryforward, but the trading creditors are not acting to obtain that property (the NOL) or to control it. They're just trading claims. In re UAL Corp., 412 F.3d 775, 778 (7th Cir. 2005).
2. Could management of the debtor seek NOL-based trading bans strategically? Besides the tax issue, management might fear that activist investors will buy up debt, control the plan of reorganization, and become the firm's principal owners.
3. The NOL carryforward is lost if historic creditors and stockholders end up owning less than 50% of the reorganized firm. Hence, a trading ban could allow for some trading but bar trading when the 50% marker is approached. But debtors who (a) don't want to come close or (b) prefer not to see large controlling creditors, would prefer an order that bars all trading, even well before the 50% level is approached.

¶ 2110: Could the Market Produce a Bankruptcy–Avoiding Security?

So debt increases the chance of a bankruptcy or financial distress. The modern understanding is that a firm structures its capital by trading off the private tax savings of the interest deduction against increased bankruptcy costs from having more debt.

For firms that would have high bankruptcy and recapitalization costs, why don't bankers and lawyers try to write bankruptcy-avoiding securities? If the prospect of a decline in the firm will create deadlocks, could the recapitalization be pre-planned to avoid the costs of deadlock?

A simple numerical example will illustrate. The firm contracts with a creditor for a loan of $500. To avoid the costly haggle if the firm declines, the two agree that in the event that the firm's stock price falls to $2 per share (from its current $10 per share), the debt will be exchanged into 250 shares of stock. No bankruptcy, no recapitalization, no difficult negotiations, and definitely no deadlocked negotiations and bankruptcy filing.

Some securities issued in past decades have similar features that automatically allow the firm to alleviate some financial stress. In some junk bond recapitalizations, the recapitalizing firms, creditors, and investment bankers are often providing that interest may be paid by the firm in shares of stock or other "payment-in-kind" (of, say, more debt securities) having a market value equal to the interest payment.[14]

A full inquiry into bankruptcy—avoiding securities requires an extended treatment elsewhere.[15] But we have covered enough similar terrain here that a summary answer can be usefully given.

1. *Rejection in bankruptcy*. A security that would accomplish an automatic recapitalization would be rejectable in bankruptcy. A bankrupt firm may reject executory contracts—contracts whose performance is incomplete under § 365 of the Bankruptcy Code. Contracts to deliver stock in exchange for debt would be executory contracts in bankruptcy. Although rejection gives rise to a claim for damages, once rejected, an exchangeable bond would be useless as a means of avoiding financial stress.

How would the exchange feature be rejected? Shareholder-managers, fearful of losing control of the firm, might launch a preemptive strike by filing for bankruptcy and seeking to reject the exchange feature. Even though the firm would decline in value because of the enhanced stress, the managers or shareholders might think that they would get a bigger slice of the diminished firm, thereby making the bankruptcy worthwhile for them.[16]

2. *Discharge-of-indebtedness tax liability*. The firm's tax liability might be increased.[17] Generally, when a creditor forgives a debtor of repayment, the debtor has taxable income to the extent debt is forgiven. Moreover, drafters would have to contemplate the instability of these

---

[14] Troubled companies have been trying to use bonds with the interest payable in common stock of the company. If the company suffers cash flow difficulties, it can then be relieved of the obligation to use up whatever cash it has left. Although the principal amount of the bond is not automatically exchangeable into common stock at the then-current market price, the obligation to pay interest *is*.

[15] Some of these ideas are developed in Note, *Distress–Contingent Convertible Bonds: A Proposed Solution to the Excess Debt Problem*, 104 Harvard Law Review 1857 (1991); Barry Adler, *Financial and Political Theories of American Corporate Bankruptcy*, 45 Stanford Law Review 311 (1993).

[16] However, this possibility could be reduced. The exchange feature could be structured so that bankruptcy could not easily be obtained before the exchange was complete. By having the exchange occur when the firm was still solvent, the potential to use bankruptcy in a preemptive strike would be doubtful.

[17] See I.R.C. § 108(e).

forgiveness sections. Five structural changes have occurred in these tax code sections since the early 1980s; recent changes have grandfathered completed recapitalizations but not future recapitalizations involving securities outstanding. In addition, NOLs are lost for some categories of change in ownership. Those crafting exchangeable bonds would have to fear that the tax rules would affect them unfavorably.[18]

Moreover, the exchange feature might induce the IRS to view the security as really an equity security, for which the corporation would not be entitled to any interest deductions.

3. *Signaling disadvantages*. Signaling theory may be relevant. Insiders have a better idea of the firms prospects than outsiders. The way the firm's capital structure is formed signals the firm's prospects. Debt, for example, signals good opportunities under one scenario, because the firm's managers would be reluctant to use excessive debt if it would measurably increase the chance of bankruptcy and disruption to the firm and the managers' careers. The effort to precook a recapitalization would be taken as an adverse signal. Similarly, some have argued that debt enhances agency benefits: managers scramble to best assure repayment. A precooked recapitalization reduces the incentives to scramble.

4. *Benefits to nonbargain creditors*. The precooked recapitalization would work only if all creditors participated or compensated other creditors for their non-participation. That is, nonparticipants would benefit because they would be better assured of being paid off in full after the participating financial creditors took stock. To make such a security work, nonparticipants would have to compensate participants ex ante. But such compensation is sometimes difficult. Not all potential creditors readily bargain over such matters. (Tort claimants, some trade creditors, and labor creditors come to mind.)

---

[18] Discharge of indebtedness income might be avoided if the deal structure gave the creditors stock with a value equal to that of the amount originally loaned. Thus the deal might have the creditors lend $500 and take 250 shares of stock if and when the stock price declined to $2 per share, from its current $10.

Chapter 22

The LBO

A. The Leveraged Buyout

¶ 2201: LBOs and the Prospect of Fraudulent Conveyance Liability

A leveraged buyout, typically called an "LBO" or a private equity transaction, is a corporate acquisition transaction, which comes in several variations with common core features: Cash from outside lenders (the leverage) is borrowed to buy up equity from the existing stockholders of the target company (the buyout). The target company's assets are typically used as collateral for the LBO loan. Sometimes the firm's own managers initiate the buyout; other times outsiders initiate it. Either way, the firm's post-buyout managers or a buyout firm usually hold much or all of the firm's stock. In one common financial structure for the LBO, institutional lenders obtain a security interest in the firm's assets and the firm issues unsecured debt, oftentimes junk bonds, for additional financing.

In one form of LBO, the acquirer forms a new empty company (a "shell" company or "acquisition vehicle") and owns all the stock of that acquisition vehicle. The acquisition vehicle borrows from the LBO to the acquisition vehicle lender and executes a merger agreement with the target. The cash from the LBO loan pays off the target company's stockholders, and the target merges with the acquisition vehicle, with the target as the surviving company—now owned by the acquirer. The assets of the target company are given as security to the LBO lender. These steps need not occur in any particular order, but in theory, they happen simultaneously.

The organizers of the LBO expect the total post-buyout value of the firm's securities to exceed their pre-buyout value. To reconcile the substance of the LBO with efficient market theory and the Modigliani–Miller irrelevance hypotheses, consider taxes, information, managerial incentives, and control:

- By substituting debt with tax-deductible interest for equity, the company reduces its tax bill, thereby increasing its private value.
- Some public firms reinvest too much of their cash in expanding their operations even though they lack good new opportunities. An LBO, with its enormous debt obligation, inhibits the managers from expanding unwisely.
- The managers of a public firm, fearing an outside attack via a hostile takeover offer, launch a preemptive strike, taking the company private (and into their own full control), thereby eluding the grasp of the hostile outside offeror.
- The managers with big equity stakes in the LBO will work harder or, more plausibly, since they already work long hours, they will make the tough but necessary decisions that they avoided when their equity stakes were smaller. When they own much of the stock themselves, they're working for themselves. And, when a buyout firm (the acquirer) owns much of the rest of the stock, the buyout firm's own managers and partners keep an eye on what the operating company's managers do. The typical, more widely dispersed pre-LBO shareholding structure of the public firm, by contrast, does not encourage the close monitoring that the buyout firm pursues.
- Inside managers of the public firm may understand that public markets are undervaluing the company. They buy the outsider's stock in an LBO deal when the stock price is low. In some cases, it's been alleged, they condition the market to value the firm low by releasing the most pessimistic information possible about the firm's prospects.

Is an LBO a fraudulent conveyance? *After* the LBO, the firm is often on the border of insolvency, and its subsequent transfers risk being classified as fraudulent. But how about the buyout itself? Can the substance of an LBO be made doctrinally to be a fraudulent conveyance, which under § 9 of the Uniform Fraudulent Conveyance Act would allow the offended creditors to annul the obligation to the creditor who received a fraudulent conveyance? (The Uniform Fraudulent Conveyance Act preceded the Uniform Fraudulent Transfer Act and was the act in place for the next decision we read, *Gleneagles*. It is substantively similar to the Uniform Fraudulent Transfer Act, which has now replaced it in most states, although not in all of them, including commercially important ones, like New York. We use the

UFCA's provisions here, because they're the ones interpreted in *Gleneagles*.)

Pre-existing creditors of the LBO company (such as the bondholders in MetLife in ¶1810) face greater risks of not being paid. But how can they succeed in having the firm's new loan obligations viewed as fraudulent conveyances? The doctrinal difficulty they face is that §§ 4 and 6 require that (1) either the LBO company be insolvent or rendered insolvent by the transaction (§ 4) or have incurred debts beyond the debtor's ability to pay (§ 6), *and* (2) that there not be fair consideration in the transaction. One can readily imagine one or the other of the *first* standards being met in an LBO, because LBOs entail near-insolvency sometimes and lots of debt usually. But both sections *also* require that the transaction not involve fair consideration, and the new lender seems to be giving fair consideration. The new lender after all writes out a big check when it lends the money. Surely from the lender's perspective, the consideration it gives is eminently fair. The LBO target takes on a big obligation to the lender, but it also got lots of cash in from the lender's loan. That cash is the fair consideration.

Section 3 of UFCA says something about fair consideration:

> **Fair consideration.** Fair consideration is given for property, or obligation,
>
> (a) When in exchange for such property, or obligation, as a fair equivalent therefor, and in good faith, property is conveyed or an antecedent debt is satisfied, or
>
> (b) When such property, or obligation is received in good faith to secure a present advance or antecedent debt in amount not disproportionately small as compared with the value of the property, or obligation obtained.

Again, the statutory text as to fair consideration at first seems satisfied when the LBO lender writes a check to the company in return for the company's obligation to repay the lender. This properly-sized check seems to be fair consideration, thereby taking the transaction out from the objective UFCA sections.

Thus those seeking to characterize the LBO as a fraudulent conveyance seem to need to satisfy the subjective, actual fraud section, § 7, which doesn't require that the consideration be unfair, but does require actual intent to hinder, delay, or defraud. But if the LBO organizers and the lender expect the firm to be better managed after the buyout or to have its tax bill lowered, then those would seem to be the primary goals of the LBO organizers and lenders, not an effort to hinder, delay, or defraud the target firm's creditors.

Yet, despite these initial difficulties in subjecting the LBO lender to liability, the lenders in the Tabor Court LBO were hit with fraudulent conveyance liability. To see how these elements of fraudulent conveyance law can govern LBOs, read *Tabor Court* below, frequently known by its lower court name, *Gleneagles*.

B. THE LBO LENDER AND FRAUDULENT CONVEYANCE LIABILITY

¶ 2202: United States v. Tabor Court Realty Corp., 803 F.2d 1288 (3d Cir. 1986)

We have consolidated appeals from litigation involving one of America's largest anthracite coal producers. . . . Ultimately, we have to decide whether the court erred in entering judgment in favor of the United States in reducing to judgment certain federal corporate tax assessments made against the coal producers, in determining the priority of the government liens, and in permitting foreclosure on the liens. To reach these questions, however, we must examine a very intricate leveraged buy-out and decide whether mortgages given in the transaction were fraudulent conveyances within the meaning of the constructive and intentional fraud sections of the Pennsylvania Uniform Fraudulent Conveyance Act (UFCA) . . . and if so, whether a later assignment of the mortgages was void as against creditors. [We so hold.]

. . . We are told that this case represents the first significant application of the UFCA to leveraged buy-out financing.

We will address [these] issues presented by the appellants and an amicus curiae, the National Commercial Finance Association, and by the United States and a trustee in bankruptcy as cross appellants:

- whether the court erred in applying the UFCA to a leveraged buy-out;
- whether the court erred in "collapsing" two separate loans for the leveraged buy-out into one transaction;
- whether the court erred in holding that the mortgages placed [by the debtor] . . . were invalid for lack of fair consideration.

* * *

We will summarize a very complex factual situation and then discuss these issues seriatim.

I.

These appeals arise from an action by the United States to reduce to judgment delinquent federal income taxes, interest, and penalties assessed and accrued against Raymond Colliery Co., Inc. and its subsidiaries (the Raymond Group) . . . and to reduce to judgment similarly assessed taxes owed by Great American Coal Co., Inc. . . .

* * *

Raymond Colliery, [at first a family-owned corporation], owned over 30,000 acres of land in Lackawanna and Luzerne counties in Pennsylvania and was one of the largest anthracite coal producers in the country. . . . Lurking in the background of the financial problems present here are two important components of the current industrial scene: first, the depressed economy attending anthracite mining in Lackawanna and Luzerne Counties, the heartland of this industry; and second, the Pennsylvania Department of Environmental Resources' 1967 order directing [one of Raymond's subsidiaries] to reduce the amount of pollutants it discharged into public waterways in the course of its deep mining operations, necessitating a fundamental change from deep mining to strip or surface mining.

[Durkin was Raymond's president. He acquired an option to buy stock from the owners of Raymond. But] Durkin had trouble in raising the necessary financing to exercise his option. He sought help from the Central States Pension Fund of the International Brotherhood of Teamsters and also from the Mellon Bank of Pittsburgh. Mellon concluded that [Raymond] was a bad financial risk. Moreover, both Mellon and Central States held extensive discussions with Durkin's counsel concerning the legality of encumbering Raymond's assets for the purpose of obtaining the loan, a loan which was not to be used to repay creditors but rather to buy out Raymond's stockholders.

After other unsuccessful attempts to obtain financing for the purchase, Durkin incorporated a holding company, Great American, and assigned to it his option to purchase Raymond's stock. Although the litigation in the district court was far-reaching, most of the central issues have their genesis in 1973 when the Raymond Group was sold to Durkin in a leveraged buy-out through the vehicle of Great American.

A leveraged buy-out is not a legal term of art. It is a shorthand expression describing a business practice wherein a company is sold to a small number of investors, typically including members of the company's management, under financial arrangements in which there is a minimum amount of equity and a maximum amount of debt. The financing typically provides for a substantial return of investment capital by means of mortgages or high risk bonds, popularly known as "junk bonds." The predicate transaction here fits the popular notion of a leveraged buy-out. Shareholders of the Raymond Group sold the corporation to a small group of investors headed by Raymond's president[, Durkin]; these investors borrowed substantially all of the purchase price at an extremely high rate of interest secured by mortgages on the assets of the selling company and its subsidiaries and those of additional entities that guaranteed repayment.

To effectuate the buy-out, Great American obtained a loan commitment from Institutional Investors Trust on July 24, 1973, in the amount of $8,530,000. The 1973 interrelationship among the many creditors of the Raymond Group, and the sale to Great American—a seemingly empty corporation which was able to perform the buyout only on the strength of the massive loan from IIT—forms the backdrop for the relevancy of the Pennsylvania Uniform Fraudulent Conveyance Act. . . .

Durkin obtained the financing through one of his two partners in Great American.[1] [Most of Raymond's assets were given as security for the buy-out loan from IIT.] We must decide whether the borrowers'

[1] Durkin owned 40% of Great American, Hyman Green owned 10%, and James R. Hoffa, Jr. owned the remaining 50%. Durkin and Green concealed Hoffa's ownership interest in Great American from IIT. Hoffa apparently came into the picture when Durkin attempted to borrow money from the Central States Pension Fund of the International Brotherhood of Teamsters to finance the purchase.

mortgages were invalid under the UFCA and whether there was consideration for the . . . mortgages.

* * *

[IIT lent money to Raymond, but t]he exchange of money and notes did not stop with IIT's advances to [Raymond]. Upon receipt of the IIT loan proceeds, [Raymond] immediately transferred a total of $4,085,000 to [Durkin's company,] Great American. In return, Great American issued to each borrowing company an unsecured promissory note with the same interest terms as those of the IIT loan agreement. In addition to the proceeds of the IIT loan, Great American borrowed other funds to acquire the purchase price for Raymond's stock[, which Raymond's other stockholders sold to Great American].

When the financial dust settled after the closing on November 26, 1973, this was the situation at Raymond: Great American paid $6.7 million to purchase Raymond's stock, the shareholders receiving $6.2 million in cash and a $500,000 note; at least $4.8 million of this amount was obtained by mortgaging Raymond's assets.

Notwithstanding the cozy accommodations for the selling stockholders, the financial environment of the Raymond Group at the time of the sale was somewhat precarious. At the time of the closing, Raymond had multi-million dollar liabilities for federal income taxes, trade accounts, pension fund contributions, strip mining and back-filling obligations, and municipal real estate taxes. The district court calculated that the Raymond Group's existing debts amounted to at least $20 million on November 26, 1983.

Under Durkin's control after the buy-out, Raymond's condition further deteriorated. Following the closing the Raymond Group lacked the funds to pay its routine operating expenses, including those for materials, supplies, telephone, and other utilities. It was also unable to pay its delinquent and current real estate taxes. Within two months of the closing, [its] deep mining operations . . . were shut down; within six months of the closing, the Raymond Group ceased all strip mining operations. Consequently, the Raymond Group could not fulfill its existing coal contracts and became liable for damages for breach of contract. . . . Within seven months of the closing, the Commonwealth of Pennsylvania and the Anthracite Health & Welfare Fund sued the Raymond Group for its failures to fulfill back-filling requirements in the strip mining operations and to pay contributions to the Health & Welfare Fund. This litigation resulted in injunctions against the Raymond Group companies which prevented them from moving or selling their equipment until their obligations were satisfied. . . .

[Raymond's properties were later sold, but the central question in the subsequent lawsuit by the United States was whether the first loans by IIT were fraudulent conveyances.]

This, then, constitutes a summary of the adjudicative facts that undergird the litigation below and the appeals before us.

II.

The instant action was commenced by the United States on December 12, 1980 to reduce to judgment certain corporate federal tax assessments made against the Raymond Group and Great American. The government sought to . . . foreclose against the property that Raymond had owned at the time of the assessments as well as against properties currently owned by Raymond. The United States argued that the IIT mortgages executed in November 1973 should be set aside under the Uniform Fraudulent Conveyance Act and further that the purported assignment of these mortgages to [the new purchasers] should be voided because at the inception [they] had purchased the mortgages with knowledge that they had been fraudulently conveyed.

. . . [T]he district court . . . concluded, inter alia, that the mortgages given by the Raymond Group to IIT on November 26, 1973 were fraudulent conveyances within the meaning of the constructive and intentional fraud sections of the Pennsylvania Uniform Fraudulent Conveyance Act. . . .

[Raymond] appealed. As heretofore stated, all these mortgages, subsequently invalidated by the district court, had been granted to IIT on November 26, 1973. . . . For the purpose of this appeal, we shall refer to the Raymond Group as "appellants," or "[the purchaser]."

* * *

III.

[The purchaser] initially challenges the district court's application of the Pennsylvania Uniform Fraudulent Conveyance Act (UFCA) . . . to the leveraged buy-out made by IIT to the mortgagors. . . . The district court determined that IIT lacked good faith in the transaction because it knew, or should have known, that the money it lent the mortgagors was used, in part, to finance the purchase of stock from the mortgagors' shareholders, and that as a consequence of the loan, IIT and its assignees obtained a secured position in the mortgagors' property to the detriment of creditors. . . .

In applying section [3(a)] of the UFCA, the district court stated:

> The initial question . . . is whether the transferee, IIT, transferred its loan proceeds in good faith. . . . IIT knew or strongly suspected that the imposition of the loan obligations secured by the mortgages and guarantee mortgages would probably render insolvent both the Raymond Group and each individual member thereof. In addition, *IIT was fully aware that no individual member of the Raymond Group would receive fair consideration within the meaning of the Act in exchange for the loan obligations to IIT.* Thus, we conclude that IIT does not meet the standard of good faith under Section [3(a)] of the Act. . . .

565 F. Supp. at 574.

[The purchaser] argues that "the only reasonable and proper application of the good faith criteria as it applies to the lender in structuring a loan is one which looks to the lender's motives as opposed to his knowledge." Br. for appellants at 17. [It] argues that good faith is satisfied when "the lender acted in an arms-length transaction without ulterior motive or collusion with the debtor to the detriment of creditors." Id.

Section [4] of the UFCA is a "constructive fraud" provision. It establishes that a conveyance made by a person "who is or will be thereby rendered insolvent, is fraudulent as to creditors, without regard to his actual intent, if the conveyance is made . . . without a fair consideration." [UFCA, § 4.] Section [3] defines fair consideration as an exchange of a "fair equivalent . . . in good faith." Because section [4] excludes an examination of intent, it follows that "good faith" must be something other than intent; because section [4] also focuses on insolvency, knowledge of insolvency is a rational interpretation of the statutory language of lack of "good faith." [The purchaser] would have us adopt "without ulterior motive or collusion with the debtor to the detriment of creditors" as the good faith standard. We are uneasy with such a standard because these words came very close to describing intent.

Surprisingly, few courts have considered this issue. [One] court held [in 1939] that because a transferee had no knowledge of the transferor's insolvency, it could not justify a finding of bad faith, implying that a showing of such knowledge would support a finding of bad faith. In [another 1971 decision, a court] set forth a number of factors to be considered in determining good faith: 1) honest belief in the propriety of the activities in question; 2) no intent to take unconscionable advantage of others; and 3) no intent to, or knowledge of the fact that the activities in question will, hinder, delay, or defraud others. Where "any one of these factors is absent, lack of good faith is established and the conveyance fails."

We have decided that the district court reached the right conclusion here for the right reasons. It determined that IIT did not act in good faith because it was aware, first, that the exchange would render Raymond insolvent, and second, that no member of the Raymond Group would [when the entire set of contemplated transactions was completed] receive fair consideration. We believe that this determination is consistent with the statute and case law.

[The purchaser] and amicus curiae also argue that as a general rule the UFCA should not be applied to leveraged buy-outs. They contend that the UFCA, which was passed in 1924, was never meant to apply to a complicated transaction such as a leveraged buy-out. The Act's broad language, however, extends to any "conveyance" which is defined as "every payment of money . . . and also the creation of any lien or incumbrance." [UFCA, § 1.] This broad sweep does not justify exclusion of a particular transaction such as a leveraged buy-out simply because it is innovative or complicated. If the UFCA is not to be applied to leveraged buy-outs, it should be for the state legislatures, not the courts, to decide.

In addition, although appellants' and amicus curiae's arguments against general application of the Act to leveraged buy-outs are not without some force, the application of fraudulent conveyance law to certain leveraged buy-outs is not clearly bad public policy.[2] In any

[2] A major premise of the policy arguments opposing application of fraudulent conveyance law to leveraged buy-outs is that such transactions often benefit creditors and that the application of fraudulent conveyance law to buy-outs will deter them in the future. See Baird and Jackson, *Fraudulent Conveyance Law and Its Proper Domain*, 38 Vand. L. Rev. 829, 855

event, the circumstances of this case justify application. . . . In the instant case, . . . the severe economic circumstances in which the Raymond Group found itself, the obligation, without benefit, incurred by the Raymond Group, and the small number of shareholders benefitted by the transaction suggest that the transaction was not entered in the ordinary course, that fair consideration was not exchanged, and that the transaction was anything but unsuspicious. The policy arguments set forth in opposition to the application of fraudulent conveyance law to leveraged buy-outs do not justify the exemption of transactions such as this.

IV.

* * *

[The purchaser] next contends that the district court erred in not crediting [it] for that portion of the IIT loan that was not passed through to Raymond's shareholders: although "the District Court acknowledged that $2,915,000, or approximately 42 percent, of the IIT loan proceeds originally went for the benefit of . . . [prior] creditors, IIT . . . received no credit therefor in regard to the partial validity of their liens." Br. for appellants at 28. [The purchaser] argues the district court determined that "the wrong committed upon the creditors . . . [was] the diversion of some 58 percent of the loan proceeds from the IIT loan to [Raymond's] shareholders." Id. at 29. It concludes that to invalidate the entire mortgage would be to provide Raymond's creditors with a "double recovery." Id. at 28. We understand the dissent to agree with [the purchaser's] analysis when noting that " 'creditors have causes of action in fraudulent conveyance law only to the extent they have been damaged.' "

[The purchaser] and, by implication, the dissent mischaracterize the district court's findings and conclusions regarding the fraudulent nature of the IIT loans. The district court did not determine that the loan transaction was only partially—or, to use [the purchaser's] formulation, 58%—fraudulent. Nor did the district court conclude that Raymond's creditors had been wronged by only a portion of the transaction. Instead, the district court stated that:

> [The purchaser's] argument rests on the incorrect assumption that some portions of the IIT mortgages are valid as against the Creditors. In Gleneagles I, this Court found that IIT and Durkin engaged in an intentionally fraudulent transaction on November 26, 1973. The IIT mortgages are therefore invalid in their entirety as to creditors. In essence, the district court ruled that the aggregate transaction was fraudulent,

(1985). An equally important premise is that creditors can protect themselves from undesirable leveraged buy-outs by altering the terms of their credit contracts. Id. at 835. This second premise ignores, however, cases such as this one in which the major creditors (in this instance the United States and certain Pennsylvania municipalities) are involuntary and do not become creditors by virtue of a contract. The second premise also ignores the possibility that the creditors attacking the leveraged buy-out (such as many of the creditors in this case) became creditors before leveraged buy-outs became a common financing technique and thus may not have anticipated such leveraged transactions so as to have been able to adequately protect themselves by contract. . . .

notwithstanding the fact that a portion of the loan proceeds was allegedly used to pay existing creditors.

. . . [M]ost of the $2,915,000 allegedly paid to the benefit of Raymond's creditors went to only one creditor—Chemical Bank. In Gleneagles I, the district court found that $2,186,247 of the IIT loan proceeds were paid to Chemical Bank in satisfaction of the mortgage that Raymond had taken to purchase . . . [a Raymond subsidiary.] The purpose of this payment is of critical significance:

> [Raymond's selling shareholders] required satisfaction of the Chemical Bank mortgage as a condition of the sale of their Raymond Colliery stock at least in part because [one of the selling shareholders] had personally guaranteed repayment of that loan. . . . [The purchaser] does not challenge this finding on appeal. Thus, of the $2.9 million allegedly paid to benefit Raymond's creditors, $2.2 million were actually intended to benefit Raymond's shareholders and to satisfy a condition for the sale. The remaining amounts allegedly paid to benefit Raymond's creditors were applied to the closing costs of the transaction. See [Gleneagles I, 565 F. Supp. at 570] (finding 133).

On this record, the district court's characterization of the transaction as a whole as fraudulent cannot reasonably be disputed. The court's consequent determination that the "IIT mortgages are . . . invalid in their entirety as to creditors" is supported by precedent. . . .

The district court determined that "[t]he Creditors . . . would not be placed in the same or similar position which they held with respect to the Raymond Group in 1973 merely by replacing the $4,085,500 of IIT loan proceeds that were misused on November 26, 1973." Gleneagles III, 584 F. Supp. at 681. We agree with the district court[.]

. . . [T]herefore, we will not disturb the district court's determination [on the extent of the fraudulent conveyance].

* * *

V.

[The purchaser], joined by the amicus, next argues that the district court erred "by collapsing two separate loans into one transaction." Br. for appellants at 30. The loan arrangement was a two-part process: the loan proceeds went from IIT to the borrowing Raymond Group companies, which immediately turned the funds over to Great American, which used the funds for the buy-out. [The purchaser] contends that the district court erred by not passing on the fairness of the transaction between IIT and the Raymond Group mortgagors. . . .

Contrary to [the purchaser's] contentions, the district court did examine this element of the transaction, stating "[W]e find that the obligations incurred by the Raymond Group and its individual members to IIT were not supported by fair consideration. The mortgages and guarantee mortgages to secure these obligations were *also* not supported by fair consideration." Gleneagles I, 565 F. Supp. at 577 (emphasis supplied).

Admittedly, in the course of its determination that the IIT–Raymond Group transaction was without fair consideration under section [3(a)], the court looked beyond the exchange of funds between IIT and the Raymond Group. But there was reason for this. The two exchanges were part of one integrated transaction. As the court concluded: "[t]he $4,085,000 in IIT loan proceeds which were lent immediately by the borrowing companies to Great American were merely passed through the borrowers to Great American and ultimately to the selling stockholders and cannot be deemed consideration received by the borrowing companies." Id. at 575.

The district court's factual findings support its treatment of the IIT–Raymond Group–Great American transaction as a single transaction. For example, Durkin, president of Great American, solicited financing from IIT for the purchase. Id. at 566 (finding 70). The loan negotiations included representatives of all three parties. Id. at 567 (findings 83–87). The first closing was aborted by IIT's counsel because of, inter alia, concern about "unknown individuals" involved with Great American. Id. at 567–68 (finding 89(a)). The $7 million loaned by IIT to the borrowing companies was "immediately placed in an escrow account"; "simultaneously" with the receipt of the IIT proceeds, the borrowing companies loaned Great American the cash for the buy-out and received in return "an unsecured note promising to repay the loans to the borrowing companies on the same terms and at the same interest rate as pertained to the loans to the borrowing companies from IIT." Id. at 570 (findings 127–29).

Appellant cannot seriously challenge these findings of fact. We are satisfied with the district court's conclusion that the funds "merely passed through the borrowers to Great American." This necessitates our agreement with the district court's conclusion that, for purposes of determining IIT's knowledge of the use of the proceeds under section [3(a)], there was one integral transaction.[3]

VI.

[The purchaser] next faults the district court's determination that the Raymond Group was rendered insolvent by "the IIT transaction and the instantaneous payment to the selling stockholders of a substantial portion of the IIT loan in exchange for their stock." Gleneagles I, 565 F. Supp. at 580. . . .

* * *

We conclude that [the purchaser] has not demonstrated that this finding [of insolvency] was clearly erroneous. . . .

VII.

[The purchaser] next argues that the district court erred in holding that the mortgages were invalid under section [7] of the UFCA. . . .

[3] Admittedly, [the purchaser's] and amicus' arguments could have some validity where the lender is unaware of the use to which loan proceeds are to be put. This is not the case here. IIT was intimately involved with the formulation of the agreement whereby the proceeds of its loan were funneled into the hands of the purchasers of the stock of a corporation that was near insolvency. . . .

. . . [S]ection [7] invalidates conveyances made with an intent to defraud creditors: "Every conveyance made and every obligation incurred with actual intent, as distinguished from intent presumed in law, to hinder, delay, or defraud either present or future creditors, is fraudulent as to both present and future creditors." [UFCA, § 7.] Under Pennsylvania law, an intent to hinder, delay, or defraud creditors may be inferred from transfers in which consideration is lacking and where the transferor and transferee have knowledge of the claims of creditors and know that the creditors cannot be paid. Direct evidence is not necessary to prove "actual intent."

* * *

B.

Appellant also objects to the district court's statement that "[i]f the parties could have foreseen the effect on creditors resulting from the assumption of the IIT obligation by the Raymond Group . . . the parties must be deemed to have intended the same." 565 F. Supp. at 581. . . . We are satisfied that this principle supports the district court's conclusion.

* * *

¶ 2203: Questions on *Gleneagles*

1. When the lender made the LBO loan to Raymond, the borrower's obligations rose by the amount of the loan and its assets rose by the amount of the loan. The loan did *not* thereby render the debtor any more insolvent than it was before the loan. What then is the basic fraudulent conveyance problem?
2. And where is the unfair consideration for the loan? The lender lent, the debtor incurred an obligation, and the debtor received fresh cash, in the full amount of its loan obligation. The consideration for the obligation to repay seems to be fair.
3. But what happens to the cash after the loan is made?
   a. LBO lender lends to the company on fair terms.
   b. The lender gets a security interest in the company's property.
   c. Then the company buys back common stock with the loan proceeds.

   Steps (a) and (b) are on fair terms. Is the court collapsing (a) and (c)? The bank lends, and money goes out to stockholders. Once (a) and (c) are collapsed, what is left is (b), which standing alone suggests that the corporation failed to *receive* fair consideration, although the lender *gave* fair consideration.

   Still, from the *lender's* perspective is the consideration unfair? Does the lender get a special, unfair deal? Or is it that from the *borrower's* perspective the entire deal (a *plus* c) yields the borrower unfair consideration?
4. Isn't the court making the LBO/lender the watchdog, the gatekeeper for the benefit of non-bargain creditors, such as the tax collector, trade creditors, tort claimants, and financial creditors who lent be-

fore the LBO became popular? Consider this description of one LBO:

> The buyout of Kaiser Steel Corporation in 1984 illustrates the potential significance of involuntary creditors. . . . Payments to stockholders were financed with cash on hand and a new $100 million loan from Citibank, secured by substantially all the company's assets. However, at closing, the company had total liabilities of approximately $750 million, of which nearly $600 million (80%) was owed to retired employees for vested medical and pension benefits. Stockholders voted to approve the LBO. The approval of retired employees was not sought. Whether they had standing to challenge the transaction prior to closing was unclear in 1984, though other employee groups have since been allowed to mount such challenges. . . .
>
> By the time Kaiser filed under Chapter 11 in 1987, Citibank had been repaid. The company's largest remaining creditors were retired employees and the Pension Benefit Guaranty Corporation[, the government-sponsored entity that guarantees some pension payments to employees]. . . . [They] had [not] approved the LBO, nor was the PBGC even a creditor at the time of the buyout.

Timothy A. Luehrman & Lance L. Hirt, *Highly Leveraged Transactions and Fraudulent Conveyance Law,* 6 Journal of Applied Corporate Finance 104, 109 (1993).

5. If you represent a lender in a future LBO, what do you want to do? Document the solvency of the company at the time of the loan? Document the company's ability to pay back its preexisting loans after the LBO transaction takes place? Document the fairness to the corporation of the entire transaction? Avoid some borderline, highly risky LBOs?

6. When the smoke cleared, Raymond had an obligation from Great American whose value was tied to Raymond's own stock. Even if Raymond's stock has value to an outsider, does it have value to Raymond? Directly, it doesn't. Indirectly, it does: Raymond could sell the stock. But Raymond could also have sold its own stock before it got the stock in this transaction. Hence, when Raymond bought its own stock, assets left Raymond, but Raymond didn't get anything of value that it didn't have before.

7. Will some stockholders be ready to engage in an LBO even if it's detrimental to the corporation? Keep in mind that the net benefit to a stockholder differs from the benefit to a corporation. A stockholder may prefer that the firm declare a dividend, even if the firm is worse off, because the dividend ends up in the stockholder's pocket. Thus the cashed-out stockholders have a reason to prefer dividends (and LBOs that buy them out) even if the company is made worse off.

   Could new manager-stockholders sometimes have a similar motivation? If they prefer to run the new company, especially if they need to put up little or no money of their own in the LBO, would they prefer the LBO result, even if the company is worse off?

   But then why would the LBO financiers participate? Would it be that with appropriate security, priority, and a high enough interest rate, their loan is expected to be profitable, but the firm would be made worse off? See the transactions diagrammed below, in ¶2204.

But how can all of these people be better off and the firm worse off? Isn't it that more risk and further losses are put on the shoulders of the preexisting creditors, with these creditors not party to the LBO transaction? And isn't that just what fraudulent conveyance law is designed to regulate?

Keep in mind that just because it's possible that the corporation is made worse off does not mean that it always is made worse off.

8. If a contract creditor anticipated the risk of an LBO that would make it worse off, what should it do in its loan agreement?

9. The proceeds of the *Gleneagles* LBO loan were partly used to pay off Chemical Bank, a preexisting creditor. To that extent, are the other preexisting creditors of Raymond harmed by the LBO loan? To that extent, was Raymond harmed?

10. Lender lends $3 million to Debtor when Debtor is insolvent. Debtor uses all the proceeds of the $3 million loan to pay off a preexisting creditor, Chemical Bank. Are other creditors of the Debtor harmed by the transaction? Under the theory in *Gleneagles*, is the loan a fraudulent conveyance? Does the Debtor receive fair consideration? If the Lender knew the Debtor would use the Lender's loan to pay $3 million to the preexisting creditor, would the new Lender be acting in good faith? If the theory of *Gleneagles* collapses the transactions, why shouldn't the court collapse the pay-off to a preexisting creditor as well?

11. If IIT wrote a check directly to Chemical Bank, which then assigned its note and security arrangement over to IIT, would that be a fraudulent conveyance? Or would it just be IIT taking over Chemical's loan? Under a "collapsed view" of the actual transaction, how would one view the new lender lending to the firm, with the firm then taking the proceeds to pay off Chemical? Isn't the "collapsed view" that IIT was just buying the loan up from Chemical?

Stockholders guaranteed the loan from Chemical. The release of the stockholders' guarantee by IIT benefitted the stockholders, but only to the extent Raymond could not pay Chemical back.

12 In related litigation, the IRS sought to have the monies that had been transferred to the old stockholders in the buyback found to be a fraudulent conveyance. (The IRS also sought to recover directly, and on behalf of the corporation apparently, on related theories of a breach of duty of care, an illegal dividend, and a breach of the duty of loyalty to creditors of an insolvent corporation.) The lawsuit was settled for $5 million. Should IIT's successors have received a "credit" for this $5 million settlement?

Many LBOs have the promoters buying back stock from public stockholders. How should the buyback from the public stockholders be analyzed under the fraudulent conveyance laws? The next decision, *Wieboldt* deals with a public company's stock buyback.

13. Fraudulent conveyance law comes in three major flavors in the United States, each descending from the medieval English Statute of 13 Elizabeth (see ¶802), as it was called. The first, the Uniform

Fraudulent Conveyance Act, has been around for decades. An updated version, the Uniform Fraudulent Transfer Act, is now more widespread. A new version, the Uniform Voidable Transfer Act, was proposed in 2014.

The bankruptcy trustee can use these state laws, via § 544, to annul fraudulently incurred corporate debts or recover fraudulently conveyed property. The trustee can also use the Bankruptcy Code's version of fraudulent conveyance law, which appears in § 548 and § 550 of the Code. Slight language differences exist among the three main versions. The typical reason for a trustee to use state law through § 544, instead of § 548 directly, has been that the state law statute of limitations is often longer than the older one-year limit for § 548. (It's now a two-year limit.)

---

§ 544. Trustee as lien creditor . . .

* * *

(b)(1) . . . [T]he trustee may avoid any transfer of an interest of the debtor in property or any obligation incurred by the debtor that is voidable under applicable law by a creditor holding an unsecured claim that is allowable under section 502 of this title. . . .

¶ 2204: Lending to an Insolvent Firm

One might think that a new lender, aware of the precariousness of the borrower, could not find it profitable to lend to the insolvent firm. Usually they do not.

But consider this sequence, which roughly corresponds to the *Gleneagles* facts. At Time 2, the company incurs the LBO debt, with an interest rate that's attractive to the lender. Later, at Time 3, the LBO target sends $8.5 million in cash to the target's stockholders and the secured creditors gets its collateral. The lender in the interim was paid an interest rate and received its principal back. The preexisting creditors would have obtained $10 million in an absolute priority bankruptcy at Time 1. They receive nothing in an absolute priority bankruptcy (with no fraudulent conveyance action) at Time 4.

The key characteristic is that the active players are taking value that would otherwise go to the preexisting creditors.

Time 1.

Assets	Liabilities
$10M Assets	$20M Debt
	SH

Time 2.

Assets	Liabilities
$10M Assets	Secured loan $8.5M at 10%
$8.5M Cash	$20M Debt
	SH

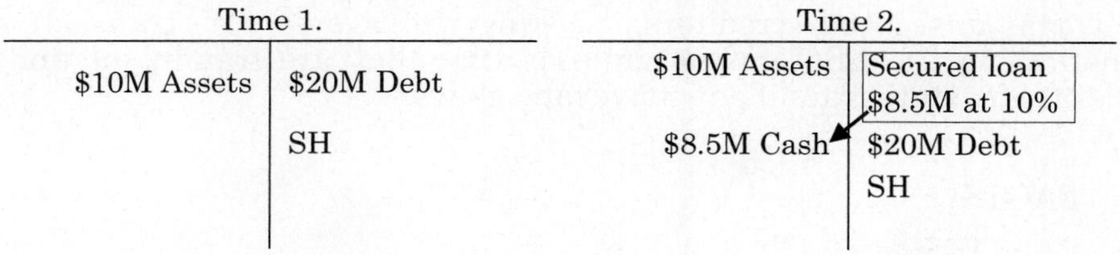

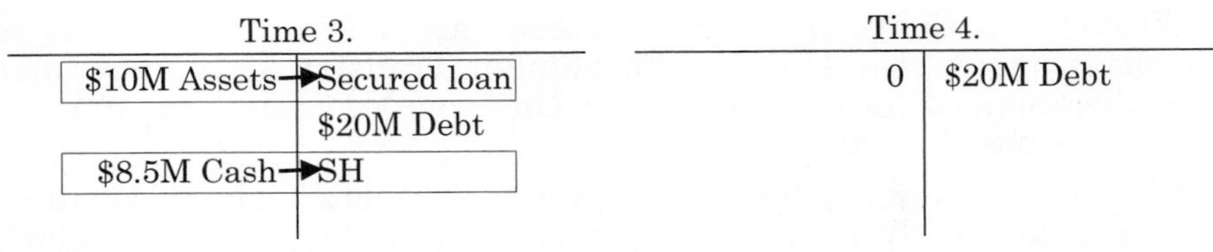

C. THE LBO STOCKHOLDERS AND FRAUDULENT CONVEYANCE LIABILITY

¶ 2205: Wieboldt Stores, Inc. v. Jerome M. Schottenstein, 94 Bankr. 488 (Bankr. N.D. Ill. 1988)

JAMES F. HOLDERMAN, District Judge:

Wieboldt Stores, Inc. ("Wieboldt") filed this [derivative] action [partly on behalf of unsecured creditors] on September 18, 1987 under the federal bankruptcy laws, 11 U.S.C. §§ 101 et seq., the state fraudulent conveyance laws, Ill. Rev. Stat. ch. 59, § 4, and the Illinois Business Corporation Act, Ill. Rev. Stat. ch. 32, para. 1.01 et seq. Pending before the court are . . . motions to dismiss this action. . . .

I. INTRODUCTION

Wieboldt's complaint against the defendants concerns the events and transactions surrounding a leveraged buyout ("LBO") of Wieboldt by WSI Acquisition Corporation ("WSI"). WSI, a corporation formed solely for the purpose of acquiring Wieboldt, borrowed funds from third-party lenders and delivered the proceeds to the shareholders in return for their shares. Wieboldt thereafter pledged certain of its assets to the LBO lenders to secure repayment of the loan.

The LBO reduced the assets available to Wieboldt's creditors. Wieboldt contends that, after the buyout was complete, Wieboldt's debt had increased by millions of dollars, and the proceeds made available by the LBO lenders were paid out to Wieboldt's then existing shareholders and did not . . . benefit . . . the corporation. Wieboldt's alleged insolvency after the LBO left Wieboldt with insufficient unencumbered assets to sustain its business and ensure payment to its unsecured creditors. Wieboldt therefore commenced this action on behalf of itself and its unsecured creditors, seeking to avoid the transactions constituting the LBO on the grounds that they are fraudulent under federal and state fraudulent conveyance laws.

II. FACTS

A. PARTIES

1. Wieboldt

. . . In 1982 Wieboldt's business was operated out of twelve stores and one distribution center in the Chicago metropolitan area. . . . Its stock was publicly traded on the New York Stock Exchange.

During the 1970s, demographic changes in Wieboldt's markets, increased competition from discount operations, and poor management caused Wieboldt's business to decline. . . .

2. Defendants

Wieboldt brings this action against 119 defendants. These defendants can be grouped into three non-exclusive categories: (1) controlling shareholders, officers and directors; (2) other shareholders of Wieboldt's common stock who owned and tendered more than 1,000 shares in response to the tender offer ("Schedule A shareholders"); and (3) entities which loaned money to fund the tender offer.

a. Controlling Shareholders, Officers and Directors

. . . Jerome Schottenstein [and related parties acquired a major block of Wieboldt stock in 1982] (collectively referred to as the "Schottenstein interests"). . . . [The] Schottenstein interests and [other connected parties] (collectively referred to as the "Trump interests" [not Donald—Roe]) each owned approximately 15 percent of Wieboldt's then outstanding shares and became Wieboldt's controlling shareholders.[4]

* * *

b. Schedule A Shareholders

In addition to the Schottenstein and Trump interests, Wieboldt had a number of shareholders as of December 20, 1985 who owned more than 1,000 shares of Wieboldt's common stock. [They are listed on] . . . "Schedule A." . . .

c. The LBO Lenders and Related Entities

On November 20, 1985 WSI commenced a tender offer for all outstanding shares of Wieboldt's common stock. . . . The tender offer was financed through three related financial transactions between Wieboldt and certain lenders and affiliated parties. These three transactions effected the LBO of Wieboldt.

[The plaintiffs have] included as defendants in this action four of the entities which were involved in these financial transactions [as lenders, including several banks, finance companies,] and General Electric Credit Corporation ("GECC").[5] . . .

B. THE TENDER OFFER AND RELATED TRANSACTIONS

By January, 1985 Wieboldt's financial health had declined to the point at which the company was no longer able to meet its obligations as they came due. On January 23, 1985 WSI sent a letter to Mr. Schottenstein in which WSI proposed a possible tender offer for Wieboldt common stock at $13.50 per share. The following day, Mr. Schottenstein informed Wieboldt's Board of Directors of the WSI proposal and the Board agreed to cooperate with WSI in evaluating the financial and operating records of the company. WSI proceeded to seek financing. . . .

[4] The Trump brothers, MBT Corporation, Mr. Schottenstein and the Schottenstein affiliates are collectively referred to in this opinion as "controlling shareholders."

[5] These entities are collectively referred to in this opinion as "State Street defendants."

During 1985 it became apparent to Wieboldt's Board that WSI would accomplish its tender offer by means of an LBO through which WSI would pledge substantially all of Wieboldt's assets . . . as collateral. . . .

* * *

. . . [B]y October, 1985 [the LBO lenders] had each agreed to fund WSI's tender offer, and each knew of the other's loan or credit commitments. These lenders were aware that WSI intended to use the proceeds of the financing commitments to . . . purchase tendered shares of Wieboldt stock. . . .

The Board of Directors was fully aware of the progress of WSI's negotiations. The Board understood that WSI intended to finance the tender offer by pledging a substantial portion of Wieboldt's assets to its lenders, and that WSI did not intend to use any of its own funds or the funds of its shareholders to finance the acquisition. . . .

Nevertheless, in October, 1985 the Board directed . . . Wieboldt's lawyers to work with WSI to effect the acquisition. During these negotiations, the Board learned that [one lender] would provide financing for the tender offer *only if Wieboldt would provide a statement from a nationally recognized accounting firm stating that Wieboldt was solvent and a going concern prior to the planned acquisition and would be solvent and a going concern after the acquisition.*[6] [However Wieboldt management] informed WSI that Wieboldt would only continue cooperating in the LBO if [the lender] agreed not to require this solvency certificate. [The lender] acceded to Wieboldt's demand and no solvency certificate was ever provided to [the lender] on Wieboldt's behalf.

On November 18, 1985 Wieboldt's Board of Directors voted to approve WSI's tender offer, and on November 20, 1985 WSI announced its offer to purchase Wieboldt stock for $13.50 per share.[7] By December 20, 1985 the tender offer was complete and WSI had acquired ownership of Wieboldt through its purchase of 99 percent of Wieboldt's stock at a total price of $38,462,164.00. All of the funds WSI used to purchase the tendered shares were provided by [the lenders]. After the LBO,

1. [Some of] Wieboldt's . . . property was [sold];
2. Substantially all of Wieboldt's remaining real estate holdings were subject to first or second mortgages to secure the [LBO] loans; and
3. Wieboldt's customer credit card accounts were conveyed to GECC and Wieboldt's accounts receivable were pledged to

[6] [Why would the lender so insist, even if the lender expected to get, say, good security? Could the lender's counsel have analyzed the *Gleneagles* situation carefully? What advice would counsel give to LBO lenders after *Gleneagles*?—Roe.]

[7] Approximately 1,900 shareholders held the 2,765,574 shares of Wieboldt common stock that were outstanding on that date. As a result of the offer, Mr. Schottenstein and his affiliates tendered at least 416,958 shares and received $5,628,933.00 from WSI. [The Trump interests] received $6,480,972.00 from WSI. . . .

GECC as security under the GECC accounts purchase agreement.

In addition, Wieboldt became liable to [an LBO lender] on an amended note in the amount of approximately $32.5 million. . . .

On September 24, 1986 . . . Wieboldt filed a voluntary reorganization proceeding pursuant to Chapter 11 of the Code. . . .

C. THE COMPLAINT

In its complaint, Wieboldt alleges that WSI's tender offer and the resulting LBO was a fraudulent conveyance under the federal bankruptcy statute and the Illinois fraudulent conveyance laws. Counts I . . . and V are based on Section 548(a)(1) of the Code, 11 U.S.C. § 548(a)(1). The essence of Count I is that the controlling and insider shareholders tendered their shares to WSI in response to WSI's offer with the actual intent to hinder, delay or defraud Wieboldt's unsecured creditors. . . . Likewise, Count V, which names GECC as defendant, claims that the pledging of Wieboldt's customer charge card accounts and other accounts receivable violated Section 548(a)(1).

Counts II, IV, VI, and VII are based on Section 548(a)(2). . . . Counts II and VII allege that the tender offer to Wieboldt shareholders (including the Schedule A shareholders) was a fraudulent conveyance because it and the resulting LBO "rendered Wieboldt insolvent or too thinly capitalized to continue in the business in which it was engaged. . . ." Count VI claims that the pledging of Wieboldt's accounts receivable violated Section 548(a)(2).

Count VIII alleges that each of the three transactions (the tender offer, the sale of [the] property, and the pledging of the Wieboldt accounts receivable) violated the Illinois fraudulent conveyance law, § 4. . . . The essence of the claim in Count VIII is that *Wieboldt did not receive* fair consideration for the property it conveyed and was insolvent at the time of the conveyances. In each of Counts I through VIII, Wieboldt seeks to avoid the transfer of assets made to the named defendants as a result of the LBO.

* * *

III. DISCUSSION

* * *

C. RULE 12(b)(6) MOTIONS TO DISMISS

The controlling shareholders, insider shareholders, Schedule A shareholders, and the State Street defendants move to dismiss the complaint on the grounds that Wieboldt has failed to state a claim under either the federal or the state fraudulent conveyance laws. . . .

* * *

1. Applicability of Fraudulent Conveyance Law

Both the federal Bankruptcy Code and Illinois law protect creditors from transfers of property that are intended to impair a creditor's ability to enforce its rights to payment or that deplete a debtor's assets at a time when its financial condition is precarious. Modern fraudulent conveyance law derives from the English Statute of Elizabeth enacted in 1570, the substance of which has been ... enacted in American statutes prohibiting such transactions. ...

The controlling shareholders, insider shareholders, and some of the Schedule A shareholders argue that fraudulent conveyance laws do not apply to leveraged buyouts. These defendants argue (1) that applying fraudulent conveyance laws to public tender offers effectively allows creditors to insure themselves against subsequent mismanagement of the company; (2) that applying fraudulent conveyance laws to LBO transactions and thereby rendering them void severely restricts the usefulness of LBOs and results in great unfairness; and (3) that fraudulent conveyance laws were never intended to be used to prohibit or restrict public tender offers.

Although some support exists for defendants' arguments, ... [t]he language of [the fraudulent conveyance] statutes in no way ... exclude[s] LBOs.

* * *

2. The Structure of the Transaction

Although the court finds that the fraudulent conveyance laws generally [apply,] ... certain defendants argue ... that they are protected by the literal language of Section 548 of the Code and the "good faith transferee for value" rule in Section 550.[8] They contend, initially, that they did not receive Wieboldt property during the tender offer and, secondarily, that, even if they received Wieboldt property, they tendered their shares in good faith, for value, and without the requisite knowledge and therefore cannot be held liable under Section 550.

The merit of this assertion turns on the court's interpretation of the tender offer and LBO transactions. Defendants contend that the tender offer and LBO were composed of a series of interrelated but independent transactions. They assert, for example, that the transfer of property from [the LBO lenders] to WSI and ultimately to the shareholders constituted one series of several transactions while the pledge of Wieboldt assets to [the LBO lenders] to secure the financing constituted a second series of transactions. Under this view, defendants did not receive the debtor's property during the tender offer but rather received WSI's property in exchange for their shares.

Wieboldt, on the other hand, urges the court to "collapse" the interrelated transactions into one aggregate transaction which had the

---

[8] While Section 548 defines the nature of the transactions that are avoidable by the debtor, Section 550 places limits on Section 548 by defining the kind of transferee from whom a debtor may recover transferred property. Section 550(a) permits a trustee to recover fraudulently transferred property from

1. the initial transferee;
2. the entity for whose benefit such transfer was made; or
3. an immediate or mediate transferee of such initial transferee (a "subsequent transferee").

11 U.S.C. § 550(a). Section 550(b) states that a trustee may not recover from

1. a subsequent transferee who takes the property for value, in good faith, and without knowledge of the voidability of the transfer; or
2. an immediate or mediate good faith transferee of such a transferee.

overall effect of conveying Wieboldt property to the tendering shareholders and LBO lenders. This approach requires the court to find that the persons and entities receiving the conveyance *were direct transferees* who received "an interest of the debtor in property" during the tender offer/buyout, and that WSI and any other parties to the transactions were "mere conduits" of Wieboldt's property. *If the court finds that all the transfers constituted one transaction, then defendants received property from Wieboldt and Wieboldt has stated a claim against them.*

Few courts have considered whether complicated LBO transfers should be evaluated separately or collapsed into one integrated transaction. However, . . . [s]ee United States v. Tabor Court Realty, 803 F.2d 1288 (3rd Cir. 1986), cert. denied, McClellan Realty Co. v. United States, 107 S. Ct. 3229 (1987).

* * *

[Although *Gleneagles* or *Tabor Court* did not involve] transactions which were identical to the WSI–Wieboldt buyout[, the *Gleneagles*] opinion [is] nonetheless significant. . . . Tabor Court found the LBO lender liable because it participated in the negotiations surrounding the LBO transactions and knew that the proceeds of its loan to Great American would deplete the debtor's assets to the point at which it was functionally insolvent under the fraudulent conveyance and bankruptcy laws. . . . [A] court should focus not on the formal structure of the transaction but rather on the knowledge or intent of the parties involved in the transaction.

Applying this principle to defendants' assertions, it is clear that, at least as regards the liability of the controlling shareholders, the LBO lenders, and the insider shareholders, *the LBO transfers must be collapsed into one transaction.* The complaint alleges clearly that these participants in the LBO negotiations attempted to structure the LBO with the requisite knowledge and contemplation that the full transaction, tender offer and LBO, be completed.[9] The Board and the insider shareholders knew that WSI intended to finance its acquisition of Wieboldt through an LBO and not with any of its own funds. They knew that Wieboldt was insolvent before the LBO and that the LBO would result in further encumbrance of Wieboldt's already encumbered assets. Attorneys for Schottenstein Stores apprised the Board of the fraudulent conveyance laws and suggested that they structure the LBO so as to avoid liability. Nonetheless, these shareholders recommended that Wieboldt accept the tender offer and themselves tendered their shares to WSI.

* * *

The court, however, is not willing to "collapse" the transaction in order to find that the Schedule A shareholders also received the debtor's

---

[9] Although many of the allegations in the complaint refer to the state of mind and activities of the Board of Directors, these allegations may fairly be imputed to the controlling shareholders. The controlling shareholders nominated a majority of the directors to their positions on the Board. In addition, many of the individuals who served on the Board were "insiders" to Schottenstein['s or Trump's corporations].

property in the transfer. While Wieboldt directs specific allegations of fraud against the controlling and insider shareholders and LBO lenders, Wieboldt does not allege that the Schedule A shareholders were aware that WSI's acquisition encumbered virtually all of Wieboldt's assets. Nor is there an allegation that these shareholders were aware that the consideration they received for their tendered shares was Wieboldt property. In fact, the complaint does not suggest that the Schedule A shareholders had any part in the LBO except as innocent pawns in the scheme. They were aware only that WSI made a public tender offer for shares of Wieboldt stock. Viewing the transactions from the perspective of the Schedule A shareholders and considering their knowledge and intent, therefore, the asset transfers to the LBO lenders were indeed independent of the tender offer to the Schedule A shareholders.

This conclusion is in accord with the purpose of the fraudulent conveyance laws. The drafters of the Code, while attempting to protect parties harmed by fraudulent conveyances, also intended to shield innocent recipients of fraudulently conveyed property from liability. Thus, although Subsection (a) of Section 550 permits a trustee to avoid a transfer to an initial transferee or its subsequent transferee, Subsection (b) of that Section limits recovery from a subsequent transferee by providing that a trustee may not recover fraudulently conveyed property from a subsequent transferee who takes the property in good faith, for value, and without knowledge that the original transfer was voidable.[10] Subsection (b) applies, however, only to subsequent transferees.

Similarly, the LBO lenders and the controlling and insider shareholders of Wieboldt are direct transferees of Wieboldt property. Although WSI participated in effecting the transactions, Wieboldt's complaint alleges that WSI was a corporation formed solely for the purpose of acquiring Wieboldt stock. The court can reasonably infer from the complaint, therefore, that WSI served mainly as a conduit for the exchange of assets and loan proceeds between LBO lenders and Wieboldt and for the exchange of loan proceeds and shares of stock between the LBO lenders and the insider and controlling shareholders. On the other hand, the Schedule A shareholders are not direct transferees of Wieboldt property. From their perspective, *WSI was the direct transferee of Wieboldt property and the shareholders were merely indirect transferees because WSI was an independent entity in the transaction.*[11]

In sum, the formal structure of the transaction alone cannot shield the LBO lenders or the controlling and insider shareholders from Wieboldt's fraudulent conveyance claims. These parties were aware that the consideration they received for their financing commitments or in exchange for their shares consisted of Wieboldt assets and not the assets of WSI or any other financial intermediary. The Schedule A shareholders, on the other hand, apparently unaware of the financing transactions, participated only to the extent that they exchanged their

---

[10] Section 550(b) also prohibits a trustee from recovering such property from a good faith transferee of such a transferee.

[11] [That is, don't collapse.—Roe.]

shares for funds from WSI. Therefore, based on the allegations in the complaint, the court concludes that:

1. the motions to dismiss filed by the LBO lenders, insider shareholders, and controlling shareholders are denied at this point because these parties received Wieboldt property through a series of integrated LBO transactions; and

2. the Schedule A shareholders' motions to dismiss are granted because these defendants did not receive Wieboldt property through the separate exchange of shares for cash.

* * *

IV. CONCLUSION

The Schedule A shareholder defendants' motions to dismiss Count VIII against them are GRANTED. The other defendants' motions to dismiss the remaining counts of the complaint are DENIED.

¶ 2206: Questions on *Wieboldt*

1. What is the structure of Wieboldt's LBO? In a typical LBO the organizers form a shell corporation, which borrows money to acquire a majority of the stock of the target corporation. The assets and operations are in the target. Once the shell acquires a majority of the target's stock, the LBO organizers merge the target with the shell, and thereby eliminate the few remaining minority stockholders (by buying up their stock). The merged entity then has both the loan obligation (from the original shell) and the assets (from the original target). The merged entity then often gives the assets as security to the LBO lenders. (The *Wieboldt* opinion doesn't state explicitly whether the merger occurred. Perhaps because the tender offer was unusually successful, with WSI getting 99% of Wieboldt's stock, the parties thought the merger not to be immediately necessary. Perhaps there was a corporate impediment to merger.)

   A key part of the LBO occurs after the usual merger, when the operating firm pledges its assets to the lender. Oftentimes the lenders, at the time they originally make the loan to the acquiring company, make it an event of default for the borrowing firm not to get control of the assets and give security interests and mortgages within a specified period of time.

   This seems to have roughly been the LBO transactional structure in *Wieboldt* (except that the formal merger seems not to have occurred; but this doesn't have any impact on the decision or the transaction).

2. The defendant stockholders claim that they never received any Wieboldt property. They didn't directly. They received a check from WSI. How then can the court conclude that the stockholders received Wieboldt property?

3. The court first talks about collapsing the entire transaction, then backs off. What in the statute makes the court wary of concluding that the public stockholders (the Schedule A stockholders, as the court calls them) took property from Wieboldt directly, in the collapsed transaction? The court says that the public stockholders on-

ly took their buyout payment indirectly. That is, the public stockholders were, in the court's view, immediate transferees of WSI, the "shell," but not of Wieboldt, the "target"? See § 550 (a)–(b):

---

§ 550. Liability of transferee of avoided transfer

(a) . . . the trustee may recover, for the benefit of the estate, the property transferred, or, if the court so orders, the value of such property, from—

(1) the initial transferee of such transfer or the entity for whose benefit such transfer was made; or

(2) any immediate or mediate transferee of such initial transferee.

(b) The trustee may not recover under section (a)(2) of this section from—

(1) a transferee that takes for value, including satisfaction or securing of a present or antecedent debt, in good faith, and without knowledge of the voidability of the transfer avoided; or

(2) any immediate or mediate good faith transferee of such transferee.

---

4. How can the inside stockholders have taken directly from Wieboldt at all? Their cash came from WSI, not Wieboldt, didn't it? True, the transaction could be collapsed: the court could say that the last step, when Wieboldt transferred security to the lenders was "really" the first step, because the lenders would never have lent had they not been reasonably sure of getting the security. So the assets were "really" dividended up to WSI and pledged to the lenders. Then the lenders turned the assets (of Wieboldt) into cash, which WSI used to buy the stock. Therefore, the stockholders are indirect recipients of Wieboldt's property; if the transaction were collapsed, they could be viewed as direct recipients of Wieboldt's property.

5. But if the transaction is collapsed, so that the court concludes that the inside stockholders got their check directly from Wieboldt, how can the court simultaneously say that the public stockholders did not also get *their* check directly from Wieboldt? One can understand the policy basis why the court reaches this result, but what is the analytic, statutory basis? Is the court in the end *not* collapsing the LBO into a single transaction?

6. Could the court have analyzed the setting more cleanly by concluding that *both public and nonpublic stockholders* only took *indirectly* from Wieboldt, through WSI? Accordingly, they were *both* subsequent transferees under § 550(a)(2). That is, the LBO is *not* fully collapsed. All the stockholders are subsequent transferees. Innocent public stockholders could avail themselves of the good faith, lack of knowledge defense of § 550(b)(1), because they knew nothing. But the insider stockholders could not, because they knew that Wieboldt would be rendered insolvent.

7. But, to go over the transaction once more, how could the stockholders be seen as indirect transferees from Wieboldt? To see how they could plausibly be indirect transferees, stay focused on the assets of Wieboldt. No LBO would happen, the Wieboldt trustee might have argued, unless Wieboldt's assets were ultimately transferred into the hands of the shareholders. How did that happen, structurally? The assets were given to WSI. That was a fraudulent transfer. The bank lenders then got the assets, and then they turned back cash to WSI. The bank lenders were subsequent transferees of WSI, the initial transferee. WSI used the cash (from the asset pledge) to buy stock from Wieboldt's stockholders. All stockholders were subsequent transferees of the original asset transfer.

   Or, the *ordering* of the steps is arbitrary. Money must flow in before any money can flow out, so the *last functional* step is the shareholder buyout.

   In this uniform reordering, all shareholders, both insiders and public, were subsequent transferees. The outside, public stockholders can avail themselves of the good faith defense in § 550(b)(1): they are transferees who took "for value, . . . , in good faith, and without knowledge of the voidability of the transfer. . . ." The inside stockholders, with knowledge, cannot use § 550(b)(1) to defend themselves.

D. THE SETTLEMENT PAYMENT SAFE HARBOR IN LBOs

¶ 2207: Kaiser Steel Corp. v. Charles Schwab: § 546(e).

Section 546(e) of the Bankruptcy Code states that "notwithstanding sections 544, 545, 547, 548(a)(1)(B), and 548(b)" a debtor may not avoid a transfer that is "a settlement payment, as defined in section 101 or 741 of this title, made by or to a stock broker, financial institution . . . or securities clearing agency, that is made before the commencement of the case, except under section 548(a)(1)[.]"

Section 741(8) defines a settlement payment as "a preliminary settlement payment, a partial settlement payment, an interim settlement payment, a settlement payment on account, a final settlement payment, or any other similar payment commonly used in the securities trade." That is, a settlement payment is a settlement payment is a settlement payment.

And securities traders know one when they see one. Clear?

Kaiser Steel went through an LBO in 1983. Kaiser purchased its own stock from customers of Charles Schwab & Co., a securities broker. Schwab held Kaiser stock in its own name (i.e., the stock was labeled as "Schwab's" stock). Schwab deposited the stock with a clearinghouse—the organization that handles the mechanics of purchases and sales, but Schwab held the stock for the benefit of its own customers. Schwab instructed the clearinghouse to send to Kaiser the Kaiser securities that the clearinghouse held for Schwab (and which Schwab held for its customers). A few days later Schwab received $450,000 from Kaiser and Schwab credited its customers with those monies for the sale of their Kaiser stock.

Kaiser's post-LBO business did poorly and Kaiser went bankrupt in 1987. The debtor brought a fraudulent conveyance action, seeking to recover payments made to stockholders, including Schwab. Schwab argued, first, that it was a "mere conduit" rather than a transferee and thus was not liable due to § 550(a). Second, it argued that § 546(e) exempted the LBO payments from constructive fraudulent conveyance liability, because the payments were settlement payments under § 546(e).

In Kaiser Steel Corp. v. Charles Schwab & Co., 913 F.2d 846 (10th Cir. 1990), the Tenth Circuit held that the payments to Schwab were settlement payments, exempt from fraudulent conveyance liability under § 546(e).

Kaiser Steel Corp. v. Charles Schwab & Co., 913 F.2d 846 (10th Cir. 1990)

Stephen H. Anderson, Circuit Judge.

Debtor-in-possession Kaiser Steel . . . , appeals from the district court's reversal of the bankruptcy court's order denying defendant Charles Schwab & Company, Inc. ("Schwab") summary judgment. We affirm.

In late 1983, the board of directors of Kaiser Steel, a publicly-traded corporation, agreed to a leveraged buyout ("LBO") by a group of outside investors ("the acquisition group"). Under the plan, a new entity owned by the acquisition group would purchase all outstanding Kaiser Steel common stock and merge with Kaiser Steel. Each share of Kaiser Steel common stock would be converted into the right to receive twenty-two dollars and two shares of preferred stock in the surviving entity. The money, which amounted to $162 million, was to come from Kaiser Steel's cash reserves and a $100 million loan from Citibank secured by the corporation's assets.

The shareholders approved the LBO on January 18, 1984. As of the effective date of the merger, February 29, 1984, holders of Kaiser Steel common stock were required to tender their shares to Kaiser's disbursing agent, Bank of America, which distributed the cash and preferred stock.

Among the holders of Kaiser Steel common stock were customers of Schwab, a securities broker. Most of the certificates were in the possession of the Depository Trust Company ("DTC"), a securities clearinghouse. DTC tendered the shares to Bank of America, and received the cash and preferred stock in the surviving entity. DTC transferred the money to Schwab through the National Securities Clearing Corporation, which sponsors Schwab's participation in DTC. . . . Schwab credited its customers' accounts within a few days of receiving the funds. . . .

In 1987, Kaiser filed for bankruptcy. The debtor-in-possession commenced this fraudulent conveyance action against a number of defendants, seeking to avoid the LBO and recover the $162 million. Schwab moved for summary judgment on two grounds: that it was not liable because it was a "mere conduit" rather than a transferee, see 11 U.S.C. § 550(a), and that the LBO payments were exempt from avoidance as settlement payments, see 11 U.S.C. § 546(e).

> A trustee or debtor-in-possession may not avoid
>
> a transfer that is . . . a settlement payment, as defined in section 741(8) of this title, made by or to a commodity broker, forward contract merchant, stockbroker, financial institution or securities clearing agency, that is made before the commencement of the case, except under section 548(a)(1) of this title."

11 U.S.C. § 546(e). Section 741(8) defines settlement payment as "a preliminary settlement payment, an interim settlement payment, a settlement payment on account, a final settlement payment, or any other similar payment commonly used in the securities trade." 11 U.S.C. § 741(8). We agree with the district court that the transfer of the consideration in the LBO was a settlement payment.

Such an interpretation "is consistent with the legislative intent behind § 546 to protect the nation's financial markets from the instability caused by the reversal of settled securities transactions." Kaiser Steel Resources, Inc. v. Jacobs, 110 B.R. at 522.

Section 546 was first enacted in 1978, and applied only to commodities markets. "Settlement payment" was not defined. . . .

In 1982, []Congress . . . extend[ed the safe harbor to securities market transactions.] . . . The protection was expanded beyond the ordinary course of business to include . . . settlement payments to and from brokers, clearing organizations, and financial institutions. Again, Congress's purpose was "to minimize the displacement caused in the commodities and securities markets in the event of a major bankruptcy affecting those industries." [H.R. Rep. No. 420, 97th Cong., 2d Sess. 1 (1982)], reprinted in 1982 U.S. Code Cong. & Admin. News at 583. The danger of a "ripple effect," id., on the entire market is at least as inherent in the avoidance of an LBO as it is in the avoidance of a routine stock sale.

Finally, interpreting "settlement payment" to include the transfer of consideration in an LBO is consistent with the way "settlement" is defined in the securities industry. Settlement is "the completion of a securities transaction." A. Pessin & J. Ross, Words of Wall Street: 2000 Investment Terms Defined 227 (1983); . . . New York Stock Exchange, Language of Investing Glossary 30 (1981) ("conclusion of a securities transaction when a customer pays a broker/dealer for securities purchased or delivers securities sold and receives from the broker the proceeds of a sale"); D. Scott, Wall Street Words 320 (1988) ("transfer of the security (for the seller) or cash (for the buyer) in order to complete a security transaction").[12] The Securities and Exchange Commission has taken the position before this court that the consummation of an LBO is a "settlement payment" exempted from avoidance by section 546(e).

Kaiser's position that section 546(e) was only intended to insulate from avoidance routine securities transactions is not without merit.

[12] Some sources limit the concept of "settlement" to the consummation of routine securities transactions. . . .

Neither LBOs nor other exceptional transactions were even mentioned in any of the discussions of the securities industry in the reports, debates, and hearings on the bill. See Bankruptcy of Commodity and Securities Brokers: Hearings Before the Subcomm. on Monopolies and Commercial Law of the House Comm. on the Judiciary, 97th Cong., 1st Sess. 238-349 (1981). However, because of the variety and scope of different securities transactions, and the absence of any restrictions in sections 546(e) and 741(8), it would be an act of judicial legislation to establish such a limitation.

. . . The LBO was a securities transaction. The transfer of money and preferred stock was the settlement of that transaction. Therefore, the transfers to Schwab were exempt from avoidance under section 546(e) as "settlement payment[s] ... to a ... stockbroker."

The judgment of the district court is AFFIRMED.

Consider Schwab's first argument—namely that the securities system transfers had Schwab and the other financial institutions involved acting as mere conduits. Doesn't this argument make sense? That is, Schwab and the other brokers do not take beneficial ownership of the security. They are delivery people. See the figures below.

Is the "transfer" to Schwab a "transfer" in terms of the statute? If it's not a "transfer," shouldn't that conclusion have ended the case? Section 101(54) says that "[t]he term 'transfer' means . . . each mode, direct or indirect, absolute or conditional, voluntary or involuntary, of disposing of or parting with . . . property . . . ." Is it plausible that Schwab didn't receive property other than as an agent of its customers?

If the case doesn't end there, with Schwab a mere conduit for the actual transfer but not an actual transferee, then what do some of the brokers have to fear? See § 550 on the exposure of the initial transferee. Presumably the initial transferee is the entity receiving the cash first from Kaiser.

Wieboldt distinguished controlling shareholders from distant shareholders. If the securities system were just a conduit to the initial transferees, what difference, if any, would there be between the exposure of individual shareholders and that of controlling shareholders? Wouldn't all securities sellers in the LBO transaction then be initial transferees of the buyer's cash? Consequence for fraudulent conveyance exposure?

* * *

Another interpretation: When Kaiser buys from a Schwab customer, do two transactions occur simultaneously? One is Kaiser's purchase from Schwab's customers of their stock. Another is the transfer of the stock through the securities clearing system. The second involve securities settlement payments. The second is settling the first transaction, making it happen. Compare the first figure below with the subsequent two figures.

LBO of Roe Industries:
The Baseline Transfer

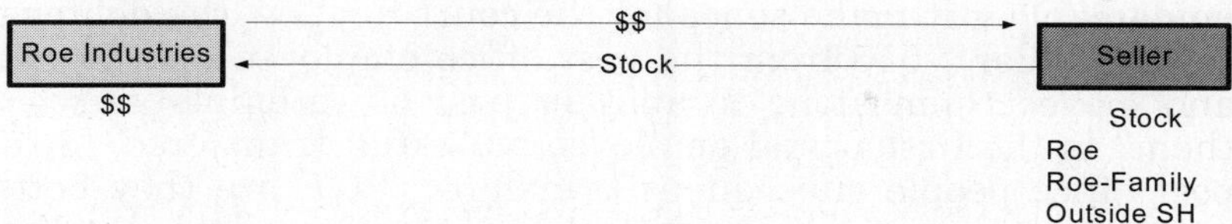

LBO of Roe Industries:
Stock Transfers Settled Through the Securities Clearing System

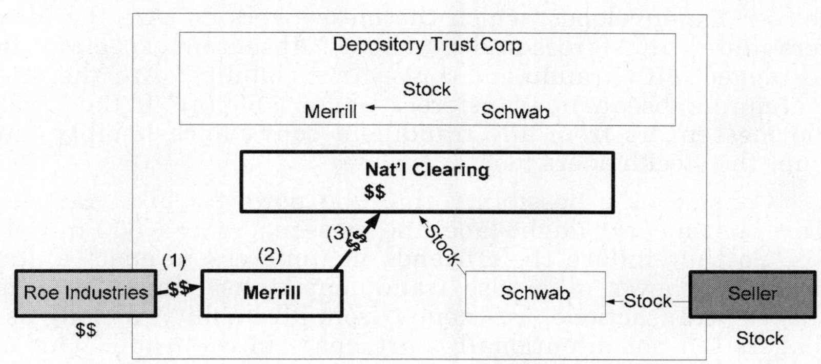

LBO of Roe Industries, Buyout Independent of Purchase Channels

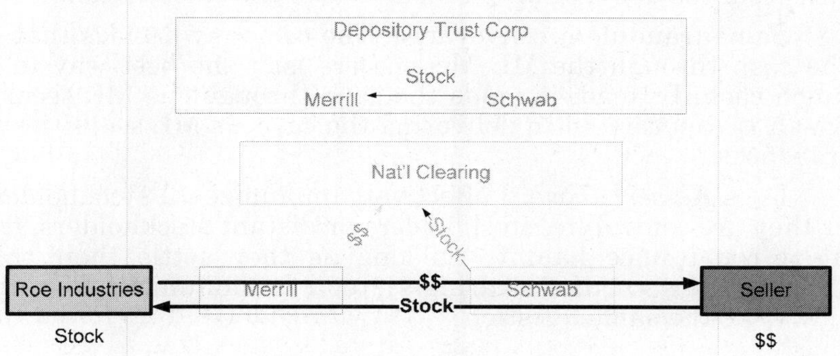

Consider the following scenarios:

A fraudulent conveyance occurs. The company sends the fraudulently conveyed funds via checks in the mail to the company's shareholders. Does it make sense for the court to allow the debtor to seek recovery under § 550 from the post office employee who took the checks and moved them along to another post office employee who delivered them? Is the first postal employee an initial transferee? Are the other post office people subsequent transferees? Or, are they better seen as mere conduits of the cash, with the real transaction being that between the company and its shareholders?

Or, a fraudulent conveyance occurs. The company pays the stockholders by putting cash into several envelopes for delivery to the shareholders. It writes the name and address of the relevant stockholder on each envelope and contracts with the ML bicycle messenger service to deliver the envelopes, which the messengers do. Are the bike messengers initial transferees under § 550(a)? Absent an exception should they be tagged with fraudulent conveyance liability? Are the stockholders therefore subsequent transferees under § 550(a)? If the Code exempts the messengers from any fraudulent conveyance liability, must it exempt the stockholders too?

Consider the possibility that the powerful bike messenger lobby fears that a court might label the messengers as § 550 initial transferees. So they induce their friends in Congress to enact a statute that says: "Whenever otherwise fraudulent transactions occur, messenger delivery transactions are exempt from all liability, as long as the messengers did not intentionally participate in the fraud." One court says that this means that a transfer of stock or cash to a messenger is exempt (of course) *and that a transfer from a messenger of stock or cash to the ultimate beneficial recipient is also exempt.* But, the court says, the transfer from buyer to seller, and vice versa, is not exempt. That buyer-to-seller transfer set is the core transfer from buyer to seller; it's separate from the delivery mechanism (which the statute exempts).

Same fraudulent conveyance. The company decides that delivering the cash through the ML Messengers isn't the best way to deliver so much cash. Instead, it sends the cash through the ML securities firm, which is experienced in delivering the cash. Is ML securities the initial transferee?

Does *Kaiser*, above, I effectively immunize all stockholders, whether they are controlling stockholders or distant stockholders, from fraudulent conveyance liability as long as they settle their transactions through the securities clearing system? It immunizes Schwab, yes, but that's not the same question.

In re Kaiser Steel, 952 F.2d 1230 (10th Cir. 1991)

Before HOLLOWAY, ANDERSON and BRORBY, Circuit Judges.

STEPHEN H. ANDERSON, Circuit Judge.

The question presented in this appeal is whether consideration paid to shareholders for their stock in connection with a leveraged buy out is exempt from the avoiding powers of a trustee under section 546(e) of the Bankruptcy Code, as "settlement payments" made "by or to a ... stockbroker, financial institution, or securities clearing agency." 11 U.S.C. § 546(e). In its order granting defendants' motion for summary judgment, the district court held that such payments fall within the exemption found in section 546(e). We agree and, therefore, affirm the judgment of the district court.

I. INTRODUCTION

This case involves a leveraged buy out gone bad. Making use of the modern counterpart of a centuries-old statute, Kaiser Steel Resources, Inc. ("Kaiser"), formerly known as Kaiser Steel Corporation ("Kaiser Steel"), seeks in the underlying action to retrieve amounts paid out to former Kaiser Steel shareholders in connection with a leveraged buy out of the company in 1984 (the "LBO"). Kaiser makes the relatively novel yet increasingly popular claim that these payments constitute a fraudulent conveyance. The current battle is much more narrow, however. It surrounds the construction of a Bankruptcy Code (the "Code") exemption that prohibits the trustee from avoiding "settlement payments" made by or to stockbrokers, financial institutions, and clearing agencies. *See* 11 U.S.C. § 546(e). Appellees, joined by the Securities and Exchange Commission ("SEC"), maintain that the section 546(e) exemption encompasses amounts paid to the shareholders in the LBO and accordingly prevents Kaiser from unwinding the transaction.

* * *

B. *History of the Case.*

In 1987, Kaiser filed a voluntary reorganization proceeding under Chapter 11 of the Code. Kaiser then commenced this fraudulent conveyance action against a number of defendants, seeking to avoid the LBO and recover the $162 million. In what amounted to a test case, Charles Schwab & Co. ("Schwab"), a broker eventually named in the action, moved for summary judgment on the grounds that it was not liable because it was a "mere conduit" rather than a transferee, *see* 11 U.S.C. § 550(a). The argument was also made by intervening defendants that the LBO payments were exempt from avoidance as settlement payments, *see* 11 U.S.C. § 546(e). Schwab's only role in the transaction was to deliver its customers' Kaiser Steel shares for payment and transfer the payments it received back to the accounts of its customers.

On appeal, . . . we held that the payments to Schwab were settlement payments exempt from recovery under section 546(e). *Kaiser Steel Corp. v. Charles Schwab & Co.,* 913 F.2d 846 (10th Cir. 1990). . . . [W]e did not decide whether Schwab was a "mere conduit" rather than a transferee. *Id.* at 848.

. . . [O]ther financial intermediaries moved for summary judgment on the basis of the section 546(e) settlement payment exemption. The district court granted summary judgment dismissing all claims asserted against the financial intermediaries and *sua sponte* dismissed the claims asserted against all other defendants, *including beneficial shareholders of Kaiser Steel stock and brokers trading on their own account.* In light of our decision in *Schwab,* Kaiser has abandoned all claims against the appellees in this case insofar as they acted in conduit/financial intermediary capacities. Therefore, all appellees remaining before us are shareholders or brokers that beneficially owned the Kaiser Steel shares tendered in connection with the LBO.

II. DISCUSSION

We now must decide whether our holding in *Schwab*—that Code section 546(e) protected payments made to the financial intermediaries—should be extended to protect payments made to the beneficial shareholders.

Section 546(e) provides as follows:

> the trustee may not avoid a transfer that is a margin payment, as defined in section 101[(38)], 741(5) or 761(15) of this title, or settlement payment, as defined in section 101[(39)] or 741(8) of this title, made by or to a commodity broker, forward contract merchant, stockbroker, financial institution, or securities clearing agency. . . .

11 U.S.C. § 546(e) . . .

Kaiser . . . insists that even if the payments are settlement payments, payments made "by or to" one of the enumerated entities are protected under section 546(e) *only* to the extent the recipient is a participant in the clearance and settlement system (i.e., a stockbroker, financial institution, clearing agency, or some other participant). Settlement payments received by an "equity security holder," according to Kaiser, are not protected.

A. *Settlement Payments.*

We cannot accept Kaiser's argument that the payments of LBO consideration to the beneficial shareholders are not settlement payments within the meaning of the statute. Our interpretation, as always, begins with the language of the statute itself. Section 546(e) refers to section 741(8) for the definition of "settlement payment." Section 741(8), in turn, defines "settlement payment" as a "preliminary settlement payment, a partial settlement payment, an interim settlement payment, a settlement payment on account, a final settlement payment, or *any other similar payment commonly used in the securities trade.*" 11 U.S.C. § 741(8) (emphasis added).

* * *

In applying this provision, our task is to apply the term "settlement payment" according to its plain meaning. ("The exceptions to our obligation to interpret a statute according to its plain language are few and far between." [Authority omitted, with the] plain language conclusive unless it produces a result "demonstrably at odds with the intention of its drafters"[]. However, since even the plain meaning of a term may depend on the context within which it is given, we must interpret the term "settlement payment" as it is plainly understood within the securities industry.

With respect to the routine purchase and sale of a security, there are at least two opportunities for "settlement." The first ("street-side settlement") takes place between the brokers and the clearing agency during the process of clearance and settlement. The brokers submit their transactions which are matched and compared. Confirmed contracts are submitted to the clearing agency's accounting functions, and the obligations created under the separate trades are netted to arrive at each clearing member's "settlement obligations." On the "settlement date" (normally five days after the trade date) the brokers and the clearing agency, which has interposed itself between the selling broker and the buying broker, will deliver securities and receive payment. "Settlement payments" are those payments made in discharge of a party's settlement obligations. . . .

In addition, a "customer-side settlement" also occurs between the broker and its customer. Logically, the term "settlement payment" may also be used to describe payments made to settle a customer's account with its broker. [Citations omitted.]

. . . Kaiser argues that the term "settlement payment" when applied to shareholders *only* applies to such routine securities transactions, not an extraordinary securities transaction like the leveraged buy out. For example, it notes that definitions used in *Schwab* to support the broad notion that "settlement" is "the completion of a securities transaction," 913 F.2d at 849, in fact refer to securities trades. . . .

* * *

Given the wide scope and variety of securities transactions, we will not interpret the term "settlement payment" so narrowly as to exclude the exchange of stock for consideration in an LBO. As the appellees and the SEC have urged, there is no reason to narrow the plain concept of "settlement" to a single type of securities transaction.

Consequently, those shareholders who tendered their shares one day after the LBO and received the LBO consideration are treated just the same under the Code as shareholders who sold their shares in the market one day prior to the LBO and received a settlement payment reflecting the market value of the LBO consideration. Neither type of investor will be forced to disgorge the payments several years later.

* * *

Kaiser apparently does not deny that these transfers were in fact made to each beneficial shareholder, either by the shareholder's stockbroker, a clearing agency, or a financial institution. Instead, relying on the legislative history and the exclusion of the word "equity security holder" among the parties listed in section 546(e) [which lists stockbrokers and other securities-handling institutions], it urges that we must interpret the . . . language in a way that only protects payments received by brokers (except those trading on their own account), financial institutions and clearing agencies, or other participants in the clearance and settlement process [and not the ultimate beneficial owner of the security]. Whether or not this formulation accurately reflects Congress' "intent", *and there is good reason to believe that it does not,* Kaiser has given us no reason to replace the unambiguous language of the provision with clues garnered from the legislative history. . . .

* * *

Accordingly, for the reasons given above, the judgment of the district court is AFFIRMED.

Kaiser II's applying § 546 to the ultimate stockholder reverses the *Wieboldt* dichotomy—saving distant stockholders but exposing controlling stockholders who engineered the LBO transaction. All stockholders participate in what the Kaiser court concludes are securities settlements.

Would one advise the controlling stockholders in Wieboldt, when engineering their next transaction to settle their buyout, even of their own, controlling stock, through a broker? See *QSI*, next.

Notice, by the way, the contrast between the potential solicitude for distant stockholders in *Kaiser II* and the extent of the solicitude elsewhere in statute. The court evinces a desire, derived it says from the statute, to protect securities markets. But does the statute reflect the same intense desire to protect securities markets in its § 510(b) subordination rule? Would a Congress that was consistently respectful of, and deferential to, securities markets have written both § 510(b) and § 546(e)? Presumably creditors wrote § 510(b) and the securities industry wrote § 546(e).

The 11th Circuit seemed unsettled by the *Kaiser II* result, holding in 1996 that payments made to the bought-out company's one-time shareholders were *not* protected by § 546(e)'s securities settlement exception. The court said that even if near-final payment in the LBO was accomplished via settlement checks "made by or to a . . . stockbroker, financial institution . . . or securities clearing agency" (this is the language of § 546), the purpose of § 546 was to protect the system of settling securities transactions, by exempting the intermediary institution from fraudulent conveyance liability; its purpose was not to exempt stockholders from fraudulent conveyance liability. "[T]he bank here was nothing more than an intermediary or conduit. Funds were deposited with the bank and when the bank received the shares from the selling shareholders, it sent funds to them in exchange. The bank never acquired a beneficial interest in either the funds or the shares." Munford, Inc. v. Valuation Research Corp., 98 F.3d 604 (11th Cir. 1996). Several bankruptcy courts were reluctant to follow the *Kaiser* result, for reasons similar to those stated in *Munford*.

However, since the *Munford* 1996 decision, the Second, Third, Sixth, and Eighth Circuits have not followed *Munford*. The Sixth Circuit extended Kaiser's domain to settlements in buyouts of private companies, if the buyout was settled through a stockbroker. QSI Holdings, Inc. v. Alford, 571 F.3d 545 (6th Cir. 2009).

QSI v. Dennis E. Alford, et al., 571 F.3d 545 (6th Cir. 2009)

Alan E. Norris, Circuit Judge.

In this appeal, we must determine whether § 546(e) of the Bankruptcy Code applies to privately traded securities. If that is indeed the case, then the settlement payments made to defendant shareholders are exempt from avoidance. This is an issue of first impression in this circuit and we now hold . . . that § 546(e) is not limited to publicly traded securities but also extends to transactions, such as the leveraged buyout at issue here, involving privately held securities.

I.

* * *

Because the facts are not in dispute, we rely upon the bankruptcy court's recitation to set the stage for our discussion:

> This adversary proceeding arises from the 1999 leveraged buyout ("LBO") of the Debtor, Quality Stores, Inc. ("Quality"). The Plaintiffs, QSI Holdings, Inc. and Quality, acting through their chief litigation officer (collectively, the "Plaintiffs"), seek to avoid payments made to approximately 170 shareholders of Quality (the "Defendants") resulting from the LBO. . . .
>
> . . .
>
> . . . Quality was a privately held corporation that operated a chain of retail stores specializing in agricultural and related products. In 1999, Quality and certain of Quality's principal shareholders entered into a merger agreement with Central Tractor Farm and Country, Inc. ("Central Tractor") and its parent company, CT Holdings, Inc. (collectively the "CT Parties"). Pursuant to the agreement, Quality was to merge with and into Central Tractor, with the surviving entity changing its name to Quality Stores, Inc. The agreement also called for Quality's shareholders to be paid, in cash or stock, for their respective equity interests. The assets of both Quality and Central Tractor were pledged as collateral for the loan that was obtained and partially utilized to pay the Quality shareholders.
>
> The total purchase price for the LBO was approximately $208 million. Of this amount, Quality's shareholders were to receive $111.5 million in cash with $91.8 million of stock in CT Holdings, Inc. Central Tractor also agreed to assume and pay $42.1 million of Quality's existing indebtedness.
>
> . . . To effectuate the securities transaction contemplated by the LBO, the CT Parties made a $111.5 cash payment to their exchange agent, HSBC Bank USA ("HSBC Bank"). HSBC Bank collected the shares of Quality stock from individual shareholders. It then transferred the securities to the CT Parties and distributed the cash, or shares in CT Holdings, Inc., to the individual shareholders.

* * *

> As a result of the merger, Quality incurred substantial integration costs. The merged company also implemented a costly expansion plan which aggressively contemplated the opening of twenty-five to fifty new stores each year. These business decisions, and others, contributed to continuing financial difficulties which eventually led a group of petitioning creditors to file an involuntary bankruptcy petition against Quality during October 2001. In response, before an order for relief was entered, Quality filed a voluntary petition under chapter 11 on November 1, 2001.
>
> The Plaintiffs filed this fraudulent conveyance action on October 31, 2003. The complaint, as amended, alleges that the Defendants gave less than reasonably equivalent value when they tendered their Quality stock for cash as part of the LBO. The complaint further alleges that the LBO left Quality with unreasonably small capital and caused it to incur debts beyond its ability to pay. The Plaintiffs seek to avoid and recover the LBO transfers as constructively fraudulent conveyances pursuant to 11 U.S.C. § 544, § 550, and the Michigan Uniform Fraudulent Transfer Act, Mich. Comp. Laws Ann. §§ 566.31 et seq. . . .

In re Quality Stores, Inc., 355 B.R. 629, 631–32 (Bankr. W.D. Mich. 2006) (footnote omitted).

II.

A. Statutes at Issue

Section 546(e) provides. . . .

Section 741(8), in turn, defines "settlement payment" as "a preliminary settlement payment, a partial settlement payment, an interim settlement payment, a settlement payment on account, a final settlement payment, or any other similar payment commonly used in the securities trade." 11 U.S.C. § 741(8).

B. Did the LBO at Issue Involve a Settlement Payment as Defined by § 546(e)?

Plaintiffs frame the central issue on appeal as "whether payments made to purchase non-public securities in a leveraged buyout can be exempted from avoidance pursuant to section 546(e) of the Bankruptcy Code by merely funneling [them through] a financial institution." In their view, Congress intended that § 546(e) "insulate the nation's public securities markets from the adverse effects of a bankruptcy, so as not to cause a ripple effect in such markets by unwinding settled securities transactions."

When construing a statute we look first to its text. Where that language is plain, "the sole function of the courts—at least where the disposition required by the text is not absurd—is to enforce it according to its terms." [Citations omitted.]

Numerous courts, including the courts below, have acknowledged that the definition of "settlement payment" set out in § 741(8) is somewhat "circular." Nonetheless, courts have recognized that the definition is "extremely broad."

With this in mind, we turn to the definition of "settlement payment." For the purposes of this appeal, the critical phrase in the definition is the final one: the payment must be one "commonly used in the securities trade." 11 U.S.C. § 741(8). . . .

. . . *Kaiser Steel*[, the prior precedent most on point,] involved publicly traded securities. The question posed here is whether its logic extends to privately traded securities. In a case involving facts similar to ours, the Eighth Circuit recently held that it does. Contemporary Indus. Corp., 564 F.3d at 986 ("Nothing in the relevant statutory language suggests Congress intended to exclude these payments from the statutory definition of 'settlement payment' simply because the stock at issue was privately held"). The court construed the phrase "commonly used in the securities trade" as "a catchall phrase intended to underscore the breadth of the § 546(e) exemption." Id.

We agree. While, like the Eighth Circuit, we recognize that other courts have reached a different conclusion, those courts stressed that Congress intended to protect publicly traded securities from market volatility caused by bankruptcy by means of § 546(e). See, e.g., In re Norstan Apparel Shops, Inc., 367 B.R. 68, 76 (Bankr. E.D.N.Y. 2007). . . .

Accordingly, we hold that nothing in the text of § 546(e) precludes its application to settlement payments involving privately held securities.

* * *

III.

The judgment is affirmed.

The *QSI* and *Kaiser* courts seem to be looking at the words of the statute. But, if plain meaning was driving the *QSI* court, one must ask how plain the meaning is. First, the words refer to securities market transactions, not explicitly the buyback by a company of its own stock. If the buyout company bought stock directly from the customer, and not through a financial institution, like Schwab or HSBC, § 546(e) wouldn't be in play. Is it possible that the statute's words do not take the beneficial transaction out from fraudulent conveyance law but do take out the delivery system?

Second, if the meaning is plain to the *QSI* and *Kaiser* courts, is it equally plain to the *Munford* court? Even if the *QSI* court felt sure of itself, should it have hesitated if another circuit court read the statute differently? If good lawyers and good judges read the words differently from the *QSI* judges, perhaps the meaning isn't so plain. Indeed, most bankruptcy courts interpreted § 546(e) differently than did *Kaiser* and *QSI*, some probably due to their policy preferences and some due to their reading of the Code. Samir D. Parikh, *Saving Fraudulent Transfer Law*, 86 American Bankruptcy Law Journal 305 (2012).

Nevertheless, even if the current interpretations of 546(e) are questionable when they exempt the ultimate beneficial owner–seller from fraudulent conveyance liability, five of the six circuits that opined on the subject pointed in the same, plain meaning interpretive direction. Hence, the trend is clear and change would come from Congress or the Supreme Court.

Consider this proposal to Congress:

NATIONAL BANKRUPTCY CONFERENCE

A Voluntary Organization Composed of Persons Interested in the Improvement of the Bankruptcy Code and Its Administration

March 15, 2010

The Honorable John Conyers, Jr.
Committee on the Judiciary
United States House of Representatives
Washington, DC 20515

Re: Proposed Amendments to the Bankruptcy Code
Concerning Exemptions for Financial Contracts

Dear Mr. Chairman:

The National Bankruptcy Conference (the "Conference") is writing to you to propose amendments to the Bankruptcy Code concerning the current exemptions in the Bankruptcy Code for financial contracts. As you may know, following amendments made to the Bankruptcy Code in 2005 and 2006, there has been a significant concern raised by bankruptcy professionals, academicians and others as to whether the current exemptions for financial contracts contained in the Bankruptcy Code are unnecessarily broad. The proposals made by the Conference in this letter would narrow the exemptions for the reasons explained below.

* * *

II. Settlement Payments

Bankruptcy Code § 546(e) was designed to protect prepetition transfers under securities contracts from avoidance as preferential transfers or fraudulent transfers. For example, . . . § 546(e) protects intermediaries in the national securities clearance and payment process from avoidance exposure with respect to the transfers for which they act as intermediaries.

There has been disagreement among the courts as to the scope of the § 546(e) protection with respect to payments to shareholders in connection with leveraged buyouts and similar transactions. Absent § 546(e), shareholders who received payouts for their stock in connection with a leveraged buyout that rendered the target company insolvent may be vulnerable to recovery of their payouts as constructive fraudulent transfers by the target company's bankruptcy estate. The recovered amounts would be available to repay the target company's unpaid creditors. Most (but not all) courts have interpreted § 546(e) sufficiently broadly as to immunize shareholders from such recoveries if they received their payouts through the national securities clearance or payment system or even merely from a bank, even though no securities contract was implicated and they are not themselves securities or payment intermediaries. The Conference believes that this result is unfair and unnecessary to protect the securities markets.

Attached hereto as Exhibit B is a draft of the suggested amendments to §§ 546 and 550 of the Bankruptcy Code to permit recourse to the beneficial holder of a security on which a settlement payment is made if the settlement payment otherwise constitutes a constructive fraudulent transfer. The proposed amendments would not affect the exemptions under those sections currently available to banks, brokers and other intermediaries who are not the beneficial holder of the security.

Yours sincerely,

Edwin E. Smith

Chair, Committee on Capital Markets

EXHIBIT B

Amend Section 546(e) as follows:

(e) Notwithstanding sections 544, 545, 547, 548(a)(l)(B), and 548(b) of this title, the trustee may not avoid a transfer that is a ... settlement payment, as defined in section 101 or 741 of this title, made by or to (or for the benefit of) a commodity broker, forward contract merchant, stockbroker, financial institution, financial participant, or securities clearing agency, ... that is made before the commencement of the case, except

(1) a transfer that is otherwise avoidable under section 548(a)(l)(A) of this title; or

(2) a transfer that is otherwise avoidable under section 544, 545, 547, 548(a)(1)(B) or 548(b) of this title, but only to the extent such transfer is a redemption payment, principal payment, dividend payment, interest payment or other distribution on or in respect of a security, made for the benefit of the beneficial holder of the security, by or on behalf of the issuer of the security or another entity obligated with respect to the security.

* * *

Add a new Subsection (g) to Section 550 as follows:

(g) The trustee may not recover any transfer of a kind described in section 546(e)(2), except from the entity that is the beneficial holder of the security on or in respect of which such transfer is made.

CHAPTER 23

MARKETS AND CHAPTER 11

¶ 2301: Robert C. Clark, *The Interdisciplinary Study of Legal Evolution*, 90 Yale Law Journal 1238 (1981)*

* * *

The fourth phase of [reorganization] development occurred ... when the equity receivership evolved to the point where ... the creditors of the insolvent business debtor [bought] ... the business ... using not cash as the means of payment, but their creditor claims, such as [their] notes, bonds, [and] debentures.... The creditors ... transform[ed] ... their debt holdings into ... new debt and stock, and at the same time [established] ... priorit[ies] among themselves and against ... the old shareholders[ ] in a way that was just as definitive as a real liquidation sale to an outside buyer. *This procedure made economic sense whenever there were no or few potential outside buyers with accurate and timely information about the true state of affairs and the future prospects of the business, and when the process of searching for and informing outside buyers would itself be very expensive.*

* * *

The [next] phase in ... corporate debtor-creditor law [established a formal,] ... structured version of the ... equity receivership ... with the ... Chandler Act in 1938. The ritual of the self-sale was dropped. All corporations in reorganization would presumptively be subjects of a reorganization plan that would primarily involve a reshuffling of the paper claims against the business assets. Furthermore, such restructuring of debt might be accomplished by a two-thirds majority

* Reprinted by permission of The Yale Law Journal Company and Fred B. Rothman & Company from The Yale Law Journal, Vol. 90, pages 1238–1274.

vote within the classes of debtors, so that a good plan might be forced on otherwise obstreperous creditors. These refinements, however, simply increased the need for careful judicial supervision of the valuation process.

[Why did these] phases . . . of creditors' remedies occur[ ] so late in the history of trade and commerce[? Perhaps] lawyers in early times simply failed to think of the legal inventions and their advantages. . . . [T]he timing of [some] legal innovations is basically a random matter, and . . . it takes time for ingenious persons to happen to be put in contact with situations that admit of improvement, and to see the solutions. An alternative, more idea-oriented explanation is that earlier lawyers were intellectually blinded by the influence of their modes of legal thought. . . .

. . . But the hypothesis that seems most powerful to me is more economic and institutional: only with the rise of very large business enterprises were there sufficiently frequent and sizable economies of scale in debt-enforcement proceedings to justify the legal innovations in question. Unless the surplus of going-concern value over liquidation value was substantial, as it might be for a large business, or the debtor business was so large and complex that it would have been impossible or quite expensive to find or to create a fair-sized pool of reasonably informed potential outside buyers, the efficiency benefits of a receivership or reorganization proceeding would not exceed the very substantial administrative, negotiating, and legal costs of the proceeding itself.[1]

¶ 2302: Mark J. Roe, Bankruptcy and Debt: A New Model for Corporate Reorganization (1983, 1987)[2]

[What if American capital markets are now so well developed that many outside investors can and do value large firms, and these investors buy and sell stock in such firms daily? And what if some of these investors buy and sell entire companies regularly?]

The core determinations made in a reorganization under chapter 11 of the Bankruptcy Code are simply stated: Who gets how much? What will the reorganized capital structure be? To resolve these simply stated questions, bankruptcy courts now loosely oversee a lengthy bargaining process that is widely thought to be cumbersome, costly, and complex. . . .

Three principal characteristics seem desirable for a corporate reorganization mechanism: speed, low cost, and a resulting sound capital structure. Other desirable characteristics are accuracy in valuation and compensation, predictability, and fairness. Accuracy and predictability diminish the uncertainty of the results of bankruptcy reorganizations, facilitating investment in risky but worthwhile

[1] These costs are high in the more advanced proceedings because of the greater need to consider valuation questions.

[2] Paper presented at a bankruptcy conference at the University of Pennsylvania Law School, October 1987. I summarize here matters that I dealt with more extensively in *Bankruptcy and Debt: A New Model for Corporate Reorganization*, 83 Columbia Law Review 527 (1983).

enterprises before a bankruptcy occurs. Speed and low cost help diminish the deadweight costs of the bankruptcy when it does occur.

Three ... mechanisms [can] ... accomplish a corporate reorganization: (1) a *bargain* among creditors and stockholders ... ; (2) litigation in which the court imposes an *administered* solution and capital structure; and (3) ... *the market*. Since 1978, Congress has preferred that the parties first attempt a bargained-for solution, and if the bargain fails, that a judicial solution be imposed. Congress and the courts have assumed that marketplace valuation for bankrupts is too inaccurate to be viable. ... [Would a sale be better?]

Anticipating an objective valuation of the firm [from a sale], the financial parties might, prior to any sale, more often than now fall into line with a settlement that would make the actual valuation sale unnecessary. If [a sale] could be successfully implemented, two major tasks of reorganization—valuation and restructuring—could take place not as now occurs over the course of years, but over a much shorter period.

... A market based reorganization [was historically] rejected by courts and others because stigma, informational impediments, uncertainty, and institutional considerations all seem likely to distort the market's expectations of the firm's long-run value. These considerations have suggested to the reorganization decisionmakers (Congress and the courts) that the pinpoint accuracy (in terms of longer-run values) in a market-based reorganization is doubtful. Usually at this juncture analysis of market-based reorganization end[ed]. ...

Empirical work now suggests, however, that some of these feared inaccuracies are unlikely to exist in a market-based system. ... On balance, the market value of a firm after reorganization seems likely to be more accurate than a judicial finding. [An increase in] ... accuracy would not necessarily in itself justify replacing the current devices with a market-based mechanism. Nevertheless, the additional possibility of quicker, cheaper reorganizations makes market-based mechanisms appropriate for serious consideration.

* * *

I. Current Doctrine and Some Game Theory: Bargaining Deadlocks and Reorganization Doctrine's Rejection of the Market

... [T]he bargaining process [in chapter 11] is likely to be a time-consuming effort to break an initial deadlock.

A. Valuation and Bargaining in Bankruptcy

Corporate bankruptcy does not correspond to the financial economist's option model. In the simple option model, when the firm value slips below the debt's face value, then the creditors take the firm. If the firm's value were above the option price, then the stockholders buy back the firm from the creditors by paying off the debt. That, however, is not what happens in a two- or three-year corporate bankruptcy.

A crucial difficulty in bankruptcy seems to be the valuation process. . . . Which creditor and stockholder layers retain an interest in the reorganized firm depends on how much the firm is deemed to be worth. Judicial valuation uncertainties create an incentive for juniors to argue that markets do not value the firm accurately and an incentive for juniors to delay. The incentive to delay springs from several related sources. First, if the valuation (or settlement) today will wipe the juniors out, they have no desire to end the proceedings. Second, if there is an operational decline because of the delay, the seniors bear the brunt of that decline. On the other hand, third, if the company has an unusual upturn by the time a later settlement were negotiated then (after the upturn), the juniors would do better.

If that were all, corporate reorganization in bankruptcy would not take two or three years. Even if the judge picked an incorrect number, the distribution would occur and the bankruptcy would be over.

But the judge cannot readily value the firm, because he or she is inexpert at such tasks and will rarely be as well-informed as the firm's managers, creditors, or major stockholders about the firm itself. Even if expert, the judge mistrusts market valuation of bankrupt enterprises. Bankruptcy doctrine says that the market values the firm too low, because of uncertainties. Rarely do bankruptcy institutions recognize that the low value is principally a function of the bankrupt firm's poor opportunities.

In most reorganizations today, the judge does not formally value the firm or its constituent capital layers. . . . [T]he parties bargain to a solution. But . . . [i]n large measure, they . . . bargain[ ] over their guess as to what the judge would accept as a valuation number. That valuation dispute may be explicit or it may exacerbate other disputes. That is, some parties may dispute the validity of a lien, the interpretation of a subordination clause, the need for equitable subordination. These may be genuine disputes, but are exacerbated by uncertainty about the valuation result if the priority were more clearly established. . . . These disputes may in fact sometimes be the strategic arguments used—subconsciously or not—to wait for a valuation determination until the affected creditor is more likely to obtain a better pay-off.

* * *

. . . While the legal process is unfolding, the firm will incur costs: lost customers and suppliers[, including skilled employees], unfinanced projects, diverted management time to dealing with the reorganization instead of the firm's operations. Transaction costs are clear; and when the firm has unique opportunities, allocative costs may also be incurred.[3]

[3] [For more ambiguous results on bankruptcy and recapitalization costs, see Robert H. Mnookin & Robert B. Wilson, *Rational Bargaining and Market Efficiency: Understanding Pennzoil v. Texaco*, 75 Virginia Law Review 295 (1989) (high indirect costs); Gregor Andrade & Steven N. Kaplan, *How Costly is Financial (not Economic) Distress?—Evidence from Highly Leveraged Transactions that Became Distressed*, 53 Journal of Finance 1443 (1998); Steven N. Kaplan, *Federated's Acquisition and Bankruptcy: Lessons and Implications*, 72 Washington University Law Quarterly 1103 (1994) (low indirect costs of pure financial stress).—Roe.]

B. Game Theory and Free–Riders

Although the particular party "causing" the deadlock incurs some of these costs, as a diminution in the value of that party's potential portion of the firm, most are borne by the other parties. The deadlock can be seen as a set of overlapping externalities. Each of the critical actors in reorganization can, by delaying, litigating, or rejecting a plan of reorganization, cause the firm and those with a claim on, or interest in, the firm to bear costs of delay. The decisionmaker bears only some of the costs that the decision triggers. A basic form of the prisoner's dilemma is at hand: the aggregation of individualistic, "rational" decisions leads to an inferior collective result.[4]

. . . [B]ecause the creditors' funds are already committed to the enterprise, the dependent relationship differs greatly from independent relationships that characterize the marketplace. The bargaining dynamic between and among dependent actors—those who must, because of continuing mutual commitments, deal with one another—provides enhanced opportunity for strategic behavior, threats, and appeals to nonmarket norms, all of which could lead to an unpredictable end to the negotiation [or to stalemates].

* * *

Historically bankruptcy courts have mistrusted market valuations. Improperly so, for the public firm, I believe.

Why did [they mistrust market values]? Several hypotheses come to mind. Bankruptcy corporate reorganization legal doctrine first developed at the beginning of [the 20th] century, when markets for bankrupt firms—and derivatively for their securities—were not highly developed. It might have made sense then to mistrust the market. The next push forward for legal doctrine in bankruptcy occurred during the Great Depression. The ideology of the time was mistrustful of the market; quick and expert valuation by the judge with the advice of the expert administrative agency, the SEC, seemed plausible.

Second, even today most bankrupt firms are small, locally owned businesses. These firms probably do face an imperfect market; even if not, judges are not sympathetic to putting the small business-owner out of business, a typical result of a market sale. The few large firm bankruptcies involve more assets, employees, and money than the aggregate of small business bankruptcies; but the legal mind adapts doctrines from the greater numbers to the fewer, but much more economically significant firms.[5]

---

[4] The process looks like the familiar common pool problem in oil recovery. Libecap & Wiggins, *Contractual Responses to the Common Pool: Prorationing of Crude Oil Production*, 74 Am. Econ. Rev. 87 (1984).

[5] A speculative additional reason: Use of market value would have compelled courts to validate an operational decision that as populist, semi-local officials they were loath to validate. A fair market value of the firm would often reveal that the firm ought to [have been] liquidated: the firm was worth more if its parts were sold off than if it were reorganized. But if the bankruptcy judge—a product of local politics—were reluctant to liquidate, he or she faced the difficult task that a fair reorganization value was less than the cash sale value offered by those who would quickly liquidate the firm. To validate the reorganization decision—which would keep the judge from approving the closing of the local factory—a reorganization value

II. A New Reorganization Paradigm

A. Using the Market

Whatever may be the reason, mistrust of the market in bankruptcy is the reality. Yet . . . a quick method of valuation [would use the market to] end the multi-year contentiousness that corporate reorganization in bankruptcy now produces: *sell the firm in its entirety or use a stock float from which firm value is extrapolated.* One prospect is to sell the firm's operations, take the cash and distribute it to the creditors. And, if that seems too radical, disruptive or transactionally costly—for good reasons or bad—why not get the valuation number from a sale of, say, 10% of the firm's stock? From that sale, a value of the firm as a whole can be extrapolated. The extrapolated value will not be perfect; sometimes the whole is worth more than the securities parts. Whichever way the value is ascertained—extrapolated value or sale in its entirety—the resultant number allows for a distribution in bankruptcy. The highest ranking creditors get paid in full—in cash if there's a sale of the entire enterprise, in stock if there's a valuation sale of only 10% of the company's stock—and so on down the capital pecking order. That effort would make the bankruptcy reality correspond to the options models that finance economists use, but which are not readily implemented in corporate bankruptcy today.

B. A Simple Illustration

Assume that the bankrupt firm has a capital structure consisting of $50 million of senior debt, $50 million of junior debt, and (old) common stock. There are no other creditors. Seniors argue the corporation is worth $50 million, juniors argue $100 million, (old) common stockholders argue $125 million. The court recapitalizes with a structure of 1,000,000 new common shares held for the parties, with the distribution of these shares to be specified later. *Uncertain as to the ease of quickly marketing all 1,000,000 shares,* it has an underwriter sell 100,000 of the shares to the public. The underwriter obtains $100 per share, indicating an extrapolated enterprise value (with the proceeds of the offering) of $100 million. The $90 million in residual value ($100 million in total enterprise value minus $10 million owned by the purchasers of the 100,000 shares) is allocated among the seniors and juniors; the old common shareholders receive nothing. The remaining 900,000 shares are then distributed: 500,000 to the seniors, 400,000 to the juniors.

Such an approach would slash through the tangled bankruptcy knots of valuation, distributional conflicts, and recapitalization. The wisdom of replacing the current means of valuation in bankruptcy with this market-based approach is initially dependent on the relative accuracy, speed, and cost of market valuation when compared to the current mechanisms.

* * *

---

had to be obtained that was higher than the cash sale, liquidation value. But that higher number was not obtainable in the market. Hence the market had to be rejected.

[C]. Bankruptcy as Other Than a Bargain Among Financial Creditors

Reorganization is not always just a question of readjusting the financial capital structure. Executory contracts such as labor agreements may give rise to critical reorganization negotiations. Suppliers may have made informal investments in the firm (by committing equipment to production for that firm) that do not appear on the firm's balance sheet and that would not formally constitute a claim in bankruptcy. These suppliers (including labor and managerial claims) may be the real subject of some reorganizations, but would be untouched in a common-stock sale and recapitalization.

That is, financial creditors may stand-off against such claimants, offering to give up a few points in interest (or exchange debt into stock) in return for a reduction of the managerial workforce or a cut in wage rates from, say, $25 per hour to $18 per hour. [A market] sale would leave these claimants untouched, reducing their incentive to participate in the reorganization give-ups, effectively make them superior in right of payment to the financial claimants [because a further reorganization would no longer be necessary and the pressure for "give-ups" would subside]. Multi-party, deadlocking negotiations might have some use if they were more likely to produce an ethic under which everyone (creditors, suppliers, labor, and management) "chips in" something.

Conclusion

. . . Bankruptcy courts [now, in the 1980s] oversee a rambling bargain that implicitly assigns a value to bankrupt public firms and then provides a capital structure that often is high in debt. If the bargain fails, litigation results. Both these processes are lengthy, costly, and, if a rapid, objective basis to value the firm is available, unnecessary. Since the post-reorganization market seems likely to value the firm more accurately than does the court, the reasons offered by bankruptcy institutions for rejection of the market in favor of judicial valuation (when bargaining fails)—incomplete information, stigma, and insufficient buyers—seem unpersuasive. . . . It is true that incompleteness of available information, costliness of available information, . . . and problems in the disparities between the value of a large block and the value of the few shares sold for purposes of extrapolating value all suggest that the post-reorganization market falls short as an *ideal* basis for accurate valuation. But judicial valuation (or the bargained-for result) faces some of these same debilities, as well as others; some debilities in the accuracy of market-based valuation can be eliminated or mitigated. More importantly, whatever the relative accuracy of the mechanisms, a market-based valuation and recapitalization via the slice-of-common-stock sale begins with the potential to be quicker *and cheaper* than the alternatives.

However, jamming the market valuation into the context of an ongoing reorganization would risk recreating the very problems that an objective market valuation might eliminate: delay and judicial inexpertise. A simple valuation sale would require determinations as to size, timing, price, and other terms. . . . While these problems are potentially resolvable, they could require judicial determinations similar to (although not as consequential as) those made in a valuation hearing. These determinations (and others, such as litigation of the validity of security interests or of contract liabilities) raise anew the specter of strategic delay by participants in the reorganizations. The question thus becomes one of judgment as to the relative severity of the defects in the three reorganization models, and the likely relative success of judicial control of the defects in each model. The choice cannot be made by economic deduction or statistical observation of market accuracy alone.

Furthermore, some bankrupt firms have substantial nonfinancial relationships with labor claimants, suppliers who have made investments specifically to sell to the bankrupt, and tort claimants. These may . . . be informal claimants in that they would continue to obtain returns were there a successful reorganization. A swift marketplace valuation would eliminate the prospect of the firm rebargaining with them, effectively making such non-Code claimants superior in right of payment to the financial claimants. Either separate mechanisms would have to be developed for bankruptcies in which such claimants were significant (and means developed to swiftly distinguish the two types) or these claimants would be conceded as superior in payment rights to Code-defined claimants.

. . . [And e]ven a simple, purely financial reorganization would be difficult to implement. Complex reorganizations with secured debt, holding companies, labor claimants, and other non-Code "investors" and suppliers would be more difficult. Nevertheless, the prospect that corporate reorganizations in bankruptcy could be speeded up, so that the transactional time corresponds with that of a securities offering or a merger, instead of the two or three years a reorganization now takes, deserves continued scrutiny.

Because many of the problems with the slice-of-common-stock sale—such as secured credit, holding company structures, creation of other sources of delay, and uncertainty associated with anything new—are possible but not necessarily present in all reorganizations, a minimal response ought to be to add the suggested reorganization method as one of the possible means of valuation and restructuring, and to clear away as much of the inhibiting statutory underbrush as possible. For example, the market-based reorganization could at least be authorized as a judicial weapon if the bargain fails to produce a result after a specified period of time. The Code could be recast to allow the bankruptcy judge to intervene and force a market-based reorganization (with judicial administrative efforts to reduce the likely distortions) if negotiations became too complex and slow.

¶ 2303: Questions on Roe

1. If bankruptcy costs are low, is a market sale better than reorganization? See Frank Easterbrook, *Is corporate bankruptcy efficient?*, 27 Journal of Financial Economics 411 (1990). The direct costs of bankruptcy are about 3% of the firm's assets. Lawrence A. Weiss, *Bankruptcy resolution: Direct costs and violation of priority of claims*, 27 Journal of Financial Economics 285 (1990). Direct costs in mergers are not low. The RJR transaction had $700 million in direct costs on a $25 billion transaction, or direct costs of about 2%. See MetLife complaint, ¶ 1810. If these are representative, the question is which transaction, sale or chapter 11, generates lower

indirect costs; for that, there's no reliable hard evidence. Indirect costs would include the bankrupt's inability to make deals with uneasy contracting parties, the diversion of management time, the flight of high-quality employees and suppliers to other firms.

2. Would the best resolution be to add a new section to chapter 11, such as the following?

[Hypothetical] § 1195. Sale of debtor

After 120 days after the petition has been filed, the court may, upon motion of any party in interest, arrange for the sale of debtor in its entirety, or arrange for the sale of stock in the debtor, thereby fixing the value of the firm for purposes of § 1129.

¶ 2304: Douglas Baird, *The Uneasy Case for Corporate Reorganization,* 15 Journal of Legal Studies 127 (1986)*

. . . Even if some kind of collective proceeding is needed to prevent a destructive race to the firm's assets, [chapter 11] could be justified only if investors before the fact would (if they could) agree to a hypothetical sale of assets instead of a real one. I argue that, as a general matter, investors taken as a group would rarely prefer the hypothetical sale to an actual one. An actual sale eliminates the potential distortions from a fictive valuation of a firm. More important, *the costs of an actual sale are likely to be less than the cost of the procedures needed to prevent manipulation and game playing by the participants in a hypothetical sale.* I argue that for this reason the entire law of corporate reorganizations is hard to justify under any set of facts and virtually impossible when the debtor is a publicly held corporation.

* * *

III

The simplest collective proceeding is a sale of the firm for cash and the distribution of the proceeds to all the investors. The common objection to such sales is that they cannot preserve the value of a firm as a going concern. Under this view, finding a third party who is willing to buy the firm as a single unit is so time-consuming and so difficult that, without a mechanism to stay the rights of all creditors and force them to become owners of the firm, the firm would be broken into small pieces that are worth less than the firm as a single unit. Only a reorganization provides the necessary "breathing space" that gives all involved a chance to sort out their affairs.

Finding buyers for firms that in fact are worth preserving as going concerns may not be more difficult, more expensive, or more error prone than [a reorganization in chapter 11]. . . .

. . . A bankruptcy judge may be less able to cast a cold eye on an enterprise and make tough decisions than someone who has put his own money on the line. He may have no effective constraint analogous to the discipline a market imposes on competing buyers who make systematic errors. Like any other individual outside such constraints, he may tend to underestimate risks.

None of this, however, is to suggest that [a] going concern sale[] of a firm [is] without cost. . . . [A] sale of the firm's assets may be difficult to orchestrate. The sale should be conducted by the residual claimants to the firm's assets because they have an incentive to obtain the best price. . . . They also suffer the consequences if they devote insufficient resources to finding a buyer or buyers, or if they waste time and money trying to sell the assets for more than anyone is willing to pay.

Ensuring that residual claimants conduct the sale (or, more precisely, ensuring that those who conduct the sale are entitled to keep the excess) is not easy. For example, the identity of the residual claimants may be uncertain. If it is not clear whether the assets are worth more than is necessary to satisfy the claims of general creditors and those senior to them, a choice must be made between allowing the general creditors (or the trustee, as their representative) to conduct the sale alone and allowing those junior to them to participate. Either decision brings difficulties. If the general creditors act alone, they may not take account of the interests of those junior to them. On the other hand, if junior owners participate, they will tend to favor any tactic that might bring a higher price—such as costly searching or endless delay—that a sole owner would reject as unjustified. These junior claimants would have the correct set of incentives *only if* they bore the additional costs of searching for a buyer who would pay more than the total amount of claims senior to their own. . . .

In addition, there may be more than one residual claimant. A firm, for example, may have dozens or thousands of general creditors. Even if they can be identified easily, it may be difficult to fashion a set of rules that enables them to work together or to appoint someone to act on their behalf. Under current law, the bankruptcy trustee is charged with acting on behalf of the general creditors, but in practice it is hard for general creditors to monitor the trustee and ensure that he heeds his obligations to them. Problems of monitoring arise whenever one person acts as the agent of others. . . .

One should not, however, exaggerate the difficulties inherent in deciding who among the investors should conduct the sale. In the case of a large firm, the residual claimants would likely hire someone with the appropriate expertise (such as an investment banker) to run the sale. It may not much matter whether the decision to hire Goldman Sachs rather than Shearman Lehman Brothers rests in one investor rather than another.

IV

. . . In a liquidation, what various claimants are entitled to receive is relatively fixed. If a firm is sold outright, substantive nonbankruptcy entitlement[s] largely determine who gets what in what order. *There is often little to argue over because rights are fixed and payments are made in cash.* In a reorganization, on the other hand, many more issues are open. One must value shares in the reorganized company and allocate them to the old owners. . . .

A threshold question is whether the complications of reorganizations and the opportunities they provide for undercompensation and strategic game playing by creditors, shareholders, and managers are worth the benefits they bring. The justification for reorganizations usually begins with the observation that many firms are worth more if kept intact (or largely intact) than if sold piecemeal. The rationale for a reorganization, however, must not be simply that some firms are worth more as "going concerns" than if liquidated. Although not common under present law, a liquidation is consistent with keeping a firm intact as a going concern. The difference between a liquidation and a reorganization is that the first involves an actual sale of all the assets of a business to a third-party buyer and the second involves a hypothetical one. Under existing law, petitions filed under Chapter 7 usually lead to a piecemeal sale of the assets, and those under Chapter 11 involve attempts (many of which fail) to keep the firm intact as a going concern. Nothing in current law, however, prevents a sale of the firm as a going concern in Chapter 7, and Chapter 11 presently allows for a piecemeal sale of the assets of the firm. *The justification for a reorganization must focus on showing the higher costs of selling the firm to a third party.*

. . . The third party acquiring the assets can bargain with the managers and obtain their services by striking separate deals with each of them. If the managers will work only if given an equity interest in the firm, the new owners can offer it to them. In this respect, new owners are in the same position as investors who continue to own the firm after a reorganization.

* * *

The owners of a firm might prefer a forced sale of assets to themselves (which a reorganization is, in effect) to an actual sale to one or more third parties *if it were cheaper*. . . . In a world in which information can be gathered and communicated quickly and in which many entrepreneurs specialize in acquiring firms in distress, the practical [business] obstacles (as opposed to the ones that are purely legal) seem quite surmountable. . . .

* * *

V

. . . [T]he owners of a . . . publicly held firm, would likely prefer a sale of the firm outright to whomever was willing to pay the most for it. A going-concern sale of assets is possible under the existing structure of Chapter 7 of the Bankruptcy Code. Such sales, however, run counter to the thinking of most bankruptcy judges and practitioners. . . .

* * *

Even though Chapter 7 permits going-concern liquidations, it was not drafted with such sales in mind. The powers of the trustee have been conceived over the years as the powers of someone who would oversee the dismantling of a firm. Were the use of Chapter 7 to change, the powers of the trustee (and the ways in which his behavior would be monitored) would also change. . . . Some tax rules provide additional examples. Under existing law, a tax-loss carryforward disappears when there is a sale of the firm for cash, but it survives a sale of the firm for securities (even if they can be readily converted into cash), and it survives when a firm is reorganized under Chapter 11.[6] The rule governing tax-loss carryforwards should be independent of what kind of bankruptcy proceeding is involved and, indeed, whether there is any bankruptcy proceeding at all. . . .

This paper has suggested that the premise underlying Chapter 11 of the Bankruptcy Code may be unsound. But in making this observation, one should not overlook the virtues of the existing law. Existing rules of corporate reorganization are a vast improvement over what preceded them. The number of cases in which the bankruptcy process has done what it is supposed to do (readjust ownership interests while at the same time respecting substantive nonbankruptcy rights without interfering with the optimum deployment of the assets) is much greater now than it was before the Bankruptcy Reform Act was passed in 1978, and courts are more sensitive to the basic principles of bankruptcy law. . . .

¶ 2305: Questions on Baird

1. Again, what if the costs of reorganization are low? What if the transaction costs of a sale are substantial?

   Even if the transaction costs of a sale are substantial and the costs of reorganization low, one would want to know if many reorganized firms merge after the chapter 11 plans are confirmed; if so, they incur both costs and would be better off if they incurred only one.

2. Do most bankrupt firms have to be better off integrated into another firm in the industry in order for a bankruptcy sale to be worthwhile? Could bidders bid to keep the firm standing alone? Could management form a bidding group if managerial skills are especially valuable?

3. Would the sale alternative be seen as fair by the average voter (or average member of Congress)?

4. Must the sale be mandatory to be viable? If mandatory, what about the problem of "informal" priority for informal claimants?

5. Stockholders always can in theory overcome an undervaluation, by paying creditors off and keeping the firm for themselves. They would be impeded only by illiquidity (either directly or via an inability to convince financiers of the under-valuation) or their own poor information (which could lead them to abandon a valuable, but undervalued firm). Could these relationships be the foundation for a new model of reorganization, for instance, by giving the stockholders a short time in which to buy the firm back or be wiped out, after which the right to buy out the seniors would pass to the next highest ranking interest or claimant?

¶ 2306: General Problems With Using the Market to Replace Chapter 11

By measuring each claim's value precisely, a sale will usually effectuate priority better than a reorganization would. The proponents

[6] See I.R.C. § 368.

of sale think that this is an advantage, but whether it is or is not depends on the value of absolute priority, which some see as costly and perhaps unfair. Absolute priority can exacerbate asset substitution incentives for equity-holders to put the firm on a risky path; on some configuration of numbers, muting absolute priority mutes the equity-holders' incentives to take unwarranted risk. Absolute priority might similarly lead equity-holders to abandon the firm, because they have no realistic chance of an upside; muting presumably reduces their incentives to abandon.

But these costs of priority arise from creditors not having an efficient mechanism to seize the firm. If we did move to "true" absolute priority, chapter 11 might become a sword for creditors to seize the firm from equityholders, rather than a shield for equityholders and managers to prevent creditors from seizing the firm.

The sale proposals would, their spokesmen claim, facilitate quicker reorganizations by fixing a value quickly and objectively; a weakness of the options proposal is that it might not be able to function *until* priorities are determined. But do the proponents of sale need a sale to get most of what they believe to be valuable? Under the Code, § 1129, the court fixes the firm's value (directly or, by confirming a negotiated plan, indirectly) *after* priorities are determined. But what if the court *immediately* determined value upon the filing of a petition, with that value determining distributions under § 1129(b)(2)? Would that not do much of what the proponents of a sale think a sale would do?

Keep in mind also that the firm when sold (or when valued via options or a slice-of-stock sale) would *not* be worth the same as when continued. We have focused on the operational costs of chapter 11, but there are also gains, such as distributional gains that the insiders can obtain from outsiders. Tax benefits, like N.O.L. carry forwards are often lost during chapter 11, but are more certain to be lost when there's a full ownership change. See ¶ 2108. The Bankruptcy Code itself shifts value from outsiders to insiders: the bankrupt can reject unprofitable contracts and assign profitable ones that it could not assign outside of bankruptcy. While looking at the total of dollars won and dollars lost to *everyone*, these rights may not add to America's *total* business value, but they are worth something to the players who would continue a chapter 11 rather than sell the firm so that they can exercise these rights.

How about perceived fairness and legitimacy? Commentators and citizens may see market-based reorganizations as too quickly shutting down firms and firing employees. Cf. Elizabeth Warren, *Bankruptcy Policy,* 54 University of Chicago Law Review 775 (1987); David Skeel, *Markets, Courts, and the Brave New World of Bankruptcy Theory,* 1993 Wisconsin Law Review 465, 497–509. Consider this excerpt from Mark Roe, *Backlash,* 98 Columbia Law Review 217, 234–38 (1998):

> Suppose we know that a harsh chapter 11—say one facilitating the quick sale or liquidation of the bankrupt firm—. . . best deployed capital and minimized . . . pain[,] because . . . we kn[e]w that chapter 11 sales or liquidations end society's bad bets quickly. Capital moves to better uses and overall employment (both in raising the number of people employed and in raising salaries at the low end) is improved.

But . . . a rule of chapter 11 sale . . . will make the employment losses [more] . . . salient in the media. This media saliency could result . . . eventually (or at least at a nontrivial level of probability) either in, say, debilitating, wealth-decreasing [other rules, or a retention of the current chapter 11]. . . .

Lest the reader think I am adding a political reason to surreptitiously buttress a case against auctions in bankruptcy . . . , I am not. I believe the best bankruptcy system, other than in the political sense of this Essay, would have some auction rule, probably as a default rule that would kick in on a creditor's motion after a few months of efforts to negotiate a reorganization plan for a public company. . . .

* * *

. . . Imagine that the 1980s wave of hostile takeovers had continued undampened into the mid–1990s . . . with continuing media saliency typified by movies like *Wall Street* and books like *Bonfire of the Vanities* and *Barbarians at the Gate;* imagine that financial operators like Michael Milken and Ivan Boesky were still front-page news; imagine a deeper militant populist tradition in the United States that was not assuaged and desiccated by a century of legislation that enacted much of the form and some substance of the populist program; . . . [imagine] that the gap between public opinion, which by a rate of 59% sees downsizings as bad for the economy, and economic opinion, which sees them as on balance good in the long run, widens and ossifie[s]; and [imagine] . . . rougher bankruptcy laws that [immediately] sold bankrupt firms into the takeover auction drama instead of sending them through two years of negotiation and reorganization. Imagine all this thrown into a heated political setting with media-salient downsizings and (contrary to fact in early 1996) a faltering economy in an election year. Fringe candidates might have become mainstream, or, to co-opt them, mainstream candidates might have adopted trade protection or *economically unwise (but politically astute) programs and made American society poorer*.

. . . One can believe in the [local] efficiency of this or that institution (freewheeling hostile takeovers, chapter 11 sales of public companies) and still doubt whether their persistence will maximize political efficiency. The dampening [such as anti-sale] rules [in bankruptcy] may enhance [the] system's adaptivity and stability, preserving the *core* efficiency tendencies of capitalism, private property, and competitive markets, by conceding a little economically unwise but politically astute regulation here and there. One could believe a set of legal institutions to be inefficient one-by-one—antitakeover rules, slow chapter 11 reorganizations, Glass–Steagall, old-style antitrust, and a list to which we could all add—and still one cannot conclude that the whole set is inefficient, because the inefficient fringe may preserve that efficient core of private property, mobility, and competition. . . .

¶ 2307: Douglas G. Baird & Robert K. Rasmussen, *Chapter 11 at Twilight,* 56 Stanford Law Review 673 (2004)

The traditional account of corporate reorganizations assumes a financially distressed business faces three conditions simultaneously: (1) It has substantial value as a going concern; (2) its investors cannot sort out the financial distress through ordinary bargaining and instead require Chapter 11's collective forum; and (3) the business cannot be readily sold in the market as a going concern. Remove any one of these conditions, and the standard account of corporate reorganization law falters. . . . It is [not] likely that all three of them will exist at the same time [for the same firm in today's world]. Hence, modern Chapter 11 practice cannot be squared with the traditional account. Regardless of whether the number of businesses entering Chapter 11 rises or falls, something different is going on.

. . . [Indeed,] traditional reorganizations have largely disappeared. Put concretely, in 84% of all large Chapter 11s from 2002, the investors entered bankruptcy with a deal in hand or used it to sell the assets of the business. In the remaining cases, going-concern value was small or nonexistent.

* * *

. . . The powers [that control creditors] enjoy reduce the work that Chapter 11 can perform as well as the powers that others (such as the board of directors) are able to exercise. . . . Even in the cases most resembling the traditional reorganization, creditor control is the dominant theme. Indeed, if the experience of large businesses leaving Chapter 11 in 2002 is any guide, those at the helm do the bidding of the creditors throughout the case. Moreover, by the end of the case, the creditors usually acquire the right to appoint a new board of directors. They commonly appoint themselves or others (such as their employees) whom they can trust to protect their interests. Corporate reorganizations today are the legal vehicles by which creditors in control decide which course of action—sale, prearranged deal, or a conversion of debt to a controlling equity stake—will maximize their return.

In 2002, 93 large businesses completed their Chapter 11 proceedings. Of these, 52 (or 56% of the sample) were sales of one sort or another. In 45 of these cases, there was a sale of assets such that the business did not even emerge in tact as an independent entity under a plan of reorganization. In addition to these clear cases of asset sales, seven other cases were in substance sales even though the business did emerge as a stand-alone enterprise under a plan of re-organization. . . .

Fruit of the Loom filed for Chapter 11 at the end of 1999. From the beginning, the senior creditors exercised control. They planned initially to take a controlling equity interest in the company, but when competing bidders appeared, they were content for the bankruptcy court to conduct a sale. Warren Buffett's Berkshire Hathaway proved to be the high bidder at $800 million in cash. . . .

In Sterling Chemicals, the court oversaw the sale of one half of the company, and the proceeds went to the secured creditors. A new investor acquired most of the equity of the remaining business, with the balance going to the unsecured creditors. The equity was wiped out, and, as provided in the plan of reorganization, the entire board of directors tendered their resignations. The new investor controlled the appointment of their successors. Similarly, a distressed-debt fund acquired control of Classic Communications in Chapter 11 and became its owners as part of the reorganization plan.

Global Crossing, one of the largest bankruptcies ever, was from the start a sale of the business to a new investor. After delays and a search for other bidders, the bankruptcy court confirmed a plan of reorganization that consisted primarily of a purchase agreement under which the prebankruptcy suitor would receive 60% of the equity in exchange for several hundred million dollars in cash.

Derby Cycle entered Chapter 11 as the second part of a plan, conceived by its investment bankers many months before, to sell its assets. The bankruptcy court approved the asset sale within five weeks of the petition. In the words of Derby's investment banker, "[B]ankruptcy can be a tool to get a transaction done. . . . This was a situation where it made a lot of sense for a lot of reasons to file for bankruptcy. But the primary reason was speed—we were just able to [do] the transaction a lot more quickly."

XO Communications filed for Chapter 11 with two alternative plans in hand. The first was a deal by which Forstmann Little would make a significant investment in exchange for control. The second was one that would wipe out equity and convert the bank debt to equity. [Forstmann] Little decided not to go through with the deal, and Carl Icahn bought a majority of the company's debt. Ownership of XO Communications passed to him upon confirmation. The company exited Chapter 11 in early 2003, and Icahn remains its owner.

* * *

[Thus], the dominant feature of the large corporate Chapter 11 today is the asset sale. A large corporation that files for bankruptcy is in play. Selling a business in Chapter 11 is no longer a last resort, but an option to be exercised at any time if it is in the creditors' interest.

Asset sales preserve a business's going-concern value in a way that undercuts the liquidation/reorganization dichotomy that marks much discussion about bankruptcy law. . . . We see sales of discrete divisions and units, but only because [discrete, division-by-division sales] are thought to maximize value. . . . [A]sset sales are a way to preserve what going concern value may exist by putting the corporation's assets into new hands.

Sales . . . do place a value on the business today, thus eliminating the option value of junior investors. When there is an asset sale, the proceeds are often less than what the most senior creditors are owed. Those junior to them are often wiped out. If the sale had not taken place, the values might have increased. Junior interests have value as long as there is no day of reckoning.

This collapsing of all future possibilities into present value, however, is not unique to asset sales. Regardless of whether there is an actual sale or the hypothetical sale that takes place in a traditional reorganization, the absolute priority rule requires a valuation in every case. This valuation collapses future values to the present and fixes everyone's rights. . . . [A pure] absolute priority rule generates strategic behavior that is hard to overcome. . . .

* * *

. . . Modern bankruptcy judges oversee auctions of going concerns and implement prenegotiated plans of reorganization. . . . Chapter 11 no longer serves anything like the role commonly ascribed to it. A court-conducted sale of Fruit of the Loom in which the high bidder is Warren Buffett bears no resemblance to an equity receivership. Even in those cases that look most like a traditional large corporate reorganization, the stakes are quite small. A collection of Marriotts and Holiday Inns is nothing like a railroad [because the hotels can be split up without demeaning their going concern value].

In examining the nature of the change in the large corporate Chapter 11s of 2002, we see that fundamental forces at work in the economy have made the traditional reorganization increasingly obsolete. Railroads had enormous going concern value and incoherent capital structures, while facing primitive capital markets. Today's businesses [differ]. . . . Any going concern surplus can be captured for creditors via a sale.

. . . For better or for worse, the role that Chapter 11 can play in today's economy has little or nothing to do with reorganizing railroads or saving factories in small towns. Traditional reorganizations are all but gone. The end of bankruptcy is indeed upon us.

APPENDIX

THE STATUTES

BANKRUPTCY ACT OF 1978
(11 U.S.C. § 101 et seq.)

§ 101. Definitions

(5) The term "claim" means—

(A) right to payment, whether or not such right is reduced to judgment, liquidated, unliquidated, fixed, contingent, matured, unmatured, disputed, undisputed, legal, equitable, secured, or unsecured;

* * *

(10) The term "creditor" means—

(A) entity that has a claim against the debtor that arose at the time of or before the order for relief concerning the debtor; . . .

* * *

(14) The term "disinterested person" means a person that—

(A) is not a creditor, an equity security holder, or an insider;

(B) is not and was not, within 2 years before the date of the filing of the petition a director, officer, or employee of the debtor; and

(C) does not have an interest materially adverse to the interest of the estate or of any class of creditors or equity security holders, by reason of any direct or indirect relationship to, connection with, or interest in, the debtor, or for any other reason.

* * *

(31) The term "insider" includes— . . .

(B) if the debtor is a corporation—

(i) director of the debtor;

(ii) officer of the debtor;

. . .

(iii) person in control of the debtor;. . .

. . .

(vi) relative of a general partner, director, officer, or person in control of the debtor;

* * *

(32) The term "insolvent" means . . . financial condition such that the sum of such entity's debts is greater than all of such entity's property, at a fair valuation . . .

* * *

(35A) The term "intellectual property" means

(A) trade secret;

(B) invention, process, design, or plant protected under title 35;

(C) patent application:

(D) . . .

(E) work of authorship protected under title 17 . . .

* * *

(40) The term "municipality" means political subdivision or public agency or instrumentality of a State.

(41) The term "person" includes individual, partnership, and corporation, but does not include governmental unit . . .

* * *

(47) The term "repurchase agreement" . . . means . . . an agreement . . . for the transfer of [specified types of securities and loans, such as mortgages and obligations of the United States] . . . with a simultaneous agreement by [the] transferee to transfer [back] to the transferor . . . at a date certain not later than 1 year after such transfer or on demand, against the transfer of funds;

* * *

(53B) The term "swap agreement"—

(A) means—

(i) any agreement, including the terms and conditions incorporated by reference in such agreement, which is—

(I) an interest rate swap. . . ;

(II) a spot, same day-tomorrow, tomorrow-next, forward, or other foreign exchange, precious metals, or other commodity agreement;

(III) a currency swap, option, future, or forward agreement;

* * *

(VI) a total return, credit spread or credit swap. . . ;

* * *

(VIII) a weather swap, option, future, or forward agreement;

. . .

(ii) any agreement or transaction that is similar to any other agreement or transaction referred to in this paragraph and that—

(I) is of a type that has been, is presently, or in the future becomes, the subject of recurrent dealings in the swap or other derivatives markets (including terms and conditions incorporated by reference therein); and

(II) is a forward, swap, future, option, or spot transaction on one or more rates, currencies, commodities, equity securities, . . .

* * *

(v) a master agreement that provides for an agreement or transaction referred to in clause (i), [or] (ii) . . . .

(54) The term "transfer" means

(A) the creation of a lien;

(B) the retention of title as a security interest;

(C) the foreclosure of a debtor's equity of redemption; or

(D) each mode, direct or indirect, absolute or conditional, voluntary or involuntary, of disposing of or parting with

(i) property; or

(ii) an interest in property.

§ 105. Power of court

(a) The court may issue any order, process, or judgment that is necessary or appropriate to carry out the provisions of this title. . . .

§ 109. Who may be a debtor

. . . [O]nly a person that resides or has a domicile, a place of business, or property in the United States . . . may be a debtor under this title.

CHAPTER 3—CASE ADMINISTRATION

§ 303. Involuntary cases

(a) . . .

(b) An involuntary case against a person is commenced by the filing with the bankruptcy court of a petition under chapter 7 or 11 of this title—

(1) by three or more entities, each of which is either a holder of a claim against such person that is not contingent as to liability or the subject of a bona fide dispute as to liability or amount, or an indenture trustee representing such a holder . . . ;

* * *

(h) . . . [A]fter trial, the court shall order relief against the debtor in an involuntary case under the chapter under which the petition was filed, only if—

> (1) the debtor is generally not paying such debtor's debts as such debts become due unless such debts are the subject of a bona fide dispute as to liability or amount;
>
> or
>
> (2) within 120 days before the date of the filing of the petition, a custodian, other than a trustee, receiver, or agent appointed or authorized to take charge of less than substantially all of the property of the debtor for the purpose of enforcing a lien against such property, was appointed or took possession.

§ 307. United States trustee

The United States trustee may raise and may appear and be heard on any issue in any case or proceeding . . .

§ 327. Employment of professional persons

(a) Except as otherwise provided in this section, the trustee, with the court's approval, may employ one or more attorneys, accountants, appraisers, auctioneers, or other professional persons, that do not hold or represent an interest adverse to the estate, and that are disinterested persons, to represent or assist the trustee in carrying out the trustee's duties under this title.

§ 361. Adequate protection

When adequate protection is required under section 362 . . . of this title of an interest of an entity in property, such adequate protection may be provided by

> (A) requiring the trustee to make a cash payment or periodic cash payments to such entity, to the extent that the stay under section 362 of this title . . . results in a decrease in the value of such entity's interest in such property;
>
> (B) providing to such entity an additional or replacement lien to the extent that such stay . . . results in a decrease in the value of such entity's interest in such property; or
>
> (C) granting such other relief . . . as will result in the realization by such entity of the indubitable equivalent of such entity's interest in such property.

§ 362. Automatic stay

(a) . . . [A bankruptcy petition] operates as a stay, applicable to all entities, of

> (1) the commencement or continuation, including the issuance or employment of process, of a judicial, administrative, or other action or proceeding against the debtor that was or could have been commenced

before the commencement of the case under this title, or to recover a claim against the debtor that arose before the commencement of the case under this title;

(2) the enforcement, against the debtor or against property of the estate, of a judgment obtained before the commencement of the case under this title;

(3) any act to obtain possession of property of the estate . . . or to exercise control over property of the estate;

(4) any act to create, perfect, or enforce any lien against property of the estate;

(5) any act to create, perfect, or enforce against property of the debtor any lien to the extent that such lien secures a claim that arose before the commencement of the case under this title;

(6) any act to collect, assess, or recover a claim against the debtor that arose before the commencement of the case under this title;

(7) the setoff of any debt owing to the debtor that arose before the commencement of the case under this title against any claim against the debtor; and

(8) the commencement or continuation of a proceeding before the United States Tax Court concerning a corporate debtor's tax liability . . .

(b) The filing of a petition . . . does not operate . . as a stay— . . .

(3) . . . of any act to perfect . . . an interest in property to the extent that the trustee's rights and powers are subject to such perfection under section 546(b) . . .

(4) under paragraph (1), (2), (3), or (6) of subsection (a) of this section, of the commencement or continuation of an action or proceeding by a governmental unit . . . to enforce such governmental unit's . . . police and regulatory power, including the enforcement of a judgment other than a money judgment, obtained in an action . . . by the governmental unit to enforce such governmental unit's . . . police or regulatory power; . . .

* * *

(6) under subsection (a) of this section, of the exercise by a . . . financial institution . . . of any contractual right . . . of any contractual right . . . to offset or net out any termination value, payment amount, or other transfer obligation arising under or in connection with 1 or more such contracts, including any master agreement for such contracts;

(7) under subsection (a) of this section, of the exercise by a repo participant or financial participant of any contractual right . . . under any security agreement or arrangement or other credit enhancement forming a part of or related to any repurchase agreement, or of any contractual right . . . to offset or net out any termination value, payment amount, or other transfer obligation. . . ;

* * *

(17) under subsection (a) of this section, of the exercise by a swap participant . . . of any contractual right (as defined in section 560) under any security agreement . . . related to any swap agreement. . . .

(d) On request of a party in interest and after notice and a hearing, the court shall grant relief from the stay provided under subsection (a) of this section, such as by terminating, annulling, modifying, or conditioning such stay

(1) for cause, including the lack of adequate protection of an interest in property of such party in interest;

(2) with respect to a stay of an act against property under subsection (a) of this section, if

(A) the debtor does not have an equity in such property; and

(B) such property is not necessary to an effective reorganization. . . .

§ 363. Use, sale, or lease of property

(a) In this section, "cash collateral" means cash, negotiable instruments . . . securities, deposit accounts, or other cash equivalents . . . and includes the proceeds, products, offspring, rents, or profits of property. . . .

(b) (1) The trustee, after notice and a hearing, may use, sell, or lease, other than in the ordinary course of business, property of the estate. . . .

* * *

(c) (1) . . . [U]nless the court orders otherwise, the trustee may enter into transactions, including the sale or lease of property of the estate, in the ordinary course of business, without notice or a hearing, and may use property of the estate in the ordinary course of business without notice or a hearing.

(2) The trustee may not use, sell, or lease cash collateral under paragraph (1) of the subsection unless

(A) each entity that has an interest in such cash collateral consents; or

(B) the court, after notice and a hearing, authorizes such use, sale, or lease in accordance with the provisions of this section.

* * *

(e) Notwithstanding any other provision of this section, at any time, on request of an entity that has an interest in property used, sold, or leased, or proposed to be used, sold or leased by the trustee, the court, with or without a hearing, shall prohibit or condition such use, sale or lease as is necessary to provide adequate protection of such interest . . . .

(k) At a sale under subsection (b) . . . of property that is subject to a lien . . . , unless the court for cause orders otherwise[,] the holder of such claim may bid . . . , and, if [it] purchases such property, [it] may offset [its] claim against the purchase price. . . .

* * *

(m) The reversal or modification on appeal of an authorization under [§ 363](b) or (c) . . . does not affect the validity of a sale . . . to an entity that purchased . . . such property in good faith, whether or not such entity knew of the pendency of the appeal, unless such authorization and such sale or lease were stayed pending appeal.

§ 364. Obtaining credit

(a) If the trustee is authorized to operate the business of the debtor under [chapter 11], the trustee may obtain unsecured credit and incur unsecured debt in the ordinary course of business allowable under section 503(b)(1) of this title as an administrative expense.

(b) The court, after notice and a hearing, may authorize the trustee to obtain unsecured credit or to incur unsecured debt other than under subsection (a) of this section, allowable under section 503(b)(1) of this title as an administrative expense.

(c) If the trustee is unable to obtain unsecured credit allowable . . . as an administrative expense, the court, after notice and a hearing, may authorize the obtaining of credit or the incurring of debt

(1) with priority over any or all administrative expenses of the kind specified in section 503(b) and 507(b) of this title;

(2) secured by a lien on property of the estate that is not otherwise subject to a lien; or

(3) secured by a junior lien on property of the estate that is subject to a lien.

(d) (1) The court, after notice and a hearing, may authorize the obtaining of credit or the incurring of debt secured by a senior or equal lien on property of the estate that is subject to a lien only if

(A) the trustee is unable to obtain such credit otherwise; and

(B) there is adequate protection of [the previously-secured creditor that is made junior].

(e) The reversal or modification on appeal of an authorization under this section to obtain credit or incur debt, or of a grant under this section of a priority or a lien, does not affect the validity of any debt so incurred, or any priority or lien so granted, to an entity that extended such credit in good faith, whether or not such entity knew of the pendency of the appeal, unless such authorization and the incurring of such debt, or the granting of such priority or lien, were stayed pending appeal.

§ 365. Executory contracts and unexpired leases

(a) . . . the trustee, subject to the court's approval, may assume or reject any executory contract or unexpired lease of the debtor.

(b) (1) If there has been a default in an executory contract or unexpired lease of the debtor, the trustee may not assume such contract or lease unless . . . the trustee

(A) cures . . . ;

(B) compensates . . . ; and

(C) provides adequate assurance of future performance. . . .

(2) Paragraph (1) of this subsection does not apply to a default that is a breach of a provision relating to

(A) the insolvency or financial condition of the debtor at any time before the closing of the case;

(B) the commencement of a case under this title;

(C) the appointment of . . . a trustee in a case under this title . . . ; or

(D) the satisfaction of any penalty rate or penalty provision relating to a default arising from any failure by the debtor to perform nonmonetary obligations under the executory contract or unexpired lease.

* * *

(c) The trustee may not assume or assign any executory contract . . . of the debtor . . . if— . . .

(2) such contract is a contract to make a loan, or extend other debt financing . . . to or for the benefit of the debtor, or to issue a security of the debtor. . . .

* * *

(e) (1) Notwithstanding a provision in an executory contract . . . an executory contract . . . of the debtor may not be terminated . . . at any time after the commencement of the case solely because of a provision in such contract . . . that is conditioned on—

(A) . . . insolvency . . . ;

(B) the commencement of a case under this title. . . .

(f) (1) . . . [N]otwithstanding a provision in an executory contract or unexpired lease of the debtor . . . that prohibits, restricts, or conditions the assignment of such contract or lease, the trustee may assign such contract or lease . . .

(2) The trustee may assign an executory contract or unexpired lease of the debtor only if

(A) . . .

(B) adequate assurance of future performance by the assignee of such contract or lease is provided . . .

* * *

(n) (1) If the trustee rejects an executory contract under which the debtor is a licensor of a right to intellectual property, the licensee under such contract may elect

(A) to treat such contract as terminated . . . ; or

(B) to retain its rights (including a right to enforce any exclusivity provision of such contract, but excluding any other right . . . to specific performance . . .) . . . to such intellectual property . . . as such rights existed immediately before the case commenced, for

(i) the duration of such contract; and

(ii) any period for which such contract may be extended by the licensee as of right under applicable nonbankruptcy law.

CHAPTER 5—CREDITORS, DEBTOR, AND THE ESTATE

§ 501 Filing of proofs of claims or interests

(a) A creditor or an indenture trustee may file a proof of claim. An equity security holder may file a proof of interest.

§ 502 Allowance of claims or interests

(a) A claim or interest . . . is deemed allowed, unless a party in interest . . . objects.

(b) . . . [T]he court, after notice and a hearing, shall determine the amount of such claim in lawful currency of the United States as of the date of the filing of the petition, and shall allow such claim in such amount, except to the extent that . . .

(2) such claim is for unmatured interest; . . .

(c) There shall be estimated for purposes of allowance under this section

(1) any contingent or unliquidated claim, the fixing or liquidation of which . . . would unduly delay the administration of the case; or

(2) any right to payment arising from a right to an equitable remedy for breach of performance.

(g) (1) A claim arising from the rejection, under section 365 or under a plan under chapter . . 11 . . . of an executory contract . . . of the debtor that has not been assumed shall be determined, and shall be allowed . . . or disallowed . . . , the same as if such claim had arisen before the date of the filing of the petition.

(2) A claim for damages calculated . . . shall be allowed under subsection (a), (b) or (c) of this section, or disallowed under subsection (d) or (e), as if such claim had arisen before the date of the filing of the petition.

(h) A claim arising from the recovery of property under section . . . 550 . . . shall be determined, and shall be allowed . . . or disallowed . . . as if such claim had arisen before the date of the filing of the petition.

§ 503. Allowance of administrative expenses

(a) . . .

(b) After notice and a hearing, there shall be allowed, administrative expenses . . . including

(1)(A) the actual, necessary costs and expenses of preserving the estate including—

(i) wages, salaries, and commissions for services rendered after the commencement of the case; and

(ii) wages and benefits awarded pursuant a judicial proceeding of a proceeding of the National Labor Relations Board as back pay attributable to any period of time occurring after commencement of the case under this title, as a result of a violation of Federal or State law by the debtor, without regard to the time of the occurrence of unlawful conduct on which such award is based . . . if the court determines that payment . . . will not substantially increase the probability of layoff or termination of current employees, . . .

* * *

(3) The actual, necessary expenses . . . incurred by—

(B) a creditor that recovers, after the court's approval, for the benefit of the estate any property transferred or concealed by the debtor;

(9) the value of any goods received by the debtor within 20 days before the date of commencement of a case under this title in which the goods have been sold to the debtor in the ordinary course of such debtor's business.

§ 506. Determination of secured status

(a) (1) An allowed claim of a creditor secured by a lien on property in which the estate has an interest . . . is a secured claim to the extent of the value of such creditor's interest in the estate's interest in such property, . . . and is an unsecured claim to the extent that the value of such creditor's interest . . . is less than the amount of such allowed claim. Such value shall be determined in light of the purpose of the valuation and of the proposed disposition or use of such property, and in conjunction with any hearing on such disposition or use or on a plan affecting such creditor's interest.

(2) . . .

(b) To the extent that an allowed secured claim is secured by property the value of which, after any recovery under subsection (c) of this section, is greater than the amount of such claim, there shall be allowed to the holder of such claim, interest on such claim, and any reasonable fees, costs, or charges provided for under the agreement or State statute under which such claim arose.

(c) The trustee may recover from property securing an allowed secured claim the reasonable, necessary costs and expenses of preserving, or disposing of, such property to the extent of any benefit to the holder of such claim, including the payment of all ad valorem property taxes with respect to the property.

§ 507. Priorities

(a) The following expenses and claims have priority in the following order:

(1) First, [unsecured claims for domestic support obligations] . . . ;

(2) Second, administrative expenses allowed under section 503(b) . . .

(b) If the trustee, under section 362, 363, or 364 of this title, provides adequate protection of the interest of a holder of a claim secured by a lien on property of the debtor and if, notwithstanding such protection, such creditor has a claim allowable under subsection (a)(2) of this section arising from the stay of action against such property under section 362 of this title, from the use, sale, or lease of such property under section 363 of this title, or from the granting of a lien under section 364(d) of this title, then such creditor's claim under such subsection shall have priority over every other claim allowable under such sub-section.

§ 510. Subordination

(a) A subordination agreement is enforceable in a case under this title to the same extent that such agreement is enforceable under applicable nonbankruptcy law.

(b) For the purpose of distribution under this title, a claim arising from rescission of a purchase or sale of a security of the debtor or of an affiliate of the debtor, for damages arising from the purchase or sale of such a security, or for reimbursement or contribution allowed under section 502 on account of such a claim, shall be subordinated to all claims or interests that are senior to or equal the claim or interest represented by such security, except that if such security is common stock, such claim has the same priority as common stock.

(c) Notwithstanding subsections (a) and (b) of this section, after notice and a hearing, the court may

(1) under principles of equitable subordination, subordinate for purposes of distribution all or part of an allowed claim to all or part of another allowed claim or all or part of an allowed interest to all or part of another allowed interest; or

(2) order that any lien securing such a subordinated claim be transferred to the estate.

§ 524. Effect of discharge

(g)(1)(A) After notice and hearing, a court that enters an order confirming a plan of reorganization . . . may issue . . . an injunction in accordance with this subsection to supplement the injunctive effect of a discharge under this section.

(B) An injunction may be issued under subparagraph (A) to enjoin entities from taking legal action for the purpose of directly or indirectly collecting, recovering, or receiving payment or recovery with respect to any claim or demand that . . . is to be paid . . . by a trust described in paragraph (2)(B)(i) . . .

(2)(A) . . . after entry of such injunction, any proceeding that involves the validity, application, construction, or modification of such injunction, . . . may be commenced only in the district court in which injunction was entered, and such court shall have exclusive jurisdiction over any such proceeding. . . .

(B) The requirements of this subparagraph are that—

(i) the injunction is to be implemented in connection with a trust that . . .—

(I) is to assume the liabilities of a debtor which . . . has been named as a defendant in personal injury, wrongful death, or property-damage actions seeking recovery for damages allegedly caused by the presence of, or exposure to, asbestos or asbestos-containing products;

(II) is to be funded in whole or part by the securities of 1 or more debtors involved in such plan and by the obligation of such debtor or debtors to make future payments, including dividends;

(III) is to own . . . a majority of the voting shares of . . . each such debtor . . . ; and

(IV) is to use its assets or income to pay claims and demands; and

(ii) . . . the court determines that—

(I) the debtor is likely to be subject to substantial future demands for payment arising out of the same or similar conduct or events that gave rise to the claims that are addressed by the injunction;

(II) the actual amounts, numbers, and timing of such future demands cannot be determined;

(III) pursuit of such demands outside the procedures prescribed by such plan is likely to threaten the plan's purpose to deal equitably with claims and future demands;

(IV) as part of the process of seeking confirmation of such plan . . . a separate class . . . of the claimants whose claims are to be addressed by a trust described in clause (i) . . . votes, by at least 75 percent of those voting, in favor of the plan. . .

(V) . . . the trust will operate through mechanisms such as structured, periodic or supplemental payments, pro rata distributions, matrices, or periodic review of estimates of the numbers and values of present claims and future demands, or other comparable mechanisms, that provide reasonable assurance that the trust will value, and be in a financial position to pay, present claims and future demands that involve similar claims in substantially the same manner.

(3)(A) If the requirements of paragraph (2)(B) are met and the order . . . was issued . . .

(i) the injunction shall be valid and enforceable . . . ;

(ii) no entity that . . . becomes a direct or indirect transferee of, or successor to any assets of, [such] a debtor or trust . . . shall be liable with respect to any claim or demand made against such entity by reason of its becoming a transferee or successor; and

(iii) . . . no entity that . . . makes a loan to such a debtor or trust or to such a successor or transferee shall, by reason of making the loan, be liable with respect to any claim or demand made against such entity, nor shall any pledge of assets made in connection with such a loan be upset or impaired for that reason;

(B) Subparagraph (A) shall not be construed to . . . relieve any such entity of the duty to comply with . . . any Federal or State law regarding the making of a fraudulent conveyance . . . ;

(4)(A) . . . such an injunction may bar any action directed against a third party who is . . . alleged to be directly or indirectly liable for the conduct of, claims against, or demands on the debtor . . . ;

(B) . . . if . . . a kind of demand . . . is to be paid . . . by a trust described in paragraph (2)(B)(i) . . . then such injunction shall be valid . . . if

(i) as part of the proceedings . . . the court appoints a legal representative for the purpose of protecting the rights of persons that might subsequently assert demands . . . ; and

(ii) the court determines, before entering the order confirming such plan, that . . . such injunction . . . is fair and equitable with respect to the persons that might subsequently assert such demands . . .

§ 525. Protection against discriminatory treatment

(a) Except as provided in [several specific statutes] a governmental unit may not deny, revoke, suspend, or refuse to renew a license, permit, charter, franchise, or other similar grant to . . . a person that is . . . a debtor under . . . the Bankruptcy Act . . . solely because such bankrupt or debtor is or has been a debtor under . . . the Bankruptcy Act, has been insolvent before the commencement . . . or has not paid a debt that is dischargeable in [chapter 11]. . . .

§ 541. Property of the estate

(c)(1) . . . [A]n interest of the debtor in property becomes property of the estate . . . notwithstanding any provision in an agreement . . . or applicable nonbankruptcy law—

* * *

(B) that is conditioned on the insolvency or financial condition of the debtor, on the commencement of a case under this title, or on the appointment of or taking possession by a trustee in a case under this title . . . and that effects . . . a forfeiture, modification, or termination of the debtor's interest in the property.

§ 544. Trustee as lien creditor . . .

(a) The trustee shall have, as of the commencement of the case . . . the rights and powers of, or may avoid any transfer of property of the debtor or any obligation incurred by the debtor that is voidable by—

(1) a creditor that extends credit to the debtor at the time of the commencement of the case, and that obtains, at such time and with respect to such credit, a judicial lien on all property on which a creditor on a simple contract could have obtained such a judicial lien, whether or not such a creditor exists;

(2) a creditor that extends credit to the debtor at the time of the commencement of the case, and obtains, at such time and with respect

to such credit, an execution against the debtor that is returned unsatisfied at such time, whether or not such a creditor exists; . . .

(b)(1) . . . [T]he trustee may avoid any transfer of an interest of the debtor in property or any obligation incurred by the debtor that is voidable under applicable law by a creditor holding an unsecured claim that is allowable under section 502 of this title. . . .

§ 545. Statutory liens

The trustee may avoid the fixing of a statutory lien on property of the debtor to the extent that such lien—

(1) first becomes effective against the debtor—

(A) when a case under this title concerning the debtor is commenced;

(B) when an insolvency proceeding other than under this title concerning the debtor is commenced;

(C) when a custodian is appointed or authorized to take or takes possession;

(D) when the debtor becomes insolvent;

(E) when the debtor's financial condition fails to meet a specified standard; or

(F) at the time of an execution against property of the debtor levied at the instance of an entity other than the holder of such statutory lien;

(2) is not perfected or enforceable at the time of the commencement of the case against a bona fide purchaser that purchases such property at the time of the commencement of the case, whether or not such a purchaser exists. . . .

§ 546. Limitations on avoiding powers

(b)(1) The rights and powers of a trustee under section[ ] 544 . . . are subject to any generally applicable [state] law that—

(A) permits perfection of an interest in property to be effective against an entity that acquires rights in such property before the date of perfection. . . .

(c)(1) . . . [S]ubject to the prior rights of a holder of a security interest in such goods or the proceeds thereof, the rights and powers of the trustee under sections 544(a), 545, 547, and 549 are subject to the right of a seller of goods that has sold goods to the debtor, in the ordinary course of such seller's business, to reclaim such goods if the debtor has received such goods while insolvent, within 45 days before the date of the commencement of a case under this title. . . .

* * *

(e) Notwithstanding sections 544, . . . , 547, 548(a)(1)(B), and 548(b) of this title, the trustee may not avoid a transfer that is . . . a settlement payment, as defined in section 101 or 741, . . . , made . . . to a . . . stockbroker, financial institution, financial participant, or securities clearing agency. . . .

(f) Notwithstanding sections . . . 547, 548(a)(1)(B), and 548(b) of this title, the trustee may not avoid a transfer made by or to (or for the benefit of) a repo participant . . . in connection with a repurchase agreement and that is made before the commencement of the case. . . .

(g) Notwithstanding sections . . . 547, 548(a)(1)(B), and 548(b) of this title, the trustee may not avoid a transfer made by or to (or for the benefit of) a swap participant . . . in connection with any swap agreement and that is made before the commencement of the case. . . .

§ 547. Preferences

(b) Except as provided in subsections (c) and (i) of this section, the trustee may avoid any transfer of an interest of the debtor in property—

(1) to or for the benefit of a creditor;

(2) for or on account of an antecedent debt owed by the debtor before such transfer was made;

(3) made while the debtor was insolvent;

(4) made—

(A) on or within 90 days before the date of the filing of the petition; or

(B) between ninety days and one year before the date of the filing of the petition, if such creditor at the time of such transfer was an insider; and

(5) that enables such creditor to receive more than such creditor would receive if—

(A) the case were a case under chapter 7 of this title;

(B) the transfer had not been made; and

(C) such creditor received payment of such debt to the extent provided by the provisions of this title.

(c) The trustee may not avoid under this section a transfer—

(1) to the extent that such transfer was—

(A) intended by the debtor and the creditor to or for whose benefit such transfer was made to be a contemporaneous exchange for new value given to the debtor; and

(B) in fact a substantially contemporaneous exchange;

(2) to the extent that such transfer was in payment of a debt incurred by the debtor in the ordinary course of business or financial affairs of the debtor and the transferee, and such transfer was—

(A) made in the ordinary course of business or financial affairs of the debtor and the transferee; or;

(B) made according to ordinary business terms;

(C) . . .

(3) that creates a security interest in property acquired by the debtor—

(A) to the extent such security interest secures new value [in the nature of a purchase-money security interest] . . .

(i) given at or after the signing of a security agreement that contains a description of such property as collateral;

* * *

(iii) given to enable the debtor to acquire such property; and

(iv) in fact used by the debtor to acquire such property; and

(B) that is perfected on or before 30 days after the debtor receives possession of such property[.]

(4) to or for the benefit of a creditor, to the extent that, after such transfer, such creditor gave new value to or for the benefit of the debtor . . .

(5) that creates a perfected security interest in inventory or a receivable or the proceeds of either, except to the extent that the aggregate of all such transfers to the transferee caused a reduction . . . to the prejudice of other creditors holding unsecured claims, of any amount by which the debt secured by such security interest exceeded the value of all security interests for such debt on [the 90-day date for the non-insiders and the 1-year date for insiders] . . .

(6) that is the fixing of a statutory lien that is not avoidable under section 545 of this title;

(7) . . .

(8) [aggregate transfers of less than $600 for an individual debtor]; or

(9) if, in a case filed by a debtor whose debts are not primarily consumer debts, the aggregate value of all property that constitutes or is affected by such transfer is less than $5000.

. . .

(f) For the purposes of this section, the debtor is presumed to have been insolvent on and during the 90 days immediately preceding the date of the filing of the petition.

(g) For the purposes of this section, the trustee has the burden of proving the avoid-ability of a transfer under subsection (b) . . ., and the creditor or party in interest against whom recovery or avoidance is sought has the burden of proving the nonavoidability of a transfer under subsection (c). . . .

* * *

(i) If the trustee avoids under subsection (b) a transfer made between 90 days and 1 year before the date of the filing of the petition, by the debtor to an entity that is not an insider for the benefit of a creditor that is an insider, such transfer shall be considered to be avoided under this section only with respect to the creditor that is an insider.

§ 548. Fraudulent transfers and obligations

(a)(1) The trustee may avoid any transfer (including any transfer to or for the benefit or an insider under an employment contract) of an interest of the debtor in property, or any obligation (including any obligation to or for the benefit or an insider under an employment contract) incurred by the debtor, that was made or incurred on or within 2 years before the date of the filing of the petition, if the debtor voluntarily or involuntarily—

(A) made such transfer or incurred such obligation with actual intent to hinder, delay, or defraud any entity to which the debtor was or became, on or after the date that such transfer was made or such obligation was incurred, indebted; or

(B)(i) received less than a reasonably equivalent value in exchange for such transfer or obligation; and

(ii)(I) was insolvent on the date that such transfer was made or such obligation was incurred, or became insolvent as a result of such transfer or obligation;

(II) was engaged in business or a transaction, or was about to engage in business or a transaction, for which any property remaining with the debtor was an unreasonably small capital;

(III) intended to incur, or believed that the debtor would incur, debts that would be beyond the debtor's ability to pay as such debts matured; or

(IV) made such transfer to or for the benefit of an insider, or incurred such obligation to or for the benefit of an insider, under an employment contract and not in the ordinary course of business.

. . .

(c) . . . a transferee or obligee of such a transfer or obligation that takes for value and in good faith has a lien on or may retain any interest transferred or may enforce any obligation incurred, as the case may be, to the extent that such transferee or obligee gave value to the debtor in exchange for such transfer or obligation.

(d)(1) . . .

(2) In this section—

(A) "value" means property, or satisfaction or securing of a present or antecedent debt of the debtor, but does not include an unperformed promise to furnish support to the debtor or to a relative of the debtor;

* * *

§ 549. Postpetition transactions

(a) . . . [the] trustee may avoid a transfer of property of the estate—

(1) that occurs after the commencement of the case; and

(2) . . . that is not authorized under this title or by the court.

§ 550. Liability of transferee of avoided transfer

(a) Except as otherwise provided in this section, to the extent that a transfer is avoided under section . . . 547, 548 . . . the trustee may recover, for the benefit of the estate, the property transferred, or, if the court so orders, the value of such property, from

(1) the initial transferee of such transfer or the entity for whose benefit such transfer was made; or

(2) any immediate or mediate transferee of such initial transferee.

(b) The trustee may not recover under section (a)(2) of this section from

(1) a transferee that takes for value, including satisfaction or securing of a present or antecedent debt, in good faith, and without knowledge of the voidability of the transfer avoided; or

(2) any immediate or mediate good faith transferee of such transferee.

(c) If a transfer made between 90 days and one year before the filing of the petition—

(1) is avoided under section 547(b) of this title; and

(2) was made for the benefit of a creditor that at the time of such transfer was an insider;

the trustee may not recover under subsection (a) from a transferee that is not an insider.

(d) The trustee is entitled to only a single satisfaction under subsection (a) of this section.

§ 553. Setoff

[T]his title does not affect any right of a creditor to offset a mutual debt owing by such creditor to the debtor that arose before the commencement of the case under this title against a claim of such creditor against the debtor that arose before the commencement of the case. . . .

(a) [T]his title does not affect any right of a creditor to offset a mutual debt except to the extent that—

(2) such claim was transferred by an entity other than the debtor to such creditor—

(A) after the commencement of the case; or

(B)(I) after 90 days before . . . ; and

(II) while the debtor was insolvent (except for a setoff of a kind described in section 362(b)(6), 362(b)(7), 362(b)(17) [and several other Code sections]). . . .

§ 554. Abandonment of property of the estate

(a) After notice and a hearing, the trustee many abandon any property of the estate that is burdensome to the estate or that is of inconsequential value and benefit to the estate.

§ 560. Contractual right to liquidate, terminate, or accelerate a swap agreement

The exercise of any contractual right of any swap participant or financial participant to cause the liquidation, termination, or acceleration of one or more swap agreements because of a condition of the kind specified in section 365(e)(1) of this title [dealing with ipso facto and similar clauses] or to offset or net out any termination values or payment amounts arising under or in connection with the termination, liquidation, or acceleration of one or more swap agreements shall not be stayed, avoided, or otherwise limited by operation of any provision of this title. . . .

CHAPTER 7—LIQUIDATION

§ 726. Distribution of property of the estate

(a) Except as provided in section 510 of this title [providing for subordination of certain claims], property of the estate shall be distributed

(1) first, in payment of claims of the kind specified in . . . Section 507 [such as administrative claims] . . . ;

(2) second, in payment of any allowed unsecured claim . . . proof of which is [in general] timely filed . . . ;

(3) third, in payment of any allowed unsecured claim proof of which is tardily filed. . . ;

(4) fourth, in payment of [certain fines];

(5) fifth, in payment of interest at the legal rate from the date of the filing of the petition, on any claim paid under paragraph (1), (2), (3), or (4) of this subsection; and

(6) sixth, to the debtor.

§ 741. Definitions for this subchapter

In this subchapter [on stock broker liquidations]—

* * *

(8) "settlement payment" means a preliminary settlement payment, a partial settlement payment, an interim settlement payment, a settlement payment on account, a final settlement payment, or any other similar payment commonly used in the securities trade. . . .

CHAPTER 9— . . . MUNICIPALITY

§ 904. Limitation on jurisdiction and powers of court

Notwithstanding any power of the court, unless the debtor consents or the plan so provides, the court may not, by any stay, order, or decree, in the case or otherwise, interfere with—

(1) any of the political or governmental powers of the debtor;

(2) any of the property or revenues of the debtor; or

(3) the debtor's use or enjoyment of any income-producing property.

CHAPTER 11—REORGANIZATION

§ 1102. Creditors' and equity security holders' committees

(a)(1) . . . [T]he United States trustee shall appoint a committee of creditors holding unsecured claims and may appoint additional committees of creditors or of equity security holders as the . . . trustee deems appropriate. . . .

(b)(1) A committee of creditors . . . shall ordinarily consist of persons, willing to serve, that hold the seven largest claims against the debtor of the kinds represented on such committee. . . .

§ 1104. Appointment of trustee or examiner

(a) . . . on request of a party in interest or the United States trustee, and after notice and a hearing, the court shall order the appointment of a trustee—

(1) for cause, including fraud, dishonesty, incompetence, or gross mismanagement of the affairs of the debtor by current management, either before or after the commencement of the case, or similar cause . . .;

(2) if such appointment is in the interests of creditors, any equity holders, and other interests of the estate . . . ;

* * *

(c) If the court does not order the appointment of a trustee . . . then . . . on request of a party in interest or the United States trustee . . . the court shall order the appointment of an examiner to conduct . . . an investigation . . . of any allegations of fraud, dishonesty, incompetence, misconduct, mismanagement, or irregularity in the management of the affairs of the debtor of or by current or former management of the debtor, if

(1) such appointment is in the interests of creditors . . . ; or

(2) the debtor's . . . debts . . . exceed $5,000,000.

§ 1107. Rights, powers, and duties of debtor in possession

(a) . . . a debtor in possession shall have all the rights . . . and powers, and shall perform all the functions and duties . . . of a trustee serving in a case under this chapter.

(b) . . . a person is not disqualified from employment under section 327 . . . by a debtor in possession solely because of such person's employment by . . . the debtor before the commencement of the case.

§ 1108. Authorization to operate business

Unless the court, on request of a party in interest and after notice and a hearing, orders otherwise, the trustee may operate the debtor's business.

§ 1109. Right to be heard

A party in interest, including the debtor, the trustee, a creditor's committee, an equity security holder's committee, a creditor, an equity security holder, or any indenture trustee, may raise and may appear and be heard on any issue in a case under this chapter.

§ 1112. Conversion or dismissal

(b)(1) . . . [O]n request of a party in interest, and after notice and a hearing, absent unusual circumstances . . . that establish that the requested conversion or dismissal is not in the best interests of creditors and the estate, the court shall convert [a chapter 11 proceeding to] chapter 7 . . . if the movant establishes cause.

(2) [Conversion or dismissal] shall not be granted absent unusual circumstances specifically identified by the court that establish that such relief is not in the best interests of creditors and the estate, if the debtor or another party in interest objects and establishes that—

(A) there is a reasonable likelihood that a plan will be confirmed . . . within a reasonable period of time; and

(B) the grounds for [conversion or dismissal] include an act or omission of the debtor other than under paragraph (4)(A) . . . for which there exists a reasonable justification for the act or omission . . . and . . . that will be cured within a reasonable period of time . . .

(3) . . .

(4) . . . [T]he term "cause" includes—

(A) substantial or continuing loss or diminution of the estate and the absence of a reasonable likelihood of rehabilitation;

(B) gross mismanagement of the estate;

(C) . . .

(D) unauthorized use of cash collateral . . . ;

* * *

(I) failure . . . to pay taxes owed . . . ;

(J) failure to file a disclosure statement . . . ;

* * *

(N) material default by the debtor with respect to a confirmed plan. . . .

§ 1113. Rejection of collective bargaining agreements

(a) The debtor in possession, or the trustee if one has been appointed . . . , may assume or reject a collective bargaining agreement only in accordance with the provisions of this section.

(b)(1)(A) Subsequent to filing a petition and prior to filing an application seeking rejection of a collective bargaining agreement, the debtor in possession or trustee (hereinafter in this section, "trustee" shall include a debtor in possession), shall—make a proposal to the authorized representative of the employees covered by such agreement, based on the most complete and reliable information available at the time of such proposal, which provides for those necessary modifications in the employees benefits and protections that are necessary to permit the reorganization of the debtor and assures that all creditors, the debtor and all of the affected parties are treated fairly and equitably; and

(B) provide, subject to subsection (d)(3), the representative of the employees with such relevant information as is necessary to evaluate the proposal.

(2) During the period beginning on the date of the making of a proposal provided for in paragraph (1) and ending on the date of the hearing provided for in subsection (d)(1), the trustee shall meet, at reasonable times, with the authorized representative to confer in good faith in attempting to reach mutually satisfactory modifications of such agreement.

(c) The court shall approve an application for rejection of a collective bargaining agreement only if the court finds that—

(1) the trustee has, prior to the hearing, made a proposal that fulfills the requirements of subsection (b)(1);

(2) the authorized representative of the employees has refused to accept such proposal without good cause; and

(3) the balance of the equities clearly favors rejection of such agreement.

* * *

(f) No provision of this title shall be construed to permit a trustee to unilaterally terminate or alter any provisions of a collective bargaining agreement prior to compliance with the provisions of this section.

§ 1121. Who may file a plan

(a) The debtor may file a plan with a petition commencing a voluntary case, or at any time in a voluntary case or an involuntary case.

(b) Except as otherwise provided in this section, only the debtor may file a plan until after 120 days after the date of the order for relief under this chapter.

(c) Any party in interest, including the debtor, the trustee, a creditors' committee, an equity security holders' committee, a creditor, an equity security holder, or any indenture trustee, may file a plan if and only if—

(1) a trustee has been appointed under this chapter;

(2) the debtor has not filed a plan before 120 days after the date of the order for relief under this chapter; or

(3) the debtor has not filed a plan that has been accepted, before 180 days after the date of the order for relief under this chapter, by each class of claims or interests that is impaired under the plan.

(d)(1) subject to paragraph (2), on request of a party in interest made within the respective periods specified in subsections (b) and (c) of this section and after notice and a hearing, the court may for cause reduce or increase the 120-day period or the 180-day period referred to in this section.

(2)(A) The 120-day period . . . may not be extended beyond a date that is 18 months after the date of the order for relief . . .

(B) The 180-day period . . . may not be extended beyond a date that is 20 months after the date of the order for relief . . .

§ 1122. Classification of claims or interests

(a) Except as provided in subsection (b) of this section, a plan may place a claim or an interest in a particular class only if such claim or interest is substantially similar to the other claims or interests of such class.

(b) A plan may designate a separate class of claims consisting only of every unsecured claim that is less than or reduced to an amount that the court approves as reasonable and necessary for administrative convenience.

§ 1123. Contents of plan

(a) Notwithstanding any otherwise applicable nonbankruptcy law, a plan shall—

(1) designate, subject to section 1122 of this title, classes of claims, other than claims of a kind specified in section 507(a)(2), 507(a)(3), or 507(a)(8) of this title, and classes of interests;

(2) specify any class of claims or interests that is not impaired under the plan;

(3) specify the treatment of any class of claims or interests that is impaired under the plan;

(4) provide the same treatment for each claim or interest of a particular class, unless the holder of a particular claim or interest agrees to a less favorable treatment of such particular claim or interest;

(5) provide adequate means for the plan's implementation, such as—

(A) retention by the debtor of all or any part of the property of the estate;

(B) transfer of all or any part of the property of the estate to one or more entities, whether organized before or after the confirmation of such plan;

(C) merger or consolidation of the debtor with one or more persons;

(D) sale of all or any part of the property of the estate, either subject to or free of any lien, or the distribution of all or any part of the property of the estate among those having an interest in such property of the estate;

(E) satisfaction or modification of any lien;

(F) cancellation or modification of any indenture or similar instrument;

(G) curing or waiving of any default;

(H) extension of a maturity date or a change in an interest rate or other term of outstanding securities;

(I) amendment of the debtor's charter; or

(J) issuance of securities of the debtor, or of any entity referred to in subparagraph (B) or (C) of this paragraph, for cash, for property, for existing securities, or in exchange for claims or interests, or for any other appropriate purpose;

(6) [amend the corporate charter in several respects]

(7) contain only provisions that are consistent with the interests of creditors and equity security holders and with public policy with respect to the manner of selection of any officer, director, or trustee under the plan and any successor to such officer, director, or trustee; . . .

(8) . . .

(b) Subject to subsection (a) of this section, a plan may—

(1) impair or leave unimpaired any class of claims, secured or unsecured, or of interests;

(2) subject to section 365 of this title, provide for the assumption, rejection, or assignment of any executory contract or unexpired lease of the debtor not previously rejected under such section;

(3) provide for—

(A) the settlement or adjustment of any claim or interest belonging to the debtor or to the estate; or

(B) the retention and enforcement by the debtor, by the trustee, or by a representative of the estate appointed for such purpose, of any such claim or interest;

(4) provide for the sale of all or substantially all of the property of the estate, and the distribution of the proceeds of such sale among holders of claims or interests;

(5) modify the rights of holders of secured claims, other than a claim secured only by a security interest in real property that is the debtor's principal residence, or of holders of unsecured claims, or leave unaffected the rights of holders of any class of claims; and

(6) include any other appropriate provision not inconsistent with the applicable provisions of this title.

(c) In a case concerning an individual, a plan proposed by an entity other than the debtor may not provide for the use, sale, or lease of property exempted under section 522 of this title, unless the debtor consents to such use, sale, or lease.

(d) Notwithstanding subsection (a) of this section and sections 506(b), 1129(a)(7), and 1129(b) of this title, if it is proposed in a plan to cure a default the amount necessary to cure the default shall be determined in accordance with the underlying agreement and applicable nonbankruptcy law.

§ 1124. Impairment of claims or interests

[Unless a holder of a claim or interest agrees to less favorable treatment] a class of claims or interests is impaired under a plan unless, with respect to each claim or interest of such class, the plan [either]—

(1) leaves unaltered the legal, equitable, and contractual rights to which such claim or interest entitles the holder of such claim or interest; [or]

(2) notwithstanding any contractual provision or applicable law that entitles the holder of such claim or interest to demand or receive

accelerated payment of such claim or interest after the occurrence of a default—

(A) cures any such default that occurred before or after the commencement of the case under this title, other than a default of a kind specified in section 365(b)(2) of this title . . . ; [and]

(B) reinstates the maturity of such claim or interest as such maturity existed before such default; [and]

(C) compensates the holder of such claim or interest for any damages incurred as a result of any reasonable reliance by such holder on such contractual provision or such applicable law; [and]

(D) if such claim or such interest arises from any failure to perform a nonmonetary obligation, . . . , compensates the holder of such claim or such interest . . . for any actual pecuniary loss incurred by such holder as a result of such failure; and

(E) does not otherwise alter the legal, equitable, or contractual rights to which such claim or interest entitles the holder of such claim or interest.

§ 1125. Postpetition disclosure and solicitation

(a) In this section—

(1) "adequate information" means information of a kind, and in sufficient detail, as far as is reasonably practicable in light of the nature and history of the debtor and the condition of debtor's books and records . . . and a hypothetical investor typical of the holders of claims or interests in the case, that would enable such a hypothetical investor of the relevant class to make an informed judgment about the plan, but adequate information need not include such information about any other possible or proposed plan . . . ; and . . .

(b) An acceptance or rejection of a plan may not be solicited after the commencement of the case [unless] there is transmitted to such holder the plan or a summary of the plan, and a written disclosure statement approved, after notice and a hearing, by the court as containing adequate information. The court may approve a disclosure statement without a valuation of the debtor or an appraisal of the debtor's assets.

* * *

(c) Whether a disclosure statement [under (b)] contains adequate information is not governed by any otherwise applicable nonbankruptcy law, rule, or regulation . . .

(d) Whether a disclosure statement [under (b)] contains adequate information is not governed by any otherwise applicable nonbankruptcy [securities] law, rule, or regulation, . . .

(e) A person that solicits acceptance or rejection of a plan, in good faith and in compliance with the applicable provisions of this title . . . is not liable, on account of such solicitation . . . for violation of any applicable law, rule, or regulation governing solicitation of acceptance or rejection of a plan. . . .

§ 1126. Acceptance of plan

(b) . . . a holder of a claim or interest that has accepted or rejected the plan before the commencement of the case under this title is deemed to have accepted or rejected such plan, as the case may be, if—

(1) the solicitation of such acceptance or rejection was in compliance with any applicable nonbankruptcy law, rule, or regulation governing the adequacy of disclosure in connection with such solicitation; or

(2) if there is not any such law, rule, or regulation, such acceptance or rejection was solicited after disclosure to such holder of adequate information. . . .

(c) A class of claims has accepted a plan if such plan has been accepted by creditors other than any entity designated under subsection (e) of this section, that hold at least two-thirds in amount and more than one-half in number of the allowed claims of such class held by creditors, other than any entity designated under subsection (e) of this section, that have accepted or rejected such plan.

(d) A class of interests has accepted the plan if such plan has been accepted by holders of such interests . . . that hold at least two-thirds in amount of the allowed interests . . . that have accepted or rejected such plan.

(e) On request of a party in interest, . . . the court may designate any entity whose acceptance or rejection of such plan was not in good faith, or was not solicited or procured in good faith. . . .

(f) Notwithstanding any other provision of this section, a class that is not impaired under a plan, and each holder of a claim or interest of such class, are conclusively presumed to have accepted the plan, and solicitation of acceptances with respect to such class from the holders of claims or interests of such class is not required.

(g) Notwithstanding any other provision of this section, a class is deemed not to have accepted a plan if such plan provides that the claims or interests of such class do not entitle the holders of such claims or interests to receive or retain any property under the plan on account of such claims or interests.

§ 1128. Confirmation hearing

(a) After notice, the court shall hold a hearing on confirmation of a plan.

(b) A party in interest may object to confirmation of a plan.

§ 1129. Confirmation of plan

(a) The court shall confirm a plan only if all of the following requirements are met:

(1) The plan complies with the applicable provisions of this title.

(2) . . .

(3) The plan has been proposed in good faith and not by any means forbidden by law.

(4) . . .

(5) . . .

(6) . . .

(7) With respect to each impaired class of claims or interests—

(A) each holder of a claim or interest of such class—

(i) has accepted the plan; or

(ii) will receive or retain under the plan on account of such claim or interest property of a value, as of the effective date of the plan, that is not less than the amount that such holder would so receive or retain if the debtor were liquidated under chapter 7 of this title on such date;

(B) . . .

(8) With respect to each class of claims or interests—

(A) such class has accepted the plan; or

(B) such class is not impaired under the plan.

(9) Except to the extent that the holder of a particular claim has agreed to a different treatment of such claim, the plan provides that—

(A) with respect to a claim of a kind specified in section 507(a)(2) [for administrative expenses] . . . on the effective date of the plan, the holder of such claim will receive on account of such claim cash equal to the allowed amount of such claim; . . . .

(10) If a class of claims is impaired under the plan, at least one class of claims that is impaired under the plan has accepted the plan, determined without including any acceptance of the plan by any insider.

(11) Confirmation of the plan is not likely to be followed by the liquidation, or the need for further financial reorganization, of the debtor or any successor to the debtor under the plan, unless such liquidation or reorganization is proposed in the plan.

(b)(1) . . . if all of the applicable requirements of subsection (a) of this section other than paragraph (8) are met with respect to a plan, the court, on request of the proponent of the plan, shall confirm the plan notwithstanding the requirements of such paragraph if the plan does not discriminate unfairly, and is fair and equitable, with respect to each class of claims or interests that is impaired under, and has not accepted, the plan.

(2) For the purpose of this subsection, the condition that a plan be fair and equitable with respect to a class includes the following requirements:

(A) With respect to a class of secured claims, the plan provides—

(i) (I) that the holders of such claims retain the liens securing such claims, whether the property subject to such liens is retained by the debtor or transferred to another entity, to the extent of the allowed amount of such claims; and

(II) that each holder of a claim of such class receive on account of such claim deferred cash payments totaling at least the allowed amount of such claim, of a value, as of the effective date of the plan, of at least the value of such holder's interest in the estate's interest in such property;

(ii) for the sale . . . of any property that is subject to the liens securing such claims, free and clear of such liens, with such liens to attach to the proceeds of such sale . . . ; or

(iii) for the realization by such holders of the indubitable equivalent of such claims.

(B) With respect to a class of unsecured claims—

(i) the plan provides that each holder of a claim of such class receive or retain on account of such claim property of a value, as of the effective date of the plan, equal to the allowed amount of such claim; or

(ii) the holder of any claim or interest that is junior to the claims of such class will not receive or retain under the plan on account of such junior claim or interest any property, . . .

(C) With respect to a class of interests—

(i) the plan provides that each holder of an interest of such class receive or retain on account of such interest property of a value, as of the effective date of the plan, equal to the greatest of the allowed amount of any fixed liquidation preference to which such holder is entitled, any fixed redemption price to which such holder is entitled, or the value of such interest; or

(ii) the holder of any interest that is junior to the interests of such class will not receive or retain under the plan on account of such junior interest any property.

§ 1141. Effect of confirmation

(a) Except as provided in subsections (d)(2) and (d)(3) of this section, the provisions of a confirmed plan bind the debtor, any entity issuing securities under the plan, any entity acquiring property under the plan [of reorganization], and any creditor, equity security holder, or general partner in the debtor, whether or not the claim or interest of such creditor, equity security holder, or general partner is impaired under the plan and whether or not such creditor, equity security holder, or general partner has accepted the plan.

(b) Except as otherwise provided in the plan or the order confirming the plan, the confirmation of a plan vests all of the property of the estate in the debtor.

(c) Except as provided in subsections (d)(2) and (d)(3) of this section and except as otherwise provided in the plan or in the order confirming the plan, after confirmation of a plan, the property dealt with by the plan is free and clear of all claims and interests of creditors, equity security holders, and of general partners in the debtor.

(d)(1) Except as otherwise provided in this subsection, in the plan, or in the order confirming the plan, the confirmation of a plan—

(A) discharges the debtor from any debt that arose before the date of such confirmation, and any debt of a kind specified in section 502(g), 502(h), or 502(i) of this title, whether or not

(i) a proof of the claim based on such debt is filed or deemed filed under section 501 of this title;

(ii) such claim is allowed under section 502 of this title; or

(iii) the holder of such claim has accepted the plan; and

(B) terminates all rights and interests of equity security holders and general partners provided for by the plan.

§ 1142. Implementation of plan

(a) Notwithstanding any otherwise applicable nonbankruptcy law, rule, or regulation relating to financial condition, the debtor . . . shall carry out the plan and shall comply with any orders of the court.

TITLE 28 OF THE UNITED STATES CODE

Judiciary and Juridical Procedure

Part I — Organization of Courts

* * *

§ 151. Designation of bankruptcy courts

In each judicial district, the bankruptcy judges in regular active service shall constitute a unit of the district court to be known as the bankruptcy court for that district. Each bankruptcy judge, as a judicial officer of the district court, may exercise the authority conferred under this chapter with respect to any action, suit, or proceeding and may preside alone and hold a regular or special session of the court, except as otherwise provided by law or by rule or order of the district court.

§ 152. Appointment of bankruptcy judges

(a) (1) Each bankruptcy judge to be appointed for a judicial district . . . shall be appointed by the court of appeals of the United States for the circuit in which such district is located. . . . Each bankruptcy judge shall be appointed for a term of fourteen years. . . . Bankruptcy judges shall serve as judicial officers of the United States district court established under Article III of the Constitution.

* * *

§ 157. Procedures

(a) Each district court may provide that any or all [cases or proceedings] arising [under] or related to a case under title 11 shall be referred to the bankruptcy judges for the district.

(b) (1) Bankruptcy judges may hear and determine all cases under title 11 and all core proceedings arising . . . in a case under title 11, referred under subsection (a) of this section, and may enter appropriate orders and judgments, subject to review under section 158 of this title.

(2) Core proceedings include, but are not limited to—

(A) matters concerning the administration of the estate;

(B) allowance or disallowance of claims against the estate . . . and estimation of claims or interests for the purposes of confirming a plan under chapter 11 . . . of title 11, but not the liquidation or estimation of contingent or unliquidated personal injury tort or wrongful death claims against the estate for purposes of distribution in a case under title 11;

(C) counterclaims by the estate against persons filing claims against the estate;

(D) orders in respect to obtaining credit;

(E) orders to turn over property of the estate;

(F) proceedings to determine, avoid, or recover preferences;

(G) motions to terminate, annul, or modify the automatic stay;

(H) proceedings to determine, avoid, or recover fraudulent conveyances;

(I) determinations as to the dischargeability of particular debts;

(J) objections to discharges;

(K) determinations of the validity, extent, or priority of liens;

(L) confirmations of plans;

(M) orders approving the use or lease of property, including the use of cash collateral;

(N) orders approving the sale of property . . . ;

(O) other proceedings affecting the liquidation of the assets of the estate or the adjustment of the debtor-creditor or the equity security holder relationship, except personal injury tort or wrongful death claims; and

(P) recognition of foreign proceedings. . . .

(3) The bankruptcy judge shall determine, on the judge's own motion or on timely motion of a party, whether a proceeding is a core proceeding under this subsection or is a proceeding that is otherwise related to a case under title 11. . . .

(5) The district court shall order that personal injury tort and wrongful death claims shall be tried in the district court in which the bankruptcy case is pending, or in the district court in the district in which the claim arose, as determined by the district court in which the bankruptcy case is pending.

* * *

§ 158. Appeals

(a) The district courts of the United States shall have jurisdiction to hear appeals—

(1) from final judgments, orders, and decrees;

(2) from interlocutory orders and decrees issued under section 1121(d) of title 11 increasing or reducing the time periods referred to in section 1121 of such title; and

(3) with leave of the court, from other interlocutory orders and decrees;

and, with leave of the court, from interlocutory orders and decrees, of bankruptcy judges entered in cases and proceedings referred to the bankruptcy judges under section 157 of this title. An appeal under this subsection shall be taken only to the district court for the judicial district in which the bankruptcy judge is serving.

* * *

Part IV — Jurisdiction and Venue

§ 1334. Bankruptcy cases and proceedings

(a) . . . [T]he district courts shall have original and exclusive jurisdiction of all cases under title 11.

* * *

(e) The district court in which a case under title 11 is commenced or is pending shall have exclusive jurisdiction . . . of all the property, wherever located, of the debtor as of the commencement of such case, and of property of the estate. . . .

* * *

§ 1408. Venue of cases under title 11

. . . [A] case under title 11 may be commenced in the district court for the district—

(1) in which the domicile, residence, principal place of business in the United States, or principal assets in the United States, of the person or entity that is the subject of such case have been located for the one hundred and eighty days immediately preceding such commencement, or for a longer portion of such one-hundred-and-eighty-day period than the domicile, residence, or principal place of business, in the United States, or principal assets in the United States, of such person were located in any other district; or

(2) in which there is pending a case under title 11 concerning such person's affiliate, general partner, or partnership.

* * *

§ 1411. Jury trials

(a) . . . [T]his chapter and title 11 do not affect any right to trial by jury that an individual has under applicable nonbankruptcy law with regard to a personal injury or wrongful death tort claim.

* * *

TRUST INDENTURE ACT OF 1939
(15 U.S.C. § 77aaa et seq.)

§ 310(b) Disqualification of trustee

If any indenture trustee has or shall acquire any conflicting interest as hereinafter defined—

(i) then, within 90 days after ascertaining that it has such conflicting interest, and if the default (as defined in the next sentence) to which such conflicting interest relates has not been cured or duly waived or otherwise eliminated before the end of such 90-day period, such trustee shall either eliminate such conflicting interest or . . . resign . . . ;

* * *

(iii) . . . any security holder who has been a bona fide holder of indenture securities for at least six months may, on behalf of himself and all others similarly situated, petition any court of competent jurisdiction for the removal of such trustee . . .

. . . an indenture trustee shall be deemed to have a conflicting interest if the indenture securities are in default (as such term is defined in such indenture . . .) and—

(1) such trustee is trustee under another indenture . . . of an obligor upon the indenture securities . . .

* * *

(10) . . . the trustee shall be or shall become a creditor of the obligor.

§ 316(a) Directions and waivers by bondholders

The indenture to be qualified—

(1) shall automatically be deemed (unless it is expressly provided therein that any such provision is excluded) to contain provisions authorizing the holders of not less than a majority in principal amount of the indenture securities . . . at the time outstanding . . . on behalf of the holders of all such indenture securities, to consent to the waiver of any past default and its consequences; . . .

(2) may contain provisions authorizing the holders of not less than 75 per centum in principal amount of the indenture securities . . . at the time outstanding to consent on behalf of the holders of all such indenture securities to the postponement of any interest payment for a period not exceeding three years from its due date. securities owned by any obligor upon the indenture securities, or by any person directly or indirectly controlling or controlled by or under direct or indirect common control with any such obligor, shall be disregarded, except that for the purposes of determining whether the indenture trustee shall be protected in relying on any such direction or consent, only indenture securities which such trustee knows are so owned shall be so disregarded.

For the purposes of this subsection . . . in determining whether the holders of the required principal amount of indenture securities have concurred in any such direction or consent, indenture

§ 316(b) Prohibition of impairment of holder's right to payment

Notwithstanding any other provision of the indenture to be qualified, the right of any holder of any indenture security to receive payment of the principal of and interest on such indenture security, on or after the respective due dates expressed in such indenture security, or to institute suit for the enforcement of any such payment on or after such respective dates, shall not be impaired or affected without the consent of such holder. . . .

UNIFORM FRAUDULENT CONVEYANCE ACT

§ 1. Definition of Terms

In this act "Assets" of a debtor means property not exempt from liability for his debts. To the extent that any property is liable for any debts of the debtor, such property shall be included in his assets.

"Conveyance" includes every payment of money, assignment, release, transfer, lease, mortgage or pledge of tangible or intangible property, and also the creation of any lien or incumbrance.

"Creditor" is a person having any claim, whether matured or unmatured, liquidated or unliquidated, absolute, fixed or contingent.

"Debt" includes any legal liability, whether matured or unmatured, liquidated or unliquidated, absolute, fixed or contingent.

§ 2. Insolvency

(1) A person is insolvent when the present fair salable value of his assets is less than the amount that will be required to pay his probable liability on his existing debts as they become absolute and matured.

(2) In determining whether a partnership is insolvent there shall be added to the partnership property the present fair salable value of the separate assets of each general partner in excess of the amount probably sufficient to meet the claims of his separate creditors, and also the amount of any unpaid subscription to the partnership of each limited partner, provided the present fair salable value of the assets of such limited partner is probably sufficient to pay his debts, including such unpaid subscription.

§ 3. Fair Consideration

Fair consideration is given for property, or obligation,

(a) When in exchange for such property, or obligation, as a fair equivalent therefor, and in good faith, property is conveyed or an antecedent debt is satisfied, or

(b) When such property, or obligation is received in good faith to secure a present advance or antecedent debt in amount not disproportionately small as compared with the value of the property, or obligation obtained.

§ 4. Conveyances by Insolvent

Every conveyance made and every obligation incurred by a person who is or will be thereby rendered insolvent is fraudulent as to creditors without regard to his actual intent if the conveyance is made or the obligation is incurred without a fair consideration.

§ 5. Conveyances by Persons in Business

Every conveyance made without fair consideration when the person making it is engaged or is about to engage in a business or transaction for which the property remaining in his hands after the conveyance is an unreasonably small capital, is fraudulent as to creditors and as to other persons who become creditors during the continuance of such business or transaction without regard to his actual intent.

§ 6. Conveyances by a Person about to Incur Debts

Every conveyance made and every obligation incurred without fair consideration when the person making the conveyance or entering into the obligation intends or believes that he will incur debts beyond his ability to pay as they mature, is fraudulent as to both present and future creditors.

§ 7. Conveyance Made with Intent to Defraud

Every conveyance made and every obligation incurred with actual intent, as distinguished from intent presumed in law, to hinder, delay, or defraud either present or future creditors, is fraudulent as to both present and future creditors.

* * *

§ 9. Rights of Creditors Whose Claims Have Matured

(1) Where a conveyance or obligation is fraudulent as to a creditor, such creditor, when his claim has matured, may, as against any person except a purchaser for fair consideration without knowledge of the fraud at the time of the purchase, or one who has derived title immediately or mediately from such a purchaser,

Have the conveyance set aside or obligation annulled to the extent necessary to satisfy his claim, or

(a) Disregard the conveyance and attach or levy execution upon the property conveyed.

(2) A purchaser who without actual fraudulent intent has given less than a fair consideration for the conveyance or obligation, may retain the property or obligation as security for repayment.

§ 10. Rights of Creditors Whose Claims Have Not Matured

Where a conveyance made or obligation incurred is fraudulent as to a creditor whose claim has not matured he may proceed in a court of competent jurisdiction against any person against whom he could have proceeded had his claim matured, and the court may,

(a) Restrain the defendant from disposing of his property,

(b) Appoint a receiver to take charge of the property,

(c) Set aside the conveyance or annul the obligation, or

(d) Make any order which the circumstances of the case may require.

UNIFORM FRAUDULENT TRANSFER ACT

§ 4. Transfers Fraudulent as to Present and Future Creditors.

(a) A transfer made or obligation incurred by a debtor is fraudulent as to a creditor, whether the creditor's claim arose before or after the transfer was made or the obligation was incurred, if the debtor made the transfer or incurred the obligation;

(1) with actual intent to hinder, delay, or defraud any creditor of the debtor; or

(2) without receiving a reasonably equivalent value in exchange for the transfer or obligation, and the debtor:

(i) was engaged or was about to engage in a business or a transaction for which the remaining assets of the debtor were unreasonably small in relation to the business or transaction; or

(ii) intended to incur, or believed or reasonably should have believed that [the transferor] would incur, debts beyond his [the transferor's] ability to pay as they became due.

(b) In determining actual intent under subsection (a)(1), consideration may be given, among other factors, to whether:

(1) the transfer or obligation was to an insider;

(2) the debtor retained possession or control of the property transferred after the transfer;

(3) the transfer or obligation was disclosed or concealed;

* * *

(5) before the transfer was made or obligation was incurred, the debtor had been sued or threatened with suit; the transfer was of substantially all the debtor's assets;

(6) the debtor absconded;

(7) the debtor removed or concealed assets;

(8) the value of the consideration received by the debtor was reasonably equivalent to the value of the asset transferred or the amount of the obligation incurred;

(9) the debtor was insolvent or become insolvent shortly after the transfer was made or the obligation incurred;

(10) the transfer occurred shortly before or shortly after a substantial debt was incurred; and

(11) the debtor transferred the essential assets of the business to a lienor who transferred the assets to an insider of the debtor.

§ 5. Transfers Fraudulent as to Present Creditors.

(a) A transfer made or obligation incurred by a debtor is fraudulent as to a creditor whose claim arose before the transfer was made or the obligation was incurred if the debtor made the transfer or incurred the obligation without receiving a reasonably equivalent value in exchange for the transfer or obligation and the debtor was insolvent at that time or the debtor became insolvent as a result of the transfer or obligation.

(b) A transfer made by a debtor is fraudulent as to a creditor whose claim arose before the transfer was made if the transfer was made to an insider for an antecedent debt, the debtor was insolvent at that time, and the insider had reasonable cause to believe that the debtor was insolvent.

§ 7. Remedies of Creditors.

(a) In an action for relief against a transfer or obligation under this Act, a creditor . . . may obtain:

(1) avoidance of the transfer or obligation to the extent necessary to satisfy the creditor's claim;

(2) an attachment or other provisional remedy against the asset transferred or other property of the transferee in accordance with the procedure prescribed by [another statute];

(3) subject to applicable principles of equity and in accordance with applicable rules of civil procedure,

(i) an injunction, against further disposition by the debtor or a transferee, or both, of the asset transferred or of other property;

(ii) appointment of a receiver to take charge of the asset transferred or of other property of the transferee; or

(iii) any other relief the circumstances may require.

(b) If a creditor has obtained a judgment on a claim against a debtor, the creditor, if the court so orders, may levy execution on the asset transferred or its proceeds.

UNIFORM COMMERCIAL CODE

§ 1-201. Scope.

(a) . . .

(b)(35) "Security interest" means an interest in personal property or fixtures which secures payment or performance of an obligation. "Security interest" includes any interest of a consignor and a buyer of accounts, chattel paper, a payment intangible, or a promissory note in a transaction that is subject to Article 9. "Security interest" does not include the special property interest of a buyer of goods on identification of those goods to a contract for sale under Section 2-505, the right of a seller or lessor of goods under Article 2 or 2A to retain or acquire possession of the goods is not a "security interest", but a seller or lessor may also acquire a "security interest" by complying with Article 9. The retention or reservation of title by a seller of goods notwithstanding shipment or delivery to the buyer under Section

2-401 is limited in effect to a reservation of a "security interest." Whether a transaction in the form of a lease creates a "security interest" is determined pursuant to Section 1-203.

§ 9-104. Control of deposit account.

(a) Requirements for control.

A secured party has control of a deposit account if:

(1) the secured party is the bank with which the deposit account is maintained;

(2) the debtor, secured party, and bank have agreed in an authenticated record that the bank will comply with instructions originated by the secured party directing disposition of the funds in the account without further consent by the debtor; or

(3) the secured party becomes the bank's customer with respect to the deposit account.

(b) Debtor's right to direct disposition.

A secured party that has satisfied subsection (a) has control, even if the debtor retains the right to direct the disposition of funds from the deposit account.

§ 9-109. Scope.

(a) Except as otherwise provided . . . this article [of the U.C.C.] applies to:

(1) a transaction, regardless of its form, that creates a security interest in personal property or fixtures by contract; . . .

(3) a sale of accounts, chattel paper, payment intangibles, or promissory notes . . .

§ 9-322. Priorities Among Conflicting Security Interests in . . . [the] Same Collateral.

(a)(1) Conflicting perfected security interests . . . rank according to priority in time of filing or perfection. . . .

§ 9-401. Alienability of Debtor's Rights.

(a) . . .

(b) [Agreement does not prevent transfer.] An agreement between the debtor and secured party which prohibits a transfer of the debtor's rights in collateral or makes the transfer a default does not prevent the transfer from taking effect.

INDEX

References are to Pages